BUSINESS

BUSINESS MATHE

SECOND EDITION

MATHEMATICS

A Collegiate Approach

NELDA W. ROUECHE

PRENTICE-HALL, INC., Englewood Cliffs, New Jersey

Library of Congress Cataloging in Publication Data

ROUECHE, NELDA W.
  Business mathematics.

  1. Business mathematics.   I. Title.
HF5691. R68 1973   513'.93   72-8464
ISBN 0-13-105056-7

BUSINESS MATHEMATICS: A COLLEGIATE APPROACH 2nd Edition

Nelda W. Roueche

© 1973, 1969 PRENTICE-HALL, INC., ENGLEWOOD CLIFFS, N.J.

Printed in the United States of America

10   9   8   7   6   5

Prentice-Hall International, Inc., *London*
Prentice-Hall of Australia, Pty. Ltd., *Sydney*
Prentice-Hall of Canada, Ltd., *Toronto*
Prentice-Hall of India Private Limited, *New Delhi*
Prentice-Hall of Japan, Inc., *Tokyo*

Contents

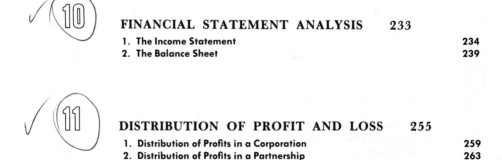

Preface

The second edition of *Business Mathematics: A Collegiate Approach* retains the distinctive features that contributed to the wide acceptance of the first edition, while introducing a number of improvements or modifications, as well as updating obsolete material. The result produces a text which, in the words of one reviewer, is "very much geared to the needs of any business student in the associate degree programs of technical and junior colleges."

As before, the primary objective of *Business Mathematics* remains to familiarize the student with a wide range of business procedures for which mathematics is required. The course serves a dual purpose of (1) sharpening the mathematical skills for a student preparing to enter business employment, and (2) providing an introduction to accounting, finance, insurance, and other more advanced, math-related business courses.

This text is intended for use in a one-term business mathematics course. It was especially designed for use in business programs in junior colleges and community colleges. The typical student in the two-year-college business program has not had extensive math preparation. However, to prepare himself for business employment, he needs to gain skill in a number of practical mathematical areas. *Business Mathematics* offers several advantages for this student:

• A brief but comprehensive review of arithmetic, equations, and per cent is included. Although such review is usually needed, many existing courses devote an unrealistic proportion of class time to review, at the expense of important business topics.

• Each topic contains an introduction describing the terminology and business aspects associated with it. I have attempted to keep these explanations as brief as possible, without sacrificing content, and have expecially endeavored to make them precise and readable.

• A large number of examples is given, including an example for every type of problem that the student might be assigned. Examples are explained in detail and all steps are included to insure that the student understands the entire solution.

• The text contains over 1,000 problems. Each section includes a combination of problems in computation designed for quick mastery of technique, as well as written problems designed to insure complete under-standing of the principle under discussion. Problems are paired (thus allowing the instructor to use one problem for classwork and to assign a similar problem for homework) and are arranged in order of increasing difficulty. My objective is to teach mathematical procedures used in busi-ness, rather than to provide tedious exercises in arithmetic. Thus the problems contain numbers that are as compatible as possible—canceling each other and/or working out to relatively whole-numbered answers.

• Easier topics, rather than being grouped together in an early chap-ter, are interspersed with related topics throughout the text. This provides a logical sequence of presentation and also allows an occasional "breather" for the student.

• Elementary algebra is used in explaining topics where it is logical and natural to do so. Chapter 2 presents a review of basic equation-solving techniques. The student may then apply these same techniques to many topics and avoid trying to memorize several variations of each formula. This approach constitutes a distinct advantage because, in attempting to memorize several similar formulas, inexperienced math students inevitably interchange variables incorrectly.

• Most graduates of junior college business programs are employed in retail businesses. Hence a major part of the book is devoted to topics related to retailing: commercial discounts, markup and markdown, profit and loss, installment buying, depreciation, taxes, insurance, payrolls, and so forth. Topics related to finance receive less emphasis, but are covered enough to familiarize the student with the basic aspects of investment and credit.

• Tables required to solve certain problems are grouped together in Appendix B at the back of the book. This enables the student to use the tables during tests without having his text open to the main body of material.

Of the new features in the second edition, the following are of par-ticular interest:

• The student problems have been extensively revised; 50% of the problems are new in this edition. Also, new types of problems are added in many chapters. For instance, new problems in the checkbook records chapter allow the student to reconcile the bank statement directly from the statement and check register.

• In keeping with the current trend toward individualized instruction, student learning objectives are included for each chapter. These learning objectives will be an advantage for both student and instructor: They specify for the student exactly which skills are to be developed and can be used in either the individualized or traditional class. For the instructor seeking ways of meeting the individual learning abilities of students, the learning objectives provide a first step in that direction; he can modify the course or identify various learning achievement levels by indicating to the student which learning objectives are required.

• The payroll chapter has been updated to include changes in legislation, as well as social security and income tax withholding tables current at the time of revision. Similarly, the section on installment loans has been extensively revised to reflect the Truth in Lending Law.

• Some changes were made because of very helpful suggestions from users. Chapter ordering was modified somewhat to accommodate the topic sequence in accounting. Also, a sizable addition in the depreciation section helps the student consolidate the basic depreciation methods.

It should be noted that the foregoing aspects, which make *Business Mathematics* especially advantageous to community colleges, should in no way detract from its use by other institutions. Thus the book may be adopted by any institution which either offers a junior-college-level business program or requires an introductory business mathematics course.

An instructor's manual for use with the text is available to the instructor. The manual contains solutions to all problems, as well as teaching suggestions.

Of the many persons who assisted with aspects of the revision, I would like to express special appreciation to the following:

• Robert H. Hosken, Jr., of Miami-Dade Junior College and R. H. Whiston of Hudson Valley Community College for their very helpful suggestions for unifying the basic depreciation methods.

• Mrs. Sarah K. Rohrer of Robert Morris College, Allen B. Roberts of Community College of Philadelphia, Mrs. Helen Scoon of Madison Area Technical College, as well as professors Hosken and Whiston, who submitted extensive suggestions for the proposed revision. Mrs. Rohrer and Mrs. Scoon also reviewed the completed revision and offered further ideas for its refinement.

• Langley Corporation, San Diego, California, for permission to reproduce its specimen stock certificate. Financial Publishing Company, Boston, Massachusetts, for permission to reproduce portions of its regular Loan Amortization Schedule and portions of *Financial Compound Interest and Annuity Tables*.

- Mrs. Judy Frieling, who typed the manuscript revision.
- Mrs. Shirley Covington of Prentice-Hall, who handled the myriad of details of editing the manuscript, securing art and illustrations, and co-ordinating final production.
- Burton Gabriel, Prentice-Hall, Editor of Quantitative Analysis for Business, who coordinated the entire revision and publication of *Business Mathematics: A Collegiate Approach.*
- And especially to my husband, John, for his continuing encouragement and enthusiasm in support of this project.

Nelda W. Roueche

BUSINESS MATHEMATICS

part one

REVIEW

1

Review of Operations

LEARNING OBJECTIVES

Upon completion of Chapter 1, the student will be able to:

1. Define and use correctly the terminology associated with each topic.

2. Multiply efficiently using
   a. Numbers containing zeroes (ex: 307 × 1400);
   b. Decimal numbers with fractions (ex: 15 × 3.5$\frac{2}{3}$); and
   c. Numbers with exponents (ex: 3^4).

3. Simplify fractions containing
   a. Decimal parts $\left(\text{ex: } \dfrac{6}{1.5}\right)$; and
   b. Fractional parts $\left(\text{ex: } \dfrac{6}{1\frac{1}{2}}\right)$.

4. Simplify expressions containing parentheses of the type $(1 - dt)$ or $S(1 + rt)$.

5. Round off numbers to a specified decimal place.

6. Round a multiplication product to an accurate number of digits, based on the digits of the original numbers.

3

THE NORMAL, day-to-day operations of most businesses require frequent computations with numbers. Many of these computations are done in modern business by machines. Some computations, however, are still performed manually. And even those processes whose final calculations will be done automatically must first be set up correctly, so that the proper numbers will be fed into the machines and the proper operation performed.

The following topics are presented in order to strengthen some of the weaknesses in working with numbers which many students often have.

MULTIPLICATION

Whenever a number is to be multiplied by some *number ending in zeroes*, the zeroes should be written to the right of the actual problem; the zeroes are then brought down and affixed to the right of the product without actually entering into the operation. If either number contains a decimal, this also does not affect the problem until the operation has been completed.

Example One

(a) 125×40—

$$
\begin{array}{r}
125 \\
\times 4\,|\,0 \\
\hline
5{,}00\,|\,0
\end{array}
$$

(b) $2.13 \times 1{,}500$—

$$\begin{array}{r} 2.13 \\ \times 15\,|\,00 \\ \hline 1,065 \\ 2\ 13 \\ \hline 3,195.\,|\,00 \end{array}$$

(c) 13,000 × 18—

$$\begin{array}{r} 18 \\ \times 13,\,|\,000 \\ \hline 54 \\ 18 \\ \hline 234,\,|\,000 \end{array}$$

When multiplying by a *number containing inner zeroes,* students often write whole rows of zeroes unnecessarily in order to assure themselves that the other digits will be correctly aligned. These useless zeroes can be eliminated if one will remember the following rule: On each line of multiplication, the first digit written down goes directly underneath the digit which was used for multiplying.

(a) 2,145 × 307—

Example Two

Wrong	Right
2,145	2,145
× 307	× 307
15 015	15 015
00 00	643 5
643 5	658,515
658,515	

(b) 1005 × 7208—

$$\begin{array}{r} 7,208 \\ \times 1,005 \\ \hline 36\ 040 \\ 7\ 208 \\ \hline 7,244,040 \end{array}$$

When multiplying a *whole number by a mixed number* (a mixed number is a whole number plus a fraction), one should first multiply by the fraction and then multiply the other numbers in the usual manner. If a decimal is involved, the decimal point is marked off in the usual way—the fraction does not affect the number of decimal places.

Example Three

(a) $24 \times 15\frac{3}{4}$ —

$$
\begin{array}{r}
24 \\
\times 15\ \frac{3}{4} \\
\hline
18\ (\frac{3}{4} \times 24 = 18) \\
120 \\
24 \\
\hline
378
\end{array}
$$

(b) $35 \times 1.3\frac{3}{7}$ —

$$
\begin{array}{r}
3\,5 \\
\times 1.3\frac{3}{7} \\
\hline
1\,5 \\
10\,5 \\
35 \\
\hline
47.0
\end{array}
$$

There are several different ways to indicate that multiplication is required. The common symbols are the "times" sign ("×") and the raised dot ("·"). Many formulas contain letters (called *variables*) which are written together; this indicates that the numbers which these variables represent are to be multiplied. A number written beside a variable indicates multiplication of the number and variable. Numbers or letters within parentheses written together should also be multiplied. A number or variable written adjoining parentheses should be multiplied by the expression within the parentheses. Thus,

$$
\begin{aligned}
3 \cdot 5 &= 3 \times 5 \\
Prt &= P \times r \times t \\
4k &= 4 \times k \\
(2.5)(4)(6.8) &= 2.5 \times 4 \times 6.8 \\
7(12) &= 7 \times 12
\end{aligned}
$$

Some few problems require the use of exponents. An *exponent* is merely a number which, when written as a superscript to the right of another number, called the *base*, indicates how many times the base is to be written in multiplying times itself.

Example Four

(a) $x^2 = x \cdot x$

exponent

base

(b) $5\overset{\text{exponent}}{^3} = 5 \cdot 5 \cdot 5 = 125$

base

(c) $2^4 = 2 \cdot 2 \cdot 2 \cdot 2 = 16$

(d) $(1.02)^3 = (1.02)(1.02)(1.02) = 1.061208$

DIVISION

Recall that a fraction indicates division—the numerator of the fraction (above the line) is to be divided by the denominator (below the line). Thus, if the denominator contains a fraction, it must be inverted and multiplied times the numerator *of the entire fraction.* If the denominator contains a decimal, it must be moved to the end of the number and the decimal in the numerator moved a corresponding number of places.

Example Five

(a) $\dfrac{3}{\frac{3}{4}} = \dfrac{3}{1} \div \dfrac{3}{4} = \dfrac{\cancel{3}}{1} \times \dfrac{4}{\cancel{3}} = \dfrac{4}{1} = 4$

(b) $\dfrac{6}{1\frac{1}{2}} = \dfrac{6}{\frac{3}{2}} = \dfrac{6}{1} \div \dfrac{3}{2} = \dfrac{\overset{2}{\cancel{6}}}{1} \times \dfrac{2}{\cancel{3}} = \dfrac{4}{1} = 4$

(c) $\dfrac{4}{.5} = \dfrac{4.0}{.5} = \dfrac{40}{5} = 8$

(d) $\dfrac{5.2}{.13} = \dfrac{5.20}{.13} = \dfrac{520}{13} = 40$

(e) $\dfrac{2.31}{.3} = \dfrac{2.31}{.3} = \dfrac{23.1}{3} = 7.7$

SUBTRACTION

Unfortunately, business expenses sometimes exceed the funds allotted to them. In this case, the *deficit* is called a *negative difference.* (Oftentimes, the account is also said to be "in the red.")

A negative difference is found by taking the numerical difference between the larger and smaller numbers. The result is indicated as being a deficit by placing a minus sign before the number.

Example Six	**(a)**	Bank balance	$598.00
		Checks written	− 650.00
		Deficit	−$ 52.00
	(b)	Profit earned	$3,500.00
		Salary owed	− 4,700.00
		Negative difference	−$1,200.00

PARENTHESES

Several formulas used in finding simple interest and simple discount contain parentheses. The student should be familiar with the correct procedure to follow in working with parentheses: If a parentheses contains both multiplication and addition or multiplication and subtraction, the multiplication should be performed first and the addition or subtraction last. (This procedure simply follows the standard rule for order of operations: Multiplication and division should always be performed before addition and subtraction. Thus, $3 \times 4 - 8 = 12 - 8 = 4$; and $9 + 16 \div 8 = 9 + 2 = 11$.)

Example Seven

(a)
$$(1 + rt) = \left(1 + \frac{\cancel{8}^{3}}{100} \cdot \frac{1}{\cancel{2}}\right)$$
$$= \left(1 + \frac{3}{100}\right)$$
$$= \left(\frac{100}{100} + \frac{3}{100}\right)$$
$$= \left(\frac{103}{100}\right)$$

(b)
$$(1 - dt) = \left(1 - \frac{\cancel{8}^{2}}{100} \cdot \frac{1}{\cancel{4}}\right)$$
$$= \left(1 - \frac{2}{100}\right)$$
$$= \left(\frac{100}{100} - \frac{2}{100}\right)$$
$$= \left(\frac{98}{100}\right)$$

(c)
$$(1 + rt) = \left(1 + \frac{\cancel{8}^{2}}{100} \cdot \frac{7}{\cancel{12}_{3}}\right)$$
$$= \left(1 + \frac{14}{300}\right)$$
$$= \left(\frac{300}{300} + \frac{14}{300}\right)$$
$$= \left(\frac{314}{300}\right)$$

If a parentheses has some number in front of it, that number is to be multiplied times the whole expression within the parentheses. That is, the terms within the parentheses should be consolidated into a single number or fraction, if possible, *before* multiplying.

Wrong

$$P(1 + rt) = \$600\,(1 + \tfrac{5}{100} \cdot \tfrac{1}{3})$$

$$= \overset{2}{\cancel{600}}(1 + \tfrac{5}{300})$$

$$= 2\,(6)$$

$$= \$12$$

Right

$$P(1 + rt) = \$600\,(1 + \tfrac{5}{100} \cdot \tfrac{1}{3})$$

$$= 600\,(1 + \tfrac{5}{300})$$

$$= 600\,(\tfrac{300}{300} + \tfrac{5}{300})$$

$$= \overset{2}{\cancel{600}}\,(\tfrac{305}{300})$$

$$= \$610$$

If it is impossible to consolidate the terms within the parentheses into a single number or fraction, then the number in front of the parentheses must be multiplied times *each* separate term within the parentheses. (Separate terms may be identified by the fact that plus or minus signs always appear between them.)

(a) $P(1 + rt) = P \cdot 1 + P \cdot rt = P + Prt$

(b) $S(1 - dt) = S \cdot 1 - S \cdot dt = S - Sdt$

(c) $S(1 - dt)$

$\$400\,(1 - \tfrac{6}{100}t)$

$$400 \cdot 1 - \overset{4}{\cancel{400}} \cdot \tfrac{6}{\cancel{100}}t$$

$$400 - 24t$$

ROUNDING OFF DECIMALS

The general rule for rounding off decimals is as follows:

1. If the last decimal place which one wishes to include is followed by a digit which is smaller than 5, the digit in question is unchanged.

2. If the last decimal place one wishes to include is followed by a digit which is 5 or larger, the digit in question is rounded off to the next higher number.

(a) Rounding off to tenths (to one decimal place):

$14.3\,)\,274 = 14.3$

(b) Rounding off to hundredths (to two decimal places):
5.37) 812 = 5.38

(c) Rounding off to thousandths (to three decimal places):
0.032) 569 = 0.033

(d) Rounding off 24.14759—
to tenths: 24.1
to hundredths: 24.15
to thousandths: 24.148

Note: A special case sometimes arises when the last decimal place one wishes to use is followed by a single 5 (and no other digits). In this case, particularly when the numbers in question should total 100 per cent, one may use the following rule: If the last digit to be included is an odd number, round it off to the next higher number; if it is even, leave it unchanged.

(e) Round to the nearest per cent:

$$
\begin{array}{rcl}
62.5\% & = & 62\% \\
+37.5\% & = & 38\% \\
\hline
100.0\% & = & 100\%
\end{array}
$$

ACCURACY OF COMPUTATION

The following rule should always be observed: The answer which one obtains from a mathematical calculation can never be more accurate than the least accurate figure used in making the calculation.

This rule requires the first solution to be rounded off in many instances. The answer must at least be rounded off so as to contain no more than the number of decimal places contained in the original figure which had the *least number of decimal places*. To be more exact, the answer should contain no more digits than the original number which had the *fewest digits*.

Example Eleven

(a) Find the area of a room 17.27 feet in length and 13.6 feet in width.

$A = lw$
$= 17.27 \times 13.6$
$= 234.872$
$= 234.9$ square feet (since 13.6 had only one decimal place)

or

$= 235$ square feet (since 13.6 had only three digits)

This rule is of particular importance in computing

amounts invested at compound interest, since tables containing many decimal places are used. The student will want to minimize work by using no more of these decimal places than is necessary; but at the same time, he must obtain an answer which is correct to the nearest cent.

To do this, one should first estimate the answer to determine the number of digits it will contain (including the cent's place). This number plus one more (to insure absolute accuracy) will determine the number of digits one needs to copy from the table.

It should be noted that any known exact amount (such as $350) is considered accurate for any number of decimal places desired.

(b) Suppose an interest problem requires that $200 be multiplied by the table value 1.48594740. We wish to use only enough digits from the table to insure that our answer is correct to the nearest cent.

First estimate the value of the tabular number: it is approximately 1.5. Therefore, the answer we obtain will be approximately $200 × 1.5 = $300.

The number $300.00 contains 5 digits; thus we must copy 5 + 1 = 6 digits from the table. (The sixth digit from the table will be rounded off using the previously discussed rules for rounding off decimals.) The number 1.48594740, rounded to six digits, equals 1.48595.

Thus $200 × 1.48595 = $297.19000 = $297.19 is the solution correct to the nearest cent.

(c) Find $1,500 times 1.86102237 correct to the nearest cent, using no more digits than necessary.

1.86102237 approximately equals 2.
2 × $1,500 = $3,000, which contains 6 digits (including the cent's digit).
6 + 1 = 7 digits are required from the table.
$1,500 × 1.861022 = $2,791.533000 = $2,791.53, correct to cents.

(d) Find $800 × 0.50752126 correct to cents, using no more digits than necessary.

0.50752126 approximately equals .5
$800 × .5 = $400, which has 5 digits.
5 + 1 = 6 digits are required from the table.
$800 × 0.507521 = $406.016800 = $406.02

Note: The zero before the decimal in the number 0.50752126 does not qualify as a significant digit (that is, as a digit which should be counted), because the zero could have been omitted without changing the value of the number.

PROBLEMS

Find the product:

1. (a) 72 × 40
   (b) 60 × 234
   (c) 138 × 500
   (d) 1,200 × 28
   (e) 2,700 × 318
   (f) 1,424 × 403
   (g) 107 × 2,766
   (h) 3,002 × 16,809
   (i) 1,080 × 526

   (j) 36 × 4.7$\frac{1}{2}$
   (k) 2.4 × 15$\frac{3}{8}$
   (l) 1.75 × 7.2$\frac{4}{5}$
   (m) 0.32 × 40$\frac{1}{4}$
   (n) 2.8 × 2.5$\frac{3}{7}$
   (o) 4^5
   (p) 2^4
   (q) 5^3
   (r) 1.05^2

2. (a) 15 × 60
   (b) 20 × 312
   (c) 400 × 37
   (d) 27 × 1,200
   (e) 2,500 × 114
   (f) 1,425 × 504
   (g) 208 × 729
   (h) 1,006 × 24,304
   (i) 2,050 × 354

   (j) 28 × 2.3$\frac{1}{4}$
   (k) 1.75 × 14$\frac{2}{5}$
   (l) 15$\frac{3}{8}$ × .24
   (m) 3.6 × 14$\frac{2}{9}$
   (n) 2.7 × 1.2$\frac{1}{3}$
   (o) 2^4
   (p) 3^5
   (q) 6^3
   (r) 1.04^2

3. Divide or subtract, as indicated:

   (a) $\dfrac{36}{\frac{4}{9}}$

   (b) $\dfrac{30}{7\frac{1}{2}}$

   (c) $\dfrac{2}{.4}$

   (d) $\dfrac{6.4}{.16}$

   (e) $\dfrac{2.16}{.6}$

   (f) Gross profit $5,000
       Expenses   −5,750

   (g) Travel allowance $450
       Travel expenses   −525

   (h) Construction contract $25,500
       Building expenses   −27,200

   (i) Gross profit $1,700
       Expenses   −2,100

4. (a) $\dfrac{9}{\frac{3}{5}}$

   (b) $\dfrac{14}{2\frac{1}{3}}$

   (c) $\dfrac{21}{.3}$

   (d) $\dfrac{9.8}{.14}$

(e) $\dfrac{2.34}{.6}$

(f) Bank balance $870
    Checks written   −925

(g) Value of stock $ 950
    Cost of stock   −1,200

(h) Advertising budget $107
    Advertising expense   −135

(i) Gross profit $3,115
    Expenses   −3,789

Find the value of each expression:

5. (a) $(1 + \frac{8}{100} \times \frac{1}{2})$
   (b) $(1 - \frac{7}{100} \cdot \frac{1}{3})$
   (c) $(1 - \frac{5}{100} \times \frac{1}{4})$
   (d) $(1 + \frac{7}{100} \cdot \frac{1}{4})$
   (e) $(1 + \frac{8}{100} \cdot \frac{1}{6})$
   (f) $(1 - \frac{6}{100} \cdot \frac{5}{12})$

   (g) $500(1 + \frac{6}{100} \cdot \frac{1}{2})$
   (h) $600(1 - \frac{8}{100} \cdot \frac{1}{3})$
   (i) $300(1 + \frac{7}{100}t)$
   (j) $640(1 - r \cdot \frac{1}{4})$
   (k) $a(1 + bc)$

6. (a) $(1 + \frac{4}{100} \cdot \frac{1}{2})$
   (b) $(1 + \frac{7}{100} \cdot \frac{1}{4})$
   (c) $(1 - \frac{8}{100} \cdot \frac{1}{4})$
   (d) $(1 - \frac{5}{100} \cdot \frac{1}{2})$
   (e) $(1 + \frac{4}{100} \times \frac{5}{12})$
   (f) $(1 - \frac{6}{100} \cdot \frac{1}{4})$

   (g) $300(1 + \frac{6}{100} \cdot \frac{1}{3})$
   (h) $200(1 - \frac{7}{100} \cdot \frac{1}{2})$
   (i) $400(1 + \frac{5}{100}t)$
   (j) $540(1 - r \cdot \frac{1}{3})$
   (k) $a(1 - bc)$

Round off each number as indicated:

7. (a) to tenths—
   24.348
   6.24
   154.65

   (b) to hundredths—
   7.475
   12.388
   0.6747

   (c) to thousandths—
   117.6339
   5.0798
   24.3072

   (d) to tenths, hundredths, and thousandths—
   7.9875
   16.6749

8. (a) to tenths—
   5.14
   319.392
   26.83

   (b) to hundredths—
   7.9348
   14.697
   121.345

   (c) to thousandths—
   59.9997
   0.4035
   6.2119

   (d) to tenths, hundredths, and thousandths—
   8.8479
   3.2595

Compute each product; round first according to the least accurate decimal and then round according to the least number of digits:

9. (a) 12.5×8.77
   (b) 4.15×7.3
   (c) 16.4×0.32
   (d) 121.1×3.72

10. (a) 8.61 × 13.5   (c) 3.45 × 7.002
    (b) 1.5 × 4.03   (d) 50.6 × .32

Compute each product, correct to the nearest cent. Use no more digits than is necessary.

11. (a) $400 × 1.6374710015   (c) $2,000 × 0.3885701998
    (b) $600 × 2.0675713052   (d) $500 × 30.1075740373

12. (a) $600 × 1.50252492   (c) $2,000 × 0.40324726
    (b) $900 × 2.00159734   (d) $40 × 16.09689554

2

Review of Equations

LEARNING OBJECTIVES

Upon completion of Chapter 2, the student will be able to:

1. Define and use correctly the terminology associated with each topic.

2. Solve basic equations that require only
   a. Combining the similar terms of the equation; and/or
   b. Using the operations of addition, subtraction, multiplication, and division.
   c. Examples: $X - 12 = 16$, $\quad 5y - 4 = 6 - 3y$, $\quad$ or $\dfrac{3x}{4} + 5 = 23$.

3. Express any written problem in a concise sentence which provides the structure for the equation that solves the problem.

4. a. Express numbers in ratios; and
   b. Use ratios to apportion numerical amounts.
   c. Ex: Divide $27,000 among three people according to a ratio of $3:4:2$.

5. Convert repeating decimals (such as $0.7777\ldots$ or $0.345345345\ldots$) to their equivalent fractions.

THE PROCEDURE REQUIRED to solve many problems in business mathematics is much more obvious if one has a basic knowledge of linear equations. (Linear equations are so named because they graph as a straight line; however, we shall not be concerned with this aspect.) Before starting to solve any actual equations, a discussion of some of the characteristics of equations may prove helpful.

1. BASIC EQUATIONS

An equation may be compared to an old-fashioned balancing scale. The "equal" marks are the center post of the scale and the two sides of the equation balance each other as do the pans of the scale.

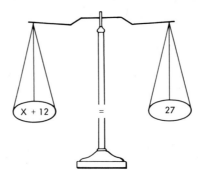

We know that one can either add weights or remove them from the pans of a scale; but so long as he makes the same changes in both pans, the scales remain in balance. The same is true of equations: In solving an equation, one may perform any operation (addition, subtraction, multiplication, or division); and so long as the same operation is performed on both sides of the equation, the balance of the equation will not be upset.

The object in solving any equation with unknowns in it is to determine what value of the unknown quantity (called the *variable*) will make the equation a true statement. Basically, this is accomplished by isolating the variable term or terms on one side of the equation and the ordinary numbers on the other side, as follows:

$$\text{Variables} = \text{Numbers}$$
$$\text{or}$$
$$\text{Numbers} = \text{Variables}$$

The terms are isolated by performing exactly the same operation on both sides of the equation.

There are only four basic equation forms—those whose solution requires a single operation of either addition, subtraction, multiplication, or division. All other equations are variations or combinations of these four forms. We shall now consider several elementary equations, beginning with the four basic forms.

In the basic equation forms to follow, there will be only one number associated with the unknown (variable) on the same side of the equation. The student should first determine which operation is involved with this number. The solution of the equation will then require that the *opposite* operation be performed on both sides of the equation.

Solve for x: $$x + 15 = 42$$

Example One

In order to isolate the variable x on the left side of the equation, we need to remove the 15. In the original equation, the 15 is added to x; therefore, we must perform the opposite of addition, or *subtract* 15 from both sides.

Subtract 15 from both sides
$15 - 15 = 0$; and $x + 0 = x$

$$x + 15 = 42$$
$$x + 15 - 15 = 42 - 15$$
$$x + 15 - 15 = 42 - 15$$
$$x = 27$$

Note: Numbers or variables in a given equation may be added or subtracted only if they are on the *same side* of the equation; thus, in Example 1, equation-solving techniques were used to get 42 and 15 on the same side of the equation before the numbers could be combined. Also, a student who has had little experience in solving equations should develop the following habit: On each succeeding line of the problem, first copy the adjusted equation resulting from the previous step; then perform the next step.

Example Two Solve for y: $\qquad\qquad\qquad\qquad\qquad y - 13 = 78$

The 13 is subtracted from y; therefore, we must *add* 13 to both sides of the equation.

$$y - 13 = 78$$

Add 13 to both sides $\qquad\qquad\qquad\qquad y - 13 + 13 = 78 + 13$

$-13 + 13 = 0 \qquad\qquad\qquad\qquad y - \underbrace{13 + 13} = \underbrace{78 + 13}$

$$y = 91$$

Example Three Solve for p: $\qquad\qquad\qquad\qquad\qquad 3p = 51$

The expression $3p$ means "3 times p" (or $3 \times p$). Any number that is multiplied times a variable is called a *coefficient*; thus, in this equation, 3 is the coefficient of p.

Since 3 is multiplied times p, we must perform the opposite of multiplication, or *divide* 3 into both sides of the equation.

$$3p = 51$$

Divide 3 into both sides $\qquad\qquad\qquad\qquad \dfrac{3p}{3} = \dfrac{51}{3}$

$$\dfrac{3}{3} = 1; \ 1p = p \qquad\qquad\qquad\qquad \dfrac{\overset{1}{\cancel{3}p}}{\cancel{3}} = \dfrac{51}{3}$$

$$p = 17$$

Example Four Solve for k: $\qquad\qquad\qquad\qquad\qquad \dfrac{k}{4} = 18$

Since 4 is divided into k, we must *multiply* both sides of the equation by 4.

$$\dfrac{k}{4} = 18$$

Multiply both sides by 4 $\qquad\qquad\qquad\qquad \dfrac{4}{1} \cdot \dfrac{k}{4} = 18 \cdot 4$

$$\dfrac{\overset{1}{\cancel{4}}}{1} \cdot \dfrac{k}{\cancel{4}} = 18 \cdot 4$$

$$k = 72$$

Now let us consider some variations and combinations of the basic equation forms.

Solve for t:

$$\frac{2t}{3} = 26$$

Just as $\dfrac{2 \times 12}{3}$ gives the same result as $\frac{2}{3} \times 12$, so $\dfrac{2t}{3}$ is the same as $\frac{2}{3}t$. In order to solve the equation for t, we need to remove the coefficient $\frac{2}{3}$ and obtain a coefficient of 1. This can be accomplished easily by multiplying by the reciprocal of $\frac{2}{3}$. The *reciprocal* of any number is the result obtained when the number is inverted (that is, the numerator and denominator are interchanged.) Thus, the reciprocal of $\frac{2}{3}$ is $\frac{3}{2}$.

$$\frac{2t}{3} = 26$$

Multiply by $\frac{3}{2}$, the reciprocal of $\frac{2}{3}$

$$\frac{\overset{1}{\cancel{3}}}{\cancel{2}} \cdot \frac{\overset{1}{\cancel{2}}}{\cancel{3}} t = \overset{13}{\cancel{26}} \cdot \frac{3}{\cancel{2}}$$

$\frac{3}{2} \cdot \frac{2}{3} = 1;\ 1t = t$

$$t = 39$$

Solve for x:

$$5x + x - 2x = 60$$

We must first combine the three x terms into a single x term. This is done by adding and/or subtracting the coefficients, whichever the signs indicate. (Recall that $x = 1x$.)

$$\underbrace{5x + x - 2x}_{} = 60$$

Combine the coefficients:
$$5 + 1 - 2 = 4$$

$$4x = 60$$

Divide both sides by 4

$$\frac{\overset{1}{\cancel{4}}x}{\cancel{4}} = \frac{60}{4}$$

$$x = 15$$

Solve for n:

$$5n - 4 = 26$$

When one side of an equation contains a variable term and a number term, it is customary to work with the number term first, in order to obtain an altered equation of the type

Variable term = Numbers

$$5n - 4 = 26$$

Add 4

$$5n - \cancel{4} + \cancel{4} = 26 + 4$$
$$5n = 30$$

Divide by 5

$$\frac{\cancel{5}n}{\cancel{5}} = \frac{30}{5}$$

$$n = 6$$

Example Eight

Solve for m:
$$17 = \frac{m}{4} + 8$$

We must first isolate the variable term so that

$$\text{Numbers} = \text{Variable term}$$

$$17 = \frac{m}{4} + 8$$

Subtract 8 from both sides $\qquad 17 - 8 = \frac{m}{4} + 8 - 8$

$$9 = \frac{m}{4}$$

Multiply by 4 $\qquad 4 \cdot 9 = \frac{m}{4} \cdot 4$

$$36 = m$$

Example Nine

Solve for x:
$$\frac{3x}{4} + 5 = 17$$

$$\frac{3x}{4} + 5 = 17$$

Subtract 5 $\qquad \frac{3x}{4} + 5 - 5 = 17 - 5$

$$\frac{3x}{4} = 12$$

Multiply by $\frac{4}{3}$ $\qquad \overset{1}{\underset{3}{\cancel{4}}} \cdot \overset{1}{\underset{4}{\cancel{3x}}} = \overset{4}{\cancel{12}} \cdot \frac{4}{\cancel{3}}$

$$x = 16$$

Example Ten

Solve for y:
$$5(y - 2) = 25$$

Recall that the coefficient 5 must be multiplied times each term within the parenthesis.

$$5(y - 2) = 25$$
$$5y - 10 = 25$$

Add 10 to both sides $\qquad 5y - 10 + 10 = 25 + 10$
$$5y = 35$$

Divide 5 $\qquad \frac{\cancel{5}y}{\cancel{5}} = \frac{35}{5}$

$$y = 7$$

Solve for c: $6c + 3 = 4c + 19$

Remember that variable terms or number terms can be added and/or subtracted only when they appear on the same side of the equation. Therefore, the first steps will involve getting all the variable terms on one side of the equation and all the number terms on the other. When the solution of an equation requires that both of these steps be done, it is customary—though not essential—to work with the variable terms first.

$$6c + 3 = 4c + 19$$

Subtract $4c$ from both sides $\quad\quad 6c - 4c + 3 = 4c - 4c + 19$

$$2c + 3 = 19$$

Subtract 3 from both sides $\quad\quad 2c + 3 - 3 = 19 - 3$

$$2c = 16$$

Divide by 2 $\quad\quad \dfrac{2c}{2} = \dfrac{16}{2}$

$$c = 8$$

PROBLEMS

Solve the following equations:

1. $1x + 18 = 32$
2. $x + 12 = 27$
3. $x - 19 = 21$
4. $y - 5 = 38$
5. $7y = 28$
6. $5x = 45$
7. $\dfrac{k}{8} = 8$
8. $\dfrac{t}{18} = 3$
9. $9r + 3 = 48$
10. $7c + 4 = 25$
11. $5p - 4 = 36$
12. $2x - 8 = 16$
13. $3t - t + 6t = 72$
14. $3y + 6y - y = 48$
15. $5n = 54 - 4n$
16. $7x = 50 - 3x$

17. $7g = 4g + 21$
18. $7v = 2v + 10$
19. $5(3x - 2) = 35$
20. $3(2k - 5) = 6$
21. $11p - 8 = 7p - 2$
22. $9m - 12 = 5m - 7$
23. $4y + 7 = 12 - y$
24. $2x + 8 = 11 - 3x$
25. $2s - 9 = 6 - 4s$
26. $4n - 7 = 8 - n$
27. $4(c - 2) = c + 9$
28. $8x - 9 = 3(x - 2)$
29. $\dfrac{r}{4} + 8 = 15$
30. $\dfrac{y}{6} + 8 = 11$
31. $\dfrac{t}{4} - 9 = 3$

32. $\dfrac{q}{5} - 4 = 5$

33. $\dfrac{5d}{6} + 7 = 22$

34. $\dfrac{4y}{7} + 9 = 17$

35. $16 = \dfrac{3k}{4} - 8$

36. $7 = \dfrac{3n}{8} - 5$

2. WRITTEN PROBLEMS

Many business problems of a mathematical nature can have no pre-determined formula applied to them. In these cases, it is necessary that the business person himself be able to set the facts of the situation into an original equation to obtain the solution.

An equation is simply a mathematical sentence. If one can express the facts of a mathematical problem into a clear, concise, English sentence, the mathematical sentence (equation) will follow in exactly the same pattern. (By the same token, it might also be said that if the student cannot express the facts into a clear, English sentence, he probably does not understand the situation well enough to be able to obtain a mathematical solution.)

One fact which helps immensely in converting English sentences into mathematical sentences is that the *verb* of the English sentences corresponds to the *equal marks* of the equations. The mathematical equivalents of several other words will be pointed out in the following examples.

Example One

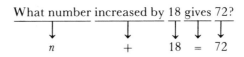

What number increased by 18 gives 72?

$$n \qquad + \qquad 18 \;=\; 72$$

Thus,

$$n + 18 = 72$$
$$n + 18 - 18 = 72 - 18$$
$$n = 54$$

Example Two

Carson's sales during Dollar Day were $5 less than Davis' sales. If Carson sold $327 worth of merchandise, what did Davis sell?

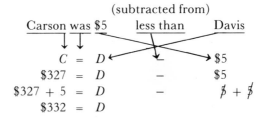

(subtracted from)

Carson was $5   less than   Davis

$$C = D \qquad \$5$$
$$\$327 = D \qquad - \qquad \$5$$
$$\$327 + 5 = D \qquad - \qquad \cancel{\$} + \cancel{\$}$$
$$\$332 = D$$

About $\frac{1}{4}$ of a family's net (spendable) income is budgeted for housing expenses (house payment, taxes, insurance, etc.).   What would their net monthly income have to be in order to afford a $25,000 home, assuming that housing expenses each month normally run 1 per cent of the purchase price?

Example Three

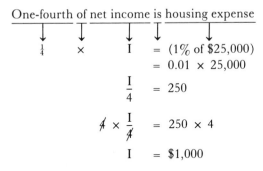

One-fourth of net income is housing expense

$$\frac{1}{4} \quad \times \quad I \quad = \quad (1\% \text{ of } \$25,000)$$
$$= \quad 0.01 \times 25,000$$
$$\frac{I}{4} \quad = \quad 250$$
$$4 \times \frac{I}{4} \quad = \quad 250 \times 4$$
$$I \quad = \quad \$1,000$$

Mr. Wilson received a stock dividend check for $675. If he owns 500 shares of stock, what was the dividend per share?

Example Four

No. shares times dividend per share equals total

$$500 \quad \times \quad D \quad = \quad \$675$$
$$500D \quad = \quad 675$$
$$\frac{500D}{500} \quad = \quad \frac{675}{500}$$
$$D \quad = \quad \$1.35$$

The city of Graham agreed to pay $\frac{3}{4}$ of the cost of a park project. The remaining cost will be paid by the county. If the city's share of the project is $18,000, what is the total cost of the project?

Example Five

Three-fourths of the total cost is the city's share

$$\frac{3}{4} \quad \times \quad C \quad = \quad \$18,000$$
$$\frac{3C}{4} \quad = \quad 18,000$$
$$\frac{4}{3} \cdot \frac{3C}{4} \quad = \quad 18,000 \times \frac{4}{3}$$
$$C \quad = \quad \$24,000$$

Adams and Baker together sold 45 cars. If Adams sold twice as many cars as Baker, how many cars did each sell?

Example Six

Note: When a problem involves two amounts, it is usually better to let the variable represent the smaller quantity.

Since Adams sold twice as many cars as Baker, Baker is the smaller quantity:

$$\underline{\text{Adams sold twice}} \quad \underline{\text{Baker}}$$
$$A \quad = \quad 2 \quad \times \quad B$$

Now,

$$\underline{\text{Adams and Baker together sold 45 cars}}$$

$$A + B = 45$$

$$2B + B = 45$$

$$\frac{3B}{3} = \frac{45}{3}$$

(Baker's sales) $\quad B = 15$ cars

(Adams' sales) $\quad A = 2B$

$$= 2 \times 15$$
$$= 30 \text{ cars}$$

Example Seven

Bananas cost $5.00 per case and grapes cost $7.00 per case. If an order of 15 cases cost $87.00, how many cases of each fruit were included?

We know there were a total of 15 cases. Suppose we knew there were 5 cases of grapes, how would we find the number of bananas? (Bananas = 15 − 5.) Suppose there were 8 cases of grapes; how many bananas would there be? (Bananas = 15 − 8.) Regardless of the actual number of cases of grapes,

$$\text{Bananas} = 15 - \text{Grapes}$$
$$\text{or} \quad B = 15 - G$$

Now,

$$\underline{\text{Cost of bananas}} \text{ plus } \underline{\text{cost of grapes}} \text{ equals } \quad \$87$$

$$\$5 \times B \quad + \quad \$7 \times G \quad = \quad 87$$

$$5(15 - G) \quad + \quad 7G \quad = \quad 87$$
$$75 - 5G \quad + \quad 7G \quad = \quad 87$$
$$75 \quad + \quad 2G \quad = \quad 87$$
$$75 - 75 \quad + \quad 2G \quad = \quad 87 - 75$$
$$2G \quad = \quad 12$$
$$\frac{2G}{2} \quad = \quad \frac{12}{2}$$

(Cases of grapes) $\quad G = 6$ Cases

(Cases of bananas) $\quad B = 15 - G$

$$= 15 - 6$$
$$= 9 \text{ Cases}$$

PROBLEMS

1. What number increased by 36 gives 60?

2. What number decreased by 36 gives 60?

3. The regular price of a coat, decreased by $12, gives a sale price of $37. What is the regular price?

4. The former price of a light fixture, increased by $2.50, gives a new price of $31. What was the old price?

5. The Harris Yard Mart charges $8 less than Phil's Motor Shop for the same lawn mower. If the Yard Mart's price is $67, what does Phil's charge?

6. Chandler's Appliances charge $15 more than the Thrifty Wholesale Company for a vacuum cleaner. If Chandler's price is $69, what would the cleaner cost at Thrifty Company?

7. One fourth of a dress shop's sales were charges. What were their total sales, if charges totaled $350?

8. One-sixth of a company's employees are women. What is the total number of employees, if there are 15 women?

9. Centex Motor Co. finds that $\frac{4}{5}$ of its new car sales include a trade-in. If 24 used cars came in last month, how many new cars were sold?

10. Approximately $\frac{2}{3}$ of the employees of a plant took no sick leave during December. If there were 120 employees without an absence, how many people does the firm employ?

11. A hardware store sold 17 drill sets for a total gross profit of $255. How much average gross profit was made on each set?

12. A salesman made 85 sales during his five-day work week. How many sales did he average each day?

13. Income from new construction totaled 2.8 times the income from repair work at Jones Plumbing. If new construction amounted to $42,000, how much income was generated by repairs?

14. The weaving department of a factory occupies 3.5 times as much floor space as the shipping department. The weaving department occupies 4,200 square feet. How large is the shipping department?

15. Depreciation and overhead together represented $3,000 on a profit and loss statement. If overhead ran four times as much as depreciation, how much was each expense?

16. Garland and White together sold 135 tickets to a civic club supper. If White sold twice as many tickets as Garland, how many tickets did each man sell?

17. A school has $11,000 allocated for building and grounds maintenance. Experience indicates that building maintenance usually costs 4.5 times as

much as grounds maintenance. How much of the allocation should be budgeted for each type of maintenance?

18. A chair company has been producing about 1,540 chairs a day, working two shifts. The second shift has produced about 1.2 times as many chairs as the first shift. How many chairs have been produced by each shift?

19. One type of yard chair costs a dealer $4 each and the matching lounge costs him $9 each. A recent shipment of 42 pieces totaled $228. How many chairs and how many lounges were included?

20. One style of shoes costs $8 wholesale in patent leather and $10 in cowhide. An invoice for $390 accompanies an order of 45 pairs of shoes. How many pairs of each style were bought?

21. Only 3 less than $\frac{2}{3}$ of the salesmen for Quality Products exceeded their quotas for the month. If 12 salesmen exceeded their quotas, how many salesmen does the firm employ?

22. According to the state policy, $1,000 more than $\frac{2}{3}$ the cost of a new school for Lincoln County will be paid by the state; the county will finance the remaining portion. If the state pays $361,000, what will be the total cost of the school?

3. RATIO

A *ratio* is a way of comparing numbers. When two numbers are being compared, the ratio may be written in any of three ways; for example, (1) 3 to 5, (2) 3:5, or (3) $\frac{3}{5}$. Thus method (3) indicates that common fractions are also ratios. If more than two numbers are being compared, the ratio is written in either of the first two ways; as, 3 to 2 to 4 or 2:3:5:3.

Ratios are often used instead of per cent in order to compare items of expense, particularly when the per cent would have exceeded 100 per cent. In this case, it is customary to reduce the ratio to a comparison to one; as 1.3 to 1 or $\frac{2.47}{1}$. (A ratio is "reduced" by expressing it as a common fraction and reducing the fraction. A ratio is reduced to "a comparison to one" by dividing the denominator into the numerator.) Ratios are also frequently used as a basis for dividing money or materials among several people.

Example One Determine the following ratios:

   (a) There are 15 licensed electricians and 25 electricians' helpers at Garrison Electric Co. What is the ratio of licensed electricians to helpers?

$$\text{Licensed electricians to helpers} = \frac{\text{Licensed}}{\text{Helpers}} = \frac{15}{25} = \frac{3}{5}$$

The ratio of licensed electricians to helpers is 3 to 5, or 3:5, or $\frac{3}{5}$.

(b) Last month, the cash sales at Jeannie's were $27,000 and the charge sales totaled $12,000. What was the ratio of cash sales to charge sales?

$$\text{Cash to charge sales} = \frac{\text{Cash}}{\text{Charge}} = \frac{\$27,000}{\$12,000} = \frac{9}{4} = 2.25 = \frac{2.25}{1}$$

The ratio may be given correctly in any of the following forms: 9 to 4 or 2.25 to 1; 9:4 or 2.25:1; $\frac{9}{4}$ or $\frac{2.25}{1}$. Since most actual business figures would not reduce to a common fraction like $\frac{9}{4}$, business ratios are usually computed by ordinary division, without attempting to reduce the fraction. Thus $\frac{\$27,000}{\$12,000} = 2.25 = \frac{2.25}{1}$ or 2.25 to 1.

A father provided in his will that his estate be divided between his wife and only child in the ratio of 5:2. How much will each receive, if the estate is valued at $21,000? **Example Two**

The numbers in a ratio are given in the same order as the corresponding elements (people, in this case) are listed. Thus, the ratio 5:2 indicates that for every $5 the wife receives, the child will get $2. The problem is solved by dividing the estate into 5 + 2 or 7 shares; the wife then receives 5 of these shares and the child receives 2 shares. If x represents one share, then

$$\text{Wife's portion} + \text{Child's portion} = \text{Total estate}$$
$$5x + \qquad\qquad 2x = \$21,000$$
$$7x = 21,000$$
$$x = 3,000$$

$$\text{Wife:}\quad 5x = 5(3,000)$$
$$= \$15,000$$

$$\text{Child:}\quad 2x = 2(3,000)$$
$$= \$6,000$$

Thus each share is $3,000, the wife's five shares total $15,000, and the child's two shares amount to $6,000. The sum of the amounts allotted to each person must equal the total amount: $15,000 + $6,000 = $21,000.

Supplies at Independence Insurance Co. are apportioned according to the number of persons in each department. The four departments employ 7, 4, 9, and 5 typists, respectively. If 200 reams of paper have just arrived, determine the number of reams to be distributed to each department. **Example Three**

The paper is to be distributed in the ratio 7:4:9:5. As before, x represents one share.

$$7x + 4x + 9x + 5x = 200$$
$$25x = 200$$
$$x = 8$$

Dept. A:	$7x =$	56 reams
Dept. B:	$4x =$	32 reams
Dept. C:	$9x =$	72 reams
Dept. D:	$5x =$	40 reams
		200 reams

Hence the four departments receive 56, 32, 72, and 40 reams, in that order.

The term "proportion" is frequently used in connection with ratio. A *proportion* is simply a mathematical statement that two ratios are equal. Thus, $\frac{6}{10} = \frac{3}{5}$ is a proportion. The same proportion could also be indicated 6:10::3:5, which is read "six is to ten as three is to five."

PROBLEMS

Reduce the following ratios and express in each of the three ratio forms:

1. (a) 18 to 54
   (b) 240 to 600
   (c) $800 to $4,800
   (d) 35 to 28
   (e) $32,000 to $20,000

2. (a) 9 to 15
   (b) $600 to $24,000
   (c) 720 to 1,200
   (d) 65 to 20
   (e) $22,000 to $5,000

3. Farnsworth Glass Co. employs 480 persons on first shift and 600 on second shift. What is the ratio of first to second shift employees?

4. Jacobs Parts Division employs 45 people in office and administrative positions and 600 people in the assembly plant. What is the ratio of "white collar" to "blue collar" workers?

5. Of the 70 persons working at Grayson Lumber Co., 42 have requested vacations during July. What is the ratio of July vacationers to those vacationing in other months?

6. Randolph & Cline employ 50 persons, of whom 36 have had at least some college training. What is the ratio of college-trained employees to non-college-trained personnel?

7. Sales of the Diversified Pool Corp. last season included $150,000 for prefab swimming pools and $350,000 for custom pools. What was the ratio of prefab sales to custom sales?

8. The Major Automobile Co. spent $6,440,000 for advertising in magazines and newspapers, and $2,800,000 for television commercials. What was the ratio of printed ad costs to TV advertising costs?

9. An insurance policy of $17,500 is to be divided between a son and mother in the ratio 2:5. How much will each receive?

10. An estate is to be divided between A and B in the ratio 2:3. What amount will each inherit, if the estate is valued at $37,000?

11. As a fund raising campaign, a civic club sold tickets to a barbeque dinner. Bob and Frank sold tickets in the ratio 5:4. If the two men together sold 108 tickets, how many did each sell?

12. The ratio of the values of dress sales to coat sales was 7:5. If total sales amounted to $900, how much was obtained from the sale of dresses and how much from coats?

13. The three top winners of a golf tournament will divide a $70,000 prize in the ratio 5:2:1. How much will each place receive?

14. Four children are to divide a $42,000 insurance benefit in the ratio 3:4:5:3. How much should each receive?

15. An advertising firm will divide an incentive bonus among four employees based on the number of new accounts each has obtained. If the personnel have signed 7, 3, 2, and 4 new accounts respectively, what is each person's share of the $12,800 bonus?

16. Three families are sharing the cost of a vacation according to the number of persons in each family. How much of the $275 trip should be paid by each family, if the families contain 3, 4, and 4 members, respectively?

4. REPEATING DECIMALS

Fractions are often easier to work with than decimals; thus, it is desirable that the student be capable of changing decimal numbers to their fractional equivalents.

Decimal numbers which terminate (or end) are easy to change to an exact fractional equivalent. The student is probably already familiar with the procedure—which is to pronounce the decimal value of the number and convert it to the fractional form. For example,

$$0.625 = 625 \text{ thousandths} = \tfrac{625}{1000} = \tfrac{5}{8}$$

Decimal numbers which neither terminate nor repeat themselves do not have an exact fractional equivalent. The only way to approximate the fractional value of such a number is to round it off at some digit and then treat it as though it had terminated. Thus,

$$0.624973\ldots = \text{approx. } 0.625$$
$$= \text{approx. } 625 \text{ thousandths}$$
$$= \text{approx. } \tfrac{625}{1000}$$
$$= \text{approx. } \tfrac{5}{8}$$

For any decimal number which does not terminate but which contains a *repeating* digit or series of digits, however, there exists a fraction which is exactly equal to the decimal number. The procedure for converting such a nonterminating, repeating decimal to its fractional equivalent employs some of the techniques of equation solving:

(a) Let N equal the nonterminating, repeating decimal number. Multiply the equation by 10, 100, 1,000, or by some multiple of 10—until the decimal point has passed to the right of *one complete repetition* of the repeating digits.

(b) Subtract some number from the number obtained in step 1 so that the difference is a *whole number*. Usually, one need only subtract N from the number obtained in step 1. However, it is sometimes necessary to multiply again by 10 or 100, so that the digits in the decimal portions of both numbers will repeat in the same order and the difference will be a whole number.

(c) Solve the difference of the two equations for N, thereby obtaining the fractional equivalent of the original decimal number.

Example One Convert $0.4444\ldots$ to its fractional equivalent.

$$\text{Let } N = 0.4444\ldots$$

(a) $$10N = 4.4444\ldots$$

(b) $$\begin{aligned} -\quad N &= -\;.4444\ldots \\ \hline 9N &= 4.0000\ldots \end{aligned}$$

(c) $$9N = 4$$
$$\frac{9N}{9} = \frac{4}{9}$$
$$N = \tfrac{4}{9}$$

Example Two What fraction is equivalent to $0.353535\ldots$?

$$\text{Let } N = 0.353535\ldots$$

(a) $\qquad 100N = \quad 35.353535\ldots$

(b) $\qquad \dfrac{-\quad N = -\ .353535\ldots}{99N = \quad 35.000000\ldots}$

(c) $\qquad 99N = 35$

$$\frac{\cancel{99}N}{\cancel{99}} = \frac{35}{99}$$

$$N = \tfrac{35}{99}$$

Find the fraction equal to $0.83333\ldots$.

Example Three

$$\text{Let } N = \quad 0.83333\ldots$$

(a) $\qquad 100N = \quad 83.3333\ldots$

(b) $\qquad \dfrac{-\ 10N = -\ 8.3333\ldots}{90N = \quad 75.0000\ldots}$

(c) $\qquad 90N = 75$

$$\frac{\cancel{90}N}{\cancel{90}} = \frac{75}{90}$$

$$N = \tfrac{5}{6}$$

Convert $0.625625625\ldots$ to a fraction.

Example Four

(a) $\qquad 1000N = 625.625625625\ldots$

(b) $\qquad \dfrac{-N = \quad -.625625625\ldots}{999N = 625.000000000\ldots}$

(c) $\qquad 999N = 625$

$$\frac{\cancel{999}N}{\cancel{999}} = \frac{625}{999}$$

$$N = \tfrac{625}{999}$$

Note: In order for a number to be classified as a repeating decimal, the *same digits* must repeat indefinitely in *the same order*. Thus $0.31313131\ldots$ is a repeating decimal; $0.31311311131111\ldots$ is not a repeating decimal.

PROBLEMS

Convert each decimal number to its fractional equivalent:

1. (a) $0.88888\ldots$
   (b) $0.696969\ldots$
   (c) $0.354354354\ldots$

(d) 0.42222 . . .
(e) 0.72666 . . .
(f) 0.171717 . . .

2. (a) 0.33333 . . .
(b) 0.181818 . . .
(c) 0.234234234 . . .
(d) 0.38888 . . .
(e) 0.71333 . . .
(f) 0.616161 . . .

3

Review of
Per Cent

LEARNING OBJECTIVES

Upon completion of Chapter 3, the student will be able to:

1. Define and use correctly the terminology associated with each topic.

2. a. Change a per cent to its equivalent decimal or fraction; or
   b. Change a decimal or fraction to its equivalent per cent.

3. Use an equation to find the missing element in a percentage relationship. (Ex: What per cent of 30 is 25?; or, 60 is 120% of what number?)

4. Use the basic equation form "___% of Original = Change?" to find the per cent of change (increase or decrease). (Ex: $33 is what per cent more than $27?)

5. Given a word problem containing per cents, express the problem in a concise sentence which translates into an equation that solves the problem.

6. Use aliquot parts of $1 and 100 in order to multiply efficiently.

No doubt, the student is familiar with the use of per cent, having studied it numerous times before. He knows that by using per cents he can compare, on the same terms, some numbers which may be quite different in size. The basis for comparing the numbers is to use a common denominator of 100 and compare the number of parts out of 100 that each is equivalent to.

Despite the fact that they have studied the topic before, per cent has proved to be a weak area for many students. Since a thorough knowledge of per cent is required in many areas of business, a review of the topic is in order.

1. BASICS

The use of per cent will be easier if the student remembers that *per cent* means *hundredths*. That is, the expression "24%" may just as correctly be read "24 hundredths." The word "hundredths" denotes either a common fraction with 100 as denominator or a decimal fraction of two decimal places. Thus

$$24\% = 24 \text{ hundredths} = \tfrac{24}{100} \text{ or } 0.24$$

Per cents must of course first be changed to either a fractional or decimal form before being used in a calculation. These conversions are simplified by applying the fact that "per cent" means "hundredths."

CHANGING A PER CENT TO A DECIMAL

When one thinks of per cent, he normally pictures the most common per cents—those between 1% and 99%. These are the per cents which occupy the first two places in the decimal representation of a per cent. (For example, $99\% = 99$ hundredths $= 0.99 =$ and $1\% = 1$ hundredth $= 0.01$.)

When converting per cents to decimals, if one always makes certain that the whole per cents between 1% and 99% are written in the first two decimal places, the other digits will naturally fall into the correct places.

Express each of the following per cents as a decimal:

(a) $7\% = 7$ hundredths $= 0.07$

(b) $63\% = 63$ hundredths $= 0.63$

(c) 32.9% (since $32\% = .32$) $= 0.329$

(d) 146% (since $46\% = .46$) $= 1.46$

(e) 115.25% (since $15\% = .15$) $= 1.1525$

(f) 3.02% (since $3\% = .03$) $= 0.0302$

(g) 0.4% (since $0\% = .00$) $= 0.004$

(h) 0.05% (since $0\% = .00$) $= 0.0005$

To change a fraction to a decimal, one must divide the numerator by the denominator: $\frac{n}{d}$ or $d\lceil n.$ When a fractional per cent is to be changed to a decimal, one may first convert the fractional per cent to a decimal per cent and then convert the decimal per cent to an ordinary decimal:

(i) $\frac{1}{8}\%$:

$$\left(\frac{1}{8} \text{ means } 8\overline{\smash{\big)}1.000} \overset{.125}{} = 0.125 \right)$$

Since $\frac{1}{8} = 0.125$

$\frac{1}{8}\% = 0.125\% = 0.00125$

(i) $\frac{2}{7}\%$:

$$\left(\frac{2}{7} \text{ means } 7\overline{\smash{\big)}2.00} \overset{.28\frac{4}{7}}{} = 0.28\tfrac{4}{7} \right)$$

Since $\frac{2}{7} = 0.28\tfrac{4}{7}$

$\frac{2}{7}\% = 0.28\tfrac{4}{7}\% = 0.0028\tfrac{4}{7}$

A fractional per cent always indicates a per cent less than 1% (or, we may say it indicates that fractional part of 1%). Thus $\frac{1}{2}\% = \frac{1}{2}$ of 1%; $\frac{3}{8}\% = \frac{3}{8}$ of 1%.

The process of converting a fractional per cent of a decimal may sometimes be shortened by writing two zeroes to the right of the decimal point (0.00) to indicate the per cent is less than 1%, and then writing the digits which one normally uses to denote the decimal equivalent of the fraction:

(k) $\frac{1}{4}\%$:

$$(\tfrac{1}{4}\% = \tfrac{1}{4} \text{ of } 1\%)$$

To show that the per cent is less than 1%, write   0.00

To indicate $\frac{1}{4}$, affix the digits 25

$$(\tfrac{1}{4} = 25 \text{ per cent}) \quad\quad 0.0025$$

Thus $\frac{1}{4}\% = 0.0025$

(l) $\frac{2}{3}\%$:

$$(\tfrac{2}{3}\% = \tfrac{2}{3} \text{ of } 1\%)$$

Indicate a per cent less than 1%   0.00

Affix the digits $66\frac{2}{3}$ $0.0066\frac{2}{3}$

CHANGING A PER CENT TO A FRACTION

After the per cent has been changed to hundredths (by dropping the per cent sign and placing the number over a denominator of 100), the resulting fraction should be reduced to lowest terms. (An improper fraction— one in which the numerator is greater than the denominator—is considered to be in lowest terms provided that it cannot be further reduced.)

Example Two   Convert each per cent to its fractional equivalent:

(a) $36\% = 36$ hundredths $= \frac{36}{100} = \frac{9}{25}$

(b) $6\% = 6$ hundredths $= \frac{6}{100} = \frac{3}{50}$

(c) $125\% = 125$ hundredths $= \frac{125}{100} = \frac{5}{4}$

Per cents containing fractions may be converted to their ordinary fractional equivalents by altering the above procedure slightly. The fact that "per cent" means "hundredths" may also be shown as

$$\% = \text{Hundredth} = \tfrac{1}{100}$$

Now let us apply this fact to change some fractional per cents to common fractions:

(d) $37\frac{1}{2}\% = 37\frac{1}{2} \times \frac{1}{100} = \frac{75}{2} \times \frac{1}{100} = \frac{75}{200} = \frac{3}{8}$

(e) $44\frac{4}{9}\% = 44\frac{4}{9} \times \frac{1}{100} = \frac{400}{9} \times \frac{1}{100} = \frac{400}{900} = \frac{4}{9}$

(f) $\frac{1}{4}\% = \frac{1}{4} \times \frac{1}{100} = \frac{1}{400}$

Decimal per cents may most easily be converted to fractions by applying the following procedure:

1. Change the per cent to its decimal equivalent.
2. Pronounce the value of the decimal; then write this number as a fraction and reduce it.

(g) 17.5%—

    1. Since $17\% = 0.17$, $17.5\% = 0.175$

    2. $0.175 = 175$ thousandths $= \frac{175}{1000} = \frac{7}{40}$

(h) 0.32%—

    Since $0\% = 0.00$, $0.32\% = 0.0032$

                      $= 32$ ten-thousandths

                      $= \frac{32}{10,000}$

                      $= \frac{2}{625}$

(i) 0.6%—

            $0.6\% = 0.006$

                   $= 6$ thousandths

                   $= \frac{6}{1000}$

                   $= \frac{3}{500}$

CHANGING A DECIMAL TO A PER CENT

Just as "per cent" means "hundredths," so *hundredths = per cent*. When a decimal number is to be changed to a per cent, the hundredths places of the decimal indicate the whole "per cents" between 1% and 99% ($0.01 = 1\%$, and $0.99 = 99\%$).

By first isolating the whole per cents between 1% and 99%, the student will have no difficulty in placing the other digits correctly.

If there is to be a decimal point in the per cent, it will come after the hundredth's place of the decimal number. (This is why it is sometimes said, "to change a decimal to a per cent, move the decimal point two places to the right.")

Express each of these decimals as a per cent:

    Example Three

(a) $0.44 = 44$ hundredths $= 44\%$

(b) $0.78\frac{1}{2} = 78\frac{1}{2}$ hundredths $= 78\frac{1}{2}\%$

(c) $0.09 = 9$ hundredths $= 9\%$

(d) 0.273 (since $0.27 = 27$ hundredths $= 27\%$) $= 27.3\%$

(e) 1.325 (given $1\widehat{3}25$; $0.32 = 32$ hundredths $= 32\%$) $= 132.5\%$

(f) 0.6 (given $0\widehat{6}$; $0.60 = 60$ hundredths $= 60\%$) $= 60\%$

(g) 0.0035 (given $0\widehat{00}35$; $0.00 = 00$ hundredths $= 0\%$) $= 0.35\%$

CHANGING A FRACTION TO PER CENT

To change a fraction to a per cent, apply the following rules:

1. Convert the fraction to its decimal equivalent by dividing the numerator by the denominator: $\frac{n}{d}$ or $d\,\overline{\rceil\,n}$.

2. Then change the decimal to a per cent, using the methods discussed above.

Example Four   Change each fraction to its equivalent per cent:

(a) $\frac{1}{8} = 8\,\overline{\rceil\,1.000}\;^{.125} = 0.125 = 12.5\%$

(b) $\frac{4}{13} = 13\,\overline{\rceil\,4.00}\;^{30\frac{10}{13}} = 0.30\frac{10}{13} = 30\frac{10}{13}\%$

(c) $\frac{8}{5} = 5\,\overline{\rceil\,8.00}\;^{1.60} = 1.60 = 160\%$

(d) $1\frac{2}{5}$ (since $\frac{2}{5} = 5\,\overline{\rceil\,2.00}\;^{.40} = 0.40$) $= 1.40 = 140\%$

or

$1\frac{2}{5} = \frac{7}{5} = 5\,\overline{\rceil\,7.00}\;^{1.40} = 1.40 = 140\%$

(e) $2\frac{1}{4}$ (since $\frac{1}{4} = 0.25$) $= 2.25 = 225\%$

or

$2\frac{1}{4} = \frac{9}{4} = 2.25 = 225\%$

PROBLEMS

Express each per cent as (1) a decimal, and (2) a fraction in its lowest terms:

1.	12%	4.	6%	7.	33.8%	10.	4.15%
2.	35%	5.	59%	8.	26.5%	11.	63.25%
3.	8%	6.	53%	9.	7.05%	12.	41.75%

13. 155%	18. 0.2%	23. $\frac{1}{4}$%	28. $22\frac{2}{9}$%
14. 145%	19. 0.72%	24. $\frac{3}{4}$%	29. $42\frac{6}{7}$%
15. 1.55%	20. 0.28%	25. $\frac{4}{5}$%	30. $83\frac{1}{3}$%
16. 1.45%	21. 162.5%	26. $\frac{3}{8}$%	31. $7\frac{1}{7}$%
17. 0.4%	22. 112.5%	27. $18\frac{2}{11}$%	32. $7\frac{1}{2}$%

Express each of the following as a per cent:

1. 0.45	9. 1.28	17. 0.008	25. $\frac{1}{6}$
2. 0.73	10. 2.35	18. 0.001	26. $\frac{3}{7}$
3. 0.05	11. 1.598	19. 0.0072	27. $\frac{8}{19}$
4. 0.07	12. 1.745	20. 0.0038	28. $\frac{12}{17}$
5. 0.813	13. 0.012	21. 2.6	29. $2\frac{1}{8}$
6. 0.395	14. 0.025	22. 4.6	30. $1\frac{3}{4}$
7. 0.067	15. 0.375	23. 0.4	31. $1\frac{7}{15}$
8. 0.028	16. 0.625	24. 0.7	32. $2\frac{5}{13}$

2. PER CENT EQUATION FORMS

All problems which involve the use of per cent are some variation of the basic per cent form: "Some per cent of one number equals another number." This basic per cent form may be abbreviated in equation form:

$$\text{\_\_}\% \text{ of } \text{\_\_} = \text{\_\_} \qquad \text{or} \qquad x\% \text{ of } y = z$$

Given in reverse order, the equation form is

$$\text{\_\_} = \text{\_\_}\% \text{ of } \text{\_\_} \qquad \text{or} \qquad z = x\% \text{ of } y$$

Since there can be only one unknown in an elementary equation, there are only three variations of the basic equation form: the unknown can be either (1) the per cent (or *rate*), (2) the first number (sometimes called the *base*), or (3) the second number (often called the *percentage*).

Equation-solving procedures which were studied earlier will be applied to solve percentage problems. Recall that before a per cent can be used in computation, it must first be changed to either a fraction or decimal. Conversely, if the unknown represents a per cent, the solution to the equation will be a decimal or fraction which must then be converted to the per cent.

(a) 30% of 24 is what number?

Example One

$$0.3 \times 24 = n$$
$$7.2 = n$$

(b) What per cent of 8 is 3?

$$r \times 8 = 3$$

or $\qquad 8r = 3$

$$\frac{\cancel{8}r}{\cancel{8}} = \frac{3}{8}$$

$$r = \tfrac{3}{8}$$

$$= 37\tfrac{1}{2}\%$$

(c) 25% of what number is 4?

$$\tfrac{1}{4} \times n = 4$$

or $\qquad \dfrac{n}{4} = 4$

$$\cancel{4} \times \frac{n}{\cancel{4}} = 4 \times 4$$

$$n = 16$$

Many of the formulas used to solve mathematical problems in business are nothing more than the basic per cent equation form with different words (or variables) substituted for the per cent and the first and second numbers. The methods used to solve the formulas are identical to those of Example One above.

One such formula is used to find "per cent of change" (that is, per cent of increase or decrease). In words, the formula can be stated, "What per cent of the original number is the change?" In more abbreviated form it is

$$\_\_\% \text{ of Original } = \text{ Change?}$$

Example Two

(a) What per cent more than 20 is 26?

1. *Original number.* To have "more than 20" implies that we originally had 20; thus 20 is the original number. In general, it can be said that the "original number" is the number which follows the words "more than" or "less than" in the stated problem.

2. *Change.* The "change" is the amount of increase or decrease which occurred. That is, the change is the numerical difference between the two numbers in the problem. (The fact that it may be a negative difference is not important to this formula.) Thus the change in this example is $26 - 20 = 6$.

$$\underline{}\% \text{ of Original} = \text{Change}$$
$$\underline{}\% \text{ of} \qquad 20 = 6$$
$$20x = 6$$
$$\frac{\cancel{20}x}{\cancel{20}} = \frac{6}{20}$$
$$x = \tfrac{3}{10}$$
$$x = 30\%$$

Thus, 26 is a 30% increase over 20.

(b) Eighteen is what per cent less than 24?

Original = 24 $\underline{}\%$ of Original = Change
Change = 24 − 18 $24r = 6$

= 6 $\frac{\cancel{24}r}{\cancel{24}} = \frac{6}{24}$

$$r = \tfrac{1}{4}$$
$$r = 25\%$$

Thus 24 decreased by 25% is 18.

This formula is often applied to changes in the prices of merchandise or stocks and to changes in volume of business from one year to the next.

PROBLEMS

1. 7% of 150 is what number?
2. 13% of 120 is what number?
3. $3\frac{1}{2}$% of 40 is what amount?
4. $7\frac{1}{2}$% of 60 is what amount?
5. 56% of 85 is how much?
6. 78% of 20 is how much?
7. How much is $\frac{1}{2}$% of 420?
8. How much is $\frac{1}{4}$% of 240?
9. What is $62\frac{1}{2}$% of 72?
10. What is $33\frac{1}{3}$% of 45?
11. 0.8% of 350 is what number?
12. 0.35% of 200 is what number?
13. What per cent of 45 is 36?
14. What per cent of 48 is 32?

15. What per cent of 36 is 45?
16. What per cent of 32 is 48?
17. What per cent of 60 is 33?
18. What per cent of 150 is 93?
19. 17 is what per cent of 68?
20. 12 is what per cent of 27?
21. 7.4 is what per cent of 185?
22. 5.4 is what per cent of 180?
23. 80 is what per cent of 50?
24. 40 is what per cent of 32?
25. 26% of what number is 39?
26. 44% of what number is 33?
27. 9% of what number is 25.2?
28. 3% of what amount is 4.5?

29. $22\frac{2}{9}\%$ of what number is 14?

30. $42\frac{6}{7}\%$ of what number is 9?

31. 9 is $1\frac{1}{2}\%$ of what amount?

32. 9 is $2\frac{1}{4}\%$ of what amount?

33. 105 is 150% of what number?

34. 27 is 135% of what number?

35. 1.4 is 0.4% of what amount?

36. 5.4 is 0.9% of what amount?

37. What per cent more than 30 is 40?

38. What per cent more than 24 is 36?

39. What per cent less than 40 is 30?

40. What per cent less than 36 is 24?

41. 87 is what per cent more than 60?

42. 63 is what per cent more than 45?

43. 30 is what per cent less than 75?

44. 32 is what per cent less than 50?

45. $42 is what per cent more than $36?

46. $54 is what per cent more than $42?

47. What per cent less than $500 is $496?

48. What per cent less than $600 is $597?

3. WORD PROBLEMS CONTAINING PER CENTS

Example One A stock which sold for $20.40 paid a $1.53 dividend. What per cent return did the stock pay?

$$\underline{\text{What per cent}} \text{ of } \underline{\text{cost}} \text{ was the } \underline{\text{dividend}}?$$

$$\underline{\quad}\% \text{ of } \$20.40 = \$1.53$$
$$20.40r = 1.53$$
$$\frac{20.40r}{20.40} = \frac{1.53}{20.40}$$
$$r = 0.075$$
$$r = 7.5\%$$

Example Two Thirty per cent of the cost of a trip was for food. If the food cost $15, what was the total cost of the trip?

$$30\% \text{ of the } \underline{\text{cost}} \text{ was } \underline{\text{food}}$$

$$30\% \times c = \$15$$
$$0.3c = 15$$
$$\frac{0.3c}{0.3} = \frac{15.0}{0.3}$$
$$c = \$50$$

Example Three Last year's sales were $25,000; this year's sales reached $26,500. What was the per cent increase in sales?

Original $= \$25,000$ $—\%$ of Original $=$ Change

Change $= \$26,500 - \$25,000$ $—\%$ of $\$25,000 = \$1,500$

$\qquad = \$1,500$ $25,000r = 1,500$

$$\frac{25,000r}{25,000} = \frac{1,500}{25,000}$$

$$r = 0.06$$

$$r = 6\%$$

What number decreased by 15% of itself gives 68?

Example Four

$$\underline{\text{What no.}} \quad \underline{\text{decreased by}} \quad \underline{(15\% \text{ of itself})} \quad \underline{\text{gives}} \quad \underline{68?}$$

$\quad\downarrow \qquad\qquad \downarrow \qquad\qquad\quad \downarrow \qquad\qquad \downarrow \quad \downarrow$

$\quad n \qquad\qquad - \qquad\qquad (0.15 \times n) \quad = \quad 68$

$\qquad\qquad\qquad\qquad\qquad n* - 0.15n \quad = \quad 68$

$\qquad\qquad\qquad\qquad\qquad\quad\; 0.85n \quad = \quad 68$

$$\frac{0.85n}{0.85} = \frac{68.00}{0.85}$$

$$n = 80$$

Tuition costs at a private college increased by 10 per cent this year. If tuition costs $\$1,045$ this year, how much was last year's tuition?

Example Five

$$\underline{\text{Old tuition}} \quad \underline{\text{increased by}} \quad \underline{10\% \text{ (of itself)}} \quad \underline{\text{equals}} \quad \underline{\text{new tuition}}$$

$\quad\downarrow \qquad\qquad \downarrow \qquad\qquad\quad \downarrow \qquad\qquad \downarrow \qquad\quad \downarrow$

$\quad T \qquad\qquad + \qquad\qquad (10\% \times T) \quad = \quad \$1,045$

$\qquad\qquad\qquad\qquad\qquad\; T + 0.1T \quad = \quad 1,045$

$\qquad\qquad\qquad\qquad\qquad\quad\; 1.1T \quad = \quad 1,045$

$$\frac{1.1T}{1.1} = \frac{1045.0}{1.1}$$

$$T = \$950$$

Note: Per cents are never used just by themselves. In an equation, any per cent used must be a per cent *of* ("times") some other number or variable.

PROBLEMS

1. There are 1,750 employees at Standard Tool & Dye Works, of which 721 belong to a union. What per cent of the total employees are union members?

    *Recall that $n = 1n$; thus $n - 0.15n = 1n - 0.15n$

$$= 1.00n - 0.15n$$

$$= 0.85n.$$

2. A realtor charges $510 to sell a house. If the sale price was $17,000, what per cent of the total purchase price is the realtor's fee?

3. In a research experiment, 18 of 50 participants had unpleasant dreams when they went to sleep immediately after a large meal. What per cent of the group had nightmares?

4. A family with a monthly spendable income of $750 averages $135 monthly for automobile expenses (car payment, insurance, gasoline, repairs, etc.). What per cent of their income is spent for car expenses?

5. An insurance salesman receives a $6\frac{1}{4}$% commission on all retirement annuity plans which he sells. When he sold a $72,000 annuity, what was his commission?

6. A construction company placed a bid of $750,000 for a college building. If they expected $8\frac{1}{3}$% of the bid to be net profit, how much net profit does the construction company hope to make on the building?

7. Sales taxes run 5% of the selling price of merchandise. If Canyon Hardware collected sales taxes totaling $367, how much total merchandise was sold?

8. Twenty per cent of graduates at a high school went to college the fall following graduation. If 55 people entered college, how many graduates were there?

9. Thirty-five per cent of the selling price of a transistor radio was gross profit. If an $8.40 gross profit was earned, what was the selling price of the radio?

10. The gross profit made on a pair of men's shoes was 15% of the cost. What had the shoes cost, if the gross profit was $3.30?

11. A down payment and closing costs amounted to 14% of the purchase price of a home. If these costs totaled $5,250, what was the purchase price?

12. A homeowner pays 1.45% of the assessed value of his home for property taxes. If his taxes were $174, what is the assessed value of his home?

13. Within the past five years, the average selling price of a car has increased from $2,500 to $3,500. By what per cent has the price increased?

14. During a clearance sale, the price of a dress was dropped from $36 to $27. What per cent reduction can the store advertise?

15. The cost-of-living index reveals that consumer expenses which cost $108 last year now cost $117 for the same items. What is the per cent increase?

16. After an efficiency study, office expenses were reduced from $5,000 a month to $4,250 a month. What per cent savings were realized?

17. A commercial property valued at $36,000 last year is listed at $28,000 on this year's balance sheet. What per cent depreciation was this?

18. Construction costs have risen so that a building which could have been built for $64,000 two years ago would now cost $72,000 to construct. What per cent rise in cost does this represent?

19. What number increased by $87\frac{1}{2}$% of itself yields 60?

20. What number increased by 40% of itself gives 49?

21. What expense decreased by 29% of itself yields $2,130?

22. What selling price reduced by 24% of itself yields $38?

23. The cost of a boat was increased by 25% of itself to obtain the selling price. If the boat sold for $2,500, what was the dealer's cost?

24. The cost of a lamp was increased by 15% of itself to get the selling price. What was the cost of the lamp, if the selling price was $23?

25. During a clearance sale, the regular price of a dress was reduced by 45% of itself. What was the regular price, if the sale price was $27.50?

26. After installing new equipment, the cost of manufacturing a machine was reduced by 10% of itself. If the new cost of manufacturing the machine is $144, what was the previous cost?

27. A sales representative's orders were 22% less than his quota. What was his quota, if his sales totaled $11,700?

28. This year's sales are 13% more than last year's sales. If the current sales are $452,000, what were last year's sales?

29. Twenty-two per cent of an employee's gross wages were withheld for income tax, social security, group insurance, etc. What were his gross wages, if $30.80 was withheld?

30. Forty-two per cent of the workers in a plant took their vacations during July. If 63 employees took July vacations, how many people are employed at the plant?

31. Rising costs, principally labor, have added $33\frac{1}{3}$% to the projected costs for the development of a new product, making the final cost $56,000. What was the initial cost estimated for the product?

32. Following a 25% reduction in price, a cookware set was sold for $36. What was the regular price of the set?

33. Because of an economic recession, a company was forced to reduce its work force from 560 employees to 350. What per cent reduction was this?

34. The value of a store's inventory increased from $30,000 to $32,400 during one six-month period. What per cent rise in value did this represent?

35. A gross profit of $225 was made on a sale of $750. What per cent of the selling price was the gross profit?

36. The salesman's commission on sales of $1,850 amounted to $148. What per cent of his sales was the commission?

4. ALIQUOT PARTS

A number which can be divided evenly (with no remainder) into another number is an *aliquot part* of that second number. Thus 3 is an aliquot part of 6 (because it divides into 6 exactly 2 times); 5 is an aliquot part of 15 (divides into 15 exactly 3 times); $8\frac{1}{3}$ is an aliquot part of 25 (divides into 25 exactly 3 times); and $12\frac{1}{2}$ is an aliquot part of 100 (divides into 100 exactly 8 times).

Strictly speaking, aliquot parts are denoted only by fractions with numerators of 1 ($\frac{1}{4}$ of \$1 = 25¢ and $\frac{1}{7}$ of 100 = $14\frac{2}{7}$). For convenience, however, multiples of aliquot parts are treated in the same manner ($\frac{2}{5}$ of \$1 = 40¢ and $\frac{7}{8}$ of 100 = $87\frac{1}{2}$).

For business applications, the aliquot parts of \$1 and of 100 are particularly useful. The following table lists some of the most frequently used aliquot parts of 100% and their multiples. The student should be certain that he has all of them memorized, for they will prove extremely useful in future chapters, as well as in this section.

The advantage of using aliquot parts is that it permits the substitution of fractions for their decimal equivalents—a substitution which usually proves to be a significant time-saver.

PER CENT EQUIVALENTS OF COMMON FRACTIONS

$\frac{1}{2} = 50\%$			
$\frac{1}{3} = 33\frac{1}{3}\%$	$\frac{2}{3} = 66\frac{2}{3}\%$		
$\frac{1}{4} = 25\%$	$\frac{3}{4} = 75\%$		
$\frac{1}{5} = 20\%$	$\frac{2}{5} = 40\%$	$\frac{3}{5} = 60\%$	$\frac{4}{5} = 80\%$
$\frac{1}{6} = 16\frac{2}{3}\%$	$\frac{5}{6} = 83\frac{1}{3}\%$		
$\frac{1}{7} = 14\frac{2}{7}\%$	$\frac{2}{7} = 28\frac{4}{7}\%$	$\frac{3}{7} = 42\frac{6}{7}\%$	
$\frac{1}{8} = 12\frac{1}{2}\%$	$\frac{3}{8} = 37\frac{1}{2}\%$	$\frac{5}{8} = 62\frac{1}{2}\%$	$\frac{7}{8} = 87\frac{1}{2}\%$
$\frac{1}{9} = 11\frac{1}{9}\%$	$\frac{2}{9} = 22\frac{2}{9}\%$	$\frac{4}{9} = 44\frac{4}{9}\%$	$\frac{5}{9} = 55\frac{5}{9}\%$
$\frac{1}{10} = 10\%$	$\frac{3}{10} = 30\%$	$\frac{7}{10} = 70\%$	$\frac{9}{10} = 90\%$
$\frac{1}{12} = 8\frac{1}{3}\%$			

Example One

(a) Multiply 376 by \$.25.

$$\$.25 = \tfrac{1}{4} \text{ of } \$1 \text{ or } \$\tfrac{1}{4}$$

Thus

$$376 \times \$.25 = 376 \times \$\tfrac{1}{4}$$
$$= \$94$$

This is accomplished in much less time than

$$
\begin{array}{r}
376 \\
\times\$.25 \\
\hline
1880 \\
752 \\
\hline
\$94.00
\end{array}
$$

(b) What is the price of 496 items at $37\frac{1}{2}$¢ each?

$$
\begin{aligned}
37\tfrac{1}{2}¢ &= \tfrac{3}{8} \text{ of } \$1 \\
&= \$\tfrac{3}{8} \\
496 \times 37\tfrac{1}{2}¢ &= 496 \times \$\tfrac{3}{8} \\
&\overset{62}{= 4\cancel{96} \times \$\tfrac{3}{8}} \\
&= \$186
\end{aligned}
$$

(c) Price 56 items @ $.42\frac{6}{7}$.

$$
\begin{aligned}
\$.42\tfrac{6}{7} &= \$\tfrac{3}{7} \\
56 \times \$\tfrac{3}{7} &\overset{8}{= \cancel{56} \times \$\tfrac{3}{7}} \\
&= \$24
\end{aligned}
$$

Sometimes, it is more convenient to consider the number of items purchased as an aliquot part of 100 items—that is, to price 100 items and then find the fractional part of that price.

Example Two

(a) Price 75 items @ $.64.

$$
75 \text{ items} = \tfrac{3}{4} \text{ of } 100 \text{ items}
$$

Thus

$$
\begin{aligned}
75 \times \$.64 &= \tfrac{3}{4} \text{ of } 100 \times \$.64 \\
&= \tfrac{3}{4} \times (100 \times \$.64) \\
&= \tfrac{3}{4} \times \$64 \\
&\overset{16}{= \tfrac{3}{4} \times \cancel{64}} \\
&= \$48
\end{aligned}
$$

(b) Find the price: 20 items @ $1.65.

$$
\begin{aligned}
20 \text{ items} &= \tfrac{1}{5} \times 100 \text{ items} \\
20 \times \$1.65 &= \tfrac{1}{5} \times 100 \times \$1.65 \\
&= \tfrac{1}{5} \times \$165 \\
&= \$33
\end{aligned}
$$

PROBLEMS

Price the following:

1. 372 @ $.25
2. 672 @ 37½¢
3. 144 @ $.62½
4. 182 @ 28⁴⁄₇¢
5. 225 @ $.33⅓
6. 36 @ 75¢
7. 126 @ $.14²⁄₇
8. 72 @ 8⅓¢
9. 576 @ $.55⅝
10. 168 @ 12½¢
11. 78 @ $.66⅔
12. 216 @ 44⁴⁄₉¢
13. 133 @ $.42⁶⁄₇
14. 120 @ 30¢
15. 84 @ $.08⅓

16. 64 @ 62½¢
17. 168 @ $.28⁴⁄₇
18. 152 @ 87½¢
19. 216 @ $.83⅓
20. 45 @ 33⅓¢
21. 324 @ $.16⅔
22. 10 @ $1.80
23. 40 @ $1.35
24. 50 @ 48¢
25. 75 @ 48¢
26. 25 @ $2.16
27. 60 @ $2.30
28. 20 @ 85¢
29. 80 @ $1.95
30. 75 @ $1.28

part two

ACCOUNTING MATHEMATICS

Basic Statistics and Graphs

LEARNING OBJECTIVES

Upon completion of Chapter 4, the student will be able to:

1. Define and use correctly the terminology associated with each topic.

2. Compute the three simple averages—mean, median, and mode.

3. Use a frequency distribution to determine mean, median, and modal class for grouped data.

4. Interpret index numbers and compute simple price relatives.

5. Construct the common types of graphs—bar, line, picture, rectangle, and circle graphs.

DECISIONS ABOUT THE FUTURE course which a business may take are rarely made without first consulting records indicating what past experience has been. When numerical records are involved, this data must be organized before it can present meaningful information. The process of collecting, organizing, tabulating, and interpreting numerical data is called *statistics*. The information presented as a result of this process is also known, collectively, as *statistics*. Statistics are invaluable to business in making comparisons, indicating trends, and analyzing facts affecting operations, production, profits, and so forth. However, the significance of statistics can often be realized more easily when the information is displayed in graph form. Thus graphs are an integral part of statistics.

1. AVERAGES

If one attempted to analyze a large group of numbers simultaneously, it would usually be impossible to obtain much useful information. Thus it is customary to condense such a group into a single number representative of the entire group. This representative number is generally some central value around which the other numbers seem to cluster; for this reason, it is called a *measure of central tendency* or an *average*. There are actually three averages: the *arithmetic mean* (or just the "mean"), the *median*, and the *mode*.

MEAN

The arithmetic mean is the common average with which the student is already familiar. It is the average referred to in everyday expressions about average temperature, average cost, the average grade on a quiz, average

age, etc. The mean is found by adding the various numbers and dividing this sum by the number of items.

Foremost Appliance Corp. had the following numbers of monthly appliance sales during 1968:

January	108	July	136
February	95	August	143
March	106	September	137
April	110	October	128
May	110	November	118
June	130	December	134

What was their average (mean) number of sales per month?

$$\frac{108+95+106+110+110+130+136+143+137+128+118+134}{12} = \frac{1455}{12}$$
$$= 121\tfrac{1}{4}$$

The mean number of sales per month was $121\tfrac{1}{4}$. Obviously, there cannot be $\tfrac{1}{4}$ of a sale, so we would say the average number of sales was 121. Notice that there was not a single month when exactly 121 sales were made. It is quite common for the "average" of a group of numbers to be a value not actually contained in the group; yet, this mean is still representative of the entire group.

WEIGHTED MEAN

The ordinary mean will present a true picture only if the data involved are of equal importance. If they are not, a weighted mean is needed. A *weighted arithmetic mean* is found by "weighting" or multiplying each number according to its importance. These products are then added and that sum is divided by the total number of weights.

A weighted average of particular importance to students is the *grade point average*:

The course credit and term grade for John Remington's fall semester are given below. At White Oaks Junior College, an A is worth 4 quality points; a B receives 3 points; a C, 2 points; and a D, 1 point. What is John's grade point average (average per credit hour) for the semester?

Credit Hours	Final Grade	Quality Points
5	A	4
3	C	2
3	B	3
2	C	2
1	D	1

If we simply found the average of John's quality points

$$\left(\frac{4 + 2 + 3 + 2 + 1}{5} = \frac{12}{5} = 2.40\right)$$

the result would be misleading because his courses are not of equal importance from a credit standpoint. We must therefore weight the quality
points for each course according to the number of credit hours each
course carries:

Credit Hours		Quality Points		
5	×	4	=	20
3	×	2	=	6
3	×	3	=	9
2	×	2	=	4
+1	×	1	=	+1
14				40

$$\tfrac{40}{14} = 2.857+ = 2.86$$

John's grade point average is thus 2.86 for the semester. This is quite
a bit better than the 2.40 obtained by the ordinary averaging method.

Example Three

Various furniture stores carry the same TV set. The price and number of
sets sold are shown below. What is (a) the average price per store and
(b) the average price per set sold?

Store	No. Sold	Price
A	60	$400
B	200	350
C	20	450
D	40	425
E	80	400

It may help first to analyze the question. The word "per" indicates
the division line of a fraction. The word following "per" tells which total
number of objects to divide by. Hence average price "per store" is found
by dividing by the total number of stores; and average price "per set" is
found by dividing by the total number of sets:

(a) Average price per store = $\dfrac{\text{Sum of prices at all stores}}{\text{Total number of stores}}$

$$\frac{\$400 + \$350 + \$450 + \$425 + \$400}{5} = \frac{\$2025}{5}$$

$$= \$405, \text{ average price per store}$$

(b) Average price per set $= \dfrac{\text{Sum of prices of all sets}}{\text{Total number of sets}}$

For this average, the various prices must be weighted according to the number of sets sold at each price.

Number		Price		
60	×	$400	=	$24,000
200	×	350	=	70,000
20	×	450	=	9,000
40	×	425	=	17,000
+80	×	400	=	+32,000
400				$152,000

$\dfrac{\$152,000}{400} = \$380$, average price per set

James Wyatt invested $2,000 in a business on January 1. On April 1, he withdrew $500; on May 1, he reinvested $1,200; and, on October 1, he invested another $1,000. What was his average investment during the year?

Example Four

$$\text{Average investment} = \frac{\text{Sum of investments of all months}}{\text{Total number of months}}$$

Before we can find the average investment, we must first determine the new balance after each change. Each succeeding balance must then be multiplied (weighted) by the number of months it remained invested.

Date	Change	Amount of Investment		Months Invested		
January 1		$2,000	×	3	=	$ 6,000
April 1	−$500	1,500	×	1	=	1,500
May 1	+1,200	2,700	×	5	=	13,500
October 1	+1,000	3,700	×	+3	=	+11,100
				12		$32,100

$\dfrac{\$32,100}{12} = \$2,675$ average investment

MEDIAN

Even when a group of numbers are of equal importance, the arithmetic mean may not convey an accurate description if the group contains a few values which differ greatly from the others. In such a case, the median may be the better average (or measure of central tendency). The *median* is the midpoint (or middle number) of a group of numbers. The median separates the group into two groups of equal size—one containing all the values larger than the median and the other containing all the values smaller than the median.

In order to find the median, the numbers must first be arranged in order of size (such an arrangement is called an *array*). If the group contains an odd number of entries, the median is the exact middle number. It may be determined quickly by dividing the number of entries by 2: the whole number next larger than the quotient indicates the position held by the median when the numbers are ordered in a series from smallest to largest.

When a group contains an even number of values, the median is also found by dividing the number of entries by 2: the median is then the arithmetic mean (average) between the number in this position and the next number when the numbers are ordered smallest to largest.

Example Five

The Wingate Insurance Agency has seven agents with the following respective years of experience: 5, 3, 22, 8, 6, 10, and 30. What is the median years' experience of these agents?

Notice that in this case the mean years' experience

$$\left(\frac{5 + 3 + 22 + 8 + 6 + 10 + 30}{7} = \frac{84}{7} = 12 \text{ years} \right)$$

does not give a very good description, since only two of the seven agents have had at least that much experience.

Since there are seven numbers in the group, divide 7 by 2: $\frac{7}{2} = 3+$;

the median is the next, or fourth number when the numbers are arranged in order of size. Hence, in the series 3, 5, 6, 8, 10, 22, 30, the median is 8 years of experience.

Example Six

The six employees of Givens Advertising Agency earn the following monthly salaries: $900; $650; $1,500; $800; $750; $700. What is the median salary?

$1,500
900
800⎫
750⎭
700
650

Since there are six employees, there is no exact middle number. The median is the arithmetic mean of the third and fourth salaries:

$\left(\frac{6}{2} = 3 \right)$

$$\frac{\$800 + \$750}{2} = \frac{\$1550}{2} = \$775$$

The median salary is $775. (The mean salary, however, is $883.33).

MODE

The *mode* of a group of numbers is the value (or values) which occurs most frequently. If all of the values in a group are different, there is no mode. A set of numbers may have two or more modes when these all occur an equal number of times (and more often than the other values).

The mode may be quite different from the mean and the median, and it does not necessarily indicate anything about the quality of the group. The mode's principal application to business, from a production or sales standpoint, is in indicating the most popular items.

The departments of Anderson Metal Works have safety records extending for the following number of weeks: 16, 23, 44, 13, 4, 23, 32, 28, 18, 36, 32, 21, 23, 40, and 27. What is the modal weeks without an accident?

Example Seven

The total weeks without an accident, arranged in order of length, are

44
40
36
32
32
28
27
23⎤
23⎬
23⎦
21
18
16
13
4

There are three departments with safety records of 23 weeks; hence 23 is the mode. If there were only two departments with 23-week records, then 23 and 32 would both be modes, since these records would be held by two departments each.

PROBLEMS

Find (1) the arithmetic mean, (2) the median, and (3) the mode for each of the following groups of numbers:

1. (a) 55, 72, 43, 81, 48, 51, 58, 72, 69, 62, 71
    (b) 5, 19, 38, 3, 10, 24, 15, 24, 41, 10, 14, 24, 19, 6
2. (a) $85; $106; $94; $110; $90; $98; $112; $105
    (b) 1,100; 1,450; 1,350; 1,500; 1,450; 250; 1,350; 1,600; 300; 1,350; 1,500; 1,450; 1,600
3. The credit hours and final grades for Nancy Hanes' five courses are listed below. She should receive 4 quality points for each A, 3 points for each B, 2 points for a C, and 1 point for a D.

(a) What are Nancy's average (mean) quality points per class?

(b) What is her quality point average for the semester (her average per credit hour)?

Credit Hours	Grade
5	B
4	A
3	C
3	B
1	C

4. A student taking five courses has made the grades listed below. The number of credit hours for each course is also indicated.

(a) What is the average (mean) grade per course?

(b) What is the mean grade per credit hour?

Credit Hours	Grade
3	86
3	88
2	95
3	90
4	77

5. Several different stores sell the same electric percolators. The number of percolators sold and the price charged by each store are shown below.

(a) What is the average price per store?

(b) What is the mean price per percolator sold?

Store	Number Sold	Price
A	8	$20.00
B	20	18.75
C	32	16.00
D	12	21.00
E	12	19.50
F	6	22.00

6. The Super Drug Store carries eight brands of toothpaste. The price per tube (family size) and number of tubes sold last month are given below.

(a) What was the mean price per brand?

(b) What was the average price per tube sold?

Brand	Tubes Sold	Price
S	60	95¢
T	90	89¢
U	100	88¢
V	75	90¢
W	40	95¢
X (sale)	400	50¢
Y	120	85¢
Z	50	98¢

7. The Standard Variety Store employs 15 people in the positions and at wages shown below.
   (a) What is the mean wage per job?
   (b) What is the mean wage per employee?

Job	No. in Job	Weekly Wages
Manager	1	$200
Cashiers	3	125
Clerks	8	80
Bookkeeper	1	105
Stockman	2	90

8. Jackson Realty Co. employs 10 persons. Their positions and weekly salaries are listed below.
   (a) Compute the mean wage per position.
   (b) What is the mean wage per person?

Position	No. in Position	Weekly Salary
Manager	1	$250
Agents	5	160
Maintenance	3	90
Bookkeeper	1	100

9. On January 1, Jim Clark invested $6,000 in a partnership. On April 1, he invested another $500 and, on June 1, he added $700. On November 1, he withdrew $200. His investment then remained the same until the end of the year. What was Clark's mean investment for the year?

10. Sam Winters invested $7,500 when he entered a partnership on January 1. On March 1, he withdrew $900. He reinvested $1,500 on August 1, but then he withdrew $300 on September 1. No other changes occurred until the end of the year. Find Winters' average (mean) investment during the year.

11. The ten employees of Greenfield Equipment earned the following monthly wages: $500, $425, $1,500, $440, $425, $400, $1,200, $450, $420, $780. What was the median wage?

12. Last week's total sales at the five branches of Richmond's were as follows: $35,700; $25,600; $72,800; $38,400; and $29,200. What was the median sales figure for the Richmond's stores?

13. The monthly sales report at Myers TV Sales showed the following models were sold: 1210, 1200, 1380, 1210, 1040, 1460, 1200, 1040, 1210, 1150, 1320, 1200, 1380, 1210, 1460, 1150, 1210, and 1460. What model represented the mode—the most popular set?

14. Employees at Empire Corp. work on production. The women sewing pockets completed the following numbers last week: 1,600, 1,580, 1,640, 1,580, 1,620, 1,640, 1,560, 1,640, 1,620, and 1,580. What was the modal number of pockets sewn?

15. The eight employees of an electrical firm are of the following ages: 55, 38, 29, 57, 33, 30, 26, and 36. What are—
    (a) the arithmetic mean,
    (b) the median, and
    (c) the mode of these ages?

16. The Smart Shop sold twelve dresses yesterday. The sales were $15, $18, $12, $20, $18, $60, $25, $20, $75, $18, $40, and $15. What was
    (a) the mean, and
    (b) the median price per dress?
    (c) Which price dress was most popular? (That is, what was the mode?)

17. Long's Shoe Store sold thirteen pairs of shoes at the following prices: $18, $25, $12, $14, $16, $22, $16, $36, $18, $28, $16, $30, and $22. Find
    (a) the mean price, and
    (b) the median price per pair.
    (c) How much is the most popularly priced style? (Or, what is the price of the modal style?)

18. The seven accountants in the Richfield Bank have had the following years of experience: 7, 4, 18, 24, 18, 6, and 10. Find
    (a) the mean,
    (b) the median, and
    (c) the mode of their years' experience.

2. AVERAGES (GROUPED DATA)

Business statistics often involve hundreds or thousands of values. If a computer is not available, it would be extremely time-consuming to arrange each value in an array. It is easier to handle large numbers of values by organizing them into groups (or *classes*). The difference between the upper and lower limits of each class is the *interval* of the class. (All classes of a problem usually have the same sized interval.) Each class is handled by first determining the number of values within the class (the *frequency*) and then using the *midpoint* (arithmetic mean) of the class as a basis for calculations. The entire process of classification and tabulation is called a *frequency distribution*.

The first step in making a frequency distribution is to decide what the class intervals shall be. For the sake of convenience, the intervals are usually round numbers. A tally is then made to classify each value; the total tally is the frequency *f* for each class. After the midpoint of each class is computed, the frequency is multiplied times the midpoint to obtain the final column of the frequency distribution.

Warren Specialties is a plant producing specialized furniture for medical and educational laboratories. Using a frequency distribution, find (a) the mean and (b) the median number of pieces processed last week by employees in the cutting department. Production was as follows:

Example One

240	209	246	247
285	225	242	261
256	227	251	239
233	260	274	245
267	219	266	282
278	250	293	248

The smallest number was 209 and the largest was 293; thus a table from 200 to 300 will include all entries. The difference between the upper and lower limits (300–200) gives a *range* of 100. We can conveniently divide this range into 5 classes. Since $\frac{100}{5} = 20$, each class interval will be 20.

Class Intervals	Tally	f	Midpoint	f × Midpoint
280–299	|||	3	290	870
260–279	++++		6	270	1,620
240–259	++++ ||||	9	250	2,250
220–239	||||	4	230	920
200–219	||	+2	210	+ 420
		24		6,080

The midpoint of each interval is the arithmetic mean of the lower limit of that class and the lower limit of the next class.

$$\left(\text{Example:} \frac{240 + 260}{2} = \frac{500}{2} = 250.\right)$$

The arithmetic mean of the frequency distribution is found by dividing the f × midpoint total by the total number of items (the frequency total). Thus

$$\frac{6,080}{24} = 253\tfrac{1}{3} \qquad \text{or} \qquad 253$$

The mean production in the cutting department was 253 pieces, to the nearest whole piece.

The median for grouped data is found as follows:

1. Divide the total number of items (total frequency) by 2. This quotient represents the position which the median holds in the tally.
2. Counting from the smallest number, find the class where this item is located, and determine how many values within this class must be counted to reach this position.
3. Using the number of values that must be counted (step 2) as a numerator, and the *total* number within the class as a denominator, form a fraction to be multiplied times the class interval.
4. Add this result to the lower limit of the interval to arrive at the median.

The median for this example is thus determined as follows:

1. $\dfrac{24}{2} = 12$: we are concerned with the twelfth item from the bottom.
2. The two bottom classes contain only $2 + 4 = 6$ items. We must therefore include 6 more items from the class 240–259.
3. There are 9 values in the class, and the class interval is 20. Hence

$$\frac{6}{9} \times 20 = \tfrac{2}{3} \times 20$$

$$= \tfrac{40}{3}$$

$$= 13\tfrac{1}{3}$$

4. $240 + 13\tfrac{1}{3} = 253\tfrac{1}{3}$ or   253

In this particular case, the median as well as the mean production in the cutting department was 253 pieces. In most instances, there will be some difference between the mean and the median.

Since a frequency distribution does not contain individual values, there is no single mode. However, the distribution may contain a modal class (the class containing the largest number of frequencies). The class interval 240–259 is the modal class of Example 1. This indicates that the most common production was between 240 and 259 pieces.

What is the median production if a frequency distribution contains 25 items and is distributed as follows?

Class Intervals	f
2,000–2,399	3
1,600–1,999	4
1,200–1,599	10
800–1,199	7
400– 799	+1
	25

The steps for solution (see Example 1) are as follows:

1. $\frac{25}{2}$ = 12.5; we must thus locate the class containing the item numbered 12.5.

2. The two bottom classes contain only 1 + 7 = 8 entries. Thus 12.5 is in the next class, 1,200–1,599, and 4.5 more values from this class complete the required 12.5.

3. The class 1,200–1,599 contains 10 items and the interval is 400. Thus

$$\frac{4.5}{10} \times 400 = 4.5 \times 40$$

$$= 180$$

4. The median production is 1,200 + 180 = 1,380 pieces.

Note: The median can also be found by counting *down from the top* to the required item, multiplying the obtained fraction times the interval in the usual manner, and then *subtracting* this product from the *upper limit* of the class. (For example, since the top two classes in Example 2 contain 3 + 4 = 7 items, 5.5 more values from class 1,200–1,599 must be included. Now, $\frac{5.5}{10} \times 400 = 220$; and 1,600 − 220 gives 1,380, as before.)

Use a frequency distribution to determine (a) the mean, (b) the median, and (c) the modal class for the following problems:

1. Use intervals of 0–19, 20–39, etc.

34	43	68	115	55	52
78	66	134	132	74	46
102	78	100	112	138	110
54	14	18	85	80	9
72	109	69	49	66	43
4	119	76	128	49	
121	36	81	23	27	
60	25	92	77	69	
85	42	99	31	135	

2. Use intervals of $50, starting with $700.

$ 870	$ 930	$1,150	$ 720	$1,000	$ 870
950	850	840	760	780	820
1,190	920	900	1,140	940	780
1,150	1,030	930	820	850	890
840	970	1,040	810	860	1,060
1,180	1,090	1,180	850	810	880

3. The following figures give the years of experience of the salesmen in district three of Nationwide Sales Corporation:

15	24	3	2	13	8
5	1	12	6	9	17
8	7	28	6	0	4
2	13	9	5	7	1
6	4	3	10	2	6
10	8	11	29	14	9

In completing a frequency distribution, use 3-year intervals to compute (a) the mean, (b) the median, and (c) the most common interval (modal class) of experience.

4. The salesmen for Top-Notch Business Forms are the following ages:

45	23	31	46	51	25
36	55	29	38	32	39
28	49	54	26	35	50
30	38	32	28	38	32
25	29	36	41	42	36
39	57	35	48	27	44

In making a frequency distribution, use intervals of 5 years (starting with 20 years) and determine (a) the mean, (b) the median, and (c) the most typical age group (modal class).

5. The following are annual salaries earned by the employees of Everett Textiles:

$ 9,700	$ 6,900	$11,700	$ 8,300	$12,200
7,500	6,400	8,500	9,200	8,200
10,100	8,200	6,200	7,600	7,400
8,600	9,800	14,000	6,700	9,800
10,900	13,900	12,500	7,200	8,900
14,100	8,800	9,200	6,700	6,300
7,800	7,100	6,900	8,000	6,800
9,200	9,000	7,100	6,900	7,300
8,500	6,700	7,800	10,200	6,900

Use intervals of $800, starting with the lowest wage, to determine (a) the mean, (b) the median, and (c) the most common wage bracket (modal class).

6. The total net weekly sales of the branches of Logan Corp. are listed below:

$23,600	$31,400	$34,300	$24,900	$24,700
28,500	39,600	26,800	33,600	37,400
36,800	36,200	29,300	35,800	31,100
34,100	27,700	39,700	32,200	24,800
24,800	22,000	34,500	25,000	36,400
27,000	30,100	39,400	28,600	28,300
35,300	25,900	27,700	34,000	35,700

Prepare a frequency distribution with $2,000 intervals, starting with the smallest sales figure. Find (a) the mean, (b) the median, and (c) the most common sales interval (modal class).

3. INDEX NUMBERS

An *index number* serves somewhat the same purpose as a per cent; that is, both are used to show the relative size or change between numbers, rather than showing the actual, numerical difference. Both allow the reader to make comparisons more easily in items over a period of time, whereas the actual, dollars-and-cents changes often could not be as readily analyzed. Index numbers are often used in business to depict long-range trends in prices or volume (of sales, production, etc.).

The simplest index number which can be computed involves a single item. Such a simple price index is sometimes called a *price relative*. This index is simply the ratio of a given year's price to the base year's price, multiplied by 100:

$$\text{Index number (or price relative)} = \frac{\text{Given year's price}}{\text{Base year's price}} \times 100$$

Example One Compute the price relatives (or index numbers) for eggs (per dozen), using 1963 as the base year:

Year	Price, in cents	Index, 1963 = 100
1963	50	
1965	49	
1968	53	

Year	Price Index
1963:	Base year = 100
1965:	$\frac{49}{50} \times 100 = 0.98 \times 100 = 98$
1968:	$\frac{53}{50} \times 100 = 1.06 \times 100 = 106$

The student should realize that this index is nothing more than a simple per cent, but written without the per cent sign. The question, "What per cent of the 1963 price was the 1968 price?" would be answered "106%."

An excellent example of the use of index numbers is the Consumer Price Index, published monthly by the U.S. Department of Labor (Bureau of Labor Statistics). The costs of a large number of goods and services are indexed for the United States as a whole and for selected cities and urban areas individually. Consider the following fictitious example. (Assume that this index is for the present year.)

Example Two

INDEX OF SELECTED EXPENSES IN SELECTED URBAN AREAS

DECEMBER, 19____
(1957–59 = 100)

Expense	U.S. Average	Atlanta	Chicago	Los Angeles	New York
Food	112.2	109.4	115.7	113.3	116.2
Housing	120.7	120.6	121.0	128.3	119.8
Medical	118.5	116.2	123.1	119.4	120.3

The index numbers presented above show the "current" cost of food, housing, and medical expenses as compared to the cost of these same expenses in each locality during the years 1957–1959. That is, the same food which cost $100 in Atlanta in 1957–59 would cost $109.40 at the present time. Similarly, medical services which cost $100 in Los Angeles in 1957–59 would now cost $119.40. (These indexes may also be read,

"Medical services which cost $10 in Los Angeles in 1957–59 would now cost $11.94.")

Various index numbers cannot be used for comparison among themselves unless they all refer to the same base amount. For instance, the table above gives the price index for housing in Chicago as 121.0 and in New York as 119.8. This means that housing which cost $100 in Chicago in 1957–59 would now cost $121.00 and that housing which cost $100 in New York in 1957–59 would now cost $119.80. It does *not* mean that $100 in 1957–59 would purchase the same quality of housing in both Chicago and New York.

Thus the table does not necessarily indicate that housing in Chicago costs more than housing in New York; it simply indicates that housing costs in Chicago have increased more rapidly since 1957–59 than have housing costs in New York. If an apartment in New York had cost substantially more in 1957–59 than did a similar apartment in Chicago, then the New York apartment would still be more expensive than the Chicago apartment (although the Chicago rent has increased faster than has the New York rent).

Hence the actual cost of living in New York as compared with the cost of living in Chicago (or any other locality) cannot be determined from the Consumer Price Index, but would have to be obtained from some other statistical source which contains an index of comparative living costs. Such an index released by the Bureau of Labor Statistics gives the following 1966 indexes, based on the U.S. urban average as 100:

Atlanta	Chicago	Los Angeles	New York
92	103	103	111

This comparative index enables us to determine that, for every $100 which the average urban family spends, the New York family spends $111, the Chicago and Los Angeles families spend $103, and the Atlanta family spends only $92—all to maintain the same standard of living.

Example 1 illustrated the computation of price relatives for only a single item—eggs. Actually, the term "index number" is often reserved for a number derived by combining several related items, each weighted according to its relative importance. For instance, the index numbers for food expenses in Example 2 are a composite of many different grocery items, each weighted according to its portion of the total food budget in a typical family (as one consideration). There are many methods for constructing such composite index numbers, all of which require more statistical knowledge than can be acquired in basic business math. Even for the same data, these composite index numbers vary significantly according to the method used; hence the best method to use depends upon careful analysis of the purpose which the index is intended to serve. Obtaining an accurate and meaningful composite index number is not a simple matter. Our "index number" problems will therefore be limited to simple price relatives.

PROBLEMS

Answer the following questions, based on the price index in Example 2:

1. (a) How much would a customer spend in Chicago today for food which cost $100 in 1957–59?
   (b) How much does the average U. S. citizen pay today for housing which cost $100 in 1957–59?
   (c) If a medical fee was $10 in 1957–59, how much should a New York resident expect to pay now for the same services?
   (d) In which area have food costs risen most rapidly?
   (e) In which area are medical expenses greatest?

2. (a) How much would the typical U.S. citizen pay today for medical expenses which cost $100 in 1957–59?
   (b) How much does a Los Angeles resident spend today for housing which cost $100 in 1957–59?
   (c) If groceries cost $10 in 1957–59, what would these same groceries cost in Atlanta now?
   (d) In which urban area have medical expenses increased most rapidly?
   (e) In which urban area is housing most expensive?

3. Compute index numbers (price relatives) for a box of bran cereal, with 1964 as the base year.

Year	Price, in cents	Index, 1964 = 100
1964	50	
1966	48	
1968	51	
1970	55	
1972	58	

4. Determine each price index for a can of frozen orange juice, using 1964 as the base year.

Year	Price, in cents	Index, 1964 = 100
1964	40	
1966	42	
1968	38	
1970	36	
1972	46	

5. Calculate each price relative for a box of detergent, using 1963 as the base year.

Year	Price, in cents	Index, 1963 = 100
1963	60	
1965	57	
1967	63	
1969	69	
1971	75	

6. Find each index number (price relative) for a pound of sirloin steak, using 1963 as the base year.

Year	Price, in cents	Index, 1963 = 100
1963	120	
1965	108	
1967	114	
1969	132	
1971	144	

4. GRAPHS

Many people read business statistics without fully realizing their significance. Statistics usually make a much stronger impression if they can be visualized. This is particularly true when the data are used to make comparisons among several items or when the statistics give the various parts that comprise a whole. The purpose of business graphs is to present such data in a manner that will be both accurate and easy to read. The most common graphs are *bar graphs*, *line graphs*, *picture graphs*, *rectangle graphs*, and *circle graphs*.

All graphs have certain things in common. Every graph should have a title so that the reader will know what facts are presented. A scale that will accurately present the information should be chosen; and the scale should be clearly labeled, starting at the point of origin (zero) for amounts of money, sales or production figures, and so on. Very large figures may be rounded off before graphing.

BAR GRAPHS

The bar graph uses either horizontal or vertical bars to compare several related values. These may be simple items (sales, production, or income, for example) over a period of years; or they may be several different items during a single time period.

Graph paper should be used whenever possible for bar graphs. (If a large graph is to be constructed for display purposes, one should first devise a scale before attempting to draw the graph.) If the data covers a period of months or years, the time factor is usually labeled on the horizontal scale.

Example One

The total amounts spent for new construction in Emerson City during the years 1968–1972 were as follows: 1968—$780,000,000; 1969—$825,000,000; 1970—$745,000,000; 1971—$793,000,000; and 1972—$840,000,000. Compare these expenditures on a bar graph.

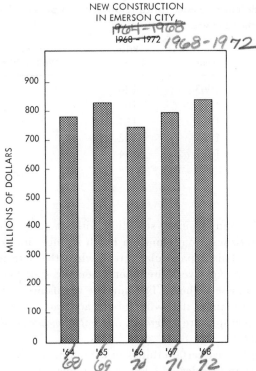

NEW CONSTRUCTION
IN EMERSON CITY,
1964–1968
1968–1972

Example Two

The U.S. Bureau of Census records the following per cents of farm and nonfarm occupations. Show these statistics in a comparative, vertical bar graph.

Year	Per Cent Farm Occupation	Per Cent Nonfarm Occupation
1920	27%	73%
1930	21	79
1940	16	84
1950	12	88
1960	9	91

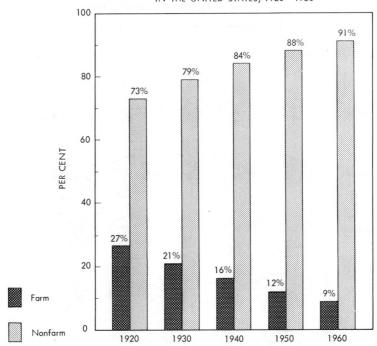

PER CENT OF FARM AND NONFARM OCCUPATIONS
IN THE UNITED STATES, 1920 - 1960

The five leading countries in the production of petroleum in 1964 were (in millions of metric tons) the United States—377; U.S.S.R.—224; Venezuela—178; Kuwait—107; and Saudi Arabia—86. Represent this production on a bar graph.

Example Three

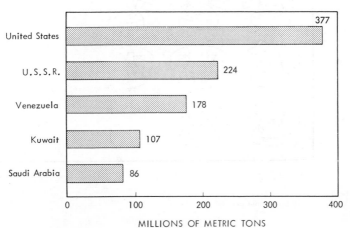

PETROLEUM PRODUCTION,

1964

MILLIONS OF METRIC TONS

COUNTRIES HAVING THE MOST TELEPHONES
PER 100 POPULATION, 1964

United States

Sweden

New Zealand

Canada

Switzerland

Denmark

Iceland

Australia

Norway

United Kingdom

 = 10 telephones per 100

Picture Graphs

The picture graph is a variation of the bar graph in which an appropriate picture is used to represent a specified quantity. The picture is then drawn the required number of times to depict each of the totals included in the graph.

Example Four

In 1964, the number of telephones per 100 persons in the countries having the most telephones was reported as follows: United States—46; Sweden— 42; New Zealand—37; Canada—36; Switzerland—36; Denmark—28; Iceland—28; Australia—24; Norway—24; United Kingdom—18. Compare these on a picture graph (see page 72).

Line Graphs

The line graph usually records change (in sales, production, income, etc.) over a period of time. The only basic difference between it and the vertical bar graph is that, instead of having bars that come up to the various values, the values are connected by a line. The line may be broken or unbroken, straight or curved. Two or more related statistics are often presented on the same line graph.

Line graphs should ordinarily be drawn on graph paper. After the scale of values has been labeled (time should be on the horizontal scale), locate the appropriate values and mark each with a dot. Finally, connect the dots with a line. (When the graph contains more than one line, be sure to make each line distinct and to identify each.)

Example Five

The net sales of Dow Manufacturing Co. for the 12 months of 1971 were as follows: January—$150,000; February—$145,000; March—$148,000; April—$155,000; May—$163,000; June—$172,000; July—$175,000; August—$169,000; September—$162,000; October—$157,000; November—$151,000; December—$158,000. Show the sales progress on a line graph.

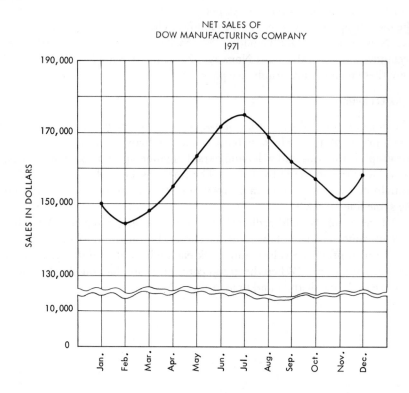

NET SALES OF
DOW MANUFACTURING COMPANY
1971

Notice in the graph of Example Five that a break in the scale was used to eliminate unused space. Every graph should show the point of origin ($0 or 0%, for example) in order to establish the scale for the reader.

Example Six

Williams Electric Co. recorded the following totals of net sales, cost of goods sold, and net profit during a five-year period:

	1968	1969	1970	1971	1972
Net sales	$70,000	$76,000	$93,000	$85,000	$88,000
Cost of goods	33,000	35,000	39,000	46,000	38,000
Net profit	3,000	5,000	10,000	4,000	9,000

Represent these business facts on a line graph.

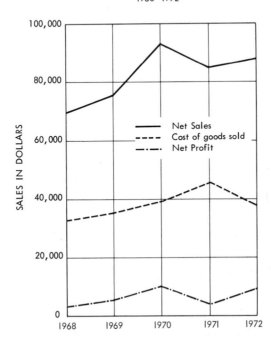

SALES ANALYSIS
WILLIAMS ELECTRIC COMPANY
1968 -1972

RECTANGLE GRAPHS

The rectangle graph presents the breakdown of a whole into its various parts. (For example, it may show what portion of a budget is spent for each item.) Thus the entire rectangle represents 100%, and each item should occupy an area proportional to its percentage of the total.

To prepare a rectangle graph, first determine what per cent of the total each item represents (if this is not given). Then draw a rectangle sufficiently large to include all items. If graph paper is used, a vertical scale of 100 is helpful in marking off the percentages. If plain paper is used, each per cent should be multiplied times the length of the rectangle to obtain the length of each part.

Example en During 1972, the various departments of A. B. Chambers Department Store accounted for the following per cents of the store's total net sales: ladies' ready to wear—25%; men's ready to wear—20%; shoes—15%; housewares—30%; accessories—10%.

A. B. CHAMBERS DEPARTMENT STORE,
Departmental Per Cents of 1972 Net Sales

25%	Ladies' Ready to Wear
20%	Men's Ready to Wear
15%	Shoes
30%	Housewares
10%	Accessories

CIRCLE GRAPHS

Like the rectangle graph, the circle graph (also called a "pie chart") depicts the relationship among the various parts that comprise a certain total.

Before constructing the graph, convert each item to its per cent of the total. Multiply each per cent times 360° to determine the number of degrees required for each item. Use a compass to draw the circle, and use a protractor to measure the number of degrees needed for each part of the graph.

Example Eight

Gaines-Howard Men's Store had the following operating expenses for October, 1971. Represent these on a circle graph.

Expense	Amount
Salaries	$6,200
Rent	1,500
Utilities	1,000
Office supplies	300
Advertising	900
Other	+ 100
Total	$10,000

Each expense must first be converted to a rate (per cent) of the total operating expense by answering the question, "What per cent of the total expense is each separate expense?"

$$\_\% \text{ of total} = \text{Each expense}$$
$$\_\% \text{ of } \$10,000 = \text{Each expense}$$
$$10,000r = \text{Each expense}$$
$$r = \frac{\text{Each expense}}{10,000}$$

Thus: Salaries $= \dfrac{6,200}{10,000} = 62\%$; Rent $= \dfrac{1,500}{10,000} = 15\%$, etc.

Each expense would require the following number of degrees:

Salaries	62% of 360° = 223.2° or	223°
Rent	15% of 360° =	54°
Utilities	10% of 360° =	36°
Office Supplies	3% of 360° = 10.8° or	11°
Advertising	9% of 360° = 32.4° or	32°
Other	+ 1% of 360° = 3.6° or	+ 4°
	100%	360°

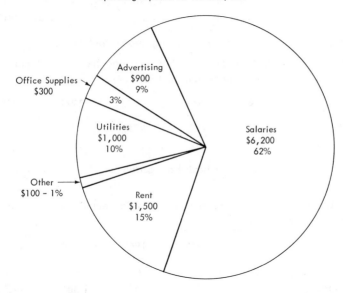

GAINES–HOWARD MEN'S STORE,
Operating Expenses for October, 1971

PROBLEMS

1. Evans Heating and Air Conditioning Distributors sold the following number of central air conditioning units over a ten-year period: 1962—52; 1963—69; 1964—65; 1965—90; 1966—98; 1967—101; 1968—133; 1969—148; 1970—165; 1971—197. Prepare a vertical bar graph to compare these sales totals.

2. The total net sales of Kost-less, Inc., during 1964–1971 were as follows:

1964	$ 78,000	1968	$173,000
1965	101,000	1969	169,000
1966	110,000	1970	171,000
1967	160,000	1971	184,000

Represent these sales on a vertical bar graph.

3. The mean wages in various job categories at Glendale Sales were as follows:

Executive	$18,500	Office	$7,000
Design	12,500	Shipping	5,000
Sales	10,000	Maintenance	4,000
Production	7,500		

Use a horizontal bar graph to depict these salary differences.

4. The ten largest cities of the world and their approximate populations are:

Shanghai	12,000,000	Moscow	6,400,000
Tokyo	8,900,000	Bombay	4,200,000
London	8,100,000	Cairo	4,000,000
New York	7,800,000	Tientsin (China)	4,000,000
Peking	7,000,000	Chicago	3,600,000

Construct a horizontal bar graph showing these populations.

5. The Majestic Corporation employed the following per cents of male and female administrative personnel during 1968–1972:

	1968	1969	1970	1971	1972
Male	98%	95%	87%	82%	78%
Female	2	5	13	18	22

Construct a comparative, vertical bar graph to show these employee per cents.

6. Great Lakes Appliance Co. records the following number of Sales to new and to repeat customers:

	1967	1968	1969	1970	1971
New	52	65	68	81	90
Repeat	18	25	33	36	42

Prepare a comparative, vertical bar graph to illustrate this indication of customer satisfaction.

7. The number of cars sold during March at the five locations of Randolph Motors was as follows:

Location	Sales
A	82
B	78
C	60
D	55
E	40

In preparing a picture graph to illustrate these sales, let each picture represent 10 sales.

8. Net sales of apples from the five warehouses of Flavor-Fresh Fruit Company were as follows:

Warehouse	Net Sales
#1	$35,000
#2	42,000
#3	30,000
#4	24,000
#5	8,000

Construct a picture graph, letting each picture symbolize $5,000 in net sales.

9. On a line graph, show the net sales each month during 1971 at Stacy's Department Store:

January	$305,000	July	$225,000
February	239,000	August	298,000
March	203,000	September	311,000
April	165,000	October	287,000
May	280,000	November	346,000
June	262,000	December	394,000

10. The total number of new cars sold by Crown Motor Corporation during a nine-year period is listed below. Present this information on a line graph.

1964	7,600	1969	10,500
1965	8,100	1970	10,200
1966	10,300	1971	11,800
1967	10,700	1972	12,900
1968	11,400		

11. The Quality Life Insurance Company issued the following number of new policies each year during a ten-year period:

	Ordinary Life	Limited Payment	Term
1963	70,500	42,000	27,000
1964	72,000	45,000	29,500
1965	76,500	38,000	30,000
1966	77,500	39,500	30,000
1967	79,000	39,500	37,500
1968	82,500	40,500	33,000
1969	96,000	43,000	32,000
1970	85,000	41,500	31,000
1971	88,500	40,500	34,500
1972	90,500	40,000	36,500

Plot these policies on the same line graph.

12. Prepare a line graph to show how a sustained advertising campaign affected net sales, cost of goods sold, and net profit for Elite Cosmetics over a six-year period.

	Net Sales	Cost of Goods	Advertising	Net Profit
1966	$120,000	$ 60,000	$ 1,000	$ 7,200
1967	126,000	65,000	5,000	8,000
1968	150,000	96,000	5,000	10,000
1969	184,000	110,000	8,000	15,600
1970	205,000	102,000	10,000	18,000
1971	210,000	120,000	12,000	15,000

13. The various departments of Food King Grocery accounted for the following per cents of their total sales.

Meat and dairy	30%
Produce	25
Canned goods	20
Frozen foods	15
Miscellaneous	10

Present this information on a rectangle graph.

14. Each dollar of income at the Westholme Gazette is derived as follows: advertising—53¢; subscription sales—32¢; news-stand sales—12¢; other —3¢. Depict this information on a rectangle graph.

15. The average consumer spends each dollar of income after taxes as follows:

Food and tobacco	25%
Clothing	10
Housing	30
Medical and personal	13
Transportation	14
Recreation	6
Other	2

Construct a circle graph showing this distribution.

16. Analysis of a baby cereal reveals the following content: protein—6%; fat—5%; carbohydrates—77%; crude fibers—1%; minerals—5%; mois- ture—6%. Make a circle graph showing this analysis.

17. Kestler Appliances, Inc. sold the following number of major appliances during 1972:

Ranges	280	Washers	210
Refrigerators	300	Dryers	120
Freezers	90		

Compare these sales on a circle graph.

18. During 1971, McCall's, Inc. had the following operating expenses. Prepare
a circle graph to compare these expenses.

Expense	Amount
Salary	$20,000
Rent	6,500
Taxes and insurance	12,000
Utilities	2,500
Depreciation	3,000
Advertising	4,000
Miscellaneous	2,000

5

Taxes

LEARNING OBJECTIVES

Upon completion of Chapter 5, the student will be able to:

1. Define and use correctly the terminology associated with each topic.

2. Compute sales tax, either
   a. Using a table, or
   b. Based on a percentage rate.

3. Find the marked price of an item, given (1) the sales tax rate and (2) the total tax or the total price.

4. Express a given (decimal) property tax rate
   a. As a per cent,
   b. As a rate per $100,
   c. As a rate per $1,000, and
   d. In mills.

5. Using the property tax formula $R \cdot V = T$ and given two of the following items, determine the unknown
   a. Property tax,
   b. Tax rate, or
   c. Assessed value of property.

INCREASED GOVERNMENT ACTIVITY (at Federal, state, and local levels) has made taxes—personal as well as business—an integral part of modern life. Two of the most common taxes are the sales tax and the property tax. The sales tax has become an everyday part of commerce. Property owners, including business organizations, must pay a property tax on their possessions. The following sections present the calculation of sales tax and property tax. (A third important tax is income tax. However, any significant study of income tax would require an entire course by itself and could not be accomplished in one unit of a business math course. A following chapter, "Wages and Payrolls," includes the taxes which must be deducted from payrolls.)

1. SALES TAX

A large majority of state legislatures has approved taxes on retail sales as a means of securing revenue. Retail merchants are responsible for collecting these taxes at the time of each sale and relaying them to the state. In some states, the legislatures have also allowed their cities the option of adopting a municipal sales tax in order to obtain local funds. The Federal government also requires the collection of an excise tax on the manufacture of certain products and the sale of some facilities and services.

There are two basic ways in which state sales taxes are established: (1) A few states have a tax which is a specified number of cents per whole dollar of the retail price, and tax on the extra cents is paid according to an arbitrarily adopted chart. (2) In most states, the sales tax is a specified per cent of the selling price. (Even in these states, however, the tax may follow a nonpercentage chart for sales under one dollar.) Most Federal taxes are also calculated on a percentage basis.

Sales taxes ordinarily apply only to sales made within the jurisdiction of the taxing body. Thus merchandise sold outside a state (such as by mail or by telephone) is not usually subject to that state's sales tax. Similarly, the municipal tax is not charged on goods delivered outside the city. In both instances, however, the tax would apply if merchandise were bought in person by a nonresident.

In areas subject to sales tax, charts are available so that the cashier may simply "look up" the tax. These charts eliminate the problem of rounding off the tax to the next cent, by listing consecutive price intervals and indicating the tax to be charged in each interval. (Sales tax charts are used whether the intervals are calculated on a percentage basis or are arbitrarily fixed.) Table 5-1 illustrates a sales tax table with arbitrarily fixed intervals, including a municipal tax. Tax intervals for sales made in the city are on the right; and intervals for sales made in the state (but outside the city limits) are on the left.

TABLE 5-1: SALES TAX

Sales Tax Intervals			
Sales Made Within State		Sales Made Within City	
Per whole dollar: 3¢		Per whole dollar: 4¢	
Tax on additional cents:		Tax on additional cents:	
Interval	Tax	Interval	Tax
$.00–$.09	0	$.00–$.09	0
.10– .39	1¢	.10– .39	1¢
.40– .69	2¢	.40– .49	2¢
.70– .99	3¢	.50– .69	3¢
		.70– .99	4¢

Seymore Lamp and Lighting Specialties made the following sales: (a) a $25.55 lamp, sold within the city; (b) a $79.65 chandelier, delivered to a resident of a neighboring city; and (c) a $16.53 lamp globe, ordered by telephone from another state. How much sales tax must be charged for each sale? (Use the tax schedule in Table 5-1.)

Example One

(a) Since this $25.55 sale was made within the city, the municipal tax applies:

$$
\begin{aligned}
25 \times 4\text{¢} &= \$1.00 \\
\$.55 \text{ (see table)} &= \underline{+.03} \\
\text{Total sales tax} &= \$1.03
\end{aligned}
$$

(b) The $79.65 chandelier is subject only to the state sales tax:

$$
\begin{aligned}
79 \times 3\text{¢} &= \$2.37 \\
\$.65 \text{ (see table)} &= \underline{+.02} \\
\text{Total sales tax} &= \$2.39
\end{aligned}
$$

(c) No sales tax will be charged on the lamp globe, since this sale was made out of state.

Example Two A 3% sales tax must be charged on all sales made by Cansler Co. (a) How much tax must be charged on a $15.44 sale? (b) The sales tax on a radio was $1.05. What was the price of the radio?

(a) The tax is 3% of the price of the merchandise. (Sales tax is always rounded to the next cent if the third decimal place is 5 or more.) Thus

$$
\begin{aligned}
\text{tax} &= 3\% \times \text{price} \\
&= 0.03 \times \$15.44 \\
&= \$.46
\end{aligned}
$$

The sales tax is $.46.

(b) The same formula is used to find the price when the sales tax is given. Since the tax was $1.05,

$$
\begin{aligned}
3\% \times \text{Price} &= \text{Tax} \\
3\% \times \text{Price} &= \$1.05 \\
.03p &= 1.05 \\
p &= \$35
\end{aligned}
$$

The radio was priced at $35; thus the total price of the radio, including the sales tax, was $36.05.

Example Three The total price of a coat, including a 4% sales tax, was $46.80. What was the marked price of the coat?

Since it is known that the sales tax was 4% of the marked price, the marked price is found as follows:

$$
\begin{aligned}
\text{Marked price} + \text{Sales tax} &= \text{Total price} \\
\text{price} + 4\% \text{ of price} &= \text{Total} \\
p + .04p &= \$46.80 \\
1.04p &= 46.80 \\
p &= \frac{46.80}{1.04} \\
p &= \$45.00
\end{aligned}
$$

The marked price of the coat was $45.00.

Note: Please observe that the sales tax is 4% of the marked price, *not* 4% of the total price. Therefore, problems of this type *cannot* be solved by taking 4% of the total price and subtracting to find the marked price. The results would be close, but they would always differ by a few cents; hence they would always be wrong. (The reader is invited to try a few examples if he is still skeptical!)

PROBLEMS

Compute the missing items in the following:

		Marked Price	Location	Sales Tax Rate	Sales Tax	Total Price
1.	(a)	$ 5.79	City	(Table 5-1)		
	(b)	18.33	State	(Table 5-1)		
	(c)	46.55	Out of State	(Table 5-1)		
	(d)	32.25	—	3%		
	(e)		—	4%	$1.10	
	(f)		—	2%	.86	
	(g)		—	5%		$71.40
	(h)		—	4%		25.83
2.	(a)	$14.59	City	(Table 5-1)		
	(b)	89.25	State	(Table 5-1)		
	(c)	32.05	Out of State	(Table 5-1)		
	(d)	16.75	—	2%		
	(e)		—	4%	$.12	
	(f)		—	5%	.95	
	(g)		—	3%		$61.80
	(h)		—	2%		26.52

3. Fire-Brite Wholesale Jewelers made the following sales:
   (a) a local sale of $125.50;
   (b) a $48.89 sale by mail from another city;
   (c) a $73.29 order by phone from an adjoining state.
   If the sales tax rates in Table 5-1 apply in this location, compute the sales tax and the total price (tax included) to be charged for each sale.

4. Wilcox TV Sales Corp. is in an area subject to the sales tax shown in Table 5-1. Find the sales tax and the total price that must be collected on the following purchases:
   (a) $219.50 within the city;
   (b) $350.20 on a telephone order from another city in the state;
   (c) $155.95 by an order from another state.

5. Find the sales tax and the total price to be charged on an item marked $28.95, if a 4% sales tax is required.

6. If a 5% sales tax is collected, determine the sales tax and the total price on a toaster marked $16.95.

7. A 3% sales tax on a purchase amounted to $1.41.
   (a) What was the marked price of the merchandise?
   (b) What was the total price including tax?

8. The 3% sales tax on a wall clock was $.54.
   (a) Find the marked price of the clock.
   (b) What was the total price of the clock, including the sales tax?

9. The import duty on a foreign camera was $9.75. If a 15% import duty was charged—
   (a) What was the original value of the camera?
   (b) What is the imported value, including the tax?

10. A sales tax of $7.30 was collected on the sale of a refrigerator. If the sales tax rate was 2%—
   (a) What was the marked price of the refrigerator?
   (b) What was the total cost, including tax?

11. The total cost of a golf bag was $33.60, including tax. If the sales tax rate was 5%—
   (a) What was the marked price of the bag?
   (b) How much sales tax was charged?

12. The total cost of an iron, including a 3% sales tax, was $21.63.
   (a) What was the marked price of the iron?
   (b) How much was the sales tax?

13. A living room chair cost $130.00, including a 4% sales tax.
   (a) What was the selling price of the chair?
   (b) What was the amount of sales tax paid?

14. After a 4% sales tax was added, the total cost of a set of stainless steel flatware was $50.96.
   (a) How much did the set cost before the tax?
   (b) How much sales tax was paid?

15. The total price for some camping equipment was $121.75, including a 3% sales tax.
   (a) Determine the marked price of the merchandise.
   (b) How much tax did the total price include?

16. The total cost of a blender was $25.74, including a 4% sales tax.
   (a) How much was the blender before the tax was added?
   (b) What amount of sales tax was required?

17. After a 5% sales tax was added, a transistor tape recorder sold for $82.47.

(a) Determine the marked price of the recorder.

(b) How much tax did the total price include?

18. The total charge for a coat, including the 4% sales tax, was $54.34.

(a) What was the marked price of the coat?

(b) What amount of sales tax was paid?

19. A telephone bill was $9.66, including a 5% state sales tax and a 10% Federal utilities tax.

(a) What was the regular monthly charge for telephone service?

(b) How much state tax was paid?

(c) What was the Federal tax?

20. An airplane ticket cost $189. This included a 3% state sales tax and a 5% Federal excise tax.

(a) What was the regular price of the ticket?

(b) How much was the state sales tax?

(c) How much Federal tax was charged?

2. PROPERTY TAX

The typical means by which counties and cities secure revenue is the property tax. This tax applies to real estate (land and the building improvements on it), as well as to personal property (cash, cars, household furnishings, appliances, jewelry, etc.). Often, the real-property tax and personal-property tax are combined into a single assessment. Two things affect the amount of tax that will be paid: (1) the assessed value of the property, and (2) the tax rate.

Property tax is normally paid on the *assessed value* of property, rather than on its market value. Assessed value in any given locality is usually determined by taking a per cent of the estimated fair market value of property. The per cent used varies greatly from locality to locality, although assessed valuations between 40% and 60% are probably most common. Thus the tax rate alone is not a dependable indication of how high taxes are in a community; one must also know how the assessed value of property is determined. Even though two towns have the same tax rate, taxes in one of the towns might be much higher if property there is assessed at a higher rate. Similarly, a community with a higher tax rate than surrounding areas might actually have lower taxes, if property there is assessed at a much lower value.

There are several ways in which the tax *rate* of an area might be expressed: as a per cent; as an amount per $100; as an amount per $1,000; or in *mills*. (Just as "per cent" means "hundredths" and indicates two decimal places, "mills" means "thousandths" and indicates three decimal places. Thus expressing a tax rate in mills is another way of expressing it as a rate per $1,000.)

The county commissioners, city councilmen, or other board responsible for establishing the tax rate uses the following procedure: After the budget (total tax needed) for the coming year has been determined, and the total assessed value of property in the area is known, the rate is computed:

$$\text{Rate} = \frac{\text{Total tax needed}}{\text{Total assessed valuation}}$$

Example One

The city of Swathmore has an annual budget of $3,000,000. If the property in Swathmore is assessed at $200,000,000, what will the tax rate be next year? Express the rate (a) as a per cent; (b) as an amount per $100; (c) as an amount per $1,000; and (d) in mills.

$$\text{Rate} = \frac{\text{Total tax needed}}{\text{Total assessed value}}$$

$$= \frac{\$3,000,000}{\$200,000,000}$$

$$\text{Rate} = 0.015$$

(a) The property tax rate is 1.5% of the assessed value of property.

(b) When the rate is to be expressed per $100, the decimal point is marked off after the hundredths place. Thus the rate is $1.50 per C (per $100).

(c) The rate per $1,000 is found by marking off the decimal point after the thousandths place. Hence the rate is $15.00 per M (per $1,000).

(d) The rate in mills is found as in (c), but is written without the dollar sign. Therefore, the rate is 15 mills.

In most instances, the tax rate does not divide out to an even quotient as in Example One. When a tax rate does not come out even, the final digit to be used is always rounded off to the next highest digit, regardless of the size of the next digit in the remainder.

Example Two

The tax rate in Anson County is 0.0174236+. Express this rate (a) as a per cent, to two decimal places; (b) per $100 of valuation (correct to cents); (c) per $1,000 of valuation (correct to cents); and (d) in whole mills.

(a) 1.75%

(b) $1.75 per C

(c) $17.43 per M

(d) 18 mills

Property tax is found using the formula

$$\text{Rate} \times \text{Valuation} = \text{Tax}$$

The same basic formula is used to find the rate or the valuation (assessed value) of property when they are unknown.

The tax rate is 2% on a home assessed at $7,000. How much property tax will be due?

Example Three

R = 2%	R × V = T
V = $7,000	2% × $7,000 = T
T = ?	$140 = T

The real property tax on this home will be $140.

The county tax rate in Somerville is $1.40 per C. Find the tax on a warehouse assessed at $8,500.

Example Four

R = $1.40 per C	R × V = T
V = $8,500	1.40 × 85 = T
= $85 hundred	$119 = T
T = ?	

The tax on this warehouse is $119.

An office building assessed at $16,400 is subject to tax at the rate of 15 mills. Calculate the real property tax.

Example Five

R = 15 mills	R × V = T
V = $16,400	15 × $16.4 = T
= $16.4 thousand	$246 = T
T = ?	

This property is taxed $246.

Note: When the tax formula is solved for valuation (V), the quotient obtained represents that many hundreds or thousands of dollars of valuation, according to whether the rate is per $100 or per $1,000. The original quotient must be converted to a complete dollar valuation. (For example, a solution of "$72" means "$72 hundred" when the rate is per $100; hence, the assessed value must be rewritten $7,200.)

The property tax on a home was $255 in a county where the tax rate was 17 mills. What was the assessed value of the property?

Example Six

$$R = 17 \text{ mills (or} \qquad\qquad R \times V = T$$
$$\$17 \text{ per } \$1,000)$$
$$V = ? \qquad\qquad\qquad 17V = \$255$$
$$T = \$255 \qquad\qquad\qquad V = \frac{255}{17}$$
$$V = 15 \text{ thousand}$$
$$V = \$15,000$$

The house was assessed at $15,000.

Example Seven Warren-Jones, Inc. paid a property tax of $216 on its building, which was assessed at $16,000. Find the rate per $1,000 in this town.

$$R = ? \qquad\qquad R \times V = T$$
$$V = \$16,000 \qquad R \times 16 = \$216$$
$$= \$16 \text{ thousand} \qquad 16R = 216$$
$$T = \$216 \qquad\qquad R = \$13.50$$

The tax rate is $13.50 per $1,000.

PROBLEMS

In the following problems, express each tax rate as indicated:

Tax Rate		Express the Rate
1. .0183472+	(a)	as a per cent with two decimal places
	(b)	as an amount per $100, correct to cents
	(c)	as an amount per $1,000, correct to cents
	(d)	in whole mills
2. .0137229+	(a)	as a per cent with one decimal place
	(b)	as an amount per $100, correct to cents
	(c)	as an amount per $1,000, correct to cents
	(d)	in whole mills
3. .0144736+	(a)	as a per cent with three decimal places
	(b)	as an amount per $100, correct to cents
	(c)	as an amount per $1,000, correct to cents
	(d)	in mills, to one decimal place
4. .0213724+	(a)	as a per cent with one decimal place
	(b)	as an amount per $100, correct to cents
	(c)	as an amount per $1,000, correct to cents
	(d)	in mills, to one decimal place

Find each missing factor relating to property tax:

		Rate	Assessed Value	Tax
5.	(a)	1.4%	$ 8,500	
	(b)	$1.68 per C	15,000	
	(c)	$13.20 per M	12,500	
	(d)	15.5 mills	16,000	
	(e)	2.6%		$325
	(f)	$2.35 per C		329
	(g)	$16.75 per M		134
	(h)	18 mills		207
	(i)	?%	15,600	390
	(j)	? per C	12,800	160
	(k)	? per M	7,500	111
	(l)	? mills	17,500	301
6.	(a)	1.8%	$10,500	
	(b)	$1.65 per C	14,000	
	(c)	$13.50 per M	9,600	
	(d)	15 mills	11,400	
	(e)	2.2%		$187
	(f)	$1.25 per C		95
	(g)	$18.75 per M		330
	(h)	16.5 mills		231
	(i)	?%	15,000	180
	(j)	? per C	12,400	217
	(k)	? per M	10,000	135
	(l)	? mills	12,500	195

7. Travis County has a property tax rate of $2.65 per $100 valuation. Determine the obligation of a homeowner whose property is assessed at $14,000.

8. Citizens of Vista Heights pay a property tax of $12.50 per $1,000 of valuation. Compute the tax assessment on a home assessed at $11,200.

9. Residents of Barton Springs are subject to a 2.4% property tax. How much tax will be due on an unimproved lot assessed at $3,500?

10. The property tax rate in Oakdale is $1.54 per C. Find the tax due on a home assessed at $15,000.

11. The property tax on a commercial building was $572. If the tax rate was $1.76 per C, what was the assessed value of the building?

12. The property tax rate in a community is 15.5 mills. What is the assessed value of a house on which the tax due is $217?

13. The property tax on a home was $391 when computed at the rate of 17 mills. Determine the assessed value of the home.

14. A resident of White Plains paid $168 property tax. If the tax rate was $1.60 per $100, what was the assessed value of his property?

15. A businessman in Greenville paid $517 in property taxes. Compute the tax rate per $100 if the assessed value of his property was $27,500.

16. A property owner in Phillips County paid $240 in property tax on an office building assessed at $16,000. What per cent is the county tax rate?

17. Property taxes cost a citizen of Glendale $299. Determine the tax rate per $1,000, if the assessed value of his property was $18,400.

18. A tax of $369 was paid on a commercial property assessed at $16,400. Find the tax rate per $100 of assessed value.

19. The property tax was $390 on a home assessed at $15,000. The following year, the tax rate was increased $.15 per $100 and the property tax was $429. Determine how much the assessed value of the house had increased the second year. (*Hint:* Solve each year separately.)

20. The property tax was $396 on a store building when the tax rate was $16.50 per $1,000. During the succeeding year, the assessed value of the building was increased by $4,000 and the property tax amounted to $476. How much had the tax rate increased?

6

Insurance

LEARNING OBJECTIVES

Upon completion of Chapter 6, the student will be able to:

1. Define and use correctly the terminology associated with each topic.

2. a. Compute fire insurance premiums.
   b. Compute the premium refund due when policy is canceled (1) by the insured, or (2) by the carrier.

3. a. Determine compensation due following a fire loss, given the coverage required for full protection.
   b. Also, find each company's share of a loss when coverage is divided among several companies.

4. a. Compute the annual premium for (1) automobile liability insurance, and (2) comprehensive-collision insurance.
   b. Find the compensation due following an accident.

5. Determine premiums for the following life insurance policies: a. term, b. straight life, c. 20-payment life, and d. endowment.

6. Calculate the following nonforfeiture values:
   a. cash value, b. paid-up insurance, and c. extended term insurance.

7. a. Determine the net cost of an insurance policy (participating or nonparticipating) over the term of the policy.
   b. Compare the costs of different policies.

8. Compare the monthly (and total) annuities that a beneficiary could receive under various settlement options.

ALL INSURANCE IS CARRIED in order to provide financial compensation should some undesirable event occur. Insurance operates on the principle of shared risk. Many persons purchase insurance protection and their payments are pooled in order to provide funds with which to pay those who experience losses. Thus rates are lower when many different people purchase the same protection and divide the risk.

The risk which a company assumes by insuring an event always influences how high the rates will be. The company determines the mathematical probability that the insured event will occur and then sets its rates accordingly. The insurance company does not know which of its clients will suffer a loss, but it knows from experience how many losses to expect. The insurance rates must be high enough to pay the expected losses, to pay the expenses of operating the company, and to provide a reserve fund should losses exceed the expected amounts during any period.

The payment made to purchase insurance coverage is called a *premium*. Insurance premiums may usually be paid either annually, semi-annually, quarterly, or monthly. The total cost of insurance is slightly higher when payments are made more frequently, in order to cover the cost of increased bookkeeping. An insurance contract, or *policy*, defines in detail the provisions and limitations of the coverage. The amount of insurance specified by the policy is the *face value* of the policy. Insurance premiums are paid in advance, and the *term* of the policy is the time period for which the policy will remain in effect. The insurance company is often referred to as the *insurer*, the *underwriter*, or the *carrier*. The person or business which purchases insurance is called the *insured* or the *policyholder*.

As indicated above, insurance is sold in order to provide financial protection to the policyholder; it is not intended to be a profit-making proposition when a loss occurs. Thus insurance settlements are always limited to either the actual amount of loss or the face amount of the policy, whichever is smaller.

1. BUSINESS INSURANCE

Certain standard forms of insurance are carried by almost all businesses; these types of insurance are discussed on the following pages. Because of its importance to private citizens as well as to business organizations, fire insurance receives particular attention.

FIRE INSURANCE

Basic fire insurance provides protection against property damage resulting from fire or lightning. (Insured property may be buildings and their contents, vehicles, building sites, agricultural crops, forest crops, etc.) Further damage resulting from smoke or from attempts to extinguish or contain a fire may be as costly as the fire damage itself. Therefore, *extended coverage* is usually included to provide protection against smoke, water, and chemical damage, as well as physical destruction caused by firemen having to break into the property or using dynamite or other means to keep a fire from spreading.

Homeowners often purchase a comprehensive "package" policy which, in addition to the above coverage, also provides protection against theft, vandalism, natural disasters, accidental loss or damage, and liability coverage in case of personal injury to visitors on the property. Similar protection may also be purchased by business firms, although it is sometimes obtained in separate policies.

PREMIUMS

Fire insurance rates are usually quoted as an amount per $100 of insurance coverage. (Separate rates are charged for insurance on the building itself, on the furniture and fixtures, and on the stock or merchandise—in that order of increasing expense.)

Each state has a fire-rating bureau which establishes its fire insurance rates. A representative of the bureau inspects every commercial property and determines the rate to be paid by each. These rates vary greatly, because they are influenced by many different factors. The primary factors which the inspector must consider are (1) the construction of the building, (2) the contents stored or manufactured therein, (3) the quality of fire protection available, and (4) the location of the buildings.

Thus a building of fireproof construction (all steel and cement, and with a fireproof roof) would have a much lower insurance rate than a frame building with a flammable roof. Similarly, property located near fire hydrants and served by a well-trained fire department in an area that receives abundant rainfall would require much lower premiums than property located in an arid region and some distance from a fire station. (The installation of fire extinguishers or sprinkler systems would reduce the rate somewhat.) A dress shop would normally have a lower rate than a paint store, because of the combustible nature of painting supplies; if the dress shop relocated to a site beside a gasoline storage area, however, its fire insurance rate would increase greatly.

Fire insurance companies ordinarily offer reduced rates when a policy is purchased for several years in advance. Table 6-1 gives typical multiples used to compute long-term rates. In actual practice, however, most policies are written for three years. (In the past, five-year fire insurance policies were common. These policies are now written only for schools or other public buildings, however.)

TABLE 6-1: LONG-TERM FIRE INSURANCE RATES

Long-Term Rates for Fire Insurance	
Years of Coverage	Multiple of Annual Premium
2	1.85
3	2.70

Example One

DeKalb Business Machines, which leases its office space, wishes to insure its inventory and equipment for $25,000 against fire. The annual rate is $.34 per $100. Compute the premium for (a) a one-year policy, and (b) a three-year policy.

Insurance premiums are computed using the procedure

$$\text{Premium} = \text{Rate} \times \text{Value of policy}$$

or simply

$$P = R \times V$$

Thus the premium for this example would be computed as follows:

(a) R = $.34 per $100   P = R × V
     V = $25,000   = $.34 × $250
         $250 hundreds   P = $85
     P = ?

The annual (one-year) premium is $85.

(b)   A three-year policy costs 2.7 times the annual premium:

$$\begin{array}{ll} \$85 & \text{Annual premium} \\ \underline{\times 2.7} & \\ \$229.50 & \text{Three-year premium} \end{array}$$

SHORT-TERM POLICIES

Sometimes a business may wish to purchase fire insurance for only a limited time in order to obtain coverage on merchandise which will soon be sold. Also, policies are sometimes canceled by the policyholder if he sells the insured property, if he moves, etc. If, for any reason, a policy is in effect for less than one year, it is considered a short-term policy. The premium to be charged for such a policy is computed according to a short-rate table, such as Table 6-2. A very short policy is relatively expensive because of the cost to the insurance company of selling, writing, and processing the policy.

TABLE 6-2: SHORT-TERM AND CANCELLATION RATES

Short-Term Rates (including cancellations by the insured)			
Months of Coverage	% of Annual Premium Charged	Months of Coverage	% of Annual Premium Charged
1	20%	7	75%
2	30	8	80
3	40	9	85
4	50	10	90
5	60	11	95
6	70	12	100

Max McConnell owned a rental home valued at $10,000, for which he had bought fire insurance at the rate of $.22 per $100. After six months, he sold the house and canceled the insurance policy. How much refund will McConnell receive? ($10,000 = 100 hundreds.) **Example Two**

$$\begin{aligned} \text{Annual premium} &= \$.22 \times 100 \\ &= \$22 \end{aligned}$$

Since the policy remained in effect for six months, 70 per cent of the annual premium will be charged.

$22	Annual premium	$22.00	Annual premium
×.7		−15.40	Short-term premium
$15.40	Six-months' premium	$6.60	Refund due

McConnell will receive a refund of $6.60.

Occasionally it becomes necessary for an insurance company to cancel a policy. This might happen because of excessive claims or a refusal of the policyholder to accept higher rates when the fire risk has increased. The company ordinarily must give advance notice that the policy will be canceled, thus allowing the policyholder time to purchase another policy before his coverage ceases. When a company cancels, it may keep only that fraction of the annual premium equivalent to the time which has elapsed. Many companies compute this time precisely, using $\dfrac{\text{Exact days}}{365}$; however, we shall use approximate time for our calculations. The insurance company is not entitled to short-term rates when it cancels the policy.

Example Three

A $75,000 fire insurance policy, sold at the rate of $.80 per $100, was canceled by the company after seven months. How much refund will the policyholder receive?

$75,000 = 750 hundreds

$.80 × 750 = Annual premium
$600 = Annual premium

7 months = $\frac{7}{12}$ year
$\frac{7}{12}$ × $600 = 7-months' premium
$350 = 7-months' premium

$600	Annual premium
−350	7-months' premium
$250	Refund due

Since the policy was canceled by the insurance company after seven months, the company is entitled to only $\frac{7}{12}$ of the annual premium, or $350. Hence, a $250 refund is due on the policy.

COMPENSATION FOR LOSS; AVERAGE CLAUSE

Experience indicates that most fires result in the loss of only a small portion of the total value of property. Realizing that total destruction is relatively rare, many people would be tempted to economize by purchasing only partial coverage. However, to pay the full amount of these damages would be extremely expensive to an insurance company if most policyholders were paying premiums on only the partial value of their property. Therefore, to maintain an economically sound business operation, as well as to encourage property-owners to purchase full insurance coverage, many policies contain an average clause. An *average clause* (or *coinsurance clause*) guarantees full payment after a loss (up to the face amount of the policy) only if the policyholder purchases coverage of at least a specified per cent of the total value of his property. (The policyholder also receives rate reductions when his fire coverage meets or exceeds the average clause requirement.) Many policies require 80% coverage, although lower coverage is sometimes allowed and higher (particularly for extended coverage policies) may often be necessary. If the required coverage is not carried, the company will pay damages equivalent only to the ratio of the required coverage that is carried; the policy-holder must bear the remaining loss himself. (In this respect, the policy-holder "coinsures" his property. The term "coinsurance" implies that the insurance company and the policy-holder each assume part of the total risk.)

A property-owner may purchase more insurance than the minimum requirement if he so desires. However, in no case will payment for damages exceed the actual value of the property destroyed, no matter how much insurance is carried. The maximum payment is always the amount of damages or the amount of the policy, whichever is smaller.

William Weldon owns a warehouse valued at $50,000. The warehouse is insured for $30,000 in a policy containing an 80 per cent average clause. (a) What part of a fire loss will the company pay? (b) How much of a $6,000 loss will the insurance company pay? (c) How much on a $28,000 loss? (d) How much on a $48,000 loss? **Example Four**

(a) According to the average clause, 80% of the property value must be insured:

$$\$50,000 \times 80\% = \$40,000 \text{ Insurance required}$$

$$\frac{\text{Insurance carried}}{\text{Insurance required}} = \frac{\$30,000}{\$40,000} = \frac{3}{4}$$

Weldon carries only $\frac{3}{4}$ of the insurance required by the average clause; therefore, the company will pay only $\frac{3}{4}$ of any loss, up to the face amount of the policy.

(b) $\frac{3}{4} \times \$6,000 = \$4,500$

The company will pay $4,500 on a $6,000 loss.

(c) $\frac{3}{4} \times \$28,000 = \$21,000$

The company will pay $21,000 toward a $28,000 loss. By his failure to carry the required coverage, the owner has indirectly agreed to coinsure the remaining portion himself.

(d) $\frac{3}{4} \times \$48,000 = \$36,000$

Preliminary calculations indicate the company's share of this loss to be $36,000. However, this exceeds the face of Weldon's policy; therefore, the company will pay only the full value of the policy, or $30,000.

MULTIPLE CARRIERS

Insurance coverage on property may often be divided among several companies. This may happen because the value of the property is so high that no single company can afford to assume the entire risk, because the owner wishes to distribute his business for public relations purposes, or simply because coverage on various portions of the property was purchased separately over a period of years.

When property is insured with multiple carriers, each company pays damages in the ratio that its policy bears to the total insurance coverage. As noted previously, the total amount paid by all carriers will never exceed the value of the damage, nor will any company's payment exceed the face value of its policy. Multiple policies may also contain average clauses.

Example Five

The Food Market suffered a $180,000 fire. They were insured under the following policies: $250,000 with company A; $150,000 with company B; and $100,000 with company C. What amount will each company pay? (The Food Market meets the coinsurance requirement necessary to receive full coverage on a loss.)

Policies

$250,000	A pays $\dfrac{\$250,000}{\$500,000}$	or	$\dfrac{1}{2}$ of the loss
150,000	B pays $\dfrac{\$150,000}{\$500,000}$	or	$\dfrac{3}{10}$ of the loss
$\dfrac{\$100,000}{\$500,000}$	C pays $\dfrac{\$100,000}{\$500,000}$	or	$\dfrac{1}{5}$ of the loss

Therefore, each company's payment is as follows:

Company	Payment
A	$\frac{1}{2} \times \$180,000 = \$\ 90,000$
B	$\frac{3}{10} \times\ \ 180,000 = \ \ \ \ 54,000$
C	$\frac{1}{5} \times\ \ \ \ 180,000 = +36,000$
	Total $= \$180,000$

Company A will pay $90,000; Company B is responsible for $54,000; and Company C will pay $36,000.

Several other types of insurance are carried by most businesses. The following paragraphs give a brief description of this additional insurance.

BUSINESS INTERRUPTION

This insurance (also called *use and occupancy*) is purchased as a supplement to fire and property insurance. Whereas fire and property insurance provides coverage for the actual physical damage resulting from a fire or natural disaster (earthquake, flood, hurricane, tornado, etc.), business interruption insurance provides protection against business lost until the physical damage can be repaired and normal business resumed. Use and occupancy insurance provides money to meet essential business expenses that continue despite the lapse in operations: interest, loan payments, mortgage or rent payments, taxes, utilities, insurance, and advertising, as well as the salaries of key members of the firm. This insurance may even pay the anticipated net profit of the firm.

LIABILITY

Businesses may be held financially liable, or responsible, for many different occurrences; general *liability* insurance is a business essential in order to provide this protection. An accident causing personal injury to a customer often results in the customer's suing the business. When firms are declared negligent of their responsibility for the customer's safety, judgments of large sums of money are often granted by the courts. Hence, no reasonable company would operate without public liability insurance. Protection from bodily injury to customers and protection from damage to customers' property while on the business premises are the principal provisions of liability insurance.

Another area in which court judgments have been quite large in recent years is bodily injury resulting from defective or dangerous products. Companies that manufacture mechanical products or food products that could conceivably be harmful can be insured by *product liability* policies.

Liability for the safety of employees is covered under *workmen's compensation* policies. This insurance provides payments to an employee who loses work time because of sickness or accidental injury resulting directly from his work responsibilities. Most workmen's compensation policies also provide death benefits in case of a fatality. The labor statutes in many states require employers to carry this insurance; and some states have a state fund for workmen's compensation, although in most cases it is purchased from commercial insurance companies. As would be expected, workmen's compensation rates vary greatly according to the occupational hazards of different jobs. These rates are usually quoted as an amount per $100 in wages. The premiums are usually based only on regular wages; that is, premiums are not paid on overtime wages.

A business firm's liability for the operation of motor vehicles is similar to that of the general public; both are included in the following section of this chapter. Business policies, however, often contain special provisions covering fleets of cars, hired cars, or the cars of employees being used in company business.

Liability for the financial obligations to contracts, such as lease agreements or mortgages, can be insured. It is also possible to protect against the financial responsibilities for completing performance contracts, such as those assumed by a building contractor to complete a construction.

MONEY AND SECURITIES

The theft of money and securities (such as checks, stocks, titles of ownership, etc.) is a constant hazard in many businesses. A number of different policies cover the various conditions under which money and valuable securities may be stolen, such as burglary from an office safe or robbery of a messenger carrying money or securities to or from the business.

General theft policies do not cover the dishonesty of employees, which must be provided for by separate policies. *Fidelity bonds* protect against embezzlement or other loss by employees who handle large sums of money. This is an essential policy in banks, retail stores, and other offices where large amounts of cash or securities are involved.

The worst financial loss experienced by most retail stores results from shoplifting, a problem of major national proportion that is increasing annually. There is presently no insurance available that adequately protects against shoplifting losses; thus, the businessman's only means of reimbursement is to pass his loss along to consumers in the form of higher prices.

LIFE INSURANCE

Particularly in small businesses, the death of a partner or a key man in the firm may jeopardize the entire business operation. Many firms, therefore, purchase life insurance on critical personnel to protect against such financial loss. Such policies also enable the firm to buy from his estate the business interest of a deceased partner. Life insurance is presented in more detail in a later section.

GROUP INSURANCE

Group insurance available at many companies provides health and accident (hospitalization) coverage—and sometimes life insurance—for employees and their families. (This coverage, unlike workmen's compensation, provides coverage for illnesses or accidents not related to occupational duties.)

The employer often pays half and sometimes all of the group insurance premiums, as a public relations gesture to build employee morale and loyalty. Even when the employee pays the entire cost, group insurance is cheaper than if he purchased similar coverage privately. Also, group policies may usually be purchased without a physical examination, which permits some people to receive insurance protection when they would not ordinarily qualify. A worker's coverage usually terminates immediately when he leaves the firm, although a group policy may often be converted to a private policy (at an increased rate, of course).

In many cases, group insurance provides standard coverage for all employees. However, certain benefits sometimes increase according to the employee's salary or years of service to the business.

PROBLEMS

Compute the premiums required to purchase the following amounts of insurance for the terms indicated. Use the multiples in Table 6-1 for long-term policies:

		Amount of Insurance	Annual Rate	Term
1.	(a)	$32,000	$.65 per $100	1 year
	(b)	15,000	.44 per $100	3 years
	(c)	40,000	.26 per $100	2 years
2.	(a)	$ 8,000	$.15 per $100	1 year
	(b)	25,000	.22 per $100	2 years
	(c)	60,000	.45 per $100	3 years

Compute the premium and/or the refund due for the following short-term policies. Use the short-term rates from Table 6-2 when applicable:

		Amount of Insurance	Annual Rate (per $100)	Term	Canceled by	Premium	Refund Due
3.	(a)	$30,000	$.57	2 months	—		—
	(b)	18,000	.40	10	Insured		
	(c)	45,000	.72	7	Carrier		
4.	(a)	$20,000	$.55	4 months	—		—
	(b)	15,000	.80	6	Insured		
	(c)	50,000	.72	5	Carrier		

Compute the compensation which will be paid under each of the following conditions:

		Property Value	Average Clause	Insurance Required	Insurance Carried	Amount of Loss	Compensation
5.	(a)	$30,000	80%		$28,000	$15,000	
	(b)	65,000	80		39,000	12,000	
	(c)	40,000	90		32,000	27,000	
	(d)	60,000	70		28,000	45,000	
	(e)	45,000	80		30,000	42,000	
6.	(a)	$10,000	80%		$10,000	$ 3,000	
	(b)	30,000	90		24,000	18,000	
	(c)	25,000	80		16,000	15,000	
	(d)	90,000	90		45,000	90,000	
	(e)	80,000	70		48,000	49,000	

Determine the compensation to be paid by each carrier (assume that average clause requirements are met):

		Company	Amount of Policy	Ratio of Coverage	Amount of Loss	Compensation
7.	(a)	A	$80,000		$35,000	
		B	60,000			
	(b)	R	25,000		80,000	
		I	40,000			
		S	15,000			
		K	20,000			
8.	(a)	C	$24,000		$15,000	
		D	16,000			
	(b)	L	12,000		20,000	
		M	30,000			
		N	18,000			

9. The inventory at Slotsky's Men's Wear is valued at $85,000. The rate for fire and extended coverage is $.78 per $100. Compute their insurance cost for—
   (a) A one-year policy.
   (b) A three-year policy.
   (c) How much savings does the three-year policy provide?

10. New Harbor Hardware purchased a $65,000 fire insurance policy on its building. The annual premium was $.52 per $100. Determine the cost of this policy for—
    (a) One year.
    (b) Two years.
    How much was saved by purchasing the two-year policy?

11. A new building constructed for Richland Drug Co. cost $75,000. The fire

insurance policy contains an 80% coinsurance clause, which Richland will meet. On that basis,

(a) How much will an annual policy cost, at $.37 per $100?

(b) What would a three-year policy cost?

(c) How much savings would be realized by taking the three-year policy?

12. Westholme Apartments are valued at $80,000. The owner purchased a fire insurance policy large enough to meet a 70% coinsurance requirement. The annual rate for this property was $.35 per $100. What was the cost of—

(a) A one-year policy?

(b) A three-year policy?

(c) How much did the owner save by purchasing the three-year term policy?

13. Snow Bound Skiwear and Equipment purchased a six-month fire insurance policy of $48,000 to protect its expanded fall and winter inventory. If the annual rate for this coverage was $.29 per $100, how much did this short-term policy cost?

14. King's Grant Plantation purchased a five-month fire insurance policy of $40,000 to insure their crops during the growing season. The annual rate for this coverage was $.15 per $100. Find the cost of the short-term policy.

15. An annual rate of $.85 per $100 was charged for a $22,000 fire insurance policy. What is the cost and the refund due if the policy is canceled after 9 months—

(a) By the policyholder?

(b) By the insurance company?

16. The annual rate for fire insurance on a $15,000 store building was $.72 per $100. Compute the premium charged and the refund due if the policy is canceled after seven months—

(a) By the insured.

(b) By the carrier.

17. The owner of a $40,000 house purchased a $35,000 fire insurance policy. If the policy contains an 85% average clause, how much settlement should the company make in case of—

(a) A $17,000 loss?

(b) A $25,000 loss?

(c) A $38,000 loss?

18. The fire insurance policy on a $90,000 manufacturing plant contains a 70% average clause. The plant is insured for $75,000. How much should the insurance company pay following—

(a) A $9,000 fire?

(b) A $27,000 fire?

(c) An $82,000 fire?

19. An $80,000 business office was insured for $56,000 with a policy requiring 80% coverage. Determine the amount to be paid if there is—
    (a) A $16,000 fire.
    (b) A $36,000 fire.
    (c) A $72,000 fire.

20. The coinsurance clause on a $150,000 plant required 80% fire coverage. The plant was insured for $100,000. What settlement should the company make following—
    (a) An $18,000 loss?
    (b) A $42,000 loss?
    (c) A total loss?

21. A building valued at $90,000 is insured for $72,000. If the fire insurance policy required 90% coverage, determine the settlement due when a fire resulted in—
    (a) $27,000 damage.
    (b) $54,000 damage.
    (c) A total loss.

22. The policy on an $80,000 office building requires 75% fire coverage. The building is insured for $48,000. What amount should the company pay following—
    (a) $3,500 fire damages?
    (b) $27,500 damages?
    (c) $65,000 damages?

23. A processing plant is insured for $20,000 with Company P; $80,000 with Company Q; and $60,000 with Company R. Compute each company's liability for—
    (a) A $72,000 fire.
    (b) A $120,000 fire.

24. A home is insured against fire under an $18,000 policy with Company M and a $12,000 policy with Company N. What settlement should each company make following—
    (a) A $7,500 fire?
    (b) A $20,000 fire?

25. A distribution center is covered by the following fire policies: $240,000 with Company A; $180,000 with Company B; $60,000 with Company C; and $120,000 with Company D. Determine each company's share following
    (a) A $200,000 fire.
    (b) A $450,000 fire.
    (c) A $750,000 fire.

26. Fire protection on a retail store is provided by the following policies: $180,000 with Company R; $120,000 with Company S; and $60,000 with

Company T. What is each company's share of
(a) A $15,000 loss?
(b) A $144,000 loss?
(c) A $420,000 loss?

2. MOTOR VEHICLE INSURANCE

Automobile and/or truck insurance is carried by responsible owners
(private or industrial) of most vehicles. Insurance policies on motor vehicles are usually written only for one-year terms. The primary reason for
the one-year policy is the alarmingly high, nation-wide accident rate,
which constantly increases rates for automobile insurance. Since insurance
rates always reflect the risk taken by the insurance company, the driving
record (and age) of the operator is another major factor in determining
the cost of vehicle insurance. This further accounts for the one-year
policies, since a driver's record may fluctuate over a period of years.

Insurance on motor vehicles is divided into two basic categories:
(1) liability coverage and (2) comprehensive-collision coverage.

LIABILITY INSURANCE

This insurance provides protection to the policyholder for damage he may
inflict to the person or property of other people. As a protection to its
citizens, some states require the owners of all vehicles registered in the state
to purchase minimum amounts of liability insurance. Liability insurance
covers *bodily injury liability* (liability for physical injury resulting from the
policyholder's negligence) and *property damage liability* (liability for damage
caused by the policyholder to another vehicle or other property.) Also
available on an optional basis is *medical payment* insurance. This insurance
will begin paying medical costs immediately, without waiting for the courts
to rule on a liability suit. "Medical pay" covers the insured himself, as
well as possible victims.

Minimum liability coverage is often quoted as "5/10/5 coverage."
This means that the policy will pay up to $5,000 for the bodily injury
caused to a single person, or, when more than one person was involved in
the accident, a maximum total of $10,000 for the injuries inflicted to all
victims. Also, a maximum of $5,000 will be paid for the property damage
resulting from a single accident. Much higher liability coverage is available at rates only slightly higher than those for minimum coverage. (Many
states require higher coverage than the minimum "5/10/5 coverage.")
Thus many drivers purchase bodily injury coverage up to $300,000/
$300,000 and property damage coverage up to $100,000.

If a court suit should result in a victim's being awarded a settlement
which exceeds the policyholder's coverage, the additional sum would have

TABLE 6-3: DRIVER CLASSIFICATIONS

(Multiples of Base Annual Automobile Insurance Premiums)

			Pleasure; Less than 3 Miles to Work Each Way	Drives to Work, 3 to 10 Miles Each Way	Drives to Work, 10 Miles or More Each Way	Used in Business
No young operators	Only operator is female, age 30–64		.90	1.00	1.30	1.40
	One or more operators age 65 or over		1.00	1.10	1.40	1.50
	All others		1.00	1.10	1.40	1.50
Young females	Age 16	DT*	1.40	1.50	1.80	1.90
		No DT	1.55	1.65	1.95	2.05
	Age 20	DT	1.05	1.15	1.45	1.55
		No DT	1.10	1.20	1.50	1.60
Young males (married)	Age 16	DT	1.60	1.70	2.00	2.10
		No DT	1.80	1.90	2.20	2.30
	Age 20	DT	1.45	1.55	1.85	1.95
		No DT	1.50	1.60	1.90	2.00
	Age 21		1.40	1.50	1.80	1.90
	Age 24		1.10	1.20	1.50	1.60

TABLE 6-3. Continued

			Pleasure; Less than 3 Miles to Work Each Way	Drives to Work, 3 to 10 Miles Each Way	Drives to Work, 10 Miles or More Each Way	Used in Business
Young unmarried males (not principal operator)	Age 16	DT	2.05	2.15	2.45	2.55
		No DT	2.30	2.40	2.70	2.80
	Age 20	DT	1.60	1.70	2.00	2.10
		No DT	1.70	1.80	2.10	2.20
	Age 21		1.55	1.65	1.95	2.05
	Age 24		1.10	1.20	1.50	1.60
Young unmarried males (owner or principal operator)	Age 16	DT	2.70	2.80	3.10	3.20
		No DT	3.30	3.40	3.70	3.80
	Age 20	DT	2.55	2.65	2.95	3.05
		No DT	2.70	2.80	3.10	3.20
	Age 21		2.50	2.60	2.90	3.00
	Age 24		1.90	2.00	2.30	2.40
	Age 26		1.50	1.60	1.90	2.00
	Age 29		1.10	1.20	1.50	1.60

* "DT" indicates completion of a certified driver training course.

to be paid by the insured. For example, suppose a driver carried 10/20/10 liability insurance and a court awards $13,000 to one victim and $2,000 to each of three other victims. Even though the total awarded to all victims

($19,000) is less than the maximum total coverage ($20,000), the insurance company will not pay the total award: Since the maximum liability for a single victim is $10,000, the insurance company is responsible only for $16,000 ($10,000 to the first victim and $2,000 each to the other three victims). The remaining $3,000 of the $13,000 judgment must be paid by the policyholder himself.

Two factors determine the standard rates charged for liability insurance: the classification of the vehicle (according to how much it is driven, whether used for business, and the age of the driver) and the territory in which the vehicle is operated. (As would be expected, rates are higher in populous areas, since traffic congestion results in more accidents.) A policyholder's rates are usually increased above the standard charge if he is at fault in an accident. A driver with a record of several accidents may be designated an *assigned risk*, at greatly increased rates, or may even have his policy canceled by the company if he is considered too great a risk.

Table 6-3 contains excerpts of the driver classifications used to determine liability insurance premiums. As one can see from the table, drivers under 21 are intricately classified according to sex, age, and whether or not they have taken a driver training course. Males under 25 are classified according to marital status and whether they are the owners or principal operators of the automobiles. Unmarried males continue to be so classified until they reach 30. Most mature drivers would be classified "all others." (An automobile is classified according to the status of the youngest person who operates the car or according to the person whose driver classification requires the highest multiple.)

Table 6-4 presents some typical base annual rates for automobile liability insurance (bodily injury and property damage) in three different territories.

Example One William Hanson is 35 years old and drives his car 8 miles (one way) to work each day. He lives in an area designated Territory 2. (a) Find the cost of basic 5/10/5 liability coverage on his automobile. (b) What would Hanson's premium be if he increased his insurance to 25/50 bodily injury and $10,000 property damage coverage?

(a) According to Table 6-4, the cost in Territory 2 of basic liability insurance ($5,000 single and $10,000 total bodily injury; $5,000 property damage) is as follows:

$33	Bodily injury (5/10)
+28	Property damage (5,000)
$61	Total base premium

TABLE 6-4: AUTOMOBILE LIABILITY INSURANCE

Base Annual Premiums

	Bodily Injury				Property Damage		
Coverage	Territory 1	Territory 2	Territory 3	Coverage	Territory 1	Territory 2	Territory 3
5/10	$25	$33	$50	$ 5,000	$20	$28	$32
10/20	28	37	55	10,000	22	30	34
15/30	30	40	60	25,000	23	31	35
25/25	33	44	65	50,000	24	32	36
25/50	35	46	70	100,000	26	34	38
50/50	36	48	72				
50/100	37	49	74				
100/100	38	50	75				
100/200	39	52	78				
100/300	40	54	80				
200/300	42	56	83				
300/300	43	58	85				

The base premium in Territory 2 is $61 for 5/10/5 liability insurance. Since Hanson is 35, he falls into the category "all others" in the vehicle classification table. Because he drives 8 miles to work, Table 6-3 indicates that the multiple 1.10 must be used to compute Hanson's annual premium:

$61   Base annual premium
×1.10
$67.10   Actual annual premium

Hanson would pay a $67.10 annual premium for basic 5/10/5 liability insurance.

(b) Increased coverage would cost as follows:

$46   25/50 bodily injury
+30 $10,000 property damage
$76   Base premium
×1.10
$83.60   Annual premium

Liability coverage of 25/50/10 would cost Hanson $83.60 for one year.

Example Two Greg Lewis of Lewis Motors was operating a company car when it struck another automobile, seriously injuring Mr. and Mrs. Warner. They sued Lewis Motors for $80,000 personal injuries and $2,500 property damage. The court awarded the Warners a $35,000 personal injury judgment and the entire property damage suit. Lewis Motors carried 10/20/10 liability coverage. (a) How much will the insurance company pay? (b) How much of the award will Lewis Motors have to pay?

(a) The insurance company will pay the maximum bodily injury coverage ($20,000) and the total award for property damage ($2,500). Thus the insurance company will pay a total of $22,500.

(b) Since the court awarded the claimants more than Lewis Motors' bodily injury coverage, Lewis Motors must pay the excess:

$35,000	Amount awarded
−20,000	Liability coverage
$15,000	Amount to be paid by Lewis Motors

Lewis Motors must pay an additional $15,000 to Mr. and Mrs. Warner.

COMPREHENSIVE AND COLLISION INSURANCE

These forms of insurance protect the policyholder against damage to his own automobile. Comprehensive insurance covers damage resulting from fire, theft, vandalism, acts of nature, falling objects, and so forth. Protection against collision or upset damage may be obtained through collision insurance. (That is, collision insurance also covers damage resulting from one-car accidents—including damage to runaway, driverless vehicles—where no collision of two vehicles occurred.) Collision insurance pays for repairs to the vehicle of the insured when he is responsible for an accident, when his car was damaged by a hit-and-run driver, or when another driver was responsible for the collision but did not have liability insurance and was unable to pay the property damage he caused.

Since comprehensive and collision insurance provides compensation only to the insured, it is not required by state law. Under certain circumstances, however, this coverage is mandatory. If an automobile is purchased by monthly installment payments, the institution financing the purchase retains legal title to the automobile until all installments are paid. In order to protect their investment, these financial agencies ordinarily require the purchaser to carry comprehensive and collision insurance.

A vehicle's owner may purchase collision insurance which pays the entire cost of repairing damage; however, such insurance is rather expensive. Most collision insurance is sold with a "deductible" clause, which means that the policyholder pays a specified part of any repair cost (an amount specified in the deductible clause). For instance, if "fifty-dollar-deductible" collision insurance is purchased, the insured must pay the first $50 in damage resulting from any one collision, and the carrier will pay the remaining cost, up to the value of the vehicle. (If damage is less than $50, the owner must pay the entire cost himself.) Collision policies are available specifying deductible amounts of $25, $50, $100, $150, or $200; however, $50-deductible and $100-deductible policies are more common. Collision coverage becomes less expensive as the policyholder pays a higher amount of the repair cost.

Recall that standard liability rates are determined by the classification of vehicle use and the territory in which the vehicle is operated. In addition to the previous considerations, comprehensive-collision rates also depend upon the make, model, and age of the vehicle (example: "Chevrolet, Bel Air, 2 years old"). Each automobile model is assigned an identification letter from A to Z. (Less expensive models are identified by letters near the beginning of the alphabet, and successive letters identify increasingly expensive models.)

The age of the automobile influences comprehensive and collision costs, since newer automobiles are more expensive to repair. Automobiles of the current model year are classified as "Age Group 1"; cars in Group 2 (the first preceding model year) and Group 3 (the second preceding model year) both pay the same rate; and models of three or more years old are classified in Group 4. Table 6-5 lists excerpts of base annual comprehensive and collision insurance rates in three territories for vehicles of various ages. As in the case of liability insurance, the base annual comprehensive-collision premiums must be multiplied by a multiple reflecting the driver's classification.

Bill Maxwell, a salesman for Apex Furniture & Fixtures, operates a company car. The automobile is a Model D, six months old, which is based in Territory 1. Maxwell is 24 and is married. Find the annual premium on comprehensive and $50-deductible collision insurance for this automobile. **Example Three**

The automobile is classified in the comprehensive and collision table (Table 6-5) under Model Class 1, Age Group 1, in Territory 1. Maxwell's driver classification in Table 6-3 (married male, 24, used in business) requires a multiple of 1.60 to find his actual annual premium:

$10	Comprehensive (Model D, Age Group 1, Territory 1)
+28	$50-deductible collision (classified as above)
$38	Base annual premium
× 1.60	Vehicle classification (married male, 24, business use)
$60.80	Total annual premium

Comprehensive and collision coverage will cost Apex Furniture & Fixtures $60.80 for this company car for one year.

TABLE 6-5: COMPREHENSIVE AND COLLISION INSURANCE

Base Annual Premiums

Model Class	Age Group	Territory 1			Territory 2			Territory 3		
			Collision			Collision			Collision	
		Compre-hensive	$50 Deductible	$100 Deductible	Compre-hensive	$50 Deductible	$100 Deductible	Compre-hensive	$50 Deductible	$100 Deductible
(1)	1	$10	$28	$18	$14	$36	$24	$20	$54	$32
A–G	2, 3	8	24	15	10	32	20	15	48	28
	4	6	20	14	8	28	18	10	40	24
(3)	1	15	38	28	18	50	36	28	75	54
J–K	2, 3	12	34	24	16	45	32	24	65	48
	4	9	28	20	12	38	28	16	55	40
(4)	1	17	43	32	22	56	44	33	85	64
L–M	2, 3	15	38	28	18	50	38	28	75	55
	4	10	33	25	15	45	32	20	65	48
(5)	1	21	50	38	28	68	50	42	100	75
N–O	2, 3	18	43	34	24	60	45	36	86	65
	4	13	38	28	18	50	38	25	75	55

Example Four James Carson is 21 and is not married. He owns a Model K automobile in Age Group 3. Carson resides in Territory 2 and drives 15 miles to work. He wishes to purchase the following automobile insurance: 25/25/5 liability coverage, comprehensive, and $100-deductible collision. What is the total annual premium for this insurance?

$ 44	25/25 bodily injury (Territory 2)
28	$5,000 property damage (Territory 2)
16	Comprehensive (Model K, Age Group 3, Territory 2)
+32	$100-Deductible collision (Model K, Age Group 3, Territory 2)
$120	Base annual premium
×2.90	Use classification (unmarried male, owner, 21, drives more than 10 miles to work)
$348	Total annual premium

Carson's automobile insurance for one year will cost a total of $348.

Example Five Sam McDowell's car struck another automobile, causing $400 damage to his own car and $700 damage to the other vehicle. McDowell carried 5/10/5 liability insurance and $100-deductible collision insurance.

(a) How much of this property damage will McDowell's insurance company pay? (b) Suppose the driver of the other car sued McDowell and was awarded $8,000 for personal injuries. How much would the insurance company pay and how much must McDowell pay the victim?

(a)   Property damage to the other car (under
          McDowell's $5,000 property-damage policy) $700
      Property damage to McDowell's car (under his
          $100-deductible collision policy: $400 − $100)   +300
                    Total property-damage settlement $1,000

McDowell's insurance company will pay a total of $1,000 toward the property damages to both vehicles. McDowell must personally pay the first $100 of repair costs for his own automobile.

(b)   Under McDowell's $5,000 single and $10,000 total bodily injury policy, the maximum amount which the insurance company will pay to any one victim is $5,000. The remaining $3,000 of this $8,000 settlement must be paid by McDowell himself.

Automobile insurance, like fire insurance, may be canceled by either the policyholder or the carrier. When this occurs, rates are computed in much the same way as for fire insurance. That is, short-term rates are charged when the insured cancels the policy. If the insurance company cancels, it may retain only a pro rata share of the annual premium, according to the length of time the policy was in force.

Problems

Compute the following motor vehicle insurance problems using the tables in this section.

Compute the liability premiums for each of the following:

		Liability Coverage	Territory	Driver Classification
1.	(a)	10/20/10	2	Age 52, drives 15 miles to work
	(b)	50/100/10	1	Unmarried male, not principal operator, 16 (driver training), drives 4 miles to work
	(c)	100/200/25	3	Unmarried male, owner, 20 (no driver training), business use
2.	(a)	15/30/5	3	Age 33, drives 7 miles to work
	(b)	50/50/25	1	Unmarried male, principal operator, 24, drives 5 miles to work
	(c)	100/300/50	2	Age 45, business use

Determine the total comprehensive-collision premiums for the following:

	Model	Age Group	Territory	Deductible on Collision	Driver Classification
3. (a)	F	2	1	$ 50	Age 48, drives 6 miles to work
(b)	L	1	2	100	Female, 35, business use
(c)	N	3	3	50	Age 68, pleasure use
4. (a)	G	1	3	$100	Age 50, drives 2 miles to work
(b)	M	3	2	50	Female, 20 (no driver training), drives 9 miles to work
(c)	J	4	2	100	Age 42, business use

5. Philip Croft, age 24, is married and lives in Territory 1. He drives 16 miles each way to work. How much must he pay for liability insurance if his coverage includes $25,000 for single bodily injuries, $50,000 for total injuries, and $25,000 for property damage?

6. Frank Belk, age 34, lives in Territory 3 some 7 miles from his work. His liability insurance covers a single bodily injury amounting to $50,000, total injuries of $50,000, and property damage of $10,000. Calculate his annual premium.

7. Lincoln-Caldwell Associates, which is located in Territory 2, owns a company station wagon, Model M, Age Group 1. All the operators are over 30. What will be the company's annual premium for comprehensive insurance and $100-deductible collision coverage?

8. Johnson-Howard-Phelps provides each salesman with a Model N automobile. These vehicles have a business-use classification and are in Age Group 4, Territory 3. How much will the company pay for comprehensive and $50-deductible insurance on each automobile, if all salesmen are in the 30–50 age bracket?

9. Carol Cohen, a career girl of 32, just purchased a new Model D automobile which she drives 5 miles from her home in Territory 3 to work. Carol wants to purchase 100/300/50 liability insurance; and her bank requires her to carry comprehensive and $50-deductible collision insurance until her automobile loan is repaid in full. How much must Carol pay for this insurance coverage?

10. Ralph Kennedy, who lives in Territory 1, owns a Model M automobile in Age Group 1. Kennedy is 24, married, and uses his car in business. His automobile insurance provides 100/300/50 liability protection as well as comprehensive and $50-deductible collision coverage. Find the annual cost of Kennedy's automobile insurance.

11. Gary Connor is 21, married, and living in Territory 1. He owns a Model L of Age Group 2, which he drives 13 miles to work. Calculate the annual

premium he must pay for 25/25/10 liability insurance, comprehensive, and $100-deductible collision.

12. Edward Ryan is 16 (with driver training) and lives in Territory 2. He is not the principal operator, using the family automobile (a Model K of Age Group 3) only for pleasure. Ryan's father just purchased a 25/50/10 liability policy, comprehensive, and $100-deductible collision insurance. How much did he pay for this coverage?

13. Greg Jones' car hit from behind a boat and trailer being towed by another car, knocking the boat off the trailer. Total damage to the boat, trailer, and other car was $8,000. The other driver sued Jones and won a judgment of $22,000 for personal bodily injuries. Jones carried 15/30/10 liability insurance.
   (a) How much of the cost of this accident will Jones' insurance cover?
   (b) How much of the expense must Jones pay personally?

14. Gary Campbell's automobile crossed the center line on a curve and struck an oncoming car occupied by a mother and two children. Damage to the victims' car totaled $1,500. Following a court suit, the court awarded a judgment of $12,000 to the mother and $3,000 to each child for injuries they sustained. Campbell's automobile insurance included 10/20/5 liability coverage.
   (a) How much of this amount will the insurance company pay?
   (b) What amount of the judgment must Campbell finance himself?

15. While Lee Dickerson was following a dump truck, a small rock bounced against his windshield and cracked it. A new windshield cost $135. Dickerson carries comprehensive and $50-deductible collision insurance.
   (a) How much of the damage will Dickerson's insurance cover?
   (b) How much must Dickerson pay?

16. Vandals stole the hubcaps from Marilyn Hahn's automobile and also broke two side windows. The loss amounted to $110. If Marilyn carried comprehensive and $100-deductible collision insurance—
   (a) How much did the insurance cover?
   (b) How much of the damage did Marilyn have to pay?

17. A truck belonging to Electrical Supply Co. failed to yield the right of way when entering a freeway and crashed into an automobile. Damage to the truck was $300 and $1,800 to the car. In addition the driver of the car was granted $28,000 because of internal injuries resulting from the collision. Electrical Supply Co. carries 25/50/10 liability, comprehensive, and $100-deductible collision insurance.
   (a) What amount is the insurance company responsible for?
   (b) What is the cost to Electrical Supply?

18. Eric Flemming's car recently skidded on ice and sideswiped another vehicle.

Damage to the other auto was $350 and $175 to his own car. The other driver suffered a neck injury; he sued Flemming for $15,000 bodily injuries and was awarded $7,500. Flemming carried 10/20/10 liability insurance, comprehensive, and $100-deductible collision insurance.

(a) For how much of the cost of Flemming's accident was the insurance company responsible?

(b) How much did Flemming have to pay?

19. Excessive speed and driving while intoxicated were the causes of an accident which left a father and child dead and a mother seriously injured. Following a court suit, the widow was awarded $60,000 on behalf of her husband, $10,000 on behalf of the child, and $2,000 because of her own injuries. Property damages were $2,500 to the victims' automobile and $1,500 to the defendant's car. The negligent driver carried 50/100/5 liability insurance, comprehensive, and $100-deductible collision insurance.

(a) How much of the cost of this accident will the insurance company pay?

(b) For how much will the guilty driver be responsible?

20. A company car belonging to Phillips Sales, Inc. went out of control, left the road, and crashed into a private home. The car was a total loss ($2,000) and damage to the house was listed at $5,800. An occupant of the car, who was not an employee, sued Phillips Sales and was awarded $30,000 by the court for personal injuries.

(a) Determine what total amount the insurance company should pay, if Phillips Sales carried 25/50/10 liability insurance, comprehensive, and $50-deductible collision insurance.

(b) How much will Phillips Sales have to pay in damages?

3. LIFE INSURANCE

The basic purpose of life insurance is to provide compensation to survivors following the death of the insured. Whereas other types of insurance pay damages only up to the actual value of the insured property, life insurance companies make no attempt to assign a maximum value to any life. A policyholder (in good health and with normal expectancy of survival) may purchase insurance of whatever amount he desires; and, when death occurs, the full value of the life insurance coverage will be paid.

The responsibility which most men feel for the financial security of their families induces them to purchase life insurance. The Institute of Life Insurance reports that approximately 90% of all married men with children under 18 are insured; and more than half own policies of at least $10,000. A majority of wives and children are also insured, at lesser amounts.

Many businesses purchase life insurance on key members of the firm whose death would cause a severe loss to the business. Partners sometimes carry insurance on each other so that, in event of a death, the surviving partners can purchase the deceased partner's share of the business from his estate.

There are four basic types of individually-owned life insurance policies. In order of increasing premium rates, they are the (1) term policy, (2) straight life policy, (3) limited payment policy, and (4) endowment policy.

TERM INSURANCE

The *term* policy is so named because it is issued for a specific period of time. The policyholder is insured during this time and, if he is still alive when the term expires, the coverage then ceases. Term insurance is considerably less expensive than the other types of policies. The reasons for the low cost are (1) since term policies are usually issued for relatively short periods of time, there is a good chance that death benefits will not be paid; and (2) unlike the other types of life insurance, term policies do not build investment value for the policyholder. (Investment values are discussed in the section, "Nonforfeiture options.")

Term policies are commonly issued for terms of 5, 10, or 15 years. Many men feel their need for insurance is greatest while they are younger and have children to support and educate. Term policies can provide maximum insurance protection during these years at a minimum cost. Another typical use of term policies is the life insurance purchased for a plane or boat trip; the term in this case is the duration of the trip.

Term policies may include the provision that, at the end of the term, the policy may be renewed for another term or converted to another form of insurance (both at increased premium rates). A variation of the ordinary term policy is *decreasing term* insurance; under this policy, the face value is largest when issued and decreases each year until it reaches zero at the end of the term.

STRAIGHT LIFE

The *straight life* (or *ordinary life*) policy is by far the life insurance coverage most often purchased in the United States. In order to maintain insurance protection, the insured must continue paying premiums for as long as he lives.

LIMITED PAYMENT LIFE

When this type of policy is purchased, the policyholder makes payments for only a limited number of years. If the policyholder survives beyond this time, he makes no further payments; however, his insurance coverage remains in force for the remainder of his life. This coverage is similar to straight life insurance, except the payments are sufficiently larger so that the policyholder will pay, during the limited payment period, an amount approximately equivalent to the total that would be paid during an average lifetime for straight life insurance.

Limited payment policies are frequently sold with payment periods of 20 or 30 years. Such policies are called "20-payment life" or "30-payment life" policies. The limited payment policy is also commonly sold with a payment period so that the policy is "paid up" at age 65.

The term *whole life policy* is often used to describe both the straight life and the limited payment life policy. The term is used because both types provide insurance protection during the entire (whole) lifetime of the insured.

ENDOWMENT

Like the term policy, the endowment policy provides insurance coverage for a specified number of years. It differs in that, if the insured is still alive when the policy period ends, the policyholder himself may receive the full face value of the policy. (Of course, his insurance protection would terminate at that time.)

Typical of endowment policies are the policies sold to "provide for the college education of your children." Naturally, the cost of these policies is quite high, because the premiums not only purchase insurance protection during the term of the policy but must also build the amount required to pay the face value at the end of that time. Stated another way, insurance companies sell endowment policies knowing that all of these policies must pay off in full at the end of the specified time period, if not before; thus endowment policies are rather expensive.

Endowment insurance is a poor means of saving money for people who already have adequate insurance, because insurance companies are conservative institutions and pay a low rate of interest. However, the policy does provide life insurance coverage not provided by commercial savings institutions; thus an individual who does not own much insurance may consider the lost interest as simply the price he pays for the insurance protection and therefore worth the cost.

Insurance policies are further classified as *participating* or *nonparticipating*. *Participating* policies are so named because the policyholders participate in the profits earned on these policies. The premium rates charged for participating policies are usually somewhat higher, because the insurance companies charge more than they expect to need in order to pay claims and operating expenses. However, the excess funds at the end of the year are then refunded to policyholders in the form of *dividends*.

At the time the policyholder purchases a participating policy, he usually selects the form in which dividends will be paid. The usual choices available to the policyholder are that the dividends may be (a) paid in cash; (b) used to help pay the premiums; (c) used to purchase additional paid-up insurance (paid-up insurance is discussed in the section, "nonforfeiture options"); or (d) left invested with the company to accumulate with interest. A fifth option sometimes available is that the dividends may be (e) used to purchase a one-year term insurance policy.

Nonparticipating policies, on the other hand, generally offer lower premium rates than participating policies; however, no dividends are paid on nonparticipating policies. Thus the actual annual cost of life insurance may be less for participating policyholders than for the owners of nonparticipating policies. A majority of the policies sold in the United States are in the participating category.

Most participating policies are sold by mutual companies. *Mutual life insurance companies* do not have stockholders, but are owned by the policyholders themselves. The companies are governed by a board of directors elected by the policyholders. Life insurance companies may also be *stock companies*, which are corporations operated for the purpose of earning profits and which are owned by stockholders. As is the usual case for corporations, the board of directors of a stock life insurance company is elected by the stockholders, and the profits earned by the company are paid to the stockholders. Thus most stock companies issue nonparticipating policies, although a few do issue some participating policies.

PREMIUMS

The risk assumed by insurance companies for other types of policies (fire or automobile, for example) is the probability that a loss will occur; and, even if a loss occurs, it may be only a partial loss. With life insurance, however, the risk is not "whether" a loss will occur, but "when" the loss will occur; for death will inevitably come to all policyholders. Thus premium rates for life insurance are higher than for corresponding amounts of coverage under other kinds of policies.

Premium rates for life insurance are computed by an *actuary*, a highly-skilled person trained in mathematical probability as well as business administration. In order to calculate premiums and benefits, the actuary uses a *mortality table*; this is an extensive table showing, for a large number of people, how many persons are alive at each age from 0 to 99 years, how many people die at each age, and the death rate for each age. The data composing a mortality table are collected over a period of years by life insurance agents in all states.

The mortality table in current use is the Commissioner's 1958 Standard Ordinary Mortality Table, which is reprinted here for the student's information as Table 6-6. If a group of people, all of the same age, take out insurance during the same year, the mortality table enables the actuary to know how many claims to expect during each succeeding year. He must set premium rates so that the total amount paid by all policy- holders is sufficient to pay all these claims, as well as to finance business expenses.

Almost all life insurance sold today is issued on the *level premium system.* This means that the policyholder pays the same premium each year for his life insurance protection. Thus the policyholders pay more than the ex- pected claims during the early years of their policies, and during the later years they pay less than the cost of the claims. The excess paid during the early years is invested by the insurance company, and interest earned on these investments pays part of the cost of the insurance. Thus the total premium cost over many years is less than if the policyholders paid each year only the amount which the company expected to need.

A physical examination is usually required before an individual life insurance policy will be issued. (Group policies, on the other hand, are generally issued without physical examinations.) Annual premiums on new policies are naturally less expensive for younger people, since their life expectancy is longer and the insurance company expects them to pay for more years than older persons would. (This emphasizes the advisabil- ity of setting up an adequate insurance program while one is still young. The high cost of insurance taken out at an older age makes new coverage too expensive for many older persons to afford.) Life insurance taken out at any given age is usually less expensive for women than for men, because women have a longer life expectancy.

Life insurance premiums on new policies are determined by the ap- plicant's age to his nearest birthday. Thus a person $26\frac{1}{2}$ would pay premiums as though he were 27 at the time when the policy was issued.

Life insurance policies are written with face values in multiples of $1,000. The tables of rates list the cost for a $1,000 policy; and this rate must be multiplied by the number of thousands of dollars in coverage that is being purchased. Table 6-7 gives typical annual premiums per $1,000 of face value for each type of life insurance policy, when taken out at various ages. (The policyholder would pay a slightly higher annual total if he paid premiums semiannually, quarterly, or monthly. Each semi- annual premium is approximately 51.5% of the annual premium; quarterly premiums are approximately 26.3% of the annual; and each monthly premium would be approximately 8.9% of the annual.) Actually, pre- miums vary greatly from company to company, as do the nonforfeiture values which will be discussed later. The premiums in Table 6-7 represent an approximate average between participating and nonparticipating rates.

TABLE 6-6: COMMISSIONERS 1958 STANDARD ORDINARY MORTALITY TABLE

Age	Number Living	Deaths Each Year	Deaths Per 1,000	Age	Number Living	Deaths Each Year	Deaths Per 1,000
0	10,000,000	70,800	7.08	50	8,762,306	72,902	8.32
1	9,929,200	17,475	1.76	51	8,689,404	79,160	9.11
2	9,911,725	15,066	1.52	52	8,610,244	85,758	9.96
3	9,896,659	14,449	1.46	53	8,524,486	92,832	10.89
4	9,882,210	13,835	1.40	54	8,431,654	100,337	11.90
5	9,868,375	13,322	1.35	55	8,331,317	108,307	13.00
6	9,855,053	12,812	1.30	56	8,223,010	116,849	14.21
7	9,842,241	12,401	1.26	57	8,106,161	125,970	15.54
8	9,829,840	12,091	1.23	58	7,980,191	135,663	17.00
9	9,817,749	11,879	1.21	59	7,844,528	145,830	18.59
10	9,805,870	11,865	1.21	60	7,698,698	156,592	20.34
11	9,794,005	12,047	1.23	61	7,542,106	167,736	22.24
12	9,781,958	12,325	1.26	62	7,374,370	179,271	24.31
13	9,769,633	12,896	1.32	63	7,195,099	191,174	26.57
14	9,756,737	13,562	1.39	64	7,003,925	203,394	29.04
15	9,743,175	14,225	1.46	65	6,800,531	215,917	31.75
16	9,728,950	14,983	1.54	66	6,584,614	228,749	34.74
17	9,713,967	15,737	1.62	67	6,355,865	241,777	38.04
18	9,698,230	16,390	1.69	68	6,114,088	254,832	41.68
19	9,681,840	16,846	1.74	69	5,859,253	267,241	45.61
20	9,664,994	17,300	1.79	70	5,592,012	278,426	49.79
21	9,647,694	17,655	1.83	71	5,313,586	287,731	54.15
22	9,630,039	17,912	1.86	72	5,025,855	294,766	58.65
23	9,612,127	18,167	1.89	73	4,731,089	299,289	63.26
24	9,593,960	18,324	1.91	74	4,431,800	301,894	68.12
25	9,575,636	18,481	1.93	75	4,129,906	303,011	73.37
26	9,557,155	18,732	1.96	76	3,826,895	303,014	79.18
27	9,538,423	18,981	1.99	77	3,523,881	301,997	85.70
28	9,519,442	19,324	2.03	78	3,221,884	299,829	93.06
29	9,500,118	19,760	2.08	79	2,922,055	295,683	101.19
30	9,480,358	20,193	2.13	80	2,626,372	288,848	109.98
31	9,460,165	20,718	2.19	81	2,337,524	278,983	119.35
32	9,439,447	21,239	2.25	82	2,058,541	265,902	129.17
33	9,418,208	21,850	2.32	83	1,792,639	249,858	139.38
34	9,396,358	22,551	2.40	84	1,542,781	231,433	150.01
35	9,373,807	23,528	2.51	85	1,311,348	211,311	161.14
36	9,350,279	24,685	2.64	86	1,100,037	190,108	172.82
37	9,325,594	26,112	2.80	87	909,929	168,455	185.13
38	9,299,482	27,991	3.01	88	741,474	146,997	198.25
39	9,271,491	30,132	3.25	89	594,477	126,303	212.46
40	9,241,359	32,622	3.53	90	468,174	106,809	228.14
41	9,208,737	35,362	3.84	91	361,365	88,813	245.77
42	9,173,375	38,253	4.17	92	272,552	72,480	265.93
43	9,135,122	41,382	4.53	93	200,072	57,881	289.30
44	9,093,740	44,741	4.92	94	142,191	45,026	316.66
45	9,048,999	48,412	5.35	95	97,165	34,128	351.24
46	9,000,587	52,473	5.83	96	63,037	25,250	400.56
47	8,948,114	56,910	6.36	97	37,787	18,456	488.42
48	8,891,208	61,794	6.95	98	19,331	12,916	668.15
49	8,829,410	67,104	7.60	99	6,415	6,415	1,000.00

TABLE 6-7: ANNUAL LIFE INSURANCE PREMIUMS
PER $1,000 OF FACE VALUE FOR MALE APPLICANTS

Age Issued	Term 10-Yr.	Straight Life	Limited Payment 20-Year	Endowment 20-Year
18	$ 6.81	$14.77	$24.69	$43.82
20	6.88	15.46	25.59	44.95
22	6.95	16.12	26.53	46.16
24	7.05	16.82	27.53	47.44
25	7.10	17.22	28.06	48.10
26	7.18	17.67	28.63	48.80
28	7.35	18.64	29.84	50.29
30	7.59	19.73	31.12	51.88
35	8.68	23.99	35.80	56.06
40	10.64	28.26	40.34	61.40
45	14.52	33.79	46.01	68.28
50	22.18	40.77	53.24	76.12
55	32.93	51.38	64.77	—
60	—	59.32	70.86	—

Example One

Jack Wilkins is 28 and wishes to purchase $5,000 of life insurance. Determine the annual cost of (a) a straight life policy, and (b) a 20-payment life policy.

In both cases, the insurance coverage is to be 5 thousand dollars. Thus each premium rate from Table 6-7 must be multiplied by 5.

(a) *Straight life*

$18.64   Premium per $1,000
  ×5
$93.20   Premium on $5,000

(b) *20-payment life*

$29.84   Premium per $1,000
  ×5
$149.20   Premium on $5,000

Wilkins would pay an annual premium of (a) $93.20 for a $5,000 straight life policy, or (b) $149.20 for the same coverage under a 20-payment life policy.

Suppose Jack Wilkins (Example 1) lived for 43 years after purchasing his life insurance. (a) How much would he pay altogether in premiums for each policy? (b) Which policy would cost more, and how much more? **Example Two**

(a)

$93.20	Annual straight life premium
×43	Number of premiums
$4,007.60	Total premium cost for straight life policy

Payments would be made on the 20-payment life policy for only 20 years.

$149.20	Annual 20-payment life premium
×20	Number of premiums
$2,984.00	Total premium cost for 20-payment life policy

The total premium cost of Wilkins' insurance would be $4,007.60 for a $5,000 straight life policy and only $2,984.00 for an equivalent 20-payment life policy. Thus—

(b)

$4,007.60	Total cost of straight life policy
−2,984.00	Total cost of 20-payment life policy
$1,023.60	Extra cost for straight life policy

The straight life policy would cost Wilkins $1,023.60 more if he lived to be 71.

Besides the basic life insurance coverage, several types of additional protection may be purchased at a slight increase in premiums. Among the additional features most frequently purchased are the *waiver of premium benefit* (the company agrees to pay the cost of the policyholder's insurance in case of total and permanent disability) and the *double indemnity benefit* (the insurance company will pay twice the face value of the policy if death results from accidental causes rather than illness.)

NONFORFEITURE OPTIONS

The most obvious benefit from an insurance policy is the death benefit: the policyholder designates a person, called the *beneficiary*, to receive the face value of the policy following his death. However, there are a number of benefits available to the insured himself which should be taken into consideration when selecting a policy.

Whereas the premiums paid for other types of insurance policies purchase only protection, the premiums paid for life insurance policies (except term policies) also build an investment for the policyholder. This investment accumulates because the level premium system has caused excess funds to be paid into the company. Due to selling and bookkeeping costs, a policyholder is not usually considered to have accumulated any investment until two or three years after the policy was written. Any time thereafter, however, the policy possesses certain values, called *nonforfeiture values* (or *nonforfeiture options*) to which the policyholder is entitled. These values may often be claimed only if the insured stops paying premiums for some reason, or if he turns in his policy (and is thus no longer insured). The principal nonforfeiture options (cash value, paid-up insurance, and extended term insurance) are outlined briefly in the following paragraphs.

Included in each life insurance policy (excluding term policies) is a table showing the *cash value* of the policyholder's investment after each year. If the insured wishes to terminate his insurance coverage, he may surrender his policy and receive this cash value. If the policyholder needs some money but prefers to maintain his insurance protection, he may borrow up to the cash value of his policy. The loan must be repaid with interest at a moderate rate, and the full amount of insurance coverage will remain in force during this time.

If the insured wishes to stop paying premiums and surrender his policy, the cash value of the policy may be used to purchase a reduced level of *paid-up insurance*. This means that the company will issue a policy which has a smaller face value but which is completely paid for. That is, without paying any further premiums, the policyholder will have a reduced amount of insurance which will remain in effect for the remainder of his life. Life insurance policies (except term policies) also contain a table showing the amount of paid-up insurance which the cash value would purchase after each year.

When a policyholder simply stops paying premiums without notifying the company of his intent and without selecting a nonforfeiture option, the company usually automatically applies the third nonforfeiture option: *extended term insurance*. Under this plan the policy remains in effect, at its full face value, for a limited period of time. Stated another way, the cash value of the policy is used to purchase a term policy with the same face value and for the maximum time period that the cash value will finance. Each policy also includes a table indicating after each year the length of time that an extended term policy would remain in force. (This provision does not apply to term policies, since they do not build cash value.)

Note: Most insurance companies allow a *grace period* (usually 31 days following the date a premium is due) during which time the overdue premium may be paid without penalty. The policy remains in effect during this time.

TABLE 6-8: NONFORFEITURE OPTIONS* ON TYPICAL LIFE INSURANCE POLICIES

(Issued at age 25)

Years in Force	Straight Life				20-Payment Life				20-Yr. Endowment			
	Cash Value	Paid-up Insur.	Ext. Term Yrs.	Ext. Term Days	Cash Value	Paid-up Insur.	Ext. Term Yrs.	Ext. Term Days	Cash Value	Paid-up Insur.	Ext. Term Yrs.	Ext. Term Days
3	$ 4	$ 14	1	174	$ 27	$ 89	10	84	$ 39	$ 104	14	42
5	26	82	9	71	68	213	19	184	90	227	23	126
10	88	243	18	46	182	502	28	186	316	515	30	131
15	157	382	20	148	314	763	32	164	590	772	35	290
20	246	530	21	137	465	1,000	Life		1,000	1,000	Life	
40	571	822	—	—	696	—	—	—	—	—	—	

*The "cash value" and "paid-up insurance" nonforfeiture values are per $1,000 of life insurance coverage. The time period for "extended term insurance" applies as shown to all policies, regardless of face value.

Bill Akron purchased an $8,000 20-payment life insurance policy at age 25. Determine the following values for his policy after it had been in force for 10 years: (a) cash value, (b) the amount of paid-up insurance which he could claim, and (c) the time period for which extended term insurance would remain in effect.

Example Three

(a) As shown in Table 6-8, the cash value per $1,000 of face value after 10 years on a 20-payment life policy issued at age 25 is $182. Therefore, the cash value of an $8,000 policy is

$182   Cash value per $1,000

× 8

$1,456   Cash value of an $8,000 policy.

The cash value of Akron's $8,000 policy would be $1,456 after the policy had been in effect for 10 years. Akron could receive this amount by turning in his policy and foregoing his insurance coverage; or he could borrow this amount and pay it back with interest without losing his insurance protection.

(b) The amount of paid-up insurance available is

$502   Paid-up insurance per $1,000

× 8

$4,016   Paid-up insurance on an $8,000 policy

If Akron surrenders his policy, he could receive a policy of $4,016 which would remain in force until his death without any premiums being required.

(c) From Table 6-8, we see that if Akron stops paying premiums, for whatever reason, extended term insurance would allow his full $8,000 coverage to remain in effect for 28 years and 186 days.

Except for term policies, the amount paid in premiums does not represent the true cost of insurance, because part of this money is building cash value for the insured and, for participating policies, part is refunded in the form of dividends. The actual cost, or net cost, of a policy is found as follows:

Nonparticipating policies

Net Cost = Premiums − Cash Value

Participating policies

Net Cost = Premiums − (Cash Value + Dividends)

The cost of different insurance policies (to date of maturity or to date of surrender) should be compared by comparing the net cost of each rather than just considering their annual premiums. (However, a policyholder who has no intention of cashing in his policy and is interested only in the insurance protection he receives might be more concerned with the relative premium rates of various policies.) When policies remain in force for many years, the cash value (plus dividends, if any) often exceeds the amount paid in premiums, thus resulting in a *net profit* or *net return* to the policyholder on his insurance.

Example Four

Oscar Longstreet purchased a $12,000 nonparticipating 20-year endowment policy from Company A when he was 25. Using Tables 6-7 and 6-8, (a) Determine the net cost of this policy after 15 years. (b) Suppose Longstreet had purchased a similar policy, but participating, from Company B at an annual premium of $50.20 per $1,000. Assume that total dividends during the 15 years were $73. What would be the net cost of policy B after 15 years, if the cash value at that time is $645 per $1,000? (c) Which policy would have been more expensive (in terms of net cost) and how much more?

(a)

Premium Cost

$48.10	Annual premium per $1,000
×12	
$577.20	Annual premium on $12,000
×15	Years
$8,658.00	Total premiums

Net Cost

Total premiums	$8,658
Less cash value ($590 × 12)	−7,080
Net Cost	$1,578

The cost of the policy from Company A was $1,578 for 15 years.

(b)

Premium Cost

$50.20	Annual premium per $1,000
×12	
$602.40	Annual premium on $12,000
×15	Years
$9,036.00	Total premiums

Net Cost

Total premiums	$9,036
Less cash value	
($645 × 12) = $7,740	
Dividends +73	
	−7,813
Net Cost	$1,223

The net cost of the policy from Company B would be $1,223 for 15 years.

(c) Thus the nonparticipating policy, which has smaller annual premiums, actually has a higher net cost for 15 years.

Policy A (nonparticipating)	$1,578
Policy B (participating)	−1,223
Additional net cost	$ 355

The net cost of the policy from Company A would be $355 more than the net cost of the policy from Company B for 15 years.

Settlement Options

When a life insurance policyholder dies, there are several ways in which the death benefits may be paid. The beneficiary may receive the face value in one lump-sum payment; more than 90% of all death benefits are paid in this way. Or the benefits may be left invested with the company in order to earn interest. An alternate method of receiving benefits, which deserves consideration, is to receive the benefits in the form of an annuity. An *annuity* is a series of payments, equal in amount and paid at equal intervals of time. (We shall consider here only annuities paid monthly.) There are several options available to the beneficiary concerning the type of annuity (or installment) he may choose; these choices are described briefly below.

1. The beneficiary may choose a monthly installment of a *fixed amount*. In this case, the specified amount will be paid each month for as long as the insurance money (plus interest earned on it) lasts. (For example, a beneficiary may decide to receive a payment of $50 per month; this will continue until the account is depleted.)

2. The beneficiary may decide he prefers the security of a monthly payment for a *fixed number of years*. (For example, the beneficiary may want to receive monthly payments for 15 years.) The insurance agent will then determine how much the beneficiary may receive monthly, in order for the funds to last the specified number of years.

3. A third choice is to take the benefits in the form of an *annuity for life*. That is, depending upon the age and sex of the beneficiary, the insurance company will agree to pay a monthly income to the beneficiary for as long as he lives.

4. The remaining possibility is to receive a *life annuity, guaranteed for a certain number of years*. (For example, if the beneficiary chooses a life annuity guaranteed for 15 years, a monthly annuity will be paid for a minimum of 15 years or as long thereafter as the beneficiary lives.) The monthly income from this annuity is somewhat lower than from the life annuity in Plan 3, but a guaranteed annuity is selected much more often than an ordinary life annuity. The reason for this is that the unqualified life annuity is payable only to the beneficiary himself; when the beneficiary dies, even if only one annuity payment has been made, no further benefits will be paid. However, the guaranteed annuity is payable to the survivors or estate of the beneficiary, if he should die before the specified time period has elapsed. Thus most people with dependents naturally choose the guaranteed annuity. Even persons without dependents often select the guaranteed annuity,

feeling that they would rather have someone receive the payments if they should die, instead of risking that most of the face value of the policy might be lost.

It should be noted that these settlement options are also available to the policyholder himself when an endowment policy matures. Also, older people often feel that they no longer need the amount of life insurance coverage carried since they were younger and had children to support. Thus many retired persons convert some of their life insurance policies to annuities in order to supplement other retirement income. (When straight life or limited payment life policies are converted to annuities, the monthly installment depends upon the cash value of the policy, rather than upon its face value.)

Table 6-9 lists the monthly income per $1,000 of face value available under the various settlement options. Life insurance policies also include tables similar to Table 6-9.

TABLE 6-9: SETTLEMENT OPTIONS

Monthly Installments per $1,000 of Face Value

Fixed Amount or Fixed Number of Years		Income for Life				
		Age When Annuity Begins			With 10 Years Certain	With 20 Years Certain
				Life Annuity		
Years	Amount	Male	Female	Annuity	Certain	Certain
10	$9.41	40	45	$3.80	$3.76	$3.64
12	8.03	45	50	4.15	4.09	3.90
14	7.05	50	55	4.58	4.50	4.18
15	6.65	55	60	5.14	5.01	4.47
16	6.31	60	65	5.86	5.61	4.75
18	5.74	65	70	6.82	6.30	4.98
20	5.29					

Example Five

Helen Remington, age 55, is the beneficiary of a $10,000 life insurance policy. Instead of taking the benefits in a single payment, Mrs. Remington wishes to receive the money in monthly installments. (a) What would be the monthly payment if she decides to receive payments for 15 years? (b) Suppose Mrs. Remington arranges to receive a monthly income of $80 per month from the insurance company. How many years would the payments continue before the funds were exhausted?

(a) Since this policy had a face value of $10,000, Mrs. Remington will receive 10 times the amount shown in Table 6-9 for any option that she might select. The table shows that for a $1,000 policy, the monthly installment for the fixed number of years (15) would be $6.65.

$6.65   Monthly installment per $1,000

×10
_____

$66.50   Monthly installment from $10,000 policy

Thus Mrs. Remington could receive the policy benefits by means of a $66.50 payment each month for 15 years.

(b) Since Mrs. Remington would receive 10 times any amount shown, we see that 10 × $8.03 will provide her approximately $80 per month. Table 6-9 indicates that Mrs. Remington could receive $80.30 per month for 12 years before the money (and interest paid by the insurance company) has been depleted.

Note: Notice that Mrs. Remington's age had no bearing on this problem, because she was not considering an annuity that would pay for the remainder of her life.

Example Six   Harry Maulson became the beneficiary of an $8,000 life insurance policy. If he was 50 at the time—(a) What monthly income would the policy finance if Maulson selected a life annuity? (b) How much would Maulson receive monthly if he chose an annuity guaranteed for 10 years?

(a) Maulson's age affects both these options because either annuity will pay until Maulson's death. (Notice an older person would receive more per month because it is not expected that he would receive payments for as many years.) According to Table 6-9, for a male age 50, the life annuity would pay

$4.58   Monthly annuity per $1,000

×8
_____

$36.64   Monthly annuity from $8,000 policy

This $8,000 policy would guarantee Maulson a monthly income of $36.64 for as long as he lives. The payments will stop immediately upon Maulson's death; no further benefits would then be paid by the insurance company, regardless of how few monthly installments may have been paid.

(b) If Maulson chooses an annuity guaranteed for 10 years, the monthly installment would be

$4.50   Monthly annuity per $1,000

×8
_____

$36.00   Monthly annuity from $8,000 policy

Under this option, Maulson can receive $36 per month for as long as he lives. Since the annuity is guaranteed for 10 years, the payments will continue for 10 years even if Maulson dies during that time.

Jane Worthington was the beneficiary of a $25,000 life insurance policy when she was 65. She chose to receive the benefits through monthly installments for 10 years. (a) What monthly installment did Mrs. Worthington receive? (b) Mrs. Worthington actually lived for 12 years. How much would she have received monthly if she had selected a life annuity guaranteed for 20 years? (c) Under which option would she have received more total income, and how much more?

Example Seven

(a) $9.41   Monthly income per $1,000 for fixed number of
       ×25   years (10)
    ─────────
     $235.25   Monthly income from $25,000 policy

Mrs. Worthington received $235.25 per month by choosing to have the benefits paid over a 10-year period.

(b) The monthly installment on a life annuity guaranteed for 20 years would have been

       $4.75   Monthly annuity per $1,000 (life annuity guar-
       ×25   anteed 20 years)
    ─────────
     $118.75   Monthly annuity from $25,000 policy

Mrs. Worthington would have received $118.75 per month had she chosen the life annuity guaranteed for 20 years.

(c) The total payments received under each policy would have been as follows:

10-Year Annuity		Life Annuity Guaranteed 20 Years	
12	Months per year	12	Months per year
×10	Years	×12	Years
120	Payments	144	Payments
$235.25	Monthly annuity	$118.75	Monthly annuity
×120	Payments	×144	Payments
$28,230.00	Total received	$17,100.00	Total received

Thus Mrs. Worthington received the full amount of the 10-year annuity or $28,230. Before her death, she would have received $17,100 from the life annuity guaranteed for 20 years. Therefore, she received $28,230 − $17,100, or $11,130 more, by selecting the 10-year annuity. (Note that payments from the guaranteed annuity would have continued to Mrs. Worthington's heirs for 8 more years.)

PROBLEMS

Unless other rates are given, use the tables in this chapter to compute the following life insurance problems. Assume each age given is the "insurable age" (age to the nearest birthday).

Using the information given and Table 6-7, compute the annual premium for each life insurance policy:

		Age	Type of Policy	Face Value
1.	(a)	55	10-year term	$30,000
	(b)	26	Straight life	25,000
	(c)	45	20-payment life	10,000
	(d)	30	20-year endowment	20,000
2.	(a)	24	Straight life	$10,000
	(b)	30	20-payment life	12,000
	(c)	35	10-year term	25,000
	(d)	50	20-year endowment	5,000

Determine the nonforfeiture values of the following policies, based on the rates in Table 6-8 (for policies issued at age 25):

		Years in Force	Type of Policy	Face Value	Nonforfeiture Option
3.	(a)	5	Straight life	$10,000	Cash value
	(b)	15	20-payment life	18,000	Extended term
	(c)	20	Straight life	50,000	Paid-up insurance
	(d)	10	20-year endowment	15,000	Cash value
4.	(a)	20	Straight life	$12,000	Extended term
	(b)	15	20-payment life	5,000	Paid-up insurance
	(c)	10	20-year endowment	10,000	Cash value
	(d)	10	20-payment life	25,000	Cash value

Use Table 6-9 to find the monthly annuity (or total years of the annuity) which the beneficiary may select in settlement of the following policies:

		Beneficiary Sex	Beneficiary Age	Face Value	Settlement Option Chosen	Monthly Annuity Years	Monthly Annuity Amount
5.	(a)	F	54	$10,000	Fixed no. of years	10	
	(b)	F	55	30,000	Fixed amt. per mo.		$240
	(c)	M	65	5,000	Life annuity	—	
	(d)	F	45	16,000	Guaranteed annuity	10	

6. (a) F   57 $10,000   Fixed amt. per mo. $70
    (b) M   60   5,000   Fixed no. of years   12
    (c) M   50   8,000   Guaranteed annuity   20
    (d) F   45   25,000   Life annuity   —

7. Charles Malina purchased a $40,000, 20-payment life policy when he was 40.
    (a) What was his annual premium?
    (b) If Malina had purchased a straight life policy of the same face value, what would his annual premium have been?
    Suppose Malina lives for 29 years after buying this insurance. How much would Malina pay before his death—
    (c) For the 20-payment life policy?
    (d) For the straight life policy?

8. The small firm of Williams Electronics wished to insure the life of its owner, Jay Williams, for 10 years, until the firm could become well established and until additional personnel could be thoroughly trained. If Williams was 35 years old—
    (a) What would the premiums on a $50,000 straight life policy cost for 10 years?
    (b) How much would an equivalent 10-year term policy cost altogether?
    (c) How much would be saved on premiums by purchasing the term policy?
    (d) What other considerations would affect the choice of policy?

9. At age 26, Lloyd Yates took out a $20,000, 10-year term policy.
    (a) Determine the total premium cost for this coverage.
    (b) If Yates had instead purchased a 20-payment life policy of the same face value, what would have been its total premium cost for the same 10-year period?
    (c) When deciding which of these policies to purchase, what besides premium cost should influence the decision?

10. Andrew Potter purchased a $30,000 straight life policy when he was 30.
    (a) How much would premiums on this policy have cost until Potter was 65?
    (b) If Potter had purchased a 20-payment life policy of the same face value, what would have been the total premiums on this policy to age 65?

11. When he was 45, Fred Watson purchased a $12,000 straight life policy.
    (a) How much would Watson have saved annually if he had taken out the policy at age 26?
    (b) How much will the premiums on the straight life policy cost until Watson reaches 65?

(c) What would the premiums have cost to age 65 if Watson had started the policy at 26?

12. Eric Johnson took out a $20,000 20-payment life policy when he was 40.
    (a) How much would he have saved on the annual premium if he had purchased this policy at age 25?
    (b) Find the total amount that would have been saved until the policy was fully paid for.

13. Harry Wallace took out a $25,000, 20-year endowment policy when he was 25.
    (a) What was his annual premium for this policy?
    (b) After 15 years, a general economic recession caused Wallace to reconsider the expense of this policy. If Wallace should decide to forego his insurance coverage, what is the cash value of his policy?
    (c) How much insurance, paid up for life, would his policy provide?
    (d) For how long could Wallace obtain the same amount of coverage under extended term insurance?

14. When he was 25, Emory Crenshaw took out a $20,000 20-payment life insurance policy.
    (a) Compute the annual cost of this policy.
    (b) After the policy had been in force for 15 years, Crenshaw decided not to continue the policy. If he relinquishes all insurance protection, how much cash could he receive?
    (c) If Crenshaw surrenders his policy in exchange for paid-up insurance, what amount of coverage would he have for the rest of his life?
    (d) For how long could he continue the $20,000 coverage under an extended term policy?

15. William Warren took out an $18,000 straight life policy when he was 25. Twenty years later, Warren is facing college expenses for his son. How much can he borrow against his policy without relinquishing his insurance coverage?

16. Richard Sutton owned a $14,000 20-payment life policy which was issued when he was 25. Ten years later, Sutton needed some money but did not want to give up his insurance protection. What amount can he borrow from the insurance company and still keep the policy in force?

17. (a) Calculate the net cost of a $30,000, 10-year term policy purchased at age 25.
    (b) Compute the net cost during the first ten years of a $30,000, 20-payment life policy (nonparticipating) issued at age 25.
    (c) Which policy would have a higher net cost for this period, and how much higher?
    (d) What besides net cost should be considered when comparing these policies?

18. Sol Aaronson, 25, is debating whether to purchase a $15,000 straight life policy (participating) or a $15,000 10-year term policy. Aaronson's agent told him that he could expect dividends of about $130 over a ten-year period on the straight life policy.
    (a) What would be the annual premium on the straight life policy?
    (b) How much would the term policy cost each year?
    (c) Compute the expected net cost of the straight life policy for 10 years.
    (d) What would be the net cost of the term policy for 10 years?
    (e) For which policy would the net cost be less, and how much less?
    (f) What in addition to net cost is a major consideration when considering a term policy?

19. Mr. X, age 25, purchased a $15,000, nonparticipating, straight life insurance policy. Mr. Y, also 25, purchased a $15,000, participating, straight life policy with an annual premium of $19.88 per $1,000.
    (a) How much was the annual premium for each policy?
    (b) What will be the net cost of Mr. X's insurance for 40 years?
    (c) Mr. Y's insurance agent told him that the company's past experience indicates he can expect to receive $1,200 in dividends over the next 40 years. The cash value of his policy at that time will be $635 per $1,000 of face value. What will be the net cost of 40 years of insurance to Mr. Y?
    (d) Which man will pay a higher net cost for his coverage, and how much higher?

20. Adolph De Silva, age 25, wishes to purchase whichever of the following policies would have a lower total net cost. Compute the net cost of—
    (a) A $12,000 20-payment life policy that is nonparticipating.
    (b) An equivalent participating policy. The annual participating premiums are $30.85 per $1,000, the cash value in 20 years will be $506 per $1,000, and the expected dividends for the 20-year period are $372.
    (c) Which policy should De Silva purchase, and how much will he save?

21. (a) What is the net cost of a $35,000 straight life policy (nonparticipating), if it is issued at age 25 and kept till age 65?
    (b) Determine the net cost of an equivalent 20-pay life policy from age 25 to age 65.
    (c) Which policy costs more, and how much more?

22. (a) Determine the net cost after 20 years of a $30,000 20-pay life policy (nonparticipating) which was issued at age 25.
    (b) What is the net cost to maturity of a $30,000 nonparticipating 20-year endowment life policy issued at age 25?
    (c) Which policy has a higher net cost, and how much higher?

23. Janet Gray, who is 45, has inherited a $20,000 life insurance policy.
   (a) If she decides to have the benefits paid in a 15-year annuity, how much will she receive monthly?
   (b) If Mrs. Gray chooses to receive a monthly annuity of about $140, how long will the payments last?

24. Grant Reid, 32, was the beneficiary of a $10,000 life insurance policy from his aunt.
   (a) If Reid chooses to receive annuity payments for 18 years, how much will he receive each month?
   (b) If Reid elects to receive a fixed annuity of approximately $95 per month, approximately how many years will the benefits last?

25. Annette Thompson has become the beneficiary of a $60,000 life insurance policy at age 50.
   (a) If Mrs. Thompson selects the settlement option of a life annuity, how much will she receive each month?
   (b) Determine the monthly payment Mrs. Thompson will receive if she chooses a life annuity guaranteed for 20 years.

26. Loretta Trammell's husband died when she was 45, leaving $35,000 in life insurance.
   (a) How much would Mrs. Trammell receive monthly if she selected a life annuity?
   (b) If she decided to receive a life annuity guaranteed for 10 years, what annuity would Mrs. Trammell receive monthly?

27. Rebecca Morton inherited a $25,000 life insurance policy when she was 55. Mrs. Morton considered a 16-year annuity and a life annuity guaranteed for 10 years, finally selecting the 16-year annuity. Mrs. Morton lived to be 75.
   (a) Determine the total amount Mrs. Morton received from her settlement.
   (b) How much would she have received had she chosen the life annuity guaranteed for 10 years?
   (c) Did Mrs. Morton gain or lose by her choice of settlement methods, and how much?

28. Lawrence Armstrong became the beneficiary of an $8,000 life insurance policy when he was 50. Armstrong gave lengthy consideration to a 20-year annuity and to a life annuity guaranteed for 10 years. Finally, Armstrong decided to be optimistic and chose the guaranteed annuity.
   (a) How much did Armstrong receive altogether, if he lived to be 75?
   (b) What total amount would he have received from the 20-year annuity?
   (c) How much did Armstrong gain by selecting the guaranteed annuity?

29. Mary Horton became the beneficiary of a $40,000 life insurance policy when she was 50. Since she had no dependents, Miss Horton decided to receive a monthly annuity for life.
   (a) What amount did the annuity pay each month?

(b) Miss Horton lived to be 85. What was the total amount she received from the annuity?

(c) Suppose Miss Horton had chosen to have the benefits paid over a 20-year period. What would her monthly annuity have been?

(d) What total amount would the 20-year annuity have paid?

(e) Did Miss Horton gain or lose by her choice of options, and how much?

30. When she was 60, Gretta Frost was the beneficiary of a $50,000 life insurance policy. Mrs. Frost selected a settlement option whereby she would receive a monthly annuity for 15 years.

(a) What was Mrs. Frost's monthly income from the insurance?

(b) If Mrs. Frost died at age 67, how much had she received at the time of her death?

(c) If Mrs. Frost had chosen a life annuity guaranteed for 10 years, how much would she have received monthly?

(d) What total amount would the guaranteed annuity have paid until her death?

(e) Did Mrs. Frost personally gain or lose by her choice of settlement methods, and how much?

35,000 annuity

7

Checkbook Records

Upon completion of Chapter 7, the student will be able to:

1. Define and use correctly the terminology associated with each topic.
2. Prepare a bank reconciliation,
   a. using given information, or
   b. using a check register and bank statement.

PRACTICALLY ALL BUSINESS obligations today are paid by check. Checks are not only more convenient and safer than cash, but the canceled check also constitutes a legal receipt. The procedures involved in a business checking account may be familiar to the student, because they are essentially the same as for personal checking accounts. However, some of the commercial check forms differ slightly from personal forms.

CHECKS

A check, like a bank note, is a *negotiable instrument*, which means it may be transferred from one party to another for its equivalent value; the second party then holds full title to the check. Most checks are written on forms printed by the individual bank. A legal check may be written on plain paper, however, provided the following requirements are met: (1) it must be dated; (2) the bank must be positively identified (with address, if

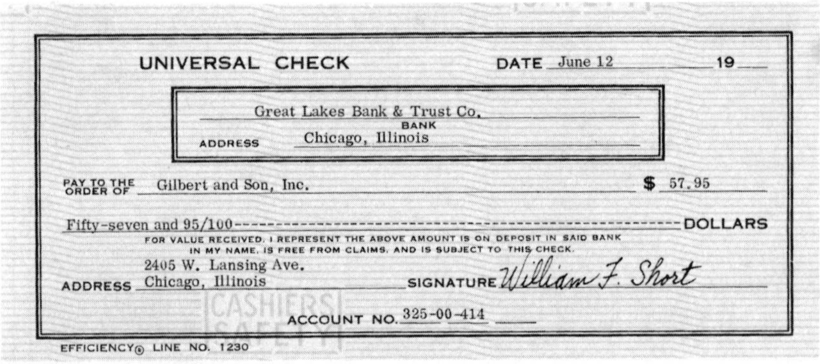
UNIVERSAL CHECK DATE June 12 19

Great Lakes Bank & Trust Co.
BANK
ADDRESS Chicago, Illinois

PAY TO THE ORDER OF Gilbert and Son, Inc. $ 57.95

Fifty-seven and 95/100 DOLLARS

FOR VALUE RECEIVED. I REPRESENT THE ABOVE AMOUNT IS ON DEPOSIT IN SAID BANK IN MY NAME, IS FREE FROM CLAIMS, AND IS SUBJECT TO THIS CHECK.

ADDRESS 2405 W. Lansing Ave. Chicago, Illinois SIGNATURE William F. Short

ACCOUNT NO. 325-00-414

EFFICIENCY® LINE NO. 1230

FIGURE 7-1: UNIVERSAL CHECK

necessary); (3) the check must name the *payee* (the person, firm, "cash," or to whomever it is payable); (4) the amount must be shown; and (5) the check must be signed by the *maker* (the person writing the check). A *universal check* is shown in Figure 7-1; this is a printed check which may be written on any bank, since it contains blanks in which all of the above information may be written.

Figure 7-2 illustrates the traditional commercial checks used by many firms. The check stub should always be kept current; all checks and deposits should be recorded immediately and the new balance computed. The check stub also provides space to record pertinent information about the check itself: what the check was for, how much sales tax (or interest) was included, how much cash discount was taken, etc.

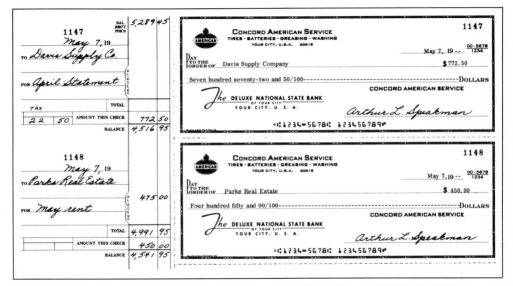

FIGURE 7-2: COMMERCIAL CHECKS

The *voucher check* (Fig. 7-3) is often used in business today (particularly by governmental, tax-financed agencies), and its popularity is gaining. The "voucher" attached to the check itself explains which invoices the check covers, itemizes any deductions, or otherwise accounts for the amount shown on the check. The voucher is not negotiable and is torn off at the perforation before the check is cashed or deposited. The company issuing the check retains one or more carbon copies of the voucher for its records.

Firms using voucher checks ordinarily also keep a *check register*, which is a concise record of checks and deposits. Figure 7-4 illustrates a typical check register.

ORIGINAL

PAYEE SHOULD DETACH TOP
AND DEPOSIT VOUCHER AT ONCE

STATE BOARD OF EDUCATION

DEPARTMENT OF. COMMUNITY COLLEGES

VOUCHER NO. / 1,308

PURCHASE ORDER NO.	DATE OF INVOICE	BUDGET POS. NO.	PARTICULARS	CODE	GROSS AMOUNT	DEDUCTIONS	NET AMOUNT
819	Sept. 23	14	30 Lab Stools	16-D	$345.00	$ 7.90	$337.10
834	Sept. 26	21	60 #243A Desks	9-A	900.00	18.00	882.00
							$1,219.10

IBAA-35

DRAWN BY (NAME AND ADDRESS OF INSTITUTION)

Blue Ridge Community College
Asheville, North Carolina

STATE BOARD OF EDUCATION - DEPARTMENT OF COMMUNITY COLLEGES

PAYABLE AT PAR THROUGH THE FEDERAL RESERVE SYSTEM

PRESENT
TO STATE TREASURER—
STATE OF NORTH CAROLINA
RALEIGH, N. C.

66-1059
512

VOUCHER NO. 1,308

DATE November 9 _____ 19____

THIS CHECK VOID AFTER 60 DAYS FROM DATE

PAY Twelve hundred nineteen and 10/100 ------------------------------- **DOLLARS** $ 1,219.10

TO THE ORDER OF

Whitman Technical Furniture, Inc.
Box 823
High Point, North Carolina

Specimen

Priscilla K. Stokes
AUTHORIZED SIGNATURE

William R. Merten
COUNTERSIGNED

G- 185

1:0512m 1059 1: 4m000m 574 1m

FIGURE 7-3: VOUCHER CHECK

Date	Check Number	Order of	For	Amount Check	Amount Deposit	Balance
19____						$ 919.81
July 16	362	The May Co.	Brass fixtures	$ 86.15		833.66
18	363	Warren's Inc.	Office supplies	15.83		817.83
18		Deposit			$840.00	1,657.83
19	364	Payroll	Weekly payroll	789.25		868.58
21	365	Carson's Inc.	Equipment Rental	27.44		841.14

FIGURE 7-4: CHECK REGISTER

Before a company can deposit or cash the checks it has received, the checks must be endorsed. There are three forms of endorsement in common use: the blank endorsement, the restrictive endorsement, and the special endorsement.

The *blank* endorsement is just the name of the person or the firm (and often the individual representing that firm) to which the check is made payable. This endorsement makes the check negotiable by anyone who has possession of it. That is, such a check could be cashed by anyone if it should become lost or stolen.

Blank   Restrictive   Special

The other two endorsements are somewhat similar. The *restrictive* endorsement is usually applied to indicate that the check must be deposited in the firm's bank account. Many firms endorse all their checks in this manner as soon as they are received, as a precautionary measure against theft. The *special* (or *full*) endorsement indicates a check is to be passed on to another person, firm, or organization. The special endorsement's great advantage over the blank endorsement is that, should the check be lost or stolen, it is negotiable only by the party named in the special endorsement.

After being endorsed, the checks are listed individually on a bank deposit slip. Checks are often listed according to the name of the bank on which they were written; however, many banks prefer that checks be listed by *bank number*. Most printed checks contain the complete identification number of the bank on which the check is written. For example,

$$\frac{66\text{-}1234}{531}$$

The "531" represents the Federal Reserve District within which the bank is located; the "66" identifies the location (state, territory, or city) of the bank; and the "1234" indicates the particular bank in that location. Some checks contain only the numbers indicating location and official bank number (for example, 66-1234). It is sufficient to use this hyphenated number when listing checks on the deposit slip. A completed deposit slip is shown in Figure 7-5.

DEPOSITED IN

FIRST-CITIZENS BANK & TRUST CO.

DATE **May 9** 19____

Checks and other items are received for deposit subject to the terms and conditions of this bank's collection agreement as stated on our signature card.

CURRENCY	134	00
COIN	12	37

CHECKS
LIST BY BANK #

1 66–1234	87	50
2 66–1312	53	43
3 66–1017	118	19
4 72–2059	69	51
5		
6		
7		
8		
9		
10		
11		
12		
13		
14		
15		
16		
17		
18		
19		
20		
21		
22		
23		
24		
25		
26		
27		
28		
29		
30		
31		

DEPOSIT TO THE CREDIT OF

Tarheel Trucking Company

C/O FIRST-CITIZENS BANK & TRUST CO.

GASTONIA, NORTH CAROLINA

LESS CASH

TOTAL DEPOSIT

$475.00

⑆0531⑉106⑆: 60 00 730⑈

FIGURE 7-5: DEPOSIT SLIP

BANK STATEMENTS

A monthly bank statement (Fig. 7-6) is sent to the owner of each checking account. The bank statement is a chronological listing of all the checks, deposits, and other charges recorded by the bank during the month. It is a rare occurrence indeed when the balance shown on the bank statement is exactly the same as the checkbook balance. This does not mean that a mistake has been made in either record; usually neither figure indicates the true balance available to spend. For this reason, the bookkeeper should always *reconcile* the bank statement. Usually both the bank statement balance and the checkbook balance have to be adjusted; when these adjusted balances coincide, the account has been reconciled and the true balance found.

The bank statement usually contains several bank charges indicated

STATEMENT OF YOUR ACCOUNT WITH

Westwood Village

CITY NATIONAL BANK

ACCOUNT NO.

009 109817

PERIOD ENDING   PAGE
May 27, 1968   1
              19

The Gates Company
Box 4490
Los Angeles Calif 90024

PLEASE NOTIFY US IMMEDIATELY
OF ANY CHANGE OF ADDRESS

CHECKS	CHECKS	CHECKS	DEPOSITS	DATE	NEW BALANCE
			BALANCE FORWARD		589:62
125:00				0430	464:62
			235:17	0501	699:79
186:45	92:07			0502	421:27
17:80	345:25			0506	58:22
			354:50	0508	412:72
118:44				0510	294:28
			649:89	0511	944:17
47:63	RT			0512	896:54
510:00	56:03	15:18			
43:67				0514	271:66
			1,359:26	0515	1,630:92
418:16	275:07			0519	937:69
106:19				0521	831:50
78:50	49:77			0523	703:23
2:40	SC			0525	700:83
27:89	345:80			0526	327:14

PLEASE EXAMINE THIS STATEMENT AND THE ENCLOSED ITEMS AT ONCE. IF NO ERROR IS REPORTED WITHIN 10 DAYS, THE STATEMENT WILL BE CONSIDERED CORRECT. ALL ITEMS CREDITED SUBJECT TO FINAL PAYMENT.
◄   **FOR YOUR CONVENIENCE, A RECONCILEMENT FORM AND KEY CODES ARE ON THE REVERSE SIDE**   ►

KEY

CM - Credit Memo	RC - Return Check Charges
CR - Credit Reversal	Bad check by depositor ($3.00 for NSF)
	RT - Return Items – Check deducted
DM - Debit Memo	SC - Service Charges
DR - Debit Reversal	SR - Reverse Service Charge

FIGURE 7-6: BANK STATEMENT

by code letters which are explained at the bottom of the statement. Typical charges are service charges for checks written, charges for printing new checks, corrections in deposits, returned checks, and so forth. (A *returned check* is one for which the writer's account did not contain sufficient funds.

Since the bank was thus unable to collect the funds, it must in turn deduct the amount from the depositor's account and return the check to the depositor. The check may be redeposited after the maker [writer] has had time to replenish the funds in his account.) Bank charges represent funds which the bank has deducted from the client's account. After the amount of these charges has been determined from the bank statement, the bookkeeper must also deduct them from the checkbook balance.

Frequently some checks and possibly a deposit (particularly those near the end of the month) will not have been processed in time to be recorded and returned with the bank statement. Such checks are known as *outstanding checks*. The bookkeeper should check the bank statement against the check-stubs to determine which checks (and deposits) are outstanding. The bookkeeper must determine the amount of the outstanding checks and deduct this amount from the bank statement balance to obtain the adjusted bank balance. (A deposit not included on the bank statement must be added to the bank statement balance to determine the adjusted bank balance.)

After these adjustments have been made, the adjusted bank balance and the adjusted checkbook balance will be the same, provided that all transactions were recorded correctly and that there has been no mathematical mistake. This adjusted balance represents the true balance in the account. Finally, an entry should be made in the checkbook to deduct the amount of the bank charges, so that the checkbook will show the adjusted balance.

Example One Reconcile the bank statement in Fig. 7-6, based on the following information: The checkbook shows a balance of $771.93; a deposit was made on May 28 in the amount of $724.35; outstanding checks are for $174.89, $53.20, $16.42, and $85.08.

BANK RECONCILIATION

Bank balance	$ 327.14	Checkbook balance	$771.93
Add: Outstanding deposit	+724.35		
	$1,051.49		
Less: Outstanding checks			
$174.89			
53.20		Less: Bank charges	
16.42		$47.63	
+85.08	−329.59	+2.40	−50.03
Adjusted balance	$ 721.90	Adjusted balance	$721.90

PROBLEMS

Prepare a bank reconciliation for each of the following:

1. The bank statement balance was $1,433.18, and the checkbook balance was $1,311.23. A bank service charge of $2.43 had been deducted. Outstanding checks were for $16.39; $42.27; $25.95; and $39.77.

2. The checkbook balance was $752.70, and the bank statement balance was $845.19. Outstanding checks were in the amounts of $18.50; $6.98; $45.00; $23.76. A service charge of $1.75 had been deducted.

3. The checkbook showed a balance of $2,019.64, while the bank statement indicated a balance of $1,741.62. A service charge was $3.75. A returned check totaled $28.13. A deposit of $369.45 was not included on the statement. Outstanding checks amounted to $7.16; $54.84; $12.09; $22.74; and $26.48.

4. The bank statement balance was $1,375.25, and the checkbook balance was $1,313.76. A deposit of $106.44 had not been entered on the bank statement. A service charge was $1.50. New checks cost $2.15. A returned check was for $25.00. Outstanding checks were for $8.95; $75.00; $47.81; $26.33; and $38.49.

5. A bank statement indicated a balance of $1,894.20, and the checkbook gave a balance of $1,827.28. Outstanding checks were in the amounts of $118.62; $9.72; $54.19; $85.12; and $37.03. An addition of $10 was made on the bank statement to correct an error in a deposit slip. A service charge was $2.50. New checks cost $1.75. A returned check was $8.79. A deposit of $234.72 was omitted from the bank statement.

6. The checkbook showed a balance of $906.73, whereas the bank statement listed a balance of $684.37. An outstanding deposit totaled $308.82. Outstanding checks were for $41.85; $30.18; $7.95; and $26.63. A charge of $1.00 was shown to correct a deposit. A service charge was $1.65. A returned check amounted to $15.00. New checks cost $2.50 to print.

7. A check register and a bank statement are given below. (a) Find the final balance for each. Determine which checks and deposits have been processed, which are still outstanding, what bank charges have been made, and (b) reconcile the bank statement. (Use the "√" column of the register to check off items that appear on the bank statement. Some have already been checked the preceding month.) Line 5 shows the adjustment made last month to balance the register. (c) How much must be deducted this month to balance the register?

CHECK REGISTER

Check No.	Date	Check Issued To	Amount of Check	√	Amount of Deposit	Balance 1,490 24
154	5/29	Dallas Service Co.	63 ¦ 18	√		
155	5/30	International Sales	13 ¦ 89			
	5/30	Deposit			245 ¦ 37	
156	5/30	Hancock Supply	88 ¦ 92			
	6/1	Adjustment for bank charges	4 ¦ 34	√		
157	6/1	Payroll	807 ¦ 84			
	6/2	Deposit			1,898 ¦ 60	
158	6/4	Community Chest	10 ¦ 00			
159	6/10	City of Austin	78 ¦ 85			
160	6/10	Wholesale Supply Co.	425 ¦ 13			
161	6/10	Welder's Supply	140 ¦ 06			
162	6/10	Southwestern Bell	15 ¦ 88			
163	6/10	Texas Realty Co.	250 ¦ 00			
164	6/10	Southwest Insurance	65 ¦ 24			
165	6/10	Phillips-Cross Co.	347 ¦ 72			
	6/12	Deposit			1,018 ¦ 61	
166	6/15	Payroll	1,124 ¦ 85			
167	6/20	Lonestar Sales	52 ¦ 94			
168	6/25	Garner & Shanks	23 ¦ 26			
	6/28	Deposit			419 ¦ 26	
169	6/29	Centex Supply	283 ¦ 55			

BANK STATEMENT

Checks and Other Debits		Deposits	Date	Balance
			5/31	1,422 ¦ 72
		245 ¦ 37	6/1	
807 ¦ 84	13 ¦ 89		6/3	
88 ¦ 92		1,898 ¦ 60	6/5	
15 ¦ 88	2 ¦ 00 DM		6/11	
347 ¦ 72	78 ¦ 85		6/12	
		1,018 ¦ 61	6/14	
425 ¦ 13			6/17	
250 ¦ 00	1,124 ¦ 85		6/18	
19 ¦ 29 RT	52 ¦ 94		6/24	
3 ¦ 50 SC	23 ¦ 26		6/29	

8. (a) Find the final balance for the check register and bank statement which follow. (b) Reconcile the bank statement. (c) What adjustment is necessary this month to balance the check register? (Line 7 of the register shows the deduction made last month to balance the register.)

CHECK REGISTER

Check No.	Date	Check Issued To	Amount of Check	√	Amount of Deposit	Balance 1,148 16
223	10/27	Allied Freight	18 53	√		1,129 63
224	10/28	Internal Revenue Service	57 49			1,072 14
225	10/28	Great Lakes Laboratories	24 21			1,047 93
	10/30	Deposit			1,476 00	2,523 93
226	11/3	Heavenly Beauty Supplies	35 89			2,488 04
227	11/4	Payroll	442 12			2,045 92
	11/5	Adjustment for bank charges	3 59	√		2,042 33
228	11/10	Midwest Realty	315 00			
229	11/10	Barton Drug Supply	207 65			
230	11/10	Commercial Sales, Inc.	45 72			
231	11/10	Protective Insurance Agency	78 33			
232	11/10	Midwestern Bell Telephone	21 41			
233	11/10	City of Chicago	86 64			
234	11/10	Health Products, Inc.	71 96			
235	11/11	Payroll	407 78			
	11/12	Deposit			891 43	
236	11/15	Great Lakes Laboratories	169 35			
237	11/17	Nationwide Sales, Inc.	262 13			
	11/18	Deposit			455 52	
238	11/18	Payroll	543 29			
239	11/23	Allied Freight	4 34			
	11/24	Deposit			509 60	
240	11/25	Payroll	428 80			
241	11/27	Milford Laboratory	50 09			
	11/28	Deposit			234 03	
242	11/29	Grange Drug Supply	361 15			

BANK STATEMENT

Checks and Other Debits				Deposits	Date	Balance
					10/31	1,126 04
24 21				1,476 00	11/5	
442 12		18 45 RT			11/8	
71 96		35 89			11/12	
86 64		315 00			11/15	
21 41					11/15	
				891 43	11/16	
407 78		45 72			11/17	
169 35				455 52	11/20	
543 29		207 65			11/21	
				509 60	11/26	
428 80		57 49			11/28	
50 09		2 40 SC			11/30	

8

Wages and Payrolls

LEARNING OBJECTIVES

Upon completion of Chapter 8, the student will be able to:

1. Define and use correctly the terminology in each topic.

2. Compute gross wages and payrolls based on
   a. salary,
   b. commission (including quota and override),
   c. production (including incentives and dockings), and
   d. hourly rates.

3. Complete the account sales and account purchase.

4. For overtime work, compute gross wages and payrolls using
   a. hourly rates (at standard overtime or overtime excess),
   b. production, or
   c. salary.

5. a. Complete net weekly payrolls based on
      (1) salary, (2) hourly rate, (3) production (each with overtime), or (4) commission.
   b. Include standard deductions for
      (1) social security, (2) federal income tax, and (3) other common deductions, as given.

6. Complete the disbursement forms required for payrolls paid in cash: the change tally and change slip.

7. a. Determine employees' quarterly FICA taxable wages.
   b. Complete the basic portion of the Employer's Quarterly Federal Tax Return.

8. a. Determine employees' taxable wages for unemployment.
   b. Compute employer's state and Federal unemployment taxes.

IN ANY BUSINESS MATH COURSE, many topics apply primarily to certain types of businesses. For instance, the study of markup and discounts applies primarily to retail businesses; the topics of both simple and compound interest have their main application in the banking profession. There is one aspect of business math, however, which applies to every conceivable type of business, no matter how small or how large—the payroll.

The importance of the payroll cannot be overemphasized. There is probably no other single factor so important to company-employee relations as the negotiation of wages and completion of the payroll. Wage negotiation within a company—whether by a union or on an individual basis—is not a responsibility of the payroll clerk, however, and thus is not included in our study. We shall be concerned with computation of the payroll, which is also a very important responsibility. To find a mistake in his pay is very damaging to an employee's morale. It is imperative, therefore, that everyone connected with the payroll exercise extreme care to insure absolute accuracy.

There are four basic methods for determining gross wages (i.e., before deductions): salary, commission, hourly rate basis, and production basis. We shall make a brief study of each.

Businesses using one of the four basic payroll methods may purchase printed forms on which to compute their payrolls. Many companies, however, use a combination of two or more of the basic plans. These firms often design their own payroll sheets to meet the particular requirements of their company.

1. COMPUTING WAGES—SALARY

Employees on a salary receive the same wages each pay period, whether this be weekly, biweekly, or monthly. Most executives, office personnel, and many professional people receive salaries.

If a salaried person misses some work time because of illness or for personal reasons, he will usually still receive the same salary on payday. However, if business conditions require a salaried person to work extra hours, the payment of additional compensation may vary according to the person's position in the firm. General office personnel who are subject to the Fair Labor Standards Act (a topic in Section 3 of this chapter) must receive extra compensation as though they were normally paid on an hourly-rate basis. However, highly paid executive and administrative personnel, whose positions are at the supervisory and decision-making level of the company, normally receive no additional compensation for extra work. Professional people (members of the medical professions, lawyers, accountants, educators, etc.) are similarly exempt from extra-pay provisions.

For the present time, we shall consider only a normal workweek. In that case, once the payroll clerk has recorded the employee's salary on his paysheet, there is no further work required to determine his gross wages. We shall, therefore, proceed directly to the next form of wage compensation.

2. COMPUTING WAGES—COMMISSION

Business people whose jobs consist of buying or selling merchandise are often compensated for their work by means of a commission. The true (or *straight*) *commission* is determined by finding some per cent of the individual's net sales. Thus we have another business formula based on the basic per cent form "__% of __ = __":

$$\text{__\% of Net sales} = \text{Commission}$$

or simply

$$\% \cdot S = C$$

Certain business people receive commissions without actually calling them *commissions*. For instance, a stockbroker's fee for buying stock is a certain percentage of the purchase price of that stock; however, his fee is called a *brokerage*. A lawyer's fee for handling the legal aspects of a real estate sale is generally some percentage of the value of the property; this constitutes a commission, although it probably will not be called one.

In addition to the straight commission, we will study several variations of the commission form of wage computation.

Example
One

(a) *Straight commission.* A salesman receives a 5% commission on his net sales. If his gross sales were $2,625 and sales returns and allowances amounted to $125, what was his commission?

Gross sales	$2,625		$\%S = C$
Less: Sales returns and			$5\% \times \$2,500 = C$
allowances	-125		$\$125 = C$
Net Sales	$2,500$		

(b) A real estate agent charges 3% of the purchase price of a home as his fee. If his commission on a sale is $540, what did the home sell for?

$$\%S = C$$
$$3\%S = \$540$$
$$\frac{0.03S}{0.03} = \frac{540.00}{0.03}$$
$$S = \$18,000$$

Travel, meals, entertainment, and similar expenses of salesmen usually remain approximately the same regardless of their sales. Thus, once a salesman has made sufficient sales to cover his expenses, the company may be willing to pay him a higher commission on additional sales. A commission rate which increases as sales increase is known as a *sliding-scale commission.*

Sometimes a salesman on straight commission is allowed a "drawing account," from which he may withdraw funds to defray business or personal expenses. The amount of his drawings will be deducted from his commission at the end of the pay period. Although a drawing account assures the salesman of a minimum income, his earned commission must consistently either equal or exceed the drawings, or else the employee will be released from the company.

(c) Herb Adams receives a 5% commission on his first $6,000 sales during the month; he receives a 5½% commission on the next $4,000 in sales, and a 6½% commission on all sales above $10,000. He is entitled to a drawing account of $400. Determine the amount due Adams for a month in which his sales were $11,600.

	$\%S = C$				
0.05 ×	6,000 = $300		Commission	$624
0.055 ×	4,000 = 220		Less: drawings	−400
0.065 ×	1,600 = 104		Amount due	$224
Sales	$11,600	$624 commission		

SALARY AND COMMISSION

Some salespeople are guaranteed a minimum income in the form of a salary. They are then paid commissions at a lower rate than is usually earned by those on straight commission.

(a) Edwina Lewis receives a $35 weekly salary plus a 2% commission on her net sales. If her gross sales for the week were $2,065 and sales returns and allowances were $65, what were her wages for the week?

Example Two

Gross sales	$2,065	%S	= C
Less: Sales returns and		0.02 × 2,000	= C
allowances	−65	$40	= C
Net Sales	$2,000		

Salary	$35
Commission	40
Wages	$75

(b) Walter White receives a salary of $40 a week plus a $1\frac{1}{2}$% commission on his net sales. If White's gross wages for the week were $130, what were his net sales?

Wages	$130
Less: salary	−40
Commission	$90

$$\%S = C$$
$$0.015S = \$90$$

$$\frac{0.015S}{0.015} = \frac{90.000}{0.015}$$

$$S = \$6,000$$

QUOTA AND COMMISSION

Many persons on commission, particularly those who also receive a salary, are required to sell a certain amount (or *quota*) before the commission starts. This plan, which is especially common in retail stores, is designed to insure the company a certain level of performance for the salary it pays.

Department heads in retail stores are often allowed a special commission on the net sales of all the clerks in their departments. This commission, called an *override*, is allowed to offset the time a department head must devote to nonselling responsibilities (such as pricing and stocking merchandise, taking inventory, placing orders, etc.).

Example Three

(a) A salesman is paid a monthly salary of $300 plus a 4% commission on all net sales in excess of $5,000. Find his wages when his net sales for the month were $13,500.

Total sales	$13,500	%S = C
Less: quota	−5,000	0.04 × $8,500 = C
		$340 = C

Sales subject to commission	$8,500	Salary	$300
		Commission	340
		Total wages	$640

(b) George Harrison is a department head in a retail store. From the following information, determine his week's wages:

Personal sales	$1,578
Returns and allowances	18
Department sales	5,485
Dept. rets. and alls.	125
Salary	75
Quota	600
Commission rate	3%
Override rate	$\frac{1}{2}$%

* * * * * * * * * *

Personal sales	$1,578	Department sales	$5,485
Less: sales returns	−18	Less: sales returns	−125
	$1,560	Sales subject to	
Less: quota	−600	override	$5,360
Sales subject to commission	$960		

	%S = C	%S = C
	0.03 × $960 = C	0.005 × $5,360 = C
	$28.80 = C	$26.80 = C

Salary	$ 75.00
Commission	28.80
Override	26.80
Total Wages	$130.60

Complete the following commission payroll:

THE STYLE SHOPPE

Payroll for week ending September 7, 19____

| Name | Net Sales | | | | | | | Comm. Rate | Gross Comm. |

Name	M	T	W	T	F	S	Total	Comm. Rate	Gross Comm.
Cobb, Edward	$330	$360	$205	$378	$443	$524	$2,240	7%	$156.80
Minkle, Ina	—	296	154	240	312	348	1,350	4	54.00
Tradd, Lois	284	315	175	302	388	416	1,880	4	75.20
Winecoff, Mary	297	325	163	318	359	428	1,890	5	94.50
								Total	$380.50

Compute the following commission payroll:

NOTIONS, INC.

Weekly Payroll
Week ending April 4, 19____

Name	Sales Gross	R & A	Net	Quota	Comm. Sales	Comm. Rate	Gross Comm.	Salary	Gross Wages
Alber, Marvin	$2,896	$36	$2,860	—	$2,860	3%	$ 85.80	$ 35.00	$120.80
Dorris, Eugene	3,524	74	3,450	$ 700	2,750	2	55.00	70.00	125.00
Norton, E. L.	2,870	10	2,860	—	2,860	4	114.40	—	114.40
Smith, William	3,747	27	3,720	1,500	2,220	5	111.00	40.00	151.00
						Total	$366.20	$145.00	$511.20

Note: The total Gross Commission plus the total Salary must equal the total Gross Wages ($366.20 + $145.00 = $511.20).

COMMISSION AGENTS

The entire operation of some agencies consists of buying and/or selling products for others. Agents employed for this purpose are known as *commission agents, commission merchants, brokers,* or *factors.* The distinguishing characteristic of such agents is that whereas they are authorized to act for another individual or firm, at no time do they become the legal owners of the property involved.

Many items—particularly foodstuffs—are produced in areas which are some distance from the market. The producer (or *consignor*) ships the goods "on consignment" to a commission agent (or *consignee*) who will sell them at the best possible price. The price obtained by the agent is the *gross proceeds*. From these gross proceeds the agent deducts his commission, as well as any other expenses incurred (such as storage, freight, insurance, etc.). The remaining sum, called the *net proceeds*, is then sent to the producer. Accompanying the net proceeds is an *account sales*, which is a detailed account of the sale of the merchandise and of the expenses involved.

Example Six

ACCOUNT SALES
J. MEADE AND SONS
1248 South Hendrix Road
Indianapolis 5, Indiana

REC'D: November 5, 19--   NO.: 1435
  VIA: C & L Railway   DATE: November 16, 19--

Shenandoah Apple Growers Asso.
891 Milford St.
Roanoke, Virginia

19-- Nov.	7 9 9	180 crates Jonathan @ $5.50 125 " Red Delicious @ $5.00 50 " Golden Delicious @ $5.60 Gross Proceeds	$990.00 625.00 280.00	 $1,895.00
		Charges: Commission, 6% of $1,895.00 Freight Storage Net Proceeds	$113.70 86.50 21.75	 221.95 $1,673.05

Other commission agents act as buyers for their clients. When a store wishes to purchase an item not regularly carried in its inventory and not obtainable through regular wholesale distributors, the store may commission an agent to secure the items. Typical examples of such items might be art objects, specialized furniture, carpets, exclusive dry goods, exotic foods, etc., which are specialties of a particular locality or country. Much international as well as domestic purchasing is accomplished in this manner.

In general, a commission agent is employed whenever it is inconvenient to send a company buyer or when a special knowledge of the product or the market conditions is required. The agent submits an itemized account of the purchase, called an *account purchase*. The account purchase includes the actual price paid by the agent (*prime cost*) plus the agent's commission on the prime cost, as well as any expenses incurred during the purchase. This total (or *gross cost*) is the actual cost of the merchandise to the company and the amount to be remitted to the commission agent.

```
                        ACCOUNT PURCHASE

                INTERNATIONAL  SPECIALTIES, INC.
                 2416 Bay Boulevard   San Francisco, California


        BOUGHT FOR THE ACCOUNT OF:

          ┌ Goldberg's                    ┐
            116 N. Main Ave.
          └ Tallahassee, Florida          ┘


        YOUR ORDER: #1439              NO.:  120337
               DATE: February 25, 19--     DATE:  March 20, 19--
```

19-- Mar.	14 19	5 bolts Japanese silk @ $175 3 bolts Thai silk @ $215 Prime Cost	$875.00 645.00	$1520.00
		Charges:		
		Shipping Freight Insurance Commission, 5% of $1520.00	$ 37.85 12.60 3.55 76.00	130.00
		Gross Cost		$1650.00

PROBLEMS

Complete the following:

		Salary	Quota	Rate	Net Sales	Commission	Total Wages
1.	(a)	—	—	4%	$5,800		—
	(b)	—	—	5		$129	—
	(c)	—	—		3,200	144	—
	(d)	$30	—	3½	3,000		
	(e)	45	—	2½			$165
	(f)	—	$ 300	6	1,800		—
	(g)	40	1,100	2	4,500		
	(h)	25	1,600	3			139
	(i)		1,000	1½	8,800		157
2.	(a)	—	—	5%	$2,100		—
	(b)	—	—	3		$ 78	—
	(c)	—	—		2,500	175	—
	(d)	$45	—	2	3,200		
	(e)	30	—		5,000		$155

(f)	—	$ 500	6	2,100	—
(g)	35	1,200	3	3,700	
(h)	40	1,000	$1\frac{1}{2}$		118
(i)		1,300	2	5,900	142

3. A retail clerk made sales totaling $11,856, with sales returns and allowances of $456. The clerk receives a 5% commission on net sales. How much are her wages?

4. A salesman in a furniture store sold furnishings totaling $11,935 during the month. Sales returns and allowances amounted to $135. What were his gross wages for the month, if his commission rate is 7%?

5. A collection agency charged $275 as their fee for securing payment from some old medical accounts. If the agency charges $12\frac{1}{2}$% of the amount collected as their fee, how much was collected?

6. The brokerage paid to a stock broker for purchasing some stock was $48. If the sale price of the stock was $6,400, what is the broker's rate?

7. Edgar Randall is a salesman for a firm manufacturing plumbing fixtures. He is allowed a drawing account of $425 and is paid on commission as follows: 2% on the first $5,000 in sales; $3\frac{1}{2}$% on the next $10,000; and 5% on all additional sales. If his sales last month were $21,760,
   (a) what is his total commission?
   (b) how much was still due at the end of the month?

8. Marshall Gaines is a salesman for a textile machine parts manufacturing company. He is allowed a monthly drawing account of $500. His commission is 3% of his first $10,000 of sales, 4% of the next $15,000, and $5\frac{1}{2}$% of all sales in excess of $25,000. Determine
   (a) his total commission;
   (b) his amount due at the end of the month, if his sales were $31,600.

9. The $116 weekly wages that Karen Grant received included a $35 salary and a commission on her net sales of $1,800. What is her commission rate?

10. Mike Nelson earned $148 for the week. This included a $50 salary and a 7% commission on his net sales. What were his net sales?

11. Bill Hudson, a cookware demonstrator, receives a weekly salary of $45 plus a $7\frac{1}{2}$% commission on all sales in excess of $800. What were his wages last week, if gross sales totaled $2,515 and returns and allowances were $75?

12. Phyllis Carpenter, a clerk in ladies ready-to-wear, earns $40 a week plus a 3% commission on all net sales in excess of $850. Determine her wages for a week in which she had gross sales of $2,922 and sales returns totaled $72.

13. As the parts manager of a large auto supply company, Tom Wallace re-

ceives a salary of $90 a week; a 3% commission on his sales in excess of $1,000; and a $\frac{1}{4}$% override on the sales of the other employees in his department. His sales last week were $2,443 with sales returns of $43. The other members of his department sold parts totaling $7,716, with sales returns of $116. Determine his total wages for the week.

14. Marilyn Lewis is head of the cosmetics and toiletries division of a large drug store. Her salary is $80 a week; in addition, she receives a $2\frac{1}{2}$% commission on her net sales in excess of $600 and a $\frac{1}{2}$% override on the net sales of the clerks working under her. Her sales last week totaled $1,800. The other employees in her department had sales of $5,617 with sales returns of $17. What were her gross wages for the week?

15. Complete the following payroll:

THE FASHION CORNER

Payroll for week ending January 6, 19___

Name	Net Sales							Comm. Rate	Gross Comm.
	M	T	W	T	F	S	Total		
Belton, Clara	$325		$360	$415	$425	$410		5%	
Cruz, Delfina	275	$305		388	416	442		6	
Mercer, Linda		389	417	427	398	436		6	
Thomas, Mary	334		376	409	512	405		7	
Wesson, Kathy	380	355	382		450	467		8	
							Total		

16. Compute the following commission payroll:

MYERS MENS SHOP

Payroll for week ending August 12, 19___

Name	Net Sales							Comm. Rate	Gross Comm.
	M	T	W	T	F	S	Total		
Ball, J. W.		$375	$412	$390	$450	$478		6%	
Connor, Bill	$272		340	366	407	453		5	
Myers, Phil	285	320	378	398	410	425		8	
Owen, Mike	234	295		360	389	415		5	
Webb, J. E.	260	352	400		395	446		6	
							Total		

17. Calculate the following commission payroll:

CARSON WHOLESALE DISTRIBUTORS

Payroll for week ending June 17, 19___

Name	Sales Gross	R & A	Net	Quota	Comm. Sales	Comm. Rate	Gross Comm.	Salary	Gross Wages
Ammons, Roy	$3,179	$49		$1,200		4%		$70.00	
Dickens, P. T.	2,853	83		—		3		55.00	
Long, Harry	3,795	75		1,000		8		—	
Perry, Joe	2,434	64		750		5		60.00	
Steele, James	2,628	58		—		7		—	
Wyatt, J. R.	2,562	82		900		5		75.00	
							Total		

18. Complete the payroll shown below:

NEWTON FURNITURE COMPANY

Payroll for week ending February 8, 19___

Name	Sales Gross	R & A	Net	Quota	Comm. Sales	Comm. Rate	Gross Comm.	Salary	Gross Wages
Bame, Henry	$2,240	$30		$1,000		3%		$60.00	
Heavner, J. R.	3,587	27		1,500		6		—	
Ingram, Jerry	3,628	18		—		3		—	
Ramsey, Dan	4,656	26		1,200		2		75.00	
Ross, Ronald	4,214	24		—		2		50.00	
Wise, L. K.	3,945	15		1,800		4		45.00	
							Total		

19. Complete the following account sales:

		ACCOUNT SALES			
		DELTA GROWERS ASSN.			
		Commission Merchants	New Orleans, Louisiana		

SOLD FOR ACCOUNT OF:

⌐ Oriental Farms ⌐
└ Monroe, Louisiana ┘

19-- Aug.					
	7	4,430 lbs. white rice @ $.12			
	7	1,525 lbs. wild rice @ $.46			
	7	2,875 lbs. brown rice @ $.18			
	11	1,570 lbs. white rice @ $.095			
			GROSS PROCEEDS		
		Charges:			
		Freight		$74.50	
		Commission, 7%			
			NET PROCEEDS		

20. Prepare an account sales for the following:

Sunshine Peach Orchards, Allendale, S. C., consigned a shipment to Empire Commission Merchants, New York, N. Y. The shipment contained 260 bu. Albertas sold on June 15 @ $6.50; 120 bu. Freestones sold on June 16 @ $6.25; 225 bu. Clings sold on June 17 @ $6.00; and 150 bu. Georgia belles sold on June 17 @ $6.50. Storage fees were $27.50 and cartage charges totaled $45. The commission agents' charge was 2%.

21. Complete the following account purchase:

		ACCOUNT PURCHASE		
		Fischer & Fischer		
		Commission Merchants		
		Los Angeles, California		
		BOUGHT FOR ACCOUNT OF		
		Midwest Import Distributors		
		St. Louis, Missouri		

19-- July	15	150 wooden sculptures (Philippines) @ $3.95		
	15	275 sets, place mats (Philippines) @ $4.80		
	18	50 rattan chairs (Hong Kong) @ $14.50		
	21	25 sets, dinnerware (Japan) @ $29.75		
	26	225 brass ornaments (India) @ $2.90		
		PRIME COST		
		Charges:		
		Freight	$157.88	
		Insurance	85.00	
		Commission, 4%		
		GROSS COST		

22.   Prepare an account purchase for the following:

> Pierre Seibert, an independent agent, was employed by The Import House, Newark, N. J., to purchase European art work. Siebert secured 240 original Roman oils on October 19 @ $45; 170 pieces of Venetian crystal on October 22 @ $8; and 50 Swiss clocks on October 30 @ $25. His charges were $370 for freight and shipping, $230 for insurance, $350 for travel expenses, and 5% commission.

3. COMPUTING WAGES—HOURLY-RATE BASIS

The hourly-rate basis for determining wages is the method under which the wages of the majority of the American working force are computed. Under this plan, the employee receives a stipulated amount for each hour's work. One or more of several factors may determine the hourly rate: the individual's ability, training, and experience, as well as Federal minimum wage laws or union contracts. Once the hourly rate has been established, however, the employee's quality of performance or amount of production in no way influence his wages.

The Fair Labor Standards Act governs the employment of approximately 50 million workers, principally those engaged in some form of interstate or international commerce and those employed by large-scale commercial enterprises. As amended in 1966, the Act prescribed a 40-hour workweek and set the minimum wage at $1.60 per hour. Many individual states have also established minimum wages (usually somewhat lower than the Federal minimum wage) which extend coverage to employees not subject to the Federal regulations.

OVERTIME

In accordance with the Federal law covering the 40-hour workweek, most employees' regular week consists of five 8-hour working days. Under the

Federal regulation, *overtime* must be paid to employees for work in excess of 40 hours. Many employers, even though not subject to the Federal Act, follow this policy voluntarily. The standard overtime rate is $1\frac{1}{2}$ times the worker's regular hourly rate ("time-and-a-half"). "Double time" is often paid for work on Sundays or on holidays, though this is not required by law.

In some instances, overtime is paid when an employee works more than 8 hours on any one day. (Some union contracts contain this provision.) As a general practice, however, a worker is required to have worked 40 hours before he receives any overtime compensation; otherwise, he might be paid some overtime without having completed the prescribed 40-hour week. If a company nonetheless pays overtime on a daily basis, the payroll clerk must keep a careful record of the employee's hours to insure that the same time is not counted twice; that is, hours which qualify as daily overtime must not be applied toward the regular 40-hour week, after which all work would be at overtime rates.

Union contracts often contain overtime provisions regarding any number of other situations, such as working two complete shifts in one day or working six or seven consecutive days.

Large firms usually have timeclocks which record on each employee's timecard his entering and leaving times. His work hours are then calculated from this record. Just as employees are compensated for overtime work, they are likewise penalized for tardiness. In smaller firms, a foreman may record his crew's hours; or, in some instances, the employee reports his own hours. Total hours worked are usually kept to the nearest quarter-hour each day.

Example One

Compute the gross wages of each employee:

ANDERSON ELECTRIC SERVICE

Weekly Payroll
Week ending May 9, 19____

Name	M	T	W	T	F	S	Total Hours	Rate per Hour	Gross Wages
Anderson, James	9	7	8	8	8	0	40	$2.20	$ 88.00
Bailey, Carl	8	8	10	0	10	4	40	1.75	70.00
Carson, W. J.	8	6	0	5	8	4	31	1.50	46.50
Davis, Willard	9	8	8	8	6	0	39	2.00	78.00
								Total	$282.50

Example Two

Compute the gross wages of each comployee of Southern Auto Repair. Overtime is paid at $1\frac{1}{2}$ times the regular rate on hours in excess of 40 per week.

SOUTHERN AUTO REPAIR

Payroll for week ending December 12, 19____

Name	M	T	W	T	F	S	Total Hours	Reg. Hrs.	Rate per Hour	Over-time Hours	Over-time Rate	Reg. Wages	Overtime Wages	Total Gross Wages
Elliott, D. R.	8	8	10	9	10	4	49	40	$2.00	9	$3.00	$ 80.00	$27.00	$107.00
Farmer, Ray	10	8	9	7	7	4	45	40	1.80	5	2.70	72.00	13.50	85.50
Givens, Troy	8	8	8	8	8	0	40	40	2.25	—	3.38	90.00	—	90.00
Harper, Tony	5	8	6	7	8	4	38	38	1.50	—	2.25	57.00	—	57.00
Ivey, Marion	9	8	6	8	9	4	44	40	2.10	4	3.15	84.00	12.60	96.60
											Total	$383.00	$53.10	$436.10

Note: The total of the Regular Wages plus the total of the Overtime Wages must equal the total Gross Wages ($383.00 + $53.10 = $436.10).

Compute James Levan's gross wages, based on the following: overtime at time-and-a-half is paid daily on work in excess of 8 hours and weekly on work in excess of 40 regular hours; double time is paid for all Sunday work. His hours each day were as follows:

Example Three

	M	T	W	T	F	S	S
Levan, James	8	9	7	10	7	5	5

		M	T	W	T	F	S	S	Total Hours	Rate per Hour	Base Wages	Total Gross Wages
	RT*	8	8	7	8	7	2		40	$1.80	$72.00	
Levan, James	1½		1		2		3		6	2.70	16.20	$106.20
	DT							5	5	3.60	18.00	

* RT indicates "Regular time"; 1½, "Time-and-a-half"; and DT, "Double time."

The following example illustrates the computation of gross wages for salaried personnel who must be paid overtime wages. This procedure is required under the Fair Labor Standards Act for salaried personnel subject to overtime provisions. (Refer also to Sec. 1, COMPUTING WAGES—SALARY, page 157).

Example Four

(a) A typist receives an $80 salary for her regular 40-hour week. What should be her gross wages for a week when she works 45 hours?

Her regular wages amount to $\dfrac{\$80}{40 \text{ hours}}$ or $2 per hour.

She is due overtime at $1\frac{1}{2}$ times this rate, or $3 per hour. Hence, her wages for a 45 hour week would be $95 ($80 for the first 40 hours plus 5 × $3 or $15 in overtime compensation.)

The same basic procedure is followed whether the normal workweek is more or less than 40 hours: The employee receives the regular rate for the first 40 hours and $1\frac{1}{2}$ times the regular rate thereafter.

(b) A secretary receives $77 weekly for a regular workweek of 35 hours. What are her gross wages when she works 43 hours?

$$\frac{\$77}{35 \text{ hours}} = \$2.20 \text{ per hour}$$

Overtime rate = $1\frac{1}{2}$ × $2.20 = $3.30 per hour

40 hours @$2.20 =	$88.00
3 hours @$3.30 =	9.90
43 hour week	= $97.90

(c) A parts manager works different hours each week, for which his base salary is $108. How much compensation should he receive during a week when he works 45 hours?

$$\frac{\$108}{45 \text{ hours}} = \$2.40 \text{ per hour}$$

Overtime rate = $1\frac{1}{2}$ × $2.40 = $3.60 per hour

40 hours @$2.40 =	$ 96.00
5 hours @$3.60 =	18.00
45 hour week	= $114.00

Observe that, for any employee whose hours vary each week as do this man's hours, the employee's regular rate per hour will also vary each week. That is, his regular rate is $2.40 per hour only during a week when he works 45 hours. If he works 54 hours the following week, then his regular rate that week will be

$\dfrac{\$108}{54}$ = \$2 per hour on the 40 hours, plus overtime for 14 hours at \$3 per hour.

All the above examples show regular rates for 40 hours and an overtime rate of $1\frac{1}{2}$ times the regular rate. An alternative method will produce the same result: calculate the total hours at the regular rate plus the overtime hours at one-half the regular rate. The additional compensation calculated by this method (overtime hours times one-half the regular rate) is called the *overtime excess*. Some firms prefer this method for their own cost accounting, and either procedure is permitted under the Fair Labor Standards Act.

A worker who earns \$2 per hour works 44 hours. Compute his earnings (a) by standard overtime and (b) by overtime excess.

Example Five

(a)   40 hours @\$2 = \$80 straight-time wages
          4 hours @\$3 =   12 overtime wages
        44 hours   = \$92 total gross wages

(b)   One-half the regular rate is $\frac{1}{2}$ of \$2 = \$1 per hour for the excess hours over 40.

      44 hours @\$2 = \$88 regular rate wages
        4 hours @\$1 =   4 overtime excess
      44 hours   = \$92 total gross wages

PROBLEMS

1. Compute the following gross earnings:

LIGHTING SUPPLY HOUSE

Payroll for week ending May 25, 19 —

Name	M	T	W	T	F	S	Total Hours	Rate per Hour	Gross Wages
Abbott, Robert	7	8	8	7	8	0		$1.90	
Davis, Jim	8	8	8	5	7	4		2.45	
Engles, A. C.	8	8	8	8	8	0		2.75	
Garcia, Al	6	7	8	8	9	0		1.85	
Melton, Tony	7	7	8	4	6	5		1.60	
Rogers, Glenn	9	8	5	5	8	4		1.80	
Slaton, Terry	7	7	7	8	7	4		2.35	
								Total	

2. Complete the following gross payroll:

ROBERTS LANDSCAPING SERVICE

Payroll for week ending October 21, 19___

Name	M	T	W	T	F	S	Total Hours	Rate per Hour	Gross Wages
Barnes, William	8	6	7	7	9	0		$2.15	
Duncan, R. C.	9	8	4	8	8	3		1.90	
Failes, John	7	7	8	6	8	3		2.05	
Hoover, J. E.	8	8	8	8	8	0		1.60	
Kelso, Michael	9	8	8	6	6	0		1.85	
Norton, Ed	8	7	7	8	6	4		1.95	
Roberts, Thomas	6	7	8	8	7	3		2.35	
								Total	

3. The employees of Centex Building Contractors receive overtime at time-and-a-half for all work in excess of 40 hours per week. Calculate their gross wages.

CENTEX BUILDING CONTRACTORS

Payroll for week ending November 4, 19___

Name	M	T	W	T	F	S	Total Hours	Reg. Hrs.	Rate per Hour	Over-time Hours	Over-time Rate	Reg. Wages	Overtime Wages	Total Gross Wages
Dempsy, Paul	8	9	8	8	7	5			$2.40					
Haight, Roger	9	9	9	9	8	0			2.80					
Mayhew, Conrad	8	8	7	7	9	3			3.10					
Norton, Jay	8	8	7	6	7	4			3.60					
Williams, Earl	9	9	8	9	8	0			3.00					
											Totals			

4. The employees of Textile Parts, Inc. are required to work a regular 40-hour week, after which they receive standard overtime for any additional hours. Compute the gross payroll.

TEXTILE PARTS, INC.

Payroll for week ending March 30, 19____

Name	M	T	W	T	F	S	Total Hours	Reg. Hrs.	Rate per Hour	Over-time Hours	Over-time Rate	Reg. Wages	Overtime Wages	Total Gross Wages
Berry, Paul	8	10	7	7	8	0			$2.50					
Horton, Ken	9	8	8	6	7	5			2.20					
Lewis, Robert	9	7	6	8	8	4			1.90					
Rogers, J. M.	7	8	5	8	6	4			1.80					
Wyatt, Paul	10	8	7	9	8	4			2.10					
											Totals			

5. The employees listed on the payroll excerpt below receive daily overtime for work in excess of 8 hours. Weekly overtime is paid after they have completed 40 regular hours. Work done on Sundays or holidays receives double-time wages. From the total hours listed each day, divide the time into the correct category and complete the gross payroll. Monday of the week shown was a national holiday.

	M	T	W	T	F	S	S
Benson, Mark	0	8	9	9	10	5	2
Everett, Bob	4	9	9	8	8	8	0
Johnson, Craig	2	9	7	8	9	5	3

Name		M	T	W	T	F	S	S	Total Hours	Rate per Hour	Base Wages	Total Gross Wages
Benson, Mark	RT									$2.00		
	$1\frac{1}{2}$											
	DT											
Everett, Bob	RT									2.30		
	$1\frac{1}{2}$											
	DT											
Johnson, Craig	RT									1.85		
	$1\frac{1}{2}$											
	DT										Total	

6. Daily overtime (in excess of 8 hours) and weekly overtime (after a 40-hour week) are paid to the employees listed below. They also receive double time for Sunday work. From the total daily hours given, determine the number of hours in each category and compute the gross wages.

	M	T	W	T	F	S	S
Coley, Jack	8	9	9	10	7	5	0
Hart, Bill	7	8	10	8	10	5	4
Puett, Ira	9	8	8	6	10	5	4

Name		M	T	W	T	F	S	S	Total Hours	Rate per Hour	Base Wages	Total Gross Wages
Coley, Jack	RT $1\frac{1}{2}$ DT									$2.10		
Hart, Bill	RT $1\frac{1}{2}$ DT									1.90		
Puett, Ira	RT $1\frac{1}{2}$ DT									2.15		
										Total		

7. Compute the gross weekly wages for the salaried employees shown below, who are all subject to the Fair Labor Standards Act:

Position	Regular Hrs. Per Week	Regular Salary	Hours Worked	Gross Wages
Secretary	40	$ 96	44	
File clerk	36	72	42	
Office assistant	(varies)	100	50	

8. The employees below earn salaries but are subject to the Fair Labor Standards Act. Determine what gross wages each should receive:

Position	Regular Hrs. Per Week	Regular Salary	Hours Worked	Gross Wages
Administrative assistant	40	$100	46	
Typist	35	91	43	
Branch manager	(varies)	154	55	

9. For each of the employees listed below, compute gross earnings (a) with overtime at time-and-a-half and (b) using overtime excess:

Employee	Hours	Rate Per Hour
A	46	$2.00
B	42	2.10
C	47	2.60

10. Determine the gross wages for the workers shown below (a) using the standard overtime method and (b) using the overtime excess method:

Employee	Hours	Rate Per Hour
X	45	$3.00
Y	43	2.20
Z	48	2.50

11. Complete the following payroll register, where the overtime excess method is used for work above 40 hours per week.

PACIFIC NORTHWEST LUMBER PROCESSING CO., INC.

Payroll for week ending August 11, 19___

Name	M	T	W	T	F	S	Total Hours	Rate per Hour	Over-time Hours	O.T. Excess Rate	Reg. Rate Wages	Over-time Excess	Total Gross Wages
Garrett, D. R.	10	8	9	12	11	5		$2.40					
Harris, A. D.	9	9	11	10	12	4		3.20					
Jones, R. N.	8	10	10	12	9	5		3.40					
Mayes, S. R.	9	11	9	9	8	5		2.80					
Wyatt, O. L.	9	10	11	12	9	4		3.60					
										Totals			

12. Use the overtime excess method in computing the following gross payroll.

MIDWEST MANUFACTURING CO., INC.

Payroll for week ending May 5, 19___

Name	M	T	W	T	F	S	Total Hours	Rate per Hour	Over-time Hours	O.T. Excess Rate	Reg. Rate Wages	Over-time Excess	Total Gross Wages
Archer, D. O.	8	9	9	10	10	6		$2.60					
Barnes, V. L.	9	9	9	9	9	4		3.00					
Doss, P. R.	9	10	12	12	9	5		3.80					
Goforth, L. L.	10	11	8	9	11	3		4.20					
Neeley, N. E.	9	11	12	9	11	4		2.80					
										Totals			

4. COMPUTING WAGES—PRODUCTION BASIS

In many factories, each employee's work consists of repeating the same task—either some step in the construction of a product, or inspecting or packing finished products. The employee's value to the company can thus be measured in terms of how often he completes his task. Therefore, instead of paying a standard rate per hour, many plants compensate employees at a specified rate per unit completed; this constitutes the *production basis* of computing wages. This type of wage computation is also known as the *piecework* or *piece-rate* plan.

Naturally, some steps in the production of a product require more time than others. Thus the rate per unit for that step would be more than the rate on another task which could be completed much more quickly. In order to keep the entire plant production moving at an even pace, more employees are hired to perform time-consuming tasks and fewer workers are employed to perform easier tasks.

On the straight production plan, the employee receives the same rate for each piece; thus

$$62 \text{ pieces @ } \$1.55 = \$96.10 \text{ wages}$$

INCENTIVES (PREMIUM RATES)

At first glance, the production plan would seem to be quite acceptable to employees, since compensation is determined entirely by individual performance. Such has not been the case however. Most companies which use the piecework plan have established quotas or minimum production standards for each job. As an extra incentive to production, workers receive a higher rate per unit on all units which they complete in excess of this minimum. It is these quotas which historically have caused such dissatisfaction with the production plan. In the past, many companies set "production" (quotas) at such high levels that only a few of the most skillful and experienced employees could attain them. Furthermore, employees complained that when they finally did master the task well enough to "make production," the company would reassign them to a new, unfamiliar task.

As a result of the general dissatisfaction over piecework plans, many union contracts now contain provisions that members must be paid on the hourly-rate basis. Those plants which do still use the production basis have tended to re-establish quotas which are more in line with the production that average employees can attain.

DOCKINGS (SPOILAGE CHARGEBACKS)

Although companies are willing to pay premium rates as incentives to high production, they also wish to discourage haste resulting in carelessness and mistakes. An employee who makes an uncorrectable mistake in his task has destroyed not only the raw materials involved, but also has wasted the work done previously by other employees. Thus an unreasonably high amount of spoilage would be quite expensive to a company. In order to discourage carelessness, many plants require employees to forfeit a certain amount for each piece they spoil. These penalty "dockings" are generally at a lower rate than the employee ordinarily receives for his task, since a small amount of spoilage is to be expected.

OVERTIME

Piecework employees who are subject to the Fair Labor Standards Act must likewise be paid time-and-a-half for work in excess of 40 hours per week. This overtime may be computed similarly to that of salaried workers (by finding the hourly rate to which their regular-time earnings are equivalent and paying $1\frac{1}{2}$ this hourly rate for overtime hours.) However, the overtime wages of a production worker may be computed at $1\frac{1}{2}$ times his regular rate per piece, provided certain standards are met to insure that the worker is indeed being paid the required minimum wage for his regular-time hours and that he is receiving time-and-a-half for his overtime hours. This method is preferred because it is simpler to compute and will therefore be used for our problems. We shall not, however, attempt to compute overtime where premium production is also involved.

Complete the following payroll, based on straight production:

Example One

COLUMBIA, INC.

Payroll for week ending April 5, 19____

Name	\multicolumn{6}{c} Net Pieces Produced						Total Net Pieces	Rate per Piece	Gross Wages Earned
	M	T	W	T	F	S			
Anderson, Frank	16	13	17	19	15	8	88	$2.00	$176.00
Carden, Ezra	35	42	35	33	32	17	194	.75	145.50
Moore, F. R.	125	138	140	131	129	65	728	.18	131.04
Thompson, Bill	84	80	87	92	83	40	466	.30	139.80
Wren, John	98	101	107	98	95	48	547	.30	164.10
								Total	$756.44

Example Two Compute the following production payroll.   All work performed on Saturday is overtime and will be paid at $1\frac{1}{2}$ times the regular piece rate.

PLAYTIME GAME CO., INC.

Payroll for week ending August 30, 19—

Name	Net Pieces Produced						Reg. Time Prod.	Rate Per Piece	Over-time Prod.	Over-time Rate	Reg. Wages	Over-time Wages	Total Gross Wages
	M	T	W	T	F	S							
Cage, R. J.	214	220	218	216	219	112	1087	$.07	112	$.105	$ 76.09	$11.76	$ 87.85
Dix, A. J.	94	90	97	99	101	51	481	.16	51	.24	76.96	12.24	89.20
Green, B. D.	68	70	72	69	71	30	350	.25	30	.375	87.50	11.35	98.85
Hines, O. L.	151	155	153	150	152	75	761	.12	75	.18	91.32	13.50	104.82
										Totals	$331.87	$48.85	$380.72

Example Three (a) Mary Wiley hems dresses in a factory.   She receives 17¢ per hem; after she exceeds the weekly production quota of 500, she receives 20¢ per hem.   Determine Mary's wages for the week when her net production was as follows:

	M	T	W	T	F	Total
Wiley, M.	105	96	104	109	99	513

	Total Net Pieces		Rate	=	Gross Wages
Base production	500	@	$.17	=	$85.00
Premium production	13	@	.20	=	2.60
				Total	$87.60

(b) Bill McDonald attaches chair arms in a furniture factory.   The production quota for his job is 240 pieces per week.   He receives a base rate of 40¢ per chair and a premium rate of 48¢ per chair. He is docked 30¢ on each chair which does not pass inspection. Compute his gross earnings for the week:

	M	T	W	T	F	Total
Gross production	51	49	55	56	50	261
Spoilage	2	0	1	3	0	6
Net Production	49	49	54	53	50	255

	Total Net Production	Rate	Gross Wages
Base production	240	$.40	$ 96.00
Premium production	15	.48	7.20
			$103.20
Spoilage chargeback	6	.30	1.80
		Total	$101.40

Complete the following production payroll, which includes incentive and penalty chargeback rates:

Example Four

GREENBURG PRODUCTS CO.

Payroll for week ending October 17, 19____

Name		Daily Production					Total Prod.	Net Quota	Production	Rate	Base Wages	Total Gross Wages
		M	T	W	T	F						
Caldwell, C. D.	GP*	159	162	152	155	158	786		Base: 750	13¢	$97.50	$100.06
	S	7	3	0	2	2	14		Premium: 22	18	3.96	
	NP	152	159	152	153	156	772	750	Chargeback: 14	10	1.40	
Phillips, R. J.	GP	126	128	131	125	129	639		Base: 632	15¢	94.80	93.96
	S	2	1	3	0	1	7		Premium: —	20	—	
	NP	124	127	128	125	128	632	650	Chargeback: 7	12	.84	
Wiggins, Myron	GP	143	141	145	142	144	715		Base: 700	14¢	98.00	99.35
	S	2	0	0	1	2	5		Premium: 10	19	1.90	
	NP	141	141	145	141	142	710	700	Chargeback: 5	11	.55	
											Total	$293.37

* GP indicates "Gross production"; S, "Spoilage"; and NP, "Net production."

PROBLEMS

1. Katrina Lewis sews darts into gym shorts. Her quota for the week is 535 pairs. Katrina receives 12¢ per pair regularly and 15¢ per pair after she has exceeded production. Determine her gross wages for a week when her production was as shown:

	M	T	W	T	F	Total
Lewis, Katrina	107	115	112	110	114	

2. Ronald Forbes works in a shipping department of a sweater factory. His base rate is 48¢ per dozen sweaters. He receives a premium rate of 55¢ per dozen when he has packed more than 200 dozen sweaters per week. Determine his wages for the following week:

	M	T	W	T	F	Total
Forbes, Ronald	42	38	36	44	43	

3. Sarah Jones sews door flaps onto canvas camping tents. She is paid 16¢ per tent on her net production up to 400 tents and an incentive of 20¢ per tent thereafter. She is docked 12¢ per tent when her work fails to pass inspection. Calculate her wages for the week when she had the following production:

	M	T	W	T	F	Total
Gross production:	84	90	92	95	91	
Spoilage:	1	0	3	2	0	
Net production:						

4. John Tyler operates a machine which bolts together two pieces of a motor. He is paid 1¢ per bolt on net production, and a premium rate of $1\frac{1}{4}$¢ per bolt in excess of 9,600 bolts per week. His spoilage chargeback rate is $\frac{3}{4}$¢ per bolt. Compute his gross wages for the following week:

	M	T	W	T	F	Total
Gross production:	2,005	1,980	1,972	1,978	1,994	
Spoilage:	12	11	8	10	11	
Net production:						

5. Complete the following production payroll:

ECKERD TOOL CO.

Weekly Payroll
Week Ending August 13, 19___

| | Net Pieces Produced ||||| Total Net Pieces | Rate per Piece | Gross Wages Earned |
Name	M	T	W	T	F			
Cary, Virginia	74	79	85	88	82		18¢	
Dobson, Arnold	98	104	108	103	110		14	
Garfield, J. R.	72	68	75	79	81		24	
Helms, Ida	28	25	30	33	34		45	
Milam, Jerry	286	291	302	295	293		7	
Stone, Max	65	67	66	64	70		32	
Yancy, Lee	110	119	117	119	122		14	
							Total	

6. Complete the following payroll based on straight production:

WARING BOLT & SCREW CO.

Payroll for week ending January 24, 19____

Name	Net Pieces Produced					Total Net Pieces	Rate per Piece	Gross Wages Earned
	M	T	W	T	F			
Bufort, Maude	157	162	165	161	169		12¢	
Duncan, Willis	301	310	315	298	307		7	
Eaves, Norris	90	93	97	94	95		20	
Norwood, E. L.	315	320	318	317	321		6	
Putnam, C. W.	270	275	268	273	269		7	
Summey, Jane	345	346	347	344	352		6	
Tillman, O. R.	278	280	275	278	283		8	
							Total	

7. Compute the following production payroll. Work performed on Saturday is overtime and should be reimbursed at $1\frac{1}{2}$ times the standard rate per piece.

MAXWELL TEXTILES, INC.

Payroll for week ending March 6, 19____

Name	Net Pieces Produced						Reg. Time Prod.	Rate Per Piece	Over-time Prod.	Over-time Rate	Reg. Wages	Over-time Wages	Total Gross Wages
	M	T	W	T	F	S							
Bell, Mary	75	78	80	81	78	38		$.20					
Hanes, Karen	107	110	108	111	119	54		.14					
Nixon, Ida	188	190	185	192	186	93		.08					
Temple, Jo	116	110	120	116	118	64		.15					
West, Kay	89	84	90	85	87	45		.18					
										Totals			

8. Complete the following production payroll. Overtime will be paid for all Saturday work.

COMFORT-KNIT SLACKS, INC.

Payroll for week ending June 23, 19___

Name	Net Daily Production						Reg. Time Prod.	Rate Per Piece	Over-time Prod.	Over-time Rate	Reg. Wages	Over-time Wages	Total Gross Wages
	M	T	W	T	F	S							
Daly, R.	90	94	93	95	98	45		$.16					
Goff, J.	155	160	161	158	156	78		.10					
Jones, B.	170	178	180	176	182	94		.09					
Land, M.	70	69	68	70	72	35		.22					
Phipps, S.	150	148	147	152	155	75		.12					
										Totals			

9. Find the gross wages for the payroll below:

CUSTOM FURNITURE CO., INC.

Payroll for week ending September 3, 19___

Name		Daily Production					Total Prod.	Net Quota	Production	Rate	Base Wages	Total Gross Wages
		M	T	W	T	F						
Ford, Michael	GP	112	115	114	116	115			Base:	17¢		
	S	2	3	2	2	3			Premium:	22		
	NP							550	Chargeback:	12		
Jansen, Lars	GP	85	90	93	90	91			Base:	24		
	S	2	0	2	1	0			Premium:	30		
	NP							425	Chargeback:	20		
McCall, Stuart	GP	79	82	86	89	88			Base:	26		
	S	3	1	0	0	1			Premium:	32		
	NP							375	Chargeback:	22		
Pouvey, Roy	GP	58	54	55	56	55			Base:	40		
	S	4	1	0	1	2			Premium:	48		
	NP							240	Chargeback:	32		
Thompson, T. G.	GP	143	156	160	152	155			Base:	15		
	S	5	3	5	4	6			Premium:	19		
	NP							600	Chargeback:	10		
											Total	

10. Complete the following gross wages:

BEST HOSIERY

Weekly Payroll
Week ending August 4, 19____

Name		Daily Production					Total Prod.	Net Quota	Production	Rate	Base Wages	Total Gross Wages
		M	T	W	T	F						
Orvin, Glenn	GP	40	42	45	48	47			Base:	45¢		
	S	3	0	1	2	0			Premium:	54		
	NP							220	Chargeback:	30		
Pealer, E. R.	GP	75	78	73	76	80			Base:	32¢		
	S	0	0	2	1	2			Premium:	39		
	NP							300	Chargeback:	22		
Rhyne, Mary	GP	108	106	103	98	110			Base:	18¢		
	S	3	5	0	1	4			Premium:	22		
	NP							525	Chargeback:	12		
St. John, Jane	GP	86	93	90	93	89			Base:	24¢		
	S	2	5	1	0	2			Premium:	30		
	NP							400	Chargeback:	16		
Watts, David	GP	56	59	65	62	64			Base:	32¢		
	S	4	2	7	2	2			Premium:	39		
	NP							300	Chargeback:	22		
										Total		

5. NET WEEKLY PAYROLLS

Employers are required by law to make certain deductions from the gross earnings of their employees. The amount remaining after deductions have been withheld is known as *net wages*. (The methods used to arrive at net wages from gross wages are the same regardless of which payroll plan may have been used to compute gross wages.)

Two compulsory, Federal deductions are made in all regular payrolls: Social Security and personal income tax. In many states, the employer is also required to withhold state income tax. Certain other deductions, either compulsory or voluntary, may also be made. The following paragraphs discuss important aspects of the various deductions.

Social Security or FICA (Federal Insurance Contributions Act)

The original Federal Insurance Contributions Act was one of the emergency measures passed during the great depression of the '30s; it has since been amended and extended many times. Social Security—as the Federal Insurance Contributions Act program has come to be called—is not a tax in the normal sense; it could more accurately be described as a compulsory savings or insurance program. Social Security funds are used to pay monthly benefits to retired or disabled workers, to pay survivor's benefits to the widow and minor children of a deceased worker, and to finance the Medicare program enacted by Congress in 1965.

Graduating Social Security rates are established by Congress for several years in advance. Historically, however, the proposed rates and the base amounts subject to withholding have both been amended frequently, causing the rates and the amounts to increase more rapidly than originally scheduled. This text uses the 1972 withholding rate for Social Security, which was 5.2% of the first $9,000 earned by each worker. All FICA deductions must be matched by an equal contribution from the employer (making the total rate 10.4%). Self-employed persons pay an FICA rate almost $1\frac{1}{2}$ times the rate paid by employees.

The following table presents future Social Security withholding rates as established by the 1971 amendment. As noted above, however, Congress may alter the law at any time; hence, some of the annual rates may be increased before they ever take effect. Similarly, the maximum taxable income of $9,000, which was scheduled to remain unchanged, may also be increased.

Social Security (FICA) Withholding Rates

Year	Rate (on first $9,000)	Maximum Contribution
1972	5.2	$468.00
1973–1975	5.65	508.50
1976–1979	5.85	526.50
1980–1986	5.95	535.50
1987 and after	6.05	544.50

The Social Security deduction to be withheld may be computed by finding 5.2% of the employee's gross wages. In order to save time, however, most payroll clerks use Social Security tax tables furnished by the government. These tables list wage intervals and the deduction to be made within each interval.

Example One

(a) William McFarlane earns a gross salary of $187.50 each week. What FICA deduction must be made?

By percentage: 5.2% of $187.50 = $9.75

By the Social Security Table (Table X, pp. 510–514): Under the "Wages" heading, consult the interval where gross earnings are "at least $187.41, but less than $187.60." The next column shows the "tax to be withheld" is $9.75.

McFarlane will pay this $9.75 tax each week for 48 weeks.

At that time, his gross earnings for the year will have reached the maximum taxable wage of $9,000 (187.50 × 48 = $9,000). During the remaining weeks of the year, no FICA deduction will be made from McFarlane's pay. His total contribution for the year will be $9.75 × 48 = $468, the maximum contribution required of any worker.

(b) John Hatfield earned gross wages of $124.72. What is his Social Security deduction?

By the table: $124.72" appears on two lines of the table. On the first line, however, Hatfield's wages appear under the heading "but less than $124.72." This does not apply, because Hatfield did not earn "less than $124.72." We must use the second line, where the wages earned were "at least $124.72." The "tax to be withheld" column indicates Hatfield's deduction will be $6.49.

FEDERAL INCOME TAX

Employers are required to make deductions from each worker's wages for Federal income tax. As in the case of Social Security, most businesses use Federal withholding tables to determine income tax deductions. Immediately after a new employee is hired, the payroll clerk should have him complete the Employee's Withholding Exemption Certificate. This form indicates the employee's marital status and the total number of dependents or exemptions (including himself) which he claims.

Married and single persons are subject to different income tax rates, the rates being higher for single persons. The Income Tax Withholding Tables (pp. 515–518) therefore contain separate listings for married and single persons. The tax to be withheld is thus dependent upon three factors: (1) the worker's gross earnings, (2) whether he is married or single, and (3) the number of exemptions he claims.

An exemption is allowed for each member of the family. The husband may claim all of these exemptions; or, if the wife works, she may claim her own exemption and also some of the children's exemptions. The principal restriction has been that the total number of exemptions claimed by both husband and wife may not normally exceed the total number of persons in the family. This total number may include a grandparent or other person who lives with the family and/or qualifies as a dependent.*

---

*To qualify, the person (1) must fall within a specified class of persons; (2) must have received more than one-half his support from the taxpayer; (3) must have earned less than a certain gross income of his own (except youths under 19 or qualified students); (4) must not have filed a joint return with a spouse; and (5) must be a citizen of the United States or of certain other specified places.

(The total number of exemptions may exceed the number in the family when the employee is past 65, suffers blindness, or for another extreme reason qualifies for additional exemptions. In another unusual instance, an employee may not have to have income tax deducted if his earnings the previous year were so low that he did not owe any income tax, and if he does not expect to owe any income tax for the current year.)

Income tax withholding tables are only approximate, and some people have owed additional tax when their income tax returns were filed. In order to help minimize this situation, the Internal Revenue Service permits workers to claim *fewer* exemptions than they are legally entitled to. By claiming fewer exemptions, the worker has more tax withheld each pay day and will thus be less likely to owe additional tax at the end of the year. The Internal Revenue Service has published tables which help the employee determine how many exemptions should be claimed in order to minimize the possibility of additional taxes.

Because of a similar but reverse situation, recent tax tables have also caused some persons to have more tax deducted than they would owe when their income tax returns were filed. Thus, in 1972, the Internal Revenue Service began allowing single persons and married persons where only one spouse was working to claim one extra exemption above their normal number of qualified exemptions. This is the first time that extra exemptions have been allowed for causes other than age or physical hardship, as cited above. This may therefore be only a temporary practice and be discontinued when more accurate income tax withholding tables are issued.

Example Two

Philip Armstrong and Edward Short both earn salaries of $140 per week; each claims only himself as a dependent. However, Armstrong is married and Short is a bachelor. How much income tax will be deducted from each man's salary?

Since Armstrong is married and claims only himself, the exemption indicated on his payroll sheet is "M-1." Using the income tax withholding table for "Married Persons" paid on a "Weekly Payroll Period," we find the gross wage interval containing wages that are "at least $140 but less than $145." The columns at the right have headings indicating the number of exemptions which may be claimed. For Armstrong, we use the column which shows "1 exemption claimed" and see that the tax to be withheld is $17.50. If Armstrong's salary does not change, he will have income tax of $17.50 withheld each week during the entire year.

Edward Short's payroll sheet indicates his exemption is "S-1." Using the income tax table for "Single Persons" paid on a "Weekly" basis, we find the same gross wage interval of "at least $140 but less than $145." In the column for "1 exemption claimed," we see that income tax of $20.20 will be deducted from Short's salary each week. Thus Short, because he is single, pays $20.20–$17.50 or $2.70 more income tax each week than Armstrong.

STATE DEDUCTIONS

In many states, state income tax is also a compulsory deduction. Withholding tables are usually available for the state tax, which is typically at a considerably lower rate than the Federal income tax.

The Social Security (FICA) Act contains provisions for an unemployment insurance tax. The funds from this tax provide compensation to ablebodied workers who are willing to work, but who have been "laid off" by their employers because there is no work available. Under the Federal Act, this unemployment tax is paid by the *employer only*, with most of the funds being collected by the individual states. (That is, no deduction is made from the worker's pay for Federal Unemployment Tax.) In a few states, however, the state has levied its own unemployment tax in addition to the Federal tax. In these states, a compulsory unemployment tax may be deducted from the worker's wages.

OTHER DEDUCTIONS

There are any number of other deductions which might be withheld from the worker's wages. One of the most common is group insurance. Many firms sponsor a group policy whereby employees may purchase health, accident, hospitalization, and sometimes even life insurance at rates substantially lower than they could obtain individually.

Union dues or dues to professional organizations may be deducted. Employees often contribute to a company or state retirement plan which will supplement their Social Security retirement benefits. Contributions to charitable causes (such as the United Fund or Community Chest) may be withheld. Some businesses participate in a payroll savings plan whereby deductions are made to purchase U. S. Savings Bonds. Numerous other examples could be cited.

Complete the net payroll of Home Entertainment Center, Inc. In addition to the standard deductions, 2% of each employee's gross wages is withheld toward a company retirement plan. **Example Three**

HOME ENTERTAINMENT CENTER, INC.
Payroll for week ending December 19, 19____

| Employee | Exemptions | Gross Wages | Deductions | | | | | Total Ded. | Net Wages Due |
			FICA	Federal Inc. Tax	Other (Ret.)	Other	Other		
Burns, Jack	M-3	$147.00	$ 7.64	$14.30	$ 2.94			$ 24.88	$122.12
Crowson, J. D.	M-4	140.00	7.28	11.50	2.80			21.58	118.42
Floyd, M. R.	M-1	137.50	7.15	16.70	2.75			26.60	110.90
Nichols, Ellen	S-1	105.00	5.46	13.80	2.10			21.36	83.64
Poston, Carl	M-2	135.00	7.02	14.70	2.70			24.42	110.58
Wright, Wilson	M-3	135.00	7.02	12.70	2.70			22.42	112.58
Totals		$799.50	$41.57	$83.70	$15.99			$141.26	$658.24

Hint: A net payroll can be completed more efficiently if all deductions of the same type are done at one time. That is, list FICA for all employees, then determine Federal income tax for all employees, etc.

Note: The totals of the individual deductions, when added together, must equal the total in the "Total Deductions" column. ($41.57 + $83.70 + 15.99 = $141.26.) The Total Gross Wages minus the Total Deductions must give the Total Net Wages Due. ($799.50 − $141.26 = $658.24.) The payroll clerk should always verify these totals before writing the paychecks.

Problems

1. Complete the following salary payroll. Withhold Social Security and income tax. Each worker also contributes 1% of his gross salary toward a company retirement plan.

WESTWOOD CONSULTANTS, INC.
Payroll for week ending April 7, 19__

Employee	Exemptions	Gross Salary	FICA	Federal Inc. Tax	Other (Ret.)	Other	Other	Total Ded.	Net Wages Due
				Deductions					
Akers, Paul	M-4	$165.00							
Engle, Richard	S-1	150.00							
Hunt, Tom	M-3	90.00							
Millsaps, Jean	M-1	110.00							
Thorne, Wm.	M-2	125.00							
Totals									

2. Compute each person's net wages due. Deduct FICA and Federal income tax. Each employee also pays $2.50 for his own group insurance (regardless of whether he claims himself as an exemption) plus $1.00 for each additional exemption.

JONES & RUDOLPH, INC.

Payroll for week ending January 3, 19____

Employee	Exemptions	Gross Salary	FICA	Federal Inc. Tax	Other (Ins.)	Other	Other	Total Ded.	Net Wages Due
				Deductions					
Garrett, Nina	M-0	$ 97.50							
Jones, Richard	M-4	150.00							
Kelly, Phyllis	S-1	90.00							
Rudolph, K. T.	M-3	150.00							
Styres, R. L.	M-3	140.00							
Totals									

3. Compute the net payroll of Maxwell Industrial Machines, Inc., whose employees are paid on an hourly basis. Deductions are made for Social

Security, income tax, and union dues. These dues are deducted according
to the employee's rate per hour as follows:

Rate per Hour	Dues
$1.60–$1.80	$2.00
1.81– 2.20	2.50
2.21– 2.60	3.00
2.61– 3.00	3.50
3.01– 3.50	4.00

MAXWELL INDUSTRIAL MACHINES, INC.
Payroll for week ending May 13, 19—

Emp. No.	Exemp- tions	Total Hours	Rate Per Hour	Gross Wages	Deductions					Net Wages Due
					FICA	Inc. Tax	Other	Other	Total Deds.	
#101	M-2	40	$1.75							
#103	M-4	38	2.85							
#105	M-3	40	2.25							
#107	S-2	40	2.50							
#109	M-3	38	3.20							
			Totals							

4. Complete the weekly payroll of the Automatic Specialties Co. The em-
    ployees are paid on an hourly basis, and deductions are withheld for FICA,
    income tax, and union dues. (These employees belong to the same union
    discussed in Problem 3—See Problem 3 for the dues rates.)

AUTOMOTIVE SPECIALTIES CO.
Payroll for week ending August 19, 19____

Emp. No.	Exemp- tions	Total Hours	Rate per Hour	Gross Wages	Deductions					Net Wages Due
					FICA	Inc. Tax	Other	Other	Total Deds.	
#121	M-2	35	$1.60							
#136	S-1	40	2.35							
#149	M-3	39	2.80							
#173	M-5	40	2.25							
#192	M-2	40	3.25							
			Totals							

5. The following commission payroll has standard deductions for FICA and Social Security. The sales representatives have each pledged 10% of their gross wages for the week as contributions to the United Fund campaign. Determine the net payroll for the week.

GENERAL SALES CORP.
Payroll for week ending January 16, 19__

Emp. No.	Exemp-tions	Net Sales	Comm. Rate	Gross Wages	FICA	Inc. Tax	Other	Other	Total Deds.	Net Wages Due
A-16	M-3	$5,700	3%							
A-20	M-1	4,500	4							
B-45	M-0	8,500	2							
C-8	S-1	8,000	2							
C-12	M-5	4,200	4							
			Totals							

6. Employees at Acme Sales Corp. are paid on the commission basis. Standard deductions are made. In addition, all employees have pledged a "day's pay" to the Community Chest. (That is, deduct $\frac{1}{5}$ or 20% of each employee's gross wages for his pledge.) Complete the net payroll.

ACME SALES CORP.
Payroll for week ending June 23, 19___

Emp. No.	Exemp-tions	Net Sales	Comm. Rate	Gross Wages	FICA	Inc. Tax	Other	Other	Total Deds.	Net Wages Due
NE-3	M-2	$3,500	4%							
NE-7	M-1	2,900	6							
MA-3	M-4	4,000	3							
MA-5	S-3	4,500	3							
SE-2	M-3	3,500	5							
			Totals							

7. Ardmore Manufacturing, Inc. pays its employees on the production basis. In addition to the standard deductions, group insurance will be deducted at the rate of $2.00 for each worker and $.50 for each additional dependent claimed. Complete the net payroll.

ARDMORE MANUFACTURING, INC.
Payroll for week ending November 5, 19__

| Emp. No. | Exemptions | Net Production | Rate per Piece | Gross Wages | Deductions | | | | | Net Wages Due |
					FICA	Inc. Tax	Other	Other	Total Deds.	
#5	M-3	1,304	7¢							
#9	M-2	650	12							
#13	M-4	835	12							
#21	S-1	868	9							
#23	M-2	712	15							
			Totals							

8. The production plan is used by Sta-rite, Inc. to pay its employees. Deductions are made for Social Security and income tax, plus a 1% withholding for the company retirement plan. Compute the net payroll.

STA-RITE, INC.
Payroll for week ending August 19, 19____

| Emp. No. | Exemptions | Net Production | Rate per Piece | Gross Wages | Deductions | | | | | Net Wages Due |
					FICA	Inc. Tax	Other	Other	Total Deds.	
#59	M-1	350	28¢							
#64	M-0	200	45							
#69	S-1	260	35							
#73	S-2	220	45							
#81	M-2	310	32							
			Totals							

9. The employees of Kiser Associates are salaried and work 40 hours during a normal week. Since end-of-the-month pressures required extra work, it will be necessary to compute overtime for the additional hours. Also, payroll records show that employee B had earned $8,980 after last week's wages were computed (and will therefore pay FICA taxes only on $9,000– $8,980 = $20 of this week's earnings.) A 1% deduction should be made for company retirement. Complete the net payroll.

KISER ASSOCIATES
Payroll for week ending December 19, 19___

Emp.	Exemp- tions	Hours Worked	Reg. Salary	Over- time Wages	Total Gross Wages	FICA	Inc. Tax	Other	Total Deds.	Net Wages Due
							Deductions			
A	M-3	45	$120.00							
B	M-5	50	180.00							
C	M-1	46	100.00							
D	M-2	44	140.00							
		Totals								

10. Sun Coast Industries pays standard overtime after 40 hours per week. Group insurance will be withheld in the amount of $5 for each worker and $1 for each additional dependent. Employee #16 had earned $8,940 after last week. Determine the company's net payroll for the week.

SUN COAST INDUSTRIES, INC.
Payroll for week ending December 14, 19___

Emp. No.	Exemp- tions	Total Hours	Rate per Hour	Reg. Wages	Over- time Wages	Total Gross Wages	FICA	Inc. Tax	Other	Total Deds.	Net Wages Due
								Deductions			
#12	M-3	42	$2.80								
#14	M-2	44	3.20								
#16	M-4	46	4.60								
#18	M-2	45	3.80								
			Totals								

11. Compute the net payroll for Dryden Sales & Service. Standard overtime will be paid. Deduct 2% for a company retirement policy. Employee #3 had earned $8,960 prior to this week.

DRYDEN SALES & SERVICE, INC.
Payroll for week ending December 3, 19___

Emp. No.	Exemp- tions	Total Hours	Rate per Hour	Reg. Wages	Over- time Wages	Total Gross Wages	FICA	Inc. Tax	Other	Total Deds.	Net Wages Due
								Deductions			
#1	M-3	42	$3.00								
#2	S-1	45	2.80								
#3	M-4	46	4.80								
#4	M-4	43	3.60								
			Totals								

12. Compute the net payroll for Bentwood Furniture Manufacturing Co. Over-time is paid at $1\frac{1}{2}$ times the regular piece rate. In addition to the standard deductions, union dues of 5% of the worker's gross wages are to be collected. Employee M had earned $8,900 before the week began.

BENTWOOD FURNITURE MANUFACTURING CO.
Payroll for week ending December 20, 19—

Emp.	Exemp-tions	Net Reg. Prod.	Over-time Prod.	Reg. Piece Rate	Reg. Wages	Over-time Wages	Total Gross Wages	Deductions				Net Wages Due
								FICA	Inc. Tax	Other	Total Deds.	
L	M-4	495	40	.30								
M	M-4	446	42	.40								
N	M-2	558	54	.20								
P	M-3	264	24	.50								
Totals												

6. DISBURSEMENT FORMS

Most businesses today pay their employees by check. This is more convenient and also eliminates the hazard of having large amounts of cash on the premises. However, there are a significant number of firms—usually smaller companies—which still pay their employees in cash. When a firm pays its employees in cash, two disbursement forms—the *change tally* and the *change slip*—must first be completed.

Before pay envelopes can be filled, the payroll clerk must determine exactly how many bills and coins of each denomination will be required for each employee. This computation is done on a *change tally*. In listing the number of bills and coins for each employee, it is customary to use the largest possible denominations that will give the correct total. (For example, $50 due should be paid in 2 twenties and 1 ten, rather than 5 tens.) This means that fewer actual pieces of money will be handled, with less likelihood of an error.

The columnar totals of each denomination of money are then transferred to a *change slip*, which verifies that these individual totals result in the correct net payroll. A single payroll check is then written for the total net wages due. This check and the change slip are presented to the bank teller, who will cash the check using the number of each denomination of money indicated on the change slip. The payroll clerk then fills the pay envelopes, using the change tally as his guide.

Compute the change tally and accompanying change slip: **Example One**

CHANGE TALLY

Name	Net Wages Due	$20	$10	$5	$1	50¢	25¢	10¢	5¢	1¢
Baker, Edwin	$ 87.36	4		1	2		1	1		1
Duke, Kathy	83.45	4			3		1	2		
Evans, Art	98.17	4	1	1	3			1	1	2
Lewis, Perry	79.69	3	1	1	4	1		1	1	4
Travis, C. L.	103.80	5			3	1	1		1	
Totals	$452.47	20	2	3	15	2	3	5	3	7

CHANGE SLIP

Denom.	No.	Amount
$20.00	20	$400.00
10.00	2	20.00
5.00	3	15.00
1.00	15	15.00
.50	2	1.00
.25	3	.75
.10	5	.50
.05	3	.15
.01	7	.07
	Total	$452.47

PROBLEMS

1. Compute the change tally for the following payroll:

CHANGE TALLY

Emp.	Net Wages	$20	$10	$5	$1	50¢	25¢	10¢	5¢	1¢
A	$ 96.18									
B	74.59									
C	108.37									
D	77.42									
E	118.91									
Totals										

2. Complete the following change tally:

CHANGE TALLY

Emp.	Net Wages	$20	$10	$5	$1	50¢	25¢	10¢	5¢	1¢
V	$ 87.18									
W	94.95									
X	102.32									
Y	86.44									
Z	98.80									
Totals										

3. Complete the change slip for Problem 1:

CHANGE SLIP

Denom.	No.	Amount
$20.00		
10.00		
5.00		
1.00		
.50		
.25		
.10		
.05		
.01		
Total		

4. Compute the change slip for Problem 2:

CHANGE SLIP

Denom.	No.	Amount
$20.00		
10.00		
5.00		
1.00		
.50		
.25		
.10		
.05		
.01		
Total		

7. QUARTERLY EARNINGS RECORDS AND RETURNS

EMPLOYEE'S EARNINGS RECORDS

Employers must keep an individual payroll record showing each employee's earnings, deductions, and other pertinent information. These records show quarterly (and sometimes monthly) totals, which are used in computing the state and Federal quarterly payroll reports that every company must file. In addition, the individual earnings record enables the payroll clerk to know when the employee's earnings reach the $9,000 cutoff point for Social Security. It also contains the yearly totals of earnings and deductions required for personal income tax purposes. Figure 8-1 presents a typical employee's earnings record.

QUARTERLY PAYROLL RETURNS

There are several payroll reports which must be completed at the end of each quarter. The exact reports vary somewhat from state to state, but there are two types which must be completed in every state: the Employer's Quarterly Federal Tax Return (#941), as well as state unemployment returns required under the Federal Insurance Contributions Act.

The Employer's Quarterly Federal Tax Return reports the amount of Social Security paid (by both the employer and employee) and the income tax that has been withheld by the company. Figure 8-2 shows a completed 941 Employer's Quarterly Federal Tax Return. At the bottom is a list of the employees who earned FICA taxable wages during the quarter. (That is, only wages *earned during that quarter* which applied toward the first $9,000 are shown here. Any employee who had already earned $9,000 before the quarter began will not be listed. If an employee's total earnings reached $9,000 during the quarter, only the first part of his earnings for the quarter will be listed.)

Lines 1–12a compose the basic part of the return. Line 1 is the total of *all* wages paid (and tips reported) during the quarter, regardless of whether this compensation was subject to FICA tax. Line 2 is the total income tax withheld from all employees (even those not listed on the lower portion of the return). Line 5 is the total of all FICA taxable wages shown on the lower part of the report; these wages are multiplied by 10.4% to obtain the total Social Security obligation from both the employees and employer. (Line 6 applies only to businesses whose employees receive tips; we shall not concern ourselves with such businesses.)

Whenever the Social Security (of both the employee and the employer) plus income tax withheld during one month exceeds $200, the employer is required to deposit these funds in an authorized commercial or Federal Reserve bank on a monthly basis, rather than waiting until the quarter ends. (Similarly, the taxes must be deposited when the cumula-

DATE OF BIRTH: 2-6-35 | JOB DESCRIPTION: Master Machinist

WORK PERIOD (DAY & HOUR) FROM Mon. 7:30 TO Fri. 4:00 | PAY PERIOD (DAY & HOUR) FROM Thur. 7:30 TO Wed. 4:00

HOW PAID: X HOURLY RATE ___ PIECE RATE ___ SALARY ___ COMMISSION ___

DATE EMPLOYED: 5-14-64 | SOCIAL SECURITY NUMBER: 123-45-6789 | FULL NAME: John Edward Baker | CLOCK OR BADGE NO.: P-2

TERMINATED: Exemptions: M-4 | DEPARTMENT: Processing | ADDRESS: 2412 E. Manor Rd.

Pay Period Ending Mo.	Wk.	19	Time Worked Regular	Time Worked Overtime	Rate Regular	Rate Overtime	Earnings Regular	Earnings Overtime	Earnings Total	Total To Date	Deductions Withholding Tax	F.I.C.A.	U.Dues	Insurance	Total Deductions	Net Amount Paid
FORWARD					4.50	6.75				4938.25	492.60	256.79	60.00	51.00	860.39	4077.86
JULY	1	5	Vacation				—	—	—		—	—				—
	2	12	40	4			180.00	27.00	207.00		21.50	10.76		8.50	40.76	166.24
	3	19	40	2			180.00	13.50	193.50		19.90	10.06			29.96	163.54
	4	26	40	3			180.00	20.25	200.25		21.50	10.41	10.00		41.91	158.34
	5															
MONTHLY TOTAL									600.75	5539.00	62.90	31.23	10.00	8.50	112.63	488.12
AUGUST	1	2	40	6			180.00	40.50	220.50		25.00	11.47			36.47	184.03
	2	9	40	1			180.00	6.75	186.75		18.30	9.71		8.50	36.51	150.24
	3	16	40	2			180.00	13.50	193.50		19.90	10.06			29.96	163.54
	4	23	40	6			180.00	40.50	220.50		25.00	11.47	10.00		46.47	174.03
	5	30	40	5			180.00	33.75	213.75		23.10	11.12			34.22	179.53
MONTHLY TOTAL									1035.00	6574.00	111.30	53.83	10.00	8.50	183.63	851.37
SEPTEMBER	1	6	32	–			144.00	–	144.00		11.50	7.49			18.99	125.01
	2	13	40	–			180.00	–	180.00		18.30	9.36		8.50	36.16	143.84
	3	20	40	4			180.00	27.00	207.00		21.50	10.76			32.26	174.74
	4	27	40	6			180.00	40.50	220.50		25.00	11.47	10.00		46.47	174.03
	5															
MONTHLY TOTAL									751.50	7325.50	76.30	39.08	10.00	8.50	133.88	617.62
QUARTERLY TOTAL									2387.25	7325.50	250.50	124.14	30.00	25.50	430.14	1957.11
OCTOBER	1	4	40	5			180.00	33.75	213.75		23.10	11.12			34.22	179.53
	2	11	40	4			180.00	27.00	207.00		21.50	10.76		8.50	40.76	166.24
	3	18	40	7			180.00	47.25	227.25		25.00	11.82			36.82	190.43
	4	25	32	8			144.00	54.00	198.00		19.90	10.30	10.00		40.20	157.80
	5															
MONTHLY TOTAL									846.00	8171.50	89.50	44.00	10.00	8.50	152.00	694.00
NOVEMBER	1	1	40	7			180.00	47.25	227.25	8398.75	25.00	11.82			36.82	190.43
	2	8	40	5			180.00	33.75	213.75	8612.50	23.10	11.12		8.50	42.72	171.03
	3	15	40	5			180.00	33.75	213.75	8826.25	23.10	11.12			34.22	179.53
	4	22	40	5			180.00	33.75	213.75	9040.00	23.10	9.01	10.00		42.11	171.64
	5	29	32	4			144.00	27.00	171.00		16.70	–			16.70	154.30
MONTHLY TOTAL									1039.50	9211.00	111.00	43.07	10.00	8.50	172.57	866.93
DECEMBER	1	6	40	6			180.00	40.50	220.50		25.00	–			25.00	195.50
	2	13	40	5			180.00	33.75	213.75		23.10	–		8.50	31.60	182.15
	3	20	40	3			180.00	20.25	200.25		21.50	–			21.50	178.75
	4	27	32	–			144.00	–	144.00		11.50	–	10.00		21.50	122.50
	5															
MONTHLY TOTAL									778.50	9989.50	81.10	–	10.00	8.50	99.60	678.90
QUARTERLY TOTAL									2664.00	9989.50	281.60	87.07	30.00	25.50	424.17	2239.83
TOTAL TO DATE									9989.50	9989.50	1024.70	468.00	120.00	102.00	1714.70	8274.80

RE-ORDER FORM W.T.R. (15-1952) (REV. 1-62) STECK DIV., STECK-WARLICK CO., AUSTIN, TEXAS

FIGURE 8-1: EMPLOYEE'S EARNINGS RECORD

FORM 941		
(Rev. Apr. 1971) Department of the Treasury Internal Revenue Service	1. TOTAL WAGES AND TIPS SUBJECT TO WITHHOLDING PLUS OTHER COMPENSATION . . . . . ➤	$12,500 00
	2. AMOUNT OF INCOME TAX WITHHELD FROM WAGES, TIPS, ANNUITIES, etc. (See instructions) . . .	1,100 00
Employer's Quarterly Federal Tax Return	3. ADJUSTMENT FOR PRECEDING QUARTERS OF CALENDAR YEAR	
	4. ADJUSTED TOTAL OF INCOME TAX WITHHELD . . . . ➤	1,100 00
	5. TAXABLE FICA WAGES PAID (Item 21) . . . $ 8,000 _____ multiplied by 10.4% = TAX	832 00
	6. TAXABLE TIPS REPORTED (Item 22) . . . $ _____ multiplied by 5.2% = TAX	
	7. TOTAL FICA TAXES (Item 5 plus Item 6) . . . . ➤	832 00
	8. ADJUSTMENT (See instructions)	
	9. ADJUSTED TOTAL OF FICA TAXES . . . . ➤	832 00

10. TOTAL TAXES (Item 4 plus Item 9) . . . . `1,932 00`

11. TOTAL DEPOSITS FOR QUARTER (INCLUDING FINAL DEPOSIT MADE FOR QUARTER) AND OVERPAYMENT FROM PREVIOUS QUARTER. LIST IN SCHEDULE B. (See instructions on page 4) . . . . `1,932 00`

Note: If undeposited taxes due at the end of the quarter are $200 or more, the entire balance must be deposited. This deposit must be entered in Schedule B and included in Item 11.

12a. UNDEPOSITED TAXES DUE (ITEM 10 LESS ITEM 11—THIS SHOULD BE LESS THAN $200). PAY TO INTERNAL REVENUE SERVICE AND ENTER HERE . . . . ➤ `-0-`

12b. IF ITEM 11 IS MORE THAN ITEM 10, ENTER EXCESS HERE ➤ $ _____ AND CHECK IF TO BE: ☐ APPLIED TO NEXT RETURN, OR ☐ REFUNDED.

13. If not liable for returns in succeeding quarters write "FINAL" here ➤ _____ and enter date of final payment of taxable wages here ➤

Under penalties of perjury, I declare that I have examined this return, including accompanying schedules and statements, and to the best of my knowledge and belief it is true, correct, and complete.

Date `10/30/72`   Signature *Arthur B. Cashwell*   Title (Owner, etc.) President

		T	
Employer's name, address, employer identification number, and calendar quarter. (If not correct, please change)	Name (as distinguished from trade name) Arthur B. Cashwell	FF	
	Date quarter ended Sep 72	FD	
	Trade name, if any Lone Star Supply Co.	FP	
	Employer Identification No. 60-1234567	I	
	Address and ZIP code Box 1190, Austin, Texas 78757	T	

-------------------- Entries must be made both above and below this line --------------------

Name (as distinguished from trade name)
Arthur B. Cashwell   Date quarter ended Sep 72

Trade name, if any
Lone Star Supply Co.   Employer Identification No. 60-1234567

Address and ZIP code
Box 1190, Austin, Texas 78757

SCHEDULE A—QUARTERLY REPORT OF WAGES TAXABLE UNDER THE FEDERAL INSURANCE CONTRIBUTIONS ACT
(FOR SOCIAL SECURITY)
IF WAGES WERE NOT TAXABLE UNDER FICA MAKE NO ENTRIES BELOW

14. (First quarter only) Number of employees (except household) employed in the pay period including March 12th. _____

15. Total pages of this return including this page and any pages of Form 941a. `1`

16. Total number of employees listed. `5`

List for each nonagricultural employee the WAGES taxable under FICA which were paid during the quarter. If you pay an employee more than $7,800 in a calendar year, report only the first $7,800 of such wages. In the case of "Tip Income," see instructions on Page 4.

Please be sure to report each employee's name and number exactly as shown on his Social Security card.

17. EMPLOYEE'S SOCIAL SECURITY NUMBER (If number is unknown, see Circular E)			18. NAME OF EMPLOYEE (Please type or print)	19. TAXABLE FICA WAGES Paid to Employee in Quarter (Before deductions)		20. TAXABLE TIPS REPORTED (See page 4) If amounts in this column are not tips check here ☐
000	00	0000	▼	▼ Dollars	Cents	Dollars Cents
111	11	1111	Charles A. Andrews	$1,200.00		
222	22	2222	Darrell W. Best	1,500.00		
333	33	3333	W. Glenn Colvert	1,800.00		
444	44	4444	S. D. Daniels	2,000.00		
555	55	5555	R. Warren Edgeworth	1,500.00		

If you need more space for listing employees, use Schedule A continuation sheets, Form 941a.
Totals for this page—Wage total in column 19 and tip total in column 20 ➤ `$8,000.00`

21. TOTAL WAGES TAXABLE UNDER FICA PAID DURING QUARTER.
(Total of column 19 on this page and continuation sheets.) Enter here and in Item 5 above . . $ `8,000.00`

22. TOTAL TAXABLE TIPS REPORTED UNDER FICA DURING QUARTER. (If no tips reported, write "None.")
(Total of column 20 on this page and continuation sheets.) Enter here and in Item 6 above . . . . ➤ $ `None`

SEE "WHERE TO FILE" ON PAGE 2.

FIGURE 8-2: EMPLOYER'S QUARTERLY FEDERAL TAX RETURN

tive total for two or three months exceeds $200.) Most firms with as many as four to six employees will have at least $200 in taxes for any one month and will thus have already deposited these taxes before the 941 Quarterly Return is completed. Line 11 of the quarterly return asks for the total of these deposits.* This deposit total is then deducted from the total taxes due for the whole quarter (line 10), to obtain the undeposited taxes still due (line 12a). (These undeposited taxes should always be less than $200; if not, a deposit should have been made. Normally, there will be a balance due on line 12a only for a very small firm or if some adjustment has been made on line 3 or line 8.) A check for the undeposited taxes must be submitted with the quarterly return. (Line 12b is used only in the event a firm has overpaid its taxes.)

Complete lines 1–12a of the Employer's Quarterly Federal Tax Return for Ashburn-Barringer, Inc., based on the following information: total wages (all taxable) for the quarter totaled $7,500; income tax of $848 was deducted; monthly deposits of $546, $504, and $578 have been made. **Example One**

The total deposits for the quarter (line 11) are $546 + 504 + $578 = $1,628.

FIGURE 8-3: EMPLOYER'S QUARTERLY FEDERAL TAX RETURN

The only part of the quarterly return that may involve more than just copying down figures already available is in determining taxable wages for FICA purposes. The following paragraphs are concerned with these taxable wages. The $9,000 base for FICA is now high enough that most workers will pay FICA taxes on all wages earned for the year. However,

*Large firms whose total taxes exceed $2,000 in less than one month are subject to special regulations and must deposit their taxes immediately after the $2,000 level is reached. Our study will not include such larger firms.

some higher paid workers and most executives will earn more than this amount and thus will not have all their earnings subject to FICA. As noted above, when employees pass the $9,000 level, the quarterly report will list only the part of their wages *earned during that quarter* which brought their total earnings to $9,000. (An employee who passes the $9,000 maximum during one quarter will be listed on the quarterly return for that quarter but will not be listed on a quarterly return of any succeeding quarter of the year.) If an employee's cumulative wages pass $9,000 during a quarter, that quarter's FICA taxable wages are found simply:

$$\$9,000 - \frac{\text{Cumulative wages at}}{\text{end of previous quarter}} = \frac{\text{FICA Taxable wages}}{\text{for current quarter}}$$

Some employee earnings records (See Fig. 8-1) include a total of the worker's cumulative earnings for the year as part of each week's payroll computations. Other earnings records compute the cumulative totals only quarterly or monthly. In any case, the payroll clerk must be careful to note when the employee's total earnings reach $9,000 and discontinue deducting FICA thereafter. The equation above can also be used by a payroll clerk to determine how much an employee can earn during a quarter before FICA should stop.

Example Two Quarterly earnings for three employees are listed below. How much can each employee earn during the next quarter before FICA deductions should stop?

Quarters	A	B	C
1st	$2,500	$2,800	$3,500
2nd	3,000	2,700	3,200
3rd	2,500	3,000	

The cumulative total for A = $8,000, for B = $8,500, and for C = $6,700. In each case,

$$\$9,000 - \frac{\text{Cumulative total at}}{\text{end of previous quarter}} = \frac{\text{FICA taxable wages}}{\text{for current quarter}}$$

Thus,

A: $9,000 − $8,000 = $1,000 of the 4th quarter's wages will be subject to FICA.

B: $9,000 - $8,500 = $ 500 of the 4th quarter's wages will be sub-
ject to FICA.

C: $9,000 - $6,700 = $2,300 of the 3rd quarter's wages will be sub-
ject to FICA. None of the 4th quar-
ter's wages will be taxable, and thus
none would be listed on the quarterly
report.

The following example illustrates the computation of FICA taxable
wages for succeeding quarters.

**Example
Three**

(a) The quarterly earnings of S. Alston, H. Barton, and J. Cohen
are shown below. Determine the FICA taxable wages for each
man during each quarter.

Name	Quarter	Quarterly Wages	Cumulative Total, End of Quarter	Qtrly. FICA Taxable Wages
S. Alston	1st	$1,500	$ 1,500	$1,500
	2nd	1,800	3,300	1,800
	3rd	2,000	5,300	2,000
	4th	1,800	7,100	1,800
H. Barton	1st	2,500	2,500	2,500
	2nd	2,500	5,000	2,500
	3rd	2,500	7,500 } *	2,500
	4th	2,500	10,000	1,500
J. Cohen	1st	3,000	3,000	3,000
	2nd	3,500	6,500 } **	3,500
	3rd	3,200	9,700	2,500
	4th	3,300	13,000	0

*The $9,000 maximum is passed during the 4th quarter, so $9,000 −
$7,500 = $1,500 FICA taxable wages for the 4th quarter.
**The $9,000 maximum is passed during the 3rd quarter, so $9,000 −
$6,500 = $2,500 FICA taxable wages for 3rd quarter. There are no taxable
wages for the 4th quarter.

(b) If Alston, Barton, and Cohen are the only employees of Midwest Radio & TV Service, what would be the company's total taxable wages during each quarter?

Name	FICA Taxable Wages			
	1st Qtr.	2nd Qtr.	3rd Qtr.	4th Qtr.
Alston, S.	$1,500	$1,800	$2,000	$1,800
Barton, H.	2,500	2,500	2,500	1,500
Cohen, J.	3,000	3,500	2,500	0
Totals	$7,000	$7,800	$7,000	$3,300

(c) Complete lines 1–12a of Midwest Radio & TV Service's quarterly return for the third quarter. They withheld income tax of $963. Their deposits for the quarter were $552, $573, and $566.

Total wages for the quarter are $2,000 + $2,500 + $3,200 = $7,700

FIGURE 8-4: EMPLOYER'S QUARTERLY FEDERAL TAX RETURN

As mentioned in Section Five, the employer's unemployment insurance tax was passed as part of the FICA Act. The funds collected under this tax are used to provide limited compensation, for a limited period of time, to workers who are unemployed because there is no work available to them. The Federal tax is levied only against employers, with most of the funds being collected by the states. (Only a few states have levied their own unemployment taxes, which may be deducted from the workers' gross earnings.) State unemployment taxes must be reported quarterly; the Federal return is submitted each January for the preceding calendar year, although deposits may be required quarterly. Since unemployment forms are not uniform from state to state, however, we shall omit any forms and study only the computation of these taxes.

Effective in 1972, employers were subject to unemployment tax if they employed one or more persons during any twenty weeks of the year or if they paid $1,500 in salaries during any quarter. The unemployment tax is similar to the FICA tax in that it applies only on wages up to a specific maximum; beginning in 1972, the tax was paid on the first $4,200 earned by each employee. The maximum rate was

$$2.7\% \quad \text{paid to the State}$$
$$\underline{.5\%} \quad \text{paid to the Federal government}$$
$$3.2\% \quad \text{total.}$$

Employers who have a good history of stable employment may have their state rates substantially reduced, while still paying only 0.5% in Federal tax, so that their total rate is well below the 3.2% maximum. The following example illustrates unemployment tax computation.

(a) The same employees and wages listed in Example Three are shown again below. Determine the amount of each man's wages that are subject to unemployment tax each quarter.

Example Four

Name	Quarter	Quarterly Wages	Cumulative Total, End of Quarter	Wages Subject to Unemployment
S. Alston	1st	$1,500	$ 1,500	$1,500
	2nd	1,800	3,300 ⎱ *	1,800
	3rd	2,000	5,300 ⎰	900
	4th	1,800	7,100	0
H. Barton	1st	2,500	2,500 ⎱ **	2,500
	2nd	2,500	5,000 ⎰	1,700
	3rd	2,500	7,500	0
	4th	2,500	10,000	0
J. Cohen	1st	3,000	3,000 ⎱ ***	3,000
	2nd	3,500	6,500 ⎰	1,200
	3rd	3,200	9,700	0
	4th	3,300	13,000	0

The wages subject to unemployment tax during a quarter can be found

$$\$4,200 - \frac{\text{Cumulative total, end}}{\text{of previous quarter}} = \frac{\text{Unemployment-taxable}}{\text{wages, current quarter.}}$$

Therefore,

*The $4,200 maximum for wages subject to unemployment tax was passed during the 3rd quarter, so

$4,200 − $3,300 = $900 subject to unemployment tax during the 3rd quarter.

**The $4,200 maximum was passed during the 2nd quarter, so

$4,200 − $2,500 = $1,700 subject to unemployment tax during the 2nd quarter. No wages are subject thereafter.

***The $4,200 maximum was passed during the 2nd quarter, so

$4,200 − $3,000 = $1,200 subject to unemployment tax during the 2nd quarter. No wages are subject during the 3rd or 4th quarters.

(b) The three men above are employed by Midwest Radio and TV. What would be the total taxable wages (for unemployment) of the firm for each quarter?

| Name | Taxable Wages for Unemployment | | | |
	1st Qtr.	2nd Qtr.	3rd Qtr.	4th Qtr.
Alston, S.	$1,500	$1,800	$900	0
Barton, H.	2,500	1,700	0	0
Cohen, J.	3,000	1,200	0	0
Totals	$7,000	$4,700	$900	0

(c) If Midwest Radio and TV Service has been assigned a reduced unemployment tax rate of 2.0% by its state, compute the firm's state unemployment taxes for each quarter and the Federal unemployment taxes due at the end of the year.

$7,000 × 2.0% = $140 due to state for 1st quarter

$4,700 × 2.0% = $ 94 due to state for 2nd quarter

$ 900 × 2.0% = $ 18 due to state for 3rd quarter

No unemployment tax will be owed to the state during the 4th quarter.

$$\$7,000 + \$4,700 + \$900 = \$12,600 \qquad \text{Total wages subject to un-}$$
$$\text{employment tax}$$

$\$12,600 \times 0.5\% = \$63$ due to Federal government for entire year

PROBLEMS

1. Complete lines 1–12a of a Federal Quarterly Return using the following facts: the total wages (all FICA taxable) were $3,640; income taxes of $320 were withheld; monthly deposits of $264.56 and $253 have been made.

2. Complete lines 1–12a of a 941 Employer's Quarterly Federal Tax Return based on the following information: the wages paid (which were all taxable) amounted to $18,000; income tax withheld was $1,985; monthly deposits of $1,286, $1,253, and $1,318 have been made.

3. Quarterly earnings for three employees are listed below. Determine how much of each employee's earnings during the following quarter will be subject to FICA tax deductions.

Quarters	X	Y	Z
1st	$2,600	$2,500	$3,300
2nd	2,200	3,000	3,500
3rd	2,400	2,800	

4. Three employees are shown below, along with their quarterly earnings. How much can each earn during the following quarter, before reaching the maximum level for FICA deductions?

Quarter	L	M	N
1st	$2,400	$2,800	$2,900
2nd	2,700	2,900	3,400
3rd	2,500	3,000	

5. The employees of Stanford Corp. are listed below, along with their total earnings and income tax deductions for each quarter.

   (a) Determine each employee's FICA taxable wages for each quarter.

   (b) Determine the corporation's total taxable wages for each quarter.

	R. Boyd		P. Caldwell		J. Dyson		F. Eaton		L. Fisher	
Quarter	Wages	Inc. Tax	Wages	Inc. Tax	Wages	Inc. Tax	Wages	Inc. Tax	Wages	Inc. Tax
1st	$1,600	$195	$2,500	$263	$2,800	$308	$2,900	$332	$3,100	$354
2nd	2,000	213	2,100	218	2,500	265	3,400	403	3,300	387
3rd	1,900	204	2,200	209	2,500	265	3,200	378	3,500	425
4th	2,200	236	2,300	245	2,900	320	3,300	385	3,400	412

6. Shown below are the employees of Gordon Sales Corp., along with their quarterly gross wages and income tax withheld each quarter.

   (a) Compute each employee's FICA taxable wages for each quarter.

   (b) Calculate the total taxable wages for the whole company for each quarter.

	S. Peters		P. Quinn		D. Royall		J. Stevens		R. Thomas	
Quarter	Wages	Inc. Tax	Wages	Inc. Tax	Wages	Inc. Tax	Wages	Inc. Tax	Wages	Inc. Tax
1st	$1,600	$168	$2,400	$267	$2,200	$241	$3,200	$406	$3,400	$448
2nd	1,800	192	2,600	284	2,400	264	2,900	366	3,200	412
3rd	1,800	192	2,500	279	2,200	241	3,200	406	3,300	425
4th	2,000	215	2,700	296	2,400	264	3,000	378	3,500	473

7. Complete lines 1-12a of the 941 Employer's Quarterly Federal Tax Return for the third quarter of Problem 5. Deposits have been made for the withheld income tax and social security in the amounts of $944, $933.60, and $841.

8. Compute lines 1–12a of the employer's quarterly return for the second quarter of Problem 6. Deposits have totaled $991.60, $945, and $923.

9. Fill in items 1–12a of the fourth quarter's Federal return for Problem 5. Monthly deposits have been made in the amounts of $794.40, $758, and $628.

10. Complete lines 1–12a of the 941 quarterly return for the fourth quarter of Problem 6. Prior deposits have been for $787, $734.80, and $697.

11. (a) Refer to Problem 3. List the taxable wages (for unemployment purposes) of employees X, Y, and Z during each quarter of the year.

    (b) What are the firm's total taxable wages for unemployment for each quarter?

    (c) If these are their company's only employees, determine the firm's state unemployment taxes for each quarter and the Federal unemployment taxes for the year. Assume the company has a reduced state rate of 1.8% (The Federal rate is never reduced.)

12. Assume the employees in Problem 4 are the only ones in their business.

    (a) Determine the taxable wages for unemployment of each worker for each quarter.

    (b) Find the total taxable wages of the company for each quarter.

    (c) What quarterly unemployment taxes will the company pay to its state? What are the annual taxes due to the Federal government? Assume the firm has a state rate of 1.5%.

13. (a) Determine the wages subject to unemployment each quarter for the employees in Problem 5.

   (b) What is the company total each quarter of wages subject to unemployment insurance tax?

   (c) If the firm has a reduced state unemployment rate of 1.2%, how much are its state unemployment taxes for each quarter? What amount is owed to the Federal government for the year's unemployment taxes?

14. (a) Refer to Problem 6. Compute the wages of each employee that are subject to unemployment tax for each quarter.

   (b) Determine the total taxable wages for unemployment of the firm for each quarter.

   (c) Assume the firm has a reduced state tax rate of 1.4%. Compute the company's state unemployment tax for each quarter and the Federal unemployment tax for the year.

Depreciation
and
Overhead

LEARNING OBJECTIVES

Upon completion of Chapter 9, the student will be able to:

1. Define and use correctly the terminology associated with each topic.

2. Compute depreciation (including additional first-year allowance and net salvage value) by the following three methods:
   a. Straight-line,
   b. Sum-of-the-digits, and
   c. Declining balance.

3. Compute overhead as a ratio of
   a. Floor space per department,
   b. Net sales, and
   c. Employees per department.

Two MAJOR BUSINESS EXPENSES are depreciation and overhead. The calculation of these expenses requires certain mathematical procedures which are the subject of the following sections.

1. DEPRECIATION

The fixed assets of a business are its buildings, machinery, equipment, and similar properties that will be used for more than one year. Such fixed assets always experience *depreciation*—loss in value because of physical deterioration (from age, use, or the effects of weather) or obsolescence (due to a change in style or because of the invention of more efficient models). Eventually, the low value, inefficiency, or maintenance required for these assets makes it necessary to replace them.

Because a fixed asset will be used for several years, the Federal Internal Revenue Service does not allow a business to list the purchase price of the asset as an expense during the year in which it was obtained. However, a business is permitted to distribute the depreciation of a fixed asset over all its years of use. Although not an item for which money is actually spent, depreciation is considered an operating expense (just as are salaries, rent, insurance, etc.) and is deducted from business profits when computing taxable income. Because depreciation is a tax-deductible item on business income tax returns, the Internal Revenue Service regulates carefully the conditions under which depreciation may be computed.

There are several acceptable methods for computing depreciation. We shall consider here the three most common methods: the *straight-line method*, the *sum-of-the-digits method*, and the *declining-balance method*. In general, a business is not required to use any particular method and may in fact depreciate different assets by different methods. The principal exception to this policy is newly acquired real estate property (buildings), which usually must be depreciated by the straight-line method. As a rule, a business must obtain prior permission in order to change its method of computing depreciation on any item; a change from the sum-of-the-digits or the declining-balance method to the straight-line method is sometimes possible without prior permission, but a change from the straight-line method to either of the others may never be made without authorization. Before depreciation can be computed, however, several aspects must be considered.

First, the *useful life* (in years) of the property to the business must be determined. This will vary from business to business, depending upon company policy. (Some firms prefer to use machinery as long as possible, whereas others prefer to replace it more frequently.) The Internal Revenue Service provides information regarding the normal life expectancy of many typical business properties.

Second, the value of the property at the end of its useful life must be estimated. This may be the *trade-in value* if the equipment will be traded, or the *scrap* or *salvage value* if it is simply to be junked after use. In order to allow for the expense of removing a machine or similar property, a business may deduct up to 10% of the cost of an item from the salvage value. Salvage, when reduced by the cost of removal, is called *net salvage*. Either salvage or net salvage may be used in determining depreciation, so long as one policy is consistently followed. (We will use salvage in all problems unless net salvage is clearly indicated.)

Finally, the *wearing value* is the difference between the original cost and the scrap value. The total amount of depreciation charged may never exceed this wearing value. (That is, a firm may never depreciate an asset below a reasonable scrap value.)

A *depreciation schedule* is kept for each asset. This is a record showing the amount of depreciation claimed each year, the total amount of depreciation claimed to date, and the current book value (calculated value) of the asset. The book value is then used in determining the company's capital assets for the year.

Note: Depreciation may not be claimed on land or on personal property (except when used for business purposes without reimbursement). Also, if a business fails to claim depreciation for a given year, that depreciation may not be claimed during any succeeding year.

STRAIGHT-LINE METHOD

The straight-line method is the simplest and most frequently used method for computing depreciation. By this method, the total wearing value is divided evenly among the years of useful life. (That is, the same amount of depreciation is charged each year.)

Example One

A delivery truck is purchased for $3,600. It is expected to last for five years and have a trade-in value of $900. Prepare a depreciation schedule by the straight-line method.

First, the wearing value must be computed and divided by the years of use to determine each year's depreciation charge.

Original cost	$3,600
Trade-in value	− 900
Wearing value	$3,600 −900 $2,700

$$\frac{\text{Wearing value}}{\text{Years}} = \frac{\$2,700}{5}$$

$$= \$540 \text{ depreciation each year}$$

Next, the depreciation schedule is completed as follows:

1. A year "0" is marked down to indicate when the asset was new, and the original cost is entered under "book value." Of course, no depreciation has yet occurred when the asset is new; thus depreciation columns have no entries on line 0.
2. Each year the "annual depreciation" is entered.
3. The "accumulated depreciation" is found each year by adding the current year's depreciation to the previous year's accumulated depreciation.
4. The "book value" is determined by subtracting the current year's (annual) depreciation from the previous year's book value.

Note: If a mistake is made at any point in a depreciation schedule, all succeeding entries will also be incorrect. Therefore, the student should use the following checks as he proceeds: (1) For any year, the sum of all the annual depreciations to that point should equal that year's accumulated depreciation. (Example: Year 3—$540 + $540 + $540 = $1,620.) (2) During any year, the book value plus the accumulated depreciation must equal the original cost. (Example: Year 4—$1,440 + $2,160 = $3,600.) (3) The final book value should equal the salvage value of the asset. (4) The final accumulated depreciation should equal the total wearing value.

DEPRECIATION SCHEDULE

(Straight-Line Method)

Year	Book Value (End of Year)	Annual Depreciation	Accumulated Depreciation
0	$3,600	—	—
1	3,060	$540	$ 540
2	2,520	540	1,080
3	1,980	540	1,620
4	1,440	540	2,160
5	900	540	2,700

SUM-OF-THE-DIGITS METHOD

The straight-line method (depreciating the same amount each year) proves satisfactory provided the asset is kept for the expected number of years. However, most machinery actually undergoes greater depreciation during its early years and less depreciation during later years. If for some reason the machine is disposed of earlier than expected, the book value on a straight-line depreciation schedule may be considerably higher than the actual market value. In order to apportion the depreciation more realistically, the sum-of-the-digits method may be used. This method distributes the wearing value unevenly among the years, with the greatest depreciation occurring during the first years. (This method is also called the *sum-of-the-years'-digits* or the *sum-of-the-periods method.*)

The fact that depreciation is a tax deductible item also accounts for the popularity of depreciation methods which offer greater depreciation during early years. (Both the sum-of-the-digits method and the declining-balance method offer this advantage.) Many firms feel that an immediate tax savings is more important than future tax savings, since money saved now can be used in the business in order to increase future income.

Prepare a depreciation schedule for Example 1 using the sum-of-the-digits method. (A $3,600 truck was expected to be worth $900 after five years.) **Example Two**

The sum-of-the-digits method derives its name from step 1 in the following procedure:

1. The digits comprising the life expectancy of the asset are added.* Thus, since the life expectancy is five years,

$$1 + 2 + 3 + 4 + 5 = 15$$

2. This sum becomes the denominator of a series of fractions. The years' digits, taken in reverse order, are the numerators of the fractions.

3. The fractions derived in step 2 are then multiplied times the wearing value to compute each year's depreciation:

Wearing value = $3,600 − $900 = $2,700

Year	Annual Depreciation
1	$\frac{5}{15} \times \$2,700 = \$900$
2	$\frac{4}{15} \times 2,700 = 720$
3	$\frac{3}{15} \times 2,700 = 540$
4	$\frac{2}{15} \times 2,700 = 360$
5	$\frac{1}{15} \times 2,700 = 180$

*The sum of the years' digits may also be found by applying the formula: (# of Years) $\times \dfrac{(\text{\# of Years} + 1)}{2}$. That is, $5 \times \dfrac{(5 + 1)}{2} = 5 \times \dfrac{6}{2} = 5 \times 3 = 15$. This formula is of great advantage when the number of years is large.

Note: In actual practice, the final year's depreciation may be found first (carrying it out to three decimal places if it does not come out even). Depreciation for the other years can then be computed, in reverse order, by multiplying the final year's depreciation by 2, 3, 4, etc.

A depreciation schedule according to the sum-of-the-digits method is then completed in the same manner described previously, and the same checks apply:

DEPRECIATION SCHEDULE

(Sum-of-the-Digits Method)

Year	Book Value (End of Year)	Annual Depreciation	Accumulated Depreciation
0	$3,600	—	—
1	2,700	$900	$ 900
2	1,980	720	1,620
3	1,440	540	2,160
4	1,080	360	2,520
5	900	180	2,700

DECLINING-BALANCE METHOD

A third method frequently used for computing depreciation is the declining-balance method (sometimes called the *constant per cent method*). This method also offers the advantage of greatest annual depreciation during the early years, progressively declining as time passes.

When the declining-balance method is used, depreciation is computed using the same rate (per cent) each year. Each year's depreciation is found by multiplying this per cent times the previous year's book value. Thus the annual depreciation decreases in direct proportion to the decrease in book value.

This method does not require estimating a salvage value in advance.* The general rule for determining the per cent to be used is to double the reciprocal of the number of years. (For example, the rate for an asset used six years would be $2 \times \frac{1}{6} = \frac{2}{6} = \frac{1}{3}$ or $33\frac{1}{3}\%$ annually.) This is the maximum rate allowed; a lower rate may be used.

Example Three Kelley Kleaners purchased new cleaning equipment at a cost of $6,000 and expect to use the equipment for eight years. Construct a declining-balance depreciation schedule.

*If one wishes to use a rate so that a specific scrap value will be obtained, the required per cent can be found using the formula $r = 1 - \sqrt[n]{\frac{s}{c}}$, where r = rate, n = number of years, s = salvage value, and c = original cost. Practical use of this formula requires a knowledge of logarithms.

Since the equipment will be used for eight years, the annual depreciation rate is twice the reciprocal of total years, or

$$2 \times \tfrac{1}{8} = \tfrac{2}{8}$$
$$= \tfrac{1}{4} \quad \text{or} \quad 25\%$$

Each succeeding book value will be multiplied by 25% (or $\tfrac{1}{4}$) to find the next annual depreciation.

DEPRECIATION SCHEDULE

(Declining-Balance Method)

Year	Book Value (End of Year)	Annual Depreciation	Accumulated Depreciation
0	$6,000.00	—	—
1	4,500.00	$1,500,00	$1,500.00
2	3,375.00	1,125.00	2,625.00
3	2,531.25	843.75	3,468.75
4	1,898.44	632.81	4,101.56
5	1,423.83	474.61	4,576.17
6	1,067.87	355.96	4,932.13
7	800.90	266.97	5,199.10
8	600.68	200.22	5,399.32

ADDITIONAL FIRST-YEAR DEPRECIATION ALLOWANCE

Recognizing the rapid early depreciation which machinery and equipment undergo, the Internal Revenue Service allows businesses to elect during the first year an extra depreciation of 20% of the cost. This extra 20% depreciation is over and above the depreciation claimed by any of the standard methods. The additional 20% first-year depreciation applies only to machinery and equipment, not to buildings. Also, the asset must have a useful life of at least six years; and the maximum cost on which the additional depreciation may be computed is $10,000, as the total of all assets which qualify.

When the 20% additional depreciation allowance is taken, this depreciation, as well as the scrap value, must be deducted from the original cost to find the base amount used for computing depreciation by the straight-line or the sum-of-the-digits method. When the declining balance method is used, only the additional first-year's depreciation is subtracted from the cost, and the remaining balance is then multiplied by the annual depreciation rate.

Example Four New processing equipment cost a dairy $5,000 and will be used for eight years, after which it is estimated to be worth $400. (a) Find the 20% additional first year's depreciation. Then compute the annual depreciation by (b) the straight-line method, (c) the sum-of-the-digits method (with depreciation schedule), and (d) the declining-balance method (with depreciation schedule).

(a) The *additional first-year depreciation* is 20% of cost:

$$\$5,000 \times 20\% = \$5,000 \times 0.2$$
$$= \$1,000$$

The additional first-year depreciation amounts to $1,000, regardless of which depreciation method is used.

(b) *Straight-line method.* The $1,000 additional first-year depreciation and the salvage value must be deducted from the cost before calculating the yearly depreciation.

Original cost	$5,000
Additional depreciation	−1,000
	$4,000
Salvage value	−400
Remaining wearing value	$3,600

The remaining wearing value of $3,600, distributed evenly among all the years, gives

$$\frac{\$3,600}{8} = \$450$$

Depreciation by the straight-line method will be $450 each year after the first year. (During the first year, the additional $1,000 depreciation will bring the total first-year depreciation to $1,450.)

(c) *Sum-of-the-digits method.* As in part b, the additional first-year's depreciation and the scrap value must first be deducted. The remaining wearing value would then be the same as in part b —$3,600.

The sum of the digits is $1 + 2 + 3 + 4 + 5 + 6 + 7 + 8 = 36$. Thus depreciation by the sum-of-the-digits method would be

Year	Annual Depreciation
1	$\frac{8}{36} \times \$3,600 = \$800 + \$1,000 = \$1,800$
2	$\frac{7}{36} \times 3,600 = 700$
3	$\frac{6}{36} \times 3,600 = 600$
4	$\frac{5}{36} \times 3,600 = 500$
5	$\frac{4}{36} \times 3,600 = 400$
6	$\frac{3}{36} \times 3,600 = 300$
7	$\frac{2}{36} \times 3,600 = 200$
8	$\frac{1}{36} \times 3,600 = 100$

During the first year, the $800 regular depreciation plus the $1,000 additional depreciation brings the total first-year's depreciation to $1,800.

DEPRECIATION SCHEDULE

**(Sum-of-the-Digits Method
with Additional First-Year Allowance)**

Year	Book Value (End of Year)	Annual Depreciation	Accumulated Depreciation
0	$5,000	—	—
1	3,200	$1,800	$1,800
2	2,500	700	2,500
3	1,900	600	3,100
4	1,400	500	3,600
5	1,000	400	4,000
6	700	300	4,300
7	500	200	4,500
8	400	100	4,600

(d) *Declining-balance method.* The balance remaining after the additional first year's depreciation is deducted from the cost is $5,000 − $1,000 = $4,000. This is the base used for computing depreciation by the declining-balance method.

Since the processing equipment will be used for eight years, it is depreciated at a maximum rate of $2 \times \frac{1}{8} = \frac{1}{4}$ or 25% per year. The normal first-year's depreciation is $4,000 × 25% or $1,000. The total first-year's depreciation is thus $2,000 ($1,000 normal depreciation plus $1,000 additional depreciation). This leaves a balance of $5,000 − $2,000 or $3,000 to be multiplied by 25% to obtain the second year's depreciation ($750).

DEPRECIATION SCHEDULE

(Declining Balance Method
with Additional First-Year Allowance)

Year	Book Value (End of Year)	Annual Depreciation	Accumulated Depreciation
0	$5,000.00	—	—
1	3,000.00	$2,000.00	$2,000.00
2	2,250.00	750.00	2,750.00
3	1,687.50	562.50	3,312.50
4	1,265.62	421.88	3,734.38
5	949.22	316.40	4,050.78
6	711.92	237.30	4,288.08
7	533.94	177.98	4,466.06
8	400.46	133.48	4,599.54

SUMMARY

The calculation of depreciation is sometimes confusing if it is thought of as three unrelated procedures; therefore, the following section is offered to help the student consolidate the straight-line, sum-of-the-digits, and declining-balance methods.

Regardless of the depreciation method employed, the annual depreciation can be thought of as the product of the depreciable value of the asset times the annual depreciation rate. That is,

Depreciable value × Rate = Annual depreciation

Before performing this operation, the depreciable value must first be determined. The depreciable value is computed identically for the straight-line and sum-of-the-digits calculations; the declining-balance calculation differs only by omitting the salvage value:

Cost − 20% 1st year allowance, − Salvage value, = Depreciable value
          if elected   if any   (or remaining
                                                                wearing value)

The depreciable value (or remaining wearing value) is then multiplied by the appropriate rate. The rate changes each year in the sum-of-the-digits method; the rate remains constant for the entire time in the straight-line and declining-balance methods. The declining-balance method further requires that, in each succeeding year, the depreciable value be reduced by the previous annual depreciation.

After each annual depreciation is computed, these amounts are then used to complete the depreciation schedules already presented.

A machine was purchased for $9,000 and will be used for 6 years, after **Example** which its salvage value will be $900. The 20% additional first-year **Five** depreciation allowance is to be used. Compare the annual depreciation that would be claimed under (a) the straight-line method, (b) the sum-of-the-digits method, and (c) the declining balance method at the maximum rate.

First, the 20% additional first-year depreciation allowance must be computed:

$$\$9,000 \times 20\% = \$1,800$$

The additional first-year depreciation is $1,800 in each case.

Next, the depreciable value is computed for each depreciation method:

	(a) Straight-line	(b) Sum-of-digits	(c) Declining-balance
Cost	$9,000	$9,000	$9,000
− 1st-year allowance	−1,800	−1,800	−1,800
	$7,200	$7,200	$7,200
− Salvage value	− 900	− 900	—
Depreciable value (or remaining wearing value)	$6,300	$6,300	$7,200

Finally, annual depreciation is computed for each depreciation method. The rate to be used in each case is as follows:

(a) The straight-line rate is always the reciprocal of the number of years; in this case, $\frac{1}{6}$.

(b) The sum-of-the-digits $1 + 2 + 3 + 4 + 5 + 6 = 21$.

(c) The maximum declining-balancing rate is twice the straight-line rate; that is, $2 \times \frac{1}{6} = \frac{2}{6} = \frac{1}{3}$.

Therefore,

(a) Straight-line:

	Depreciable Value	× Rate =	Annual Depreciation
(1)	$6,300.00 ×	$\frac{1}{6}$ =	$1,050.00 + 1,800.00 = $2,850.00
(2)	6,300.00 ×	$\frac{1}{6}$ =	1,050.00
⋮			
(6)	6,300.00 ×	$\frac{1}{6}$ =	1,050.00

Each year is the same, after year one.

(b) Sum-of-the-digits:

(1)	$6,300.00 ×	$\frac{6}{21}$	=	$1,800.00 + 1,800.00 = $3,600.00	
(2)	6,300.00 ×	$\frac{5}{21}$	=	1,500.00	
(3)	6,300.00 ×	$\frac{4}{21}$	=	1,200.00	
(4)	6,300.00 ×	$\frac{3}{21}$	=	900.00	
(5)	6,300.00 ×	$\frac{2}{21}$	=	600.00	
(6)	6,300.00 ×	$\frac{1}{21}$	=	300.00	

(c) Declining balance:

(1)	$7,200.00 × $\frac{1}{3}$ = $2,400.00 + 1,800.00 = $4,200.00			
	−2,400.00			
(2)	4,800.00 × $\frac{1}{3}$ = 1,600.00			
	−1,600.00			
(3)	3,200.00 × $\frac{1}{3}$ = 1,066.67			
	−1,066.67			
(4)	2,133.33 × $\frac{1}{3}$ = 711.11			
	− 711.11			
(5)	1,422.22 × $\frac{1}{3}$ = 474.07			
	− 474.07			
(6)	948.15 × $\frac{1}{3}$ = 316.05*			
	− 316.05			
	$ 632.10*			

*Notice that the straight-line and the sum-of-the-digits methods both depreciate the machinery to its stated salvage of $900, but the declining-balance method computes a final value of $632.10. If $900 is an accurate salvage value, the maximum declining balance rate may not be used for this machinery, since a business is not permitted to depreciate an asset below its actual value; the maximum allowable depreciation for year six would be $48.15.

The following example illustrates an asset whose purchase price exceeds the $10,000 maximum allowable for the 20% additional first-year depreciation, and also includes net salvage value.

Example Six A processing machine that cost a foundry $12,000 new will be used for 9 years, after which its second-hand value will be $2,200.

(a) Compute the 20% additional first-year depreciation.

(b) Determine the *net* salvage value for the machine and use this to

(c) compute the annual depreciation by the straight-line method.

(a) The additional first-year depreciation on this $12,000 machine is the maximum allowable: 20% of $10,000 = $2,000.

(b) Net salvage is found by reducing the normal salvage by 10% of the cost.

Salvage	$2,200
10% of cost (10% of $12,000)	−1,200
Net Salvage	$1,000

(c) The $2,000 additional first-year depreciation and the $1,000 net salvage value must be deducted from the cost of the machine before the annual depreciation can be determined:

Original cost	$12,000
Additional depreciation	− 2,000
	$10,000
Net salvage value	− 1,000
Remaining wearing value (or Depreciable value)	$ 9,000

The remaining wearing value of $9,000, distributed evenly among the years, gives

Depreciable Value	× Rate =	Annual Depreciation
$\dfrac{\$9,000}{9} = \$1,000$ or	$\$9,000 \times \tfrac{1}{9} =$	$\$1,000$

The depreciation will be $1,000 annually for each year after the first year. Depreciation for the first year will be $3,000 (the $1,000 annual amount plus the $2,000 additional allowance.)

The depreciation problems in this text each pertain to a single item. It should be noted, however, that it is now acceptable for a number of assets with the same or even different useful lives to be combined into one account, using a single rate of depreciation for the entire account. These *multiple asset accounts* are usually broken down as (1) *group accounts*—similar assets having approximately the same useful lives; (2) *classified accounts*—assets classified according to use, but without regard to useful life; and (3) *composite accounts*—assets combined without regard to their character or useful lives. For group accounts, the depreciation rate is determined from the average of the useful lives of the assets. For classified and

composite accounts, however, a rate is usually determined by first computing one year's depreciation on each item; the total of this depreciation is
then divided by the total cost of the items to obtain an average rate which
will be applied to the account each year.

PROBLEMS

Compute the annual depreciation and complete a depreciation schedule for
each of the following, using the data and method indicated:

		Cost	Scrap Value	Useful Life	Depreciation Method
1.	(a)	$3,000	$600	4 yrs.	straight-line
	(b)	3,000	600	4	sum-of-digits
	(c)	5,000	—	5	declining balance
2.	(a)	$2,200	$700	5 yrs.	straight-line
	(b)	2,200	700	5	sum-of-digits
	(c)	4,800	—	4	declining balance

If the additional 20% first-year depreciation allowance were elected, compute
the annual depreciation that would be charged during (1) the first year, and
(2) the second year:

		Cost	Scrap Value	Useful Life	Depreciation Method
3.	(a)	$8,000	$800	7 yrs.	straight-line
	(b)	5,500	800	8	sum-of-digits
	(c)	9,000	—	6	declining balance
4.	(a)	$7,500	$600	6 yrs.	straight-line
	(b)	8,000	800	7	sum-of-digits
	(c)	6,000	—	8	declining balance

5. The Children's Clinic paid $2,400 for its waiting room furnishings. The
   furniture will be worth $400 after 8 years of use. Prepare a straight-line
   depreciation schedule for these furnishings.

6. The building in which Warwick Paint Co. is located cost $80,000. They
   estimate that in 30 years it will be worth approximately $5,000 and will
   have to be replaced. What will be the annual depreciation charge by the
   straight-line method during this time?

7. A typewriter with electronic memory cost Harrington Advertising Associates
   $2,000. Newer models will probably make this machine obsolete within
   six years, when it will be worth $320. Construct a depreciation schedule
   for the machine by the sum-of-the-digits method in order to determine how
   much income tax deduction can be claimed each year.

8. Chateau Restaurant purchased a new, high-speed, electronic oven for $1,200. They plan to use the oven for five years, after which they expect to receive about $300 on a trade-in. Complete a depreciation schedule for the oven using the sum-of-the-digits method.

9. Carter Electrical Co. paid $3,500 for a new salesman's car, which they expect to use for three years.
   (a) Depreciate the car on a declining balance schedule, using a constant yearly rate of 40%.
   (b) What will be the value of the car when it is traded?

10. A new television camera cost station WXYZ $4,800. Such cameras are usually obsolete in 4 years.
   (a) Make a depreciation schedule using the declining-balance method at a constant yearly rate of 30%.
   (b) How much will the camera supposedly be worth on trade-in at that time?

11. A photoprocessing machine cost Color Corp. $3,000. After six years of use, the machine's value will be $600. Construct a depreciation schedule by the straight-line method, including the 20% additional first-year depreciation allowance.

12. The knitting machine at Lytton Fabrics cost $6,500. After seven years, Lytton expects to receive approximately $1,000 when they trade in on a newer model. Using the straight-line method and claiming the additional 20% first-year allowance, construct a depreciation schedule for the machine.

13. A metal stamping machine at Playworld Toys cost $10,000. The company expects to use the machine for eight years, after which it will be worth approximately $800. In order to obtain more tax savings during early years, Playworld decided to claim the 20% additional first-year allowance and to depreciate the stamping machine using the sum-of-the-digits method. Prepare this depreciation schedule.

14. Gardner's Sheet Metal Shop paid $4,000 for a machine used to construct ducts. The machine is expected to last for seven years, and it will then be valued at $400. Complete a depreciation schedule by the sum-of-the-digits method, and elect the 20% additional first-year allowance.

15. The Steck Printing Co. purchased a new quick-set machine for $6,000. The machine is expected to operate for six years. Make a depreciation schedule for the machine using the declining balance method at the maximum rate and including the additional first-year allowance.

16. Dr. William Pendleton purchased $8,000 worth of new dental equipment for his office. The equipment will be used for ten years. Dr. Pendleton wants to claim the additional first-year allowance and thereafter to depreciate at the maximum yearly rate. Prepare this depreciation schedule.

In each of the following problems, determine (a) the 20% additional first-year depreciation allowance, (b) the *net* salvage value of the asset, and (c) compute the annual depreciation by the straight-line method for the first year and for succeeding years. (Depreciation schedules are not necessary.)

17. A packaging machine cost $17,000 new and will be used for 15 years, when its salvage value will be $4,700.

18. Processing equipment at a cannery cost $11,000. After 13 years of use, the machinery will be worth $3,600 secondhand.

19. A box factory paid $14,000 for the equipment and installation of an automatic assembly machine. If the machine is used 12 years, the factory can expect $2,600 on a trade-in.

20. A machine to mold hand tools cost a manufacturer $18,000. The machine's salvage value will be $5,300 after 10 years.

2. OVERHEAD

In addition to the cost of materials or merchandise, other expenses are incurred in the operation of any business. Examples of such operating expenses are salaries, rent, utilities, office supplies, taxes, depreciation, insurance, and so on. These additional expenses are known collectively as *overhead*.

Overhead contributes indirectly to the actual total cost of the merchandise being manufactured or sold by the concern. In order to determine the efficiency of various departments, to determine the total cost of manufacturing various items, or to determine whether certain items are being sold profitably, a portion of the total plant overhead is assigned to each department. From the many methods of distributing overhead, we shall consider three: according to total floor space, according to total net sales, and according to the number of employees in each department.

Example One Eric Manufacturing Co. wishes to distribute its mean monthly overhead of $80,000 among the various departments *according to the total floor space* of each department. The floor space of each department is as follows:

Department	Floor Space
A—Office	500 sq. ft.
B—Receiving and raw materials	2,500
C—Cutting and sewing	5,000
D—Inspecting and shipping	+ 2,000
Total =	10,000 sq. ft.

Each department therefore has the following ratio of floor space and is assigned the following amount of overhead expense:

Department	Ratio of Floor Space	Overhead Charge
A	$\dfrac{500}{10,000} = \dfrac{1}{20}$	$\frac{1}{20} \times \$80,000 = \ \$\ 4,000$
B	$\dfrac{2,500}{10,000} = \dfrac{1}{4}$	$\frac{1}{4} \times \ 80,000 = \ \ 20,000$
C	$\dfrac{5,000}{10,000} = \dfrac{1}{2}$	$\frac{1}{2} \times \ 80,000 = \ \ 40,000$
D	$\dfrac{2,000}{10,000} = \dfrac{1}{5}$	$\frac{1}{5} \times \ 80,000 = +16,000$
		Total overhead = $\ \$80,000$

The $15,000 October overhead of Mathews Co. is to be distributed *accord-ing to the total net sales* of each department. These sales were as follows: **Example Two**

Department	Net Sales
Ladies'	$25,000
Men's	15,000
Shoes	10,000
Sports and toys	5,000
Housewares	+20,000
Total net sales =	$75,000

The overhead charged to each department on the basis of net sales is as follows:

Department	Ratio of Sales	Overhead Charge
Ladies'	$\dfrac{\$25,000}{\$75,000} = \dfrac{1}{3}$	$\frac{1}{3} \times \$15,000 = \ \$\ 5,000$
Men's	$\dfrac{\$15,000}{\$75,000} = \dfrac{1}{5}$	$\frac{1}{5} \times \ 15,000 = \ \ 3,000$
Shoes	$\dfrac{\$10,000}{\$75,000} = \dfrac{2}{15}$	$\frac{2}{15} \times \ 15,000 = \ \ 2,000$
Sports & toys	$\dfrac{\$5,000}{\$75,000} = \dfrac{1}{15}$	$\frac{1}{15} \times \ 15,000 = \ \ 1,000$
Housewares	$\dfrac{\$20,000}{\$75,000} = \dfrac{4}{15}$	$\frac{4}{15} \times \ 15,000 = +\ 4,000$
		Total overhead = $\ \$15,000$

Example
Three

The Randall Pharmacy plans to distribute its annual overhead of $144,000 *according to the total number of employees* in each department. These are as follows:

Department	Employees
#1—Drugs	3
#2—Patent medicines	5
#3—Health and beauty aids	4
#4—Fountain and tobacco	2
#5—Sundries	+2
Total =	16

Distributing overhead according to the number of employees results in the following charge to each department:

Department	Ratio of Employees	Overhead Charge
#1	$\frac{3}{16}$	$\frac{3}{16} \times \$144,000 = \$ 27,000$
#2	$\frac{5}{16}$	$\frac{5}{16} \times 144,000 = 45,000$
#3	$\frac{4}{16} = \frac{1}{4}$	$\frac{1}{4} \times 144,000 = 36,000$
#4	$\frac{2}{16} = \frac{1}{8}$	$\frac{1}{8} \times 144,000 = 18,000$
#5	$\frac{2}{16} = \frac{1}{8}$	$\frac{1}{8} \times 144,000 = + 18,000$
		Total overhead = $144,000

PROBLEMS

In each of the following problems, distribute overhead according to floor space, net sales, or number of employees, depending on the information given:

	Dept.	Floor Space (in sq. ft.)	Total Overhead		Dept.	Floor Space (in sq. ft.)	Total Overhead
1. (a)	A	2,000	$24,000	(b)	#20	2,000	$80,000
	B	3,000			#30	1,000	
	C	2,500			#40	1,500	
	D	4,500			#50	2,500	
					#60	3,000	
2. (a)	V	7,500	$90,000	(b)	#1	500	$40,000
	W	2,500			#2	3,500	
	X	3,000			#3	5,000	
	Y	1,500			#4	1,000	
	Z	500					

	Dept.	Net Sales	Total Overhead		Dept.	Net Sales	Total Overhead
3. (a)	#1	$ 5,000	$5,000	(b)	P	$16,000	$4,800
	#2	15,000			Q	8,000	
	#3	20,000			R	24,000	
	#4	10,000			S	12,000	
					T	4,000	
4. (a)	R	$15,000	$8,000	(b)	1B	$20,000	$18,000
	S	8,000			2D	15,000	
	T	12,000			3G	25,000	
	U	5,000			4M	30,000	
					5S	10,000	

	Dept.	No. Employees	Total Overhead		Dept.	No. Employees	Total Overhead
5. (a)	#1	8	$72,000	(b)	A	10	$135,000
	#2	3			B	25	
	#3	4			C	5	
	#4	9			D	20	
					E	15	
6. (a)	H	10	$120,000	(b)	B-1	4	$14,000
	I	20			B-2	5	
	J	5			B-3	9	
	K	10			B-4	2	
	L	25					
	M	30					

7. The Family Mart, a discount department store, allocates overhead expenses according to the total floor space occupied by each department. Determine the overhead to be assigned to each department, if total overhead for October was $18,000.

Department	Floor Space (in sq. ft.)
Women's wear	6,000
Men's wear	4,500
Children's wear	3,000
Hardware	1,500
Home furnishings	5,000
Garden supplies	7,500
Patent medicines	2,000
Offices	500

8. Jensen Manufacturing Co. wishes to distribute their annual overhead of $150,000 among their separate departments according to floor space allotted to each. Divide their overhead among the following departments:

Department	Floor Space (in sq. ft.)
Office	800
Raw materials	1,200
Casting	2,500
Assembling	4,000
Warehouse	1,500

9. Ashdale Hardware Co. charges overhead to its various departments according to each department's ratio of total net sales. If the July operating expenses were $6,400, what was each department's share of the overhead?

Department	Net Sales
Equipment	$ 4,000
Appliances	12,000
Housewares & gifts	8,000
Sporting goods	15,000
Lighting fixtures	1,000

10. The Little Something (a ladies' clothing store) wishes to distribute its September overhead of $9,600 according to each department's portion of the total net sales. Compute the operating expense to be assigned each of the following departments:

Department	Net Sales
Dresses and coats	$16,000
Sportswear	12,000
Shoes	6,000
Hats	2,000
Accessories	4,000
Lingerie	8,000

11. The Home Bakery charges operating expenses according to the number of employees in each department. Overhead during March totaled $16,000. Assign the overhead expense to each department:

Department	Number of Employees
Mixing	4
Baking	2
Decorating	6
Sales	5
Administrative	3

12. Expenses at Garden Fresh Grocers are distributed according to the number of people working in each department. If their December overhead was $18,000, how much should be charged to each department?

Department	Number of Employees
Meat & dairy	6
Produce	3
Grocery items	4
Frozen foods	2
Bakery products, dietary and gourmet foods	1
Cashiers, bagboys, and management	8

10

Financial
Statement
Analysis

LEARNING OBJECTIVES

Upon completing Chapter 10, the student will be able to:

1. Define and use correctly the terminology in each topic.

2. On an income statement with the individual amounts given,
   a. Compute the net profit, and
   b. Find the per cent of net sales that each item represents.

3. On comparative income statements, compute
   a. Subtotals and totals;
   b. Per cents of net sales for each year; and
   c. Increase or decrease between years (amounts and %).

4. On a balance sheet with individual amounts given, compute
   a. Total assets,   c. Net worth, and
   b. Total liabilities,   d. Per cent each item represents.

5. On comparative balance sheets, compute the
   a. Subtotals and totals,
   b. Per cents of total assets, for each year, and
   c. Increase or decrease between years (amounts and %).

6. Select from income statements and balance sheets the amounts required to compute common business ratios:
   a. Working capital ratio,
   b. Acid-test ratio,
   c. Ratio of net income (after taxes) to average net worth,
   d. Ratio of net sales to average total assets,
   e. Accounts receivable turnover,
   f. Average age of accounts receivable, and
   g. Other percentage relationships where the items required are specifically named.

AT LEAST ONCE each year (sometimes more often), the bookkeeping records of every business are audited to determine the financial condition of the business: what the volume of business was, how much profit (or loss) was made, how much these things have changed in the past year, how much the business is actually worth, and so on. As a means of presenting this important information, two financial statements are normally prepared and analyzed: the *income statement* and the *balance sheet*.

1. THE INCOME STATEMENT

The *income statement* shows a business' sales, expenses, and profit (or loss) during a certain period of time. (The time might be a month, a quarter, six months, or a year.) The basic calculations of an income statement are these:

$$
\begin{array}{l}
\text{Net sales} \\
-\text{Cost of goods sold} \\
\hline
\text{Gross profit} \\
-\text{Operating expenses} \\
\hline
\text{Net profit (or net loss)}
\end{array}
$$

Notice that *gross profit* (also known as *margin*) is the amount that would remain after the merchandise has been paid for. Out of this gross profit must be paid all the *operating expenses* (*overhead* such as salaries, rent, utilities, supplies, insurance, etc.). Whatever amount then remains is the clear or spendable profit — the *net profit*.

In order effectively to analyze expenses or to compare an income statement with preceding ones, it is customary to convert the dollar amounts to per cents of the total net sales. These per cents are computed as follows:

$$—\% \text{ of Net sales} = \text{Each amount}$$

$$\frac{—\% \times \text{Net sales}}{\text{Net sales}} = \frac{\text{Each amount}}{\text{Net sales}}$$

$$—\% = \frac{\text{Each amount}}{\text{Net sales}}$$

During June, 1972, Johnson Grocery had net sales of $50,000. Its groceries cost $37,500 wholesale, and operating expenses totaled $7,500. How much profit was made during June, and what was the per cent of net sales for each item?

Example One

JOHNSON GROCERY

Income Statement for Month Ending June 30, 1972

base

Net sales	$50,000	100%
Cost of goods sold	37,500	75
Gross profit	$12,500	25%
Operating expenses	7,500	15
Net profit	$ 5,000	10%

The above per cents were obtained as follows:

$$—\% = \frac{\text{Each amount}}{\text{Net sales}}$$

(1) $\dfrac{\text{Cost of goods}}{\text{Net sales}} = \dfrac{\$37,500}{\$50,000} = 75\%$

(2) $\dfrac{\text{Gross profit}}{\text{Net sales}} = \dfrac{\$12,500}{\$50,000} = 25\%$

(3) $\dfrac{\text{Operating expenses}}{\text{Net sales}} = \dfrac{\$7,500}{\$50,000} = 15\%$

(4) $\dfrac{\text{Net profit}}{\text{Net sales}} = \dfrac{\$ 5,000}{\$50,000} = 10\%$

Thus we see that 75% of the income from sales was used to pay for the merchandise itself, leaving a gross profit ($12,500) of 25% of sales. Another 15% of the income from sales must be used to pay the $7,500 operating expenses. This leaves a clear, net profit of $5,000, which is 10% of the sales income.

Note: Observe that the cost of goods, the overhead, and the net profit account for all of the income from sales. Also, the overhead (operating expenses) and the net profit comprise the margin (gross profit). In equation form,

$$
\begin{array}{llll}
\text{Cost} & +\ \text{Overhead} + \text{Net profit} & = \text{Sales} \\
\$37{,}000\ + & \underbrace{\$7{,}500\ \ +\ \ \$5{,}000} & = \$50{,}000 \\
\\
\text{Cost}\ + & \text{Margin} & = \text{Sales} \\
\$37{,}000\ + & \$12{,}500 & = \$50{,}000
\end{array}
$$

This fundamental relationship is the basis for the equation $C + M = S$, which is applied by merchants to determine the selling price of their merchandise. (This is the subject of Chapter 13.)

These relationships, which are true for the amounts of money shown on the income statement, are also true of the per cents for each item:

$$
\begin{array}{llll}
\text{Cost} + \text{Overhead} + \text{Net profit} & = \text{Sales} \\
75\%\ + & \underbrace{15\%\ \ +\ \ 10\%} & = 100\% \\
\\
\text{Cost}\ + & \text{Margin} & = \text{Sales} \\
75\%\ + & 25\% & = 100\%
\end{array}
$$

The foregoing income statement was a highly simplified example. In actual practice, the basic topics used to calculate profit (net sales, cost of goods sold, and operating expenses) are broken down in detail, showing the contributing factors of each. The next example presents a more complete income statement.

Of the various topic breakdowns, only cost of goods sold needs particular mention. To the value of the inventory on hand at the beginning of the report period is added the total of all merchandise bought during the period (less returned merchandise and plus freight charges paid separately). This gives the total value of all merchandise which the company had available for sale during the period. Since some of this merchandise is not sold, however, the value of the inventory on hand at the end of the period must be deducted, in order to obtain the value of the merchandise which was actually sold.

Notice that, just as the individual amounts are added or subtracted to obtain subtotals, so may their corresponding per cents be added or subtracted to obtain the per cents of the subtotals. This is possible because each amount is represented as a per cent of the same number (net sales).

The per cents indicated in the right-hand column are the ones of particular interest to management and potential investors: (1) What per cent of sales was the cost of goods? (2) What per cent of sales was the gross profit (margin)? (3) What per cent of sales was the operating expense (overhead)? But most important by far to the owners and possible investors is the final per cent: (4) What per cent of sales was the net profit? This is usually the first question asked by anyone considering investing money in a business.

WALFIELD VARIETY STORE

Example
Two

Income Statement for Year ending December 31, 1971

Income from sales:				
Total sales		$102,500		102.5%
Less: Sales returns and				
allowances		2,500		2.5
Net sales			$100,000	100.0%
Cost of goods sold:				
Inventory, January 1		$ 25,700		
Purchases	$71,500			
Less: Returns and				
allowances	1,200			
Net purchases	$70,300			
Add: Freight in	500			
Net purchase cost		70,800		
Goods available for sale		$ 96,500		
Inventory, December 31		26,500		
Cost of goods sold			70,000	70.0
Gross profit on sales			$ 30,000	30.0%
Operating expenses:				
Salaries		$ 12,500		12.5%
Rent		3,500		3.5
Utilities		700		.7
Office supplies		200		.2
Depreciation		1,500		1.5
Insurance		900		.9
Miscellaneous		700		.7
Total operating expense			20,000	20.0
Net profit			$ 10,000	10.0%

The per cents derived in the foregoing examples represent *vertical analysis*. That is, each separate item is represented as a per cent of the total during a *single* time period. In order to analyze business progress and potential more effectively, however, recent figures should be compared with corresponding figures from the previous period (or periods). When comparisons are made between corresponding items during a *series* of two or more time periods, this is known as *horizontal analysis*.

The following example illustrates horizontal analysis. On this comparative income statement, both the dollar increase (or decrease) and the per cent of change are shown. Figures for the earlier year are used as the basis for finding the per cent of change, using the formula "—% of original = change?"

Example Three

GLEASON-WHITTIER, INC.

Comparative Income Statements
for Fiscal Years Ending June 30, 1972 and 1971

	1972	1971	Increase (or Decrease) Amount	%	% of Net Sales 1972	1971
Income:						
Net sales	$220,000	$200,000	$20,000	10.0%	100.0%	100.0%
Cost of goods sold:						
Inventory, July 1	$ 15,000	$ 20,000	($ 5,000)	25.0%	6.8%	10.0%
Purchases	178,000	155,000	23,000	14.8	80.9	77.5
Net goods available for sale	$193,000	$175,000	$18,000	10.3%	87.7%	87.5%
Inventory, June 30	18,000	15,000	3,000	20.0	8.2	7.5
Cost of goods sold	175,000	160,000	15,000	9.4	79.5	80.0
Gross margin	$ 45,000	$ 40,000	$ 5,000	12.5%	20.5%	20.0%
Expenses:						
Administration	$ 18,000	$ 15,000	$ 3,000	20.0%	8.2%	7.5%
Occupancy	7,500	5,000	2,500	50.0	3.4	2.5
Selling	9,000	8,000	1,000	12.5	4.1	4.0
Miscellaneous	1,500	2,000	(500)	25.0	0.7	1.0
Total expenses	36,000	30,000	6,000	20.0	16.4	15.0
Net income (before taxes)	$ 9,000	$ 10,000	($ 1,000)	10.0%	4.1%	5.0%

This example (for net sales) is typical of how all per cents of change were found. Net sales increased from $200,000 to $220,000, a "change" of $20,000. The "original" is the first year, 1971. Thus

$$\text{—% of Original} = \text{Change}$$
$$\text{—%} \times \$200,000 = \$20,000$$
$$\frac{200,000x}{200,000} = \frac{20,000}{200,000}$$
$$x = \tfrac{1}{10}$$
$$x = 10\%$$

Notice that, whereas the "amounts" of increase or decrease may be added or subtracted to obtain the amounts of the subtotals, the "per cents" of increase or decrease *cannot* be added or subtracted to obtain the per cents of change in the subtotals. This is because each per cent of change is based on a different number (the 1971 amount of that particular item).

2. THE BALANCE SHEET

The purpose of a *balance sheet* is to give an overall picture of what a business is worth at a specific time: how much it owns, how much it owes, and how much the owners' investment is worth. On a balance sheet are listed all of a business' *assets* (possessions and money owed to the business) and all its *liabilities* (money which the business owes to someone else). The balance remaining after the liabilities are subtracted from the assets is the *net worth* of the business. Thus the assets must balance the liabilities and net worth; or

Assets = Liabilities + Net worth

The general headings of a balance sheet are ordinarily broken down as follows: Assets are divided into *current assets* and *fixed assets*. Among the current assets are cash, bank accounts, accounts receivable (accounts owed to the business by customers who have bought merchandise "on credit"), notes receivable (money owed to the business by customers who have signed a written promise to pay by a certain date), and the merchandise inventory. Fixed assets are the buildings, furnishings, machinery, equipment (listed at their current book value after depreciation) and land (which may not be depreciated).

The liabilities of a business are separated according to *current liabilities* and *fixed liabilities*. Current liabilities include the accounts payable (accounts owed elsewhere for goods bought on credit), notes payable, and interest and taxes due within a short time. Fixed liabilities are such long-term debts as mortgages and bonds.

Other common terms used instead of net worth are *net ownership, net investment, proprietorship* (for an individually owned business), *owner's equity,* and *stockholders' equity* (for a corporation).

The following balance sheet again illustrates vertical analysis. That is, each asset is represented as a per cent of the total assets; and each liability, as well as the net worth, is presented as a per cent of the total liabilities plus net worth (which is the same as the total assets).

WILLIAM C. RYAN, INC.

Balance Sheet, December 31, 1971

	Assets		%
Current assets:			
Cash on hand	$ 200		.2%
Cash in bank	4,200		3.5
Accounts receivable	32,400		27.0
Inventory	13,200		11.0
Total current assets		$ 50,000	41.7%
Fixed assets:			
Plant site	$12,600		10.5%
Building	33,000		27.5
Equipment	19,000		15.8
Delivery trucks	5,400		4.5
Total fixed assets		70,000	58.3
Total assets		$120,000	100.0%
	Liabilities and Net Worth		
Current liabilities:			
Accounts payable	$26,400		22.0%
Notes payable	4,800		4.0
Total current liabilities		$ 31,200	26.0%
Fixed liabilities:			
Mortgage		34,800	29.0
Total Liabilities		$ 66,000	55.0%
Net Worth		54,000	45.0
Total Liabilities and Net Worth		$120,000	100.0%

Just as horizontal analysis was helpful in studying the income statement, so is it useful in determining the significance of a balance sheet. The next example presents such a balance sheet.

Net Worth = Total assets minus Total Liabilities

Assets = Net worth plus Total Liabilities

GRAHAM-CHAMBERS, INC.
Comparative Balance Sheet
for Fiscal Years Ending January 31, 1971 and 1970

	1971	1970	Increase (or Decrease)		% of Total Assets	
			Amount	%	1971	1970
Assets						
Cash	$ 26,000	$ 22,000	$ 4,000	18.2%	16.8%	14.7%
Accounts receivable	22,000	18,000	4,000	22.2	14.2	12.0
Inventory	27,000	25,000	2,000	8.0	17.4	16.7
Current assets	$ 75,000	$ 65,000	$10,000	15.4%	48.4%	43.3%
Fixed assets	80,000	85,000	(5,000)	(5.9)	51.6	56.7
Total assets	$155,000	$150,000	$ 5,000	3.3%	100.0%	100.0%
Liabilities and stockholders' equity						
Current liabilities	$ 36,000	$ 40,000	($ 4,000)	(10.0%)	23.2%	26.7%
Fixed liabilities	37,000	35,000	2,000	5.7	23.9	23.3
Total liabilities	$ 73,000	$ 75,000	($ 2,000)	(2.7%)	47.1%	50.0%
Common stock	$ 55,000	$ 50,000	$ 5,000	10.0%	35.5%	33.3%
Retained earnings	27,000	25,000	2,000	8.0	17.4	16.7
Total stockholders' equity	$ 82,000	$ 75,000	$ 7,000	9.3%	52.9%	50.0%
Total liabilities and stockholders' equity	$155,000	$150,000	$ 5,000	3.3%	100.0%	100.0%

In addition to the analysis possible from single or comparative financial statements, a number of other business ratios are commonly used to provide a more thorough indication of a business' financial condition. These ratios are computed using figures readily available from the income statement and the balance sheet. The next example contains an explanation and example of some of the more common ratios.

The ratios *a* through *f* given below are based on the balance sheet of Graham-Chambers, Inc. in Example Five. Their income statement for 1971 was as follows:

GRAHAM-CHAMBERS, INC.

**Condensed Income Statement
for Fiscal Year Ending January 31, 1971**

Net sales	$200,000	100.0%
Cost of goods sold	140,000	70.0
Gross margin	$ 60,000	30.0%
Operating expenses	48,000	24.0
Net income (before taxes)	$ 12,000	6.0%
Income taxes	2,000	1.0
Net income (after taxes)	$ 10,000	5.0%

(a) _Working capital ratio._ This ratio is often called the _current ratio_, because it is the ratio of current assets to current liabilities. Thus

$$\frac{\text{Current assets}}{\text{Current liabilities}} = \frac{\$75,000}{36,000}$$

$$= \frac{2.1}{1} \qquad \text{or} \qquad 2.1 \text{ to } 1$$

The current ratio is 2.1 to 1 for Graham-Chambers. A ratio of 2:1 is generally considered the minimum acceptable ratio; bankers would probably hesitate to lend money to a firm whose working capital ratio was lower than 2:1.

(b) _Acid-test ratio._ The current ratio included all current assets. In order to provide some measure of a firm's ability to obtain funds quickly, the _acid-test_ or _quick ratio_ is computed. This is a ratio of the quick assets to the current liabilities. _Quick assets_ (sometimes called _liquid assets_) are those which can be easily and quickly converted to cash; for example, accounts receivable and notes receivable, as well as cash itself. (The inventory is not included in the acid-test ratio, because it often proves difficult to convert the inventory to cash quickly.)

$$\frac{\text{Quick assets}}{\text{Current liabilities}} = \frac{\$48,000}{36,000}$$

$$= \frac{1.3}{1} \qquad \text{or} \qquad 1.3 \text{ to } 1$$

As an indication of a firm's ability to meet its obligations, the acid-test ratio should be at least 1:1.

(c) *Net income (after taxes) to average net worth.* Since businesses are organized to make profits, of primary concern to the owners is the return on their investment. This ratio indicates the rate of return on the average owners' equity.

$$\text{Average net worth} = \frac{\$75,000 + \$82,000}{2}$$

$$= \frac{\$157,000}{2}$$

$$= \$78,500$$

$$\frac{\text{Net income (after taxes)}}{\text{Average net worth}} = \frac{\$10,000}{78,500}$$

$$= 12.7\%$$

(d) *Net sales to average total assets.* This ratio gives some indication of whether a business is using its assets to best advantage—that is, of whether its sales volume is in line with what the company's capital warrants. This ratio (sometimes called the *total capital turnover*) would indicate inefficiency if it is too low. (*Note:* The "total assets" used here should exclude any assets held by the company which do not contribute to the business operation.)

$$\text{Average total assets} = \frac{\$150,000 + \$155,000}{2}$$

$$= \frac{\$305,000}{2}$$

$$= \$152,500$$

$$\frac{\text{Net sales}}{\text{Average total assets}} = \frac{\$200,000}{\$152,500}$$

$$= \frac{1.3}{1} \quad \text{or} \quad 1.3 \text{ to } 1$$

The ratio of net sales to average total assets is 1.3 to 1; or, the turnover of total capital was 1.3 times.

(e) *Accounts receivable turnover.* Accounts receivable turnover is the ratio of net sales to average accounts receivable. (Notes receivable, if they are held, should also be included with the accounts receivable.)

$$\text{Average accounts receivable} = \frac{\$18,000 + \$22,000}{2}$$

$$= \frac{40,000}{2}$$

$$= \$20,000$$

$$\frac{\text{Net sales}}{\text{Average accounts receivable}} = \frac{\$200,000}{\$20,000}$$

$$= 10 \text{ times}$$

Accounts receivable are not actually an asset to a business until they are collected. Prompt collection of the accounts receivable makes funds available to the business to meet its own obligations and to take advantage of cash discounts and special offers. Furthermore, the older an account becomes, the less likelihood that it will be collected. Thus a minimum of the firm's assets should be tied up in the receivables, and they should turn over frequently.

(f) *Average age of accounts receivable.* This ratio, in conjunction with the preceding one, indicates whether a business is keeping its accounts receivable up to date. The average age in days is found by dividing 365 days by the turnover in accounts receivable.

$$\frac{365}{\text{Accounts receivable turnover}} = \frac{365}{10}$$

$$= 36.5 \text{ days}$$

The average age of the accounts receivable is 36.5 days. If Graham-Chambers has an allowable credit period of 30 days, this average age of 36.5 days indicates that they are not keeping up with collections.

There are quite a few other ratios of interest to owners and management. One of these, the equity ratio, is already indicated on the balance sheet; the equity ratio is the ratio of owners' equity to total assets (52.9%). The ratio of current liabilities to net worth and the ratio of total liabilities to net worth are ratios based on balance sheet figures. Other common ratios relating to net sales are the ratio of net sales to net worth, the fixed property turnover (the ratio of net sales to fixed assets), the ratio of net sales to net working capital $\left(\frac{\text{Net sales}}{\text{Current assets} - \text{Current liabilities}} \right)$, and the inventory turnover (the ratio of net sales to average inventory, which is discussed in Chapter 14 on Markdown and Turnover).

Additional ratios involving net income are the ratio of net income to total assets and

$$\left(\frac{\text{Net income after} \ldots}{\text{Average common} \ldots}\right.$$

book value of the stock

$$\text{puted:} \left(\frac{\text{Owners' equi} \ldots}{\text{Number of shares of s} \ldots}\right.$$

computed if it were thought they

Although the financial statem

puted from them are of great value in

financial condition of a business, such r

information from other businesses of the sa

economic condition of the country as a whol

consideration as part of any thorough analysis

potential investor. On this basis, reports which ori

able might appear less acceptable or might indicat

unusually well in comparison with competing firms.

the rate (per cent) of return per share of common stock

taxes – Preferred dividends).

stockholders' equity). Of interest also is the

(when there is only one type of stock, this is com-

ock). Any number of other ratios could be

would be useful.

ments and the ratios that can be com-

evaluating the overall efficiency and

ports are not foolproof. Similar

ne type, as well as the general

must also be taken into

by management or by a

inally seemed accept-

the business did

Office supplies	6,500	1.3
Insurance	5,000	1.0
Advertising	10,000	2.0
Depreciation	7,000	1.4
Other	2,500	.5
Total operating expenses	140,000	28.0
Net profit on operations	$60,000	12.0%
Income taxes	35,000	7.0
Net income	$25,000	5.0%

expenses

equals

net profit

minus

taxes

equals

net income

2. ARDMORE WHOLESALERS, INC.

Income Statement for Fiscal Year Ending March 31, 1972

			%	
Income from sales:				
Gross sales		$615,000	————%	
Sales returns and allowances		15,000	————	
Net sales		$600,000	————	100.0 %
Cost of goods sold:				
Inventory, April 1, 1968		$200,000		
Purchases	$432,500			
Less: Returns and allowances	6,000			
Net purchases	$426,500			
Add: Freight in	3,500	430,000		
Net purchase cost				
Goods available for sale		$630,000		
Inventory, March 31, 1969		180,000	450,000	
Cost of goods sold			————	
Gross margin on sales		$150,000	————%	
Operating expenses:		2		
Office salaries		$ 20,000	————%	
Occupancy		25,000	————	
Selling		45,000	————	
Buying		15,000	————	
Insurance		6,000	————	
Depreciation		12,000	————	
Miscellaneous		3,000	————	
Total operating expense		126,000	————	
Net income on operations		$24,000	————%	
Income taxes		5,000	————	
Net income (after taxes)		$19,000	————%	

3. **W. D. CRENSHAW CO.**

Balance Sheet, September 30, 1972

			%
Assets			
Current assets:			
Cash	$ 4,000		———%
Accounts receivable	22,000		———
Notes receivable	2,000		———
Merchandise inventory	20,000		———
Total current assets	$———		———%
Fixed assets:			
Building (less depreciation)	$16,000		———%
Furnishings and fixtures			
(less depreciation)	3,200		———
Delivery truck	2,800		———
Land	10,000		———
Total fixed assets			
Total assets	$———		———%
Liabilities and proprietorship			
Current liabilities:			
Accounts payable	$20,000		———%
Taxes payable	1,600		———
Note payable	2,400		———
Total current liabilities	$———		———%
Fixed liabilities:			
Mortgage (due 1978)		$32,000	———
Total liabilities	$———		———%
Proprietorship:			
W. D. Crenshaw, capital	———		———
Total liabilities and proprietorship	$———		———%

4. **SMITH PENCIL CO.**

Balance Sheet, April 1, 1972

		%	
Assets			
Current assets:			
Cash	$14,000	———%	
Accounts receivable	36,000	———	
Stock on hand	70,000	═══	
Total current assets		$———	———%
Fixed assets:			
Plant	$40,000		
Land	15,000		
Equipment	25,000		
Total fixed assets		———	———
Total assets		$═══	═══%
Liabilities and *net worth*			
Current liabilities:			
Accounts payable	$33,000	———%	
Note payable	6,000	———	
Interest payable	1,000	═══	
Total current liabilities		$———	———%
Fixed liabilities:			
Bonds (due 1973)	25,000	———	
Total liabilities		$———	———%
Net worth:			
Retained earnings	$35,000	———%	
6% preferred stock	54,000	———	
Common stock	46,000	═══	
Total net worth		———	———
Total liabilities and net worth		$═══	═══%

5. **SANFORD AND GRIER ELECTRONICS**

Comparative Income Statement
for Years Ending June 30, 1972 and 1971

	1972	1971	Increase (or Decrease) Amount	%	% of Net Sales 1972	1971
Income:						
Net Sales	$480,000	$400,000				
Cost of goods:						
Inventory, July 1	$ 40,000	$ 60,000				
Purchases	320,000	240,000				
Goods available for sale	$———	$———				
Inventory, June 30	60,000	40,000				
Cost of goods sold	———	———				
Gross profit	$———	$———				
Expenses:						
Salaries	$ 60,000	$ 48,000				
Occupancy	32,000	28,000				
Promotion	24,000	12,000				
Depreciation	12,000	16,000				
Miscellaneous	12,000	8,000				
Total expenses	———	———				
Net profit on operations	$———	$———				

6.   SIMS UPHOLSTERY SHOP

**Comparative Income Statements
for Fiscal Years Ending March 31, 1972 and 1971**

	1972	1971	Increase (or Decrease)		% of Net Sales	
			Amount	%	1972	1971
Income from sales:						
Net sales	$66,000	$60,000				
Cost of goods sold:						
Inventory, April 1	$24,000	$20,000				
Purchases	42,000	44,000				
Goods available for sale	$———	$———				
Inventory, March 31	21,000	24,000				
Cost of goods sold	———	———				
Gross margin	$———	$———				
Operating expenses:						
Salaries	$12,000	$10,000				
Occupancy	3,300	3,000				
Depreciation	400	600				
Insurance	300	500				
Other	500	900				
Total expenses	———	———				
Net income on operations	$———	$———				

7. **GEM APPLIANCE SALES, INC.**

Comparative Balance Sheet
for Years Ending December 31, 1971 and 1970

	1971	1970	Increase (or Decrease) Amount	%	% of Total Assets 1971	1970
Assets						
Cash	$ 24,000	$ 30,000				
Accounts receivable	48,000	40,000				
Inventory	143,000	130,000				
Current assets	$———	$———				
Fixed assets	105,000	100,000				
Total assets	$———	$———				
Liabilities and net worth						
Current liabilities	$60,000	$ 75,000				
Fixed liabilities	45,000	40,000				
Total liabilities	$———	$———				
Retained earnings	$50,000	$ 50,000				
Common stock	———	———				
Total net worth	———	———				
Total liabilities and net worth	$———	$———				

8. **ARDMORE WHOLESALERS, INC.**

Comparative Balance Sheet
for Fiscal Years Ending March 31, 1972 and 1971

	1972	1971	Increase (or Decrease) Amount	%	% of Total Assets 1972	1971
Assets						
Cash	$ 40,000	$ 32,000				
Accounts receivable	60,000	48,000				
Inventory	180,000	200,000				
Current assets	280,000	280,000				
Fixed assets	120,000	100,000				
Total assets	$400,000	$380,000				
Liabilities and owner's equity						
Current liabilities	$ 80,000	$ 70,000				
Fixed liabilities	140,000	170,000				
Total liabilities	$230,000	$				
J. D. Ardmore, equity	180,000	140,000				
Total liabilities and owner's equity	$	$				

9. Compute the following ratios or per cents, based on the balance sheet in Problem 3:
   (a) Working capital ratio
   (b) Acid-test ratio
   (c) What per cent of total assets are current assets?
   (d) What per cent of total assets are fixed assets?
   (e) What per cent of total assets are the total liabilities?
   (f) What per cent of total assets is the owners' equity?

10. Determine the ratios or per cents in Problem 9(a–f), based on the balance sheet in Problem 4.

11. Calculate the ratios or per cents requested below, which pertain to the 1971 business year of Gem Appliance Sales, Inc. Use the income statement in Problem 1 and the balance sheet in Problem 7.
   (a) Working capital ratio
   (b) Acid-test ratio
   (c) Ratio of net income (after taxes) to average net worth
   (d) Ratio of net sales to average total assets

(e) Accounts receivable turnover

(f) Average age of accounts receivable

(g) What per cent of net sales was the cost of goods?

(h) What per cent of net sales was the gross profit?

(i) What per cent of net sales were the operating expenses?

(j) What per cent of net sales was net profit (both before and after taxes)?

(k) What per cent of total assets were current assets?

(l) What per cent of total assets were fixed assets?

(m) What per cent of total assets were total liabilities?

(n) What per cent of total assets was total net worth?

12. Compute the ratios or per cents listed in Problem 11 (a–n), concerning the fiscal year ending March 31, 1972, of Ardmore Wholesalers, Inc. The figures needed to compute these ratios are found in Problems 2 and 8.

Distribution of Profit and Loss

LEARNING OBJECTIVES

Upon completion of Chapter 11, the student will be able to:

1. Define and use correctly the terminology associated with each topic.

2. Compute the dividend to be paid per share of common and preferred stock, given the total dividend declared and information about the number and types of stock.

3. Distribute profits (or losses) to the members of a partnership, given the total profit (or loss) and information about each partner's investment. Distributions will be according to
   a. Agreed ratios,
   b. Salaries,
   c. Interest on investments,
   d. Average investments per month, and
   e. Combinations of these methods.

WITHIN OUR SYSTEM of free enterprise, businesses are operated for the ultimate purpose of making a profit. After the amount of net profit (or loss) of a business has been determined, it is necessary to apportion that amount among the owners. Methods of distribution depend largely upon the type of business. In general, there are three categories of private business organization: (1) sole proprietorship, (2) partnership, and (3) corporation.

SOLE PROPRIETORSHIP

This is the simplest form of business. A single person makes the initial investment and bears the entire responsibility for the business. If a profit is earned, the entire profit belongs to the individual owner. By the same token, the sole proprietor must assume full responsibility for any loss incurred. (One principal disadvantage of this form of business is that the owner's liability extends even to his personal possessions not used in business; for instance, his home might have to be sold to discharge business debts.)

Sole proprietorships are usually small businesses, since they are limited to the resources of one person. There often is no formal organization or operating procedure; an individual with sufficient skill or financial resources simply goes into business by making his services available to potential clients.

Since all profit (or loss) resulting from a sole proprietorship belongs to the individual owner, there is no mathematical distribution required. Hence the problems in this section will be limited to those concerning partnerships and corporations.

A partnership is an organization in which two or more persons engage in business as co-owners. A partnership may provide the advantages of increased investments and more diversified skills, as well as more manpower available to operate the business. (For example, Partners A, B, and C might form a partnership because A had the funds to start the business, B had the skill and experience required to manufacture their product, and C was an expert in salesmanship and marketing. Thus, by pooling their resources, both financial and personal, a profitable business can be formed; however, none of the partners could have established a profitable business independently.) Partnerships often include a *silent partner*—one who takes no active participation in the business operations, whose contribution to the partnership is entirely financial, and whose very existence as a partner may not be known outside the business.

A partnership may be entered into simply by mutual consent. To avoid misunderstanding and disagreement, however, all partners should sign a legal agreement (called *articles of copartnership*) setting forth the responsibilities, restrictions, procedures, method of distribution of profits and losses, etc., of the partnership. (For instance, the abrupt withdrawal of a partner, if not prohibited by written agreement, might place the entire partnership in bankruptcy.)

Taking into consideration the contribution made by each partner, a partnership is permitted to distribute profits or losses in any way that is acceptable to the partners involved. In the absence of any formal written agreement, the law would require that profits be shared equally among the partners. Despite whatever agreement the partners may have among themselves, however, in most states the partners are responsible jointly and separately for the liabilities of the partnership. This means that if the personal resources of the partners together (jointly), when calculated according to their terms of agreement, are not sufficient to meet the partnership's liabilities, then a single partner with more personal wealth will have to bear the liabilities of the partnership individually (separately). Also, a business commitment made by any partner, even if it is not within his agreed area of responsibility, is legally binding upon the entire partnership.

A partnership is automatically dissolved whenever there is any change in the partners involved, such as when a partner withdraws from the business, sells his share to another person, or dies, or when an additional person enters the partnership. However, a new partnership may be created immediately to reflect the change, without any lapse in business operations.

CORPORATIONS

The corporation is the most complex form of business. It is considered to be an artificial person, created according to state laws. Its capital is derived from the sale of *stock certificates*, which are certificates of ownership in the business. A person's ownership in a corporation is measured according to the number of shares of stock which he owns. Figure 11-1 illustrates a stock certificate.

The corporation offers a distinct advantage over both the sole proprietorship and the partnership in that its liability extends only to the amount invested in the business by the stockholders. That is, the personal property of the owners (*stockholders*) may not be confiscated to meet business liabilities. (It should be noted that even small businesses may be incorporated in order to provide this protection. However, the ethics of certain professions—legal, medical, accounting, and others—permit only partnerships, not corporations.) The corporation also differs from the sole proprietorship and the partnership in that the firm must pay income taxes on its net operating income.

When a corporation is formed, it receives a *charter* from the state, authorizing the operation of business, defining the privileges and restrictions of the firm, and specifying the number of shares and type of stock which may be issued. The stockholders elect a *board of directors*, which selects the *administrative officers* of the corporation. Although it is ultimately responsible to the stockholders, the board actually makes decisions regarding policy and the direction which the business will take, and the officers are responsible for carrying out the board's decisions. The board of directors also makes the decision to distribute profits to the stockholders; the income declared on each share of stock is called a *dividend*.

When a corporation issues stock, the certificates are usually assigned some value, called the *par value* or *face value*. The par value may be set at any amount, although it is typically some round number. Stock is usually sold at par value when a corporation is first organized. After the firm has been in operation for some time, the *market value* (the amount for which stockholders would be willing to sell their stock) will increase or decrease, depending upon the prosperity of the business. Stock is sometimes issued without any face value, in which case it is known as *no-par-value* or *nonpar-value* stock.

There are two main categories of stock: *common stock* and *preferred stock*. Since there are fewer methods for distributing profits to stockholders than to partners, we shall consider first the distribution of corporate profits.

1. DISTRIBUTION OF PROFITS IN A CORPORATION

DISTRIBUTION OF PROFITS: COMMON STOCK

This type of stock carries no guaranteed benefits in case a profit is made or the corporation is dissolved. It does entitle its owner to one vote in a stockholders' meeting for each share he owns. Many corporations issue only common stock. In this case, distributing the profits is simply a matter of dividing the profit to be distributed by the *outstanding stock* (the number of shares of stock which have been issued).

The board of directors of Impact Corp. authorized $187,000 of the net profit to be distributed among their stockholders. If the corporation has issued 100,000 shares of common stock, what is the dividend per share?

Example One

$$\frac{\text{Total dividend}}{\text{Number of shares}} = \frac{\$187,000}{100,000} = \$1.87 \text{ per share}$$

A dividend of $1.87 per share of common stock will be declared.

DISTRIBUTION OF PROFITS: PREFERRED STOCK

The charters of many corporations also authorize the issuance of preferred stock. This stock has certain advantages over common stock; most notably, preferred stock carries the provision that dividends of a specified per cent of par value (or of a specified amount per share, on nonpar-value stock) must be paid to preferred stockholders before any dividend is paid to common stockholders. For example, a share of 6%, $100 par-value stock would be expected to pay a $6 dividend each year.

Also, in event the corporation is dissolved, the corporation's assets may first have to be applied toward refunding the par value of preferred stock, before any compensation is returned to common stockholders. Holders of preferred stock usually do not have a vote in the stockholders' meeting. Also, most preferred stock is *nonparticipating*, which means it cannot earn dividends above the specified rate. (However, some preferred stock is *participating*, which permits dividends above the stated per cent when sufficient profits exist. Such participating stock is frequently restricted so that additional earnings above the specified rate are permitted only after the common stockholders have received a dividend equal to the specified preferred dividend.)

Even when a net profit exists, a board of directors may not think it advisable to declare a dividend. Thus the owners of a corporation may receive no income on their investment during some years. *Cumulative preferred stock* provides an exception to this situation, however. As the name implies, unpaid dividends accumulate; that is, dividends due from previous years, when no dividend was declared, must first be paid to owners of cumulative preferred stock before any dividends are paid to other stockholders.

Example Two

Rider Corp. has 1,000 shares of $100 par-value common stock outstanding and 500 shares of 5%, $100 par-value preferred stock. The board just declared a $7,000 dividend. What dividend will be paid on each class of stock?

Dividends on the preferred stock are always computed first.

$$5\% \times \$100 \text{ par value} = \$5 \text{ dividend on each share of preferred stock}$$

$$\$5 \text{ per share} \times 500 \text{ shares} = \$2,500 \text{ required to pay dividends on all preferred stock}$$

$7,000	Total dividend
−2,500	Dividend on all preferred stock
$4,500	Dividend allotted to common stock

$$\frac{\text{Total common stock dividend}}{\text{Number of common shares}} = \frac{\$4,500}{1,000} = \$4.50 \text{ dividend per share of common stock}$$

Hence the preferred stockholders receive their full dividend of $5 per share; and a dividend of $4.50 per share will be paid to common stockholders.

During the previous two years, Matsun, Inc. paid no dividend. This year, a dividend of $325,000 was declared. Stockholders of the corporation own 100,000 shares of nonpar-value common stock and 20,000 shares of 6%, $50 par-value cumulative preferred stock. How much dividend will be paid on each share of stock?

Example Three

Since no dividends were paid during the past two years, dividends for three years are now due on the cumulative preferred stock.

6% × $50 par value = $3 Dividend per year on each share of cumulative preferred stock

$\underline{\times 3}$ Years

$9 Dividend due on each share of cumulative preferred stock

$9 per share × 20,000 shares = $180,000 payable to preferred stockholders

$325,000	Total dividend
−180,000	Dividend on preferred stock
$145,000	Total dividend on common stock

$$\frac{\$145,000}{100,000 \text{ shares}} = \$1.45 \text{ Dividend per share of common stock}$$

Thus a three-year dividend of $9 per share will be paid to owners of the cumulative preferred stock, and $1.45 per share will go to the common stockholders.

PROBLEMS

Determine the dividend that should be paid on each share of stock:

		No. of Shares	Type of Stock	Total Dividend Declared
1.	(a)	50,000	$10 par-value common	$175,000
	(b)	15,000	no-par-value common	$52,500
		5,000	6%, $50 par-value preferred	
	(c)	200,000	$100 par-value common	$1,000,000
		10,000	7%, $100 par-value preferred, cumulative for 2 years	
2.	(a)	80,000	$5 par-value common	$28,000
	(b)	10,000	nonpar-value common	$60,000
		2,000	8%, $50 par-value preferred	

	No. of Shares	Type of Stock	Total Dividend Declared
(c)	400,000	$10 par-value common	$380,000
	10,000	6%, $100 par-value preferred, cumulative for 3 years	

3. After a successful business year, the board of directors of Jones-Frazier, Inc. declared a $190,000 dividend. The firm has 40,000 shares of nonpar-value stock outstanding. What will be the dividend on each share?

4. The board of directors of Sigfield Corp. declared a $150,000 dividend. What is the dividend per share for their 60,000 shares of $50 par-value common stock?

5. Allied Motor Corporation has 100,000 outstanding shares of $10 par-value common stock and 35,000 shares of 6%, $100 par-value preferred stock. The board of directors has declared a $725,000 stock dividend. Determine the amount to be paid on each share.

6. There are 50,000 shares of no-par-value common stock and 5,000 shares of 7%, $100 par-value preferred stock outstanding at Transit Freight. If the board declared a $410,000 dividend, how much will be paid on each share of stock?

7. The Garringer-Mecklenburg Corp. has issued 80,000 shares of $100 par-value common stock and 15,000 shares of 8%, $100 par-value preferred stock. The board voted to pay $640,000 in dividends to all stockholders of record. What dividend will each share earn?

8. Golden West Sales, Inc. approved a $160,000 dividend. Determine the dividend per share for their 150,000 outstanding shares of nonpar-value common stock and 20,000 shares of 5%, $100 par-value preferred stock.

9. Centex Manufacturing, Inc., has 75,000 shares of $5 par-value common stock outstanding and 8,000 shares of 7%, $50 par-value cumulative preferred stock. No dividend was declared during the past year. This year, a $176,000 dividend was approved by the board. Compute the earnings for each share of stock.

10. Due to the costs of plant expansion, Lyttaker Corp. declared no dividend during the past two years. This year, a $53,000 dividend was declared. Compute the dividend payable on each share of the 80,000 shares of no-par-value common stock and 5,000 shares of 6%, $10 par-value cumulative preferred stock.

11. In order to increase its retained earnings, the board of Wyatt Distributors, Inc. has not declared a dividend during the previous two years. This year, however, a dividend of $366,000 has been approved. What dividend per share will be paid, if there are 55,000 shares of nonpar-value common stock and 6,000 shares of 5%, $150 par-value cumulative preferred stock?

12. A decline in sales resulted in no dividend being declared last year by

Macomb, Inc. This year, however, a $46,000 dividend was declared. What dividend per share will be paid on each category of stock, if there are 10,000 shares of no-par-value common stock and 1,000 shares of 8%, $100 par-value cumulative preferred stock?

2. DISTRIBUTION OF PROFITS IN A PARTNERSHIP

There are numerous ways in which the profits or losses of a partnership may be divided. We shall consider some of the typical methods. Recall that profits and losses are shared equally among partners unless another specific agreement is made.

The partnership of Ables, Baldwin, and Connors earned a net profit of $18,000. Ables had $10,000 invested, Baldwin had $5,000 invested, and Connors had $7,500 invested. No formal agreement was reached concerning the distribution of profits. How much should each partner receive? **Example One (Equal distribution)**

$$\frac{\$18,000}{3} = \$6,000 \text{ each}$$

Each partner would receive $6,000.

Considering the capital investment and time devoted to the business by each partner, partners X, Y, and Z agree to share profits (or losses) in the ratio $3:5:2$. Divide a profit of $25,000. **Example Two (Agreed ratio)**

The sum of $3 + 5 + 2 = 10$ indicates the profit will be divided into 10 shares; X will receive 3 of the 10 shares, Y will receive 5 shares, and Z will receive 2 shares. Thus X gets $\frac{3}{10}$ of the profit; Y receives $\frac{5}{10}$ or $\frac{1}{2}$ of the profit; and Z gets $\frac{2}{10}$ or $\frac{1}{5}$ of the profit.

X	$\frac{3}{10}$ ($25,000) =	$ 7,500
Y	$\frac{1}{2}$ ($25,000) =	12,500
Z	$\frac{1}{5}$ ($25,000) =	+5,000
	Total profit =	$25,000

Partner X will receive $7,500, Y will receive $12,500, and Z will receive $5,000. Note that the sum of all partners' profits equals the total profit of the partnership. This must always be true; therefore, the student should always check his calculations to be certain that the amounts he allots to the various partners will equal the total profit (or loss).

Partners L and M began operations with a $6,000 investment from L and a $4,000 investment by M. Partner M later invested $3,000 more. They agreed to divide profits or losses according to the ratio of their original investments. What part of a $4,500 profit would each partner receive? **Example Three (Original investment)**

$6,000 + $4,000 = $10,000 total original investment

L had $\dfrac{\$6,000}{\$10,000}$ or $\dfrac{3}{5}$ of the original investment

$$\text{M had} \quad \frac{\$4,000}{\$10,000} \quad \text{or} \quad \frac{2}{5} \quad \text{of the original investment}$$

Therefore, L will receive $\frac{3}{5}$ of the profit and M will get the other $\frac{2}{5}$:

$$
\begin{array}{lll}
\text{L} & \frac{3}{5}\,(\$4,500) = & \$2,700 \\
\text{M} & \frac{2}{5}\,(\$4,500) = & +1,800 \\
& & \overline{\$4,500} \qquad \text{Total profit}
\end{array}
$$

L's share of the profit is $2,700 and M will receive $1,800.

Example Four (Investment at beginning of the year) During their second year of operations, partners L and M (Example 3) revised their agreement so that profits would be distributed according to each partner's investment at the beginning of the year. If their second year's profit was $26,000, how much of this belongs to each partner?

At the beginning of their second year,

$$
\begin{array}{lr}
\text{L's investment was still} & \$6,000 \\
\text{M had } \$4,000 + \$3,000 \text{ or} & +7,000 \text{ invested} \\
\text{Total investment} = & \overline{\$13,000}
\end{array}
$$

Thus

$$\text{L will receive} \quad \frac{\$6,000}{\$13,000} \quad \text{or} \quad \frac{6}{13} \text{ of the profit.}$$

$$\text{M will receive} \quad \frac{\$7,000}{\$13,000} \quad \text{or} \quad \frac{7}{13} \text{ of the profit.}$$

$$
\begin{array}{lll}
\text{L} & \frac{6}{13}\,(\$26,000) = & \$12,000 \\
\text{M} & \frac{7}{13}\,(\$26,000) = & +14,000 \\
& & \overline{\$26,000} \qquad \text{Total profit}
\end{array}
$$

L gets $12,000 of the second year's profit, and M receives $14,000.

Example Five (Average investment per month) C and D are partners. C invested $4,900 on January 1; on April 1, he withdrew $400; and on September 1, he reinvested $1,200. D invested $4,000 on January 1 and did not change this during the year. If profits are to be shared according to each partner's average investment per month, how much of a $10,800 profit should each receive?

Since D's investment did not change during the year, his average investment was $4,000. C's average investment is as follows:

Date	Change	Amount of Investment		Months Invested		
January 1	—	$4,900	$\times$	3	=	$14,700
April 1	−$400	4,500	$\times$	5	=	22,500
September 1	+$1,200	5,700	$\times$	+4	=	+22,800
				$\overline{12}$		$\overline{\$60,000}$

$$\frac{\$60,000}{12} = \$5,000 \text{ average investment per month}$$

$$
\begin{array}{ll}
\$5,000 & \text{C's average investment} \\
+4,000 & \text{D's average investment} \\
\hline
\$9,000 & \text{Total of average investments}
\end{array}
$$

Therefore, C receives $\dfrac{\$5,000}{\$9,000}$ or $\dfrac{5}{9}$ of the profit. D's investment earns $\dfrac{\$4,000}{\$9,000}$ or $\dfrac{4}{9}$ of the profit.

$$
\begin{array}{lll}
\text{C} & \frac{5}{9}(\$10,800) = & \$\ 6,000 \\
\text{D} & \frac{4}{9}(\$10,800) = & +4,800 \\
& & \hline \\[-1.5ex]
& \$10,800 & \text{Total profit}
\end{array}
$$

C receives $6,000 of the total profit and D receives the remaining $4,800.

Partners R, S, and T agreed to pay S a salary of $5,000, to pay T a salary of $3,000, and to divide the remaining profit or loss in the ratio of 3:1:2. If a net profit of $20,000 was earned, how much would be due each partner?

Example Six (Salary and agreed ratio)

The salaries must be deducted first, and the remaining profit divided into $3 + 1 + 2 = 6$ shares:

$$\$5,000 + \$3,000 = \$8,000 \text{ in salaries}$$

$$
\begin{array}{ll}
\$20,000 & \text{Total net profit} \\
-8,000 & \text{Salaries} \\
\hline
\$12,000 & \text{To be divided in the ratio } 3:1:2
\end{array}
$$

$$
\begin{array}{lll}
\text{R receives } \frac{3}{6} \text{ or } \frac{1}{2} \text{ of the } \$12,000 & \frac{1}{2}(\$12,000) = & \$\ 6,000 \\
\text{S earned } \frac{1}{6} \text{ of the } \$12,000 & \frac{1}{6}(\$12,000) = & 2,000 \\
\text{T gets } \frac{2}{6} \text{ or } \frac{1}{3} \text{ of the } \$12,000 & \frac{1}{3}(\$12,000) = & +4,000 \\
& & \hline \\[-1.5ex]
& & \$12,000
\end{array}
$$

Thus the total amount to be paid each partner is

	R	S	T	Check
Salary	—	$5,000	$3,000	$ 6,000
Ratio	+$6,000	+2,000	+4,000	7,000
Total	$6,000	$7,000	$7,000	
				+7,000
				$20,000 Total net profit

R's share of the net profits is $6,000; and S and T each receive $7,000.

**Example
Seven
(Interest
on in-
vestment,
salary,
and agreed
ratio)**
H and K organized a partnership with an investment of $5,000 by H and $7,500 from K (a silent partner). They agreed to pay 6% interest on each partner's investment, to pay H a salary of $9,000, and to divide the remaining profit or loss equally.

(a) Distribute a profit of $15,750.

(b) Divide a $9,350 net profit.

(a) The various methods of distribution must be taken in the order indicated by the agreement. Thus the interest payment to each partner will be

	H	K
Investment	$5,000	$7,500
Interest rate	×6%	×6%
Interest	$300	$450

After the interest is deducted from the net profit, then the salary is paid:

Interest

$300	$15,750 Total profit
+450	−750 Interest
$750 Total interest	$15,000
	−9,000 Salary
	$6,000 To be shared equally

$$\frac{\$6,000}{2} = \$3,000 \text{ additional profit due each partner}$$

Hence the total profit earned by each partner is

	H	K	Check
Interest	$ 300	$ 450	$12,300
Salary	9,000	—	3,450
Ratio	+3,000	+3,000	$15,750 Total net profit
Total	$12,300	$3,450	

H receives $12,300 as his share of the profits, and K would get $3,450.

(b) The interest due each partner and the salary would be the same as in part a. Hence, the remaining calculations would be

$9,350	Total profit
−750	Interest
$8,600	
−9,000	Salary
−$400	Shortage to be shared equally

The partners lack by $400 having enough profits to pay the interest and salary due them. According to the terms of their agreement, this shortage will be shared equally. Thus

$$\frac{\$400}{2} = \$200 \text{ of the amount due each partner will not be paid.}$$

So, each partner's share is as follows:

	H	K	Check	
Interest	$ 300	$450	$9,100	
Salary	9,000	—	250	
	$9,300	$450	$9,350	Total net profit
Ratio (shortage)	−200	−200		
Total	$9,100	$250		

H would be paid $9,100 and K would receive $250.

PROBLEMS

Divide the net profit among the partners according to the conditions given:

		Partners	Investment	Method of Distribution	Net profit
1.	(a)	A	$15,000	Ratio of 2:3	$20,000
		B	8,000		
	(b)	C	$ 8,000	Ratio of their investments	$18,000
		D	12,000		
		E	4,000		
	(c)	F	$ 7,500	6% interest on investment; and ratio of 4:3:2	$28,200
		G	8,000		
		H	4,500		
	(d)	I	$ 9,000	8% interest on investment; $7,000 salary to J; and the remainder in ratio of their investments	$28,200
		J	6,000		

2. (a) Q $ 4,000   Ratio of 5:3:4 $18,000
        R   9,000
        S   7,000

   (b) T $ 6,000   Ratio of their investments $24,000
        U   10,000

   (c) V $ 7,000 $5,000 salary to V; $16,000
        W   8,000 $3,000 salary to W; and
                         remainder divided equally

   (d) X $ 6,000   7% interest on investment; $14,330
        Y   8,000 $4,000 salary to Z; and
        Z   5,000   remainder in ratio 3:4:2

3. G and K entered into a partnership without making specific arrangements regarding the distribution of profits or losses. G invested $8,000 and K contributed $10,000. How much of their $17,000 profit will go to each partner?

4. P, Q, and R entered into a partnership without making any arrangement for the distribution of profits. P invested $5,000 as a silent partner. Q invested $3,000 and devoted his full time to the business. R invested $6,000 and worked half-time in the business. How much of a $13,500 net profit should each partner receive?

5. Partners I, O, and U formed a partnership and decided to share profits or losses in the ratio 7:3:5.
   (a) What is each partner's share of an $18,000 net profit?
   (b) How much obligation for a $4,500 loss would each partner assume?

6. Partners A, B, C, and D agreed on a ratio of 3:4:5:4 to distribute profits or losses.
   (a) Divide a net profit of $19,200.
   (b) How much of a $9,600 loss must be assumed by each partner?

7. M and D entered into partnership. M invested $8,000 in the enterprise. D invested $6,000 initially and several months later invested $4,000 more. Their partnership agreement stated that the net profit or loss would be divided according to the ratio of their original investments. What is each partner's share of a $28,000 profit?

8. X and Y are partners. X's original investment was $5,000, and he later invested $3,000 more. Y invested $7,000 in the partnership. If their agreement was to distribute profits and losses according to the ratio of their original investments, how much of a $16,800 net profit should go to each partner?

9. During the second year of M and D's partnership (see Problem 7), their agreement was changed as follows: M would receive an $8,500 salary; D would draw a $7,000 salary; and the remaining profit or loss would be

divided in the ratio of their investments at the beginning of the second year. Disburse their second year's profit of $42,500.

10. Partners X and Y (see Problem 8) amended their agreement so that during the second year their net profit was divided as follows: X would get a salary of $4,500; Y received a $6,500 salary; the remaining profit or loss was to be divided in the ratio of their investment at the beginning of the second year. How much of a $26,000 profit would each partner receive?

11. Partners X and L decided to distribute profits or losses according to average investment per month. X invested $4,000 and did not change his investment. L invested $8,400 on January 1. On June 1, he withdrew $900. On October 1, he reinvested $500 and left his investment unchanged thereafter.
    (a) Compute L's average investment.
    (b) Distribute their profit of $16,200 between X and L.

12. S and T agreed to divide profits from their partnership according to their average investments. On January 1, S invested $5,000. On June 1, he withdrew $1,000. On September 1, he reinvested $550 and did not change his investment thereafter. T's original investment of $5,400 remained unchanged.
    (a) What is S's average investment per month?
    (b) What part does each partner get of their $15,000 profit?

13. P and Q are partners. P had $8,000 invested for the entire year. Q had $10,000 invested on January 1. On March 1, he withdrew $1,400; and on September 1, he reinvested $500.
    (a) What average investment per month did Q maintain?
    (b) The partnership agreement states that P and Q will receive 7% interest on their average investments and that the remaining profit or loss will be divided equally. If a profit of $17,190 was earned for the year, how much will each partner receive?

14. P and T are partners. P had $6,000 invested and did not change his investment. On January 1, T had $5,100 invested; on May 1, he withdrew $600; and on October 1, he reinvested $1,200.
    (a) What was T's average investment?
    (b) P and T agreed to distribute profits by paying 6% interest on their average investments and dividing the remaining profit or loss equally. What is each partner's share of a $17,660 net profit?

15. A invested $9,500 into a partnership, and Z contributed $10,500. The terms of their agreement are that each will receive 8% interest on investment; Z will receive a $6,000 salary; and the remaining profit or loss will be shared equally.
    (a) Determine each partner's share of a $22,600 profit.
    (b) Distribute a $6,800 profit.

16. T and V are partners, T having invested $6,000 and V having $8,000 invested. They agreed to pay 7% interest on investment, to pay T a salary of $7,500, and to divide the remaining profit or loss equally.

    (a) Divide a net profit of $16,480.

    (b) What would be each partner's share of an $8,240 profit?

17. Q invested $12,500 and T added $10,000 to fund their partnership. They agreed to pay 6% interest on investment; to pay Q a salary of $8,000; to pay T a salary of $11,000; and to divide the remaining profit or loss in the ratio of 5:3.

    (a) What is each partner's share of a $26,750 profit?

    (b) How much would Q and T each receive from an $18,750 profit?

18. H and J are partners. H invested $7,200 and J invested $8,400. They agreed to pay 5% interest on investment; to pay H a salary of $4,000 and J a salary of $5,000; and to distribute the remaining profit or loss in the ratio 3:4.

    (a) Divide a net profit of $13,280.

    (b) What is each partner's share of an $8,380 net profit?

part three

RETAIL MATHEMATICS

12

Commercial Discounts

LEARNING OBJECTIVES

Upon completion of Chapter 12, the student will be able to:

1. Define and use correctly the terminology associated with each topic.

2. When a series of trade discount per cents are given,
   a. Find net cost rate factor, and
   b. Use it to compute
      (1) Net cost, and
      (2) Single equivalent discount per cent.

3. Using the trade discount formula "% Paid × List = Net" and given two of the following amounts, find the unknown
   a. Net cost,
   b. List price, or
   c. Discount per cent.

4. Use sales terms given on an invoice to determine
   a. Cash discount, and
   b. Net payment due.

5. Use sales terms and the formula "% Paid × List = Net" to find list price when net payment is given.

A BUSINESS WHICH PURCHASES merchandise that is then sold directly to the *consumer* (user) is known as a *retail* business or store. The retailer may have purchased this merchandise either from the manufacturer or from a *wholesaler* (a business which buys goods for distribution only to other businesses and does not sell to the general public). The purchasing, pricing, and sale of merchandise in a retail store requires a certain kind of mathematics, which is the subject of this unit.

Competition for the customer has led to a widespread use of discounts, both in wholesale and retail sales. The following sections examine two of these commercial discounts—*trade discounts* and *cash discounts*.

1. TRADE DISCOUNTS

Manufacturers and wholesalers usually issue catalogs to be used by retailers. These catalogs are often quite bulky, containing photographs, diagrams and/or descriptions of all items sold by the company. As would be expected, the prices of items shown in the catalogs are subject to change periodically. To reprint an entire catalog each time there is a price change would be unduly expensive; thus several methods have been developed whereby a business can keep the customer informed of current prices without having to reprint the entire catalog.

Some catalogs are issued in looseleaf binders, and new pages are printed to replace only those pages where a price change has occurred. Other catalogs contain no prices at all; instead, a separate price list, which is revised periodically, accompanies the catalog.

We shall be concerned in this course with a third type of catalog. The prices shown in this catalog are the *list prices* or *suggested retail prices*, usually the prices which the consumer pays for the goods. The retailer buys these goods at a reduction of a certain percentage off the catalog price. This reduction is known as a *trade discount*. The actual cost to the retailer, after the trade discount has been subtracted, is the *net cost* or *net price* of the item. The per cents of discount that are to be allowed (which may vary from item to item in the catalog) may be printed on a discount sheet which supplements the catalog, or they may be quoted directly to a company placing a special order.

It should be noted that these discounts apply only to goods; the full amount must be paid for freight, telephone, or other charges.

The list price of a lamp is $20. The discount sheet indicates a trade discount of 30% is to be allowed. What is the net price?

Example One

(a)

List	$20
Less trade discount (30% × $20)	−6
Net price	$14

Now, saying that a 30% reduction is allowed means that the retailer is still paying the other 70% of the list price. Indeed, the per cent of discount subtracted from 100% (the whole list) will always indicate what per cent of the list price is still being paid for the goods. For example,

25% discount means $100\% - 25\% = 75\%$ paid

40% discount means $100\% - 40\% = 60\%$ paid

16% discount means $100\% - 16\% = 84\%$ paid

Knowing this allows us to work the previous problem in a shorter way, using the formula *% Paid × List = Net*. (Keep in mind that per cents must be converted to their decimal or fractional equivalent before being used. Many problems can be worked more conveniently when per cents are changed to fractions.)

(b) A 30% discount on the above lamp means that $100\% - 30\% = 70\%$ of the list price is still being paid.

Using decimals	Using fractions
% Paid × List = Net	% Paid × List = Net
70% × $20 = Net	70% × $20 = Net
0.7 × 20 = Net	$\frac{7}{10}$ × 20 = Net
$14 = Net	$14 = Net

Two or more trade discounts on the same goods are often quoted;

these multiple discounts are known as *series* or *chain discounts*. If discounts of 25%, 20%, and 10% (often written 25/20/10) are offered, the net price may be found by calculating each discount in succession. (However, the order in which the discounts are taken does not affect the result.)

Example Two

A radio is advertised at $50 less 25%, 20%, and 10%. Find the net cost to the retailer.

(a)
List	$50.00	
Less 25%	−12.50	(25% × $50 = $12.50)
	$37.50	
Less 20%	−7.50	(20% × $37.50 = $7.50)
	$30.00	
Less 10%	−3.00	(10% × $30 = $3)
Net Cost	$27.00	

This problem may be worked much more quickly using the % Paid × List = Net method:

(b) 25%, 20%, and 10% discounts are equivalent to 75%, 80% and 90% paid.

$$\% \ Pd \times L = N$$
$$(0.75)(0.8)(0.9)(\$50) = N$$
$$(0.54)50 = N$$
$$\$27 = N$$

The number that is the product of all the "per cents paid" is very significant and is called the *net cost rate factor*. The net cost rate factor is a number which can be multiplied times the list price to determine the net cost. All items subject to the same discounts have the same net cost rate factor. Thus, instead of reworking the entire problem for each item, the buyer determines which net cost rate factor applies and uses it to find the net price of all the items.

Example Three

A framed mirror subject to the same discount rates as the radio in Example 2 lists for $35. What is the net cost?
From Example 2, the net cost rate factor = 0.54

$$0.54 \times \$35 = \$18.90 \ net \ cost$$

For purposes of cost comparison, it is often desirable to know what single discount rate is equivalent to a series of discounts. This can be done by subtracting the per cent paid (the net cost rate factor) from 100% as follows:

What single discount rate is equivalent to the series 25/20/10 offered in Example 2?
    The net cost rate factor, 0.54, means 54% of the list price was paid.

$$100\% - 54\% = 46\%, \text{ single equivalent discount rate}$$

    Observe that series discounts of 25%, 20%, and 10% are *not* the same as a single discount of 55%.

After discounts of 20% and 5% have been granted, the net cost of a bedroom suite is $380. (a) What was the list price? (b) What is the net cost rate factor? (c) What single discount per cent is equivalent to discounts of 20% and 5%?

(a) $\% \text{ Pd} \times \text{L} = \text{N}$
    $(0.8)(0.95)\text{L} = 380$
    $.0.76\text{L} = 380$

$$\frac{0.76\text{L}}{0.76} = \frac{380}{0.76}$$

$$\text{L} = \$500$$

(b)   Net cost rate factor $= 0.76$

(c)   The single discount equal to discounts of 20% and 5% is $100\% - 76\% = 24\%$.

The list price of a record player is $150. If the net cost is $120, what single discount rate was offered?

$\% \text{ Pd} \times \text{L} = \text{N}$ The price changed by $150 - $120 = $30:
    $x \cdot 150 = 120$ ____% of Original $=$ Change?

$$\frac{150x}{150} = \frac{120}{150} \quad \text{or} \quad x \cdot 150 = 30$$

$$\frac{150x}{150} = \frac{30}{150}$$

    $x = \frac{4}{5}$
    $x = 80\%$ $x = \frac{1}{5}$
                                     $x = 20\%$ discount

But $x = \%$ Pd. Thus a 20% discount was given.

A yard chair lists for $12. Originally, a 15% discount was allowed. In order to meet competition, the wholesaler added a second discount, thus bringing the net price down to $8.16. Find the second discount per cent.

$$\% \text{ Pd} \times \text{L} = \text{N}$$
$$(0.85)(x)(12) = 8.16$$
$$10.2x = 8.16$$
$$x = 0.8$$

But x represents 80% paid. Thus $100\% - 80\% = 20\%$ additional discount.

PROBLEMS

Complete the following:

		Trade Discounts	% Paid (or Net Cost Rate Factor)	List	Net Cost	Single Equivalent Discount %
1.	(a)	10%		$20		—
	(b)	35%		40		—
	(c)	25%			$42	—
	(d)		55%		33	—
	(e)	20%, 10%		50		
	(f)	$12\frac{1}{2}\%$, $14\frac{2}{7}\%$		68		
	(g)	30%, 15%			11.90	
	(h)	30%, 20%, 10%			47.88	
2.	(a)	20%		$15		—
	(b)	15%		40		—
	(c)	30%			$31.50	—
	(d)		76%		38.00	—
	(e)	25%, 20%		55		
	(f)	$14\frac{2}{7}$, $33\frac{1}{3}\%$		35		
	(g)	40%, 15%			43.35	
	(h)	20%, 15%, 10%			91.80	

3. Compute the net cost of the following items:
   (a) A ledger set listed at $7.50, less 40%.
   (b) A wall map listed at $16, less 15%.
   (c) A dictionary listed at $9.60, less $37\frac{1}{2}\%$.
   (d) A duplicator listed at $81, less $22\frac{2}{9}\%$.

4. Determine net cost on the following items:
   (a) A pencil sharpener listed at $9.60, less 20%.
   (b) A desk lamp listed at $12.00, less 35%.
   (c) A typewriter table listed at $27.00, less $33\frac{1}{3}\%$.
   (d) A typewriter chair listed at $36.00, less $16\frac{2}{3}\%$.

5. Complete the following invoice:

SOUTHLAND HARDWARE SUPPLY
P. O. Box 2390
Los Angeles, Calif. 90064

To: Handy Hardware Co.
1241 Post Dr.
Culver City, Calif.

INVOICE NO.: 24118
DATE: May 9, 19 __

YOUR ORDER NO.	RECEIVED	SHIPPED	VIA	TERMS
1842	5/2/ __	5/8/ __	Truck	Net

QUANTITY	CAT. NO.	DESCRIPTION	LIST	EXTENSION
12	S411	Aluminum grills	$ 8.50	
5	R380	10" tricycles	12.40	
5	R519	24" bicycles	32.60	
24	D210	Folding chairs	6.75	
8	D211	Lounge chairs	11.50	
10	D220	Folding chairs	B.O. *	
4 doz.	D040	Rewebbing kits	3.50 doz.	
2 doz.	R060	Replacement pedals	10.00 doz.	
		Total		
		Less 20% discount		
		Net		
		Freight		$7.80
		Total		

* "B.O.," indicating "Back Order," means that although the item listed is not currently in stock, the order will be held and the item will be shipped as soon as it becomes available.

6. Find the total cost of the following goods. All are subject to a 15% discount. Freight charges are $4.75.

> 5 doz. aspirin @ $4.50 per doz.
> 3 doz. lozenges @ $4.20 per doz.
> 2 doz. boxes adhesive tape @ $4.80 per doz.
> $\frac{1}{2}$ doz. elastic arch supports @ $1.50 each
> 3 sets aluminum crutches @ $10.00 each

7. Determine (1) the net cost for each of the following items. Also find (2) the net cost rate factor and (3) the single equivalent discount rate.
   (a) A fan listed for $25, less 20% and 20%.
   (b) A drill listed for $48, less $22\frac{2}{9}$% and $14\frac{2}{7}$%.

(c) A hand saw listed for $15, less 20%, 15%, and 10%.
(d) A wrench set listed for $20, less 30%, 10%, and 10%.

8. Find (1) the net cost on each of the following items. Also tell (2) the net cost rate factor and (3) the single equivalent discount rate.
(a) A pair of pliers listed for $2, less 20% and 25%.
(b) A hand saw listed for $10, less 20%, and 12½%.
(c) A tool box listed for $12, less 30%, 20%, and 5%.
(d) An electric drill listed for $30, less 20%, 10%, and 10%.

9. The National Distributing Co. offers discounts of 30% and 15%. Columbia Wholesale advertises 20/20/5. Which company offers the better discount? (Hint: compare single equivalent discount rates.)

10. Williams Company advertises discounts of 20/10/5. Young, Inc., offers 15% and 20%. Which company sells at the lower price?

11. After discounts of 30% and 10%, the net price of an article was $25.20. Find the list price.

12. The net price of an article is $18 after discounts of 20% and 10% have been allowed. What was the list price?

13. Find the list price of a mower, if the net price was $51 after discounts of 20% and 15%.

14. Find the list price of a garden rake if, after discounts of 30% and 20%, the net cost is $2.80.

15. What single discount has been allowed, if a fireplace screen which lists for $63 is sold for $45?

16. What single discount per cent has been allowed if a garden tractor which lists for $84 is sold for $70?

17. Acme Wholesalers has been selling edgers for $80 less 25%. Their competitors are now selling the edgers for $48. What additional discount will Acme have to offer in order to match their competitor's price? What single discount would produce the same price?

18. Jones Hardware Distributors have their best sprinklers listed at $15, less 20%. In order to reduce their net price to $10.20, what extra discount per cent must they now offer? What single discount rate would give the same net price?

19. Green Distributors have clock radios listed for $50 less 20%. The Haynes Wholesale Co. lists the same radio for $60 less 40%.
(a) What net price does each company offer now?
(b) What additional discount will Green have to allow in order to meet Haynes' price?

20. Crown Jewelers have watches listed for $50 less 40% and 20%. The Jewel Box carries the same watches for $45 less 33⅓%.

(a) What are the net prices offered by each company?

(b) What further discount per cent must The Jewel Box allow so that their net price will be the same as the Crown Jewelers?

21. Electric Supply House carries a crystal chandelier for $80 less 25% and 10%. State Wholesale, Inc., lists the same fixture for $75 less 20/20/10.

(a) Find the current net price of each firm.

(b) What further discount rate must be offered by the higher company in order to meet the competitor's price?

22. Williams Company carries a yard furniture group at $30, less 20%. Young, Inc., advertises the same group for $36, less $33\frac{1}{3}$% and 10%.

(a) What are the net prices offered by each company?

(b) What additional discount rate must be allowed by the higher company in order to meet the competitor's price?

2. CASH DISCOUNTS

Merchants who sell goods on credit often offer the buyer a reduction on the amount due as an inducement to prompt payment. This reduction is known as a *cash discount*. The cash discount is a certain percentage of the price of the goods, but it may be deducted only if the buyer pays his account within a stipulated time period.

The invoice or the monthly statement contains *sales terms*, which indicate the per cent of discount and the time period within which the account must be paid if the cash discount is to apply. A typical example would be "Terms: 2/10, n/30." These sales terms are read "two ten, net thirty." This means a 2% discount may be taken if payment is made within ten days from the invoice date; from the eleventh to thirtieth days, the net amount is due; after thirty days, the account is overdue and may be subject to interest charges.

Contrary to the way it sounds, "cash discount" does not generally refer to a discount allowed only for the payment of cash on the day of purchase. On the other hand, cash discounts may be taken only on the cost of goods, not on freight or other charges.

Some monthly statements, sent out during the last week of a month, contain terms such as "1/10, E.O.M." This means the 1% discount can be taken if paid within ten days following the "end of the month"; that is, if paid by the tenth of the coming month. In actual practice, many businesses assume this to be the meaning of sales terms on a statement of account, even though the initials E.O.M. may not be included.

Determine the amount due on the following statement of account:

Example One

```
┌─────────────────────────────────────────────────────────────────────┐
│                         STATEMENT                                     │
│                                                                       │
│  Phone:              CROWN JEWELERS                                    │
│  312-809-6108          1421 West Thorpe                                │
│                        St. Louis, Missouri                            │
│                                                                       │
│  ┌─────────────────────┐                                              │
│   Sheldon Jewelry Store          Date: September 28, 19___            │
│   Box 655                        Terms: 3/10, E.O.M.                  │
│   Hannibal, Missouri │                                                │
│  └─────────────────────┘                                              │
└─────────────────────────────────────────────────────────────────────┘
```

Date	Invoice No.	Charges	Credits	Balance
9/1				$255.00
9/5	14319	$185.60		440.60
9/12			$255.00	185.60
9/20	14401	79.35		264.95
9/23	14437	80.05		345.00
9/23	*Ppd. Fgt.	7.50		$352.50

PAY LAST
AMOUNT IN
THIS COLUMN

*"Ppd. Fgt." indicates "prepaid freight."

If paid by October 10, the 3% discount may be taken. Recall that the cash discount does not apply to freight.

Goods	$345.00	Due on goods	$334.65
Less discount (3% × $345)	−10.35	Freight	+7.50
Payment due on goods	$334.65	Total amount due	$342.15

A check for $342.15 will be mailed with the explanation that a $10.35 discount has been taken. The next statement will show a credit for the full $352.50. If the statement is paid October 11 or after, a check for the entire $352.50 must be sent.

Example Two

Three invoices from the same company are to be paid on October 15. Each invoice has terms 3/15, 1/30, n/60. The invoices are dated September 7 for $75.80, September 20 for $90.00, and September 30 for $109.00. What amount must be paid to retire the entire obligation?

No discount may be taken on the first invoice since it is more than 30 days old: $75.80

The second invoice is less than 30 days old, so a 1% discount may be taken:

$$\begin{array}{r} \$90.00 \\ (1\% \times \$90) \quad -.90 \\ \hline 89.10 \end{array}$$

The third invoice is exactly 15 days old; therefore, the 3% discount may be taken:

$$\begin{array}{r} \$109.00 \\ (3\% \times \$109) \quad -3.27 \\ \hline 105.73 \end{array}$$

Total payment due $\quad \$270.63$

On occasion it may not be possible to pay an entire invoice during the discount period. Whatever payment is made, however, is considered to be the net payment due after the discount had been calculated on some part of the debt. These partial payment problems may be solved using the formula % Paid × List = Net (Payment).

An invoice dated December 10 for $250 has terms 2/10, n/30. What payment must the buyer make to reduce his obligation by $100, if paid by December 20? **Example Three**

This $100 obligation is subject to a 2% discount, just as in previous problems.

2% discount means 98% was paid:

$100		% Pd × L = N
Less (2% × $100) −2	or	0.98 × $100 = N
Net Payment $ 98		$98 = N

Thus a payment of $98 will deduct $100 from the balance due. That is, after paying $98 of the $250 account within the discount period, $150 remains to be paid.

An invoice dated November 3 for $340 contains sales terms 3/15, n/30. If a $194 payment is made on November 18, by how much has the debt been reduced? What amount remains to be paid? **Example Four**

3% discount means 97% was paid:

$$\% \text{ Pd} \times \text{L} = \text{N}$$
$$0.97\text{L} = \$194$$
$$\text{L} = \$200$$

Since $200 has been deducted from the debt by a $194 payment, $340 − $200 or $140 remains to be paid.

PROBLEMS

Determine the amount due on each invoice if paid on the date indicated:

		Date of Invoice	Amount	Sales Terms	Date Paid
1.	(a)	Sept. 17	$230	2/10, n/30	Sept. 23
	(b)	Jan. 5	180	3/15, n/30	Jan. 20
	(c)	May 28	125	1/10, n/30	June 9

		Date of Invoice	Amount	Sales Terms	Date Paid
	(d)	Oct. 24	458.75	3/15, 1/30, n/60	Nov. 3
	(e)	Feb. 20	283.90	2/10, 1/20, n/30	March 6
	(f)	July 18	521.19	2/15, n/30, E.O.M.	Aug. 5
2.	(a)	June 16	$320	3/10, n/30	June 24
	(b)	July 19	650	2/15, n/30	Aug. 4
	(c)	Aug. 27	175	1/10, n/30	Sept. 3
	(d)	Sept. 25	485.40	2/15, 1/30, n/60	Oct. 9
	(e)	Nov. 29	247.35	3/10, 1/20, n/30	Dec. 11
	(f)	Feb. 25	538.42	2/10, n/30, E.O.M.	Mar. 10

Find the following, if partial payment was made on each invoice within the discount period:

		Amount of Invoice	Sales Terms	Credit Toward Account	Net Payment Made	Amount Still Due
3.	(a)	$340	2/10, n/30	$250		
	(b)	420	3/10, n/30	120		
	(c)	600	2/15, n/30			$200
	(d)	280	2/10, n/30		$147	
	(e)	370	3/15, n/60		261.90	
4.	(a)	$400	3/10, n/30	$250		
	(b)	670	2/10, n/30	335		
	(c)	800	4/10, n/20			$200
	(d)	765	2/10, n/30		$392	
	(e)	580	3/15, n/30		368.60	

5. The following items were on an invoice dated April 11. The order is subject to trade discounts of 20% and 10%. The invoice includes prepaid freight of $5 and contains sales terms of 2/10, n/30. Find the remittance due on April 21.

> 12 doz. flashbulbs @ $1.50 doz.
> 10 doz. flashcubes @ $.60 each
> 8 replacement lamps @ $4.50 each
> 25 packages, color film @ $3.60 each
> 20 slide trays @ $1.20 each

6. Trade discounts of $33\frac{1}{3}$% and 10% are to be allowed on the following items. The items were listed on an invoice dated September 24 and which contained terms 3/10, n/30. Find the amount due if paid on October 4. Prepaid freight and insurance totaled $5.45.

15 doz. packages drapery pins @ $7.00 doz.
15 doz. packages drapery hooks @ $.40 each
150 yd. drapery cord @ $.25 yd.
200 yd. pleating tape @ $.30 yd.
10 doz. curtain rods @ $.75 each

7. Three invoices from The Rodgers Co. contain sales terms of 2/10, 1/20, n/30. The invoices total $360 on May 5, $530 on May 17, and $420 on May 22. If the invoices are all paid on June 1, how much is due?

8. The Wilson Company decides to pay four invoices simultaneously on May 12. Each contains sales terms 3/15, 1/30, n/60. What amount does Wilson owe, if the invoices are dated March 20 for $225, April 15 for $170, April 21 for $405, and April 27 for $618?

9. On August 27, Powers Appliance Sales received an invoice for $740 and containing sales terms of 3/15, n/60, E.O.M. Powers decided to pay enough on September 15 to reduce the obligation by $400. What amount must be paid?

10. Jones Furniture wants to reduce a $600 debt by $300. The charge was on an invoice dated June 17 and containing terms 3/10, 2/30, n/30. How much must Jones remit on July 1 in order to receive the $300 credit?

11. An invoice dated October 20 for $720 contains terms 3/15, 2/30, n/60. On November 3, the buyer wishes to make a payment of sufficient amount so that he receives credit for half his obligation.
   (a) How much should he remit on November 3?
   (b) On November 22, he finds he can pay the remainder of the debt. How much is this second payment?
   (c) What is the total amount that was paid to discharge the $720 obligation?

12. Wilson, Inc., owes Grant Distributors $1,200, according to Grant's August 26 statement with terms 2/10, 1/20, n/30, E.O.M.
   (a) What must be the amount of Wilson's payment on September 10 in order to credit his account for two-thirds of his debt?
   (b) If Wilson finds he can pay the remainder of the account on September 18, what will be his second payment?
   (c) What will be the total he has paid to discharge his $1,200 debt?

13. Watts Plumbing Co. owes Wilson Supply $630, according to a March 7 invoice with terms 2/10, n/30.
   (a) If Wilson Supply receives $441 from Watts Plumbing on March 17, how much credit should they give the Watts account?
   (b) How much does Watts still owe?

14. On March 3, Drexel Mills received a $735 partial payment from Jones

Furniture Company. Drexel had sent an invoice for $1,500 on February 22, with terms 2/10, n/30.

(a) How much credit on account will Jones Furniture receive for this partial payment?

(b) How much more does Jones owe Drexel?

Markup

LEARNING OBJECTIVES

Upon completing Chapter 13, the student will be able to:

1. Define and use correctly the terminology in each topic.

2. Given a percentage markup (based on cost or on selling price), use the formula "C + M = S" to find
   a. Selling price,
   b. Cost, and
   c. Dollar markup.

3. a. Determine per cent of markup based on cost using the formula " ? % of C = M."
   b. Similarly, compute per cent of markup based on selling price using the formula " ? % of S = M."

4. a. Calculate selling price factor (Spf).
   b. Use "Spf × C = S" to find selling price or cost.

5. Use "C + M = S," "%Pd × L = N," and "__%S = M" to find
   a. Regular selling price,
   b. Reduced sale price,
   c. Per cent of sale or regular markup, and/or
   d. Net cost (when trade discounts are offered).
   (The order in which the formulas are used depends on which information is given and which must be computed.)

6. a. Find the selling price required on perishable items so that the goods expected to sell will provide the desired profit on the entire purchase.
   b. Similarly, determine the regular selling price when some of the items will be sold at a given reduced price.

In accordance with the American economic philosophy, merchants offer their goods for sale with the intention of making a profit. If a profit is to be made, the merchandise must be marked high enough so that the cost of the goods and all selling expenses are recovered. On the other hand, a merchant cannot mark his goods so as to include an unreasonably high profit, or else he will not be able to meet his competition from other merchants in our free enterprise system. In order to stay within this acceptable range, therefore, it is important that business people have a thorough understanding of the factors involved and the methods used to determine the selling price of their merchandise. The first step in this direction should be to become familiar with the terms involved.

The actual *cost* of a piece of merchandise includes not only its catalog price but also sales tax, freight, and any other charges incurred during the process of getting the merchandise to the store.

The difference between this cost and the selling price is known as *gross profit*. Other names for gross profit are *markup* and *margin*.

Gross profit is not all clear profit, however, for out of it must be paid business expenses, or *overhead*. Examples of overhead are salaries, rent, office equipment, lights and water, heat, advertising, taxes, insurance, etc. Whatever remains after these expenses have been paid constitutes the clear or *net profit*. The net profit remaining is often quite small; indeed, expenses sometimes exceed the margin, in which case there is a loss.

The following diagram illustrates the breakdown on selling price:

Selling Price		
Cost	Markup	
	Overhead	Net Profit

Markup (or gross profit) may be computed as a percentage of cost, or it may be based on sales. But regardless of which method is used, the same relationship between cost and markup always exists as shown in the diagram; specifically, Cost plus Markup (or margin or gross profit) always equals Selling price. From this relationship we obtain our fundamental selling price formula:

$$C + M = S$$

where C = cost, M = markup, and S = selling price.

Since the Margin is composed of Overhead plus net Profit, the same formula can be restated

$$C + (OH + P) = S$$

where OH = overhead and P = net profit.

1. MARKUP BASED ON COST

Before attempting to calculate selling price, let us consider the following examples.

Suppose a dress shop bought a dress for $20 and sold it for $25. Assume the store's expenses (overhead) run 15% of cost. (a) How much margin (or gross profit) did the store obtain? (b) What were the shop's expenses on the sale? (c) How much profit was made?

Example One

(a)
$$C + M = S$$
$$\$20 + M = \$25$$
$$M = \$5$$

The markup (or margin) on the sale was $5.

(b) Overhead is 15% of cost; or

$$15\% \times C = OH$$
$$0.15\,(\$20) = OH$$
$$\$3 = OH$$

The shop's expenses for this sale were $3.

(c) Since the overhead plus net profit make up the margin, then

$$OH + P = M$$
$$\$3 + P = \$5$$
$$P = \$2$$

A net profit of $2 was obtained on this dress.

Example Two The wholesale cost of a hi-fi set was $85. A music store sold the set for $100. The store's last income statement showed that expenses were 20% of sales. (a) What was the markup on the hi-fi? (b) How much overhead should be charged to this sale? (c) How much profit or loss was made on the hi-fi set?

(a)
$$C + M = S$$
$$\$85 + M = \$100$$
$$M = \$15$$

The selling price included a markup of $15.

(b) The overhead was 20% of the selling price; thus

$$20\% SP = OH$$
$$0.2\,(\$100) = OH$$
$$\$20 = OH$$

Business expenses on this sale totaled $20.

(c) One can immediately see that, if expenses were $20 while only $15 was brought in by the sale, there was obviously a $5 loss on the transaction. This calculation is as follows:

$$OH + P = M$$
$$\$20 + P = \$15$$
$$\$20 - \$20 + P = \$15 - \$20$$
$$P = -\$5$$

The calculation results in a negative difference. Hence, a negative profit $(-\$5)$ indicates a $5 loss on the sale.

This last example illustrates a vital fact about selling—just because an item sells for more than it cost does not necessarily mean that any profit is made on the sale. Thus it is essential that business people have the mathematical ability to take their expenses into consideration and price their merchandise to obtain exactly the required markup.

Now let us consider some examples where the markup is based on cost.

Example Three A merchant has found that his expenses plus the net profit he wishes to make usually run $33\frac{1}{3}\%$ of the cost of his goods. For what price should he sell a dress which cost him $24?

(a) We know the markup equals $33\frac{1}{3}\%$ or $\frac{1}{3}$ of the cost. Since $\frac{1}{3}$ of $\$24 = \$8$, then

$$C + M = S$$
$$\$24 + \$8 = S$$
$$\$32 = S$$

(b) This same problem can be computed in another way: Since markup equals $\frac{1}{3}$ of the cost ($M = \frac{1}{3}C$), by substitution

$$C + M = S$$
$$C + \tfrac{1}{3}C = S$$
$$\tfrac{4}{3}C = S$$

but since cost equals $24,

$$\tfrac{4}{3}(\$24) = S$$
$$\$32 = S$$

It is customary in business to price merchandise as shown in Example 3(b), above, primarily because this is quicker than the method in Example 3(a), where markup was computed separately and then added to the cost (an extra step). In using method (b), the student should form the habit of combining the C's before substituting the dollar value of the cost. Another advantage of method (b) is that it allows one to find the cost when the selling price is known. The following example illustrates how cost is found (as well as why the C's should be combined before substituting for cost).

A business marks up its merchandise 20% of cost. (a) What would be the selling price of an item costing $15? (b) What was the cost of an item selling for $30? **Example Four**

(a) Markup is 20% of Cost, or 0.2C

$$C + M = S$$
$$C + 0.2C = S$$
$$1.2C = S$$
$$1.2(\$15) = S$$
$$\$18 = S$$

The item should sell for $18 in order to obtain a gross profit (markup) of 20% on cost.

(b)
$$C + M = S$$
$$C + 0.2C = S$$
$$1.2C = S$$
$$1.2C = \$30$$
$$C = \$25$$

The item cost $25.

One can quickly see that markup based on cost is quite different from margin based on sales. For instance, suppose an article cost $1.00 and sold for $1.50. The 50¢ markup is 50% of the cost but only $33\frac{1}{3}$% of the selling price.

A merchant may wish to know what margin based on sales is equivalent to his margin based on cost, or vice versa. To find the percent markup based on cost, he would use the formula

$$\underline{}\% \text{ of } C = M$$

where C = cost and M = margin. To determine the per cent of margin based on selling price, he would use the formula

$$\underline{}\% \text{ of } S = M$$

where S = selling price and M = markup.

Example Five

An electric mixer cost $36 and required $4 postage and insurance. It sold for $50. (a) What per cent markup on cost did this represent? (b) What was the per cent of margin based on selling price?

The actual cost of the mixer is $36 + 4 = $40; therefore,

$$C + M = S$$
$$M = S - C$$
$$M = \$50 - \$40$$
$$M = \$10$$

(a)
$$\underline{}\%C = M$$
$$\underline{}\% \times \$40 = \$10$$
$$40x = 10$$
$$x = \tfrac{1}{4}$$
$$x = 25\% \text{ markup, based on cost}$$

(b)
$$\underline{}\%S = M$$
$$\underline{}\% \times \$50 = \$10$$
$$50x = 10$$
$$x = \tfrac{1}{5}$$
$$x = 20\% \text{ markup, based on selling price}$$

Note: In all cases where the same markup is used, the beginning calculations would be the same. Suppose the markup is 25% of cost $(M = \tfrac{1}{4}C)$; then,

$$C + M = S$$
$$C + \tfrac{1}{4}C = S$$
$$\tfrac{5}{4}C = S$$

When the margin is 25% of cost, the basic calculation would always yield

$\frac{5}{4}C = S$. This $\frac{5}{4}$ is called the selling price factor. The *selling price factor* (Spf) is a number which can be multiplied times the cost to obtain the selling price. This definition can be expressed by the formula

$$Spf \times C = S$$

Thus, in actual practice, a retail store would not price each item by the complete process, starting with $C + M = S$. Rather, any store which uses a markup of 25% on cost would know that its selling price factor is $\frac{5}{4}$. (The selling price factor of $\frac{5}{4}$ could be expressed in any equivalent form: $1\frac{1}{4}$, 1.25, or 125%.) Hence the store would eliminate the first steps of the markup formula and start with the selling price factor. Thus, in order to price an item which cost $24, the store would perform only the following calculation, based on $Spf \times C = S$:

$$\frac{5}{4}C = S$$
$$\frac{5}{4}(\$24) = S$$
$$\$30 = S$$

The item should sell for $30.

After trying a few examples, the student will observe that, when markup is based on cost, the selling price factor can be found simply by adding "1" ("one") to the decimal or fractional equivalent of the markup. (This is *not* true when markup is a per cent of sales.)

A word to the wise: Don't forget that many per cents can be handled easier when converted to fractions instead of to decimals.

PROBLEMS

Answer the following questions about each problem:

(1) How much markup does each sale include? (2) How much are the overhead expenses? (3) Is a profit or loss made on the sale, and how much?

		Cost	Selling Price	Overhead
1.	(a)	$12	$18	25% of Cost
	(b)	25	29	20% of Cost
	(c)	30	40	$12\frac{1}{2}$% of Selling price
	(d)	65	70	10% of Selling price
	(e)	45	54	$22\frac{2}{9}$% of Selling price
2.	(a)	$40	$48	15% of Cost
	(b)	25	28	20% of Cost
	(c)	30	36	$11\frac{1}{9}$% of Selling price
	(d)	10	12	25% of Selling price
	(e)	65	72	$16\frac{2}{3}$% of Selling price

Find the missing information. (Compute the selling price before finding markup.)

		% Markup on Cost	Cost	Selling Price	Markup	% Markup on Selling Price
3.	(a)	25%	$48			
	(b)	60	35			
	(c)	33⅓	57			
	(d)	30		$32.50		
	(e)	11⅑		70		
	(f)		56	64		
	(g)			84	$12	
4.	(a)	50%	$18			
	(b)	20	45			
	(c)	12½	56			
	(d)	40		$35		
	(e)	22⅔		55		
	(f)		63	81		
	(g)			60	$12	

5. (a) What would be the selling price factor for a markup of 38% on cost?
   (b) What would be the selling price of an item costing $50?
   (c) What dollar markup does this yield?

6. (a) If a markup of 35% on cost is used, what would be the selling price factor?
   (b) What would be the selling price of an article which cost $80?
   (c) How much gross profit would be made?

7. Some men's shirts cost $72 per dozen and sold for $9 each.
   (a) What per cent of cost was the markup?
   (b) What per cent of selling price was the markup?

8. Hosiery costs a department store $9 per dozen and sells for $1.00 a pair.
   (a) What per cent of cost is the margin?
   (b) What per cent of selling price is the margin?

9. (a) Find the selling price factor corresponding to a 60% markup on cost.
   (b) Price items which cost as follows: $3.50; $5.00; $7.75; $4.45.
   (c) What per cent markup on selling price does this correspond to?

10. (a) What selling price factor is equivalent to a margin of 40% on cost?
    (b) Determine what selling price should be marked on goods which have the following costs: $3.95; $7.90; $5.45; $4.85.
    (c) What per cent markup on selling price does this correspond to?

11. (a) An item selling for $34.80 was marked to obtain a gross profit of 45% on cost. Find the cost of this item.

(b) After an article was marked up $12\frac{1}{2}$% on cost, it sold for $3.60. What was its cost; and what was the equivalent per cent markup on sales?

12. (a) Using a margin of 35% on cost, a store priced an article at $3.24. What was the cost of this item?

(b) A markup of $42\frac{6}{7}$% on cost was used to price an item which sold for $3.00. Find the cost of this item; and find what per cent markup on sales this represents.

13. The catalog list price of a vacuum cleaner is $120. The Family Center buys the cleaners at a 50% discount and sells them at a 25% discount off the list price. Find

(a) the cost and the selling price;

(b) the per cent markup based on cost;

(c) the per cent markup based on sales.

14. A lawnmower has a catalog list price of $60. The Discount Barn buys the mowers at a 40% discount.

(a) What is their per cent markup on cost, if they sell the mowers at a 25% discount off this list price?

(b) What per cent markup on sales does this represent?

15. A shipment of six identical gold-framed mirrors cost $200. Freight and insurance on the shipment amounted to $16.

(a) At what price should each mirror be marked in order to obtain a margin of $33\frac{1}{3}$% on cost?

(b) What per cent markup on selling price does this represent?

16. Freight on a shipment of ten lamps was $8; the catalog price of the ten lamps was $172.

(a) If the merchant is to make a gross profit of 25% on cost, what should be the selling price of each lamp?

(b) What would be the equivalent per cent markup on selling price?

2. MARKUP BASED ON SELLING PRICE

Many business expenses are calculated as a per cent of net sales. For example, salesmen's commissions are based on their sales. Sales taxes, of course, are based on sales. When deciding how much to spend for advertising or research and development, a firm may designate a certain per cent of sales. Many companies take inventory at its sales value. The income statement, which is one of two key reports used to indicate the financial condition of a company, lists the firm's sales, all its expenses, and its net profit; each of these items is then computed as a per cent of net sales.

With so many other items calculated on the basis of sales, it is not surprising, then, that most businesses prefer to price their merchandise so that markup will be a certain per cent of the selling price. (The student may also have observed that, for any given dollar markup, the per cent based on sales is smaller than the per cent based on cost. This creates a better impression of the business—that the merchant is not trying to make such a high profit at the customers' expense.) Markup based on sales also offers a merchant the added advantage of being able to refer to his daily cash register tape and immediately calculate his gross profit.

Example One
Using a markup of 30% on sales, price an item which cost $35.

As before, we start with the equation $C + M = S$. We know that the markup equals 30% of sales, or $M = \frac{3}{10}S$. Thus we substitute $\frac{3}{10}S$ for M in the formula $C + M = S$:

$$C + M = S$$
$$C + \tfrac{3}{10}S = S$$
$$C + \tfrac{3}{10}S - \tfrac{3}{10}S = S - \tfrac{3}{10}S$$
$$C = \tfrac{7}{10}S$$

It is essential that the student understand the above calculations. When $\frac{3}{10}S$ is substituted for M, there are then S's on both sides of the equation. When an equation contains the same variable on both sides of the equal marks, the variables cannot be combined directly. So, in order to combine the S's, "$\frac{3}{10}S$" has to be subtracted from both sides of the equation. (When markup is based on selling price, it will always be necessary to subtract on both sides of the equation. This should be done before the actual dollar value is substituted for the cost.)

Now we are ready to find the selling price. The $35 is substituted for the cost C:

$$C = \tfrac{7}{10}S$$
$$\$35 = \tfrac{7}{10}S$$

In order to find S, we must eliminate the $\frac{7}{10}$. This is accomplished by multiplying both sides of the equation by the reciprocal, $\frac{10}{7}$:

$$\$35 = \tfrac{7}{10}S$$
$$\tfrac{10}{7}(\$35) = \tfrac{10}{7}(\tfrac{7}{10}S)$$
$$\$50 = S$$

Thus the selling price is $50. (In this example, $\frac{10}{7}$ was the selling price factor, because $\frac{10}{7}$ multiplied times the cost, $35, produced the selling price, $50.)

Sometimes it is more convenient to convert the markup per cent to a decimal than to a fraction. The following example illustrates such a problem.

A hardware store prices its merchandise to obtain a gross profit of 16% of the selling price. For how much should they sell a light fixture which cost $42? **Example Two**

The markup is to be 16% of sales (M = 0.16S). Recall that S = 1S = 1.00S; thus

$$C + M = S$$
$$C + 0.16S = S$$
$$C + \cancel{0.16S} - \cancel{0.16S} = S - 0.16S$$
$$C = 0.84S$$
$$\$42 = 0.84S$$
$$\frac{\$42}{0.84} = \frac{\cancel{0.84}S}{\cancel{0.84}}$$
$$\$50 = S$$

The fixture should sell for $50.

An iron sold for $25. Expenses were 14% of sales and net profit was 6% of sales. (a) What was the cost of the iron? (b) What per cent markup on cost does this represent? **Example Three**

(a) Recall that gross profit (markup) equals expenses plus net profit. Thus

$$M = OH + P$$
$$M = 14\%S + 6\%S$$
$$M = 20\%S$$

Since M = ⅕S, then

$$C + M = S$$
$$C + \tfrac{1}{5}S = S$$
$$C + \tfrac{1}{5}S - \tfrac{1}{5}S = S - \tfrac{1}{5}S$$
$$C = \tfrac{4}{5}S$$
$$C = \tfrac{4}{5}(\$25)$$
$$C = \$20$$

(b) Markup equals $25 − $20 or $5.

$$\underline{\quad}\%C = M$$
$$\underline{\quad}\%20 = 5$$
$$20x = 5$$
$$x = \tfrac{5}{20}$$
$$x = \tfrac{1}{4}$$
$$x = 25\% \text{ markup on cost}$$

PROBLEMS

Complete the following:

		% Markup on Selling Price	Cost	Selling Price	Markup	% Markup on Cost
1.	(a)	40%	$18			
	(b)	$33\frac{1}{3}$	48			
	(c)	20		$80		
	(d)	$37\frac{1}{2}$		72		
	(e)		70		$14	
2.	(a)	$33\frac{1}{3}$%	$18			
	(b)	$22\frac{2}{9}$	49			
	(c)	25		$52		
	(d)	$14\frac{2}{7}$		84		
	(e)		21		$9	

3. (a) What would be the selling price factor for a markup of $28\frac{4}{7}$% on selling price?
   (b) Find the selling price of an item which cost $35.
   (c) How much dollar markup does this yield?

4. (a) If a markup of 10% on sales is used, what would be the selling price factor?
   (b) What would be the selling price of an article which cost $54?
   (c) What gross profit would be made?

5. A gross profit of $9.50 is made on a sale. If the margin was 38% on selling price,
   (a) What was the selling price?
   (b) What was the cost?

6. A margin of 45% on selling price resulted in a gross profit of $54.
   (a) What was the selling price?
   (b) What was the cost?

7. (a) Find the selling price factor corresponding to a 20% markup on sales.
   (b) Price items which cost as follows: $3.60; $6.00; $5.20; $4.80.
   (c) What per cent markup on cost does this represent?

8. (a) What selling price factor is equivalent to a margin of $33\frac{1}{3}$% on sales?
   (b) Determine the selling price of goods which cost as follows: $4.90; $7.50; $2.85; $5.00.
   (c) What per cent markup on cost does this correspond to?

9. The Art Mart purchased 150 prints for a total cost of $600. They sold

10 prints for $10 each, 75 for $6 each, 40 for $5 each, and the remaining 25 were sold on special for $2 each.
(a) How much gross profit was made on the entire transaction?
(b) What per cent markup on cost was made?
(c) What per cent markup on selling price was made?

10. The Chapeaux bought 250 spring hats at a total cost of $1,500. They sold 25 for $14 each, 50 for $11 each, 80 for $10 each, 75 for $8 each, and the remaining 20 were reduced and sold at $5 each.
(a) How much gross profit was made on the entire transaction?
(b) What was the per cent of margin based on cost?
(c) What per cent markup on selling price did they make?

11. (a) Which would give a better markup, 20% on cost or 20% on selling price? (Hint: Compare selling price factors.)
(b) Which is better, 45% on cost or $37\frac{1}{2}$% on selling price?

12. (a) Would 25% on cost or 25% on selling price yield a larger gross profit?
(b) Which is better, 40% on cost or 30% on selling price?

13. An item selling for $72 was priced using a markup of 50% of sales.
(a) What was the selling price factor?
(b) What was the cost of the item?
(c) What is the equivalent per cent markup on cost?

14. Using a margin of $28\frac{4}{7}$% on sales, a company sold an item for $49. Find their—
(a) selling price factor;
(b) cost;
(c) corresponding per cent markup based on cost.

15. A housewares manager wants to buy ovenware that can retail for $35. She must obtain a gross profit of $42\frac{6}{7}$% on sales.
(a) What is her selling price factor?
(b) What is the most she can pay for the ovenware sets she buys?

16. The Grande Shoppe requires a margin of $16\frac{2}{3}$% on sales.
(a) What is their selling price factor?
(b) What is the most they could pay for some roll brim hats which will sell for $18?

17. Capital Furniture Co. paid $630 less $33\frac{1}{3}$% for a bedroom suite. Their expenses are 20% on sales and they would like to obtain a net profit of 10% on sales. At what price should Capital sell the bedroom suite?

18. The Old Gate Antiques figures its expenses to be 20% of sales and wants to make a net profit of $13\frac{1}{3}$% of sales. At what price should they sell a picture frame which cost them $40 less 30%?

3. MARKUP BASED ON SELLING PRICE (CONTINUED)

Few, if any, retail merchants are able to sell their entire stock at its regular marked prices. Clearance sales and "store-wide discounts" are common. The following problems involve markup when merchandise is sold at a sale or discount price.

Example One

The regular marked price on an heirloom bedspread is $24, which includes a markup of 20% on *cost*. During a special sale, the price was reduced so that the store obtained a 10% markup on the sale price. What was (a) the cost? (b) the sale price?

(a)   When M = 20% of cost, then

$$C + M = S$$
$$C + 0.2C = S$$
$$1.2C = S$$
$$1.2C = \$24$$
$$C = \$20$$

(b)   When M = $\frac{1}{10}$ of sales, then

$$C + M = S$$
$$C + \tfrac{1}{10}S = S$$
$$C + \tfrac{1}{10}S - \tfrac{1}{10}S = S - \tfrac{1}{10}S$$
$$C = \tfrac{9}{10}S$$
$$\$20 = \tfrac{9}{10}S$$
$$\tfrac{10}{9}(\$20) = \cancel{\tfrac{10}{9}}(\cancel{\tfrac{9}{10}}S)$$
$$\$22.22 = S$$

The sale price was $22.22.

For situations in which a "sale" price is involved, the student may often find it helpful to think through the entire pricing process from the time an item enters the store until it is sold "on sale."

Example Two

Willson Department Store uses a markup of 30% of selling price to obtain its regular marked prices. During a clearance sale, a coat which originally cost $28 was reduced by 20% of the marked price. (a) What was the regular marked price of the coat? (b) What was the sale price? (c) What per cent markup on sales was made at the sale price?

(a)   First, the coat is priced, using a markup of 30% on sales (M = $\frac{3}{10}$S):

$$C + M = S$$
$$C + \tfrac{3}{10}S = S$$
$$C = S - \tfrac{3}{10}S$$
$$C = \tfrac{7}{10}S$$
$$\$28 = \tfrac{7}{10}S$$
$$\tfrac{10}{7}(\$28) = \tfrac{\cancel{10}}{\cancel{7}}(\cancel{\tfrac{7}{10}}S)$$
$$\$40 = S$$

The regular selling price (marked price) of the coat was $40.

(b) Later, the price was reduced: A 20% discount means 80% (or $\tfrac{4}{5}$) of the regular price was paid:

$$\%\,Pd \times L = \text{Net sale price}$$
$$\tfrac{4}{5}(\$40) = N$$
$$\$32 = N$$

The clearance sale price of the coat was $32.

(c) In order to find the per cent markup on sales at the sale price, we must first determine the actual dollar markup at the sale price:

$C + M = S$	$\underline{\quad ?\quad} \%\,S = M$
$M = S - C$	$\underline{\quad ?\quad} \%\,\$32 = \$4$
$M = \$32 - \$28$	$32x = 4$
$M = \$4$	$x = \tfrac{4}{32} \text{ or } \tfrac{1}{8}$
	$x = 12\tfrac{1}{2}\%$

Thus $12\tfrac{1}{2}\%$ of the sale price was gross profit.

Example Three

During a clearance sale, Erwin Department Store marked a dress down 25%, selling it for $12. Even at this reduced price, Erwin's still made a gross profit of $16\tfrac{2}{3}\%$ on sales. What per cent markup on sales would Erwin's have made if the dress had sold at its regular marked price?

Before we can use the formula $\underline{\quad\quad}\%\,S = M$ to determine the regular per cent markup on sales (d), we must know S (the regular list or selling price) and M. Thus we must first calculate the cost (a) and the regular selling price (b). From these we can determine the regular margin (c).

(a) At the sale price, $M = \tfrac{1}{6}S$:

$$C + M = S$$
$$C + \tfrac{1}{6}S = S$$
$$C = S - \tfrac{1}{6}S$$
$$C = \tfrac{5}{6}S$$
$$C = \tfrac{5}{6}(\$12)$$
$$C = \$10$$

The dress cost $10.

(b)   The dress was reduced 25% off regular price:

$$\%\,Pd \times List = Net\ selling\ price$$
$$\tfrac{3}{4}L = \$12$$
$$L = \$16$$

The regular list (selling) price was $16.

(c)   The dress regularly sold for $16; thus the regular margin was $16 − $10 or $6.

(d)

$$\underline{\quad}\%\,S = M$$
$$\underline{\quad}\%\,16 = 6$$
$$16x = 6$$
$$x = \tfrac{6}{16}\ or\ \tfrac{3}{8}$$
$$x = 37\tfrac{1}{2}\%$$

The regular markup, based on sales, was $37\tfrac{1}{2}\%$.

Many businesses deal in discounts every day. These merchants must price their goods very carefully, so they can allow the customer a "discount" off the marked price and still make their desired margin on the sale.

Example Four   Jones Furniture paid a wholesale company $350 less 20% and 10% for a French provincial couch. Jones must obtain a 20% markup on sales. At what price must Jones mark the couch so they can allow 30% and 10% off this marked price and still make their 20% margin?

The solution involves three parts: (a) to find the cost; (b) to determine what their actual selling price will be; and (c) to determine what marked price, less discounts of 30% and 10%, will leave the net selling price Jones wants.

(a)

$$\%\,Pd \times L = Net\ cost$$
$$(0.8)(0.9)(\$350) = N\ cost$$
$$0.72(350) = N\ cost$$
$$\$252 = N\ cost$$

The couch cost $252.

(b)   A 20% markup on sales $(M = \frac{1}{5}S)$ is used to determine the actual selling price:

$$C + M = S$$
$$C + \tfrac{1}{5}S = S$$
$$C = S - \tfrac{1}{5}S$$
$$C = \tfrac{4}{5}S$$
$$\$252 = \tfrac{4}{5}S$$
$$\tfrac{5}{4}(\$252) = \tfrac{5}{4}(\tfrac{4}{5}S)$$
$$\$315 = S$$

Jones will actually sell the couch for $315.

(c)
$$\% \, Pd \times L = \text{Net selling price}$$
$$(0.7)(0.9)L = \$315$$
$$0.63\,L = 315$$
$$L = \$500$$

The marked (or list) price of the couch will be $500.

PROBLEMS

Compute the missing items in the following problems:

		Cost	% Regular Markup	Reg. List	% Discount	Sale Price	% Sale Markup
1.	(a)		45% of C	$58	—		20% of S
	(b)		$37\frac{1}{2}$% of C	33	—		$14\frac{2}{7}$% of S
	(c)	$36	40% of S		25%		?% of S
	(d)	50	$33\frac{1}{3}$% of S		20%		?% of S
	(e)		?% of S		10%	$45	$22\frac{2}{9}$% of S
	(f)		?% of S		$22\frac{2}{9}$%	49	$28\frac{4}{7}$% of S
	(g)	$540 less 25/20 = ?	—		20/10		25% of S
	(h)	$425 less 20/20 = ?	—		20/15		20% of S
2.	(a)		25% of C	$90	—		10% of S
	(b)		35% of C	54	—		$16\frac{2}{3}$% of S
	(c)	$32	20% of S		10%		?% of S
	(d)	60	25% of S		20%		?% of S
	(e)		?% of S		20%	32	$12\frac{1}{2}$% of S
	(f)		?% of S		25%	45	20% of S
	(g)	$400 less 30/10 = ?	—		20/10		30% of S
	(h)	$250 less 20/10 = ?	—		25/20		$33\frac{1}{3}$% of S

3. The regular price of top coats at The Clothes Closet was $87, which in-included a 45% markup on cost. During a pre-inventory sale, the coats were reduced so that the sale price produced a $16\frac{2}{3}$% gross profit on sales.
   (a) What did the coats cost?
   (b) What was the sale price?

4. The Style Shoppe sold coats for $49, representing a margin of 40% on cost. At a clearance sale, the coats are to be remarked with a new price giving a margin of $12\frac{1}{2}$% on selling price.
   (a) What did the coats cost?
   (b) What will be the sale price?

5. The usual selling price at The Fashion Center includes a markup that is 30% of the selling price. During a sale, a suit which cost $56 received a 20% reduction off its regular price.
   (a) What was the marked price of the suit?
   (b) How much did the suit cost on sale?
   (c) What per cent markup on sales did the store make during its sale?

6. A raincoat which cost $24 was marked up to make a gross profit of 40% of the regular selling price. The marked price was later reduced by 25% before the coat was sold.
   (a) What was the regular price of the raincoat?
   (b) What was the sale price of the raincoat?
   (c) What per cent of the sale price was the margin?

7. During a clearance sale, a jeweler marked a diamond ring down $12\frac{1}{2}$%, making the sale price $350. At this sale price, the jeweler made a $28\frac{4}{7}$% gross profit on sales. Find—
   (a) the list price;
   (b) the cost;
   (c) the per cent markup on sales he makes at the regular list price.

8. A merchant marked a cookware set down 30%, clearing it out on sale for $35. At this sale price, he still obtained a margin of $14\frac{2}{7}$% on sales. What were his—
   (a) list price?
   (b) cost?
   (c) per cent of gross profit based on sales at the regular list price?

9. A color television console cost a dealer $500 less 25/20. After marking the set so that he could allow a "20/20 discount," the dealer still obtained a markup of $37\frac{1}{2}$% of the actual selling price. What had been—
   (a) the cost?
   (b) the actual selling price?
   (c) the marked price?

10. A chair cost a dealer $150 less 20% and 15%. He marked the chair so that he could allow a "discount" of 20% off his marked price; but he still

made a gross profit of 25% on sales. What had been—
(a) the cost?
(b) the selling price?
(c) the marked price?

4. MARKUP ON PERISHABLES

A number of businesses handle products which perish in a short time if they are not sold. Examples of such businesses would be produce markets, bakeries, florists, dairies, and so forth. To a lesser extent, many other businesses would fall into this category, since styles and seasons change and the demand for a certain product diminishes. Clothing stores, appliance stores, and automobile dealers would be typical of this category.

These merchants know that not all of their goods will sell at their regular prices. The remaining items will have to be sold at a reduced price or else discarded altogether. Experienced businessmen know approximately how much of their merchandise will sell. They must, therefore, price the items high enough so that those which do sell will bring in the gross profit required for the entire stock.

One might wonder why the merchant does not buy only the amount he expects to sell. The main reason is this: If a customer came to buy an item and found that it had been sold out, he might never return to that store. Consequently, wise businessmen purchase a small amount more than they expect to sell. Then, if they have more customers than usual, they retain the customer's good will and make additional profits at the same time.

A grocer bought 100 lbs. of grapes at 15¢ per pound. He expects about 10% of these to spoil. At what price per pound must he mark the grapes in order to have a margin of 40% on cost?

Example One

The grapes cost 100 lb. × 15¢ or $15. Since he wishes a margin of 40% on cost ($M = 0.4C$), then

$$C + M = S$$
$$C + 0.4C = S$$
$$1.4C = S$$
$$1.4\,(\$15) = S$$
$$\$21 = S$$

He must get at least $21 from the sale of the grapes.

He expects 10% or 10 lbs. of grapes to spoil; so his necessary $21 in sales must come from the sale of the other 90 pounds. Now if x = price per pound of grapes, then

$$90x = \$21$$
$$x = 23\tfrac{1}{3} \quad \text{or} \quad 24\text{¢ per pound}$$

When a fraction of a cent remains, retail merchants customarily mark the item to the next penny even though the fraction may have been less than one-half cent. It should also be noted that, in this example, on all sales above the expected ninety pounds, the entire selling price will be additional profit.

Example Two

A bakery made 50 packages of buns at a cost of 20¢ each. About 10% of these will be sold "three days old" at 12¢ each. Find the regular price in order that the bakery may make 32% on cost.

The buns cost 50 × 20¢ or $10 to make, and the bakery uses a markup of 32% on cost (M = 0.32C). Thus

$$C + M = S$$
$$C + 0.32C = S$$
$$1.32C = S$$
$$1.32 (\$10) = S$$
$$\$13.20 = S$$

Now, 10% or 5 packages will be sold at 12¢ each, which means 60¢ will be earned at the reduced price. This leaves 45 packages to be sold at the regular price. The regular sales and the "old" sales together must total the $13.20; hence, if x = regular price per package,

$$\text{Regular} + \text{Old} = \text{Total}$$
$$\text{Regular} + 60¢ = \$13.20$$
$$\text{Regular} = \$12.60$$
$$45x = \$12.60$$
$$x = 28¢ \text{ per package}$$

PROBLEMS

Find the missing information:

		No. Bought	Cost Each	Total Cost	Markup on Cost	Total Sales	Amount to Spoil	No. to Sell	Selling Price Each
1.	(a)	100 lbs.	30¢		20%		10%		
	(b)	75 doz.	$2		40%		4%		
	(c)	250	$1.60		$37\frac{1}{2}\%$		6%		
2.	(a)	100 lb.	40¢		50		4		
	(b)	25	$16		30		8		
	(c)	30 doz.	$5		$33\frac{1}{3}$		10		

Complete the following, which involves part of the goods being sold at the regular price and the remainder at the reduced price:

		No. Bought	Cost Each	Total Cost	Markup on Cost	Total Sales	No. at Reg. Pr.	Amt. at Red. Pr.	No. at Red. Pr.	Red. Pr.	Reg. S.P.
3.	(a)	400 lb.	30¢		20%		5%			17¢	
	(b)	50	$4		44%		6%			$2	
4.	(a)	20 doz.	$4		25		10			$2.75	
	(b)	120 lb.	15¢		35		5			6¢	

5. Suppose in Example 1 (Section 4), that 95 pounds of grapes actually sold.
   (a) How much gross profit would the grocer make?
   (b) What per cent markup on cost would he obtain?
   (c) What per cent markup on selling price would that be?

6. Suppose that in Example 2 (Section 4), the bakery actually sold 48 packages of buns at the regular price, and the remainder at 12¢ each.
   (a) What gross profit would be obtained?
   (b) What per cent markup on cost does that represent?
   (c) What per cent markup on selling price does that represent?

7. The Garden Fresh Market purchased 125 pounds of bananas at 12¢ per pound. Experience indicates that 4% of the bananas probably will not sell. At what price per pound would the market make 20% on cost?

8. Supreme Florists purchased 40 chrysanthemum plants at $2.00 each. Previously, about 5% have remained unsold. What must they charge per plant in order to make 30% on cost?

9. A grocery bought 5 crates of cherries at $7.20 per crate. Each crate contains 12 boxes of cherries. Approximately 10% of the fruit will spoil before it sells. At what price should each box be marked to realize a gross profit of 25% on cost?

10. A grocery purchased 10 crates of berries at $4.80 per crate. Each crate contained 24 boxes of strawberries. The grocer has found that about 10% of the berries spoil and do not sell. What should he charge for each box of berries to realize a gross profit of 25% on cost?

11. The Smart Shop purchased 80 pants suits at a cost of $25 each. The buyer expects 15% of these suits eventually to be sold on sale at $20 each. What must be the regular price of the pants suits in order to make 65% on cost for the entire purchase?

12. The Sunshine Dairy purchased 200 quarts of Jersey milk at a cost of 25¢ each. Their operating margin is 22% of cost. If $7\frac{1}{2}$% of the milk has to be sold after four days at a reduced price of 18¢ per quart, what is their regular price per quart?

Markdown and Turnover

LEARNING OBJECTIVES

Upon completion of Chapter 14, the student will be able to:

1. Define and use correctly the terminology associated with each topic.

2. a. Using "_____% of Original = Change," compute
   (1) Amount of markdown, and
   (2) Per cent of markdown.
   b. When necessary, first use the markup formulas of Chapter 13 to determine
   (1) Cost,
   (2) Regular selling price, or
   (3) Regular markup

3. When a markdown has occurred, determine the amount and per cent of
   a. Operating profit,
   b. Operating loss, or
   c. Gross loss.

4. Complete the following cash forms:
   a. Daily cash record, and
   b. Over-and-short summary.

5. Compute (both at cost and at retail)
   a. Average inventory, and
   b. Stock turnover.

Two other significant aspects of retail business are markdown and turnover. Almost all retail concerns must sell at least some of their merchandise at a reduced selling price, while stock turnover reflects the selling efficiency of an organization. The following sections explain the mathematics required to compute markdown and turnover.

1. MARKDOWN

In the previous chapter, we saw that merchandise must often be sold at a reduced price. This reduction may be expected and planned for well in advance, as in the case of seasonal clearance sales on clothing. Other reductions may be less predictable, as when the merchants' association decides to have a special city-wide promotion or when the competition has unexpectedly lowered its price.

Regardless of what motivates a price reduction, there are guidelines which merchants generally follow in determining how much to mark down their merchandise. Businessmen prefer to recover both the actual cost and the overhead on an item if possible; in this case, no net profit would be made, but there would be no loss either. If they recover the wholesale cost but not all of the operating expenses, there has been an *operating loss*. If not even the wholesale cost of the article was recovered, the transaction resulted in a *gross loss* (sometimes called *absolute loss*). We will be interested here in determining whether or not any profit was made following a markdown, as well as relative percentages.

Example One A coat which sold for $48 was reduced to $32.

   (a) What was the markdown on the coat?

310

(b) By what per cent was the price reduced?
   (a) The coat was reduced by $48 − $32 or $16.

(b) $\underline{?\,\%}$ of original selling price = change.

$$\underline{?\,\%}\text{ of }\$48 = \$16$$
$$48x = 16$$
$$x = \tfrac{16}{48} \quad \text{or} \quad \tfrac{1}{3}$$
$$x = 33\tfrac{1}{3}\%\text{ reduction on selling price}$$

The coat in Example 1 had cost the department store $30. The store's operating expenses are 20% of cost.
   Was an operating profit (net profit) or an operating loss made on the coat?

Example Two

(a) (Required) Markup = M = 0.2C; cost = C = $30; S = selling price.

$$C + M = S$$
$$C + 0.2C = S$$
$$1.2C = S$$
$$1.2(\$30) = S$$
$$\$36 = S$$

In order to recover the operating expenses, the selling price should have been $36; that is, $36 was the total cost of handling the coat. Thus the operating loss on the coat was the difference between total handling cost and selling price: $36 − $32 or $4.

A group of living room tables sells regularly for $120. The group cost the company $90; selling expenses are $15. If the tables are marked down by 30%—(a) What is the operating loss? (b) What is the absolute loss? (c) What was the per cent of gross loss (based on cost)?
   The actual cost of handling the tables was $90 + $15 or $105. The selling price of the tables will be

Example Three

$$\%\text{ Paid} \times \text{List} = \text{Net}$$
$$0.7\,(\$120) = \text{Net}$$
$$\$84 = \text{Net selling price}$$

(a)

Total handling cost	$105
Selling price	−84
Operating loss	$ 21

(b) The gross or absolute loss is the difference between wholesale cost and selling price.

$$\begin{array}{lr} \text{Wholesale cost} & \$90 \\ \text{Selling price} & -84 \\ \hline \text{Gross loss} & \$\ 6 \end{array}$$

(c)   What per cent of wholesale cost was the gross loss?

$$\underline{\ ?\ }\% \text{ of } \$90 = \$6$$
$$90x = 6$$
$$x = \tfrac{6}{90}$$
$$x = 6\tfrac{2}{3}\% \text{ gross loss}$$

Example Four   An antique picture cost a dealer $60; his operating expenses are 20% of cost and his net profit is usually $13\tfrac{1}{3}\%$ of cost. (a) What is his regular selling price on the picture? (b) What is the maximum per cent of markdown that he can offer without taking an operating loss?

(a)   His regular margin is overhead plus net profit:

$$\begin{array}{ll} \text{Overhead} & 20\% \text{ of Cost} \\ \text{Net profit} & +13\tfrac{1}{3}\% \text{ of Cost} \\ \hline \text{Markup} & 33\tfrac{1}{3}\% \text{ of Cost} \end{array}$$

Therefore, M $= \tfrac{1}{3}$C and C $= \$60$; thus

$$C + M = S$$
$$C + \tfrac{1}{3}C = S$$
$$\tfrac{4}{3}C = S$$
$$\tfrac{4}{3}(\$60) = S$$
$$\$80 = \text{Regular selling price}$$

(b)   The operating expenses are 20% or $\tfrac{1}{5}$ of cost;

$$\tfrac{1}{5}(\$60) = \$12 \text{ in Operating expenses}$$

$$\begin{array}{ll} \text{Cost} & \$60 \\ \text{Overhead} & +12 \\ \hline \text{Total handling cost} & \$72 \end{array} \qquad \begin{array}{lr} \text{Regular Selling Price} & \$80 \\ \text{Total Cost} & -72 \\ \hline \text{Markdown} & \$\ 8 \end{array}$$

The lowest sale price the merchant could offer without taking any operating loss would be $72. This means he would mark the picture down $8 from its regular selling price.

$$\underline{\ ?\ }\% \text{ of Original} = \text{Change}$$
$$\underline{\ ?\ }\% \text{ of } \$80 = \$8$$
$$80x = 8$$
$$x = \tfrac{8}{80} \quad \text{or} \quad \tfrac{1}{10}$$
$$x = 10\% \text{ reduction in price}$$

Complete the following:

		Regular Selling Price	Markdown %	Markdown Amount	Sale Price	Whole-sale Cost	Operating Expenses	Total Han-dling Cost	Operating Profit or Loss*
1.	(a)	$45	20%			$28	$ 6		
	(b)	60		$20		36	12		
	(c)	24			18		3		$3
	(d)	16					4	$15	(5)
	(e)			15		32		39	(4)
	(f)		28$\frac{4}{7}$		25		4		1
2.	(a)	$36		$ 8		$24	$ 3		
	(b)	20	15%				4	$19	
	(c)	75			$60	50			(5)
	(d)	32			24	20		25	
	(e)			9	21		5		(4)
	(f)		20				3	10	2

Determine the following:

		Regular Selling Price	Markdown %	Markdown Amount	Sale Price	Whole-sale Cost	Operat-ing Expenses	Total Han-dling Cost	Operat-ing Loss	Gross Loss Amount	%
3.	(a)	$48		$12		$40	$5				
	(b)	70	20%			63		$68			
	(c)		32		$17	4	24				
	(d)		50		18		9			($3)	
4.	(a)	$24	33$\frac{1}{3}$%			$20	$3				
	(b)	5		$ 2		3		$ 4			
	(c)	50			$37	5	45				
	(d)		25		30		4			($2)	

5. During a preinventory clearance, a $45 pair of men's boots was advertised at a 40% reduction. If the boots cost $24 originally and selling expenses were 25% of cost, how much operating profit or loss was made on the boots?

6. A 33$\frac{1}{3}$% discount was offered on a tape recorder which usually sold for $96. The recorder cost $50 and operating expenses were 15% of cost. How much operating profit or loss was made on this sale?

7. A portable television which usually retails for $108 was sold on sale for $72.

(a) What per cent markdown was the store allowing?

(b) If the TV had cost the store $90 less 20% and $22\frac{2}{3}$%, and selling expenses had been $10, how much operating profit or loss was made?

8. A $120 rotary antenna was closed out for $75.

(a) What per cent markdown did this represent?

(b) The dealer had paid $100 less 30% and 10% for the antenna, and operating expenses are 10% of the regular selling price. How much operating profit or loss was made?

9. A jewelry store paid $25 for a silverplated water pitcher. Their expenses are 20% of regular sales and they expect to make a net profit of $17\frac{1}{2}$% of sales. During an Anniversary Sale, they offered the pitcher at a 45% discount.

(a) What is the regular price of the pitcher?

(b) How much operating loss did they have?

(c) How much and what per cent gross or absolute loss did they have?

10. A hardware store paid $40 for a set of Teflon-coated aluminum cookware. On regular sales, their overhead is 15% of sales and the net profit is $13\frac{4}{7}$% of sales. For a Dollar Days special, the store sold the set at a 40% discount.

(a) What would be the regular price of the cookware?

(b) What was the operating loss on this sale?

(c) How much and what per cent gross or absolute loss did the store suffer?

11. Silk neckties cost a men's store $105 per dozen, less 20% and 20%. The shop marks the ties up to cover expenses of 30% on cost and a net profit of $12\frac{5}{9}$% on cost.

(a) What is the regular selling price of a necktie?

(b) What is the maximum markdown which the store could allow without taking any operating loss?

(c) What per cent markdown would this be?

12. A shoe store buys textured hosiery for $18 per dozen, less $33\frac{1}{3}$% and 10%. The marked price of the hose includes 20% on cost for expenses and 30% on cost for net profit.

(a) What does a pair of hose regularly sell for?

(b) What is the largest markdown which would be allowed on the hose without experiencing an operating loss?

(c) What per cent markdown would this represent?

13. A hardware store sold 180 garden hoses for $3.50 each. This price included a markup of 15% on cost for overhead and 10% on cost for net profit. Another 20 of the hoses were sold during a special promotion for $2 each.

(a) What were the total wholesale cost, total handling cost, and total sales?

(b) Was a net profit, operating loss, or gross loss made on the 200 hoses?

(c) How much was it, and what per cent of wholesale cost did it represent?

14. A cloth store bought 120 pairs of scissors. They sold 100 pairs for $1.95 each, which included 10% on cost for expenses and 20% on cost for net profit. The remaining 20 pairs were sold on Dollar Day for $1 each.

(a) What were the total wholesale cost, total handling cost, and total sales?

(b) Was a net profit, operating loss, or gross loss made on the entire transaction?

(c) How much was it, and what per cent of wholesale cost did it represent?

2. TURNOVER

CASH RECORDS

There is some variation, of course, but one good indication of business stability is the consistency of sales. These sales are recorded daily on the cash register tapes of a business and are given careful attention by officials of the company.

At the beginning of the business day, a stipulated amount is placed in each cash register drawer; this is the *change fund* which must be available so that early customers may receive correct change. The fund (usually $20 to $50) will contain a certain number of the various denominations of money.

At the close of the business day, the clerk completes a *daily cash record*. He counts each denomination of money separately, lists each check separately, and finds the total. The original change fund is then deducted from this total and the remaining sum (the *net cash receipts*) should equal the total day's sales shown on the cash register tape.

Human error being what it is, however, it frequently occurs that the cash receipts and the cash register total are not equal. If the cash receipts are smaller than the total sales, the cash is *short*. If there is more cash than the total of sales, the cash is *over*.

A summary of these daily cash records, commonly called an *over-and-short summary*, may be kept by the week or by the month. Over a period of time, the totals of the amounts in the "cash over" and in the "cash short" usually tend nearly to cancel each other.

Example One

JONES DEPARTMENT STORE

Daily Cash Record

Date: January 10, 1967

Register: 13 - E

Clerk: Phyllis Drum

Pennies .... $	.83
Nickels	2.55
Dimes	4.20
Quarters	7.50
Halves	9.50
Ones	22.00
Fives	55.00
Tens	120.00
Twenties	80.00

Other currency
Checks (list separately): $ 4.95
18.34
12.50
40.00
15.75   91.54

Total $393.12

Less: Change fund   25.00
Net cash receipts $368.12
Cash over (subtract)
Cash short (add)   .10
Cash register total $368.22

Example Two

JONES DEPARTMENT STORE

Over – and – Short Summary

Date	Cash Register Totals	Net Cash Receipts	Cash Over	Cash Short
Jan. 10, 1967	$ 1,587.35	$ 1,586.73		$ .62
11	1,548.06	1,548.90	$ .84	
12	1,516.63	1,517.19	.56	
13	1,594.42	1,592.98		1.44
14	1,630.25	1,631.25	1.00	
15	1,789.67	1,788.50		1.17
Totals	$ 9,666.38	$ 9,665.55	$ 2.40	$ 3.23

Total cash receipts $ 9,665.55
Total cash short (add)   3.23
$ 9,668.78
Total cash over (subtract)   2.40
Total cash register readings $ 9,666.38

1. Prepare a daily cash report for clerk Mary Danos of Sally's Dress Shop on today's date. The number of each denomination of money is as follows: pennies, 76; nickels, 54; dimes, 61; quarters, 85; halves, 7; ones, 28; fives, 16; tens, 9; twenties, 3; other currency—one $50. Checks were for $19.95; $12.43; $24.78; $22.13; $36.57; $45.25; and $32.00. Her change fund is $30.00. The cash register total for the day is $505.47.

2. Assume you work at Wylder Hardware. Prepare your own daily cash report for today. The number of each denomination of money in your register drawer is as follows: pennies, 72; nickels, 58; dimes, 36; quarters, 28; halves, 7; ones, 21; fives, 9; tens, 9; twenties, 4; other currency—none. Checks were for $18.75; $6.50; $9.18; $4.75; $11.37; and $22.53. Your change fund is $20. The cash register total for the day is $306.70.

3. Waring's Department Store has had total sales and net cash receipts as follows:

Date	Total Sales	Net Cash Receipts
April 16, 1972	$1,246.18	$1,246.43
17	988.52	987.52
18	1,061.73	1,061.83
19	1,455.27	1,455.74
20	1,885.95	1,885.36
21	2,009.60	2,009.28

Complete the store's weekly over-and-short summary.

4. Compute the weekly over-and-short summary for Greene Garden Store. Each day's cash register totals and net cash receipts are as follows:

Date	Cash Register Totals	Net Cash Receipts
Sept. 18, 1972	$ 943.52	$ 943.38
19	869.10	869.10
20	911.74	911.47
21	935.36	935.46
22	1,008.14	1,008.27
23	898.06	898.18

STOCK TURNOVER

Another indication of a business's stability and efficiency is the number of times per year that its inventory is sold—its *stock turnover*. This varies greatly with different types of businesses. For instance, a florist might maintain a relatively small inventory but sell his complete stock every few days. A furniture dealer, on the other hand, might stock a rather large inventory and have a turnover only every few months.

Regardless of what might be considered a desirable turnover for a business, the methods used to calculate this turnover are similar. One business statistic which is used in this calculation is the average value of the store's inventory. Inventory may be evaluated at either its cost or its retail value, although it is perhaps more often valued at retail.

Average inventory for a period is found by adding the various inventories and dividing by the number of times the inventory was taken.

Example Three

Inventory at retail value of the Crescent Gift Shop was $12,680 on January 1; $10,980 on June 30; and $13,840 on December 31. Find the average inventory.

$12,680
10,980
13,840
3⟌$37,500 = $12,500 average inventory (at retail) for the year

Stock turnover is found as follows:

$$\text{Turnover (at retail)} = \frac{\text{Net sales}}{\text{Average inventory (at retail)}}$$

$$\text{Turnover (at cost)} = \frac{\text{Cost of goods sold}}{\text{Average inventory (at cost)}}$$

Turnover is more frequently computed at retail than at cost. Many modern stores mark their goods only with retail prices, which makes it almost impossible to take inventory at cost. Another reason is that turnover at cost does not take into consideration the markdown on merchandise which was sold at a reduced price or the loss on goods which were misappropriated by shoplifters—a constant problem in many retail businesses. Turnover at retail and at cost will be the same only if all merchandise is sold at its regular price; ordinarily, the turnover at retail is slightly less than at cost.

Example Four

The gift shop in Example 3 above had net sales during the year of $43,750. What was the stock turnover for the year at retail?

$$\text{Turnover} = \frac{\text{Net sales}}{\text{Average inventory (at retail)}} = \frac{\$43,750}{\$12,500}$$

Turnover = 3.5 at Retail

Example Five

The gift shop above had used a markup of 20% on sales to price its merchandise. Find the turnover at cost, when the cost of goods sold during the year was $35,200.

The average inventory at sales price was $12,500. The markup was 20% or $\frac{1}{5}$ of selling price. To find the cost of this inventory,

$$C + M = S$$
$$C + \tfrac{1}{5}S = S$$
$$C = \tfrac{4}{5}S$$
$$C = \tfrac{4}{5}(\$12,500)$$
$$C = \$10,000$$

The average inventory at cost was $10,000. Now turnover at cost is

$$\text{Turnover} = \frac{\text{Cost of goods}}{\text{Average inventory (at cost)}} = \frac{\$35,200}{\$10,000}$$

$$\text{Turnover} = 3.52 \text{ at Cost}$$

PROBLEMS

1. Inventories at cost were as follows: $35,418; $37,025; $35,882; and $35,675. Find the average inventory.

2. The following inventories were taken during the year: $19,170; $17,840; $15,990; $16,870; and $20,130. What was the average inventory?

3. A store had taken inventory of $16,260 at cost. The new manager decided to take future inventories at retail. Later inventories were $21,870 and $20,950. If the store used a regular markup of $33\frac{1}{3}\%$ on cost, find the average inventory at retail.

4. A store uses a markup of 25% on cost to price its merchandise. Having taken an inventory of $14,200 at cost, a store took subsequent inventories at retail. If later inventories were for $16,820 and $17,330, what was the average inventory at retail?

5. The store in Problem 1 had net sales of $171,000; their merchandise had cost $138,600. Find their turnover at cost.

6. Net sales at the shop in Problem 2 were $66,000 and the cost of goods sold had been $50,400. What was the shop's turnover at cost?

7. The store in Problems 1 and 5 had used a markup of 20% on selling price for all its merchandise. What was its turnover at retail?

8. The shop discussed in Problems 2 and 6 priced all its merchandise using a markup of 25% on selling price. Find its turnover at retail.

part four

MATHEMATICS OF FINANCE

15

Simple Interest

LEARNING OBJECTIVES

Upon completing Chapter 15, the student will be able to:

1. Define and use correctly the terminology in each topic.
2. Use the simple interest formula $I = Prt$ to find any variable, when the other items are given.
3. a. Use the amount formula $S = P + I$ to find amount or interest.
   b. Use the amount formula $S = P(1 + rt)$ to find amount or principal.
4. Compute ordinary or exact interest using ordinary or exact time.
5. Predict how a given change in rate or time will affect the amount of interest.
6. Apply the 6%, 60-day method of interest calculation.
7. Given information about a simple interest note, use any of the above formulas required to compute the unknown
   a. Interest,
   b. Maturity value,
   c. Rate,
   d. Time, or
   e. Principal.
8. Compute present value of a simple interest note, either
   a. On the original day, or
   b. On some other given day prior to maturity.

The borrowing and lending of money is a practice which dates far back into history. Never, however, has the practice of finance been more widespread than it is today. Money may be loaned at a simple interest or a simple discount rate. The loan may be repaid in a single payment or a series of payments, depending upon the type of loan. When money is invested with a financial institution, compound interest is usually earned on the deposits. The following chapters explain the basic types of loans, important methods of loan repayment, and fundamental investment procedures.

1. BASIC SIMPLE INTEREST

Persons who rent buildings or equipment expect to pay for the use of someone else's property. Similarly, those who borrow money must pay rent for the use of that money. Rent paid for the privilege of borrowing another's money is called *interest*. The amount of money that was borrowed is the *principal* of a loan.

A certain percentage of the principal is charged as interest. The per cent or *rate* is quoted on a yearly (per annum) basis, unless otherwise specified. The *time* is the number of days, months, or years for which the money will be loaned. (In order to make rate and time correspond, time is always converted to years, since rate is always given on a yearly basis.) When simple interest is being charged, interest is calculated on the whole principal for the entire length of the loan. Simple interest is found using the formula

$$I = Prt$$

where I = interest, P = principal, r = rate, and t = time. The *amount* due at the end of the loan (also called *maturity value*) is the sum of the principal plus the interest. This is expressed by the formula

$$S = P + I$$

where S = amount (or maturity value or sum), P = principal, and I = interest.

A loan of $600 is made at 4% for 7 months. Find (a) the interest, and (b) the maturity value on this loan.

Example One

(a) $P = \$600$

$$r = 4\% = 0.04 \quad \text{or} \quad \frac{4}{100}$$

$$t = 7 \text{ mos.*} = \frac{7}{12} \text{ yr.}$$

$I = Prt$

$$= \$6\overset{2}{\cancel{00}} \times \frac{\cancel{4}}{\cancel{100}} \times \frac{7}{\cancel{12}}$$
$$ \overset{}{\underset{3}{}}$$

$$I = \$14$$

(b)

$$S = P + I$$
$$= \$600 + \$14$$
$$S = \$614$$

The two formulas in Example 1 can be combined, allowing the maturity value to be found in one step. Since $I = Prt$, by substitution in the formula

$$S = P + I$$
$$= P + Prt$$
$$S = P(1 + rt)$$

If the formula $S = P(1 + rt)$ is used to calculate the amount, the interest may be found by taking the difference between maturity value and principal.

Rework Example 1 using the maturity value formula $S = P(1 + rt)$.

Example Two

$P = \$600$

$r = \frac{4}{100}$

$t = \frac{7}{12}$ yr.

$$S = P(1 + rt)$$

$$= 600\left(1 + \frac{\cancel{4}}{100} \times \frac{7}{\underset{3}{\cancel{12}}}\right)$$

$$= 600\left(1 + \frac{7}{300}\right)$$

$$= 600\left(\frac{300}{300} + \frac{7}{300}\right)$$

*Keep in mind that, for periods less than one year, time must be expressed as a fraction of a year.

$$= \cancel{600}^{2}\left(\frac{\cancel{307}}{\cancel{300}}\right)$$

$$S = \$614$$

$$P + I = S$$
$$I = S - P$$
$$I = \$614 - 600$$
$$I = \$14$$

Example Three At what rate will $450 earn $18 in interest after 8 months?

$$P = \$450 \qquad\qquad I = Prt$$

$$r = ? \qquad\qquad \$18 = \$450r \times \frac{2}{3}$$

$$t = \tfrac{8}{12} = \tfrac{2}{3} \text{ yr.} \qquad 18 = \overset{150}{\cancel{450}}\left(\cancel{\frac{2}{3}}\right)r$$

$$I = \$18 \qquad\qquad 18 = 300r$$

$$r = \tfrac{18}{300} \quad \text{ or } \quad \tfrac{6}{100} \quad \text{ or } \quad 0.06$$

$$r = 6\%$$

Example Four How long will it take for $240 to amount to $245 at a simple interest rate of 5%?

This problem may be worked using the maturity value formula $S = P(1 + rt)$. However, the simple interest formula $I = Prt$ is easier to work with and should be used whenever possible. The student should notice that the formula $I = Prt$ may be used to find a missing variable whenever the *interest* is given or can be found quickly.

In this case, the interest may be computed easily, since

$$I = S - P \qquad\qquad I = Prt$$

$$= \$245 - \$240 \qquad \$5 = \$2.40\left(\frac{5}{100}\right)t$$

$$I = \$5 \qquad\qquad\qquad 5 = 12t$$

$$P = \$240 \qquad\qquad\qquad \tfrac{5}{12} = t$$

$$r = 5\% = \tfrac{5}{100} \qquad\qquad t = \tfrac{5}{12} \text{ yr.} \quad \text{ or } \quad 5 \text{ months}$$

$$t = ?$$

Example Five What principal would have a maturity value of $309 in 9 months if the interest rate is 4%?

In this problem the interest is not given and is impossible to determine because the maturity value and principal are not both known. Thus the amount formula $S = P(1 + rt)$ must be used to find the principal.

$P = ?$

$r = 4\% = \frac{4}{100}$

$t = \frac{9}{12}$ or $\frac{3}{4}$ yr.

$S = \$309$

$S = P(1 + rt)$

$\$309 = P\left(1 + \dfrac{\cancel{4}}{100} \times \dfrac{3}{\cancel{4}}\right)$

$\$309 = P\left(\dfrac{100}{100} + \dfrac{3}{100}\right)$

$\$309 = P\left(\dfrac{103}{100}\right)$

$\dfrac{100}{\cancel{103}} \times \cancel{309}^{\,3} = P\left(\dfrac{\cancel{103}}{\cancel{100}}\dfrac{\cancel{100}}{\cancel{103}}\right)$

$\$300 = P$

PROBLEMS

Find the interest and amount—

1. (a) $600 at 5% for 1 year
   (b) $600 at 5% for 6 months
   (c) $360 at 6% for 7 months
   (d) $450 at 7½% for 4 months
   (e) $760 at 7% for 9 months

2. (a) $400 at 6% for 6 months
   (b) $400 at 3% for 6 months
   (c) $630 at 4% for 9 months
   (d) $840 at 6½% for 7 months
   (e) $540 at 8% for 3 months

3. Find the interest and amount of parts (a), (c), and (e) in Problem 1, using the maturity value formula $S = P(1 + rt)$.

4. Using the amount formula $S = P(1 + rt)$, find both interest and amount of parts (a), (c), and (e) of Problem 2.

5. What is the interest rate if $36.40 interest is due on a $780 loan after 8 months?

6. What was the interest rate if the interest due on a 10-month loan of $780 was $32.50?

7. How long will it take for $800 to amount to $824 at a 6% interest rate?

8. How long would it take for a loan of $1,200 at 7% to acquire a maturity value of $1,270?

9. If $600 is worth $613 after 4 months, what interest rate was charged?

10. If $600 is worth $609 after 4 months, what was the interest rate?

11. What principal will have a maturity value of $1,270 after 10 months at 7%?

12. What principal will amount to $832 after 8 months at 6%?

13. At what simple interest rate will an investment double itself in 12 years? (Hint: Choose any principal; what is the interest after 12 years?)

14. How long would it take for an investment to double at 6% simple interest?

2. ORDINARY TIME AND EXACT TIME

The problems given in Section 1 were limited to those with time periods of even months or years. This is not always the case, as many loans are made for a certain number of days. Suppose a loan is made on July 5 for 60 days: Do we consider 60 days to be two months and consider the loan due on September 5, or do we take the 60 days literally and consider the amount due on September 3? Suppose this loan made on July 5 is for a time of two months: would we consider the time to be $\frac{2}{12} = \frac{1}{6}$ year or should we use the actual 62 days between July 5 and September 5? The answers to these questions depend upon whether ordinary time or exact time is being used.

When *ordinary time* is being used, each month is considered to have 30 days. Thus any five-month period would be considered as $5 \times 30 = 150$ days. Similarly, 90 days would be considered as three months. In actual practice, however, ordinary time is seldom used, as we shall see later.

If *exact time* is being used, the specific number of days within the time period is calculated. Thus 90 days would usually be slightly less than three months. Exact time may be calculated most conveniently using Table XII: The Number of Each Day of the Year (p. 519). In this table, each day of the year is listed in consecutive order and assigned a number from 1 to 365. The following examples demonstrate use of the table.

Example One Using exact time, find (a) the due date of a loan made March 12 for 180 days, and (b) the time between February 24 and October 9.

(a) From the table of each day of the year, we see that March 12 is the 71st day. Thus

$$
\begin{array}{r}
\text{March 12} = \quad 71 \text{ day} \\
+ \ 180 \text{ days} \\
\hline
251\text{st day}
\end{array}
$$

The 251st day is September 8; thus the note is due on September 8, using exact time.

(b) From February 24 to October 9:

$$\begin{array}{rl} \text{October 9} = & 282 \text{ day} \\ \text{February 24} = & -55 \text{ day} \\ \hline & 227 \text{ days} \end{array}$$

There are 227 days between February 24 and October 9, using exact time.

A loan is made on April 15 for four months. Find (a) the due date and (b) the number of days in the term of the loan using both ordinary and exact time.

Example Two

(a) Four months after April 15 is August 15. The amount will be due on August 15 regardless of which kind of time is used.*

(b) From April to August 15:

Ordinary time

4 months = 4 × 30   or   120 days between April 15 and August 15.

Exact time

$$\begin{array}{rl} \text{August 15} = & 227 \text{ day} \\ \text{April 15} = & 105 \text{ day} \\ \hline & 122 \text{ days} \end{array}$$

There are 122 exact days between April 15 and August 15.

Sometimes the time period of a loan includes a leap year. This does not affect the calculation of ordinary time, of course, since all months are considered to have 30 days. The leap year must be given consideration, however, when exact time is being used. During a leap year, February 29 becomes the 60th day of the year; thus, from March 1 on, the number of each day is one greater than is shown in the table. That is, during a leap year, March 15 is the 75th day instead of the 74th as the table shows. This change in the number of the day must be made before the exact time is calculated.

A simple test allows one to determine whether any given year is a leap year: Leap year always falls on a year evenly divisible by the num-

---

*Note: If the given number of months ends on a day which does not exist, the due date would be the last day of the month. For example, a loan made on March 31 for eight months would be due on November 30, since there is no November 31.

ber 4. That is, 1972 is divisible by 4; so 1972 was a leap year. The year 1975 is not divisible by 4; thus 1975 is not a leap year. Presidential election years also fall on leap years.

Example Three

Find the exact time between January 16, 1972, and May 7, 1972.

Since 1972 is a leap year, May 7 is the 128th day.

$$
\begin{array}{rcl}
\text{May 7} & = & 128 \text{ day} \\
\text{January 16} & = & \underline{16 \text{ day}} \\
& & 112 \text{ days}
\end{array}
$$

There are 112 days between January 16, 1972, and May 7, 1972.

Example Four

Find the exact time between November 16 of one year and April 3 of the next.

We must find the remaining days in the present year and then add the days in the following year.

$$
\begin{array}{rcl}
\text{Present Year} & = & 365 \text{ days} \\
-\text{November 16} & = & \underline{320 \text{ day}} \\
& & 45 \text{ days remaining in present year} \\
+ \text{ April 3} & = & \underline{93 \text{ day}} \\
& & 138 \text{ days}
\end{array}
$$

There are 138 exact days between November 16 and April 3.

PROBLEMS

Find the exact time from the first date to the second date—

1. (a) March 4 to October 23
    (b) June 10 to November 21
    (c) April 19 to August 5
    (d) July 29 to November 12
    (e) February 11, 1972 to May 18, 1972
    (f) January 10, 1980 to September 3, 1980
    (g) July 4, 1973 to February 15, 1974
    (h) October 14, 1975 to May 25, 1976

2. (a) March 15 to November 26
    (b) January 4 to April 19
    (c) May 26 to October 17
    (d) August 16 to December 1
    (e) January 16, 1972 to May 20, 1972
    (f) February 20, 1980 to April 8, 1980
    (g) September 12, 1973 to January 30, 1974
    (h) November 23, 1975 to March 17, 1976

Determine the due date, using both ordinary and exact time—

3. (a) 30 days after August 25
   (b) 90 days after April 10
   (c) 150 days after June 3

4. (a) 60 days after August 13
   (b) 180 days after June 10
   (c) 120 days after July 23

Find the due date and both the ordinary and exact times (in days) for loans made on the given dates—

5. (a) September 15 for 3 months
   (b) May 19 for 6 months
   (c) February 16, 1972, for 9 months
   (d) January 8, 1973, for 8 months
   (e) June 10, 1974, for 10 months

6. (a) April 24 for 5 months
   (b) January 17 for 7 months
   (c) February 20, 1976, for 6 months
   (d) January 31, 1973, for 3 months
   (e) October 25, 1977, for 4 months

3. ORDINARY INTEREST AND EXACT INTEREST

It has been seen that the time of a loan is frequently a certain number of days. As stated previously, a time of less than one year must be expressed as a fraction of a year. The question then arises: When converting days to fractional years, are the days placed over a denominator of 360 or 365? It is this question that ordinary and exact interest is concerned with.

Just as ordinary time indicated 30 days per month, *ordinary interest* indicates 360 days per year. Similarly, *exact interest* indicates 365 days per year. (A 366-day year is never used, even for leap year.)

We have now discussed two ways of determining time and two types of interest. There are four possible combinations of these to obtain t for the interest formula:

1. Ordinary time over ordinary interest: $t = \dfrac{\text{Approximate days}}{360}$

2. Ordinary time over exact interest: $t = \dfrac{\text{Approximate days}}{365}$

3. Exact time over ordinary interest: $t = \dfrac{\text{Exact days}}{360}$

4. Exact time over exact interest: $t = \dfrac{\text{Exact days}}{365}$

Example One
On $730 at 6% for 144 days, compute (a) the ordinary interest, and (b) the exact interest.

(a) $P = \$730$

$r = \frac{6}{100}$

$t = \frac{144}{360}$ or $\frac{2}{5}$

$I = Prt$

$= \$\cancel{730} \times \dfrac{\cancel{6}}{\cancel{100}} \times \dfrac{2}{\cancel{5}}$ (with 1.46 over 730)

$I = \$17.52$

(b) $P = \$730$

$r = \frac{6}{100}$

$t = \frac{144}{365}$

$I = Prt$

$= \$\cancel{730} \times \dfrac{\cancel{6}}{\cancel{100}} \times \dfrac{1.44}{365}$ (with 2 over 730)

$I = \$17.28$

Example Two
A three-month loan of $720 with interest at 5% is originated on June 12. Compute the interest due on the loan using (a) ordinary time, and (b) exact time. (Use ordinary interest—360-day year—for both examples.)

(a) Three months using ordinary time is 90 days:

$P = \$720$

$r = \frac{5}{100}$

$t = \frac{90}{360}$ or $\frac{1}{4}$

$I = Prt$

$= \$\cancel{720} \times \dfrac{\cancel{5}}{\cancel{100}} \times \dfrac{1}{\cancel{4}}$ (with 1.80 over 720)

$I = \$9.00$

(b) Three months after June 12 is September 12:

$$\begin{aligned} \text{September 12} &= 255 \text{ day} \\ \text{June 12} &= 163 \text{ day} \\ \hline &\quad 92 \text{ days} \end{aligned}$$

$P = \$720$

$r = \frac{5}{100}$

$t = \frac{92}{360}$

$I = Prt$

$= \$\cancel{720} \times \dfrac{\cancel{5}}{\cancel{100}} \times \dfrac{\cancel{92}}{\cancel{360}}$ (with 2 over 720)

$I = \$9.20$

Example 1 showed that for the same number of days, *ordinary interest* (360-day year) results in more interest due on a loan. Using ordinary interest in both cases, Example 2 demonstrated that *exact time* brings more interest on a loan. Thus, of the four possible combinations, the combination of exact time and ordinary interest results in the most interest due to the lender and is, therefore, the combination most often used.

This combination of exact time and ordinary interest (number 3 in our list) is known as the *Bankers' Rule*, a name derived from the fact that all banks generally compute their interest in this way.

Since the Bankers' Rule is the combination used most frequently by financial institutions, the student will be expected to use the Bankers' Rule at all times, unless he is given other directions or unless it is impossible to compute exact time from the information given. (For example, if a problem involves a three-month loan but no date is included, it is impossible to compute exact time; thus ordinary time would have to be used. However, if a problem states that a three-month loan began on some specific date, then the exact days during that particular three-month interval would be used.)

PROBLEMS

Find the ordinary interest and exact interest—

1. (a) on $1,460 for 90 days at 8%
   (b) on $730 for 60 days at 6%

2. (a) on $730 for 120 days at 6%
   (b) on $1,095 for 160 days at 9%

3. If $365 was loaned on July 9 for 4 months at 6%, determine the interest due by each of the four combinations of time and interest.

4. A loan of $365 was made on April 2 for 6 months at 5%. Calculate the interest on this loan using each of the four combinations of time and interest.

5. Find the ordinary interest on $900 for 183 days at each of the following interest rates—
   (a) 8%
   (b) 4%
   (c) 2%
   (d) 6%
   Observe carefully the relationships of your answers to each other.

6. Compute ordinary interest on $720 for 152 days at the following rates—
   (a) 10%
   (b) 5%
   (c) $2\frac{1}{2}$%
   (d) 7.5%
   Study your answers carefully.

7. Find the ordinary interest on a $1,200 loan at 7% for each of the following time periods—
   (a) 120 days
   (b) 60 days
   (c) 30 days
   (d) 180 days
   Notice the relationship between the change in time and the change in interest due.

8. Compute the interest on a $600 loan at 4% for each of the given time periods—
    (a)   90 days
    (b)   45 days
    (c)   30 days
    (d)   120 days
    Observe carefully the relationship between time and interest due.

9. The ordinary interest on a loan for a certain number of days at 4% was $12.60. Using what you learned in Problem 5, compute the ordinary interest on this loan for the same time at—
    (a)   2%
    (b)   6%
    (c)   3%

10. The ordinary interest on a sum of money for a certain number of days at 6% was $6.40. Applying what you discovered in Problem 6, find the ordinary interest on this sum for the same number of days at—
    (a)   3%
    (b)   9%
    (c)   4.5%

11. When interest was computed at a certain rate, the interest due on a 180-day loan was $18.30. Using your conclusions from Problem 7, find the interest due on the same principal and at the same rate if the time were—
    (a)   90 days
    (b)   120 days
    (c)   270 days

12. Interest of $9.30 was due on a 150-day loan at a certain rate. Applying what you learned in Problem 8, compute the interest on the same principal and at the same rate, if the time was—
    (a)   50 days
    (b)   120 days
    (c)   180 days

4. THE 6%, 60-DAY METHOD

The 6%, 60-day method is actually a shortcut for computing interest which can be used quite frequently. To illustrate, consider the following examples:

Example One   Find the interest on $430 at 6% for 60 days.

$$P = \$430 \qquad\qquad I = Prt$$

$$r = \tfrac{6}{100} \qquad\qquad = \$4.30 \times \frac{6}{100} \times \frac{1}{6}$$

$$t = \tfrac{60}{360} = \tfrac{1}{6} \qquad\qquad I = \$4.30$$

When the time of a loan is 60 days and the interest rate is 6%, the time and rate will always cancel each other; thus the interest will always be exactly $\frac{1}{100}$ or 1% of the principal. The interest on a 6%, 60-day loan can therefore be calculated very quickly by mentally moving the decimal point of the principal two places to the left.

Find the interest on $430 at 6% for 60 days, using the 6%, 60-day method: **Example Two**

1. The interest at 6% for 60 days is 1% of the principal.
2. 1% of $430 = $4.30 interest.

The problems in Section 3 pointed out that, if the interest rate is halved, the interest will be cut in half. The same is true of time: if time is reduced to one-third as long, the interest will be only one-third as much. These facts are also employed as part of the 6%, 60-day method.

(a) Find the interest on $300 at 3% for 60 days. **Example Three**
    Interest at 6% for 60 days is $I_{6-60} = \$3.00$.
    Since 3% is $\frac{3}{6} = \frac{1}{2}$ of 6%, the interest due is

$$\tfrac{1}{2}(\$3.00) = \$1.50$$

(b) Find the interest on $400 at 6% for 90 days.

$$I_{6-60} = \$4.00$$

Since 90 days is $\frac{90}{60} = \frac{3}{2}$ of 60 days, the interest due is

$$\tfrac{3}{2}(\$4.00) = \$6.00$$

(c) Find the interest on $560 at 4.5% for 120 days.

$$I_{6-60} = \$5.60$$

$$4.5\% = \frac{4.5}{6} = \frac{4.5}{6.0} = \frac{45}{60} = \frac{3}{4}$$

$$120 \text{ days} = \frac{120}{60} = 2$$

$$\left(\frac{3}{\cancel{4}}\right)\left(\frac{\cancel{2}}{1}\right)(\$\cancel{5.60}) = \$8.40$$

PROBLEMS

Use the 6%, 60-day method to find the interest, and also find the amount on each of the following:

	Principal	Rate	Time
1.	$ 535	6%	60 da.
2.	1,850	6	60
3.	680	3	60
4.	1,200	4	60
5.	640	6	45
6.	750	6	30
7.	350	6	108
8.	380	6	180
9.	540	4	75
10.	450	8	20
11.	1,665	8	40
12.	600	4	30
13.	600	5	150
14.	360	9	45
15.	596	4.5	120
16.	436	7	90
17.	1,275	9	48
18.	780	7.5	80
19.	764.36	8	45
20.	664.73	4	90
21.	339.24	4.5	80
22.	206.25	7.5	48

5. SIMPLE INTEREST NOTES

When a person borrows money, he usually signs a written promise to repay the loan; this document is called a *promissory note*, or just a *note*. The quantity of money that appears on a note is the *face value* of the note. If an interest rate is mentioned in the note, the face value of this simple interest note is the principal of the loan. Interest is computed on the whole principal for the entire length of the loan, and the *maturity value* (principal plus interest) is repaid in a single payment on the *due date* (or maturity date) stated in the note. If no interest is mentioned, the face value is the maturity value of the note. The person who borrows the money is called the *maker* of the note, and the one to whom the money will be repaid is known as the *payee*.

The use of simple interest notes varies from state to state; the banks in some states issue simple interest notes, whereas others normally use another type of note. Figure 15-1 shows a simple-interest bank note. (The face value of this note is $500. Notice that the maturity value ($510) is entered in the margin for the bank's convenience.) Notes between individuals are usually simple interest notes also.

NAME George D. Rogers   DUE DATE Oct. 5 NO. 08335 $510.00

PRIN $500

INT $10

INS X

Austin, Texas, _____ July 7 _____, 19 —

ON DEMAND, or if no demand is made, then ____ 90 days ____ after date, without grace, for value received, I, we, and each of us, as principals, promise to pay to the order of NORTH AUSTIN STATE BANK, at Austin, Texas, the sum of ____ Five hundred and no/100 _____DOLLARS, with a FINANCE CHARGE of $10 which is an ANNUAL PERCENTAGE RATE of ____ 8 ____% from ____ July 7 ____ until maturity, and if not then paid, at the rate of 10% per annum until paid.

In the event of default in the payment of this note, when due, or in the performance of any agreement contained in the security agreement if any is taken to secure payment hereof, or in the event the holder deems itself insecure, then the holder of this note shall have the option, without demand or notice, to declare the principal and interest at once due and payable and to exercise any and all other rights or remedies provided in this note and in the security agreement, if any, including the right to set off against this note and all other liabilities of the undersigned to the holder, all money or other property in its possession held for or owed to the undersigned.

Each maker, surety, endorser, and guarantor of this note hereby waives presentment for payment or acceptance, notice of non-payment or dishonor, protest, notice of protest, and diligence in the collection hereof or in filing suit hereon and agrees that liability for the payment hereof shall not be affected or impaired by any release of or change in the security, if any, or by any extension in the time for payment; and further agrees to pay all costs and expenses of collection incurred by the holder, and if this note is placed in the hands of an attorney for collection after maturity, or is collected by legal proceedings of any kind, to pay a reasonable attorney's fee, which shall not in any event be less than the sum of $50.00 and shall bear interest at the rate of 10% per annum from the date of its accrual.

Payment of this note is secured by all money or other property of the undersigned now or at any time hereafter in the possession of the holder in any capacity and also

by _____

INSURANCE AGREEMENT

CREDIT LIFE INSURANCE is not required to obtain this loan. No charge is made for credit insurance and no credit insurance is provided unless the borrower checks the appropriate statement below:

(a) The cost for Credit Life Insurance alone will be $_____ for the term of credit.

☐ I desire Credit Life Insurance.
☒ I do not desire Credit Life Insurance.

Signature for Insurance Acknowledgment

Date _____   _George D. Rogers_

Address 4206 Running Brook Lane

Phone: Bus. 472-8911   Res. _____

Age ____ Filing Fee ____ CO-SIGNERS ARE EXPECTED TO PAY IN THE EVENT THE BORROWER DOES NOT.

FIGURE 15-1: INTEREST-BEARING PROMISSORY NOTE

Another use is that of a customer giving a creditor a note and promising to pay his account on a specified date, either with or without interest. Figure 15-2 illustrates a customer's promise to pay without interest.

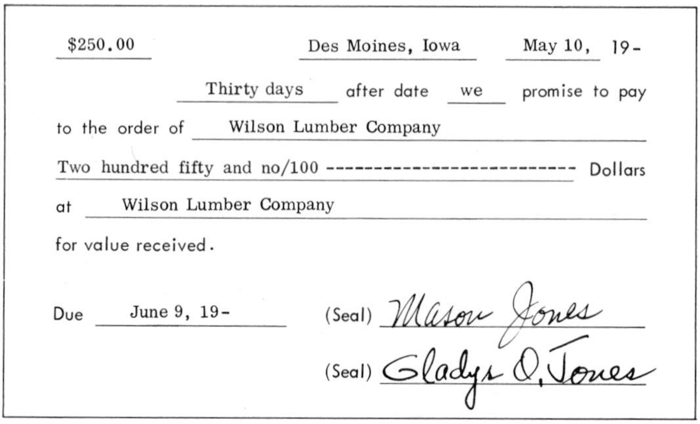
$250.00 Des Moines, Iowa May 10, 19-

Thirty days after date we promise to pay

to the order of Wilson Lumber Company

Two hundred fifty and no/100 ------------------------ Dollars

at Wilson Lumber Company

for value received.

Due June 9, 19- (Seal) Mason Jones

(Seal) Gladys O. Jones

FIGURE 15-2: NON-INTEREST-BEARING PROMISSORY NOTE

Before loaning money, a bank may require the borrower to provide *collateral*—some item of value which is used to secure the note. Thus, if the loan is not repaid, the bank is entitled to obtain its money by selling the collateral. (Any excess funds above the amount owed would be returned to the borrower.) Some items commonly used as collateral are cars, real estate, insurance policies, stocks and bonds, as well as savings accounts. Figure 15-3 illustrates a simple interest note in which a savings account is the collateral.

Most promissory notes are short-term notes—for one year or less. In many localities, short-term loans from banks are almost exclusively either installment loans or simple discount loans. For an installment loan, the maturity value is calculated as for a simple interest loan; however, this amount is repaid in weekly or monthly payments rather than being repaid in one lump sum, as is the case for simple interest notes. (The simple discount loan and the installment loan are both discussed in detail in later topics.)

Example One A $420 three-month note, dated August 3, was repaid on the due date with interest at 6%. Find (a) the due date, and (b) the amount repaid.

(a) The due date is November 3.

(b) Using the Bankers' Rule,

DATE	**CREDITS**	**BALANCE**

DUE Oct. 13   **No.** 10411   **$** 1,242.00

COLLATERAL NOTE

Austin, Texas, _____ April 16 _____ 19--

ON DEMAND, or if no demand be made, then _____ 180 days _____ after date, without grace, for value received, the undersigned (including all makers, endorsers, sureties, and guarantors) promise(s) to pay to the order of NORTH AUSTIN STATE BANK, at Austin, Texas

the sum of $ 1,200.00 with a FINANCE CHARGE of 342.00 which is an ANNUAL PERCENTAGE RATE OF 7% from April 16 until maturity, and if not then paid, at the rate of 10% per annum until paid.

The undersigned has pledged and deposited herewith as collateral security for the payment of this and any other liability or liabilities, joint or several, contingent or absolute, to the holder hereof, now due or to become due or that may hereafter be contracted or incurred, and hereby creates in favor of holder, a security interest in the following property, including all income and all cash, stock, and other dividends paid thereon, all securities received in addition thereto or in exchange therefor, and all rights to subscribe for securities incident to such property, hereinafter called collateral:

Savings account #42-6749

INSURANCE AGREEMENT

CREDIT LIFE INSURANCE is not required to obtain this loan. No charge is made for credit insurance and no credit insurance is provided unless the borrower checks the appropriate statement below:

    (a) The cost for Credit Life Insurance alone will be $_____ for the term of credit.
    ☐ I desire Credit Life Insurance.
    ☒ I do not desire Credit Life Insurance.

_____ Date _____   Signature for Insurance Acknowledgment

Also hereby giving to, and creating in favor of, the holder hereof a security interest for the amount of all of the aforesaid liabilities, in any other property, securities, or moneys of the undersigned, which may at any time be delivered to, or be in the possession of, the holder hereof, and authorizing said holder at holder's option at any time to apply to the payment of any of said liabilities any and all moneys now or hereafter in the hands of said holder on deposit, or otherwise, belonging to the undersigned, whether such liability or liabilities be then due or not, as hereinafter provided; with the further right in holder hereof, whenever in the opinion of the holder either the market value or the actual value of the collateral shall be or become insufficient to provide an ample margin of security, to call for additional security, and the undersigned agrees to deposit such additional security within such time as may be specified in said call. The surrender of this note, upon payment or otherwise, shall not affect the right of the holder to retain the collateral for any other liability of the undersigned to the holder.

The holder shall be deemed to have exercised reasonable care with respect to the collateral if it takes such action for that purpose as the undersigned shall reasonably request in writing; but no omission to do any act not requested by the undersigned shall be deemed a failure to exercise reasonable care, and no omission to comply with a request of the undersigned shall of itself be deemed a failure to exercise reasonable care. The undersigned shall take all steps necessary to preserve rights against prior parties to instruments or chattel paper constituting the collateral and shall be responsible generally for its preservation. The holder, or its nominee, need not collect interest on or principal of any collateral or give any notice with respect thereto.

All liabilities of the undersigned shall at the option of the holder, on the happening of any of the following events, each of which shall constitute a default hereunder, become immediately due and payable without notice or demand:

    (a) The failure of the undersigned to perform any agreement hereunder, or to pay any liability above mentioned, or the interest due and owing thereon;
    (b) The entry of a judgment against, or the issuance of any attachment or garnishment against, or the filing of any lien against any property of, the undersigned;
    (c) The taking of possession of any substantial part of the property of the undersigned at the instance of any governmental authority or anyone else;
    (d) The death, dissolution, termination of existence, insolvency, assignment for the benefit of creditors, or the commencement of any bankruptcy, reorganization, receivership, or insolvency proceedings of, by or against any of the undersigned;
    (e) The determination by holder that a material adverse change has occurred in the financial condition of the undersigned;
    (f) The assignment by the undersigned of any equity in any of the collateral without the written consent of the holder;
    (g) The failure of the undersigned to deposit additional collateral when called for hereunder;
    (h) The failure to pay when due any premium on any life insurance policy held as collateral, or upon any other default in the terms of such policy of life insurance or under the terms of any assignment thereof.

Upon the occurrence of any default hereunder, the holder of this note shall have the authority:

    (a) To declare all other of the undersigned's liabilities immediately due and payable;
    (b) To exercise any and all other rights and remedies provided by the Uniform Commercial Code of Texas, or any other applicable law; and,
    (c) To set off against this note, and all other liabilities of each of the undersigned to the holder, all money owed by the holder in any capacity to each of the undersigned; and the holder shall be deemed to have exercised such right of set off and to have made a charge against any such money immediately upon occurrence of such default, even though such charges are made or entered on the books of the holder subsequent thereto.

The holder shall have, without being limited to, the following rights, each of which may be exercised at any time:

    (a) To pledge and transfer this note and the collateral securing the same, and any pledge or transferee shall have all rights of the holder hereunder, and the holder shall be thereafter relieved from any liability with respect to any collateral so pledged to transferee;
    (b) To transfer the whole or any part of the collateral into the name of itself or its nominee;
    (c) To vote the collateral;
    (d) To notify the obligors of any collateral to make payment to the holder of any amount due thereon;
    (e) To take control of any proceeds of collateral.

All costs to obtain, preserve, and enforce this note, and to maintain and preserve the collateral, including a reasonable attorney's fee, which shall not in any event be less than $50.00 and shall bear interest at the rate of 10% per annum from the date of its accrual, and the expenses incurred by the holder shall become part of the liability secured hereby; and in the event of a deficiency, after application of the proceeds of the collateral to the liabilities secured hereby, borrower shall be liable therefor and shall pay the same to the holder upon demand.

It is understood and agreed that this note has been entered into under and pursuant to the Uniform Commercial Code of Texas, and that the holder hereof has all rights and remedies of a secured party thereunder. If any provision hereof shall, for any reason, be held invalid or unenforceable, such invalidity or unenforceability shall not affect any other provision hereof, but this note shall be construed as if such invalid or unenforceable provision had never been contained therein.

All of the foregoing promises are the joint and several promises of the undersigned and shall bind the undersigned, its respective heirs, personal representatives, successors and assigns. Each maker, surety, endorser, and guarantor of this note, hereby waives presentment for payment or acceptance, notice of non-payment or dishonor, protest, notice of protest and diligence in the collection thereof, or in filing suit hereon, and agrees that liability for the payment hereof shall not be affected or impaired by any release of or change in the security or by any extension of time for payment.

ADDRESS 7808 Silverlake Drive   _James J. Wasson_

PHONE: BUS. _____ RES. 345-7741   _Karen R. Wasson_

FILING FEE _____ AGE _____

FIGURE 15-3: INTEREST-BEARING PROMISSORY NOTE WITH COLLATERAL

$$\begin{aligned}
\text{November 3} &= 307 \\
\text{August 3} &= \underline{215} \\
t &= 92 \text{ da.} \qquad \text{or} \qquad \tfrac{92}{360} \\
r &= 6\% \\
P &= \$420
\end{aligned}$$

$$I = Prt$$

$$= \$4\cancel{20} \times \frac{\cancel{6}}{\cancel{100}} \times \frac{92}{\cancel{360}}_{60}$$

$$\overset{.07}{}$$

$$I = \$6.44$$

$$S = P + I$$

$$= \$420 + \$6.44$$

$$S = \$426.44$$

Example Two The maturity value of a 90-day simple interest note is $648. If interest of 5% was charged, what was the face value of the note?

$$S = \$648 \qquad\qquad S = P(1 + rt)$$

$$r = \tfrac{5}{100} \qquad\qquad \$648 = P\left(1 + \frac{5}{100} \times \frac{1}{4}\right)$$

$$t = \tfrac{90}{360} \text{ or } \tfrac{1}{4} \qquad 648 = P\left(1 + \frac{5}{400}\right)$$

$$P = ? \qquad\qquad 648 = P\left(\frac{405}{400}\right)$$

$$\left(\frac{400}{405}\right)648 = P\left(\frac{\cancel{405}}{\cancel{400}}\right)\left(\frac{\cancel{400}}{\cancel{405}}\right)$$

$$\$640 = P$$

Example Three A $720 note at 7% interest had a maturity value of $737.64. What was the time of the note?

$$S = \$737.64 \qquad\qquad I = Prt$$

$$P = \underline{720.64} \qquad \$17.64 = \$7.20 \times \frac{7}{\cancel{100}} \times t$$

$$I = \$17.64$$

$$r = \tfrac{7}{100} \qquad\qquad 17.64 = 50.4t$$

$$t = ? \qquad\qquad 0.35 \text{ yr.} = t$$

$$t = .35 \text{ yr.} \times 360 \text{ days per yr.}$$

$$t = 126 \text{ days}$$

Remember: The Bankers' Rule should be used in all cases where it is possible to do so. The 6%, 60-day method may also be used wherever it is convenient.

PROBLEMS

1. Identify each part of the first note (Figure 15-1) shown above—
   (a) face value   (f) principal
   (b) maker   (g) rate
   (c) payee   (h) time
   (d) date   (i) interest
   (e) due date   (j) maturity value

2. Identify each part of the third note (Figure 15-3) shown above—
   (a) face value   (f) principal
   (b) maker   (g) rate
   (c) payee   (h) time
   (d) date   (i) interest
   (e) due date   (j) maturity value

Compile the missing information:

	Principal	Rate	Date	Due Date	Time	Interest	Maturity Value
3. (a)	$780	6%	4/8	10/5			
(b)	450	4	7/15		123 da.		
(c)	720	5	1/30		8 mos.		
(d)		8		8/20	144 da.	$48	
4. (a)	$600	4%	3/27	8/24			
(b)	480	6	4/17		6 mos.		
(c)	288	5	10/23		61 da.		
(d)		4.5		9/23	140 da.	$7	

5. A note dated February 25, 1973, calls for payment on July 25, 1973. Find the interest and the amount due, if the principal is $480 and the interest is at 7%.

6. A note dated May 15, 1973, reads: "Three months from date, I promise to pay $450 with interest at 8%." What will be the interest on the note and the maturity value?

7. A note dated March 1, 1972, reads: "Nine months from date, I promise to pay $300 with interest at 6%." Find the maturity value.

8. A note dated January 20, 1972, is due on April 9, 1972, with interest at 7%. If the principal is $270, what amount will be due?

9. A six-month note is drawn for $270 with interest at 5%. What amount will be due on the maturity date?

10. Find the maturity value of a 4%, 7-month note with a face value of $720.

11. A note dated January 15 was due on May 15. If the face value of the note

was $375 and interest of $10 was required, what interest rate was charged?

12. Find the interest rate charged if $307.50 was paid on October 17, 1966, to cancel a $300 debt incurred on April 20, 1966.

13. How much time is required for $500 to earn $14 interest at 7% interest?

14. How long will it take $400 to earn $10 at 6% interest?

15. How long will it take $800 to amount to $842 at 9% interest?

16. What time is required for $300 to amount to $304.50 at 5% interest?

17. A ten-month note dated February 1 has interest at 8%. If the interest due is $30.30, what was the face value of the note?

18. The interest on a 183-day note is $12.81. If interest was computed at 6%, find the principal of the note.

19. If $545.49 is paid on June 17, 1972, to discharge a note dated April 17, 1972, find the face value of the 6% note.

20. A six-month note dated May 5, 1973, is discharged on the due date by a payment of $923. What was the principal of the note, if 5% interest was charged?

6. PRESENT VALUE

In the last two problems of the previous section, we were told the maturity value of a note and asked to find what principal had been loaned. When the principal is being found, this is often referred to as finding the *present value*. Present value can also be explained by answering the question: What amount would have to be invested today (at the present) in order to obtain a given maturity value? This "X" amount that would have to be invested is the present value.

Present value at simple interest can be found using the same maturity value formula that has been used previously: $S = P(1 + rt)$. However, when present value is to be found repeatedly, the formula is usually altered slightly by dividing by the parentheses:

$$S = P(1 + rt)$$

$$\frac{S}{1 + rt} = \frac{P(1 + rt)}{(1 + rt)}$$

$$\frac{S}{1 + rt} = P$$

$$\text{or} \quad P = \frac{S}{1 + rt}$$

The formula can be used more conveniently in this form, since it is set up to solve for the principal or present value. However, Example One illustrates a present value problem solved with both versions of the formula, and either form may be used for this type of problem.

If the maturity value of a 6%, 3-month note dated March 11 was $609.20, find the present value (or principal, or face value) of the note.

Example One

$S = \$609.20$

$r = \dfrac{6}{100}$

$t = \dfrac{92}{360}$

6% – 92 da.

P = ?   S = $609.20

March 11   June 11

$$S = P(1 + rt)$$

$$\$609.20 = P\left(1 + \frac{\overset{}{\cancel{6}}}{\cancel{100}} \times \frac{\overset{.92}{\cancel{92}}}{\cancel{360}}\right)$$
$$\phantom{\$609.20 = P\left(1 + \frac{6}{100}\right)}60$$

$$\$609.20 = P\left(1 + \frac{0.92}{60}\right)$$

$$609.20 = P\left(\frac{60}{60} + \frac{0.92}{60}\right)$$

$$609.20 = P\left(\frac{60.92}{60}\right)$$

$$\left(\frac{60}{\cancel{60.92}}\right)\overset{10}{\cancel{609.20}} = P\left(\frac{\cancel{60.92}}{\cancel{60}} \times \frac{\cancel{60}}{\cancel{60.92}}\right)$$

$$\$600 = P$$

$$P = \frac{S}{1 + rt}$$

$$= \frac{\$609.20}{1 + \dfrac{\overset{}{\cancel{6}}}{\cancel{100}} \times \dfrac{\overset{.92}{\cancel{92}}}{\cancel{360}}}$$
$$\phantom{= \frac{\$609.20}{1}}60$$

$$= \frac{609.20}{\dfrac{60}{60} + \dfrac{0.92}{60}}$$

$$= \frac{609.20}{\dfrac{60.92}{60}}$$

$$= \overset{10}{\cancel{609.20}}\left(\frac{60}{\cancel{60.92}}\right)$$

$$P = \$600$$

The present value of the note is $600.

Example 1 involved only one interest rate. Many investments, however, involve two interest rates. To illustrate present value at two interest rates, consider the following case:

Suppose I find a place where I can earn 10% on my investment. The most I have been offered any other place is 6%, so I immediately invest $1,000 in this "gold mine." On the way home, I meet a friend who offers to buy this investment for the same $1,000 I just deposited. Would I sell the investment for $1,000, knowing I could not earn 10% interest on any other investment I might make? No! My $1,000 is really worth more than

$1,000 to me, because I would have to deposit more than $1,000 elsewhere in order to earn the same amount of interest.

This case demonstrates that an investment is not always worth its exact face value; it may be worth more or less than its face value, when compared to the average rate of interest being paid by most financial institutions. This typical, or average, interest rate is referred to as the "rate money is worth." Thus, if most financial institutions are paying 5%, then money is worth 5%.

If an investment is made at a rate that is not the prevailing rate money is worth, then the present value of the investment is different—either greater or less—than the principal. One must find the size of the investment that would have to be made at the rate money is worth in order to achieve a maturity value equal to the maturity value of the investment in question. The size of this "rate-money-is-worth investment" is the present or true value of the actual investment.

Example Two

A 90-day note for $1,000 is drawn on June 12 at 4%. If money is worth 6%, find the present value of this note on the day it was drawn.

The solution to this kind of problem involves two steps: (1) Find the actual *maturity value of the note*, and (2) find the *present value at the rate money is worth* of that calculated amount.

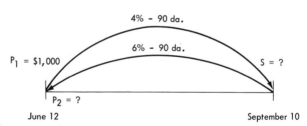

1. $P_1 = \$1,000$ $S = P(1 + rt)$

       $r = 4\%$

       $t = \frac{90}{360} = \frac{1}{4}$ $= 1,000 \left(1 + \frac{\cancel{4}}{100} \cdot \frac{1}{\cancel{4}}\right)$

       $S = ?$

                        $= 1,000 \left(\frac{101}{100}\right)$

                        $S = \$1,010$

2. $S = \$1,010$ $P = \dfrac{S}{1 + rt}$

       $r = 6\%$

       $t = \frac{90}{360} = \frac{1}{4}$ $= \dfrac{1,010}{1 + \dfrac{\cancel{6}}{100} \times \dfrac{1}{\cancel{4}}}$

       $P_2 = ?$

$$= \frac{1,010}{1 + \dfrac{3}{200}}$$

$$= \frac{1,010}{\dfrac{203}{200}}$$

$$= 1,010 \left(\frac{200}{203}\right)$$

$$P_2 = \$995.07$$

The present value of the note on the day it was drawn was $995.07. This means that the lender (payee) would have earned just as much interest on $995.07 invested elsewhere at the rate money is worth (6%) as he earned on this $1,000 note lent at only 4%. That is, the lender's $1,000 is really only worth $995.07 to him.

When one wishes to find the exact present value of an investment where two interest rates are involved, he should know beforehand whether the present value is more or less than the principal. This can be determined as follows:

Suppose an investment is made at 7% when money is worth 4%. First, consider the maturity value that would result from the same principal invested at the two rates:

Example Three

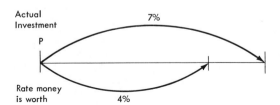

The maturity value of the 7% investment would exceed the amount of the 4% investment. Now realign the "rate-money-is-worth" arrow so that both maturity value arrows fall at the point of the *actual* maturity value:

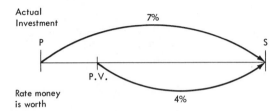

This realignment shows that, at the rate money is worth, a larger sum would have to be invested in order to obtain the same maturity value.

It also indicates that the present value of the investment is larger than the principal.

Whether the present value is greater or smaller than the principal can be determined for any investment by following the same procedure:

1. Compare the maturity values of the same principal invested at the actual rate of investment and at the rate money is worth.

2. Realign the arrow representing the rate money is worth so that it coincides with the maturity value at the actual rate given.

3. Locate the origin of the line representing the rate money is worth to determine whether the present value is more or less than the principal.

Previous examples have required finding the present value on the day a note was drawn. It is often desirable to know the worth of an investment on some day nearer the due date. The worth of an investment on any day prior to the due date is also called present value. The procedure for finding this present value is the same as that already discussed, except that in the second step the time as well as the rate will be different.

Example Four Find the (present) value on August 17 of a $720, six-month note taken out on March 16 at 5%, if money is worth 6%.

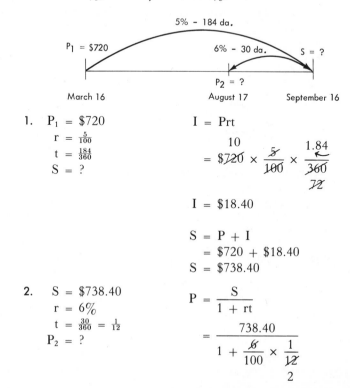

1. $P_1 = \$720$
    $r = \frac{5}{100}$
    $t = \frac{184}{360}$
    $S = ?$

    $I = Prt$

    $$= \$720 \times \frac{5}{100} \times \frac{1.84}{360}$$

    $I = \$18.40$

    $S = P + I$
    $= \$720 + \$18.40$
    $S = \$738.40$

2. $S = \$738.40$
    $r = 6\%$
    $t = \frac{30}{360} = \frac{1}{12}$
    $P_2 = ?$

    $$P = \frac{S}{1 + rt}$$

    $$= \frac{738.40}{1 + \frac{6}{100} \times \frac{1}{12}}$$

$$= \frac{738.40}{1 + \dfrac{1}{200}}$$

$$= \frac{738.40}{\dfrac{201}{200}}$$

$$= 738.40 \left(\frac{200}{201}\right)$$

$$P_2 = \$734.73$$

This means that if the note were sold on August 17, it would have to be sold for $734.73 so that the money could be invested at 6% and on September 16 the maturity value of the new investment would also be $738.40.

The difference between maturity value and present value is known as *true discount.* Stated differently, true discount is equal to the interest that would be earned on the present value if it were invested at the rate money is worth. True discount is used infrequently, however. When any discount is considered, it is usually bank discount, which will be studied in the following chapter.

Note: Any convenient method may be used to find the amount in the following problems: $I = Prt$ and $S = P + I$; the 6%, 60-day method; or $S = P(1 + rt)$.

PROBLEMS

Complete the following:

		Maturity Value	Rate	Time	Present Value
1.	(a)	$614	7%	120 da.	
	(b)	842	9	210	
2.	(a)	$820	6%	150 da.	
	(b)	357	8	90	

Complete the following, finding the present value on the day of investment:

		Principal	Rate	Time	Maturity Value	Rate Money Is Worth	Present Value
3.	(a)	$ 900	8%	60 da.		6%	
	(b)	1,000	5	180		7	
4.	(a)	$1,000	7%	72 da.		5%	
	(b)	800	3	45		6	

Find the present value on the day indicated:

		Principal	Rate	Time	Maturity Value	Rate Money Is Worth	Days Before Maturity Date	Present Value
5.	(a)	$300	6%	180 da.		9%	90 da.	
	(b)	600	8	270		5	36	
6.	(a)	$500	5%	72 da.		6%	20 da.	
	(b)	200	9	100		4	30	

7. The maturity value was $465.30 on an 8% note. If the five-month note was dated June 10, find its face value.

8. On April 12, $605 was paid in settlement of a note dated January 27. If the interest at 4% was paid, what was the principal of the note?

9. A ten-month note for $600 was drawn on January 15 at 6%. If money is worth 9%, find the present value of the note on the day it was issued.

10. On June 1, a four-month note for $450 is drawn at 4%. If money is worth 8%, find the present value of the note on the day it was drawn.

11. Determine whether present value is more or less than principal—
    (a) actual investment rate is 5%; money is worth 8%
    (b) actual investment rate is 7%; money is worth 5%
    (c) From this and previous problems: What is the correlation between the actual rate to the rate money is worth and the present value to the principal?

12. Find whether present value is greater or smaller than principal—
    (a) actual investment rate is 6%; money is worth 5%
    (b) actual investment rate is 4%; money is worth 7%
    (c) Based on your answers to this and to previous problems: How does the relationship between the actual rate and the rate money is worth compare to the relationship between present value and principal?

13. A six-month note dated March 8 is made at 5% for $720. What is the present value of the note on July 10, if money is worth 6%?

14. On April 10, a three-month note for $450 is taken out at 8%. If money is worth 5%, find the present value of the note on June 4.

15. A realtor received the following bids on a lot he was offering: $9,900 cash right now; $10,200 in four months; or $10,500 in 12 months. What is the best offer, if money is worth 6%? (Hint: Compare the present values of the three amounts.)

16. The following offers were made on a house: $16,000 cash; $16,300 in three months; or $16,500 in six months. Which offer should be accepted, if money is worth 4%?

Bank
Discount

LEARNING OBJECTIVES

Upon completion of Chapter 16, the student will be able to:

1. Define and use correctly the terminology associated with each topic.

2. a. Determine the proceeds of a simple discount note, using the simple discount formulas
   (1) $D = Sdt$, and
   (2) $p = S - D$.
   b. Also, apply $p = S(1 - dt)$ to compute
   (1) Proceeds, or
   (2) Maturity value.

3. a. Rediscount a simple discount note (or a simple interest note) on a given day prior to the maturity date.
   b. Also, determine the amount of interest made
   (1) By the original lender, and
   (2) By the second lender.

4. Compute the savings gained by signing a discount note on the last day allowed by invoice sales terms, in order to take advantage of the cash discount. (The bank note will be repaid on the same due date specified by the sales terms.)

5. Explain the similarities and differences of simple interest and discount notes.

THE PRECEDING CHAPTER discussed the simple interest note. Many banks, however, use the simple discount note for short-term loans (one year or less). There are some similarities and several major differences between the two types which it is imperative that the student understand.

1. SIMPLE DISCOUNT NOTES

The student will recall that the face value of the simple interest note was the principal of the loan. Interest was computed on this principal and added to it to obtain the maturity value.

The *face value* of a discounted note, however, is the *maturity value* that will be repaid to the payee. As in the case of the simple interest note, the maturity value is repaid in a single payment at the end of the loan.

The interest on a discounted note is called *bank discount*. Bank discount is computed on the *maturity value* (face value) of the note and is then *subtracted* from the maturity value. (As opposed to simple interest, which is computed on the *principal* and then *added* to the principal to *obtain* the maturity value.) The amount remaining after the bank discount has been subtracted from the maturity value of the note is called *proceeds*. The proceeds is the actual amount for which the borrower will receive the bank's check and which he will be able to spend. Because the bank discount is subtracted from the face value before the borrower receives his money, this is often referred to as paying "interest in advance."

To re-emphasize: the distinguishing aspect of the simple discount note is that interest is charged on the amount that is to be paid back, rather than on the amount that was actually borrowed.

Figures 16-1 and 16-2 illustrate typical simple discount notes. Figure

Int. = $20.00

$ 1,000.00 _____ March 19 _____, 19 --

_____ 90 days _____ after date, for value received and with interest discounted to maturity

at ___8___ % per annum, the undersigned promise(s) to pay

to **NORTH CAROLINA NATIONAL BANK** or Order

One thousand and no/100 --Dollars

PAYABLE AT ANY OFFICE OF THE NORTH CAROLINA NATIONAL BANK IN NORTH CAROLINA. INTEREST HEREON SHALL ACCRUE AFTER MATURITY OR DEMAND, UNTIL PAID, AT THE RATE STATED ABOVE.

The holder of this note may accelerate the due date hereof or require the pledging of collateral as security herefor, or both, at any time the holder deems itself insecure. In the event the indebtedness evidenced hereby be collected by or through an attorney at law after maturity, the holder shall be entitled to collect reasonable attorneys' fees. The Bank is hereby authorized at any time to charge against any deposit accounts of any parties hereto any and all liabilities hereunder whether due or not.

All persons bound on this obligation, whether primarily or secondarily liable as principals, sureties, guarantors, endorsers or otherwise, hereby waive the benefits of all provisions of law for stay or delay of execution or sale of property or other satisfaction of judgment against any of them on account of liability hereon until judgment be obtained and execution issued against any other of them and returned unsatisfied or until it can be shown that the maker or any other party hereto has no property available for the satisfaction of the debt evidenced by this instrument, or until any other proceedings can be had against any of them, also their right, if any, to require said Bank to hold as security for this note any collateral deposited by any of said persons as security for this demand, or any other demands. Demand, presentment, protest, notice of protest and notice of dishonor waived by all parties bound hereon. Witness my/our hand(s) and seal(s)

Address ___3016 N. Enfield Drive___ _____Charles N. Offord_____ (Seal)

Due ___June 17___ No. ___20842___ _____ (Seal)

NCNB 2151 REV 10-69

FIGURE 16-1: SIMPLE DISCOUNT NOTE

$INT = 30

$ 2,400.00   September 20   , 19--

60 days   after date, for value received and with interest discounted to maturity

at 7.5 % per annum, the undersigned promise(s) to pay

to   **NORTH CAROLINA NATIONAL BANK**   or Order

Two thousand four hundred and no/100------------------------Dollars

PAYABLE AT ANY OFFICE OF THE NORTH CAROLINA NATIONAL BANK IN NORTH CAROLINA. INTEREST HEREON SHALL ACCRUE AFTER MATURITY OR DEMAND, UNTIL PAID, AT THE RATE STATED ABOVE.

To secure the payment of this note and liabilities as herein defined, the parties hereto hereby pledge and grant to said Bank (the word "Bank" wherever used herein shall include any holder or assignee of this note) a security interest in the collateral described as follows:

10 shares - IBM stock

and any collateral added thereto or substituted therefor, including shares issued as stock dividends and stock splits and dividends representing distribution of capital assets. The Bank is hereby authorized at any time to charge against any deposit accounts of any party hereto any and all liabilities whether due or not. The Bank may declare all liabilities due at once in the event any party hereto becomes subject to any proceedings for the relief of creditors including but not limited to proceedings under the Bankruptcy Act or otherwise, or if in the judgment of Bank the collateral decreases in value so as to render Bank insecure and Bank demands additional collateral which is not furnished, or if Bank at any time otherwise deems itself insecure. In the event the indebtedness evidenced hereby or liabilities as defined herein be collected by or through an attorney at law, the holder shall be entitled to collect reasonable attorneys' fees.

Upon failure to pay any liability when due, Bank may sell the collateral at public or private sale, for cash or on credit, as a whole or in parcels, without notice, and Bank may at any such sale purchase the collateral or any part thereof for its own account, and the proceeds of any such sale shall be applied first to the costs of such sale and the expenses of collection, including reasonable attorneys' fees, and then to the outstanding balance due on said liabilities, the application to be made in the manner and proportions as Bank elects. The Bank may forbear from realizing on the collateral or any part thereof, by sale or otherwise, all as the Bank may decide, and the liabilities of the parties hereto shall not be released, discharged or in any way affected by any such forbearance, nor shall any of the parties hereto have any rights or recourse against the Bank by reason of any action the Bank may take under this note, by reason of any deterioration, waste, or loss of any of the collateral unless such deterioration, waste, or loss be caused by the willful act or willful failure to act of the Bank. Upon payment of this note the Bank may release the collateral but shall have the right to retain the same to secure any unpaid liabilities. Upon any transfer of this note and the collateral, the Bank shall be fully relieved of responsibility with reference thereto. "Liabilities" or "Liability," as herein used, shall include this note and all obligations of every kind of any party hereto in whatever capacity to Bank, now or hereafter existing, whether arising directly or acquired from others as collateral or otherwise, whether absolute or contingent, joint or several, secured or unsecured, due or not due, direct or indirect, including, but not limited to, liabilities arising by operation of law, contractual or tortious, liquidated or unliquidated or otherwise.

All persons bound on this obligation, whether primarily or secondarily liable as principals, sureties, guarantors, endorsers or otherwise, hereby waive presentment, protest, notice of dishonor and of acceleration of maturity and any right to require the Bank to retain any collateral pledged as security for this note or any other liabilities and agree that any extension of time for payment with or without notice shall not affect their joint and several liabilities.

Witness our/my hand(s) and seal(s).

John M. Somes (Seal)

Patricia L. Somes (Seal)

Address 619 Winding Way

Due November 19   No. 62275

NCNB 2185 REV. 10-69

FIGURE 16-2: COLLATERAL DISCOUNT NOTE

16-1 is an unsecured or signature note; that is, the loan is made simply on the basis of the borrower's good credit standing. Banks often establish some maximum amount which they will lend on an unsecured note. Figure 16-2 illustrates a collateral note, which requires the maker (borrower) to secure the note with some item of value.

Bank discount is computed using the formula

$$D = Sdt$$

where D = discount, S = maturity value (face value) of the discount note, d = discount rate, and t = time. As would be expected, the Bankers' Rule is used for all discount notes.

Proceeds p are then found using the formula

$$p = S - D$$

Let us consider the difference between the amount of money one would be able to spend if he borrows at a discount rate and the amount available to spend if he borrows at an interest rate.

The face values of two notes are $1,000 each. The discount rate and interest rate are both 6%, and the time of each is 60 days. **Example One**

Interest Note	Discount Note
$P = \$1,000$	$S = \$1,000$
$r = 6\%$	$d = 6\%$
$t = \frac{60}{360}$ or $\frac{1}{6}$	$t = \frac{60}{360}$ or $\frac{1}{6}$
$I = Prt$	$D = Sdt$
$= \$1,000 \times \frac{6}{100} \times \frac{1}{6}$	$= \$1,000 \times \frac{6}{100} \times \frac{1}{6}$
$I = \$10$	$D = \$10$
$S = P + I$	$p = S - D$
$= \$1,000 + \$10$	$= \$1,000 - \$10$
$S = \$1,010$	$p = \$990$

Notice that on the simple interest note, the borrower pays $10 for the use of $1,000. On the simple discount note, the borrower pays $10 for the use of only $990. Thus, for the actual amount the borrower will have available to spend, he pays more interest at a discount rate than at an interest rate. Or stated another way: the borrower is really paying slightly more than 6% on the money he actually uses, since 6% of $990 for 60 days would be only $9.90 interest due, not $10.

From this example, we can conclude that, when a borrower obtains money at a discount rate, he will always be paying somewhat more than the stated rate on the money he actually receives. In addition, the Truth in

Lending Law, enacted in 1969, enables the borrower to be more informed about the true rate he is paying. The law requires the lender to reveal both the amount of interest and the annual percentage rate charged on the money received, correct to the nearest $\frac{1}{4}\%$. Banks have available tables which enable them to determine this true rate very easily. We will not study this procedure here, but will cover Truth in Lending rates more thoroughly in Chapter 17 as part of our study of installment buying. (The difference between the stated rate and the true rate is much greater when multiple payments are involved.) However, it will be of interest here to know the true rate required under the Truth in Lending Law for the examples above. The true rate for Example One, although somewhat larger than 6%, is still 6% to the nearest $\frac{1}{4}\%$. Figure 16-3 shows the Truth in Lending disclosure statement which corresponds to the note in Figure 16-1. We see that the true annual percentage rate paid for the $980 which the borrower received is actually 8.25%. For the note in Figure 16-2, the true rate is the stated rate of 7.5%, correct to the nearest $\frac{1}{4}\%$.

The bank discount formulas given above can be combined into a single formula for finding proceeds. By substituting Sdt for D, we have

$$p = S - \underset{\downarrow}{D}$$
$$= S - Sdt$$
$$p = S(1 - dt)$$

Example Two

A $1,600 note is discounted at 5% for 108 days. Find the bank discount and proceeds using (a) D = Sdt, (b) the 6%, 60-day method, and (c) p = S(1 - dt).

$$S = \$1,600$$
$$d = \tfrac{5}{100}$$
$$t = \tfrac{108}{360} \quad \text{or} \quad \tfrac{3}{10}$$

(a)

$$D = Sdt$$

$$= \$\overset{8}{\underset{}{1\overset{16}{6\cancel{0}0}}} \times \frac{\overset{5}{\cancel{5}}}{\cancel{100}} \times \frac{3}{\underset{\underset{2}{\cancel{}}}{\cancel{10}}}$$

$$D = \$24$$

$$p = S - D$$
$$= \$1,600 - \$24$$
$$p = \$1,576$$

TRUTH IN LENDING DISCLOSURE STATEMENT
NORTH CAROLINA NATIONAL BANK
COMMERCIAL BANKING DEPARTMENT

DATE OF NOTE
March 19

BORROWER'S NAME
Charles N. Oxford

AMOUNT OF NOTE
$ 1,000.00

FINANCE CHARGES			AMOUNT FINANCED	
Interest	$ 20.00	Paid to Borrower	$ 980.00
Fees	$ --	Credit life Insurance Prem. (if any)	$ --
	$	Financing Statement Filling Fee (if any)	$ --
	$		$
Total FINANCE CHARGE	$ 20.00		$
ANNUAL PERCENTAGE RATE	8.25 %		$
Prepaid Finance Charge (if any)	$ --	TOTAL AMOUNT FINANCED	$ 980.00

No. of Payments	Due Dates or Periods	Amount of Regular Payment	Amount of Final Payment	Balloon Payment (if any)	Total of Payments
1	June 17	--	--	--	$ 1,000.00

SECURITY INTEREST IN THE FOLLOWING COLLATERAL (if applicable) _____

NOTE: The Security Agreement will secure future or other indebtedness and will cover after-acquired property.

☐ If checked, the collateral includes the principal residence of the borrower, and two (2) copies of the Notice of Right to Rescind are attached hereto.

REBATE OF UNEARNED FINANCE CHARGE IN EVENT OF PREPAYMENT: ☐ NO REBATE ☐ OTHER (specify)_____

PROPERTY INSURANCE, IF REQUIRED, MAY BE PURCHASED FROM ANY REPUTABLE INSURER SELECTED BY THE BORROWER.

ADDITIONAL INFORMATION_____

Receipt of the foregoing statement fully completed and any attachments referred to therein is hereby acknowledged.

Charles N. Oxford
Customer's Signature

CREDIT LIFE INSURANCE ELECTION (if applicable):
I understand that Credit Life insurance is not required as a condition of this loan but may be purchased at a cost of $_____ . I hereby affirm my desire to purchase such insurance.

NCNB 2260 REV. 2—70

Date _____

Customer's Signature for Credit Life Insurance _____

FIGURE 16-3: TRUTH IN LENDING DISCLOSURE STATEMENT (FOR FIGURE 16-1)

(b)

$$\text{rate} = \tfrac{5}{6}$$
$$\text{time} = \tfrac{108}{60} \quad \text{or} \quad \tfrac{9}{5}$$
$$D_{6\text{-}60} = \$16$$

$$\frac{\$\cancel{16}^{8}}{1}\left(\frac{5}{\cancel{6}}\right)\left(\frac{\cancel{9}^{3}}{5}\right)_{\cancel{2}}$$

$$D = \$24$$

$$p = S - D$$
$$= \$1{,}600 - \$24$$
$$p = \$1{,}576$$

(c)

$$p = S(1 - dt)$$
$$= 1{,}600\left(1 - \frac{\cancel{5}}{100} \times \frac{3}{\cancel{10}^{2}}\right)$$

$$= 1{,}600\left(1 - \frac{3}{200}\right)$$

$$= 1{,}600\left(\frac{200}{200} - \frac{3}{200}\right)$$

$$= \cancel{1{,}600}^{8}\left(\frac{197}{\cancel{200}}\right)$$

$$p = \$1{,}576$$

$$D = S - p$$
$$= \$1{,}600 - \$1{,}576$$
$$D = \$24$$

Although both bank discount and proceeds may be found either way, as a general rule one would probably use method (a) or (b), since the computation would be easier.

Example Three Find the proceeds on a three-month note for $720 dated July 1, if bank discount at 5% is deducted.

$$S = \$720 \qquad D = Sdt$$
$$d = \tfrac{5}{100} \qquad \quad = \$720 \times \tfrac{5}{100} \times \tfrac{92}{360}$$
$$t = \tfrac{92}{360} \qquad D = \$9.20$$

$$p = S - D$$
$$= \$720 - \$9.20$$
$$p = \$710.80$$

It was shown in Example 1 that, when interest and bank discount are equal, the borrower has less spendable money from a discounted note. In that example, however, the maturity values of the two notes were not the same. We will now consider a simple interest and a simple discount note which both have the same maturity value, and compare the amounts which the borrower would have available to spend.

Example Four

A simple interest note and a simple discount note both have a maturity value of $1,000. If the notes both had interest computed at 6% for 120 days, find (a) the principal of the simple interest note, and (b) the proceeds of the discount note.

(a) Simple Interest Note

$$S = \$1,000$$
$$r = \tfrac{6}{100}$$
$$t = \tfrac{120}{360} \quad \text{or} \quad \tfrac{1}{3}$$
$$P = ?$$

$$P = \frac{S}{1 + rt}$$

$$= \frac{\$1,000}{1 + \dfrac{\cancel{6}}{100} \times \dfrac{1}{\cancel{3}}}$$

$$= \frac{1,000}{\dfrac{100}{100} + \dfrac{2}{100}}$$

$$= \frac{1,000}{\dfrac{102}{100}}$$

$$= 1,000\left(\frac{100}{102}\right)$$

$$P = \$980.39$$

(b) Simple Discount Note

$$S = \$1,000$$
$$d = \tfrac{6}{100}$$
$$t = \tfrac{120}{360} \quad \text{or} \quad \tfrac{1}{3}$$
$$p = ?$$

$$p = S(1 - dt)$$

$$= \$1,000\left(1 - \frac{\overset{2}{\cancel{6}}}{100} \times \frac{1}{\cancel{3}}\right)$$

$$= 1,000\left(1 - \frac{2}{100}\right)$$

$$= 1,000\left(\frac{100}{100} - \frac{2}{100}\right)$$

$$= \cancel{1,000}\left(\frac{\overset{10}{98}}{\cancel{100}}\right)$$

$$p = \$980$$

In this case, the maker of the note would have 39¢ more to spend if the note were a simple interest note. If $980.39 were invested at 6% for 120 days, the maturity value would be $1,000. The $1,000 − $980.39 = $19.61 interest that would be earned is called the *true discount*. This is 39¢ less than the $20 *bank discount* charged on the simple discount note.

Example Five

The proceeds on a note discounted for 90 days were $643.50. If the face value were $650, what discount rate was charged?

$$S = \$650.00$$
$$p = \underline{643.50}$$
$$D = \$6.50$$

$$D = Sdt$$
$$\$6.50 = \$650 \times d \times \tfrac{1}{4}$$

$$\frac{6.50}{162.50} = \frac{162.50d}{162.50}$$

$$t = \tfrac{90}{360} \quad \text{or} \quad \tfrac{1}{4}$$
$$d = ?$$

$$0.04 = d$$
$$d = 4\%$$

PROBLEMS

1. Identify the parts of the first discounted note (Fig. 16-1) shown above—
    (a) face value   (f) rate
    (b) maker   (g) time
    (c) payee   (h) bank discount
    (d) date   (i) proceeds
    (e) due date   (j) maturity value

2. Identify each part of the second discounted note (Fig. 16-2) shown above—
    (a) face value   (f) rate
    (b) maker   (g) time
    (c) payee   (h) bank discount
    (d) date   (i) proceeds
    (e) due date   (j) maturity value

Complete the following:

		Maturity Value	Discount Rate	Date	Due Date	Time	Bank Discount	Proceeds
3.	(a)	$400	9%	3/18		180 da.		
	(b)	800	6	7/25		30		
	(c)	720	7.5	9/30	11/29			
	(d)	550	8		8/14	90		
4.	(a)	$800	6%	3/5	6/3			
	(b)	640	4.5	1/10		150 da.		
	(c)	300	5	7/19		120		
	(d)	450	8		12/16	60		

Use the 6%, 60-day method to find bank discount, and also find proceeds—

5. (a) $450 at 8% for 40 days
    (b) 280 at 7.5% for 72 days
    (c) 640 at 5% for 180 days

6. (a) $400 at 5.5% for 90 days
    (b) 240 at 6% for 135 days
    (c) 840 at 7% for 30 days

Complete the following:

		Maturity Value	Discount Rate	Date	Due Date	Time	Proceeds
7.	(a)	$900	8%	3/10		6 mos.	
	(b)	480	5	5/18		60 da.	
	(c)	540	6	2/25		9 mos.	
	(d)	320	9	7/8		4 mos.	
8.	(a)	$420	6%	1/14		5 mos.	
	(b)	600	7	4/19		120 da.	
	(c)	240	3	2/4		7 mos.	
	(d)	450	4	6/9		3 mos.	

9. A bank discounts notes at 7%. If a borrower signs a $400 note for 180 days, how much does he receive from the bank?

10. A borrower signs a 120-day note for $600. If the bank discounts the note at 5%, what will be the amount of the check he receives from the bank?

11. The bank discount on a note was $40. If the note had a maturity value of $1,200 and the discount rate was 8%, what was the time of the note?

12. A note had a face value of $800. When the note was discounted at 6%, the bank discount was $12. What was the time of the note?

13. The face value of a note was $640 and the proceeds were $632. What interest rate was charged on this 90-day note?

14. The proceeds of a 60-day note were $296. If the discount was computed on a maturity value of $300, what discount rate was used?

15. An eight-month note dated January 26 is discounted at 6%. If the face value is $600, what are the proceeds?

16. A note with maturity value of $900 is dated March 10 for six months. If bank discount at 4% is deducted, what are the proceeds?

17. The maturity values of two three-month notes are both $714. Compare the present value at 8% interest with the proceeds at 8% discount.

18. Two six-month notes both have maturity values of $510. Compare the present value at 4% interest with the proceeds at 4% discount.

2. MATURITY VALUE (AND REDISCOUNTING NOTES)

It often happens that the proceeds of a simple discount note are known and one wishes to find the maturity value of the note. When problems of this type are to be computed, it is customary to use an altered version of the basic discount formula $p = S(1 - dt)$. The formula is altered by dividing both sides of the equation by the expression in parentheses:

$$p = S(1 - dt)$$

$$\frac{p}{1 - dt} = \frac{S(\cancel{1} - \cancel{dt})}{(\cancel{1} - \cancel{dt})}$$

$$\frac{p}{1 - dt} = S \quad \text{or} \quad S = \frac{p}{1 - dt}$$

Thus the formula is set up to solve for the maturity value S. Example One, however, shows a problem worked by both versions of the discount formula, and either form may be used to solve the assignment problems.

Example One

The proceeds of a three-month note dated June 17 at 4% were $445.40. What is the maturity value?

$p = \$445.40$

$d = \frac{4}{100}$

$t = \frac{92}{360}$

$S = ?$

$$p = S(1 - dt)$$

$$\$445.40 = S\left(1 - \frac{4}{100} \times \overset{\overset{92}{\cancel{\,}}}{\underset{90}{\cancel{360}}}\right)$$

$$445.40 = S\left(1 - \frac{0.92}{90}\right)$$

$$445.40 = S\left(\frac{90}{90} - \frac{0.92}{90}\right)$$

$$445.40 = S\left(\frac{89.08}{90}\right)$$

$$\left(\frac{90}{89.08}\right) \overset{5}{\cancel{445.40}} = S\left(\frac{\cancel{89.08}}{\cancel{90}}\right)\left(\frac{\cancel{90}}{\cancel{89.08}}\right)$$

$$450 = S$$

$$S = \$450$$

$$S = \frac{p}{1 - dt}$$

$$= \frac{\$445.40}{1 - \frac{4}{100} \times \overset{92}{\underset{90}{\cancel{360}}}}$$

$$= \frac{445.40}{1 - \frac{0.92}{90}}$$

$$= \frac{445.40}{\frac{90}{90} - \frac{0.92}{90}}$$

$$= \frac{445.40}{\frac{89.08}{90}}$$

$$= \overset{5}{\cancel{445.40}}\left(\frac{90}{\cancel{89.08}}\right)$$

$$S = \$450$$

The maturity value is $450 on September 17.

A promissory note, like a check or currency, is a negotiable instrument. That is, it can be sold to another person or it can be used to purchase something or to pay a debt.

If the payee of a discounted note (usually some financial institution) sells the note to another bank, the note has been *rediscounted*. That is, the second bank uses the maturity value of the note as the basis for determining the proceeds which it will pay for the note. It should be observed that the discount rates which financial institutions charge each other are somewhat lower than those which banks ordinarily charge businesses and individuals.

When a note has been rediscounted, the actual interest made by the original payee is the difference between the amount received when the note is sold (the rediscounted proceeds) and the amount which was originally loaned (the original proceeds).

Chemical City Savings Bank was the holder (payee) of a $1,500, 180-day note discounted at 6%. Sixty days before the note was due, the Chemical City Bank rediscounted (or sold) the note at First Savings at 4%. (a) How much did the Chemical City Bank receive for the note? (b) How much did they make on the transaction? **Example Two**

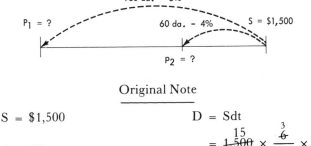

180 da. – 6%

$P_1 = ?$ 60 da. – 4% $S = \$1,500$

$P_2 = ?$

Original Note

$S = \$1,500$

$d = 6\%$

$t = \frac{180}{360}$ or $\frac{1}{2}$

$p_1 = ?$

$D = Sdt$

$$= 1{,}500 \times \frac{\overset{15}{\cancel{6}}}{\cancel{100}} \times \frac{1}{\cancel{2}}$$

$D = \$45$

$p = S - D$
$= 1{,}500 - 45$
$p_1 = \$1{,}455$

The proceeds of the original note (the amount which Chemical City Bank had loaned to the maker) were $1,455.

Rediscounted Note

$S = \$1,500$

$d = 4\%$

$t = \frac{60}{360}$ or $\frac{1}{6}$

$p = S(1 - dt)$

$$= 1{,}500 \left(1 - \frac{\overset{2}{\cancel{4}}}{100} \times \frac{1}{\underset{3}{\cancel{6}}}\right)$$

$$= 1{,}500 \left(1 - \frac{2}{300}\right)$$

$$P_2 = ? \qquad\qquad = \cancel{1,500}^{5} \left(\frac{298}{\cancel{300}}\right)$$
$$P_2 = \$1,490$$

(a) The proceeds of the rediscounted note were $1,490. That is, Chemical City Bank received $1,490 when they sold the note to First Savings.

(b) Chemical City Bank made $1,490 − $1,455 or $35 on the transaction. This is only $10 less than the entire $45 interest Chemical City Bank would have made had they not sold the note, although only $\frac{2}{3}$ of the time of the note had elapsed.

It is also possible that the payee of a simple interest note may wish to sell it at a bank before the due date. The amount which the bank would pay is determined as follows:

1. Find the maturity value of the simple interest note.

2. Discount the maturity value of the note using the bank's rate and the time until the due date. The proceeds remaining is the amount which the bank would pay for the note.

3. The interest which the original payee has made is the difference between what he sold the note for (the discounted proceeds) and the original amount loaned (the principal of the simple interest note).

Example Three James Jones was the payee of a $600, 90-day note with interest at 4%. Thirty days before the due date, Jones' banker discounted the note at 6%. (a) How much did Jones receive for the note? (b) How much did he make on the transaction?

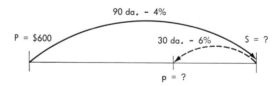

Simple Interest Note (Finding Maturity Value)

P = $600	I = Prt
r = 4%	$= \cancel{600} \times \dfrac{\cancel{4}}{\cancel{100}} \times \dfrac{1}{4}$
$t = \frac{90}{360}$ or $\frac{1}{4}$	I = 6
S = ?	S = P + I
	= 600 + 6
	S = $606

Discount Note (Finding Proceeds)

S = $606	D = Sdt
d = 6%	$= \cancel{606} \times \dfrac{\cancel{6}}{\cancel{100}} \times \dfrac{1}{\cancel{12}}$
$t = \frac{30}{360}$ or $\frac{1}{12}$	D = $3.03
p = ?	p = S − D
	= $606 − $3.03
	p = $602.97

(a) Jones received $602.97 for the note.

(b) Since he had loaned $600 originally, Jones made $2.97 in interest. This is slightly less than half the $6 interest which the maker will pay for the loan, even though $\frac{2}{3}$ of the time has elapsed.

PROBLEMS

Complete the following:

		Proceeds	Discount Rate	Date	Due Date	Time	Maturity Value
1.	(a)	$594	6%	Aug. 20		60 da.	
	(b)	624	5	Mar. 18		180 da.	
	(c)	780	7.5	Feb. 23		4 mos.	
	(d)	375.70	9	Jan. 7		8 mos.	
2.	(a)	$714	5%	Jan. 25		60 da.	
	(b)	785	4.5	July 12		150 da.	
	(c)	295.40	6	Aug. 4		3 mos.	
	(d)	437.80	8	Apr. 25		4 mos.	

Find the additional information:

		Original Note				Rediscounted Note			Net Interest Earned
		Maturity Value	Rate	Time	Proceeds	Rate	Time	Proceeds	
3.	(a)	$ 600	5%	60 da.		4%	30 da.		
	(b)	1,200	8	150		6	90		
	(c)	1,500	6	72		5	48		
4.	(a)	$ 400	6%	270 da.		5%	72 da.		
	(b)	900	7	120		4	40		
	(c)	1,200	9	180		5	90		

Find the net interest made on the following:

		Simple Interest Note				Discounted Note			
		Principal	Rate	Time	Maturity Value	Discount Rate	Time	Proceeds	Net Interest Earned
5.	(a)	$ 500	6%	120 da.		9%	40 da.		
	(b)	600	5	180		8	75		
6.	(a)	$1,200	3%	90 da.		8%	45 da.		
	(b)	800	4	45		5	18		

7. On January 19, the proceeds of a ten-month note were $839.20. If "interest in advance" had been deducted at 8%, what was the face value of the note?

8. The proceeds of a six-month note dated March 19 were $264.48. If the discount rate was 4%, what was the maturity value of the note?

9. A four-month note was discounted at 6% on May 20. If the proceeds of the note were $411.39, what was the maturity value?

10. On August 10, the proceeds of a two-month note were $356.95. If the bank discount had been computed at 5%, what was the face value of the note?

11. On June 1, the First State Bank issued a 150-day note for $450, discounted at 8%. On September 19, First State rediscounted the note with the Bank of the West at 6%.
    (a) What amount had First State loaned the maker?
    (b) How much did First State receive when they rediscounted the note?
    (c) How much did First State make on the transaction?
    (d) How much more would First State have received if they had kept the note?

12. Citizens Loan and Trust was the payee of a $1,200, 90-day note dated September 30 and discounted at 5%. On December 14, the note was rediscounted at Second National Bank at 3%. Find—
    (a) the amount originally loaned;
    (b) the amount received when the note was sold;
    (c) the amount that Citizens Loan and Trust made on the transactions;
    (d) how much less this was than the interest Citizens would have earned had they kept the note.

13. Raleigh Appliance Center was the payee of a $720, 180-day note dated October 1, with interest at 5%. On February 13, Raleigh Appliance discounted the note at their bank at 8%.
    (a) How much did Raleigh Appliance receive for the note?
    (b) How much interest did Raleigh Appliance make?

    (c)   How much interest did Raleigh Appliance lose by not keeping the note?

14.   Andrew Gaines was the holder of a $400, 108-day note dated June 21, with interest at 5%. On September 7, Gaines' banker discounted the note at 6%.

    (a)   How much did Gaines receive when he sold the note?

    (b)   How much interest did Gaines make on the note?

    (c)   How much interest did Gaines lose by selling the note before the due date?

15.   The Merchants Bank and Trust was the payee of a $600, 60-day note dated August 15 and discounted at 7%. On September 14 the note was sold to Ohio Savings and Loan at a 4% discount rate.

    (a)   What amount did The Merchants Bank lend to the maker of the note?

    (b)   What amount did The Merchants Bank receive when they sold the note?

    (c)   How much interest did The Merchants Bank earn on the note?

    (d)   How much interest did The Merchants Bank lose by not keeping the note to maturity?

16.   Blackman Furniture Co. was the payee of a $1,500, 120-day note dated April 30, with interest at 4%. On June 29, Blackman Furniture discounted the note at their bank at 6%.

    (a)   How much did the bank pay Blackman Furniture for the note?

    (b)   How much interest did Blackman Furniture earn on the note?

    (c)   How much more interest would Blackman Furniture have made by keeping the note until maturity?

3. DISCOUNTING NOTES TO TAKE ADVANTAGE OF CASH DISCOUNT

In Chapter 12, we learned that many merchants offer cash discounts as inducements to buyers to pay their accounts promptly. These discounts typically are a full 1% to 2% in only 10 days. When a businessman does not have sufficient cash available on the last day of the cash discount period, he often signs a bank note in order to take advantage of the cash discount. Although the bank charges interest on the note, the businessman still "comes out ahead" if he borrows for only a short term. Remember that a bank rate of 6% means 6% for an entire year; for a 20-day note, the actual interest charge would be only $\frac{1}{3}$%. Thus the businessman would still save $1\frac{2}{3}$% by borrowing to take advantage of a 2% cash discount.

    The businessman would save money by borrowing, provided that he borrowed for a short enough period of time so that the bank discount he must pay is less than the cash discount. However, we will consider only the situation when the maximum amount will be saved: On the *last* day of the cash discount period, a note is discounted so that the proceeds exactly equal the amount required to take advantage of the cash discount. The note will be for only the time remaining until the net amount of the invoice would have been due.

Example One An invoice dated October 4 is for goods of $485 and freight of $3.10. The terms are 2/10, n/30. If a note is discounted at 6%, in order to take advantage of the cash discount—

(a) What will be the face value of the note?

(b) How much will be saved by borrowing the necessary cash?

The last day of the cash discount period is October 14; the net amount is due twenty days later on November 3. Therefore, the discounted note will be taken out on October 14 for 20 days.

(a)

$485
×0.02
———
$9.70 cash discount

$485.00 goods
− 9.70 cash discount
————
$475.30
+ 3.10 freight
————
$478.40 amount needed to
take advantage of
cash discount

$p = \$478.40$

$r = 6\%$

$t = 20 \text{ days}$

$$= \tfrac{20}{360} = \frac{1}{18}$$

$S = ?$

$$S = \frac{p}{1 - dt}$$

$$= \frac{478.40}{1 - \dfrac{\cancel{6}}{100} \times \dfrac{1}{\cancel{18}}\,_{3}}$$

$$= \frac{478.40}{1 - \dfrac{1}{300}}$$

$$= \frac{478.40}{\dfrac{299}{300}}$$

$$= 478.40 \left(\frac{300}{299}\right)$$

$$S = \$480$$

A note with face value of $480 would have to be signed.

(b) $485.00 goods
  + 3.10 freight
  $488.10 amount due November 3 if a note is not signed
  − 480.00 maturity value of note due November 3
  $ 8.10 amount saved by discounting a note

Complete the following:

		Amount of Invoice	Sales Terms	Amount Needed (Proceeds)	Time of Note	Discount Rate	Face Value of Note	Amount Saved
1.	(a)	$ 610.20	2/10, n/30			6%		
	(b)	1,828.57	2/10, n/30			8		
	(c)	987.63	3/15, n/30			5		
2.	(a)	$ 366.12	2/10, n/30			6%		
	(b)	814.29	2/15, n/30			6		
	(c)	925.77	3/10, n/30			4		

3. An invoice for $1,626.53 has terms 2/15, n/30. If a bank note is discounted at 9% in order to take advantage of the cash discount—
   (a) What will be the face value of the note?
   (b) How much will be saved by taking out the note?

4. A bank note is discounted at 5% in order to take advantage of the cash discount on an invoice for $987.63 with terms 3/15, n/30.
   (a) What is the maturity value of the note?
   (b) How much will be saved?

5. Freight and extra charges totaled $12.20 on an invoice for merchandise of $719.39. The invoice contains sales terms of 2/10, n/30.
   (a) What would be the amount of a bank note discounted at 7% in order to take advantage of the cash discount?
   (b) How much will be saved by borrowing in order to pay within the discount period?

6. An invoice contains merchandise of $908.67 and freight of $7.50. A 4% bank note is discounted in order to take advantage of the 2/10, n/30 sales terms.
   (a) What will be the face value of the note?
   (b) How much will be saved?

4. SUMMARY OF SIMPLE INTEREST AND SIMPLE DISCOUNT

It is essential that the student understand the identifying characteristics of both the simple interest and simple discount notes, as well as the differences between the two. Both kinds of *Promissory Notes* are:

1. generally for one year or less;
2. repaid in a single payment at the end of the time.

As for their differences, the following are characteristic of the *Simple Interest Note:*

1. The face value is the principal of the note. The face value is the actual amount which was loaned.
2. Interest is computed on the face value of the note at the rate and for the time which appear on the note.
3. The maturity value of the simple interest note is the sum of the face value plus interest.
4. A simple interest problem will contain one or more of these identifying characteristics: *"interest* rate of $x\%$"; "with *interest* at $x\%$"; a maturity value which exceeds the face value; *"amount".*
5. The solution of simple interest problems requires one or more of the following formulas: (a) I = Prt; (b) S = P + I; (c) S = P(1 + rt); (d) P = $\dfrac{S}{1 + rt}$.

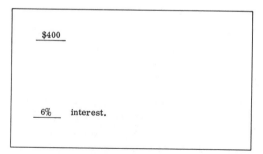

$400

6% interest.

FIGURE 16-4: SIMPLE INTEREST NOTE

The following are characteristic of the *Simple Discount Note:*

1. The face value of the simple discount note is the maturity value—the amount which will be repaid.
2. Discount notes may contain a rate quoted as a certain per cent "discounted to maturity." The interest (called "bank discount") is computed on the face value of the note. (That is, the borrower pays interest on the amount he will repay rather than on the amount he has borrowed.)
3. The actual amount which the borrower (maker) receives from the lender (payee) is called the "proceeds." The proceeds are found

by subtracting the bank discount from the face value. This is often called paying interest in advance.

4. Simple discount problems may be distinguished from simple interest problems by the use of one or more of the following terms: "*discount* rate of $x\%$"; *discounted* at $x\%$; "*proceeds*"; maturity value equals the face value; "interest in advance."

5. The solution of simple discount problems requires one or more of the following formulas: (a) $D = Sdt$; (b) $p = S - D$; (c) $p = S(1 - dt)$; (d) $S = \dfrac{p}{1 - dt}$.

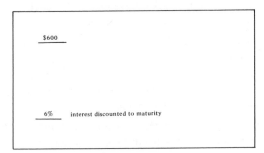

$600

6%   interest discounted to maturity

FIGURE 16-5: SIMPLE DISCOUNT NOTE

PROBLEMS

1. Find the interest and amount on a $600 note for 90 days at 8%.

2. A $900 note is taken out for 120 days at 5%. Find the interest and amount.

3. A bank discounts a 180-day note for $1,000 at 9%. Find the bank discount and the proceeds.

4. The face value of a 150-day note is $300. If the discount rate is 4%, find the bank discount and the proceeds.

5. A simple interest and a simple discount note both have face values of $450. Both notes are for 60 days, and both have interest charged at 8%.
   (a) Find the interest which will be paid on each.
   (b) Find the amount the borrower will actually receive on each note.
   (c) Find the maturity value of each note.

6. The face value is $840 on both a simple interest and a simple discount note. If both notes are for 90 days and have interest of 5% charged—
   (a) How much interest will be charged on each note?
   (b) How much will each maker have to spend?
   (c) How much will the payee receive on the maturity date in each case?

7. Find the face value of a 7%, 120-day note if the proceeds are $586.

8. The proceeds of a 6%, 75-day note are $790. Find the maturity value; the face value.

9. The maturity value is $509 on a 72-day note with interest at 9%. What is the face value of the note? How much did the maker receive on the loan?

10. A 144-day note with interest at 7% has a maturity value of $514. Find the principal of the loan. What is the face value of the note?

11. The maturity values of two six-month notes are both $820.
    (a) Compare the present value at 5% interest with the proceeds at 5% discount.
    (b) How much would the maker have to spend in each case?
    (c) What amount of interest is paid on each?

12. Two nine-month notes both have maturity values of $721.
    (a) Compare the present value at 4% interest with the proceeds at 4% discount.
    (b) What amount does the maker receive from each note?
    (c) How much interest is paid on each note?

13. A $540 note was issued on May 30 for two months at 6% interest. If money is worth 9%, what was the (present) value of the note on the day it was drawn?

14. On March 18, a $600, 6-month note is drawn with interest at 6%. If money is worth 4%, what is the (present) value of the note on the day it was drawn?

15. On January 13, a $720, eight-month note is drawn with interest at 4% to be charged. Find the present value of the note 90 days before it is due, if the standard rate of interest is 8%.

16. A $450 note with interest at 8% is signed on April 8 for 5 months. If the standard rate of interest is 5%, find the present value of the note 36 days before it is due.

17. William Lacy was the holder of a five-month, $600 note dated April 20 with interest at 6%. Forty-five days before the note was due, Lacy discounted the note at his bank at 8%.
    (a) How much did Lacy receive for the note?
    (b) How much interest did he earn?
    (c) How much interest did the bank make?

18. Andrew Hines was the payee of a $288, two-month note dated August 29 with interest at 5%. Thirty days before it was due, Hines sold the note to his banker, who discounted it at 6%.
    (a) What did Hines receive for the note?
    (b) How much did Hines make on the note?
    (c) How much interest did the bank make?

19. Citizens Bank was the payee of an $800 note dated June 9 for six months, discounted at 9%. The Citizens Bank rediscounted the note at 6% at another bank 60 days before it was due.
    (a) What amount had the Citizens Bank loaned to the maker?
    (b) How much did Citizens Bank receive when they sold the note?
    (c) How much interest did Citizens Bank earn?
    (d) How much interest did the second bank make?

20. On May 10, the Capital City Bank became the payee of a $360, four-month note discounted at 7%. Forty days before the note was due, the Capital City Bank rediscounted the note at a Trust company at 5%.
    (a) How much were the proceeds loaned to the maker of the note?
    (b) How much did Capital City receive when they sold the note?
    (c) How much interest did the Capital City Bank make on the note?
    (d) How much interest did the trust company earn?

17

Multiple Payment Plans

LEARNING OBJECTIVES

Upon completion of Chapter 17, the student will be able to:

1. Define and use correctly the terminology associated with each topic.

2. Apply the United States rule to
   a. Compute the credit to be given for partial payments made on a note, and
   b. Find the balance due on the maturity date.

3. a. Compute the interest due monthly on a charge account, and
   b. Determine the total amount required to pay off the account.

4. Determine for an installment plan purchase the
   a. Down payment,
   b. Finance charge, and
   c. Regular monthly or weekly payment.

5. a. Compute "finance charge per $100" (or "rate × time"), and
   b. Consult a table to determine the annual percentage rate charged on an installment purchase.

6. Construct a table to verify that the annual percentage rate (Objective 5) would actually result in the amount of interest charged.

THE SIMPLE INTEREST and simple discount notes studied earlier are normally repaid in a single payment at the end of the time period. However, a borrower may prefer to repay part of his debt before the entire loan is due. The lender, in order to give the borrower proper credit for his payments prior to the maturity date, should apply the United States rule. Also, many firms, when extending credit, feel that the entire debt will more likely be repaid if the borrower is required to make regular installment payments which begin immediately, rather than a single payment which is not due for some time. Partial payments may thus be made under the *United States rule* or on basic *installment plans*, both of which are discussed in the following sections.

1. UNITED STATES RULE

A person who has borrowed money on a note may sometimes wish to pay off part of the debt before the due date, in order to reduce the amount of interest he must pay. Such partial payments are not required (as they would be for an installment loan) but may be made whenever the borrower's financial condition permits. There were formerly two methods commonly used to calculate the credit which should be given for partial payments and to determine how much more is owed on the debt; these are the *United States rule*, which we shall study, and the *merchants' rule*. The merchants' rule is the simpler of the two methods (which probably accounts for the popularity it once enjoyed), and the results obtained by the two methods are nearly the same. However, widespread acceptance of the United States rule has made the merchants' rule now obsolete; hence, our study of partial payments will be limited to the United States rule.

374

The United States rule derives its name from the fact that this method has been upheld by the United States Supreme Court, as well as by a number of state courts. It is the method used by the Federal government in its financial transactions. The Banker's Rule should be used to determine "time" for the interest calculations.

Basically, the rule is applied in the following manner:

1. Interest is computed on the principal from the first day until the date of the first partial payment.

2. The partial payment is used first to pay the interest, and the remaining part of the payment is deducted from the principal.

3. The next time a payment is made, interest is calculated on the adjusted principal from the date of the previous payment up to the present. The payment is then used to pay the interest due and to reduce the principal, as before. (This step may be repeated as often as additional payments warrant.)

4. The balance due on the maturity date is found by computing interest due since the last partial payment and adding this interest to the unpaid principal.

William Farrish was the maker of a 180-day, $2,000 note bearing interest at 6%. The note was dated March 5. On April 4, Farrish paid $800 toward his obligation; and on June 3, he paid another $500. How much remains to be paid on the due date?

Example One

(a) Using the 6%, 60-day method of interest calculation, interest is computed on the full $2,000 from March 5 until the first partial payment (April 4):

April 4	94	$I = \$20 \times \frac{1}{2}$
March 5	−64	$I = \$10$
	30 days	

$$I_{6\text{-}60} = \$20$$
$$30 \text{ days} = \tfrac{30}{60} = \tfrac{1}{2}$$

(b) The $800 is applied to the interest, and the remaining payment ($800 − $10 = $790) is deducted from the principal.

Principal	$2,000
Less: payment to principal	−790
Adjusted principal	$1,210

(c) Interest is computed on the $1,210 adjusted principal from April 4 until June 3. The $500 payment pays this interest first, and the remainder is subtracted from the current principal:

June 3	154	Partial payment	$ 500.00
April 4	−94	Less: interest	− 12.10
	60 days	Payment to principal	$ 487.90

$I_{6\text{-}60} = \$12.10$

Current principal	$1,210.00
Payment to principal	− 487.90
Adjusted principal	$ 722.10

(d) Since no other payment is made until the maturity date, interest is computed on $722.10 from June 3 until September 1:

September 1	244
June 3	−154
	90 days

$I = \$7.22 \times \tfrac{3}{2}$

$I = \$10.83$

$I_{6\text{-}60} = \$7.22$

$90 \text{ days} = \tfrac{90}{60} = \tfrac{3}{2}$

$S = P + I$

$= \$722.10 + \$10.83$

$S = \$732.93$

The entire process involved in the foregoing application of the United States rule is condensed below:

Interest Period	Prt	=	I	Part. Pmt. −	I	=	Pmt. to P	Current P	−	Pmt. to P	=	Adj. P
3/5–4/5	$2,000 × .06 × $\frac{30}{360}$ = $10			$800 − $10		=	$790	$2,000 − $790			=	$1,210
4/5–6/3	1,210 × .06 × $\frac{60}{360}$ = 12.10			500 − 12.10		=	487.90	1,210 − 487.90			=	722.10
6/3–9/1	722.10 × .06 × $\frac{90}{360}$ =		10.83	Interest due, 9/1								
			+722.10	Principal								
			$732.93	Balance due, 9/1								

On September 1, $732.93 remains to be paid.

Complications arise from the United States rule if the partial payment is not large enough to pay the interest due. The unpaid interest cannot be added to the principal, for then interest would be earned on interest; this would constitute compound interest, and the charging of compound interest on loans is illegal. This problem is solved simply by holding the payment or payments (without giving credit for them) until the sum of these partial payments is large enough to pay the interest due to that date. The procedure then continues as usual. (Note that the borrower does not save any interest unless his partial payment is sufficiently large to pay the interest due and reduce the principal somewhat.)

Using the United States rule, compute the balance due on the maturity date of each of the following notes:

		Note			Partial Payments	
		Principal	Rate	Time	Amount	Day
1.	(a)	$1,000	9%	120 da.	$415	60th day
					203	80th
	(b)	1,500	6	150	410	40th
					511	100th
	(c)	1,200	8	205	320	75th
					46Ɛ	165th
2.	(a)	$1,800	6%	180 da.	$612	40th day
					716	120th
	(b)	1,000	6	360	310	60th
					514	180th
	(c)	1,800	7	120	907	20th
					307	60th

3. On March 3, Andrew Myer signed a $3,000 note with interest at 8% for 270 days. Myer made payments of $680 on July 1 and $932 on August 30. How much will he owe on the due date?

4. Bill Ramsey borrowed $1,800 on a 6%, 180-day note dated April 16. He paid $609 toward the note on May 16 and $610 on July 5. What will he owe on the maturity date?

5. Garfield Associates borrowed $3,200 on a 4.5% note dated July 12 for 150 days. The firm made partial payments of $1,016 on August 21 and $622 on November 9. Find the balance due on the maturity date.

6. On February 20, Albert Rogers borrowed $1,200 by signing a 7.5%, 240-day note. He made a $415 partial payment on April 21 and paid $210 on June 20. Determine the amount he still owes at the end of the loan period.

2. INSTALLMENT PLANS

The student undoubtedly already has some knowledge of that uniquely American tradition, the *installment plan*. Almost all department stores, appliance stores, and furniture stores, as well as finance companies and banks, offer some form of installment plan whereby a customer may take possession of a purchase immediately and, for an additional charge, pay for it later by a series of regular payments. Americans pay exorbitant rates, as we shall see, for the privilege of buying on credit; but, because the dollar amounts involved are not extremely large, many people are willing to pay them.

The installment plan actually provides a great boost to the American economy, because the typical family buys many things on the spur of the moment on the installment plan that they would never buy were they compelled to save the money required for a cash purchase. The lure of the sales pitch—"nothing down; low monthly payments," "budget terms," "go now, pay later," "buy now; no payment for sixty days," "small down payment; three years to pay," "consolidate all your bills into one low, monthly payment"—has caused many families to feel that they will never miss that small extra amount each month. The result is that many families soon find themselves saddled with so many of these "small monthly payments" that they cannot make ends meet and are in danger of bankruptcy. The Chamber of Commerce or the Family Service Agency in many cities provides inexpensive counseling to help such families learn to budget their incomes and "get back on their feet" financially.

The Truth in Lending Law, which took effect in 1969, now enables the consumer to determine how much the privilege of credit buying actually costs, thereby allowing him to make an intelligent decision when faced with the question of when to buy on the installment plan. Indeed, the question has become "when to buy" rather than "whether to buy," because almost all Americans take advantage of time-payment plans at one time or another. The single item most often purchased in this way (other than homes) is the automobile, which is followed by other durable items, such as furniture and appliances. Even realizing the expense of these plans, most people feel that the added convenience at times justifies the additional cost.

The high rate of interest charged by companies offering installment plans is not without justification. The merchant incurs numerous additional operating expenses as a result of the installment plan: the costs of investigating the customer's credit standing, discounting bank notes, buying extra insurance, paying cashiers and bookkeepers for the additional work, collection costs necessitated by buyers who do not keep up with payments, as well as "bad debts" loss from customers who never finish paying. And, of course, the merchant is entitled to interest, since he has capital invested in the merchandise being bought on the time-payment plan. Thus the installment plan is expensive for the seller as well as the buyer.

Basically, there are two types of installment plans. (1) The first plan is called *open end credit*, because the time period of the credit account is not definite and the customer may receive additional credit before the first credit is entirely repaid. Under this plan, interest is computed each month (or other payment period) on the unpaid balance. Each payment is applied first toward the interest and then toward the balance due, in accordance with the United States rule of partial payments.

This plan is used by most department stores and other retail businesses offering "charge accounts" and "credit cards." The monthly interest rate is usually 1% (= 12% per year) to 1½% (= 18% per year). Customer accounts at these stores usually vary quite a bit from month to month, because the account results from a number of small purchases rather than one large purchase. Many accounts of this type are never actually paid off, because new purchases continue to be made. There may be a limit to the amount a customer is entitled to charge; and a pre-scribed minimum monthly payment may be required according to the amount owed. (For instance, the maximum balance which Mrs. Jones' charge account may reach is $200. She must pay at least $10 per month if her balance is under $100 and must pay at least $15 per month if she owes $100 or more.) These accounts are often called "revolving charge accounts."

The balance of Mrs. Paulsen's charge account at Steinway, Inc. is $80. The store charges 1% per month interest on customer charge accounts. Mrs. Paulsen decided to pay off this account in monthly payments of $20. (a) Determine how much of each payment will be interest and how much will apply toward her account. (b) Find the total amount she will pay. (c) Find the total interest included.

Example One (Installment plan having monthly rate)

The following schedule computes the interest and payment that ap-plies toward the balance due each month. "Interest" is found by taking 1% of the "balance due." This interest must then be deducted from the "monthly payment" in order to determine the "payment (that applies) toward the balance due." The "payment toward balance due" is then subtracted from the "balance due" to find the "adjusted balance due," which is carried forward to the next line as the "balance due."

(a)

Payment Number	Balance Due	Interest (1%)	Monthly Payment	Payment toward Balance Due	Adjusted Balance Due
1	$80.00	$ .80	$20.00	$19.20	$60.80
2	60.80	.61	20.00	19.39	41.41
3	41.41	.41	20.00	19.59	21.82
4	21.82	.22	20.00	19.78	2.04
5	2.04	.02	2.06	2.04	.00
	Totals	$2.06	$82.06	$80.00	

(b) During the last month, Mrs. Paulsen paid only the remaining balance due plus the interest due. Thus she paid a total of $82.06 in order to discharge her $80 obligation.

(c) The amount in (b) included $2.06 in interest.

(2) The other type of installment plan is used when a single purchase (automobile, suite of furniture, washing machine, etc.) is made. In this case, the account will be paid in full in a specified number of payments; hence, finance charges for the entire time are computed and added to the cost at the time of purchase.

The typical procedure for an installment purchase is as follows: The customer makes a *down payment* (sometimes including a trade-in) which is subtracted from the cash price to obtain the *outstanding balance.* A *carrying charge* (or *time payment differential*) is then added to the outstanding balance. The resulting sum is divided by the number of payments (usually weekly or monthly) to obtain the amount of each installment payment.

This second type of time-payment plan is also used by finance companies and by banks in their installment-loan, personal-loan, and/or automobile-loan departments. The only variations in the plan as described above are that there is no down payment made (the amount of the loan becomes the outstanding balance) and the interest charged corresponds to the carrying charge. Bank interest rates are usually lower, because banks will lend money only to people with acceptable credit ratings. Finance companies cater to persons whose credit ratings would not qualify them for loans at more selective institutions. Many states allow these small-loan agencies to charge up to $3\frac{1}{2}\%$ per month (or 42% per year). Their profits are not so high as their rates might indicate, however, for these companies have a high percentage of bad debts from uncollected loans.

As noted above, high-powered advertising has often misled buyers into making financial commitments that were substantially greater than they realized beforehand. The Truth in Lending Law protects against false impressions by requiring that if a business mentions one feature of credit in its advertising (such as the amount of down payment), it must also mention all other important features (such as the number, amount, and frequency of payments that follow.) If an advertisement states "Only $2 down," for example, it must also state that the buyer will have to pay $10 a week for the next two years.

The principal accomplishment of the law is that it enables the buyer to know both the finance charge (the total amount of extra money he pays for buying on credit) and the annual percentage rate to which this is equivalent. Some merchants may require a carrying charge, a service charge, interest, insurance, or other special charges levied only upon credit sales; the finance charge is the sum of all these items. The annual percentage rate correct to the nearest quarter of a per cent must then be determined by one of the two methods approved in the law. Tables are available from the government which enable the merchant to determine the correct percentage rate without extensive mathematical calculations.

It is important to understand the distinction between the interest rates required under the law and simple interest rates such as we have studied previously. Formerly, merchants often advertised a simple interest rate, and interest was computed on the original balance for the entire payment period. Consider the following, however: On a simple interest note, the borrower keeps all the money until the end of the time; thus he rightfully owes interest on the original amount for the entire period. On an installment purchase at simple interest, on the other hand, the buyer must immediately begin making payments. As the credit period expires, therefore, he has repaid most of the obligation and then owes very little, yet his payments would still include just as much interest as the early payments did. This means he would be paying at a much higher interest rate than on the early payments. A simple interest rate would thus be deceiving; however, the Truth in Lending Law permits the buyer to know the true rate he is paying. (Examples in this section will illustrate the differences in these rates.) Since the rates required under the law are quite complicated to compute, the Federal Reserve System publishes tables which merchants can use to determine annual percentage rates. These tables contain rates corresponding to both monthly and weekly payments; however, this text will include tables only for monthly payments.

It should be pointed out that the law does not establish any maximum interest rates or maximum finance charges or otherwise restrict what a seller may charge for credit. Neither are there restrictions on what methods the seller may use to determine the finance charge. The law only requires that the merchant fully inform the buyer what he is paying for the privilege of credit buying. In addition to the finance charge and the annual percentage rate, other important information must also be itemized for the buyer, including penalties he must pay for not conforming to the provisions of the credit contract.

Note: The term "installment plan," as used in this section, describes high-interest payment plans which run for a limited number of years. (The maximum time is usually three years.) The chapter on amortization includes the periodic payments made to repay home loans or other real estate loans, to repay long-term personal bank loans, or to repay other loans when a relatively low interest rate is computed only on the balance due at each payment (such as credit union loans or loans on insurance policies).

The following examples all pertain to installment plans of the second category, where the finance charge (carrying charge, interest, etc.) is calculated at the time the contract is made.

Lakeland Jewelry Store (which specializes in small appliances) will sell an electric mixer for $45 cash or on the following "easy-payment" terms:

Example Two

$\frac{1}{3}$ down payment, a full 10% carrying charge, and monthly payments for six months. (a) What is the monthly payment? (b) What is the total cost of the mixer on the installment plan? (c) How much more than the cash price will be paid on the installment plan?

Cash	$45.00	
Down payment	−15.00	($\frac{1}{3}$ of $45)
Outstanding balance	$30.00	
Carrying charge	+ 3.00	(10% of $30)
Total of payments	$33.00	

$$\frac{\$33.00}{6} = \$5.50 \text{ monthly payment}$$

(a) A payment of $5.50 per month is required. Notice the finance (carrying) charge was 10% of the outstanding balance. The merchant may use this or any convenient method for determining his finance charge; however, this 10% rate is much lower than the rate he is required to disclose to the credit buyer. Since these payments cover only half a year, this rate is equivalent to simple interest at 20% per year. However, the rate which the merchant must reveal to the buyer is the rate that applies when interest is computed only on the balance due at the time each payment is made. Thus the merchant must tell the buyer that an annual percentage rate of $33\frac{1}{2}$% is being charged. (Later examples will further illustrate these rates.)

The student should also observe the following: If the finance charge is given as a fraction or a per cent, the finance charge is found by multiplying this rate times the outstanding balance remaining *after* the down payment has been made.

(b)
Down payment	$15.00
Total of monthly payments	+33.00
Total installment plan cost	$48.00

The actual total cost of the mixer, when bought on the installment plan, is $48.

(c) The carrying charge of $3 represents the additional cost to the credit customer. This may also be shown as follows:

Total installment plan price	$48.00
Cash price	−45.00
Time payment differential	$ 3.00

This $3 finance charge, along with the $33\frac{1}{2}\%$ annual percentage rate, represent the two most important items the merchant must disclose to the credit buyer under the Truth in Lending Law, although several other things are also required.

William Herrscher bought a new car that was priced at $3,200. He received a $900 trade-in allowance on his old car and also paid $200 cash. He arranged a two-year automobile loan on which the lender computed 6% simple interest.

**Example
Three**

(a) What is Herrscher's monthly payment?

(b) What will he pay altogether for his car?

(c) How much extra is he paying for the privilege of credit buying?

(d) What annual percentage rate must the lender disclose under the Truth in Lending law?

(a) Herrscher's regular payment is $98 per month.

Cash price	$3,200	
Down payment	−1,100	($900 trade-in + $200 cash)
Outstanding balance	$2,100	$I = Prt$
Finance charge	252	$= \$2,100 \times \frac{6}{100} \times \frac{2}{1}$
	$2,352	

$$\frac{\$2,352}{24} = \$98 \text{ per month}$$

(b) The total cost of his new car will be $3,452; this is shown as follows:

Down payment:	Trade-in	$ 900
	Cash	200
Total of monthly payments		2,352
Total cost		$3,452

(c) This total cost includes an extra $252 interest (or finance or carrying) charge above the cash price.

(d) The annual percentage rate which the lender must disclose is found using Table XXI (pages 542–548). The instructions indicate that the finance charge should be divided by the amount financed (the outstanding balance) and the result multiplied by 100.

This gives the finance charge per $100 of amount financed.

$$\frac{\text{Finance charge}}{\text{Amount financed}} \times 100 = \frac{\$252}{\$2,100} \times 100 = .12 \times 100 = 12$$

Thus the lender pays $12 interest for each $100 being financed. (Note that this result is also the total simple interest per cent charged; that is, the "rate × time": 6% × 2 years = 12%. This relationship will always exist, so either method could be used to determine the table value.)

To use Table XXI, look in the left-hand column headed "Number of Payments" and find line 24, since this problem includes 24 monthly payments. Look to the right until you find the column containing the value nearest to the 12.00 we just computed. The per cent at the top of that column will then be the correct annual percentage rate. In this example, our 12.00 is exactly midway between two entries (11.86 and 12.14); in that case, the larger value is always used. Thus, the per cent at the top of the column indicates the annual percentage rate is $11\frac{1}{4}\%$.

For practical purposes, this means that if interest were computed at $11\frac{1}{4}\%$ only on the remaining balance each month and the United States rule were used so that the $98 applied first to the interest due and then to reduce the principal, then 24 payments of $98 would exactly repay the $2,100 loan and the $252 interest.* Thus it is the $11\frac{1}{4}\%$ rate that the merchant must state is being charged.

When simple interest is calculated on the *original balance* for the entire length of a loan, this rate is sometimes called a *nominal interest* rate. By contrast, an annual rate which is applied only to the *balance due at the time of each payment* is called an *effective interest* rate. The annual rates determined for the Truth in Lending law by Table XXI are known as *actuarial* rates and are almost identical to effective rates. It is this actuarial (or effective) rate which must be disclosed to the buyer by the merchant.

Example Four

(a) What actuarial (or effective) interest rate is equivalent to a nominal (or simple) interest rate of 8%, if there are six monthly installments?

---

*Strictly speaking, there is a mathematical distinction between the annual percentage rates in Table XXI and the annual rates that one should use to apply the United States rule (as was done here), although either rates are acceptable under the Truth in Lending law. The U. S. rule computes interest on the amount financed from the original date until the day payments are made. The rates in Table XXI, however, are applied in the opposite direction: the present value on the original day of all the payments must equal the amount financed. While this is a distinct difference in mathematical procedure, the difference in the actual percentage rates is insignificant for our purposes. Thus, since a table of rates applicable to the U. S. rule was not available, we shall use the rates from Table XXI in applying the U. S. rule.

(b) How much simple interest would be due on a $300 loan at a nominal 8% rate for six months?

(c) Verify that the actuarial rate would produce the same amount of interest, if 6 monthly payments were made.

(a) Multiplying "rate × time" gives the value we look for in the Table:

$$8\% \times \tfrac{1}{2}\,\text{year} = 4$$

This means the interest due is 4% of the amount borrowed. It also means the borrower pays $4 interest for each $100 borrowed.

Since this is a six-month loan, we look on line 6 for the column containing the value nearest to 4.00. The nearest value is 3.97. We now see that a simple (nominal) interest rate of 8% for six months corresponds to an actuarial (effective) rate of 13.50 or $13\tfrac{1}{2}\%$, correct to the nearest $\tfrac{1}{4}\%$.

(b) A $300 loan at 8% simple interest for six months would require interest as follows:

$$I = Prt$$
$$= \$300 \times \underbrace{8\% \times \tfrac{1}{2}}$$
$$= 300 \times 4\% \qquad [\text{as in part (a)}]$$
$$I = \$12$$

OR

At $4 per $100 financed,
3 hundreds
×$4 per $100
$12 interest

(c) If the $300 principal plus $12 interest were repaid in 6 monthly payments, the monthly payment is

$$\frac{\$312}{6} = \$52 \text{ per month.}$$

The United States rule is then used to verify the $13\tfrac{1}{2}\%$ actuarial rate. The interest due is subtracted from the $52 payment first. Then the rest of the payment is deducted from the outstanding principal to obtain the adjusted principal upon which interest will be calculated at the time of the next payment.

Month	$Prt = I$	Payment to Principal
1st	$\$300.00 \times \dfrac{13.5}{100} \times \dfrac{1}{12} = \$\ 3.38$	$\$\ 48.62$
2nd	$251.38 \times \dfrac{13.5}{100} \times \dfrac{1}{12} = \quad 2.83$	49.17
3rd	$202.21 \times \dfrac{13.5}{100} \times \dfrac{1}{12} = \quad 2.27$	49.73
4th	$152.48 \times \dfrac{13.5}{100} \times \dfrac{1}{12} = \quad 1.72$	50.28
5th	$102.20 \times \dfrac{13.5}{100} \times \dfrac{1}{12} = \quad 1.15$	50.85
6th	$51.35 \times \dfrac{13.5}{100} \times \dfrac{1}{12} = \quad .58$	51.42

$$\$11.93 + \$300.07 = \$312.00$$

Thus we see that a rate of 13.5%, applied only to the unpaid balance each month, would result in interest of $11.93 over six months' time. This is 7¢ less than the $12 simple interest that would be due at an 8% nominal rate. (The difference results from rounding and from the use of Table XXI in applying the U.S. rule. Recall that Table XXI is correct only to the nearest quarter of a per cent.)

Example Five The Thrif-T-Loan Co. requires six monthly payments of $43.50 to repay a loan of $240. Find (a) the amount of interest that will be paid and (b) the annual (actuarial) percentage rate charged. (c) Verify that the annual percentage rate would actually result in the amount of interest charged.

(a) The six payments of $43.50 will total $261.00 altogether. The interest charged will therefore be $21.00:

$\$\ 43.50$	Total of payments	$\$261.00$
$\underline{\times 6}$	Amount of loan	$\underline{-240.00}$
$\$261.00$	Interest (finance charge)	$\$\ 21.00$

(b) Before finding the actuarial rate, we first find the finance charge per $100 of amount financed:

$$\frac{\text{Finance charge}}{\text{Amount financed}} \times 100 = \frac{\$21}{\$240} \times 100 = .0875 \times 100 = 8.75$$

Now on line 6 of the table we find the nearest value to 8.75 is 8.78. Thus the Thrif-T-Loan Co. must inform the borrower he is paying interest at an annual percentage rate of 29.5%.

(c) As before, the monthly payment applies first to the interest due, and the remainder of the payment is then deducted from the outstanding principal.

Month	Prt = Interest		Payment to Principal
1st	$240.00 \times \dfrac{29.5}{100} \times \dfrac{1}{12} =$	\$ 5.90	\$ 37.60
2nd	$202.40 \times \dfrac{29.5}{100} \times \dfrac{1}{12.} =$	4.97	38.53
3rd	$163.87 \times \dfrac{29.5}{100} \times \dfrac{1}{12} =$	4.03	39.47
4th	$124.40 \times \dfrac{29.5}{100} \times \dfrac{1}{12} =$	3.06	40.44
5th	$83.96 \times \dfrac{29.5}{100} \times \dfrac{1}{12} =$	2.06	41.44
6th	$42.52 \times \dfrac{29.5}{100} \times \dfrac{1}{12} =$	$\dfrac{1.05}{\$21.07\ +}$	$\dfrac{42.45}{\$239.93}\ = \$261.00$

Thus we see that an effective rate of 29.5%, applied only to the unpaid balance each month, would require $21.07 in interest on a $240 loan. (Again, this contains a 7¢ error.) The $21.00 interest in this problem would be equivalent to simple interest at the rate of only 17.5%, which illustrates well how misleading installment rates could be before the Truth in Lending law was passed.

Note: In verifying rates as in part (c), the "rate × time" will be the same each month $\left(\text{in this case, } \dfrac{29.5}{100} \times \dfrac{1}{12}.\right)$ In working problems of this kind, therefore, it is easiest to find the product $\left(\dfrac{29.5}{100} \times \dfrac{1}{12} = .02458\right)$ and use this factor to multiply times the principal each month. (Be sure you carry the factor out to enough places to obtain correct cents. Review Section 1, Accuracy of Computation, in Chapter 1.)

As a general rule, the shorter the period of time, the higher installment rates tend to be. Customers seem to be willing to pay these very high rates, since the actual dollar amounts for shorter periods are not as large.

PROBLEMS

Find the total amount of interest that would be paid while paying off the following charge accounts:

		Amount of Account	Monthly Payment	Interest per Month
1.	(a)	$ 60	$10	1 %
	(b)	120	30	$1\frac{1}{2}$
2.	(a)	$ 70	$15	$1\frac{1}{2}\%$
	(b)	220	50	1

Find the regular (monthly or weekly) payment required to pay for the following installment purchases:

		Cash Price	Down Payment Required	Finance Charge	Time Period
3.	(a)	$230	$30	$16	9 months
	(b)	160	25%	6	36 weeks
	(c)	900	$\frac{1}{3}$	12% simple interest	24 months
4.	(a)	$165	none	$15	15 months
	(b)	120	30%	$12	32 weeks
	(c)	400	10%	8% simple interest	36 months

For the following installment problems, determine the annual (actuarial) percentage rate charged:

		Amount Financed	Finance Charge	Months
5.	(a)	$ 50	$ 6	15
	(b)	375	60	18
	(c)	—	10% simple interest	24
	(d)	—	12% simple interest	4
6.	(a)	$100	$16	12
	(b)	280	70	24
	(c)	—	8% simple interest	36
	(d)	—	18% simple interest	6

Verify that the following annual percentage rates would produce the given interest:

	Principal	Interest	Monthly Payment	Months	Annual Rate
7.	$400	$20	$105	4	23.75%
8.	200	12	53	4	28.50

9. Paul Williams purchased a $90 cassette tape recorder and charged it to his account at Reed Music Store. He is paying $18 per month and the store charges 1% per month on his unpaid balance. How much interest will he pay?

10. Oakdale Department Store charges 1% per month interest on charge accounts. David Anderson charged a $70 suit and agreed to pay $13 monthly toward his account. How much interest will he pay?

11. A refrigerator-freezer sells for $720 cash; or $\frac{1}{4}$ down, a finance charge of $60, and the balance in 24 monthly installments. What is the monthly payment?

12. A portable color television sells for $240 cash; or a $\frac{1}{3}$ down payment, a carrying charge of $20, and the balance in 12 payments. What is the monthly installment payment?

13. A bedroom suite is priced at $450. On the time-payment plan, a 20% down payment is required, and the 18 monthly payments include a $54 finance charge. What is the amount of each payment?

14. A washing machine sells for $260; or 15% down, a carrying charge of $25, and the balance in 12 equal installments. What amount is required each month?

15. The cash price of a piano is $1,000. The piano may be purchased for a 10% down payment and 18 monthly payments. For convenience, the manager computes the finance charge at 8% simple interest.
    (a) How much is the finance charge on the piano?
    (b) What is the monthly payment?
    (c) What is the total cost of the piano on the installment plan?
    (d) What annual percentage rate must the seller disclose to the buyer?

16. A stereo is priced at $500. The time-payment plan requires a 10% down payment and 24 monthly payments. For simplicity, the finance charge is computed at 6% nominal (simple) interest.
    (a) How much is the finance charge?
    (b) Determine the monthly payment on the stereo.
    (c) What is the total cost of the stereo when bought on the installment plan?
    (d) Find the annual percentage rate that the seller must reveal under the Truth in Lending law.

17. A loan of $50 is repaid in 12 monthly payments of $5 each. Find—
    (a) the finance charge on the loan;
    (b) the annual percentage rate the lender must disclose.

18. Eighteen monthly payments of $5.75 are required to repay a $90 loan. Determine—
    (a) the finance charge the borrower pays;
    (b) the annual percentage rate charged on the loan.

19. A $450 loan is repaid in 18 monthly payments of $31 each.
    (a) What is the finance charge on the loan?
    (b) At what annual percentage rate is interest paid?

20. Monthly payments of $23.60 are required for one year in order to repay $240.
    (a) How much interest is charged?
    (b) What is the annual percentage rate at which the borrower pays interest?

21. A console color television costs $800 cash. It may also be purchased for $80 down and 36 equal payments of $26.
    (a) What is the total cost of the television on the installment plan?
    (b) How much does the buyer pay to finance his purchase?
    (c) What annual percentage rate does he pay for the privilege of credit buying?

22. A room air conditioner sells for $550. On the time-payment plan, after a down payment of $50, 12 monthly installments of $45 each are required.
    (a) How much is the total cost of the air conditioner when purchased on credit?
    (b) What is the carrying charge?
    (c) At what annual percentage rate is interest paid?

23. Al Watley received a $600 allowance for his old car when he traded for a $3,000 economy compact. His payments were $126 per month for 24 months.
    (a) How much did Watley pay altogether for his new car?
    (b) How much was the finance charge on his purchase?
    (c) What annual percentage rate must the dealer reveal to Watley?

24. Dennis Jones made 18 monthly payments of $46.60 to pay for a used car. The car had originally been priced to sell for $1,000, and Jones made a cash down payment of $280.
    (a) What was the total cost of the car?
    (b) How much extra did Jones pay in order to finance the car?
    (c) At what annual percentage rate was interest paid?

25. For their own convenience, the Domestic Finance Co. computes interest on loans at 10% simple interest. What annual rate must they reveal under the Truth in Lending law on

(a) a one-year loan?

(b) a 24-month loan?

(c) a six-month loan?

26. The State Appliance Co. finds it easiest to determine finance charges by computing 12% simple interest. Determine the rate they must disclose under the Truth in Lending law for

(a) a 12-month installment purchase;

(b) an 18-month installment purchase;

(c) an eight-month installment purchase.

27. A loan company computes 8% nominal interest on a loan of $84 to be repaid in seven monthly payments.

(a) How much interest will the borrower pay?

(b) What is the monthly payment required?

(c) At what annual actuarial rate is interest paid?

(d) Verify that the actuarial rate you found will result in the same amount of interest.

28. (a) What amount of interest would be due on a five-month loan of $200 if a nominal rate of 6% were charged?

(b) How much will the monthly payment be?

(c) What annual actuarial rate is charged on the loan?

(d) Verify that this actuarial rate is correct.

29. Assume that $100 was borrowed at the rate and time of problem 5(d).

(a) How much interest would the borrower pay?

(b) What amount is his monthly payment?

(c) Verify that the annual rate you found in 5(d) would actually result in the correct amount of interest.

30. Suppose that $600 was borrowed under the conditions in problem 6(d).

(a) How much interest would be charged?

(b) How much is the monthly payment?

(c) Verify that the annual rate determined in 6(d) would produce the required amount of interest.

Compound
Interest

LEARNING OBJECTIVES

Upon completion of Chapter 18, the student will be able to:

1. Define and use correctly the terminology associated with each topic.

2. Compute compound amount without use of a table for short periods.

3. Compute compound interest and amount using the formula $S = P(1 + i)^n$ and the compound amount table.

4. a. Find compound interest and amount at institutions paying interest compounded daily from date of deposit to date of withdrawal, including deposits that earn from the first of a month if deposited by the tenth.
   b. Also, compare this with interest and amount that would be earned if interest were not compounded daily.
   c. The formulas $I = P \times \text{Dep. tab.}$ and $I = W \times \text{W/D tab.}$ are used for computing interest compounded daily.

5. Compute present value at compound interest (on the original day or on another given day) of investments made at either simple or compound interest. The formula $P = S(1 + i)^{-n}$ and the present value table will be used.

IT WAS previously noted that money invested with a financial institution earns compound interest. Compound interest is more profitable than simple interest to the investor because, at compound interest, "interest is earned on interest." That is, interest is earned, not only on the principal, but also on all previously accumulated interest. Most compound interest is calculated using prepared tables. To be certain he clearly understands compound interest, however, the student should compute a few problems himself.

1. COMPOUND INTEREST (BY COMPUTATION)

Recall that for a simple interest investment, interest is paid on the *original principal* only; at the end of the time, the maturity value is the total of the principal plus the simple interest. Now consider the following example.

Example One

Suppose investor A invests $1,000 for three years at 6% simple interest. Then,

$P = \$1,000$	$I = Prt$	$S = P + I$
$r = 6\%$ or $\frac{6}{100}$	$= \$1,000 \times \frac{6}{100} \times \frac{3}{1}$	$= \$1,000 + \$180$
$t = 3$ years	$I = \$180$	$S = \$1,180$

Mr. A would earn $180 interest on the money he invested, making his total maturity value $1,180.

Now suppose Mr. B invests $1,000 for only six months, also at 6% interest. Then,

$P = \$1,000$	$I = Prt$	$S = P + I$
$r = 6\%$ or $\frac{6}{100}$	$= \$1,000 \times \frac{6}{100} \times \frac{1}{2}$	$= \$1,000 + \$30$
$t = 6$ months or $\frac{1}{2}$ yr.	$I = \$30$	$S = \$1,030$

Mr. B would have $1,030 at the end of his six-month investment.

Then suppose Mr. B reinvests this $1,030 for another six months at 6%; Mr. B would earn $30.90 interest on his second investment, making his total amount $1,060.90. If this total were then deposited for six months, the interest would be $32.78 and Mr. B would have $1,125.51. If this procedure were repeated each six months until three years had passed, Mr. B would have made six investments and the computations would be as follows:

1st 6 months	$I = Prt$ $= \$1,000 \times \frac{6}{100} \times \frac{1}{2}$ $I = \$30$	$S = \$1,030$
2nd 6 months	$I = Prt$ $= \$1,030 \times \frac{6}{100} \times \frac{1}{2}$ $I = \$30.90$	$S = \$1,060.90$
3rd 6 months	$I = Prt$ $= \$1,060.90 \times \frac{6}{100} \times \frac{1}{2}$ $I = \$31.83$	$S = \$1,092.73$
4th 6 months	$I = Prt$ $= \$1,092.73 \times \frac{6}{100} \times \frac{1}{2}$ $I = \$32.78$	$S = \$1,125.51$
5th 6 months	$I = Prt$ $= \$1,125.51 \times \frac{6}{100} \times \frac{1}{2}$ $I = \$33.76$	$S = \$1,159.27$
6th 6 months	$I = Prt$ $= \$1,159.27 \times \frac{6}{100} \times \frac{1}{2}$ $I = \$34.78$	$S = \$1,194.05$

Thus, after three years, Mr. B's original principal would have amounted to $1,194.05. Since Mr. A had only $1,180 after his single, three-year investment, Mr. B made $1,194.05 − $1,180 or $14.05 more interest by making successive, short-term investments.

The above example illustrates the idea of *compound interest:* each time that interest is computed, the interest is added to the previous principal; that total then becomes the principal for the next interest period. Thus money accumulates faster at compound interest because *interest is earned on interest*, as well as on the principal.

Interest is said to be "compounded" whenever interest is computed and added to the previous principal. This is done at regular intervals known as *conversion periods* (or just *periods*). Interest is commonly compounded annually (once a year), semiannually (twice a year), quarterly (four times a year), or monthly. The total value at the end of the investment (original principal plus all interest) is the *compound amount*. The *compound interest* earned is the difference between the compound amount and the original principal. The length of the investment is known as the *term*. The quoted interest rate is always the nominal (or yearly) rate.

Before compound interest can be computed, (1) the term must be expressed as its total number of periods; and (2) the interest rate must be converted to its corresponding rate per period.

Example Two

Determine the number of periods for each of the following investments: (a) five years compounded annually; (b) three years compounded semi-annually; (c) four years compounded quarterly; (d) two years compounded monthly.

In general, the number of periods is found in this way:

Years × Number of periods per year = Total number of periods

Thus

    (a)   5 years compounded annually

                  = 5 years × 1 period per year = 5 periods

    (b)   3 years compounded semiannually

                  = 3 years × 2 periods per year = 6 periods

    (c)   4 years compounded quarterly

                  = 4 years × 4 periods per year = 16 periods

    (d)   2 years compounded monthly

                  = 2 years × 12 periods per year = 24 periods

Example Three

Determine the rate per period for each investment: (a) 5% compounded annually; (b) 7% compounded semiannually; (c) 6% compounded quarterly; (d) 6% compounded monthly.

Keep in mind that the stated interest rate is always the yearly rate. Thus, if the rate is 4% compounded quarterly, the rate per period is 1% (since 1% paid four times during the year is equivalent to 4%). One may find rate per period as follows:

$$\frac{\text{Yearly rate}}{\text{Number of periods per year}} = \text{Rate per period}$$

Hence

    (a)   5% compounded annually $= \dfrac{5\%}{1 \text{ period per year}}$

                  = 5% per period (or 5% each year)

    (b)   7% compounded semiannually $= \dfrac{7\%}{2 \text{ periods per year}}$

                  = $3\frac{1}{2}$% per period (or $3\frac{1}{2}$% each six months)

(c) 6% compounded quarterly $= \dfrac{6\%}{4 \text{ periods per year}}$

$= 1\frac{1}{2}\%$ per period (or $1\frac{1}{2}\%$ each quarter)

(d) 6% compounded monthly $= \dfrac{6\%}{12 \text{ periods per year}}$

$= \frac{1}{2}\%$ per period (or $\frac{1}{2}\%$ each month)

Now let us compute a problem at compound interest:

Find the compound amount and the compound interest for the following investments:

Example Four

(a) $100 for three years at 5% compounded annually:

3 years × 1 period per year = 3 periods

$\dfrac{5\%}{1 \text{ period per year}} = 5\%$ per period

1st period	Principal	$100.00	
	Interest	+5.00	(5% of $100)
2nd period	Principal	$105.00	
	Interest	+5.25	(5% of $105)
3rd period	Principal	$110.25	
	Interest	+5.51	(5% of $110.25)
	Compound amount	$115.76	

Compound amount	$115.76
Less: original principal	100.00
Compound interest	$ 15.76

(b) $100 for one year at 8% compounded quarterly:

1 year × 4 periods per year = 4 periods

$\dfrac{8\%}{4 \text{ periods per year}} = 2\%$ per period

1st period	Principal	$100.00	
	Interest	+2.00	(2% of $100)
2nd period	Principal	$102.00	
	Interest	+2.04	(2% of $102)
3rd period	Principal	$104.04	
	Interest	+2.08	(2% of $104.04)
4th period	Principal	$106.12	
	Interest	+2.12	(2% of $106.12)
	Compound amount	$108.24	

Compound amount	$108.24
Less: original Principal	100.00
Compound interest	$ 8.24

PROBLEMS

Determine the number of periods and the rate per period for each of the following:

		Rate	Compounded	Years
1.	(a)	6%	monthly	5
	(b)	4	quarterly	7
	(c)	7	semiannually	10
	(d)	8	annually	14
	(e)	$5\frac{1}{2}$	semiannually	8
2.	(a)	8%	annually	12
	(b)	5	semiannually	15
	(c)	3	monthly	5
	(d)	4	quarterly	7
	(e)	$4\frac{1}{2}$	semiannually	4

Find the compound amount and the compound interest for each of the following:

3. $100 invested for two years at 4% —
   (a) compounded semiannually;
   (b) compounded quarterly.

4. $100 invested for two years at 4% —
   (a) compounded annually;
   (b) compounded quarterly.

5. $400 invested for three years at 8% —
   (a) compounded annually;
   (b) compounded semiannually.

6. $400 invested for one year at 8% —
   (a) compounded semiannually;
   (b) compounded quarterly.

7. $600 invested for one year at 6% —
   (a) compounded annually;
   (b) compounded quarterly.

8. $600 invested for three years at 6% —
   (a) compounded annually;
   (b) compounded semiannually.

9. $200 invested for one-half year at 6% —
   (a) compounded quarterly;
   (b) compounded monthly.

10. $1,000 invested for six months at 9% —
    (a) compounded quarterly;
    (b) compounded monthly.

11. Study carefully your answers to parts (a) and (b) of the preceding problems. What conclusion seems to be indicated?

12. Suppose you are given the principal, rate, and years of a compound interest problem. What else must you know in order to work the problem?

2. COMPOUND AMOUNT (USING TABLES)

Example 1 in the previous section illustrated the advantage of a compound interest investment over a simple interest investment. All banks and savings institutions in the United States pay compound interest on savings accounts. There are several factors besides rate, however, that the investor should consider before opening an account.

The problems in the last section demonstrated the advantage of more frequent compounding. Thus, if two banks offer 5% interest, but one compounds quarterly and the other compounds semiannually, the depositor would earn more interest at the bank offering quarterly interest.

Many institutions pay interest only upon the lowest balance that has been on deposit for the entire conversion period. That is, if an account is opened in the middle of a quarter, no interest will be earned that quarter because the funds have not been on deposit for an entire quarter. Similarly, if money is withdrawn during the quarter, no interest will be paid on the withdrawn funds for that quarter (even if they are redeposited the next day); rather, interest will be paid only on the lowest balance that remained after any withdrawal. If only deposits—no withdrawals—are made during a quarter, the account would still earn interest only on its balance on the first day of the quarter.

While computing the problems in Section 1, it no doubt became obvious to the student that this procedure can become quite long and tedious. Compound amount may also be found using the formula

$$S = P(1 + i)^n$$

where S = compound amount, P = original principal, i = interest rate per period, and n = number of periods.

(a) Using the formula for compound amount, compute the compound amount and compound interest on $1,000 invested for three years at 6% compounded semiannually. **Example One**

$P = \$1,000$ $S = P(1 + i)^n$
$i = 3\%$ per period $= \$1,000(1 + 3\%)^6$
$n = 6$ periods $= 1,000(1 + 0.03)^6$
$S = ?$ $= 1,000(1.03)^6$

Recall that the exponent—i.e., "6"—tells how many times the factor 1.03 should be written down before being multiplied. Thus 1.03 should be used as a factor 6 times:

$$S = \$1,000(1.03)^6$$
$$= 1,000(1.03)(1.03)(1.03)(1.03)(1.03)(1.03)$$
$$= 1,000(1.19405230\ldots)$$
$$= 1,000(1.19405230\ldots)$$
$$S = \$1,194.05$$

Therefore, the maturity value (compound amount) would be $1,194.05. The compound interest is $1,194.05 − $1,000 or $194.05.

Even using this formula, however, the calculation of compound amount would still be quite tedious if the number of periods (the exponent) were very large. The computation is greatly simplified through the use of a compound amount table—a list of the values obtained when the parenthetical expression $(1 + i)$ is used as a factor for the indicated numbers of periods.

(b) Using the compound amount formula and table, rework part (a).

$$P = \$1,000 \qquad\qquad S = P(1 + i)^n$$
$$i = 3\% \qquad\qquad\qquad = \$1,000(1 + 3\%)^6$$
$$n = 6$$

To find compound amount, turn to Table XIII: Amount of 1 (at Compound Interest, pp. 520–539). Various interest rates per period are given at the top outside margin of each page; find the page headed by 3%. The lines of the columns correspond to the number of periods, and these are numbered on both the right-hand and left-hand sides of the page. Go down to line 6 of the Amount column on the 3% page and there read "1.1940522965"; this is the value of $(1.03)^6$. Now,

$$S = P(1 + i)^n \qquad\qquad I = S - P$$
$$= \$1,000(1 + 3\%)^6 \qquad\qquad = \$1,194.05$$
$$= 1,000(1.1940522965) \qquad\qquad -1,000.00$$
$$S = \$1,194.05 \qquad\qquad I = \$\quad 194.05$$

Note: The value in the table includes the "1" from the parenthetical expression $(1 + i)$. It is *not* correct to add "1" to the tabular value before multiplying by the principal. (The student should now review Section 1, Accuracy of Computation, in Chapter 1, which demonstrates how many digits from the table must be used in order to insure an answer correct to the nearest penny.)

Example Two Find the compound amount and compound interest of $600 invested at 5% compounded quarterly for twelve years.

$$P = \$600 \qquad S = P(1 + i)^n \qquad\qquad I = S - P$$

$$i = 1\tfrac{1}{4}\% \qquad\quad = \$600(1 + 1\tfrac{1}{4}\%)^{48} \qquad = \$1,089.21$$

$$n = 48 \qquad\qquad = 600(1.815355) \qquad\quad -600.00$$

$$\qquad\qquad\qquad = 1,089.2130 \qquad\qquad I = \$\ \ \ 489.21$$

$$\qquad\qquad S = \$1,089.21$$

Thus, after twelve years, the $600 investment would be worth $1,089.21, of which $489.21 is interest.

David Schultz opened a savings account on January 1, 1971, with a deposit of $500. The bank paid 4% compounded quarterly. On October 1, 1971, he deposited enough more money to bring his account up to $700. (a) How much was David's deposit on October 1? (b) What was the value of David's account on April 1, 1972? (c) What was the total amount of interest earned?

This is basically a two-part problem. We must first find the amount in David's account on the day he made his second deposit. That amount plus the deposit then becomes the principal which draws interest for the remaining time.

$P_1 = \$500$, $i = 1\%$, $n = 3$ $\qquad\qquad\qquad$ $P_2 = \$700$, $i = 1\%$, $n = 2$

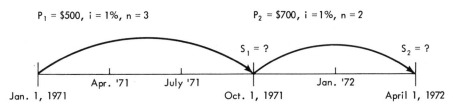

(a) Banking quarters usually begin on the first days of January, April, July, and October. This means that David's $500 deposit earned interest for three quarters before he made another deposit. Hence

$$P_1 = \$500 \qquad S = P(1 + i)^n \qquad\qquad \$700.00$$

$$i = 1\% \qquad\quad = \$500(1 + 1\%)^3 \qquad -515.15$$

$$n = 3 \qquad\qquad = 500(1.03030) \qquad\quad \overline{\$184.85} \ \ \text{Deposit}$$

$$\qquad\qquad\qquad = 515.15000$$

$$\qquad\qquad S_1 = \$515.15$$

David's deposit on October 1 was $184.85.

(b) On October 1, David's account contained $515.15. He had to make a $184.85 deposit in order to bring his account up to $700. There were two more quarters until April 1, during which his $700 principal earned interest.

$$P_2 = \$700 \qquad\qquad\qquad\qquad S = P(1 + i)^n$$

$$i = 1\% \qquad\qquad\qquad\qquad\quad = \$700(1 + 1\%)^2$$

$$n = 2 \qquad\qquad\qquad\qquad\quad = 700(1.02010)$$

$$\qquad\qquad\qquad\qquad\qquad\quad = 714.07000$$

$$\qquad\qquad\qquad\qquad\qquad S_2 = \$714.07$$

David's account was worth $714.07 on April 1, 1972.

(c) The total interest earned may be found in either of two ways: (1) by adding the interest paid on each of the principals, or (2) by finding the difference between the final balance and the total of all deposits.

(1) $I = S - P$ $I = S - P$ $15.15 interest
        $= \$515.15$ $= \$714.07$ 14.07 interest
        -500.00 -700.00 $\overline{\$29.22}$ *total interest*
        $I_1 = \$\ \ 15.15$ $I_2 = \$\ \ 14.07$

(2) 500.00 714.07 final balance
        $+184.85$ -684.85 total deposits
        $\overline{\$684.85}$ total deposits $\overline{\$\ \ 29.22}$ *total interest*

Example Four On July 1, 1969, Bill Dotson deposited $3,000 in a savings bank that paid 5% compounded semiannually. On January 1, 1971, the bank began paying $5\frac{1}{2}\%$ interest. (a) What was the value of Bill's account on January 1, 1973? (b) How much interest had been earned?

This is also a two-part problem. We must first find the amount when the 5% rate ended. This amount then becomes the principal for the term of the $5\frac{1}{2}\%$ rate.

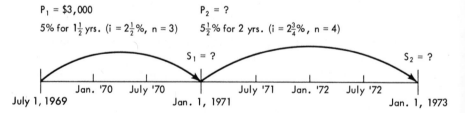

$P_1 = \$3,000$ $P_2 = ?$
5% for $1\frac{1}{2}$ yrs. ($i = 2\frac{1}{2}\%$, n = 3) $5\frac{1}{2}\%$ for 2 yrs. ($i = 2\frac{3}{4}\%$, n = 4)

$S_1 = ?$ $S_2 = ?$

Jan. '70 July '70   July '71 Jan. '72 July '72
July 1, 1969   Jan. 1, 1971   Jan. 1, 1973

(a) Bill's $3,000 deposit earned 5% interest compounded semi-annually for one-and-a-half years (July 1, 1969–January 1, 1971). Thus

$P_1 = \$3,000$ $S = P(1 + i)^n$
$i = 2\frac{1}{2}\%$ $= \$3,000(1 + 2\frac{1}{2}\%)^3$
$n = 3$ $= 3,000(1.076891)$
                        $= 3,230.673000$
                $S_1 = \$3,230.67$

There was $3,230.67 in Bill's account on January 1, 1971. This became the principal which earned interest at $5\frac{1}{2}\%$ compounded semiannually for two years (until January 1, 1973). So,

$$P_2 = \$3,230.67$$
$$i = 2\tfrac{3}{4}\%$$
$$n = 4$$

$$S = P(1 + i)^n$$
$$= \$3,230.67(1 + 2\tfrac{3}{4}\%)^4$$
$$= 3,230.67(1.114621)$$
$$= 3,600.9726\ldots$$
$$S_2 = \$3,600.97$$

(b)   On January 1, 1973, Bill's account was worth \$3,600.97. During the entire three-and-a-half years, his total interest earned was

$$I = S - P$$
$$= \quad \$3,600.97$$
$$\underline{-3,000.00}$$
$$I = \$ \quad 600.97$$

PROBLEMS

1.–8.   Rework Problems 3–10 of the previous section, using the compound amount formula and table. (Some answers may vary by a few cents because the tables are not rounded off after each period.)

Compute the compound amounts and compound interest:

		Principal	Rate	Compounded	Years
9.	(a)	$1,000	5%	monthly	6
	(b)	800	7	semiannually	12
	(c)	1,600	6	quarterly	11
	(d)	450	4	monthly	8
	(e)	2,400	$4\tfrac{1}{2}$	semiannually	13
10.	(a)	$ 600	5%	semiannually	7
	(b)	950	6	monthly	4
	(c)	1,500	8	quarterly	15
	(d)	2,400	7	quarterly	9
	(e)	400	$5\tfrac{1}{2}$	semiannually	20

11.   Find compound amount and compound interest on the following at 4% compound monthly for five years—
(a) $500;
(b) $1,000;
(c) $2,000.
(d)   What conclusion can be reached about the principal?

12.   Compute compound amount and interest on the following at 5% compounded monthly for seven years—
(a) $100;
(b) $200;
(c) $400.
(d)   What is your conclusion regarding the principal?

13. Determine compound amount and interest on $1,000 with interest compounded semiannually for ten years at the following rates—
    (a) 3%;
    (b) 6%;
    (c) 12%.
    (d) Is there a predictable outcome when rate is doubled?

14. Calculate compound amount and interest (compounded quarterly for thirteen years) on $1,000 at—
    (a) 4%;
    (b) 8%;
    (c) 16%.
    (d) Do you find a definite relationship when rate is doubled?

15. Compute compound amount and compound interest on $1,000 at 7% compounded quarterly for—
    (a) 4 years;
    (b) 8 years;
    (c) 16 years.
    (d) Do you find a predictable relationship when time is doubled?

16. Determine compound amount and interest on $1,000 at 6% compounded semiannually for—
    (a) 6 years;
    (b) 12 years;
    (c) 24 years.
    (d) Does doubling the time produce a predictable effect?

17. Gilbert Novarro opened a savings account on January 1, 1971, with a deposit of $1,000. On July 1, 1971, he deposited enough money to make his account total $1,400. If the bank paid 5% compounded quarterly,
    (a) What was the total in his account on July 1, 1971, before his deposit was added?
    (b) What amount did he deposit on that day?
    (c) How much was Novarro's account worth on July 1, 1972?
    (d) How much total interest had been earned?

18. On July 1, 1971, Sharon White deposited $1,000 in a savings bank. The institution paid 5% compounded semiannually.
    (a) What was the value of Sharon's account on January 1, 1972?
    (b) On that day, Sharon made a deposit which brought the balance in her account to $1,200. What was the amount of her deposit?
    (c) What was Sharon's account worth on January 1, 1973?

19. Ronald Gleason deposited $300 on January 1, 1970. The bank paid $4\frac{1}{2}$% compounded semiannually. On July 1, 1971, Ronald deposited another $200.
    (a) What was the value of Gleason's account on July 1, 1971, before his deposit?

(b) What was his account worth on January 1, 1973?

(c) What total amount of interest was earned?

20. Robert Cox had $500 on deposit on October 1, 1971. The bank paid 4% compounded quarterly. On July 1, 1972, he made a deposit of $300.

    (a) Find the value of Cox's account on July 1 before he made the deposit.

    (b) Determine the value of his account on April 1, 1974.

    (c) How much interest will the account have earned?

21. On July 1, 1970, Marilyn Ross' savings account contained $1,000. Her bank paid $5\frac{1}{2}$% compounded semiannually.

    (a) How much did her account contain on July 1, 1971?

    (b) On July 1, 1971, the bank reduced the rate to 5% compounded semiannually. How much did her account contain on January 1, 1973?

    (c) What total amount of interest was earned?

22. On July 1, 1971, Bill Williams had $1,000 on deposit at a bank paying 4% compounded semiannually. On January 1, 1972, the bank began paying $4\frac{1}{2}$% compounded semiannually.

    (a) What was the value of Williams' account on January 1, 1972?

    (b) How much was his account worth on January 1, 1973?

    (c) How much total interest had his account earned?

23. Rita Watson had $1,000 in her savings account on January 1. The bank was paying 6% compounded quarterly. On April 1, the bank began paying 6% compounded monthly.

    (a) What was the balance in her account on April 1?

    (b) What was Rita's account worth at the end of the year?

    (c) How much interest did she earn that year?

24. Michael Shelton had $1,000 on deposit on January 1 at a bank paying 5% compounded quarterly. On July 1, Michael moved his account to a bank paying $5\frac{1}{2}$% compounded semiannually.

    (a) With what amount did Michael open his new account on July 1?

    (b) How much was his account worth at the end of the year?

    (c) How much interest was earned during the year?

3. INTEREST COMPOUNDED DAILY

It is becoming increasingly popular for financial institutions to pay "daily interest" (interest compounded daily). Some institutions pay interest for the exact number of days that money has been on deposit, while many others offer the added inducement of interest paid from the first of the month for all deposits made by the tenth of the month.

    Interest on deposits is compounded daily; but to eliminate excessive bookkeeping, most institutions enter interest in the depositor's account only once each quarter. (For this reason, the daily interest table contains factors for one quarter. In accordance with the practice followed by most savings institutions, it is a 90-day quarter; deposits made on the 31st of any month earn interest as if they were made on the 30th. Recall that quarters begin in January, April, July, and October.)

In the previous section, it was pointed out that depositors lose interest at many institutions because deposits or withdrawals are made sometime during an interest period. The primary advantage of interest compounded daily is that interest is never lost—money earns interest for every day it is on deposit, regardless of when it is deposited or withdrawn.

Our study will be limited to 5% interest compounded daily. Interest is found by multiplying the principal (deposit) times the appropriate value from Table XIX: Interest from Date of Deposit (p. 540). So,

$$\text{Interest} = \text{Principal} \times \text{Deposit table}$$

which might be abbreviated

$$I = P \times \text{Dep. tab.}$$

In the daily interest deposit table, there is a column for each of the three months of the quarter; each column (month) contains entries for 30 days. To use the table, one looks for the date on which a deposit was made; the factor beside that date is the number to be multiplied times the amount of deposit in order to obtain the interest (provided the money remained on deposit until the quarter ended). If interest is paid from the first of the month and a deposit was made by the tenth of the month, then one should use the factor given beside the first day of the month rather than beside the actual day of deposit.

Example One

Find the interest which would be earned at 5% compounded daily, if $1,000 were deposited in a savings and loan association paying interest from the first on deposits made by the tenth (a) on April 15, and (b) on November 6.

(a) April 15 is the first month of the quarter; therefore, we refer to the "1st Month" column of the deposit table and to the 15th line under that heading:

$$\begin{aligned} I &= P \times \text{Dep. tab.} \\ &= \$1,000(0.010611) \\ &= 10.611 \\ I &= \$10.61 \end{aligned}$$

When the quarter ends, interest of $10.61 will be added to the depositor's account. (Notice that the deposit would have earned no interest at all in most institutions paying 5% quarterly interest, because the deposit was made after the quarter had already begun.)

(b)   November is the second month of the quarter. Since the deposit
      was made by the tenth of November, we use the factor beside
      the "1" (the first) under "2nd Month":

$$I = P \times \text{Dep. tab.}$$
$$= \$1,000(0.008368)$$
$$= 8.368$$
$$I = \$8.37$$

The deposit will earn interest of $8.37 during the remaining part of
the quarter.

Example Two

William Midler has a savings account in a savings and loan association
where deposits made by the tenth earn interest from the first at 5% compounded daily. When the quarter began in July, Midler's account contained $800. During the quarter, he made the following deposits: $200 on
July 9; $50 on August 20; and $100 on September 8. (a) How much interest will the account earn during the quarter? (b) How much will the account contain at the end of the quarter?

If a deposit is made by the tenth of the first month of a quarter, that
deposit can be added to the beginning balance and interest computed on
that principal for the entire quarter. For deposits made after the tenth of
the first month, interest should be computed separately for each deposit.
The total interest for the quarter is the sum of all interest of the various
deposits.

(a)   Since $800 was on deposit July 1 and the $200 deposit was made
      before July 10, Midler will earn interest on $1,000 for the whole
      quarter:

$$I = P \times \text{Dep. tab.}$$
$$= \$1,000(0.012578)$$
$$= 12.578$$
$$I = \$12.58$$

August is the second month; thus the interest on the $50 deposit
made on the 20th is:

$$I = P \times \text{Dep. tab.}$$
$$= \$50(0.00571)$$
$$= .28550$$
$$I = \$ .28$$

The $100 deposit made September 8 would earn interest from the
first of the third month:

$$I = P \times \text{Dep. tab.}$$
$$= \$100(0.00418)$$
$$= \quad .418$$
$$I = \$ \quad .42$$

Thus the transactions for the quarter would be as follows:

Principal	Interest
$800⎱ 200⎰	$12.58
50	.28
100	.42
$1,150	+ $13.28 = $1,163.28 balance, end of quarter

The account would earn total interest of $13.28 during the quarter.

(b) The balance in Midler's account at the end of the quarter would be $1,163.28.

When withdrawals are involved, interest may be calculated in the following manner:

1. Subtract the withdrawals from the opening principal. Compute interest on this remaining balance for the entire quarter.
2. Determine the interest which would be earned on the withdrawn funds until the date they were withdrawn. This interest is found as follows, using Table XX: Interest to Date of Withdrawal (p. 541):

$$\text{Interest} = \text{Withdrawal} \times \text{Withdrawal table}$$

which may be abbreviated

$$I = W \times W/D \text{ tab.}$$

(The daily interest withdrawal table is similar to the daily interest deposit table in that it is divided into the three months of the quarter, and one uses the factor beside the appropriate date.)

3. Total interest for the quarter is the sum of the various amounts of interest found in steps 1 and 2.

Example Three An account contained $1,300 on October 1. On December 13, a withdrawal of $300 was made. (a) How much interest did the account earn for the quarter, if interest was paid at 5% compounded daily? (b) What was the balance in the account after the quarter ended?

(a) Since $300 was withdrawn from the $1,300 account, only $1,000 will earn interest for the entire quarter. In Example 2, we found that the interest on $1,000 for one quarter is $12.58.

Next, we need to compute the interest that will be earned on the $300 between the start of the quarter and December 13, when the $300 was withdrawn. Since December is the third month of the quarter, we use the 13th line in the "3rd Month" column in the withdrawal table:

$$I = W \times W/D \text{ tab.}$$
$$= \$300\,(0.01019)$$
$$= 3.05700$$
$$I = \$3.06$$

The $300 will earn interest of $3.06 before it is withdrawn on December 13.

Interest
___

$12.58
+3.06
_____
$15.64   total interest for the quarter

(b)   The balance in the account at the end of the quarter was

Opening balance	$1,300.00
Withdrawal	− 300.00
	$1,000.00
Interest	+15.64
	$1,015.64 Balance, end of quarter

Compute (a) the interest and (b) the balance at the end of the quarter for the following transactions at 5% interest compounded daily:

Example Four

Balance	January 1	$1,200
Deposit	January 10	300
Withdrawal	February 23	100
Deposit	March 15	400
Withdrawal	March 20	100

(a)   Since a $300 deposit was made on January 10, the account would have earned interest on $1,200 + $300 or $1,500 for the entire quarter, if there had been no withdrawals. Since two withdrawals of $100 were made, only $1,500 − $200 or $1,300 will earn interest for the entire quarter.

Withdrawals
___

February 23	$100
March 20	+100
	$200

Opening balance	$1,200
Deposit, January 10	+300
Effective opening balance	$1,500
Withdrawals	−200
Principal earning interest for entire quarter	$1,300

$$I = P \times \text{Dep. tab.}$$
$$= \$1,300\,(0.012578)$$
$$= 16.351400$$
$$I = \$16.35$$

The interest on the $400 deposit made on the 15th of March (third month) is

$$I = P \times \text{Dep. tab.}$$
$$= \$400\,(0.00222)$$
$$= .88800$$
$$I = \$.89$$

Interest on the $100 withdrawal made the 23rd of February (second month) is

$$I = W \times \text{W/D tab.}$$
$$= \$100\,(0.00739)$$
$$= .739$$
$$I = \$.74$$

Interest on the $100 withdrawal made the 20th of March (third month) is

$$I = W \times \text{W/D tab.}$$
$$= \$100\,(0.01117)$$
$$= 1.117$$
$$I = \$1.12$$

Thus total interest for the quarter is

	Interest
Interest on funds on deposit for the entire quarter	$16.35
Interest on $400 deposited March 15	.89
Interest on $100 withdrawn February 23	.74
Interest on $100 withdrawn March 20	1.12
Total interest for quarter	$19.10

(b)   The balance after the quarter ended was

Deposits	Withdrawals		
$300	$100	Opening balance	$1,200.00
+400	+100	Deposits	+700.00
$700	$200		$1,900.00
		Withdrawals	−200.00
			$1,700.00
		Interest	+19.10
		Balance, end of quarter	$1,719.10

The savings account contained $1,719.20 after the quarter ended.

The following problems are all for interest paid at 5% compounded daily. Unless otherwise stated in the problem, interest is to be paid from the first of the month on deposits made by the tenth of the month.

Find (1) the amount of interest and (2) the balance at the end of the quarter for the following deposits:

1. (a) $1,000 on April 15
   (b)   500 on September 6
   (c)   1,800 on February 21
   (d)   4,000 on October 4

2. (a) $ 100 on May 17
   (b)   2,000 on January 7
   (c)   1,500 on December 3
   (d)   400 on July 29

In the following problems, compute the interest that would be earned (1) if interest is paid from the exact date of deposit and (2) if interest is paid from the first of the month on deposits made by the tenth:

3. (a) $1,000 on March 5
   (b)   800 on May 10
   (c)   3,000 on July 7

4. (a) $1,000 deposited November 6
   (b)   5,000 deposited January 8
   (c)   700 deposited June 4

In the following problems, compute the interest that would be earned for one quarter (1) at 5% compounded daily, and (2) at 5% compounded quarterly on the given principals:

5. (a) $1,000
   (b)   4,500

6. (a) $10,000
   (b)   2,500

Find (1) the total amount of interest and (2) the balance after the quarter ended for the following accounts:

	Opening Balance	Deposits
7. (a)	$3,000 on July 1	$ 400 on July 20 1,000 on August 8 200 on September 15
(b)	$1,600 on April 1	$ 400 on April 4 300 on May 28 100 on June 12

8. (a) $2,500 on January 1 $ 500 on January 7
                                         50 on February 27
                                       400 on March 6

     (b) $4,000 on October 1 $ 80 on October 20
                                         200 on November 2
                                 1,000 on December 10

Compute (1) the interest for the quarter and (2) the balance when the quarter ended for the following problems:

	Opening Balance	Withdrawals
9. (a)	$1,200 on October 1	$200 on November 14
(b)	$4,700 on January 1	$300 on February 2
		400 on March 18
10. (a)	$3,400 on July 1	$400 on August 16
(b)	$1,800 on April 1	$500 on May 1
		300 on June 7

Transactions for an entire quarter are given below. Calculate (1) the total interest each account would earn and (2) the balance in each account after the quarter ends. (*Hint:* Be alert for deposits made before the tenth of a month.)

	Opening Balance	Deposits	Withdrawals
11. (a)	$1,800 on July 1	$400 on July 9	$200 on August 20
(b)	$3,200 on April 1	$300 on April 27	$100 on April 14
		100 on May 13	100 on June 10
(c)	$2,400 on January 1	$400 on January 5	$500 on February 4
		80 on March 7	300 on March 28
12. (a)	$ 900 on January 1	$300 on January 10	$200 on March 25
(b)	$2,400 on October 1	$200 on November 18	$300 on October 3
		50 on December 6	100 on December 13
(c)	$4,700 on April 1	$400 on April 8	$200 on April 27
		70 on May 9	900 on June 20

4. PRESENT VALUE (AT COMPOUND INTEREST)

It often happens that one wishes to know how much he would have to deposit now (at the present) in order to obtain a certain maturity value. The principal that would have to be deposited is the *present value*.

The formula for obtaining present value at compound interest is a variation of the compound amount formula. The formula is rearranged to solve for P rather than S, by dividing both sides of the equation by the parenthetical expression:

$$S = P(1 + i)^n$$

Divide by $(1 + i)^n$:

$$\frac{S}{(1 + i)^n} = \frac{P\cancel{(1 + i)^n}}{\cancel{(1 + i)^n}}$$

$$\frac{S}{(1 + i)^n} = P$$

or

$$P = \frac{S}{(1 + i)^n}$$

Therefore, present value could be found by dividing the known maturity value S by the appropriate value from the compound amount table (Table XIII) which we have already been using. However, division using such long decimal numbers would be an extremely long and cumbersome operation; hence present value tables have been developed which allow present value to be computed by multiplication.

Just as $\frac{12}{3} = 12 \cdot \frac{1}{3}$, so

$$\frac{S}{(1 + i)^n} = S \cdot \frac{1}{(1 + i)^n}$$

The entries in Table XVI: Present Worth of 1 (pp. 520–539) are the quotients obtained when the numbers from the compound amount table are divided into "1." These quotients (the present value entries) may then be multiplied by the appropriate maturity value to obtain the present value.

Since present value is usually computed using multiplication, the formula is commonly written in a form that indicates multiplication and uses a negative exponent. Recall that a negative exponent indicates the factor actually belongs in the opposite part of the fraction. (That is, $3x^{-2}$ means $\frac{3}{x^2}$.) Thus

$$P = \frac{S}{(1 + i)^n}$$

is usually written

$$P = S(1 + i)^{-n}$$

The following example will illustrate that present value may be found using either the compound amount table (Table XIII) or the present value table (Table XVI). As a general rule, however, the student should use the present value table (Table XVI) when computing present value at compound interest.

Example One

The maturity value of an investment is to be $1,000 after five years at 4% compounded quarterly. Compute the present value (a) using the compound amount table (Table XIII) and (b) using the present value table (Table XVI). (c) Also determine how much interest will be earned.

(a)

$S = \$1,000$
$i = 1\%$
$n = 20$
$P = ?$

$$P = \frac{S}{(1 + i)^n}$$

$$= \frac{\$1,000}{(1 + 1\%)^{20}}$$

$$= \frac{1,000}{1.220190}$$

$$= 819.544$$

$$P = \$819.54$$

(b)

$$P = S(1 + i)^{-n}$$
$$= \$1,000(1 + 1\%)^{-20}$$
$$= 1,000(0.819544)$$
$$P = \$819.54$$

(c)

$$I = S - P$$
$$= \$1,000.00$$
$$\underline{-819.54}$$
$$I = \$ \ \ 180.46$$

So, $819.54 invested now will earn $180.46 interest and mature to $1,000 after five years at 4% compounded quarterly.

Example Two

Ralph Akins wants to have $5,000 in three years for a down payment on a home. (a) What single deposit would have this maturity value, if money is worth 5% compounded monthly? (b) How much interest will be earned during the three years?

(a)

$S = \$5,000$
$n = 36$
$i = \frac{5}{12}\%$
$P = ?$

$$P = S(1 + i)^{-n}$$
$$= \$5,000(1 + \frac{5}{12}\%)^{-36}$$
$$= 5,000(0.8609762)$$
$$= 4,304.881$$
$$P = \$4,304.88$$

(b)

$$I = S - P$$
$$= \$5,000.00$$
$$\underline{-4,304.88}$$
$$I = \$ \ \ 695.12$$

If Akins deposits $4,304.88 now, it will earn $695.12 interest in three years at 5% compounded monthly and have a $5,000 maturity value.

As was true of simple interest problems, present value (or present worth) may on occasion differ from principal. The actual amount of money that is invested is always the principal; it may or may not be invested at the interest rate currently being paid by most financial institutions. The present value of the investment is the amount which would have to be invested at the rate money is worth (the rate being paid by most financial institutions) in order to obtain the same maturity value that the actual investment will have. If an investment is sold before its maturity date, it should theoretically be sold for its present value at that time.

William Baxter has made an $8,000 investment that is earning interest at the rate of 8% compounded semiannually. Baxter expects the investment to continue paying for ten years. If money is worth 6% compounded quarterly, what is the least amount for which Baxter would sell his investment?   **Example Three**

This is a two-part problem. We must first determine the maturity value of the $8,000 investment. Then, using the rate money is actually worth, we must compute the present worth of the maturity value obtained by step one.

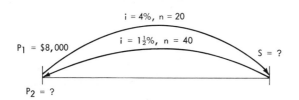

$$i = 4\%, \ n = 20$$
$$P_1 = \$8,000 \qquad i = 1\tfrac{1}{2}\%, \ n = 40 \qquad S = ?$$
$$P_2 = ?$$

1.

$$P_1 = \$8,000$$
$$i = 4\%$$
$$n = 20$$
$$S = ?$$

$$S = P(1 + i)^n$$
$$= \$8,000(1 + 4\%)^{20}$$
$$= 8,000(2.1911231)$$
$$= 17,528.9848000$$
$$S = \$17,528.98$$

2.

$$S = \$17,528.98$$
$$i = 1\tfrac{1}{2}\%$$
$$n = 40$$
$$P_2 = ?$$

$$P = S(1 + i)^{-n}$$
$$= \$17,528.98(1 + 1\tfrac{1}{2}\%)^{-40}$$
$$= 17,528.98(0.5512623)$$
$$= 9,663.065\ldots$$
$$P_2 = \$9,663.07$$

Baxter should not sell his $8,000 investment for less than $9,663.07, for this is the amount he would have to deposit in a bank paying 6% quarterly interest in order to have $17,528.98 in ten years.

PROBLEMS

Compute present value at compound interest for the following. Also determine the amount of interest that will be earned before maturity.

		Maturity Value	Rate	Compounded	Years
1.	(a)	$1,000	6%	quarterly	4
	(b)	600	5	monthly	6
	(c)	1,500	8	semiannually	12
	(d)	4,000	4½	semiannually	20
	(e)	2,400	6	monthly	7
2.	(a)	$1,000	7%	quarterly	15
	(b)	2,800	5	semiannually	18
	(c)	500	3	monthly	8
	(d)	1,400	6	quarterly	11
	(e)	2,000	8	semiannually	10

3. Roger Moffitt wants to have $10,000 in his savings account in 17 years when his young daughter will be ready for college. If the savings and loan association pays 6% compounded semiannually on long-term certificates of deposit—
   (a) How much would Moffitt have to deposit now in order to reach his goal?
   (b) How much interest will the account earn during this time?

4. Watkins Associates expects to need $5,000 in eight years to replace some machinery. If they can make an investment which pays 7% compounded semiannually—
   (a) How much should Watkins invest in order to have this maturity value?
   (b) What amount of interest will their investment earn?

5. Far West Motor Freight Lines expect to replace a van in five years at a cost of $8,000. If they can make an investment now at 6% compounded monthly—
   (a) How much must be deposited now to obtain the desired maturity value?
   (b) How much of the $8,000 will be interest?

6. Arnold Douglas wants to have $1,000 in two years for a down payment on a new car.
   (a) What single deposit now will mature to $1,000 at 4% compounded monthly?
   (b) How much interest will the deposit earn?

7. A business firm plans to expand its offices in four years at a cost of $20,000.
   (a) What single deposit made now will have a maturity value of $20,000, if money earns 8% compounded quarterly?
   (b) How much interest will be earned?

8. William Farmer will retire in 15 years, and he would like to have $10,000 at that time.
   (a) What single deposit made now will mature to $10,000 if money is worth 6% compounded quarterly?
   (b) How much interest will the deposit earn in 15 years?

9. A $3,000 investment is made at 5% compounded quarterly, to continue for 15 years.
   (a) What is the maturity value of the investment?
   (b) If money is generally worth $5\frac{1}{2}$% compounded semiannually, what is the present worth of the investment?

10. A seven-year, $6,000 investment was made at $5\frac{1}{2}$% compounded semi-annually.
    (a) What is the maturity value of this investment?
    (b) What is the present worth of the investment, if money usually earns 5% compounded quarterly?

11. George Martin holds a four-year, $7\frac{1}{2}$% simple interest note for $1,000. Money is worth 6% compounded quarterly.
    (a) How much will the borrower repay on the due date of the note?
    (b) If Martin had sold the note on the day it was drawn, how much should he have received?

12. Wayne Redmond is the payee of a $500 note at 6% simple interest for three years. Most financial institutions pay 5% compounded monthly.
    (a) What maturity value must the maker repay?
    (b) How much should Redmond have received if he had sold the note on the day it was issued?

13. An $800, simple interest note was drawn at $6\frac{1}{4}$% for two years.
    (a) What will be the total amount due when the note matures?
    (b) If money is worth 7% compounded semiannually, what was the present worth of the note on the day it was drawn?

14. A $1,000 note was issued for two years at 5% simple interest.
    (a) How much will be owed on the maturity date of the note?
    (b) What was the present worth of this note on the day it was drawn, if money is worth 4% compounded monthly?

19

Annuities

LEARNING OBJECTIVES

Upon completion of Chapter 19, the student will be able to:

1. Define and use correctly the terminology associated with each topic.

2. Determine amount and compound interest earned on an annuity, using $S = \text{Pmt.} \times \text{Amt. ann. tab.}_{\overline{n}|i}$ and the amount of annuity table.

3. a. Compute present value of an annuity, using $\text{P.V.} = \text{Pmt.} \times \text{P.V. ann. tab.}_{\overline{n}|i}$ and the present value of annuity table. (That is, determine the original value required in order for one to withdraw the given annuity payments.)
   b. Also, determine
   (1) The total amount received, and
   (2) The interest included.

4. Use the same procedure (Objective 3) to determine
   a. The total amount paid for a real estate purchase, and
   b. The equivalent cash price.

NOTICE THAT the compound interest problems in the previous chapter basically involved making a *single deposit* which remained invested for the entire time. There are few people, however, who have large sums available to invest in this manner. Most people must attain their savings goals by making a series of regular deposits. This leads to the idea of annuities.

An *annuity* is a series of payments (normally equal in amount) which are made at regular intervals of time. Most people typically think of an annuity as the regular payment received from an insurance policy when it is cashed in after retirement. This is one good example, but there are many other everyday examples that are seldom thought of as annuities. Besides savings deposits, other common examples are rent, salaries, Social Security payments, installment plan payments, loan payments, insurance payments—in fact, any payment made at regular intervals of time.

There are several time variables that may affect an annuity. For instance, some annuities have definite beginning and ending dates; such an annuity is called an *annuity certain*. Examples of an annuity certain are installment plan payments or the payments from a life insurance policy converted to an annuity of a specified number of years.

If the beginning and/or ending date are uncertain, the annuity is called a *contingent annuity*. Monthly Social Security retirement benefits and the payments on an ordinary life insurance policy are examples of contingent annuities for which the ending dates are unknown, because both will terminate when the person dies. If a person provides in his will that following his death a beneficiary is to receive an annuity for a fixed number of years, this is a contingent annuity for which the beginning date is uncertain. A person with a large estate might provide that his surviving wife receive a specified yearly income for the remainder of her life and that the balance then be donated to some charity; this contingent annuity would then be uncertain on both the beginning and ending dates.

Another factor affecting annuities is whether the payment is made at the beginning of each time interval (such as rent or insurance premiums, which are normally paid in advance) or at the end of the period (such as salaries or Social Security retirement benefits). An annuity for which payments are made at the beginning of each period is known as an *annuity due*. When payments come at the end of each period, the annuity is called an *ordinary annuity*.

We shall be studying *investment annuities*—annuities which are earning compound interest (rather than rent or installment payments, for example, which are earning no interest). An annuity is said to be a *simple annuity* when the date of payment coincides with the conversion date of the compound interest.

The study of contingent annuities requires some knowledge of probability, which is not within the scope of this text. Thus, since our purpose is just to give the student a basic introduction to annuities, our study of annuities will be limited to simple, ordinary annuities certain—annuities for which both the beginning and ending dates are fixed, and for which the payments are made on the conversion date at the end of each period.

1. AMOUNT OF AN ANNUITY

The *amount of an annuity* is the maturity value which an account will have after a series of equal payments into it. (The actual formula for amount of an annuity is rather involved and would probably not be very meaningful to the student.) As in the case of other compound interest problems, amount of an annuity is usually found by using the appropriate table for the appropriate rate per period and number of periods. Thus we shall compute amount of an annuity by using Table XIV: Amount of 1 per Period (pp. 520–539) and the following procedure:

$$\text{Amount} = \text{Payment} \times \text{Amount of annuity table}_{\overline{n}|i}$$

where n = number of periods and i = interest rate per period. For simplicity, the procedure* might be abbreviated,

$$S = \text{Pmt.} \times \text{Amt. ann. tab.}_{\overline{n}|i}$$

(In the table title "Amount of 1 per Period," the "1 per Period" indicates this is an annuity table, since an annuity involves a payment for each conversion period. The "1" means a payment of "$1", and we multiply the tabular value by the number of dollars in any given problem.)

---

*Many texts give the procedure for amount of an annuity in the form $S = Ps_{\overline{n}|i}$, where S = maturity value, P = payment, and $s_{\overline{n}|i}$ indicates use of the amount of an annuity table. Strictly speaking, $S = Ps_{\overline{n}|i}$ is also a procedure, not a formula.

The total amount of deposits is found by multiplying the periodic payment times the number of periods. Total interest earned is then the difference between the maturity value and the total deposits made into the account.

Example One
(a) Find the amount of an annuity of $100 paid each six months for ten years into an account paying 6% compounded semiannually. (b) How much was actually deposited during the time of the annuity? (c) How much interest did the account earn during the time of the annuity?

(a) (Notice that the deposits are made each six months to coincide with the conversion date of the bank; we would not be able to compute the annuity if they were otherwise.)

$$Pmt. = \$100 \qquad S = Pmt. \times Amt.\ ann.\ tab._{\overline{n}|i}$$
$$n = 20 \qquad\qquad = \$100 \times Amt.\ ann.\ tab._{\overline{20}|3\%}$$
$$i = 3\% \qquad\qquad = 100(26.87037)$$
$$\qquad\qquad\qquad = 2,687.037$$
$$\qquad\qquad S = \$2,687.04$$

(b) Since 20 deposits of $100 each will be made, the total deposits will be 20 × $100 or $2,000.

(c) The interest earned during the annuity is

Amount of annuity	$2,687.04
Total deposits	−2,000.00
Interest	$ 687.04

Example Two
Nancy Anderson deposits $20 into her savings account each month. (a) How much will her account contain in five years, if the bank pays 5% compounded monthly? (b) How much will Nancy have deposited herself? (c) How much interest will have been earned?

(a) $$Pmt. = \$20 \qquad S = Pmt. \times Amt.\ ann.\ tab._{\overline{n}|i}$$
$$n = 60 \qquad\qquad = \$20 \times Amt.\ ann.\ tab._{\overline{60}|\frac{5}{12}\%}$$
$$i = \tfrac{5}{12}\% \qquad\qquad = 20(68.00608)$$
$$\qquad\qquad\qquad = 1,360.12160$$
$$\qquad\qquad\qquad = \$1,360.12$$

(b) Since 60 deposits of $20 each totals $1,200,

(c) The interest earned will be $1,360.12 − $1,200 or $160.12.

PROBLEMS

Using the amount-of-an-annuity procedure, find the maturity value that would be obtained if one makes the payments given below. Also determine the total deposits and the total interest earned.

		Periodic Payment	Rate	Compounded	Years
1.	(a)	$1,000	6%	quarterly	5
	(b)	200	4	semiannually	11
	(c)	50	7	quarterly	15
	(d)	700	5	monthly	4
	(e)	1,400	$4\frac{1}{2}$	semiannually	9
2.	(a)	$ 100	4%	monthly	7
	(b)	1,500	7	semiannually	8
	(c)	80	6	quarterly	16
	(d)	600	5	quarterly	5
	(e)	2,000	$5\frac{1}{2}$	semiannually	19

3. A grandfather deposited $100 into his grandson's savings account on each birthday until the grandson was 21.
   (a) How much did the grandfather deposit?
   (b) What amount was in the account on the boy's 21st birthday, if the account earned 8% annual interest?
   (c) How much interest was earned during the time of the annuity?

4. A "rich uncle" gave his niece $100 each Christmas until the niece was 18. If the savings bank paid 7% annual interest—
   (a) What was the value of the account at the last Christmas?
   (b) How much had actually been deposited?
   (c) How much was interest?

5. Grace Evans deposits $300 each quarter in her savings account. Money is worth 5% compounded quarterly.
   (a) What will be the value of Grace's account after six years?
   (b) What will be the total of Grace's deposits?
   (c) How much interest will her account contain?

6. Each month Harry Wise deposits $50 into his savings and loan account. The association has been paying 5% compounded monthly.
   (a) How much will Harry's account be worth in seven years?
   (b) How much of this total will Harry have deposited?
   (c) How much will be interest?

7. Benson Textiles, Inc. is saving $3,000 each six months in order to purchase new knitting machines in three years. Their savings certificates pay 6% compounded semiannually.
   (a) How much will the firm deposit during the three years?
   (b) What will be the value of their savings certificates then?
   (c) How much of the maturity value will be interest?

8. Lytle Industries are investing $5,000 each six months with the intention of expanding their plant facilities in five years. The money is being invested in a mutual fund paying 8% compounded semiannually.

(a) How much will Lytle invest during the five years?

(b) What will be the amount of their account?

(c) How much interest will the account have drawn?

2. PRESENT VALUE OF AN ANNUITY

Observe that our study of amount of an annuity involved starting with an empty account and making payments into it so that the account contained its largest amount at the end of the term. The study of present value of an annuity is exactly the reverse: The account contains its largest balance at the beginning of the term and one receives payments from the account until it is empty. This balance which an account must contain at the beginning of the term is the *present value* or *present worth of an annuity*.

Rather than studying the actual formula for present value of an annuity, we will use an informal procedure as we did for amount of an annuity. By consulting Table XVII: Present Worth of 1 per Period (pp. 520–539), present value may be computed as follows:

$$\text{Present value} = \text{Payment} \times \text{Present value of annuity table}_{\overline{n}|i}$$

where, as before, n = number of payments and i = interest rate per period. The procedure* may be abbreviated

$$\text{P.V.} = \text{Pmt.} \times \text{P.V. ann. tab.}_{\overline{n}|i}$$

(Again, the words "1 per Period" in the table title tell us that this is an annuity table. The table gives the present value of a payment of $1 each conversion period, and we multiply by the number of dollars in the given problem.)

The total amount to be received from an annuity is found by multiplying the payment times the number of periods. As long as there are still funds in the account, it will continue to earn interest; thus, even though the balance of the account is declining during the term of the annuity, the account will still continue to earn some interest until the final payment is received. The total interest which the account will earn is the difference between the beginning balance (the present value) and the total payments to be received.

Example One
(a) Find the present value of an annuity of $100 received each six months for ten years from an account earning 6% compounded semiannually. (b) How much will the owner actually receive from the annuity? (c) How much of these payments was interest on the account?

---

*The procedure for present value of an annuity is often indicated as $A = Pa_{\overline{n}|i}$, where A = present value, P = payment, and $a_{\overline{n}|i}$ indicates use of the present-value-of-an-annuity table.

(a) Pmt. = $100   P.V. = Pmt. × P.V. ann. tab.$_{\overline{n}|i}$
     n = 20   = $100 × P.V. ann. tab.$_{\overline{20}|3\%}$
     i = 3%   = 100(14.87747)
                                = 1,487.747
                       P.V. = $1,487.75

(b) The owner of the annuity will receive 20 payments of $100 each for a total of $2,000.

(c) The account will earn interest of

Total payments	$2,000.00
Present value	− 1,487.75
Interest	$ 512.25

Thus, from an account containing $1,487.75, one may withdraw $100 each six months until a total of $2,000 has been withdrawn. During this time, the declining fund will have earned $512.25 interest. After the final payment is received, the balance of the account will be exactly $0.

Glen Marr wishes to receive $20 each month during the four years while he is in college. If his money is invested in a savings bank paying 4% compounded monthly—(a) How much must Glenn's account contain when he starts to college? (b) How much will the annuity pay during his years in college? (c) How much of the annuity is interest?   **Example Two**

(a) Pmt. = $20   P.V. = Pmt. × P.V. ann. tab.$_{\overline{n}|i}$
     n = 48   = $20 × P.V. ann. tab.$_{\overline{48}|\frac{1}{3}\%}$
     i = $\frac{1}{3}$%   = 20(44.2888)
                              = 885.7760
                     P.V. = $885.78

He must have $885.78 in his account when he starts to college.

(b) Glenn will receive 48 payments of $20 each, for a total of $960.

(c) The annuity will include interest totaling

Total payments	$960.00
Present value	− 885.78
Interest	$ 74.22

George Hensen would like to receive an annuity of $300 each quarter for 15 years after he retires; he will retire in ten years. Money is worth 5% compounded quarterly. (a) How much must George have when he retires in order to receive this annuity? (b) What single deposit would he have to make now in order to provide the funds for the annuity? (c) How much   **Example Three** will the annuity actually pay? (d) How much total interest will the deposit earn until the annuity ends?

This is a two-part problem. The first step is to find what beginning balance (present value) would be required for the 15-year annuity; the second step is to determine what single deposit (present value at compound interest) would result in a maturity value equal to the answer obtained in the first step.

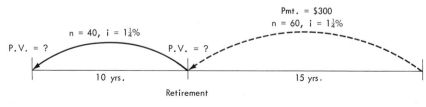

(a) Pmt. = $300
     n = 60
     i = $1\frac{1}{4}\%$

$$P.V. = Pmt. \times P.V. \text{ ann. tab.}_{\overline{n}| i}$$
$$= \$300 \times P.V. \text{ ann. tab.}_{\overline{60}| 1\frac{1}{4}\%}$$
$$= 300(42.034592)$$
$$= 12,610.377600$$
$$P.V. = \$12,610.38$$

George would have to have $12,610.38 in his account when he retires in order to receive an annuity of $300 each quarter for 15 years.

(b) We must now determine what single deposit, made now, would reach a maturity value of $12,610.38 when George retires in ten years.

$$S = \$12,610.38$$
$$n = 40$$
$$i = 1\frac{1}{4}\%$$

$$P = S(1 + i)^{-n}$$
$$= \$12,610.38(1 + 1\frac{1}{4}\%)^{-40}$$
$$= 12,610.38(0.6084133)$$
$$= 7,672.322\ldots$$
$$P = \$7,672.32$$

A single deposit of $7,672.32 now will be worth $12,610.38 after ten years at 5% quarterly.

(c) George will receive 60 payments of $300 each for a total of $18,000 during the time of his annuity.

(d) The total interest is the difference between what he will actually receive from the annuity ($18,000) and the original amount invested ($7,672.32):

Total receipts	$18,000.00
Principal invested	−7,672.32
Interest	$10,327.68

The original $7,672.32 investment will result in $10,327.68 interest before the annuity expires 25 years later. The original principal will have considerably more than doubled itself.

Keep in mind that "present value" often refers to the value of an investment on the first day of the term. (It always refers to the value on some day prior to the maturity date.) This fact will help clarify the following example.

The purchaser of a house paid $5,000 down and agreed to pay $1,000 every six months for nine years. Money is worth 6% compounded semiannually. (a) What would have been the equivalent cash price of the house? (b) How much did the buyer actually pay for the house? **Example Four**

(a) The "cash price" of the house would have been its cost on the original day; thus, since we are discussing the value on the beginning day of the term, we know that present value is required.

Cash price = Down payment
          + Present value of the periodic payments

$$\text{Pmt.} = \$1,000 \qquad \text{P.V.} = \text{Pmt.} \times \text{P.V. ann. tab.}_{\overline{n}| i}$$
$$n = 18 \qquad\qquad = \$1,000 \times \text{P.V. ann. tab.}_{\overline{18}| 3\%}$$
$$i = 3\% \qquad\qquad = 1,000(13.753513)$$
$$\qquad\qquad\qquad = 13,753.513$$
$$\qquad\quad \text{P.V.} = \$13,753.51$$

Thus

Down payment	$5,000.00
Present value of periodic payments	+13,753.51
Cash price	$18,753.51

(b) The buyer actually paid a down payment of $5,000 plus 18 payments of $1,000 each for a total cost of $23,000:

Down payment	$5,000.00
Total of periodic payments	+18,000.00
Total cost	$23,000.00

The equivalent cash price was $18,753.51 because that sum, invested in an account earning 6% semiannual interest, would have had a maturity value equal to the maturity value that would be obtained if the $5,000 down payment and each semiannual payment were deposited at the same rate.

PROBLEMS

Hint: Remember that the basic problems of amount and present value at compound interest involve a *single* deposit for some period of time, whereas the annuity problems involve a *series* of payments.

Using the present-value-of-an-annuity procedure, determine (1) the present value required in order to receive each of the annuities given below, (2) the total amount that each annuity would pay, and (3) how much interest would be included.

		Payment	Rate	Compounded	Years
1.	(a)	$ 100	6%	monthly	6
	(b)	500	8	quarterly	10
	(c)	1,000	7	semiannually	12
	(d)	60	5	monthly	4
	(e)	1,400	10	semiannually	15
2.	(a)	$ 100	7%	quarterly	7
	(b)	50	6	monthly	8
	(c)	1,500	4	semiannually	10
	(d)	400	6	quarterly	18
	(e)	80	5	monthly	5

(1) Calculate the *maturity value* and the interest included if one makes deposits in the amounts shown below. (2) Then determine the *present value* of an account required in order to receive these annuity payments, along with the total amount of interest that will be included in the annuity.

		Payment	Rate	Compounded	Years
3.	(a)	$ 100	9%	monthly	3
	(b)	1,000	6	quarterly	8
	(c)	2,000	5	semiannually	10
4.	(a)	$100	5%	quarterly	10
	(b)	500	6	semiannually	15
	(c)	60	4	monthly	4

5. Sid Ward wishes to establish an annuity that will pay him $1,000 each six months for nine years. If money is worth 6% compounded semiannually—
   (a) What amount must be in his account when the annuity starts?
   (b) How much will the annuity pay?
   (c) How much interest will the account earn during the term of the annuity?

6. James Carson wishes to purchase an annuity of $100 monthly for three years. If the current interest rate is 6% compounded monthly—
   (a) How much would be required to finance the annuity?

    (b)   How much will Carson actually receive from the annuity?

    (c)   How much interest will the annuity include?

7.   Burt Allen would like to provide an annuity to pay him $3,000 quarterly for 15 years after he retires.

    (a)   What amount must Allen have when he reaches retirement, if money earns 7% compounded quarterly?

    (b)   How much will Allen receive during the 15 years?

    (c)   How much interest will the account earn before his funds are exhausted?

8.   Gary Post would like to receive a $50 monthly annuity during the four years he is in college. If his savings and loan association pays 5% compounded monthly—

    (a)   How much would Gary have to have on deposit when he starts to college, in order to be able to withdraw $50 each month?

    (b)   What will be the total of Gary's withdrawals?

    (c)   How much interest will be earned during his college years?

9.   A father wants to set up an annuity that will pay $100 quarterly during the four years his child attends college. He can invest his money at 9% compounded quarterly.

    (a)   What must be the balance in the account when the child enters college?

    (b)   The child will be college age in 8 years. What single deposit could he make today that will provide the funds for the annuity?

    (c)   How much interest will the initial deposit earn before the annuity expires?

10.   A man would like to receive $1,000 each six months for ten years after he retires. He can invest his money at 5% compounded semiannually.

    (a)   How much money must he have when he retires in order to receive the annuity?

    (b)   The man will retire in 20 years. What deposit could he make today that will provide the funds for the annuity?

    (c)   How much interest would this deposit earn before the annuity ends?

11.   Max Warren will retire in 13 years. He wants to fund an annuity that will pay $4,000 each six months for 14 years after retirement. Money is worth 7% compounded semiannually.

    (a)   How much will be required at retirement in order to provide the annuity?

    (b)   How much would Warren have to deposit now in order to finance the annuity?

    (c)   How much interest would this deposit eventually earn?

12.   William Jennings' son will be ready for college in 12 years. Jennings wants

to provide for an annuity of $400 quarterly during his son's four years in college. His money can be invested at 7% compounded quarterly.

   (a) What amount must be on deposit when the son enters college, in order to receive this annuity?

   (b) How much would Jennings have to deposit today in order to provide for the annuity?

   (c) How much total interest will this deposit earn before the son finishes college?

13. A business property was purchased for $15,000 down and monthly payments of $1,000 for six years.

   (a) What was the total cost to the buyer?

   (b) What would have been the equivalent cash price, if money is worth 9% compounded monthly?

14. A tract of land was obtained for a $5,000 down payment and quarterly payments of $500 for ten years.

15. Mr. and Mrs. Horton purchased a home for $12,000 down and semiannual payments of $2,000 for 20 years.

   (a) How much will the Hortons pay altogether?

   (b) What cash price could the seller have deposited at 8% compounded semiannually in order to have the same maturity value after 20 years that he can have by depositing the Hortons' payments?

16. Fred Blanton purchased a small business for $4,000 down and monthly payments of $100 for five years.

   (a) How much did Blanton pay altogether for the business?

   (b) What cash price could the former owner have invested at 4% compounded monthly and had the same total after five years that he will have from depositing Blanton's payments?

Sinking Funds and Amortization

LEARNING OBJECTIVES

Upon completion of Chapter 20, the student will be able to:

1. Define and use correctly the terminology associated with each topic.

2. Using Pmt. $= S \times$ S.F. tab.$_{\overline{n}|i}$ and the sinking fund table, determine
   a. The regular payment required to finance a sinking fund,
   b. The total amount deposited, and
   c. The interest earned.

3. Prepare a sinking fund schedule to verify that the payments (Objective 2) will result in the required maturity value.

4. Using Pmt. $=$ P.V. $\times$ Amtz. tab.$_{\overline{n}|i}$ and the amortization table, compute
   a. The periodic payment required to amortize a loan,
   b. The total amount paid, and
   c. The interest included.

5. Prepare an amortization schedule to verify that the payments (Objective 4) pay off the loan correctly.

6. Explain the characteristics of the six basic types of compound interest and annuity problems.

Far-sighted investors may wish to establish a savings plan so as to achieve a specified savings goal by a certain time. An account of this type is known as a sinking fund.

The loan plans studied in previous chapters involved either simple interest or simple discount. For large loans which take many years to repay, however, ordinary simple interest would not be profitable to lenders, as later examples will show. Thus long-term loans must be repaid in a series of payments which include the interest due since the previous payment. This loan repayment procedure is known as amortization. Sinking funds and amortization are the subject of the following sections.

1. SINKING FUNDS

The section in the preceding chapter on amount of an annuity dealt with making given periodic payments into an account (at compound interest) and finding what the maturity value of that account would be. It frequently happens that businessmen know what amount will be needed on some future date and are concerned with determining what periodic payment would have to be invested in order to obtain this amount. When a special account is established so that the maturity value (equal periodic deposits plus compound interest) will exactly equal a specific amount, such a fund is called a *sinking fund*.

Sinking funds are often used to finance the replacement of machinery, equipment, facilities, and so forth, after depreciation, or to finance the redemption of bonds. (Bonds are somewhat similar to promissory notes in that they are written promises to repay a specified debt on a certain date. The primary difference is that interest on bonds is typically paid periodically, whereas the interest on a note is all repaid on the maturity date. Large corporations, municipalities, and state governments usually finance long-term improvements by selling bonds. The study of bonds themselves is not within the scope of this text; we shall be concerned here only with setting up a sinking fund to redeem the bonds at maturity.)

The object of a sinking fund problem, then, is to determine what periodic payment, invested at compound interest, will produce a given maturity value. Since amount-of-annuity problems also involve building a fund that would contain its largest amount at maturity, we can see that sinking fund problems are a variation of amount-of-annuity problems. The difference is that in this case we are concerned with finding the periodic payment of the annuity rather than the maturity value. (The periodic payment to a sinking fund is often called the *rent*.)

The periodic payment can be found using the amount-of-annuity procedure and Table XIV. The formula is easily altered to solve for the periodic payment by dividing both sides by the value from the table:

$$S = \text{Pmt.} \times \text{Amt. ann. tab.}_{\overline{n}|i}$$

$$\frac{S}{\text{Amt. ann. tab.}_{\overline{n}|i}} = \frac{\text{Pmt.} \times \cancel{\text{Amt. ann. tab.}_{\overline{n}|i}}}{\cancel{\text{Amt. ann. tab.}_{\overline{n}|i}}}$$

$$\frac{S}{\text{Amt. ann. tab.}_{\overline{n}|i}} = \text{Pmt.}$$

or

$$\text{Pmt.} = \frac{S}{\text{Amt. ann. tab.}_{\overline{n}|i}}$$

Since use of this procedure would involve long and tedious division, however, the student will normally find the periodic payment by using Table XV: Payment to a Sinking Fund (pp. 520–539) and the following procedure:

$$\text{Payment} = \text{Maturity value} \times \text{Sinking fund table}_{\overline{n}|i}$$

where n = number of payments and i = interest rate per period. This procedure* may be abbreviated

$$\text{Pmt.} = S \times \text{S.F. tab.}_{\overline{n}|i}$$

*The procedure for finding the payment to a sinking fund is often given as $P = S \times \dfrac{1}{S_{\overline{n}|i}}$, where P = payment, S = maturity value, and $\dfrac{1}{S_{\overline{n}|i}}$ indicates use of the sinking fund table. (This table is often denoted "Annuity Whose Amount is 1.") The procedure $P = S \times \dfrac{1}{S_{\overline{n}|i}}$ indicates that it is a variation of the amount-of-annuity procedure $S = P s_{\overline{n}|i}$.

Find the periodic payment which must be made into a sinking fund invested at 6% compounded annually in order for the fund to be worth $1,000 after five years, using (a) the amount of an annuity table and (b) the sinking fund procedure. (c) How much of this maturity value will actually have been deposited? (d) How much interest will the sinking fund have earned?

(a) $S = \$1,000$
$n = 5$
$i = 6\%$

$$\text{Pmt.} = \frac{S}{\text{Amt. ann. tab.}_{\overline{n}|i}}$$

$$= \frac{\$1,000}{\text{Amt. ann. tab.}_{\overline{5}|6\%}}$$

$$= \frac{\$1,000}{5.63709}$$

$$= 177.396\ldots$$

$$\text{Pmt.} = \$177.40$$

(b)

$$\text{Pmt.} = S \times \text{S.F. tab.}_{\overline{n}|i}$$
$$= \$1,000 \times \text{S.F. tab.}_{\overline{5}|6\%}$$
$$= \$1,000\,(0.177396)$$
$$= 177.396$$
$$\text{Pmt.} = \$177.40$$

A payment of $177.40 would have to be deposited into the sinking fund annually in order to have $1,000 at maturity.

(c) There will be five payments of $177.40 each, making the total deposits $877.00.

(d) The interest earned is thus

Maturity value	$1,000.00
Total deposits	− 887.00
Interest	$ 113.00

Note: Many business math books do not include a separate sinking fund table because of the relationship that exists between the sinking fund table and the amortization table (to be studied later). Each value in the sinking fund table can be determined by consulting the corresponding value in the amortization table and subtracting i. (For example, the amortization table for $n = 5$ and $i = 6\%$ gives 0.23739640. Then, 0.237-39640 − 0.06 gives 0.17739640, which is the value given in the sinking fund table for $n = 5$ and $i = 6\%$.)

West Bellevue issued bonds totaling $200,000 in order to extend its water facilities. The city council set up a sinking fund at 8% compounded semi-annually in order to provide for redemption of the ten-year bonds. (a) What semiannual rent will have to be deposited in the sinking fund? How much (b) actual investment and (c) interest will the sinking fund contain at maturity?

Example Two

(a) $S = \$200,000$

 $n = 20$

 $i = 4\%$

Pmt. $= S \times$ S.F. tab.$_{\overline{n}|i}$

$= \$200,000 \times$ S.F. tab.$_{\overline{20}|4\%}$

$= 200,000 (0.03358175)$

$= 6,716.35000000$

Pmt. $= \$6,716.35$

The city must deposit $6,716.35 into the sinking fund each six months.

(b) There will be 20 semiannual rent payments of $6,716.35 each, for a total of $134,327.00.

(c) The sinking fund will earn interest of

Maturity value	$200,000.00
Total deposits	− 134,327.00
Interest	$ 65,673.00

When a sinking fund is in progress, businesses often keep a *sinking fund schedule*. The schedule shows how much interest the fund has earned during each period and what the current balance is. The schedule also verifies that the periodic payments will result in the desired maturity value.

Prepare a sinking fund schedule for Example 1, in which five annual payments of $177.40 each are made into a fund paying 6% compounded annually.

Example Three

 The "interest" earned each period is found by multiplying the previous "balance at end of period" by the periodic interest rate i (example: $365.44 × 6% = $21.93). The "interest" plus the "amount of periodic payment" gives the "total increase" (example: $21.93 + $177.40 = $199.33). The "balance at end of period" is then found by adding this "total increase" to the previous "balance at end of period" (example: $199.33 + $365.44 = $564.77).

Payment	Periodic Interest	Periodic Payment	Total Increase	Balance, End of Period
1	$ 0	$177.40	$177.40	$ 177.40
2	10.64	177.40	188.04	365.44
3	21.93	177.40	199.33	564.77
4	33.89	177.40	211.29	776.06
5	46.56	177.40	223.96	1,000.02
Totals	$113.02	$887.00		

$1,000.02 Final balance

Notice that the final balance in the sinking fund will be 2¢ more than the $1,000 required. This happens because the periodic payment ($177.40), as well as the periodic interest, had been rounded off.

PROBLEMS

Using the sinking fund table, determine the periodic payment necessary to finance the sinking fund. Also calculate the total deposits and the total amount of interest contained in the maturity value.

		Maturity Value	Rate	Compounded	Years
1.	(a)	$ 10,000	5%	quarterly	8
	(b)	50,000	7	semiannually	10
	(c)	8,000	6	monthly	6
	(d)	120,000	8	annually	14
	(e)	90,000	7	quarterly	9
2.	(a)	$100,000	8%	semiannually	12
	(b)	20,000	7	annually	5
	(c)	5,000	4	annually	3
	(d)	75,000	5	semiannually	8
	(e)	150,000	6	quarterly	12

3. Manifold Corporation is planning a $600,000 expansion in four years. The firm can establish a sinking fund at 10% compounded semiannually.
   (a) What payment will Manifold have to make each six months in order to finance the sinking fund?
   (b) How much of the maturity value will be company investments?
   (c) How much interest will the mature fund contain?

4. Bearington and Styres, Inc. expects to need $10,000 in five years to purchase new office equipment.
   (a) What quarterly rent would have to be paid into a sinking fund invested at 8% compounded quarterly?

   (b)   What part of the maturity value would be deposits?

   (c)   How much interest will the fund draw?

5. The Grabar Tire and Appliance Store will need $100,000 in order to open a second location. If they establish a three-year fund earning 9% compounded monthly—

   (a)   What monthly rent will provide the funds?

   (b)   How much of the maturity value will be interest?

6. The voters of Kensington passed an $80,000 bond referendum for new playground equipment for its parks. An eight-year sinking fund was established at 7% compounded annually to redeem the bonds.

   (a)   What annual payment must be made to finance the fund?

   (b)   How much interest will the account contain at maturity?

7. The City of Scottsdale sold bonds worth $700,000 at maturity in order to modernize its water treatment plant. To prepare for redemption of the bonds, a sinking fund was established at 6% compounded quarterly for six years.

   (a)   What quarterly payment must be made to provide the $700,000 needed to retire the bonds?

   (b)   How much of the maturity value will be interest on the deposits?

8. The citizens of Bradley Heights voted to issue bonds totaling $100,000 to build an addition to the high school. The bonds will mature in ten years. If a sinking fund is set up earning 5% compounded semiannually—

   (a)   How much must be deposited each six months to finance the fund?

   (b)   How much of the final amount will be interest?

Find the periodic payment necessary to finance each of the following sinking funds. Then prepare a sinking fund schedule to verify that these periodic payments will result in the desired maturity value.

		Maturity Value	Rate	Compounded	Years
9.	(a)	$10,000	6%	annually	4
	(b)	4,000	8	quarterly	2
10.	(a)	$1,000	5%	annually	4
	(b)	5,000	6	semiannually	3

2. AMORTIZATION

BANK LOANS

In our study of simple interest, it was pointed out that simple interest notes are usually for short periods of time—a year or less. Example 1 in Section 1 of Chapter 18 (page 394) was given to illustrate the advantage to the depositor of compound interest over simple interest. The same example can be used to illustrate that simple interest notes for periods longer than one year are not profitable to bankers. Suppose the investors in that example are replaced by bankers who are each lending $1,000.

Banker A lends $1,000 at 6% simple interest for three years. Thus,

$$P = \$1,000 \qquad\qquad I = Prt$$
$$r = 6\% \qquad\qquad\qquad = \$1,000 \times \tfrac{6}{100} \times \tfrac{3}{1}$$
$$t = 3 \text{ yrs.} \qquad\qquad I = \$180$$

Banker A would receive $180 interest on his money.

Banker B, on the other hand, lends $1,000 at 6% for only six months. When the borrower repays the loan after six months, Banker B then lends both the principal and the interest for another six months. This process is repeated for three years; so, in effect, Banker B earns compound interest on the $1,000 he originally lent. Therefore,

$$P = \$1,000 \qquad S = P(1 + i)^n \qquad\qquad I = S - P$$
$$n = 6 \qquad\qquad = \$1,000(1 + 3\%)^6 \qquad = \$1,194.05$$
$$i = 3\% \qquad\qquad = 1,000(1.194052) \qquad\quad -1,000.00$$
$$\qquad\qquad\qquad = 1,194.052 \qquad\qquad I = \$\ \ \ 194.05$$
$$\qquad\qquad S = \$1,194.05$$

Banker B would earn total interest of $194.05.

Thus Banker A would earn $180 interest on his single three-year note. Banker B, by making a series of six-month loans, would receive a total of $194.05 interest or $14.05 more than Banker A. One can easily understand that banks would prefer to invest their money in successive short-term loans rather than tying it up in single long-term loans. If carried to its logical conclusion, the result would be that no one could borrow money for long-term projects such as building a home or starting a business.

Therefore, when a borrower receives a large bank loan, he makes periodic, partial payments. (That is, at regular intervals he makes a payment that includes both a payment to reduce the principal and also the interest due on the principal still owed.) This procedure is the same as paying on the installment plan at an annual percentage rate required by the Truth in Lending law (that is, an effective interest rate—interest paid only on the balance due.) At the same time, it enables the bank, in effect, to earn compound interest (by reloaning the interest just repaid).

Note: It should be pointed out that financial institutions are prohibited from *charging* compound interest on a single loan. That is, a single borrower could not be charged $194.05 "interest" for a $1,000, three-year loan at 6%.

As mentioned above, it is usual to repay a large loan by making a series of equal periodic payments that include both principal and interest; this process is known as *amortization*. Perhaps the best example of amortization is the monthly payment homeowners make to pay off real estate mortgages. However, equal periodic payments may be used to amortize a long-term loan taken out for any purpose—such as to start a business, to purchase equipment or machinery, to modernize facilities, and so on.

Note: It should be emphasized that the interest rates associated with amortization are effective rates; that is, the interest rate each period is applied to the outstanding balance only. To put it another way: The borrower receives credit for the principal which has been repaid, and he pays interest only on the amount he still owes.

Since the bulk of the debt exists at the beginning of the time period, and the problem is to determine what periodic payment is necessary to discharge the debt, amortization is thus a variation of the present-value-of-an-annuity problem already studied. The debt itself is the present (beginning) value of the annuity. The payment may be found by altering the present-value-of-annuity procedure slightly and using the present-value-of-an-annuity table (Table XVII). Thus

$$\text{P.V.} = \text{Pmt.} \times \text{P.V. ann. tab.}_{n \rceil i}$$

$$\frac{\text{P.V.}}{\text{P.V. ann. tab.}_{n \rceil i}} = \frac{\text{Pmt.} \times \cancel{\text{P.V. ann. tab.}}_{n \rceil i}}{\cancel{\text{P.V. ann. tab.}}_{n \rceil i}}$$

$$\frac{\text{P.V.}}{\text{P.V. ann. tab.}_{n \rceil i}} = \text{Pmt.}$$

or

$$\text{Pmt.} = \frac{\text{P.V.}}{\text{P.V. ann. tab.}_{n \rceil i}}$$

This procedure, however, necessitates dividing by a number from the present-value-of-an-annuity table. In order to simplify the calculations, financial institutions usually use Table XVIII: Partial Payment (pp. 520–539), which is an amortization table for regular payments scheduled each period. This table can be used in the following procedure:

$$\text{Payment} = \text{Present value} \times \text{Amortization table}_{n \rceil i}$$

As before, n = number of periods and i = interest rate per period. The procedure* may be abbreviated

---

*If it seems preferable, the procedure in this section could be indicated

$$\text{Payment} = \text{Present value} \times \text{Partial payment table}_{n \rceil i}$$

abbreviated.

$$\text{Pmt.} = \text{P. V.} \times \text{Part. Pmt. tab.}_{n \rceil i}$$

$$\text{Pmt.} = \text{P. V.} \times \text{Amtz. tab.}_{\overline{n}|\,i}$$

The total amount paid to amortize a loan is found by multiplying the periodic payment by the number of payments. The total amount of interest is then the difference between the total paid and the original loan (present value).

Example One Compute the semiannual payment required to amortize a $1,000 loan made at 6% for four years using (a) the present-value-of-an-annuity table and (b) the amortization table. Also determine (c) the total amount that will be paid, and (d) how much interest this total includes.

(a) P.V. = $1,000

$$\text{Pmt.} = \frac{\text{P.V.}}{\text{P.V. ann. tab.}_{\overline{n}|\,i}}$$

$$n = 8$$

$$= \frac{\text{P.V.}}{\text{P.V. ann. tab.}_{\overline{8}|\,3\%}}$$

$$i = 3\%$$

$$= \frac{\$1,000}{7.01969}$$

$$= 142.456\ldots$$

$$\text{Pmt.} = \$142.46$$

(b)

$$\text{Pmt} = \text{P.V.} \times \text{Amtz. tab.}_{\overline{n}|\,i}$$
$$= \$1,000 \times \text{Amtz. tab.}_{\overline{8}|\,3\%}$$
$$= 1,000(0.142456)$$
$$= 142.456$$
$$\text{Pmt.} = \$142.46$$

A payment of $142.46 made each six months will repay both the principal and the interest due on the $1,000 loan.

(c) There will be eight payments of $142.46 each, making a total (principal plus interest) of $1,139.68.

(d) The interest included is

However, it is essential to keep in mind that this table applies only to regularly scheduled amortization payments and cannot be used for irregular partial payments such as we studied under the United States rule in Chapter 17.

This procedure may also be indicated by $P = A \times \dfrac{1}{a_{\overline{n}|\,i}}$, where P = payment, A =

present value and $\dfrac{1}{a_{\overline{n}|\,i}}$ denotes use of the amortization table. (This table is often entitled

"Annuity Whose Present Value is 1".) The form $P = A \times \dfrac{1}{a_{\overline{n}|\,i}}$ indicates that it is a variation

of the present-value-of-an-annuity procedure $A = P a_{\overline{n}|\,i}$.

Amount paid	$1,139.68
Principal	− 1,000.00
Interest	$ 139.68

Interest would be computed each six months on the balance still owed. The total of this interest would be $139.68.

Persons making payments to amortize a loan are often given an *amortization schedule*, which is a period-by-period breakdown showing how much of each payment goes toward the principal, how much is interest, the total amount of principal and interest that has been paid, the principal still owed, and so forth. Figure 20-1 illustrates an actual amortization schedule of a $20,000 loan at 6% interest for 30 years, which will be repaid in monthly payments of $119.92.

Since our amortization table (Table XVIII) contains only 100 periods, we are only able to determine monthly payments for loans with terms no longer than $8\frac{1}{3}$ years. However, the following table will enable the student to compare the monthly payments required at various prevailing rates for mortgages of the most common lengths—20, 25, and 30 years.

MONTHLY PAYMENT PER $1,000 OF MORTGAGE
(Including principal and interest)

Rate	20 Years	25 Years	30 Years
$6\frac{1}{2}$%	$7.46	$6.75	$6.32
$6\frac{3}{4}$	7.61	6.91	6.49
7	7.76	7.07	6.66
$7\frac{1}{4}$	7.91	7.23	6.83
$7\frac{1}{2}$	8.06	7.39	7.00
$7\frac{3}{4}$	8.21	7.56	7.17
8	8.37	7.72	7.34
$8\frac{1}{4}$	8.53	7.89	7.52
$8\frac{1}{2}$	8.68	8.06	7.69

The following example demonstrates for the student the basic calculations required for drawing up an amortization schedule and also shows that the payment obtained in Example 1 is correct.

Example Two

Prepare a simplified amortization schedule for Example 1, which found that a semiannual payment of $142.46 would amortize a $1,000 loan at 6% for four years.

The "interest" due each period is found by multiplying the "princi-

Schedule of Direct Reduction Loan

RATE %	PAYMENT $	LOAN $	TERM: YEARS	MONTHS	PERIODS
6.00	119.92	20,000.00	30		360

Prepared by Financial Publishing Company, Boston

PAYMENT NUMBER	PAYMENT ON INTEREST	PRINCIPAL	BALANCE OF LOAN	PAYMENT NUMBER	PAYMENT ON INTEREST	PRINCIPAL	BALANCE OF LOAN
1	100.00	19.92	19,980.08	61	93.05	26.87	18,583.30
2	99.90	20.02	19,960.06	62	92.92	27.00	18,556.30
3	99.80	20.12	19,939.94	63	92.78	27.14	18,529.16
4	99.70	20.22	19,919.72	64	92.65	27.27	18,501.89
5	99.60	20.32	19,899.40	65	92.51	27.41	18,474.48
6	99.50	20.42	19,878.98	66	92.37	27.55	18,446.93
7	99.39	20.53	19,858.45	67	92.23	27.69	18,419.24
8	99.29	20.63	19,837.82	68	92.10	27.82	18,391.42
9	99.19	20.73	19,817.09	69	91.96	27.96	18,363.46
10	99.09	20.83	19,796.26	70	91.82	28.10	18,335.36
11	98.98	20.94	19,775.32	71	91.68	28.24	18,307.12
12	98.88	21.04	19,754.28	72	91.54	28.38	18,278.74
13	98.77	21.15	19,733.13	73	91.39	28.53	18,250.21
14	98.67	21.25	19,711.88	74	91.25	28.67	18,221.54
15	98.56	21.36	19,690.52	75	91.11	28.81	18,192.73
16	98.45	21.47	19,669.05	76	90.96	28.96	18,163.77
17	98.35	21.57	19,647.48	77	90.82	29.10	18,134.67
18	98.24	21.68	19,625.80	78	90.67	29.25	18,105.42
19	98.13	21.79	19,604.01	79	90.53	29.39	18,076.03
20	98.02	21.90	19,582.11	80	90.38	29.54	18,046.49
21	97.91	22.01	19,560.10	81	90.23	29.69	18,016.80
22	97.80	22.12	19,537.98	82	90.08	29.84	17,986.96
23	97.69	22.23	19,515.75	83	89.93	29.99	17,956.97
24	97.58	22.34	19,493.41	84	89.78	30.14	17,926.83
25	97.47	22.45	19,470.96	85	89.63	30.29	17,896.54
~~	~~~	~~~	~~~	~~~	~~~	~~~	~~~
267	44.85	75.07	8,895.06	327	18.66	101.26	3,631.52
268	44.48	75.44	8,819.62	328	18.16	101.76	3,529.55
269	44.10	75.82	8,743.80	329	17.65	102.27	3,427.28
270	43.72	76.20	8,667.60	330	17.14	102.78	3,324.50
271	43.34	76.58	8,591.02	331	16.62	103.30	3,221.20
272	42.96	76.96	8,514.06	332	16.11	103.81	3,117.39
273	42.57	77.35	8,436.71	333	15.59	104.33	3,013.06
274	42.18	77.74	8,358.97	334	15.07	104.85	2,908.21
275	41.79	78.13	8,280.84	335	14.54	105.38	2,802.83
276	41.40	78.52	8,202.32	336	14.01	105.91	2,696.92
277	41.01	78.91	8,123.41	337	13.48	106.44	2,590.48
278	40.62	79.30	8,044.11	338	12.95	106.97	2,483.51
279	40.22	79.70	7,964.41	339	12.42	107.50	2,376.01
280	39.82	80.10	7,884.31	340	11.88	108.04	2,267.97
281	39.42	80.50	7,803.81	341	11.34	108.58	2,159.39
282	39.02	80.90	7,722.91	342	10.80	109.12	2,050.27
283	38.61	81.31	7,641.60	343	10.25	109.67	1,940.60
284	38.21	81.71	7,559.89	344	9.70	110.22	1,830.38
285	37.80	82.12	7,477.77	345	9.15	110.77	1,719.61
286	37.39	82.53	7,395.24	346	8.60	111.32	1,608.29
287	36.98	82.94	7,312.30	347	8.04	111.88	1,496.41
288	36.56	83.36	7,228.94	348	7.48	112.44	1,383.97
289	36.14	83.78	7,145.16	349	6.92	113.00	1,270.97
290	35.73	84.19	7,060.97	350	6.35	113.57	1,157.40
291	35.30	84.62	6,976.35	351	5.79	114.13	1,043.27
292	34.88	85.04	6,891.31	352	5.22	114.70	928.57
293	34.46	85.46	6,805.85	353	4.64	115.28	813.29
294	34.03	85.89	6,719.96	354	4.07	115.85	697.44
295	33.60	86.32	6,633.64	355	3.49	116.43	581.01
296	33.17	86.75	6,546.89	356	2.91	117.01	464.00
297	32.73	87.19	6,459.70	357	2.32	117.60	346.40
298	32.30	87.62	6,372.08	358	1.73	118.19	228.21
299	31.86	88.06	6,284.02	359	1.14	118.78	109.43
300	31.42	88.50	6,195.52	360	.55	109.43	109.98*

The final payment is usually somewhat different from the regular
payment, and is shown starred on the last line.

Figure 20-1: Amortization Schedule

pal owed" times i (example: $1,000 × 3\% = \$30$). Each "payment toward principal" is found by subtracting the interest from the total payment (example: $\$142.46 - \$30.00 = \$112.46$). The next "principal owed" is then found by subtracting the previous "payment toward principal" from the previous "principal owed" (example: $\$1,000.00 - \$112.46 = \$887.54$).

Notice that there is a 2¢ difference in the total amounts of interest and principal derived in this example and in Example 1. This is because the periodic payment ($142.46), as well as the periodic interest, had been rounded off; eight payments of $142.46 result in a 2¢ overpayment of principal. In actual practice, the final payment of an amortization is usually slightly different from the regular payment, in order to have the total amounts come out exact.

Payment	Principal Owed	Interest	Each payment = $142.46 Payment Toward Principal
1	$1,000.00	$30.00	$112.46
2	887.54	26.63	115.83
3	771.71	23.15	119.31
4	652.40	19.57	122.89
5	529.51	15.89	126.57
6	402.94	12.09	130.37
7	272.57	8.18	134.28
8	139.29	4.15	138.31
	Totals	$139.66	$1,000.02

Total amount paid $1,139.68

Fred Jackson bought a $25,000 home by making a $5,000 down payment and making equal quarterly payments for ten years. If he had a 5\% loan— (a) What was his quarterly payment? (b) How much interest did he pay? (c) How much did he pay altogether for the home?

Example Three

$$\begin{array}{ll} \text{Cash price} & \$25,000 \\ \text{Down payment} & -5,000 \\ \text{Principal (or present} & \\ \text{value) of loan} & \$20,000 \end{array}$$

(a) P.V. = $20,000   Pmt. = P.V. × Amtz. $\text{tab}_{\overline{n}|i}$
      n = 40   = $20,000 × Amtz. $\text{tab.}_{\overline{40}|1\frac{1}{4}\%}$
      i = $1\frac{1}{4}\%$ = 20,000(0.0319214)
                    = 638.4280000
            Pmt. = $638.43

(b) Mr. Jackson will make 40 payments of $638.43 to amortize his loan. This $25,537.20 total will include interest of

Total payments	$25,537.20
Principal	−20,000.00
Interest	$ 5,537.20

(c) So, the total cost of the house to Mr. Jackson, including the down payment, is

Total cost of loan	$25,537.20
Down payment	+5,000.00
Total cost of home	$30,536.20

Note: The advantage to the borrower of effective interest over simple interest is obvious when one considers the following case: Suppose Mr. Jackson's loan of $20,000 had been at 5% simple interest for ten years. His interest then would have been

$$P = \$20,000 \qquad I = Prt$$
$$r = 5\% \qquad = \$20,000 \times \tfrac{5}{100} \times \tfrac{10}{1}$$
$$t = 10 \text{ years} \qquad I = \$10,000$$

Mr. Jackson's simple interest would have been $10,000 instead of $5,537.20, or nearly twice as much! Furthermore, the simple interest would have been fully half the amount he borrowed. This loan was only for ten years; suppose his loan had been for 20 or 30 years—how much simple interest would he have paid then? It is easy to see that no one could afford to buy a home or start a business if he had to borrow money at simple interest.

The illustration at the beginning of this section pointed out that long-term simple interest notes (with a single payment at maturity) would not be profitable to bankers. We now see that such notes would also be un-reasonably expensive to borrowers. Thus effective interest with periodic payments works to the advantage of both the borrower and the lender. (If financial institutions could charge simple interest and also receive periodic payments—as is frequently done on installment purchases and loans (although the Truth in Lending Act does require that the equivalent effective annual percentage rate be disclosed)—this would be the most profit-able arrangement for the lender; however, this is not done on long-term loans from banking institutions.)

Problems

Using the amortization table (Table XVIII), find the payment necessary to amortize each loan. Also compute the total amount that will be repaid and determine how much interest is included.

		Principal (P.V.)	Rate	Compounded (Paid)	Years
1.	(a)	$10,000	9%	monthly	6
	(b)	40,000	5	quarterly	10
	(c)	90,000	8	semiannually	16
	(d)	6,000	6	monthly	4
	(e)	75,000	7	semiannually	30
2.	(a)	$100,000	6%	semiannually	25
	(b)	30,000	5	monthly	8
	(c)	8,000	4	quarterly	3
	(d)	25,000	7	quarterly	20
	(e)	70,000	5	annually	12

3. Eric Grayson borrowed $60,000 in order to go into business for himself. His loan was at 8% with semiannual payments for 23 years.
   (a) How much will he pay each six months?
   (b) How much total interest will Grayson pay?

4. Gary Smith borrowed $5,000 in order to remodel his home. His payments were made monthly for six years. If Smith had a 4% loan—
   (a) What was his monthly payment?
   (b) How much interest did his payments include?

5. Beauty-Craft Mills took out a $30,000, four-year loan at 9% in order to purchase new processing equipment. Quarterly payments will be made to amortize the loan.
   (a) What is the amount of each payment?
   (b) How much interest will Beauty-Craft pay?

6. A $70,000 loan at 6% was signed by Apex Corp. in order to build a new warehouse. If payments were made quarterly for 10 years—
   (a) What payment was necessary to discharge the loan?
   (b) How much interest was included in the payments?

7. Mr. and Mrs. Smith purchased a $48,000 home by making an $8,000 down payment and financing the balance at 7% for 25 years. If payments are made semiannually—
   (a) How much is each payment?
   (b) How much interest will the Smiths pay?
   (c) What will be the total cost of their home?

8. Mr. and Mrs. Garrison paid $3,000 down on a $33,000 house and made quarterly payments for 25 years on a 5% loan.
   (a) What payment did the Garrisons make each quarter?
   (b) How much interest did their loan include?
   (c) What was the total cost of their home to the Garrisons?

9. Handcrafted Furniture Manufacturers paid $17,000 immediately and made monthly payments for five years in order to amortize the cost of a $97,000 plant expansion. The loan was drawn at 5%.
   (a) What was the amount of each payment?
   (b) How much interest was paid on the loan?
   (c) What was the actual total cost of the expansion?

10. The contractor's price for a new building was $63,000. Snyder, Inc. paid $13,000 down and financed the balance for six years at 6%. If their payments were made monthly—
   (a) What payment was necessary to repay the loan?
   (b) How much interest was included in the payments?
   (c) What was the actual total cost of the building to Snyder, Inc.?

Find the periodic payment required for each of the following loans. Then verify your answer by preparing an amortization schedule similar to the one in Example 2 above, showing how much of each payment is interest and how much applies toward principal.

		Principal (P.V.)	Rate	Compounded (Paid)	Years
11.	(a)	$ 1,000	6%	annually	4
	(b)	6,000	8	semiannually	2
12.	(a)	$10,000	5%	annually	5
	(b)	8,000	6	semiannually	3

3. REVIEW

The following criteria may help enable the student to distinguish between the basic types of problems studied in Chapters 18 through 20. The first step is to determine whether the problem is a compound interest problem or an annuity problem. (If a series of regular payments is involved, it is an annuity; otherwise it is a compound interest problem.) The next step is to decide whether amount or present value is required. (In general, if the *question* in the problem refers to the *end* of the time period, it is an *amount* problem; if the question relates to the *beginning* of the time period, it is a *present value* problem.)

Note: This review includes only the basic problems of each type so that the student can confidently identify each without its being listed under a section heading. This is not intended to be a complete review of the entire unit; the student's personal review should also include the variations of the basic problems studied in each section.

Compound Interest	Annuity
The basic problem involves a *single* deposit invested for the entire time.	The problem involves a *series* of *regular* payments (or deposits).

<table>
<tr><td>

1. *Amount* at compound interest: a deposit is made and one wishes to know how much it will be worth at the *end* of the time.
$$[S = P(1 + i)^n]$$

</td><td>

1. *Amount* of an annuity: regular deposits are *made* and one wishes to know the value of the account at the *end* of the time.
$$[S = \text{Pmt.} \times \text{Amt. ann. tab.}_{\overline{n}|\, i}]$$

</td></tr>
<tr><td>

2. *Present value* at compound interest: one wishes to determine how much must be invested at the *beginning* of the time period in order to obtain a given maturity value. $[P = S(1 + i)^{-n}]$

</td><td>

2. *Present value* of an annuity: regular payments are to be *received* and one wants to find how much must be on deposit at the *beginning* from which to withdraw the payments.
$$[\text{P.V.} = \text{Pmt.} \times \text{P.V. ann. tab.}_{\overline{n}|\, i}]$$

If the problem involves finding a periodic payment, one of the following applies:

3. *Sinking fund:* one is asked to find what regular payment must be made to *build up* an account to a given amount.
$$[\text{Pmt.} = S \times \text{S.F. tab.}_{\overline{n}|\, i}]$$

4. *Amortization:* one is asked to determine what regular payment must be made to *discharge* a debt.
$$[\text{Pmt.} = \text{P.V.} \times \text{Amtz. tab.}_{\overline{n}|\, i}]$$

</td></tr>
</table>

PROBLEMS

Find the compound amount and compound interest:

		Principal	Rate	Compounded	Years
1.	(a)	$1,000	8%	semiannually	9
	(b)	500	5	monthly	6
2.	(a)	$ 100	6%	quarterly	7
	(b)	2,000	$5\frac{1}{2}$	semiannually	10

Compute the present value and compound interest:

		Maturity Value	Rate	Compounded	Years
3.	(a)	$ 4,000	9%	quarterly	10
	(b)	10,000	5	semiannually	4
4.	(a)	$ 1,000	7%	quarterly	3
	(b)	5,000	6	monthly	8

(1) Determine the maturity value if one makes the following periodic payments. (2) How much would be deposited during the time period? (3) How much of the maturity value is interest?

		Periodic Payment	Rate	Compounded	Years
5.	(a)	$1,000	8%	quarterly	12
	(b)	100	6	monthly	7
6.	(a)	$1,000	5%	semiannually	6
	(b)	100	4	quarterly	13

7.–8.   Rework Problems 5 and 6. This time—
   (1) find the present value required in order to receive the annuity payment given.
   (2) How much would be received during the time of the annuity?
   (3) How much interest would be earned during this time?

(1) Find the periodic payment required to finance a sinking fund with the maturity value given below. (2) How much of the final value will be actual deposits? (3) How much interest will be included?

		Maturity Value	Rate	Compounded	Years
9.	(a)	$10,000	9%	monthly	5
	(b)	8,000	6	quarterly	8
10.	(a)	$ 1,000	8%	quarterly	3
	(b)	50,000	7	semiannually	15

(1) Compute the periodic payment required to amortize each of the following debts. (2) What total amount will be paid to discharge each obligation? (3) How much interest will be included?

		Debt	Rate	Paid	Years
11.	(a)	$10,000	5%	monthly	8
	(b)	30,000	6	quarterly	20
12.	(a)	$10,000	7%	quarterly	14
	(b)	4,000	6	monthly	3

13. Harry Banks wants to have $6,000 available in three years in order to remodel his home. Money is worth 6% compounded monthly.
   (a) How much must he deposit now in order to achieve his savings goal?
   (b) How much interest will the account earn?

14. Mary Willis plans to redecorate her office in five years and expects to spend $3,000. Her savings and loan association pays $4\frac{1}{2}$% compounded semi-annually.
   (a) How much would Mary need to deposit now in order to have $3,000 in five years?
   (b) How much of the $3,000 will be interest?

15. Brown and Williams, Inc. is investing $2,000 each quarter, planning to expand their operations in six years. Their investment earns 7% compounded quarterly.
   (a) How much will the account contain in six years?
   (b) How much of this amount will be interest?

16. Samuel Green deposits $100 each month into his savings account, which earns 5% compounded monthly.
   (a) How much will Sam have after five years?
   (b) How much of this amount will be interest?

17. Tiemann Associates purchased a $50,000 plant site by signing an 18-year loan and making semiannual payments. Money is worth 8% compounded semiannually.
   (a) What semiannual payment does Tiemann Associates make?
   (b) How much interest will they pay over the 18-year-loan term?

18. In order to purchase a $5,000 boat, Fred Graham made quarterly payments for four years. He had a 6% loan.
   (a) What was the amount of each payment?
   (b) How much total interest did Fred's payments include?

19. Warren Abrams would like to receive $2,000 each six months for 20 years after he retires. He can invest his money in a fund paying $5\frac{1}{2}$% compounded semiannually.
   (a) How much must Abrams' fund contain at retirement in order to provide these payments?

(b) How much would he receive before the fund is exhausted?

(c) How much interest would be earned during this time?

20. Instructor Myers plans to return to graduate school for three years and would like to receive $1,000 each six months during this time. He can invest his money at 7% compounded semiannually.

(a) What amount must Mr. Myers' account contain when he returns to school if he is to receive these payments?

(b) How much will he receive while in school?

(c) What part of these payments will be interest?

21. Bob and Carol Daly want to have $4,000 in four years in order to make a trip to Europe. If money is worth 5% compounded monthly—

(a) How much must the Dalys save each month in order to obtain their goal?

(b) How much of the $4,000 will be deposits?

(c) How much of the $4,000 will be interest?

22. In order to extend curb and gutter facilities, the town of Roxbury sold bonds worth $100,000 at maturity. The city council plans to make deposits for 15 years in order to provide the $100,000 to redeem the bonds. If money is worth 8% compounded quarterly—

(a) What quarterly payment will the town have to make to finance the fund?

(b) How much of the $100,000 will be actual deposits?

(c) How much interest will the $100,000 include?

23. Jason Wright invested $10,000 in a fund that was earning 9% compounded quarterly. If the fund continues to earn at the same rate—

(a) What will be the value of his investment after 10 years?

(b) How much interest will the account contain then?

24. Hiram and Jones invested $3,000 in savings certificates which pay 6% compounded monthly.

(a) How much will the certificates be worth after seven years?

(b) How much interest will the certificates earn?

APPENDICES

Appendix A
Arithmetic

LEARNING OBJECTIVES

Upon completing Appendix A, the student will be able to:

1. Define and use correctly the terminology in each topic.
2. a. Identify the place value associated with each digit in a whole number or a decimal number.
   b. Pronounce the complete number.

3. a. Express the basic number properties:
      (1) Commutative for addition and multiplication,
      (2) Associative for addition and multiplication, and
      (3) Distributive.
   b. Verify each property using
      (1) Whole numbers,
      (2) Common fractions, and
      (3) Decimal fractions.

4. Perform accurately the arithmetic operations (addition, subtraction, multiplication, and division) using whole numbers, common fractions, and decimal fractions.

5. Manipulate common fractions accurately:
   a. Reduce,
   b. Change to higher terms,
   c. Convert mixed numbers to improper fractions, and
   d. Convert common fractions to their equal decimal value.

6. Manipulate decimal fractions accurately:
   a. Convert to common fractions (including decimals with fractional remainders); and
   b. Multiply and divide by powers of 10 by moving the decimal point.

ALTHOUGH ARITHMETIC COMPUTATION in most businesses is done with machines, the student should possess a certain facility with computation. The following topics are presented in order to provide practice where necessary in the arithmetic skills.

1. READING NUMBERS

The Hindu-Arabic number system which we use is known as the "base ten" system. This means that it is organized by 10 and powers of 10. Any number can be written using combinations of ten basic characters called *digits*: 0, 1, 2, 3, 4, 5, 6, 7, 8, and 9. When combined in a number, each digit represents a particular value according to its rank in the order of digits and to the position it holds in the number (this latter is known as its *place value*). The following chart shows what place value (and power of 10) is represented by each place in a number. Larger place values are on the left and smaller values are toward the right.

Note: Each power of 10 is indicated (or abbreviated) by an *exponent*, which is a small number written after the 10 in a raised position. The exponent indicates the number of tens that would have to be multiplied together in order to obtain the unabbreviated place value. Thus, in the expression 10^4, the exponent "4" indicates the complete number is found by multiplying together four 10's: $10^4 = 10 \times 10 \times 10 \times 10 = 10,000$. It should also be observed that the exponent indicates the number of zeroes that the complete number contains. That is, 10^5 is equal to a "1" followed by 5 zeroes: $10^5 = 10 \times 10 \times 10 \times 10 \times 10 = 100,000$.

The "2" in the number in the chart, because of the place it occupies, represents "two 10's" or 20. Similarly, the "4" represents "four 10,000's"

BILLIONS			MILLIONS			THOUSANDS			HUNDREDS		
Hundred billions: 10^{11}	Ten billions: 10^{10}	Billions: 10^9	Hundred millions: 10^8	Ten millions: 10^7	Millions: 10^6	Hundred thousands: 10^5	Ten thousands: 10^4	Thousands: 10^3	Hundreds: 10^2	Tens: 10^1	Units: 10^0
		1	3	7	6	0	4	9	5	2	8

or 40,000. The last three digits above, "528," are read "five hundred twenty-eight."

For convenience in reading, large numbers are usually separated with commas into groups of three digits, starting at the right. Each three-digit group is then read as the appropriate number of hundreds, tens, and units, followed by the family name of the groupings. Thus, the digits "376" above are read "three hundred seventy-six million." The entire number above, written with commas, would appear 1,376,049,528 and would be read "one billion, three hundred seventy-six million, forty-nine thousand, five hundred twenty-eight." Commas in a number have no mathematical significance and are used merely to separate the family groupings and indicate the point at which one should pronounce the family name.

When preparing to read a large number, the student should never have to name every place value (smallest to largest) in order to determine the largest value; rather, one should point off the groups of three, reading the family names as he proceeds, until the largest family grouping is reached. Thus the largest value of the number 207,XXX,XXX,XXX is quickly identified, reading right to left:

$$\underset{207,}{\overset{B}{\frown}} \; \underset{XXX,}{\overset{M}{\frown}} \; \underset{XXX,}{\overset{T}{\frown}} \; \underset{XXX}{\overset{H}{\frown}}$$

The 207 represents "two hundred seven billion," and succeeding values would be read in decreasing order.

In reading the value of a number, it is incorrect to use the word "and" except to designate the location of a decimal point. The number 16,000,003 is pronounced "sixteen million, three."

PROBLEMS

In the number 47,315,809,062, identify the place of the following digits:

1. (a) 1
   (b) 2

2. (a) 5
   (b) 6

(c) 3   (c) 7
(d) 4   (d) 8
(e) 5   (e) 9

Write in words the values of the following numbers:

3. (a)   55,218,349   4. (a)   6,411,293,857
    (b)   4,623,352,787   (b)   123,625,819,743
    (c)   83,004,260,409   (c)   205,100,416
    (d)   625,780,211,007   (d)   15,063,008,760
    (e)   36,500,004,708   (e)   9,301,000,065
    (f)   203,000,700,695   (f)   620,000,090,050
    (g)   74,000,000,030   (g)   30,000,000,700

2. WHOLE NUMBERS

The simplest set of numbers in our number system are those used to
identify a single object or a group of objects. These are the *counting numbers*
or *natural numbers* or positive *whole numbers*. The counting numbers, along
with zero and the negative whole numbers (whole numbers less than zero),
comprise the set known as the *integers*. Earliest "mathematics" consisted
simply of using the integers to count one's possessions—sheep, cattle, tents,
wives, and so on. As civilization advanced and became more complex, the
need for more efficient mathematics also increased. This led to the perfection of the four arithmetic *operations:* addition, subtraction, multiplication, and division. (This review includes operations only with nonnegative
numbers.)

ADDITION

This operation provides a shortcut which eliminates having to count each
item consecutively until the total is reached. The names of the numbers
in an operation of addition are as follows:

$$
\begin{array}{lr}
\text{Addend} & 23 \\
\text{Addend} & +16 \\
\hline
\text{Sum} & 39
\end{array}
$$

Addition functions under two basic mathematical laws, expressed as
(1) the commutative property of addition, and (2) the associative property
of addition. The *commutative property of addition* means that the *order* in which
two addends are taken does not affect the sum. More simply, if two numbers are to be added, it does not matter which is written down first. The
commutative property is usually written in general terms (terms which apply to all numbers) as

$$\text{CPA:} \qquad a + b = b + a$$

The commutative property of addition can be illustrated using the numbers 2 and 3:

$$2 + 3 \overset{?}{=} 3 + 2$$
$$5 = 5$$

The *associative property of addition* applies to the *grouping* of *three* numbers; it means that, when three numbers are to be added, the sum will be the same regardless of which two are grouped together to be added first. The associative property is expressed in the following general terms:

APA: $(a + b) + c = a + (b + c)$

The associative property can be verified as follows: Suppose the numbers 2, 3, and 4 are to be added. By the associative property,

$$(2 + 3) + 4 \overset{?}{=} 2 + (3 + 4)$$
$$5 \quad + 4 \overset{?}{=} 2 + \quad 7$$
$$9 = 9$$

By applying both the commutative and associative properties of addition, one can verify other groupings or the addition of more addends.

An excellent way in which the student can speed addition is by adding in groups of numbers which total 10. The student should be thoroughly familiar with the combinations of two numbers which total 10 ($1 + 9$; $2 + 8$; $3 + 7$; $4 + 6$; $5 + 5$) and should be alert for these combinations in problems. For example,

3   This should not be added "3 plus 7 is 10 plus 6 is 16
7   plus 4 is 20." Rather, one should immediately recog-
6   nize the two groups of 10 and add "10 plus 10 is 20,"
4   as:

$$
\begin{array}{l}
3 \,\rangle \; 10 \\
7 \\
6 \,\rangle \; 10 \\
\underline{4} \\
20
\end{array}
$$

Most problems do not consist of such obvious combinations, but the device may frequently be employed if one is alert for it. For instance,

$$
\begin{array}{l}
8 \,\rangle \; 10 \\
4 \\
2 \,\rangle \; 10 \\
\underline{6} \\
20
\end{array}
$$

4   (added "4 plus 10
5   is 14 plus 9 is 23,"
9   or "4 plus 9 is 13
5   plus 10 is 23")

$$\overline{23}$$

```
9⌐    (added "10      8     (added "8 plus 10
6 )   plus 6 is 16    6⌐    is 18 plus 10 is 28
1⌐    plus 10 is      4⌐    plus 5 is 33")
4⌐    26")            3⌐
6⌐                    5 )
—                    7⌐
26                   ——
                     33
```

This technique, like many others, can be carried to extremes. It is intended to be a time-saver; it will be provided the student is alert for combinations adding up to 10 when they are conveniently located near each other. However, a problem may take longer to add if one wastes time searching for widely separated combinations. Also, it is easy to miss a number altogether if one is adding numbers from all parts of the problem rather than adding in nearly consecutive order. Therefore, the student should use the device when he can, but should not expect it to apply to every problem.

If a first glance at a problem reveals that the same digit appears several times in a column, the following device is useful: Count the number of times the digit appears and multiply this number by the digit itself; the remaining digits are then added to this total. For example,

```
7     (added "four 7's
4     are 28 plus 4 is
7     32 plus 8 is 40")
7
8
7
——
40
```

As the student probably knows, addition problems may be checked either by adding upward in reverse order or simply by re-adding the sum.

Horizontal addition problems seem harder because the numbers being added are so far apart. More mistakes are made in horizontal problems because a digit from the wrong place is often added. However, many business forms require horizontal addition. The following hint may make such addition easier:

1. A right-handed person should use his left index finger to cover all the larger digits in the first number, down to the digit currently being added. (Unfortunately, left-handed persons will have to forego this aid.)

2. As digits from succeeding numbers are added, place the pencil point beneath the digit currently being added. Mentally repeat the current subtotal frequently as you proceed.

For example, while the tens' digits are being added in the following problem, the left index finger should cover the digits "162" of the first number. The pencil point should be placed under the 5, 1, 2, and 7 as each is added.

$$16,2 \overline{)83} + 22,054 + 40,611 + 7,927 + 19,670 = \underline{\dots.45}$$

SUBTRACTION

This operation is the opposite of addition. (Since subtraction produces the same result as when a negative number.is added to a positive, subtraction is sometimes defined as an extension of addition.) The parts of a subtraction operation have the following names:

Minuend	325
Subtrahend	−198
Difference or Remainder	127

A subtraction problem can be checked mentally by adding together the subtrahend and difference; if the resultant sum equals the minuend, the operation is verified.

The student can easily determine that neither the commutative nor the associative property applies to subtraction. For example, it makes a great deal of difference whether we find $17 − $8 or $8 − $17. And any example will show that the associative property does not hold:

$$(7 - 5) - 2 \stackrel{?}{=} 7 - (5 - 2)$$
$$2 \quad - 2 \stackrel{?}{=} 7 - \quad 3$$
$$0 \neq 4$$

As the student knows, subtraction often necessitates "borrowing," or regrouping of the place values. For example, the number 325 in our first example of subtraction—which represents three 100's, two 10's, and five 1's—had to be regrouped into two 100's, eleven 10's, and fifteen 1's. Both groupings equal 325, as the following examples show:

Original	Regrouped		Subtraction
300	200	(two 100's)	(two 100's)
20	110	(eleven 10's)	(eleven 10's)
5	15	(fifteen 1's)	(fifteen 1's)
325	325		

$$\begin{array}{r} 2 \;\; 11 \;\; 1 \\ \cancel{3} \;\; \cancel{2} \;\; 5 \\ -1 \;\; 9 \;\; 8 \\ \hline 1 \;\; 2 \;\; 7 \end{array}$$

The student is also aware that addition problems often contain many numbers, whereas subtraction problems contain only two numbers. Subtraction problems could just as well contain more numbers were it not for the fact that regrouping becomes so complicated. Many office calculators, which can regroup repeatedly when necessary, can perform a series of subtractions before indicating a total. (This is not possible with multiplication or division.)

MULTIPLICATION

This operation was developed as a shortcut for addition. Suppose a student has three classes on each of five days; the week's total classes could be found by addition:

$$\frac{M \quad T \quad W \quad T \quad F}{3 + 3 + 3 + 3 + 3} = \frac{\text{Total}}{15}$$

This approach to the problem would become quite tedious, however, if we wanted to know the total receipts at a grocery store from the sale of 247 cartons of soft drinks at $.67 each.

Thus multiplication originated when persons learned from experience what sums to expect following repeated additions of small numbers, and the actual addition process then became unnecessary. Perfection of the operation led to the knowledge that any two numbers, regardless of size, could be multiplied if one had memorized the products of all combinations of the digits 0–9. (The frequent occurrence in business situations of the number 12 makes knowledge of its multiples quite valuable also.) The following table lists the products of the digits 2–9, as well as the numbers 10–12. The student should be able to recite instantly all products up through the multiples of 9. A knowledge of products through the multiples of 12 is also very useful.

MULTIPLICATION TABLE

	2	3	4	5	6	7	8	9	10	11	12
2	4	6	8	10	12	14	16	18	20	22	24
3	6	9	12	15	18	21	24	27	30	33	36
4	8	12	16	20	24	28	32	36	40	44	48
5	10	15	20	25	30	35	40	45	50	55	60
6	12	18	24	30	36	42	48	54	60	66	72
7	14	21	28	35	42	49	56	63	70	77	84
8	16	24	32	40	48	56	64	72	80	88	96
9	18	27	36	45	54	63	72	81	90	99	108
10	20	30	40	50	60	70	80	90	100	110	120
11	22	33	44	55	66	77	88	99	110	121	132
12	24	36	48	60	72	84	96	108	120	132	144

The numbers of an operation of multiplication have the following names:

Multiplicand (or Factor)	18
Multiplier (or Factor)	$\times 4$
Product	72

There are three properties affecting the operation of multiplication: (1) the commutative property of multiplication, (2) the associative property of multiplication, and (3) the distributive property.

The *commutative property of multiplication*, like the commutative property of addition, applies to the *order* in which *two* numbers are taken. The commutative property asserts that either factor can be written first, and the product will be the same. In general terms, the commutative property of multiplication is written

$$\text{CPM:} \qquad a \cdot b = b \cdot a$$

It can be illustrated using the factors 4 and 7:

$$4 \cdot 7 \overset{?}{=} 7 \cdot 4$$
$$28 = 28$$

The *associative property of multiplication* is similar to the associative property of addition in that it applies to the *grouping* of any *three* numbers. That is, if three numbers are to be multiplied, the product will be the same regardless of which two are multiplied first. The associative property of multiplication is expressed in general terms as:

$$\text{APM:} \qquad (a \cdot b)c = a(b \cdot c)$$

Using the numbers 2, 5, and 3, the associative property is verified as follows:

$$(2 \cdot 5)3 \overset{?}{=} 2(5 \cdot 3)$$
$$(10)3 \overset{?}{=} 2(15)$$
$$30 = 30$$

The third property applies to the combination of multiplication and addition. It is the *distributive property*, sometimes called the *distributive property of multiplication over addition*. This property means that the product of the sum of two numbers equals the sum of the individual products. Stated differently, this means that if two numbers are added and their sum is multiplied by some other number, the final total is the same as if the two numbers were first separately multiplied by the third number and the products then added. The distributive property is expressed for all numbers as

$$\text{DP:} \qquad a(b + c) = ab + ac$$

Using 2 for the multiplier and the numbers 3 and 5 for the addends, the distributive property can be verified as follows:

$$2(3 + 5) \overset{?}{=} 2 \cdot 3 + 2 \cdot 5$$
$$2(8) \overset{?}{=} 6 \quad + 10$$
$$16 = 16$$

Note: The distributive property has frequent application in business. One of the best examples is sales tax: When several items are purchased, the sales tax is found by adding all the prices and then multiplying only once by the applicable sales tax per cent. This is much simpler than multiplying the tax rate by the price of each separate item and then adding to find the total sales tax, although the total would be the same by either method.

While other methods are sometimes used, the easiest, quickest, and most reliable check of a multiplication problem is simply to repeat the multiplication. (If convenient, the factors may be reversed for the checking operation.)

Students often waste time and do much unnecessary work when *multiplying by numbers which contain zeros.* When multiplying by 10, 100, 1,000, etc., the product should be written immediately simply by affixing to the original factor the same number of zeroes as contained in the multiplier. Thus

$$54 \times 10 = 540; 2{,}173 \times 100 = 217{,}300; \text{ and } 145 \times 1{,}000 = 145{,}000.$$

When multiplying numbers ending in zeroes, the factors should be written with the zeroes to the right of the problem as it will actually be performed. After multiplication with the other digits has been completed, affix the zeroes to the basic product. For example,

(a)

$$148 \times 60$$

$$\begin{array}{r} 148 \\ \times 6\,|\,0 \\ \hline 8{,}88\,|\,0 \end{array}$$

(b)

$$6{,}700 \times 52$$

$$\begin{array}{r} 52 \\ \times 67\,|\,00 \\ \hline 364 \\ 312 \\ \hline 348{,}4\,|\,00 \end{array}$$

(c)
$$130 \times 1,500$$

13	0	Note here that
15	00	all three zeroes
65		are affixed to
13		the product.
195,	000	

When a multiplier contains zeroes within the number, many people write whole rows of useless zeroes in order to be certain that the significant digits remain properly aligned.   These unnecessary zeroes should be omitted; the other digits will still be in correct order if the student practices this basic rule of multiplication: On each line of multiplication, the first digit to be written down is placed directly beneath the digit in the multiplier (second factor) being multiplied at the time:

(a)
$$671 \times 305$$

Wrong	Right
671	671
×305	×305
3355	3355
000	2013
2013	204,655
204,655	

(b)
$$4,386 \times 6,004$$

4,386
×6,004
17 544
26316
26,333,544

DIVISION

This operation is the reverse of multiplication. The numbers in an operation of division are identified as follows:

$$\begin{array}{r} 4 \quad \text{Quotient} \\ \text{Divisor} \quad 18 \overline{)77} \quad \text{Dividend} \\ 72 \\ \hline 5 \quad \text{Remainder} \end{array}$$

That is,

$$\text{Divisor} \overline{)\text{Dividend}}^{\text{Quotient}} \quad \text{or} \quad \text{Dividend} \div \text{Divisor} = \text{Quotient}$$

Division is neither commutative, associative, nor distributive, as can be determined by brief experiments. Obviously, $4\,\overline{\smash{\big)}\,16}$ yields quite a different quotient from $16\,\overline{\smash{\big)}\,4}$. An example to test the associative property reveals different quotients:

$$(36 \div 6) \div 3 \overset{?}{=} 36 \div (6 \div 3)$$
$$6 \quad \div 3 \overset{?}{=} 36 \div \quad 2$$
$$2 \neq 18$$

Similarly, a test of the distributive property reveals that it does not apply either:

$$60 \div (4 + 6) \overset{?}{=} 60 \div 4 + 60 \div 6$$
$$60 \div \quad 10 \quad \overset{?}{=} \quad 15 \quad + \quad 10$$
$$6 \neq 25$$

Division by one-digit divisors should be carried out mentally and the quotient written directly; this method is commonly called *short division*. The student may find it helpful to write each remainder in front of the next number as the operation progresses. For example,

$$7\,\overline{\smash{\big)}\,9422} \qquad \text{written} \qquad 7\,\overline{\smash{\big)}\,9^2 4^3 2^4 2}^{\,1\ 3\ 4\ 6}$$

Division involving divisors of two or more digits is usually performed by writing each step completely. Division performed in this manner is known as *long division*. The following general rules apply to both long and short division and cover aspects of division where mistakes are often made:

1. The first digit of the quotient should be written directly above the last digit of the partial dividend which the divisor divides into. For example, when dividing $25\,\overline{\smash{\big)}\,17628}$, the first digit of the quotient should be written above the 6:

$$\begin{array}{r} 7 \\ 25\,\overline{\smash{\big)}\,17628} \\ \underline{175} \end{array}$$

2. The amount remaining after each succeeding step in division must always be smaller than the divisor. Otherwise, the divisor would have divided into the dividend at least one more time. (If a remainder is larger than the divisor, the previous step should be repeated to correct the corresponding digit in the quotient.) For example, if the first step had been

$$\begin{array}{r} 6 \\ 25\overline{)17,628} \\ \underline{150} \\ 26 \end{array}$$ ◄——— remainder is
more than 25

the quotient should be corrected:

$$\begin{array}{r} 7 \\ 25\overline{)17,628} \\ \underline{175} \\ 1 \end{array}$$ ◄——— remainder is
less than 25

3. Succeeding digits of the dividend should be brought down one at a time. For example,

$$\begin{array}{r} 7 \\ 25\overline{)17,628} \\ \underline{175} \\ 1\,2 \end{array}$$

4. Each time a digit is brought down, a new digit must be affixed to the quotient directly over the digit that was just brought down. Thus a zero is affixed to the quotient when a brought-down digit does not create a number large enough for the divisor to divide into at least one whole time. For example,

$$\begin{array}{r} 70 \\ 25\overline{)17,628} \\ \underline{175} \\ 12 \end{array}$$

The next digit is then brought down and the division process continued as follows:

$$\begin{array}{r} 705 \\ 25\overline{)17,628} \\ \underline{175} \\ 128 \\ \underline{125} \\ 3 \end{array}$$

5. The final remainder may be written directly after the quotient as follows:

$$
\begin{array}{r}
705 \ \text{R3} \\
25\overline{)17{,}628} \\
\underline{175} \\
128 \\
\underline{125} \\
3
\end{array}
$$

Division problems can be checked by multiplying the divisor by the quotient and adding the remainder (if any). This result should equal the original dividend. For example, for the above division problem,

$$
\begin{array}{r}
705 \\
\times 25 \\
\hline
17{,}625 \\
+3 \\
\hline
17{,}628
\end{array}
$$

PROBLEMS

1. (a) Express the commutative property of addition, using g and h.
   (b) Write and then verify the commutative property of addition, using 15 and 47.
   (c) Express the associative property of addition, using d, e, and f.
   (d) Write and verify the associative property of addition, using 9, 28, and 16.
   (e) Express the commutative property of multiplication, using x and y.
   (f) Write and then verify the commutative property of multiplication, using 38 and 25.
   (g) Express the associative property of multiplication, using l, m, and n.
   (h) Write and verify the associative property of multiplication, using 7, 3, and 9.
   (i) Express the distributive property, using r, s, and t.
   (j) Write and then verify the distributive property, using 5, 3, and 6.

2. (a) Express the commutative property of addition, using k and l.
   (b) Write and then verify the commutative property of addition, using 45 and 18.
   (c) Express the associative property of addition, using r, s, and t.
   (d) Write and verify the associative property of addition, using 9, 6, and 13.
   (e) Express the commutative property of multiplication, using v and w.
   (f) Write and then verify the commutative property of multiplication, using 12 and 26.
   (g) Express the associative property of multiplication, using p, q, and r.
   (h) Write and verify the associative property of multiplication, using 4, 9, and 3.

(i)   Express the distributive property, using x, y, and z.

(j)   Write and then verify the distributive property, using 8, 2, and 5.

The following problems were especially designed to provide practice in adding by combinations which total 10:

3.	(a)	(b)	(c)	(d)	(e)
	6	4	2	7	3
	5	7	8	5	4
	4	9	5	6	7
	5	3	1	5	2
			9	4	8

	(f)	(g)	(h)	(i)
	5	5	49	25
	6	7	47	67
	8	5	95	56
	4	2	33	23
	1	4	15	54
	9	8		

4.	(a)	(b)	(c)	(d)	(e)
	9	8	4	7	2
	2	7	6	5	9
	1	3	8	9	8
	8	5	5	5	3
			2	1	7

	(f)	(g)	(h)	(i)
	8	6	44	67
	8	9	43	35
	1	4	86	28
	2	9	69	75
	9	6	21	52
	4	1		

Add the following, using time-saving techniques where possible.   Check your answers.

5.	(a)	(b)	(c)	(d)	(e)
	7	3	7	4	42
	9	8	4	9	38
	5	9	7	4	75
	8	2	5	4	18
	4	6	3	5	94
			5	4	

	(f)	(g)	(h)	(i)
	32	12	57	74
	29	73	82	65
	55	47	67	56
	63	85	37	21
	46	59	97	33
			28	49

6. (a) 243　　(b) 308　　(c) 418
　　 658　　　　 475　　　　 37
　　 291　　　　 632　　　　295
　　 445　　　　 487　　　　646
　　　　　　　　 729　　　　 95

　 (d) 4,272　 (e) 4,616　 (f)　 285
　　 3,060　　　 3,872　　 3,656
　　 7,355　　　 9,524　　　 125
　　 9,298　　　 6,636　　　 47
　　　　　　　　 2,518　　 7,389

　 (g) 58,036　 (h) 63,316　 (i) $4,391.54
　　 21,845　　　 37,845　　　 29.18
　　 37,544　　　 20,437　　　105.15
　　 83,621　　　 78,055　 2,436.77
　　　　　　　　 48,672　　　　 7.05
　　　　　　　　　　　　　 455.93

7. (a)　　　 29 +　　 48 +　　 31 +　　 55 +　　 74 = _____
　 (b)　　　 78 +　　 24 +　　 45 +　　 52 +　　 63 = _____
　 (c)　　 338 +　　 609 +　　 241 +　　 585 +　　 311 = _____
　 (d)　　 937 +　　 428 +　　 883 +　　 725 +　　 236 = _____
　 (e)　 5,200 + 7,751 + 3,929 + 4,066 +　 6,628 = _____
　 (f)　 23,489 + 8,601 +　　 321 + 6,658 + 13,876 = _____

8. Subtract in each of the following. Check by adding:

　 (a) 465　　(b) 954　　(c) 809
　　 382　　　　 688　　　　538

　 (d) 2,537　 (e) 4,086　 (f) 7,545
　　 1,698　　　 2,918　　 4,763

　 (g) 25,400　 (h) 75,811　 (i) 450,933
　　 9,396　　　 37,609　　 378,416

9. Multiply:

　 (a)　　 247 × 　10　　 (g)　 5,800 ×　　 650
　 (b)　 1,000 × 　39　　 (h)　 1,450 ×　 7,200
　 (c)　　 463 × 100　　 (i)　　 711 ×　　 609
　 (d)　　 42 × 190　　 (j)　 7,542 ×　　 405
　 (e)　 1,700 × 258　　 (k)　 9,321 ×　 5,006
　 (f)　 24,000 × 315　　 (l)　 123,046 × 40,803

10. Multiply:

　 (a) 48　　(b) 546　　(c) 717
　　 52　　　　 27　　　　 83

(d) 2,506   (e) 8,693   (f) 9,325
    317   274   7,109

(g) 28,069   (h) 531,728   (i) 7,328,619
   2,635   3,057   2,745

Divide. Check, using multiplication:

11. (a) 6 ⟌ 3,588   (c) 5 ⟌ 13,545   (e) 7 ⟌ 34,828
   (b) 3 ⟌ 2,244   (d) 8 ⟌ 48,032   (f) 9 ⟌ 43,226

12. (a) 36 ⟌ 3,420   (f) 248 ⟌ 153,512
   (b) 72 ⟌ 24,912   (g) 3,518 ⟌ 207,562
   (c) 537 ⟌ 13,425   (h) 157 ⟌ 468,500
   (d) 806 ⟌ 51,584   (i) 4,785 ⟌ 29,108,110
   (e) 627 ⟌ 183,711   (j) 78,362 ⟌ 9,804,530

13. The following table shows the sales made by various departments of a discount department store during one week. Find the total sales of the store for each day and the total sales of each department for the entire week. (This final total serves as a check of your addition: The sum of the weekly totals from each department must equal the sum of the daily totals for the whole store. That is, the sum of the totals in the right-hand column must equal the sum of the totals across the bottom.)

DISCOUNT MART

Sales for week of August 4

Dept.	Monday	Tuesday	Wednesday	Thursday	Friday	Saturday	Dept. Totals
#1	$345.68	$406.29	$323.76	$386.91	$459.85	$481.86	$
#2	562.09	438.88	475.45	424.18	582.37	519.12	
#3	445.21	459.16	398.06	437.75	493.46	418.25	
#4	293.34	302.28	285.37	356.11	374.04	380.84	
#5	322.66	289.55	314.42	349.23	352.58	334.17	
#6	488.49	419.37	392.76	407.33	469.87	493.66	
Daily Totals	$	$	$	$	$	$	$____

14. Complete the following check record, which shows the checks written and deposits made in a personal checking account. Add the deposits to the balance in account and subtract the checks from this balance. Check as follows:

Original balance	$	_____
Add: total deposits	+	_____
	$	_____
Subtract: total checks	−	_____
Final balance	$	_____

CHECK RECORD

CHECK NO.	DATE	CHECK ISSUED TO	AMOUNT OF CHECK		√	AMOUNT OF DEPOSIT		BALANCE 215	69
144	11/18	Food Fair	37	27					
145	11/18	Thrifty Cleaners	8	45					
−	11/20	DEPOSIT				155	78		
146	11/23	Kendall Drug Co.	12	65					
147	11/25	Food Fair	26	19					
148	11/27	General Telephone	9	53					
149	11/29	Fidelity Insurance Co.	48	17					
−	12/1	DEPOSIT				786	29		
150	12/2	Cansler Realty	195	00					
151	12/2	Dept. of Water & Power	12	37					
152	12/2	Dr. Mason	28	00					
153	12/2	Food Fair	27	49					
154	12/4	Eastover Dept. Store	78	28					
155	12/6	Williams Furniture Co.	174	19					

15. Complete the following sales invoice. Multiply the cost of each item by the number of items purchased. Add to find the total cost of the purchase.

OFFICE SUPPLY HOUSE
Invoice

No. Purchased	Description	Cost per Item	Total
14	X-22 pencil sharpeners	$ 3.12	$
12	X-25 pencil sharpeners	3.55	
25	B-13 reams bond stationery	2.46	
15	K-46 reams onion skin	1.95	
26	R-12 reams duplicating paper	2.88	
175	PY-8 erasers	.03	
125	TG-2 clips	.04	
6	TC-32 typewriter covers	.75	
72	C-28 pencils	.07	
46	L-4 ballpoint pens	.42	
8	RF-10 typewriters	79.50	
5	P-7 addressographs	95.27	
3	A-IV calculators	168.38	
2	HD-5 electric typewriters	209.95	
17	RP-34 ledger sets	15.88	
		Total	$

16. Using the following breakdown, find the average amount of life insurance sold to clients in various states. (That is, divide the value of insurance sold in each state by the number of policies written.) Add to find the total value

of all policies sold and the total number of policies; then find the average value per policy sold by the company (to the nearest dollar.)

THE ATLANTIC INSURANCE CO.

Average Value of Policy by State

STATE	TOTAL VALUE OF POLICIES SOLD	NO. OF POLICIES	AVERAGE VALUE PER POLICY
Connecticut	$ 72,816,000	3,552	
Delaware	22,388,000	965	
Florida	108,480,000	8,475	
Georgia	100,011,000	6,290	
New Jersey	171,236,000	9,256	
New York	428,856,000	25,680	
North Carolina	94,461,000	6,845	
Pennsylvania	252,396,000	14,760	
South Carolina	51,794,000	3,572	
Virginia	89,333,000	5,690	
Total	$		$

3. COMMON FRACTIONS

The system of fractions was developed to meet the need for measuring quantities which are not whole amounts. The parts of a fraction are identified by the following terms:

$$\begin{array}{cc} \text{Numerator} & 3 \\ \text{Denominator} & \overline{5} \end{array}$$

A *common fraction* is an indicated division—a short method of writing a division problem. That is, if $3 is to be divided among five persons, each person's share is indicated

$$\$3 \div 5 \qquad \text{or} \qquad \$\tfrac{3}{5}$$

Thus the fraction line indicates division (the numerator is to be divided by the denominator), and the entire fraction represents each person's share. We now see why common fractions are often known as "rational numbers." A *rational number* is any number which can be expressed as the quotient of two integers. The fraction $\tfrac{3}{5}$ is a rational number because it is expressed as the quotient of the integers (whole numbers) 3 and 5. The entire fraction represents the quotient—the value of 3 divided by 5.

A common fraction is called a *proper fraction* if its numerator is smaller than the denominator (for example, $\tfrac{4}{5}$) and if the indicated division would result in a value less than 1. The numerator of an *improper fraction* is equal to or greater than the denominator (for example, $\tfrac{7}{7}$ or $\tfrac{15}{7}$) and thus has a value equal to or greater than 1.

REDUCING FRACTIONS

Two fractions are equal if they represent the same quantity. When writing fractions, however, it is customary to use the smallest possible numbers. Thus it is often necessary to *reduce* a fraction—to change it to a fraction of equal value but written with smaller numbers.

The fraction $\frac{3}{3}$ represents $3 \div 3$ or 1. Obviously, any number written over itself as a fraction equals one $\left(\frac{x}{x} = 1\right)$. We also know from multiplication that 1 times any number equals that same number ($1 \cdot x = x$). These facts are the mathematical basis for reducing fractions. A fraction can be reduced if the same number is a factor of both the numerator and the denominator. For example,

$$\frac{6}{15} = \frac{2 \times 3}{5 \times 3} \quad \text{(the factors of 6 are 2 and 3)}$$
$$\text{(the factors of 15 are 5 and 3)}$$

But since $\frac{3}{3} = 1$, then

$$\frac{6}{15} = \frac{2 \times 3}{5 \times 3} = \frac{2}{5} \times \frac{3}{3} = \frac{2}{5} \times 1 = \frac{2}{5}$$

Hence, $\frac{2}{5}$ represents the same quantity as $\frac{6}{15}$.

In actual practice, one reduces a fraction by testing mentally the numerator and denominator to determine the *greatest* factor which they have in common (that is, to determine the largest number which will divide into both evenly). The reduced value is then indicated by writing these quotients in fraction form:

$$\frac{20}{15} \quad \text{(think: 5 divides into 20 \textit{four} times and into 15 \textit{three} times)} \qquad \text{Write:} \qquad \frac{20}{15} = \frac{4}{3}$$

Sometimes, however, the greatest common factor may not be immediately obvious. When the greatest common factor is not apparent, a fraction may be reduced to its lowest terms by performing a series of reductions:

$$\frac{60}{84} = \frac{2}{2} \times \frac{30}{42} = \frac{30}{42} = \frac{2}{2} \times \frac{15}{21} = \frac{15}{21} = \frac{3}{3} \times \frac{5}{7} = 1 \times \frac{5}{7} = \frac{5}{7}$$

The end result will be the same whether the reduction is performed in one step or in several steps. It should be noted that if a series of reductions is used, the product of these several common factors equals the number which would have been the greatest single common factor. For example, the fraction $\frac{60}{84}$ was reduced above by 2, 2, and 3; the product of these factors is 12, which is the greatest common factor:

$$\frac{60}{84} = \frac{2}{2} \times \frac{2}{2} \times \frac{3}{3} \times \frac{5}{7} = 1 \times 1 \times 1 \times \frac{5}{7} = \frac{5}{7} \quad \text{or} \quad \frac{60}{84} = \frac{12}{12} \times \frac{5}{7} = 1 \times \frac{5}{7} = \frac{5}{7}$$

Therefore, the student should divide by the largest number that he recognizes as a factor of both the numerator and denominator. However, one should always examine the result to determine whether it still contains another common factor.

CHANGING TO HIGHER TERMS

Suppose we wish to know whether $\frac{5}{8}$ or $\frac{7}{9}$ is larger. In order to compare the size of fractions, as a practical matter one must rewrite them using the same denominator. The process of rewriting fractions so that they have a common denominator (which is usually larger than either original denominator) is called *changing to higher terms*.

The product of the various denominators will provide a common denominator. However, it is customary to use the *least common denominator*, which is the smallest number which all the denominators will divide into evenly. Thus the least (or lowest) common denominator is often a number which is smaller than the product of all the denominators. In fact, one of the given denominators may be the least common denominator.

When finding the least common denominator, the student should first consider the multiples of the largest given denominator. If this method does not reveal the least common denominator quickly, the student should find the product of the denominators. Before using this product as the common denominator, though, he should first consider $\frac{1}{2}$, $\frac{1}{3}$, or even $\frac{1}{4}$ of this product to determine if that might be the lowest common denominator. If not, then the product itself probably represents the lowest common denominator.

Consider the fractions $\frac{2}{3}$, $\frac{1}{6}$, and $\frac{3}{8}$. In order to find the least common denominator, examine the multiples of 8 (the largest denominator). The multiples of 8 are 8, 16, 24, 32, 40, etc. Neither 8 nor 16 is divisible by 3 or 6. However, 24 is divisible by both 3 and 6 (and, of course, by 8). Hence, 24 is the least common denominator of $\frac{2}{3}$, $\frac{1}{6}$, and $\frac{3}{8}$.

Next, consider the fractions $\frac{5}{6}$, $\frac{3}{7}$, and $\frac{5}{8}$. The product of the denominators is $6 \times 7 \times 8$ or 336. However, $\frac{1}{2}$ of 336 or 168 represents the smallest number which 6, 7, and 8 will all divide into evenly. Thus 168 is the least common denominator. Also consider the fractions $\frac{1}{6}$, $\frac{2}{7}$, and $\frac{2}{9}$. The product of these denominators is $6 \times 7 \times 9$ or 378. One-half of 378 is 189, which is not divisible by 6. However, $\frac{1}{3}$ of 378 is 126, which is divisible by 6, 7, and 9 all. Hence 126 is the least common denominator.

Changing to higher terms is based on the same principles as reducing fractions, but applied in reverse order. That is, the procedure is based on the facts that any number over itself equals 1 $\left(\dfrac{x}{x} = 1\right)$, and that any number multiplied by 1 equals that same number $(x \cdot 1 = x)$. Thus, once the least common denominator has been determined, one must then find how many times the given denominator divides into the common denominator. This result (written as a fraction equal to 1) is used to convert the fraction to higher terms. For example, suppose we have already determined that 12 is the lowest common denominator for $\frac{3}{4}$ and $\frac{1}{6}$. To convert $\frac{3}{4}$ to higher terms, think, "4 divides into 12 *three* times." Thus $\frac{3}{3}$ is used to change $\frac{3}{4}$ to higher terms:

$$\frac{3}{4} = \frac{3}{4} \times 1 = \frac{3}{4} \times \frac{3}{3} = \frac{3 \times 3}{4 \times 3} = \frac{9}{12}$$

We have multiplied $\frac{3}{4}$ by a value, $\frac{3}{3}$, equal to 1. Therefore, we know that the value of the fraction remains unchanged and that $\frac{3}{4} = \frac{9}{12}$. Similarly, 6 divides into 12 *two* times. Thus

$$\frac{1}{6} = \frac{1}{6} \times 1 = \frac{1}{6} \times \frac{2}{2} = \frac{1 \times 2}{6 \times 2} = \frac{2}{12}$$

Hence $\frac{1}{6} = \frac{2}{12}$.

In actual practice, it is unnecessary to write out this entire process. Rather, one mentally divides the denominator into the lowest common denominator and multiplies that quotient times the numerator to obtain the numerator of the converted fraction. Therefore, to change $\frac{3}{4}$ to twelfths, think: "4 divides into 12 *three* times; that *three* times the numerator 3 equals 9; thus $\frac{3}{4} = \frac{9}{12}$." Or, when changing $\frac{1}{6}$ to twelfths, think: "6 divides into 12 *two* times; *two* times 1 equals 2; therefore, $\frac{1}{6} = \frac{2}{12}$."

Now let us compare $\frac{5}{6}$ and $\frac{7}{9}$ to determine which is larger.

$$\frac{5}{6} = \frac{15}{18} \qquad \text{and} \qquad \frac{7}{9} = \frac{14}{18}$$

Thus, comparing the fractions on the same terms, $\frac{15}{18}$ is larger than $\frac{14}{18}$. Hence $\frac{5}{6}$ is larger than $\frac{7}{9}$.

ADDITION AND SUBTRACTION

The same terminology and properties of operation that apply to integers apply to common fractions as well. Thus the parts of each operation have the following names:

Addend	$\frac{3}{7}$		Minuend	$\frac{3}{7}$
Addend	$+\frac{2}{7}$		Subtrahend	$-\frac{2}{7}$
Sum	$\frac{5}{7}$		Difference or Remainder	$\frac{1}{7}$

The commutative property of addition and the associative property of addition also apply to common fractions:

$$\text{CPA:} \quad a + b = b + a$$
$$\frac{3}{7} + \frac{2}{7} \overset{?}{=} \frac{2}{7} + \frac{3}{7}$$
$$\frac{5}{7} = \frac{5}{7}$$

$$\text{APA:} \qquad (a + b) + c = a + (b + c)$$

$$(\tfrac{3}{7} + \tfrac{2}{7}) + \tfrac{1}{7} \overset{?}{=} (\tfrac{2}{7} + \tfrac{1}{7})$$

$$\tfrac{5}{7} + \tfrac{1}{7} \overset{?}{=} \tfrac{3}{7} + \tfrac{3}{7}$$

$$\tfrac{6}{7} = \tfrac{6}{7}$$

As in the case of whole numbers, neither of the above properties applies for subtraction.

Before common fractions can be either added or subtracted, the fractions must first be written with a common denominator. The numerators are then added or subtracted (whichever is indicated). The result is then written over the *same* common denominator. (The student should be certain this fact is firmly impressed in his mind, for mistakes are frequently made in this operation.) The answer should then be reduced, if possible. Consider the following examples:

(a)

$$\frac{3}{5} = \frac{9}{15}$$
$$+\frac{2}{3} = \frac{10}{15}$$
$$\frac{19}{15}$$

(b)

$$\frac{3}{4} = \frac{9}{12}$$
$$\frac{2}{3} = \frac{8}{12}$$
$$+\frac{5}{6} = \frac{10}{12}$$
$$\frac{27}{12} = \frac{9}{4}$$

(c)

$$\frac{1}{4} + \frac{3}{8} + \frac{1}{6} = \frac{6}{24} + \frac{9}{24} + \frac{4}{24}$$

$$= \frac{6 + 9 + 4}{24}$$

$$= \frac{19}{24}$$

(d)

$$\frac{9}{16} = \frac{9}{16}$$
$$-\frac{3}{8} = \frac{6}{16}$$
$$\frac{3}{16}$$

(e)

$$\frac{5}{7} = \frac{15}{21}$$
$$-\frac{1}{3} = \frac{7}{21}$$
$$\frac{8}{21}$$

(f)

$$\frac{1}{2} - \frac{1}{6} = \frac{3}{6} - \frac{1}{6}$$

$$= \frac{3 - 1}{6}$$

$$= \frac{2}{6}$$

$$= \frac{1}{3}$$

MULTIPLICATION AND DIVISION

As would be expected, the terms previously used to identify the parts of multiplication and division with whole numbers also apply to those operations with fractions.

$$
\begin{array}{ll}
\text{Multiplicand or Factor} & \text{Dividend} \\
\quad\text{Multiplier or Factor} & \quad\text{Divisor} \\
\qquad\text{Product} & \qquad\text{Quotient} \\
\downarrow\quad\downarrow\quad\downarrow & \downarrow\quad\downarrow\quad\downarrow \\
\tfrac{3}{4} \times \tfrac{1}{2} = \tfrac{3}{8} & \tfrac{1}{8} \div \tfrac{2}{3} = \tfrac{3}{16}
\end{array}
$$

The commutative and associative properties of multiplication apply to fractions as they did to integers; and the distributive property of multiplication over addition holds for fractions as it did for whole numbers. (As before, none of these properties is true for division.)

CPM:
$$a \times b = b \times a$$
$$\tfrac{1}{2} \times \tfrac{3}{5} \overset{?}{=} \tfrac{3}{5} \times \tfrac{1}{2}$$
$$\tfrac{3}{10} = \tfrac{3}{10}$$

APM:
$$(a \times b)c = a(b \times c)$$
$$(\tfrac{1}{4} \times \tfrac{3}{5}) \times \tfrac{1}{2} \overset{?}{=} \tfrac{1}{4} \times (\tfrac{3}{5} \times \tfrac{1}{2})$$
$$\tfrac{3}{20} \times \tfrac{1}{2} \overset{?}{=} \tfrac{1}{4} \times \tfrac{3}{10}$$
$$\tfrac{3}{40} = \tfrac{3}{40}$$

DP:
$$a(b + c) = ab + ac$$
$$\tfrac{1}{3}(\tfrac{1}{4} + \tfrac{2}{5}) \overset{?}{=} \tfrac{1}{3} \times \tfrac{1}{4} + \tfrac{1}{3} \times \tfrac{2}{5}$$
$$\tfrac{1}{3}(\tfrac{5}{20} + \tfrac{8}{20}) \overset{?}{=} \tfrac{1}{12} \quad + \tfrac{2}{15}$$
$$\tfrac{1}{3}(\tfrac{13}{20}) \overset{?}{=} \tfrac{5}{60} \quad + \tfrac{8}{60}$$
$$\tfrac{13}{60} = \tfrac{13}{60}$$

When multiplying fractions, the various numerators are multiplied together to obtain the numerator of the product, and the denominators are multiplied together to obtain the denominator of the product. Where possible, the product should be reduced.

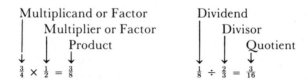

$$\tfrac{2}{5} \times \tfrac{2}{3} = \tfrac{2}{5} \times \tfrac{2}{3} = \frac{2 \times 2}{5 \times 3} = \tfrac{4}{15}$$

When one fraction is to be divided into another, the divisor (second fraction) must first be inverted (that is, the numerator and denominator must be interchanged). Then, proceed as in multiplication. When a fraction is inverted, the new fraction is called the *reciprocal* of the original fraction. Hence the reciprocal of $\tfrac{3}{5}$ is $\tfrac{5}{3}$. Thus it is often said that one divides by "multiplying by the reciprocal."

$$\tfrac{3}{4} \div \tfrac{2}{3} = \tfrac{3}{4} \times \tfrac{3}{2} = \frac{3 \times 3}{4 \times 2} = \tfrac{9}{8}$$

(To divide by $\tfrac{2}{3}$, *multiply* by the *reciprocal* $\tfrac{3}{2}$)

The student may be accustomed to "canceling" when multiplying or dividing fractions. When one uses cancellation, he is actually just reducing the problem rather than waiting and reducing the answer. We know that the value of a fraction remains unchanged when it is reduced. Thus cancellation is permissible because it is a reduction process and does not change the value of the answer.

Consider the problem $\tfrac{3}{4} \times \tfrac{1}{3}$. If multiplied in the standard manner, the product would be $\tfrac{3}{12}$, which reduces to $\tfrac{1}{4}$. The following operations illustrate how the problem itself may be reduced before the answer is obtained:

$$\tfrac{3}{4} \times \tfrac{1}{3} = \frac{3 \times 1}{4 \times 3}$$

Since multiplication is commutative, we can reverse the order of the numbers:

$$\frac{3 \times 1}{4 \times 3} = \frac{1 \times 3}{4 \times 3}$$
$$= \tfrac{1}{4} \times \tfrac{3}{3}$$
$$= \tfrac{1}{4} \times 1$$
$$= \tfrac{1}{4}$$

Thus, $\tfrac{3}{4} \times \tfrac{1}{3} = \tfrac{1}{4}$. However, one would not usually reduce by rewriting the problem to make the 3's form the fraction $\tfrac{3}{3}$ and thereby reduce to 1. Rather, seeing that there is one 3 in the numerator and another in the denominator, one would cancel the 3's (or reduce $\tfrac{3}{3}$ to 1) as follows:

$$\tfrac{3}{4} \times \tfrac{1}{3} = \frac{\overset{1}{\cancel{3}}}{4} \times \frac{1}{\underset{1}{\cancel{3}}} = \tfrac{1}{4}$$

Two numbers may be reduced even though they may be widely separated in the problem, provided one is in the numerator and the other in the denominator:

$$\tfrac{4}{5} \times \tfrac{3}{5} \times \tfrac{7}{8} = \frac{\overset{1}{\cancel{4}}}{5} \times \tfrac{3}{5} \times \frac{7}{\underset{2}{\cancel{8}}} = \tfrac{1}{5} \times \tfrac{3}{5} \times \tfrac{7}{2} = \tfrac{21}{50}$$

Now consider the division problem $\tfrac{4}{5} \div \tfrac{8}{15}$. If this problem were divided before it is reduced, the operation would be as follows:

$$\tfrac{4}{5} \div \tfrac{8}{15} = \tfrac{4}{5} \times \tfrac{15}{8}$$
$$= \tfrac{60}{40}$$
$$= \tfrac{3}{2}$$

The problem could also be reduced prior to the actual division:

$$\frac{4}{5} \div \frac{8}{15} = \frac{4}{5} \times \frac{15}{8}$$

$$= \frac{4}{5} \times \frac{5 \times 3}{4 \times 2}$$

$$= \frac{4 \times 5 \times 3}{5 \times 4 \times 2}$$

Because multiplication is commutative and associative, we may rearrange the numbers:

$$\frac{4 \times 5 \times 3}{5 \times 4 \times 2} = \frac{5 \times 4 \times 3}{5 \times 4 \times 2}$$

$$= \frac{5}{5} \times \frac{4}{4} \times \frac{3}{2}$$

$$= 1 \times 1 \times \frac{3}{2}$$

$$= \frac{3}{2}$$

Hence, $\frac{4}{5} \div \frac{8}{15} = \frac{3}{2}$ by either method. In actual practice, however, neither method is normally used. Rather, after the divisor has been inverted, cancellation would be used to reduce the fractions. That is, the fraction $\frac{4}{8}$ would be reduced to $\frac{1}{2}$, and $\frac{15}{5}$ would be reduced to $\frac{3}{1}$ as follows:

$$\frac{4}{5} \div \frac{8}{15} = \frac{4}{5} \times \frac{15}{8}$$

$$= \frac{\overset{1}{\cancel{4}}}{\cancel{5}_{1}} \times \frac{\overset{3}{\cancel{15}}}{\cancel{8}_{2}}$$

$$= \frac{1}{1} \times \frac{3}{2}$$

$$= \frac{3}{2}$$

Thus we see that cancellation is a method of reducing fractions and therefore produces the same answers as ordinary reduction. However, cancellation may be used only under the following conditions: Cancellation may be performed only in a multiplication problem, or in a division problem *after* the divisor has been inverted; and a number in the *numerator* and another number in the *denominator* must contain a common factor (that is, must comprise a fraction which can be reduced). The numbers being reduced are slashed with a diagonal mark; the quotient obtained when dividing by the common factor is written above the number in the numerator and below the number in the denominator. These reduced values are then used in performing the multiplication.

Mixed Numbers

A number composed of both a whole number and a fraction is known as a *mixed number* (for example, $3\frac{1}{2}$). Multiplication and division involving mixed numbers is easier if the mixed number is first converted to a common fraction.

Mixed numbers may be converted to fractions by applying the same basic principles we have used to reduce fractions or to change to higher terms—namely, that any number over itself equals $1 \left(\dfrac{x}{x} = 1 \right)$ and that multiplying any number by 1 equals that same number $(x \cdot 1 = x)$. The student will recall that a whole number may be written in fraction form using a denominator of one. (That is, $5 = \frac{5}{1}$. This is correct because $\frac{5}{1}$ means $5 \div 1$, which equals the original 5.) Now consider the mixed number $3\frac{1}{2}$:

$$
\begin{aligned}
3\tfrac{1}{2} &= 3 &+ \tfrac{1}{2} \\
&= 3 \times 1 + \tfrac{1}{2} \\
&= 3 \times \tfrac{2}{2} + \tfrac{1}{2} \\
&= \tfrac{3}{1} \times \tfrac{2}{2} + \tfrac{1}{2} \\
&= \tfrac{6}{2} + \tfrac{1}{2} \\
&= \tfrac{7}{2}
\end{aligned}
$$

Thus we see that $3\frac{1}{2}$ may be converted to the common fraction $\frac{7}{2}$ by multiplying the whole-number part by a fraction equal to 1 and then adding the fraction from the mixed number. (The "fraction equal to 1" is always composed of the denominator from the fraction in the mixed number over itself—in this case, $\frac{2}{2}$. Thus the mixed number $4\frac{2}{3}$ would be converted by substituting $\frac{3}{3}$ for 1.) Any mixed number always equals an improper fraction.

The familiar procedure used to convert a mixed number to a common fraction is to "multiply the denominator times the whole number and add the numerator." This total over the original denominator (in the fraction part) is the value of the common fraction equivalent to the mixed number. Thus

$$
3\tfrac{1}{2} = 3 \overset{+}{\underset{\times}{\diagdown}} \tfrac{1}{2} = \begin{array}{r} 3 \\ \times 2 \\ \hline 6 + 1 \end{array} = \tfrac{7}{2}
$$

If the whole number is so large that the product is not immediately obvious, the multiplication can be performed digit by digit and the numerator added in the same way as are numbers which have been "carried." For example,

$16\frac{3}{8} = \dfrac{?}{8}$ Think: "8×6 is 48 plus 3 is 51"—Write

1 and carry the 5 $\left(16\frac{3}{8} = \dfrac{\cdots 1}{8} \right)$. Then,

"8×1 is 8 plus 5 is 13." So,

$$16\tfrac{3}{8} = \tfrac{131}{8}$$

The following examples demonstrate how mixed numbers are handled in multiplication and division problems:

(a)
$$4\tfrac{1}{2} \times 3\tfrac{1}{3} = \tfrac{9}{2} \times \tfrac{10}{3}$$
$$= \tfrac{\overset{3}{\cancel{9}}}{\underset{1}{\cancel{2}}} \times \tfrac{\overset{5}{\cancel{10}}}{\underset{1}{\cancel{3}}}$$
$$= \tfrac{3}{1} \times \tfrac{5}{1}$$
$$= \tfrac{15}{1}$$
$$= 15$$

(b)
$$5\tfrac{2}{5} \div 3\tfrac{3}{5} = \tfrac{27}{5} \div \tfrac{18}{5}$$
$$= \tfrac{27}{5} \times \tfrac{5}{18}$$
$$= \tfrac{\overset{3}{\cancel{27}}}{\underset{1}{\cancel{5}}} \times \tfrac{\overset{1}{\cancel{5}}}{\underset{2}{\cancel{18}}}$$
$$= \tfrac{3}{1} \times \tfrac{1}{2}$$
$$= \tfrac{3}{2}$$

(c)
$$4\tfrac{7}{8} \div 1\tfrac{11}{16} = \tfrac{39}{8} \div \tfrac{27}{16}$$
$$= \tfrac{39}{8} \times \tfrac{16}{27}$$
$$= \tfrac{\overset{13}{\cancel{39}}}{\underset{1}{\cancel{8}}} \times \tfrac{\overset{2}{\cancel{16}}}{\underset{9}{\cancel{27}}}$$
$$= \tfrac{13}{1} \times \tfrac{2}{9}$$
$$= \tfrac{26}{9}$$

Notice in division that a mixed-number divisor should be converted to an improper fraction before the divisor is inverted.

In certain instances, it is necessary to change an improper fraction to a mixed number. This operation simply reverses the former procedure. Suppose $\tfrac{19}{8}$ is to be converted to a mixed number. The numerator may first be broken down into a multiple of the denominator plus a remainder. The familiar properties of $1 \left(\dfrac{x}{x} = 1 \text{ and } x1 = x \right)$ may then be applied as before:

$$\tfrac{19}{8} = \frac{2(8) + 3}{8}$$
$$= \frac{2(8)}{8} + \tfrac{3}{8}$$
$$= \tfrac{2}{1} \times \tfrac{8}{8} + \tfrac{3}{8}$$
$$= \tfrac{2}{1} \times 1 + \tfrac{3}{8}$$
$$= 2 \quad + \tfrac{3}{8}$$
$$= 2\tfrac{3}{8}$$

Thus $\tfrac{19}{8} = 2\tfrac{3}{8}$. In actual practice, however, the procedure used to convert improper fractions to mixed numbers applies the fact that a fraction is an indicated division. That is, $\tfrac{19}{8}$ means $19 \div 8$, which equals 2 with a remainder of $\tfrac{3}{8}$. Hence, $\tfrac{19}{8} = 2\tfrac{3}{8}$.

Addition may be performed using mixed numbers (without changing them to improper fractions). Although it is generally considered acceptable to leave answers as improper fractions, it is not correct to leave a mixed number which includes an improper fraction. The improper fraction should be changed to a mixed number and this amount added to the whole number to obtain a mixed number which includes a proper fraction (reduced to lowest terms). Thus, if the sum of an addition problem is $7\frac{14}{6}$, this result must be converted as follows:

$$
\begin{aligned}
7\tfrac{14}{6} &= 7 + \tfrac{14}{6} \\
&= 7 + 2\tfrac{2}{6} \\
&= 9\tfrac{2}{6} \\
&= 9\tfrac{1}{3}
\end{aligned}
$$

The following operations are examples of addition with mixed numbers:

(a)
$$
\begin{aligned}
& 7\tfrac{5}{9} \\
+ & 3\tfrac{1}{9} \\
\hline
& 10\tfrac{6}{9} = 10\tfrac{2}{3}
\end{aligned}
$$

(b)
$$
\begin{aligned}
6\tfrac{5}{8} &= 6\tfrac{15}{24} \\
+9\tfrac{2}{3} &= 9\tfrac{16}{24} \\
\hline
15\tfrac{31}{24} &= 16\tfrac{7}{24}
\end{aligned}
$$

(c)
$$
\begin{aligned}
16\tfrac{2}{3} &= 16\tfrac{4}{6} \\
+17\tfrac{5}{6} &= 17\tfrac{5}{6} \\
\hline
33\tfrac{9}{6} &= 34\tfrac{3}{6} = 34\tfrac{1}{2}
\end{aligned}
$$

Subtraction may also be performed using mixed numbers. The student will recall that subtraction usually requires regrouping (or borrowing). This procedure, when applied to fractions, means that improper fractions must often be created where they did not exist.

Consider the problem $7\frac{3}{8} - 4\frac{7}{8}$. Although the mixed number $4\frac{7}{8}$ is smaller than $7\frac{3}{8}$, the fraction $\frac{7}{8}$ cannot be subtracted from $\frac{3}{8}$. In order to perform the operation, one must regroup the $7\frac{3}{8}$. Mixed numbers are regrouped by borrowing one unit from the whole number, converting this unit to a fraction (the common denominator over itself), and adding this fractional "1" to the fraction from the mixed number. Using this procedure, $7\frac{3}{8}$ is regrouped as follows:

$$
\begin{aligned}
7\tfrac{3}{8} &= 7 && + \tfrac{3}{8} \\
&= 6 + 1 && + \tfrac{3}{8} \\
&= 6 + \tfrac{8}{8} && + \tfrac{3}{8} \\
&= 6 + && \tfrac{11}{8} \\
&= 6\tfrac{11}{8}
\end{aligned}
$$

Thus $7\frac{3}{8}$ equals $6\frac{11}{8}$. In actual practice, the procedure of borrowing 1 and adding it to the existing fraction may be done mentally, with only the result being written. The following operations illustrate the above subtraction problem and others:

(a)
$$5\frac{5}{6}$$
$$-1\frac{1}{6}$$
$$\overline{4\frac{4}{6}} = 4\frac{2}{3}$$

(b)
$$7\frac{3}{8} = 6\frac{11}{8}$$
$$-4\frac{7}{8} = 4\frac{7}{8}$$
$$\overline{2\frac{4}{8}} = 2\frac{1}{2}$$

(c)
$$15\frac{1}{3} = 15\frac{4}{12} = 14\frac{16}{12}$$
$$-8\frac{3}{4} = 8\frac{9}{12} = 8\frac{9}{12}$$
$$\overline{6\frac{7}{12}}$$

Notice that the fractions in mixed numbers are first changed to fractions with a common denominator before regrouping for subtraction (c).

PROBLEMS

Express each of the properties requested, using the variables or numbers indicated. Verify the properties when numbers are used.

1. (a) Commutative property of addition, using p and q.
    (b) Commutative property of addition, using $3\frac{1}{2}$ and $5\frac{2}{3}$.
    (c) Associative property of addition, using d, e, and f.
    (d) Associative property of addition, using $\frac{3}{4}$, $\frac{1}{2}$, and $\frac{3}{5}$.
    (e) Commutative property of multiplication, using r and s.
    (f) Commutative property of multiplication us $4\frac{4}{5}$ and $3\frac{3}{4}$.
    (g) Associative property of multiplication, using u, v, and w.
    (h) Associative property of multiplication, using $\frac{5}{6}$, $\frac{2}{7}$, and $\frac{7}{8}$.
    (i) Distributive property, using j, k, and l.
    (j) Distributive property, using $\frac{2}{3}$, $\frac{3}{4}$, and $\frac{6}{5}$.

2. (a) Commutative property of addition, using g and h.
    (b) Commutative property of addition, using $\frac{2}{9}$ and $\frac{1}{6}$.
    (c) Associative property of addition, using l, m, and n.
    (d) Associative property of addition, using $\frac{1}{5}$, $\frac{5}{6}$, and $\frac{2}{3}$.
    (e) Commutative property of multiplication, using h and k.
    (f) Commutative property of multiplication, using $3\frac{1}{5}$ and $4\frac{3}{8}$.
    (g) Associative property of multiplication, using x, y, and z.
    (h) Associative property of multiplication, using $\frac{5}{7}$, $\frac{3}{5}$, and $\frac{1}{6}$.
    (i) Distributive property, using t, u, and v.
    (j) Distributive property, using $\frac{1}{3}$, $\frac{6}{7}$, and $\frac{3}{5}$.

3. Reduce the following fractions to lowest terms (that is, reduce as much as possible):

(a) $\frac{14}{21}$ (c) $\frac{21}{36}$ (e) $\frac{26}{78}$ (g) $\frac{63}{84}$ (i) $\frac{231}{273}$

(b) $\frac{18}{8}$ (d) $\frac{45}{75}$ (f) $\frac{72}{48}$ (h) $\frac{128}{80}$ (j) $\frac{140}{336}$

4. Convert the following fractions to fractions having least common denominators:

(a) $\frac{1}{2}$ and $\frac{2}{5}$ (g) $\frac{5}{6}$, $\frac{5}{12}$, and $\frac{4}{9}$

(b) $\frac{2}{3}$ and $\frac{5}{7}$ (h) $\frac{3}{8}$, $\frac{5}{9}$, and $\frac{1}{6}$

(c) $\frac{3}{8}$ and $\frac{1}{4}$ (i) $\frac{4}{5}$, $\frac{3}{4}$, and $\frac{2}{3}$

(d) $\frac{5}{12}$ and $\frac{3}{8}$ (j) $\frac{7}{16}$, $\frac{5}{6}$, and $\frac{3}{8}$

(e) $\frac{7}{9}$ and $\frac{3}{5}$ (k) $\frac{3}{4}$, $\frac{4}{5}$, and $\frac{5}{6}$

(f) $\frac{1}{4}$, $\frac{2}{3}$, and $\frac{5}{8}$ (l) $\frac{3}{5}$, $\frac{1}{6}$, and $\frac{4}{9}$

5. Compare the following fractions by converting to a common denominator. Then arrange the original fractions in order of size, starting with the smallest.

(a) $\frac{2}{3}$, $\frac{4}{5}$, $\frac{7}{12}$, $\frac{7}{15}$, $\frac{5}{6}$, $\frac{3}{4}$ (b) $\frac{5}{8}$, $\frac{3}{4}$, $\frac{11}{18}$, $\frac{5}{6}$, $\frac{17}{24}$, $\frac{5}{9}$

6. Change the following mixed numbers to improper fractions:

(a) $7\frac{1}{2}$ (c) $3\frac{4}{9}$ (e) $12\frac{4}{5}$ (g) $8\frac{2}{3}$ (i) $26\frac{4}{7}$

(b) $8\frac{3}{5}$ (d) $5\frac{5}{6}$ (f) $6\frac{5}{11}$ (h) $18\frac{5}{9}$ (j) $37\frac{7}{8}$

7. Convert the following improper fractions (and improper mixed numbers) to mixed numbers. Reduce if possible:

(a) $\frac{21}{6}$ (d) $\frac{44}{12}$ (g) $\frac{105}{9}$ (j) $9\frac{10}{4}$

(b) $\frac{38}{8}$ (e) $\frac{59}{7}$ (h) $\frac{72}{16}$ (k) $4\frac{11}{7}$

(c) $\frac{80}{15}$ (f) $\frac{58}{14}$ (i) $\frac{63}{11}$ (l) $16\frac{21}{9}$

8. Find the sums of the following addition problems, reducing where possible:

(a) $\frac{3}{4}$ (e) $\frac{5}{7}$ (i) $\frac{8}{15}$ (m) $9\frac{1}{4}$ (q) $7\frac{2}{3}$
$\frac{1}{2}$ $\frac{3}{5}$ $\frac{2}{5}$ $6\frac{7}{9}$ $5\frac{3}{8}$
  $\frac{1}{2}$ $\frac{1}{4}$ $2\frac{1}{6}$
   $\frac{1}{3}$

(b) $\frac{7}{8}$ (f) $\frac{5}{12}$ (j) $\frac{5}{6}$ (n) $2\frac{1}{2}$ (r) $4\frac{5}{6}$
$\frac{2}{3}$ $\frac{2}{9}$ $\frac{2}{3}$ $5\frac{3}{8}$ $3\frac{1}{2}$
  $\frac{3}{4}$ $\frac{7}{10}$ $8\frac{1}{3}$
  $\frac{1}{6}$ $\frac{3}{5}$ $1\frac{2}{7}$

(c) $\frac{2}{5}$ (g) $\frac{1}{4}$ (k) $5\frac{1}{3}$ (o) $7\frac{1}{2}$ (s) $6\frac{3}{7}$
$\frac{1}{3}$ $\frac{1}{8}$ $7\frac{3}{4}$ $8\frac{2}{3}$ $\frac{1}{2}$
$\frac{3}{10}$ $\frac{5}{6}$ $8\frac{1}{4}$
  $\frac{2}{3}$ $4\frac{3}{4}$

(d) $\frac{3}{4}$ (h) $\frac{1}{6}$ (l) $3\frac{5}{6}$ (p) $6\frac{3}{8}$ (t) $2\frac{3}{5}$
$\frac{2}{3}$ $\frac{7}{8}$ $9\frac{1}{2}$ $4\frac{5}{16}$ $7\frac{1}{4}$
$\frac{1}{6}$ $\frac{11}{24}$ $3\frac{1}{4}$ $\frac{5}{8}$
  $\frac{5}{9}$ $5\frac{1}{2}$

9. Subtract in each of the following, reducing where possible:

(a) $\frac{3}{4}$ (d) $\frac{5}{8}$ (g) $12\frac{4}{7}$ (j) $17\frac{3}{8}$ (m) 24

$\frac{5}{12}$ $\frac{2}{5}$ $5\frac{2}{5}$ $8\frac{5}{7}$ $15\frac{5}{11}$

(b) $\frac{5}{8}$ (e) $\frac{3}{4}$ (h) $14\frac{5}{16}$ (k) $25\frac{2}{7}$ (n) $36\frac{5}{14}$

$\frac{1}{4}$ $\frac{2}{3}$ $8\frac{7}{8}$ $18\frac{5}{9}$ $14\frac{5}{8}$

(c) $\frac{5}{7}$ (f) $7\frac{5}{8}$ (i) $21\frac{1}{6}$ (l) $36\frac{2}{3}$ (o) $42\frac{2}{9}$

$\frac{1}{3}$ $4\frac{1}{6}$ $13\frac{8}{9}$ $28\frac{5}{6}$ $28\frac{3}{4}$

10. Multiply, reducing wherever possible:

(a) $\frac{3}{4} \times \frac{7}{9}$ (k) $6 \times 1\frac{2}{3}$

(b) $\frac{6}{7} \times \frac{2}{3}$ (l) $5\frac{1}{4} \times 2\frac{2}{3}$

(c) $\frac{2}{3} \times \frac{5}{6}$ (m) $2\frac{1}{2} \times 3\frac{1}{3}$

(d) $\frac{9}{16} \times \frac{4}{15}$ (n) $7\frac{1}{5} \times 3\frac{1}{8}$

(e) $\frac{5}{12} \times \frac{8}{15}$ (o) $6\frac{2}{5} \times 2\frac{1}{12}$

(f) $\frac{7}{8} \times 5\frac{1}{3}$ (p) $\frac{6}{7} \times \frac{5}{8} \times \frac{3}{10}$

(g) $\frac{5}{6} \times 2\frac{2}{5}$ (q) $2\frac{4}{5} \times \frac{3}{7} \times 3\frac{3}{4}$

(h) $3\frac{1}{8} \times \frac{8}{15}$ (r) $3\frac{1}{7} \times \frac{3}{8} \times 3\frac{1}{2} \times 1\frac{5}{11}$

(i) $4\frac{1}{2} \times \frac{10}{21}$ (s) $3\frac{1}{5} \times \frac{1}{18} \times \frac{3}{4} \times 5\frac{5}{6}$

(j) $3\frac{1}{16} \times \frac{2}{7}$

11. Divide, reducing to lowest terms:

(a) $\frac{1}{2} \div \frac{5}{6}$ (f) $14 \div 3\frac{1}{2}$ (k) $2\frac{1}{4} \div 1\frac{7}{8}$

(b) $\frac{7}{8} \div \frac{3}{4}$ (g) $3\frac{3}{4} \div 5$ (l) $4\frac{1}{6} \div 3\frac{1}{2}$

(c) $\frac{5}{7} \div \frac{2}{3}$ (h) $6\frac{2}{5} \div 12$ (m) $7\frac{3}{4} \div 8\frac{2}{3}$

(d) $\frac{3}{8} \div \frac{5}{12}$ (i) $2\frac{5}{8} \div \frac{7}{16}$ (n) $5\frac{3}{5} \div 15\frac{3}{4}$

(e) $\frac{7}{10} \div \frac{7}{15}$ (j) $\frac{5}{12} \div 5\frac{5}{6}$ (o) $12\frac{4}{7} \div 4\frac{2}{5}$

4. DECIMAL FRACTIONS

As the developing number system became more sophisticated, a method was devised for expressing parts of a whole without writing a complete common fraction; this is the system of *decimal notation*. Decimal values are actually abbreviated fractions. That is, the written number is only the numerator of an indicated fraction. The denominator of the indicated fraction is some power of 10. This denominator is not written, but is indicated by the location of the decimal point. Thus, since decimal values represent fractional parts of a whole, they are known as *decimal fractions*.

Decimal fractions are an extension of the whole number system, both because they are based on powers of 10 and also because the value of any digit is determined by the position it holds in the number. The following chart shows the value and power of 10 that is associated with each place in a decimal number. (Some whole-number places are included to show that decimal values are an extension of whole-number place values. Notice that the names for decimal place values repeat, in reverse order, the names of integer place values—except that the letters "-ths" are added to indicate that these are decimal values.

A decimal point (or period) is used in a number to show where the whole amount ends and the fractional portion begins. A whole number is usually written without a decimal point, but every integer is understood to have a decimal point after the units place. Thus 15 could be written "15." (or "15.0," or "15.00" etc.) and would be just as correct.

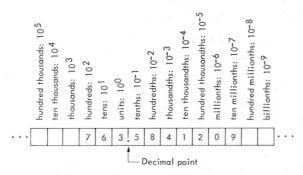

The student will recall from our study of integers that 10^2 represents 100 and the digit 7 in the chart above thus has the value 7×100 or 700. Similarly, 10^{-2} represents $\frac{1}{100}$, and the digit 8 above has the value $8 \times \frac{1}{100}$ or $\frac{8}{100}$. In the same manner, the digit 5 above represents "5 tenths" or $\frac{5}{10}$; the digit 4 represents "4 thousandths" or $\frac{4}{1000}$. Hence any digit in the first place following a decimal represents that number divided by 10 $\left(\frac{x}{10}\right)$; any number in the second place represents that number over 100 $\left(\frac{y}{100}\right)$; any number in the third decimal place represents that number over 1,000 $\left(\frac{z}{1000}\right)$; etc.

As pointed out previously, a decimal is actually an abbreviated fraction. Thus the decimal fraction 0.475 (the zero is placed before the decimal point purely for clarity) represents a common fraction with a numerator of 475 and (since the decimal contains three digits to the right of the decimal point) a denominator of 1,000. Therefore, the decimal fraction 0.475 could be written $\frac{475}{1000}$. This illustrates why decimal fractions, like common fractions, are known as *rational numbers*, since they can be expressed as the quotient of two integers.

Decimal fractions are written (or spoken) by writing the digits as if they represented a whole number and then writing the place value associated with the furthest place to the right of the decimal point. Thus

Number	Written (or spoken) form
0.9	"nine tenths"
0.14	"fourteen hundredths"
0.007	"seven thousandths"
0.3024	"three thousand twenty-four ten-thousandths"
0.00508	"five hundred eight hundred-thousandths"
25.6	"twenty-five and six tenths"
2.03	"two and three hundredths"
4,070.035	"four thousand seventy and thirty-five thousandths"

Notice that zeroes between the decimal point and the first significant digit do not affect the written form. (For example, 0.007 is written "*seven* thousandths.") Also, the word "and" is written (or spoken) solely to indicate the location of the decimal point. (Thus 2.03 is pronounced "two *and* three hundredths.") Zeroes to the right of a decimal fraction (with no other digits following) do not affect its value. (Thus 0.4, 0.40, 0.400, and 0.4000 are equal in value, because $\frac{4}{10} = \frac{40}{100} = \frac{400}{1000} = \frac{4,000}{10,000}$.)

CONVERTING COMMON FRACTIONS TO DECIMAL FRACTIONS

Manual computation can often be accomplished efficiently using common fractions, although at times common fractions become cumbersome. Most computation in modern offices, however, is done on electric machines, which are equipped to handle decimal values rather than common fractions. Thus business efficiency requires a knowledge not only of common fractions and decimal fractions separately but also of how to convert each form to the other.

The student will recall that a common fraction is an indicated division. Hence, $\frac{2}{5}$ means 2 ÷ 5. This principle is the basis for converting common fractions to decimal fractions. That is, a common fraction is converted to a decimal fraction by dividing the denominator into the numerator:

$$\frac{n}{d} = n \div d = d\overline{\smash{\big)}n}$$

This procedure applies to improper as well as to proper fractions. If a mixed number is to be converted to a decimal number, the fractional part of the mixed number is converted in this same manner, and the decimal equivalent is then affixed to the whole number of the mixed number. The following examples illustrate these procedures:

(a)

$$\begin{array}{r} .4 = 0.4 \\ \tfrac{2}{5} = 5\overline{\smash{\big)}2.0} \\ \underline{2.0} \end{array}$$

(b)
$$\frac{3}{40} = 40\overline{\smash{\big)}\ 3.000} \quad \frac{.075}{} = 0.075$$
$$\underline{2\ 80}$$
$$200$$
$$\underline{200}$$

(c)
$$\frac{9}{8} = 8\overline{\smash{\big)}\ 9.000} \quad \frac{1.125}{} = 1.125$$

(d)
$$2\tfrac{8}{25}: \quad \frac{8}{25} = 25\overline{\smash{\big)}\ 8.00} \quad \frac{.32}{} = 0.32$$
$$\text{so} \quad 2\tfrac{8}{25} = 2.32$$

The student is no doubt aware that many fractions do not have an exact decimal equivalent. This will always be the case (unless the fraction represents a whole number) if the denominator is 3 or is divisible by 3, or if the denominator is a prime number larger than five. (A *prime number* is any number that is divisible by no numbers except itself and 1—for example 7, 11, 17, 23, 31, to name but a few.)

The student may not always recognize whether a fraction has an exact decimal equivalent. The recommended procedure when converting fractions is first to divide to the hundredths place (two decimal places). If further inspection reveals that the quotient will come out to an exact whole number after one more division, then include the third decimal place. If it is obvious that the quotient would not be exact even with three decimal places, then stop dividing after two decimal places and express the remainder as a fraction. Consider the following examples:

(e)
$$\frac{3}{8} = 8\overline{\smash{\big)}\ 3.000} \quad \frac{.375}{} = 0.375$$

(f)
$$\frac{13}{200} = 200\overline{\smash{\big)}\ 13.000} \quad \frac{.065}{} = 0.065$$

(g)
$$\frac{3}{7} = 7\overline{\smash{\big)}\ 3.00} \quad \frac{42\tfrac{6}{7}}{} = 0.42\tfrac{6}{7}$$

(h)
$$\frac{16}{29} = 29\overline{\smash{\big)}\ 16.00} \quad \frac{.55\tfrac{5}{29}}{} = 0.55\tfrac{5}{29}$$

CONVERTING DECIMAL FRACTIONS TO COMMON FRACTIONS

The standard procedure for converting a decimal fraction to a common fraction is to pronounce the value of the decimal, write this value in fraction form, and then reduce this fraction. Therefore,

(a) 0.2 $=$ 2 tenths $=$ $\frac{2}{10}$ $= \frac{1}{5}$

(b) 0.12 $=$ 12 hundredths $=$ $\frac{12}{100}$ $= \frac{3}{25}$

(c) 0.336 $=$ 336 thousandths $=$ $\frac{336}{1000}$ $= \frac{42}{125}$

(d) 0.0045 $=$ 45 ten-thousandths $=$ $\frac{45}{10,000}$ $= \frac{9}{2000}$

If a decimal fraction also contains a common fraction, the conversion procedure is similar but requires additional steps. This process applies the fact that a fraction is an indicated division. Since a fraction within a fraction cannot be reduced directly, the fraction is reduced by first performing an operation of division and then reducing the quotient. Suppose $0.83\frac{1}{3}$ is to be converted to a fraction. Then

(e)
$$0.83\frac{1}{3} = \frac{83\frac{1}{3}}{100}$$

$$= 83\frac{1}{3} \div 100$$

$$= 83\frac{1}{3} \times \frac{1}{100}$$

$$= \frac{250}{3} \times \frac{1}{100}$$

$$= \frac{250}{300}$$

$$= \frac{5}{6}$$

Hence $0.83\frac{1}{3}$ is equivalent to $\frac{5}{6}$. A similar example is given below:

(f)
$$0.31\frac{1}{4} = \frac{31\frac{1}{4}}{100}$$

$$= 31\frac{1}{4} \div 100$$

$$= 31\frac{1}{4} \times \frac{1}{100}$$

$$= \frac{125}{4} \times \frac{1}{100}$$

$$= \frac{125}{400}$$

$$= \frac{5}{16}$$

As noted previously, many computations can be done more easily by using fractional equivalents for decimal numbers, especially if the decimals are as complicated as those above. In order to save time, however, the student should be able to recognize when a decimal is the equivalent of one of the common fractions most often used—without having actually to convert it. These equivalents are listed on page 46, and the student should memorize all that he does not already know.

ADDITION AND SUBTRACTION

Addition and subtraction with decimals are extremely similar to addition and subtraction with integers. The same names apply to the parts of each problem:

Addend	0.36	Minuend	0.73
Addend	+0.58	Subtrahend	−0.46
Sum	0.94	Difference or Remainder	0.27

The basic properties of addition (the commutative and associative properties of addition) also apply when decimal fractions are used:

CPA:
$$a + b = b + a$$
$$0.3 + 0.5 \overset{?}{=} 0.5 + 0.3$$
$$0.8 = 0.8$$

APA:
$$(a + b) + c = a + (b + c)$$
$$(0.3 + 0.4) + 0.2 \overset{?}{=} 0.3 + (0.4 + 0.2)$$
$$0.7 + 0.2 \overset{?}{=} 0.3 + 0.6$$
$$0.9 = 0.9$$

As for addition and subtraction with whole numbers, decimal numbers must also be arranged so that all the digits of the same place are in the same column. That is, all the tenths' places must be in a vertical line, all the hundredths' places in one column, and so forth. In so arranging decimal numbers, the decimal points will always fall in a straight line. Therefore, in actual practice, it is customary to arrange the numbers by aligning the decimal points.

The actual addition or subtraction of decimal fractions is performed in exactly the same way as with integers; the decimal points have no effect on the operations. The decimal point in the answer is located directly under the decimal points of the problem.

It was pointed out earlier that appending zeros to the right of a decimal number does not alter its value. (That is, $3.7 = 3.70 = 3.700$, etc.). Thus, if the numbers of a problem contain different numbers of decimal places, the student may wish to add zeroes so that all will contain the same number of decimal places. This is particularly helpful in subtraction problems where the subtrahend contains more decimal places than the minuend.

(a) Add: $0.306 + 9.8 + 14.65 + 6.775 + 24 + 0.09$.   (b) Subtract: $18.6 - 5.897$

(a)
$$
\begin{array}{r}
0.306 \\
9.8 \\
14.65 \\
6.775 \\
24. \\
0.09 \\
\hline
55.621
\end{array}
$$

(b)
$$
\begin{array}{r}
18.600 \\
-5.897 \\
\hline
12.703
\end{array}
$$

Notice that zeroes were inserted in the minuend to facilitate the subtraction.

MULTIPLICATION

The standard terminology is used to identify decimal numbers in a multiplication problem:

$$
\begin{array}{ll}
\text{Multiplicand or Factor} & 0.3 \\
\text{Multiplier or Factor} & \times 0.4 \\
\hline
\text{Product} & 0.12
\end{array}
$$

The commutative and associative properties of multiplication and the distributive property of multiplication over addition also hold for decimal fractions:

CPM:
$$a \times b = b \times a$$
$$0.7 \times 0.4 \overset{?}{=} 0.4 \times 0.7$$
$$0.28 = 0.28$$

APM:
$$(a \times b)c \quad = \quad a(b \times c)$$
$$(0.7 \times 0.3) \times 0.5 \overset{?}{=} 0.7 \times (0.3 \times 0.5)$$
$$0.21 \times 0.5 \overset{?}{=} 0.7 \times 0.15$$
$$0.105 = 0.105$$

DP:
$$a(b + c) = \quad ab \quad + \quad ac$$
$$0.3(0.4 + 0.5) \overset{?}{=} 0.3 \times 0.4 + 0.3 \times 0.5$$
$$0.3(0.9) \overset{?}{=} 0.12 + 0.15$$
$$0.27 = \quad 0.27$$

Decimal numbers are written down for multiplication in the same arrangement that would be used if there were no decimal points. The actual multiplication of digits is also performed in the same way as for integers. The only variation comes in the placing of a decimal point in the product. In order to determine how this is done, consider the problem 12.4 × 3.13:

12.4	Observe that this multiplication problem is approxi-	12.4
×3.13	mately 12 × 3; therefore, the product must be ap-	×3.13
327	proximately 36. This indicates that the decimal	372
124	point must be located between the 8's. Thus	124
372		372
38812		38.812

The correct position of the decimal point in every multiplication product could thus be determined by approximating the answer and locating the decimal point accordingly. However, the product would invariably contain the same number of decimal places as the total number of decimal places in the factors. Therefore, as a time-saving device, it is customary to count the total number of decimal places in the factors and place the decimal point accordingly, rather than to estimate the product. (In the preceding problem, 12.4 contained one decimal place and 3.13 contained two decimal places; thus the product contained three decimal places —38.812.)

Sometimes basic multiplication produces a number containing fewer digits than the total number of decimal places required for the product. In this case, the student must insert a zero or zeroes between the decimal point and the first significant digit so that the product will contain the correct number of decimal places. Consider the example, 0.04 × 0.2:

0.04	The factors require a three-digit product. Thus two	0.04
×0.2	zeroes must be inserted after the decimal point:	×0.2
8		0.008

The student can readily understand that 0.008 is the correct answer, because 0.04 × 0.2 is equal to $\frac{4}{100} \times \frac{2}{10} = \frac{8}{1000}$.

Some additional examples are given below:

(a)

$$
\begin{array}{r}
41.8173 \\
\times 2.36 \\
\hline
2509038 \\
1254519 \\
836346 \\
\hline
98.688828
\end{array}
$$

(b)
$$\begin{array}{r} 0.0547 \\ \times 3.6 \\ \hline 3282 \\ 1641 \\ \hline 0.19692 \end{array}$$

(c)
$$\begin{array}{r} 7.38 \\ \times 0.004 \\ \hline 0.02952 \end{array}$$

(d)
$$\begin{array}{r} 0.24 \\ \times 0.03 \\ \hline 0.0072 \end{array}$$

Multiplication by powers of 10 presents a special case. Study the following operations:

(a)
$$\begin{array}{r} 25.13 \\ \times 10 \\ \hline 251.30 \end{array}$$

(b)
$$\begin{array}{r} 65.8 \\ \times 100 \\ \hline 6,580.0 \end{array}$$

(c)
$$\begin{array}{r} 78 \\ \times 100 \\ \hline 7,800 \end{array}$$

(d)
$$\begin{array}{r} 3.9471 \\ \times 1000 \\ \hline 3,947.1000 \end{array}$$

Observe that each product contains the same digits as the multiplicand (along with some zeroes appended) and that each decimal point has been moved to the right the same number of places as there were zeroes in the power of 10. By applying this information, the student should never actually have to multiply by a power of 10. Instead, he should obtain the product simply by moving the decimal point as many places to the right as there are zeroes in the power of 10. Thus

(a)
$$25.13 \times 10 = 25\underset{\curvearrowright}{\cancel{.}}13$$
$$= 251.3$$

(b)
$$65.8 \times 100 = 65\underset{\curvearrowright}{\cancel{.}}80.$$
$$= 6,580$$

(c)
$$78 \times 100 = 78\underset{\curvearrowright}{x}0\underset{\curvearrowright}{0}.$$
$$= 7,800$$

(d)
$$3.9471 \times 1,000 = 3\underset{\curvearrowright}{x}947.1$$
$$= 3,947.1$$

DIVISION

Decimal numbers in a division problem are identified by the terms previously learned:

$$\begin{array}{r} 5.3 \quad \text{Quotient} \\ \text{Divisor} \quad 1.5 \overline{)7.95} \quad \text{Dividend} \end{array}$$

The basic operation of division is performed in the same manner for decimal numbers as for whole numbers. The decimal points do not affect the division process itself, but only the location of the decimal point in the quotient. In order to understand how the decimal points are handled, consider the following example:

$$\begin{array}{r} 51 \\ 3.02 \overline{)15.402} \\ \underline{15\ 10} \\ 302 \\ \underline{302} \end{array}$$

Notice that this division is approximately $3 \overline{)15}$; therefore, the quotient must be approximately 5. This indicates the decimal point in the quotient must be located after the 5.

$$\begin{array}{r} 5.1 \\ 3.02 \overline{)15.402} \\ \underline{15\ 10} \\ 302 \\ \underline{302} \end{array}$$

It would be possible to position the decimal point in every quotient by first estimating the result and then placing the decimal point accordingly. However, this requires additional time and effort; hence some quick, easy method for determining the correct location of the quotient decimal is necessary. The student is no doubt familiar with the method commonly used to position the decimal quickly; that is, to "move the decimal point to the end of the divisor and move the decimal in the dividend the same number of places." Let us see why this procedure is permissible.

It was observed that the decimal point of the quotient is always located directly above the decimal point of the dividend if the divisor is a whole number. For example,

$$\begin{array}{r} 2\ 13 \\ 12 \overline{)25.56} \\ \underline{24} \\ 15 \\ \underline{12} \\ 36 \\ \underline{36} \end{array}$$

Since this problem is approximately $12 \overline{)25}$, the result must be approximately 2. Thus the decimal point of the quotient should be located directly above the decimal point in the operation:

$$\begin{array}{r} 2.13 \\ 12 \overline{)25.56} \\ \underline{24} \\ 15 \\ \underline{12} \\ 36 \\ \underline{36} \end{array}$$

Thus the student knows exactly where the decimal point belongs if the divisor is a whole number. With this in mind, let us apply three familiar principles—namely, that a fraction is an indicated division; that any number over itself equals $1 \left(\dfrac{x}{x} = 1 \right)$; and that multiplying any number by 1 equals that same number $(x \cdot 1 = x)$. Now suppose we have the division problem $3.2 \overline{\smash{\big)}\ 9.28}$. This is the division indicated by the fraction $\frac{9.28}{3.2}$. Then,

$$\frac{9.28}{3.2} = \frac{9.28}{3.2} \times 1$$

$$= \frac{9.28}{3.2} \times \tfrac{10}{10}$$

$$\frac{9.28}{3.2} = \frac{92.8}{32}$$

Now, since

$$\frac{9.28}{3.2} = \frac{92.8}{32}$$

then the divisions indicated by each fraction are equal; or

$$3.2 \overline{\smash{\big)}\ 9.28} = 32 \overline{\smash{\big)}\ 92.8}$$

But we know the correct location for the decimal point when dividing by a whole number:

$$
= \begin{array}{r}
2.9 \\
32 \overline{\smash{\big)}\ 92.8} \\
\underline{64} \\
28\ 8 \\
\underline{28\ 8}
\end{array}
$$

Therefore, the other quotient must also be 2.9:

$$
\begin{array}{r}
2.9 \\
3.2 \overline{\smash{\big)}\ 9.28} \\
\underline{6\ 4} \\
2\ 88 \\
\underline{2\ 88}
\end{array}
\quad = \quad
\begin{array}{r}
2.9 \\
32 \overline{\smash{\big)}\ 92.8}
\end{array}
$$

Thus we can always position the decimal easily by "making the divisor a whole number," so to speak. But when we "move the decimal point to the end of the divisor and move the decimal point in the dividend a corresponding number of places," we are, in effect, multiplying by 1, which does not change the value. Stated differently, moving both decimals one place to the right is the same as multiplying a fraction by $\frac{10}{10}$; moving the decimals two places is equivalent to multiplying by $\frac{100}{100}$; moving the decimals three digits is equivalent to multiplying by $\frac{1,000}{1,000}$; and so forth.

Having determined why it is permissible to "move the decimal points," let us now consider some special cases. The decimal point in a dividend must often be moved more places to the right than there are digits. In this case, the student must append zeroes to the dividend in order to fill in the required number of places. (Suppose the decimal point in the number 14.3 must be moved three places. This is the same as multiplying 14.3 times 1,000; so, $14{\times}3\underrightarrow{}.\ = 14,300.$) If the dividend is a whole number, the student obviously must first insert a decimal point before moving it to the right. (For example, if a divisor must be multiplied by 10 to become a whole number and the dividend is 17, then 17 must also be multiplied by 10. That is, the decimal point must be moved one place to the right: $17 \times 10 = 17. \times 10 = 17\underrightarrow{}.\ = 170.$)

It has been pointed out that appending zeroes to the right of a decimal number does not change its value. (That is, $0.52 = 0.520 = 0.5200 = 0.52000$, etc.) When a division problem does not terminate (or end) within the number of digits contained in the dividend, the operation may be continued by appending zeroes to the dividend. The process may be continued until the quotient terminates or until it contains as many decimal places as required.

Once the decimal point has been located in the quotient, each succeeding place must contain a digit. If normal division skips some of the first decimal places, these places must be held by zeroes. (This procedure is similar to that in multiplication, when zeroes must be inserted after the decimal point in order to complete the required number of decimal places.)

The following examples show how these procedures apply:

(a) $3.02\overline{\smash{\big)}15.402}$:

$$
\begin{array}{r}
5.1 \\
3.02\underrightarrow{}\,\overline{\smash{\big)}\,15.40\,2} \\
15\ 10 \\
\hline
30\ 2 \\
30\ 2 \\
\hline
\end{array}
$$

(b) $4.725\overline{\smash{\big)}37.8}$:

$$
\begin{array}{r}
8.\ = 8 \\
4.725\underrightarrow{}\,\overline{\smash{\big)}\,37.800.} \\
37\ 800 \\
\hline
\end{array}
$$

(c) $0.72\overline{\smash{)}36}$:

```
                    50
        0.72 ) 36.00
               36 0
                  0
                  0
```

(d) $62.5\overline{\smash{)}23.95}$:

```
                    .3832
        62.5 ) 23.9.5000
               18 7 5
                5 2 00
                5 0 00
                  2 000
                  1 875
                   1250
                   1250
```

(e) $4.5\overline{\smash{)}0.0279}$:

```
                   .0062
        4.5 ) 0.0.279
               270
                90
                90
```

A special case develops when the divisor of a problem is a power of 10:

(a) $10\overline{\smash{)}13.6}$:

```
                 1.36
        10 ) 13.60
             10
              3 6
              3 0
               60
               60
```

(b) $100\overline{)245.3}$:

$$
\begin{array}{r}
2.453 \\
100\overline{)245.300} \\
200 \\
\hline
45\ 3 \\
40\ 0 \\
\hline
5\ 30 \\
5\ 00 \\
\hline
300 \\
300 \\
\hline
\end{array}
$$

(c) $100\overline{)7.31}$:

$$
\begin{array}{r}
.0731 \\
100\overline{)7.3100} \\
7\ 00 \\
\hline
310 \\
300 \\
\hline
100 \\
100 \\
\hline
\end{array}
$$

(d) $1{,}000\overline{)629}$:

$$
\begin{array}{r}
.629 \\
1{,}000\overline{)629.000} \\
600\ 0 \\
\hline
29\ 00 \\
20\ 00 \\
\hline
9\ 000 \\
9\ 000 \\
\hline
\end{array}
$$

In each operation directly above, the quotient contains the same digits as the dividend, but the decimal point is moved to the left the same number of places as there were zeroes in the divisor. Knowing this, the student should never actually have to perform a division by a power of 10. Rather, he should obtain the answer simply by moving the decimal point to the left. Thus

(a)
$$13.6 \div 10 = 1\underset{\curvearrowleft}{.3}\times 6$$
$$= 1.36$$

(b)
$$245.3 \div 100 = 2\underset{\curvearrowleft}{.45}\times 3$$
$$= 2.453$$

(c)
$$7.31 \div 100 = .\underset{\curvearrowleft}{\_7}\times 31$$
$$= 0.0731$$

(d)
$$629 \div 1,000 = .\underset{\curvearrowleft}{629}$$
$$= 0.629$$

Note: Students often confuse multiplication and division by powers of 10 and forget which way to move the decimal point. If this happens, the student can quickly determine the correct direction by making up an example using small numbers. For example, $4 \times 10 = 40$ (that is, $4.0 \times 10 = 40.$). The decimal point of the 4 moved to the right; therefore, the decimal point moves toward the right for all multiplication by powers of 10. Hence, the decimal point obviously moves to the left for division.

PROBLEMS

Express each of the properties requested, using the variables or numbers indicated. Verify the properties when numbers are used:

1. (a) Commutative property of addition, using r and f.
    (b) Commutative property of addition, using 4.82 and 7.35.
    (c) Associative property of addition, using $x, y,$ and z.
    (d) Associative property of addition, using 1.3, 5.2, and 0.6.
    (e) Commutative property of multiplication, using m and n.
    (f) Commutative property of multiplication, using 0.6 and 0.9.
    (g) Associative property of multiplication, using $g, h,$ and k.
    (h) Associative property of multiplication, using 0.3, 0.4, and 0.7.
    (i) Distributive property, using $b, d,$ and g.
    (j) Distributive property, using 0.5, 0.3, and 0.8.

2. (a) Commutative property of addition, using v and w.
    (b) Commutative property of addition, using 8.73 and 9.48.
    (c) Associative property of addition, using $f, g,$ and h.
    (d) Associative property of addition, using 0.27, 0.55, and 0.84.
    (e) Commutative property of multiplication, using s and t.
    (f) Commutative property of multiplication, using 0.7 and 0.8.
    (g) Associative property of multiplication, using $p, q,$ and r.
    (h) Associative property of multiplication, using 0.4, 0.7, and 0.2.
    (i) Distributive property, using $k, l,$ and m.
    (j) Distributive property, using 0.3, 0.5, and 0.7.

3. In the number 9,735.24186, identify the place value associated with each of the following digits:
    (a) 1   (d) 4   (g) 7
    (b) 2   (e) 5   (h) 8
    (c) 3   (f) 6   (i) 9

4. Write in words the values of the following numbers:
   - (a) 0.368
   - (b) 0.08
   - (c) 0.075
   - (d) 0.2066
   - (e) 18.8
   - (f) 76.63
   - (g) 300.708
   - (h) 4.0016

5. Convert the following common fractions (and mixed numbers) to their decimal fraction equivalents:
   - (a) $\frac{3}{5}$
   - (b) $\frac{1}{4}$
   - (c) $\frac{7}{20}$
   - (d) $\frac{18}{25}$
   - (e) $\frac{17}{40}$
   - (f) $\frac{29}{250}$
   - (g) $\frac{3}{8}$
   - (h) $\frac{3}{7}$
   - (i) $\frac{4}{11}$
   - (j) $\frac{5}{12}$
   - (k) $\frac{5}{14}$
   - (l) $\frac{7}{32}$
   - (m) $\frac{19}{6}$
   - (n) $\frac{147}{8}$
   - (o) $\frac{107}{20}$
   - (p) $15\frac{4}{9}$
   - (q) $6\frac{2}{7}$
   - (r) $5\frac{123}{250}$

6. Find the common fraction equivalent to each of the following decimals:
   - (a) 0.72
   - (b) 0.4
   - (c) 0.375
   - (d) 0.35
   - (e) 0.424
   - (f) 0.06
   - (g) 0.2575
   - (h) $0.14\frac{2}{7}$
   - (i) $0.63\frac{7}{11}$
   - (j) $0.08\frac{1}{3}$
   - (k) $0.27\frac{7}{9}$
   - (l) $0.45\frac{5}{6}$

7. Multiply or divide, as indicated, by moving the decimal point:
   - (a) $14.62 \div 10$
   - (b) 3.752×100
   - (c) $227.1 \div 1,000$
   - (d) 72.33×10
   - (e) $0.4188 \times 1,000$
   - (f) $35.89 \div 100$
   - (g) 49.8×100
   - (h) $16 \div 10$
   - (i) 0.728×10
   - (j) $3.827 \div 1,000$
   - (k) $0.615 \div 100$
   - (l) $125 \times 1,000$
   - (m) $52.9 \times 10,000$
   - (n) $0.04 \div 100$
   - (o) $13.8 \div 10,000$

8. Add. (Arrange problems j–m in columns before adding.)

(a)	(d)	(g)
3.85	12.371	0.92
7.09	17.859	59.6
5.53	23.076	7.483
8.76	38.944	385.2
		16.793
		154.87

(b)	(e)	(h)
0.455	475.821	5.6
0.937	795.044	128
0.246	608.149	7.79
0.118	597.624	13.855
		0.738
		358.68

(c)   0.2676   (f)   17.931   (i)   15.79
      0.4395   4.09   139.9
      0.8479   124.8   46.432
      0.6071   0.796   5.91
                  38.5   347.8
                  0.005   269.917

(j)   127.9 + 0.485 + 16.76 + 145.269 + 7.382 + 119.65
(k)   45.18 + 7.934 + 318.6 + 275 + 8.55 + 139.7
(l)   6.791 + 403.84 + 25.633 + 381.069 + 0.648 + 57.29
(m) 93.711 + 253 + 7.09 + 76.6 + 125.27 + 208.719

9. Subtract. (Arrange problems n–q in columns before subtracting.)

(a) 128.84   (i) 43.4007
      69.39   8.052

(b) 7.622   (j) 295.4
      4.885   68.17

(c) 18.351   (k) 73.28
      9.783   35.079

(d) 547.805   (l) 157.6
     328.498   85.923

(e) 63.8472   (m) 46
     36.9903   19.254

(f) 85.007   (n) 48.8 – 7.26
      56.328   (o) 153 – 78.35

(g) 324.050
      60.538   (p) 307.9 – 60.409

(h) 19.721   (q) 5.4 – 0.3721
      12.35

10. Multiply:

(a) 4.73   (f) 0.324
      7.6   0.26

(b) 15.8   (g) 0.148
      6.4   0.62

(c) 7.64   (h) 0.0316
      0.82   2.47

(d) 324.9   (i) 0.078
      0.075   0.016

(e) 0.563   (j) 0.0138
     5.41   0.43

11. Divide. (When quotients are not exact whole numbers, follow the pro-
     cedure recommended in this section for changing fractions to decimals.)

(a) 5.72 ⟌ 80.08   (i) 8.25 ⟌ 264
(b) 17.6 ⟌ 59.84   (j) 1.475 ⟌ 831.9
(c) 0.283 ⟌ 7.5844   (k) 12.64 ⟌ 15.8
(d) 0.768 ⟌ 0.39936   (l) 0.0375 ⟌ 30.6
(e) 4.71 ⟌ 0.10833   (m) 31.2 ⟌ 147.696
(f) 4.32 ⟌ 0.269136   (n) 4.32 ⟌ 2.82
(g) 13.5 ⟌ 0.083295   (o) 0.528 ⟌ 25.84
(h) 0.2749 ⟌ 0.098964   (p) 4.032 ⟌ 14.8

Appendix B
Tables

Table I: Sales Tax Intervals

Sales Tax Intervals	
Sales Made Within State	Sales Made Within City
Per whole dollar: 3¢	*Per whole dollar:* 4¢
Tax on additional cents:	*Tax on additional cents:*

Interval	Tax	Interval	Tax
$.00–$.09	0	$.00–$.09	0
.10– .39	1¢	.10– .39	1¢
.40– .69	2¢	.40– .49	2¢
.70– .99	3¢	.50– .69	3¢
		.70– .99	4¢

Table II: Long-Term Fire Insurance Rates	
Long-Term Rates for Fire Insurance	
Years of Coverage	Multiple of Annual Premium
2	1.85
3	2.70

Table III: Short-Term and Cancellation Rates

Short-Term Rates (including cancellations by the insured)			
Months of Coverage	% of Annual Premium Charged	Months of Coverage	% of Annual Premium Charged
1	20%	7	75%
2	30	8	80
3	40	9	85
4	50	10	90
5	60	11	95
6	70	12	100

Table IV: Driver Classifications

(Multiples of Base Annual Automobile Insurance Premiums)

			Pleasure; Less than 3 Miles to Work Each Way	Drives to Work, 3 to 10 Miles Each Way	Drives to Work, 10 Miles or More Each Way	Used in Business
No young operators	Only operator is female, age 30–64		.90	1.00	1.30	1.40
	One or more operators age 65 or over		1.00	1.10	1.40	1.50
	All others		1.00	1.10	1.40	1.50
Young females	Age 16	DT*	1.40	1.50	1.80	1.90
		No DT	1.55	1.65	1.95	2.05
	Age 20	DT	1.05	1.15	1.45	1.55
		No DT	1.10	1.20	1.50	1.60
Young males (married)	Age 16	DT	1.60	1.70	2.00	2.10
		No DT	1.80	1.90	2.20	2.30
	Age 20	DT	1.45	1.55	1.85	1.95
		No DT	1.50	1.60	1.90	2.00
	Age 21		1.40	1.50	1.80	1.90
	Age 24		1.10	1.20	1.50	1.60

Table IV, continued

			Pleasure; Less than 3 Miles to Work Each Way	Drives to Work, 3 to 10 Miles Each Way	Drives to Work, 10 Miles or More Each Way	Used in Business
Young unmarried males (not principal operator)	Age 16	DT	2.05	2.15	2.45	2.55
		No DT	2.30	2.40	2.70	2.80
	Age 20	DT	1.60	1.70	2.00	2.10
		No DT	1.70	1.80	2.10	2.20
	Age 21		1.55	1.65	1.95	2.05
	Age 24		1.10	1.20	1.50	1.60
Young unmarried males (owner or principal operator)	Age 16	DT	2.70	2.80	3.10	3.20
		No DT	3.30	3.40	3.70	3.80
	Age 20	DT	2.55	2.65	2.95	3.05
		No DT	2.70	2.80	3.10	3.20
	Age 21		2.50	2.60	2.90	3.00
	Age 24		1.90	2.00	2.30	2.40
	Age 26		1.50	1.60	1.90	2.00
	Age 29		1.10	1.20	1.50	1.60

* "DT" indicates completion of a certified driver training course.

Table V: Automobile Liability Insurance

Base Annual Premiums

	Bodily Injury				Property Damage		
Coverage	Territory 1	Territory 2	Territory 3	Coverage	Territory 1	Territory 2	Territory 3
5/10	$25	$33	$50	$ 5,000	$20	$28	$32
10/20	28	37	55	10,000	22	30	34
15/30	30	40	60	25,000	23	31	35
25/25	33	44	65	50,000	24	32	36
25/50	35	46	70	100,000	26	34	38
50/50	36	48	72				
50/100	37	49	74				
100/100	38	50	75				
100/200	39	52	78				
100/300	40	54	80				
200/300	42	56	83				
300/300	43	58	85				

Table VI: Comprehensive and Collision Insurance

Base Annual Premiums

Model Class	Age Group	Territory 1			Territory 2			Territory 3		
		Compre-hensive	Collision		Compre-hensive	Collision		Compre-hensive	Collision	
			$50 Deductible	$100 Deductible		$50 Deductible	$100 Deductible		$50 Deductible	$100 Deductible
(1)	1	$10	$28	$18	$14	$36	$24	$20	$54	$32
A–G	2, 3	8	24	15	10	32	20	15	48	28
	4	6	20	14	8	28	18	10	40	24
(3)	1	15	38	28	18	50	36	28	75	54
J–K	2, 3	12	34	24	16	45	32	24	65	48
	4	9	28	20	12	38	28	16	55	40
(4)	1	17	43	32	22	56	44	33	85	64
L–M	2, 3	15	38	28	18	50	38	28	75	55
	4	10	33	25	15	45	32	20	65	48
(5)	1	21	50	38	28	68	50	42	100	75
N–O	2, 3	18	43	34	24	60	45	36	86	65
	4	13	38	28	18	50	38	25	75	55

Table VII: Annual Life Insurance Premiums
Per $1,000 of Face Value for Male Applicants

Age Issued	Term 10-Yr.	Straight Life	Limited Payment 20-Year	Endowment 20-Year
18	$ 6.81	$14.77	$24.69	$43.82
20	6.88	15.46	25.59	44.95
22	6.95	16.12	26.53	46.16
24	7.05	16.82	27.53	47.44
25	7.10	17.22	28.06	48.10
26	7.18	17.67	28.63	48.80
28	7.35	18.64	29.84	50.29
30	7.59	19.73	31.12	51.88
35	8.68	23.99	35.80	56.06
40	10.64	28.26	40.34	61.40
45	14.52	33.79	46.01	68.28
50	22.18	40.77	53.24	76.12
55	32.93	51.38	64.77	—
60	—	59.32	70.86	—

Table VIII: Nonforfeiture Options* on Typical Life Insurance Policies

(Issued at age 25)

Years in Force	Straight Life				20-Payment Life				20-Yr. Endowment			
	Cash Value	Paid-up Insur.	Ext. Term Yrs.	Ext. Term Days	Cash Value	Paid-up Insur.	Ext. Term Yrs.	Ext. Term Days	Cash Value	Paid-up Insur.	Ext. Term Yrs.	Ext. Term Days
3	$ 4	$ 14	1	174	$ 27	$ 89	10	84	$ 39	$ 104	14	42
5	26	82	9	71	68	213	19	184	90	227	23	126
10	88	243	18	46	182	502	28	186	316	515	30	131
15	157	382	20	148	314	763	32	164	590	772	35	290
20	246	530	21	137	465	1,000	Life		1,000	1,000	Life	
40	571	822	—	—	696	—	—	—	—	—	—	—

*The "cash value" and "paid-up insurance" nonforfeiture values are per $1,000 of life insurance coverage. The time period for "extended term insurance" applies as shown to all policies, regardless of face value.

Table IX: Settlement Options

Monthly Installments per $1,000 of Face Value

Fixed Amount or Fixed Number of Years		Income for Life				
		Age When Annuity Begins		Life Annuity	With 10 Years Certain	With 20 Years Certain
Years	Amount	Male	Female			
10	$9.41	40	45	$3.80	$3.76	$3.64
12	8.03	45	50	4.15	4.09	3.90
14	7.05	50	55	4.58	4.50	4.18
15	6.65	55	60	5.14	5.01	4.47
16	6.31	60	65	5.86	5.61	4.75
18	5.74	65	70	6.82	6.30	4.98
20	5.29					

Table X: Social Security Employee Tax Table

Social Security Employee Tax Table

5.2 percent employee tax deductions

Wages At least	But less than	Tax to be withheld	Wages At least	But less than	Tax to be withheld	Wages At least	But less than	Tax to be withheld	Wages At least	But less than	Tax to be withheld
$0.00	$0.10	$0.00	$12.41	$12.60	$.65	$24.91	$25.10	$1.30	$37.41	$37.60	$1.95
.10	.29	.01	12.60	12.79	.66	25.10	25.29	1.31	37.60	37.79	1.96
.29	.49	.02	12.79	12.99	.67	25.29	25.49	1.32	37.79	37.99	1.97
.49	.68	.03	12.99	13.18	.68	25.49	25.68	1.33	37.99	38.18	1.98
.68	.87	.04	13.18	13.37	.69	25.68	25.87	1.34	38.18	38.37	1.99
.87	1.06	.05	13.37	13.56	.70	25.87	26.06	1.35	38.37	38.56	2.00
1.06	1.25	.06	13.56	13.75	.71	26.06	26.25	1.36	38.56	38.75	2.01
1.25	1.45	.07	13.75	13.95	.72	26.25	26.45	1.37	38.75	38.95	2.02
1.45	1.64	.08	13.95	14.14	.73	26.45	26.64	1.38	38.95	39.14	2.03
1.64	1.83	.09	14.14	14.33	.74	26.64	26.83	1.39	39.14	39.33	2.04
1.83	2.02	.10	14.33	14.52	.75	26.83	27.02	1.40	39.33	39.52	2.05
2.02	2.22	.11	14.52	14.72	.76	27.02	27.22	1.41	39.52	39.72	2.06
2.22	2.41	.12	14.72	14.91	.77	27.22	27.41	1.42	39.72	39.91	2.07
2.41	2.60	.13	14.91	15.10	.78	27.41	27.60	1.43	39.91	40.10	2.08
2.60	2.79	.14	15.10	15.29	.79	27.60	27.79	1.44	40.10	40.29	2.09
2.79	2.99	.15	15.29	15.49	.80	27.79	27.99	1.45	40.29	40.49	2.10
2.99	3.18	.16	15.49	15.68	.81	27.99	28.18	1.46	40.49	40.68	2.11
3.18	3.37	.17	15.68	15.87	.82	28.18	28.37	1.47	40.68	40.87	2.12
3.37	3.56	.18	15.87	16.06	.83	28.37	28.56	1.48	40.87	41.06	2.13
3.56	3.75	.19	16.06	16.25	.84	28.56	28.75	1.49	41.06	41.25	2.14
3.75	3.95	.20	16.25	16.45	.85	28.75	28.95	1.50	41.25	41.45	2.15
3.95	4.14	.21	16.45	16.64	.86	28.95	29.14	1.51	41.45	41.64	2.16
4.14	4.33	.22	16.64	16.83	.87	29.14	29.33	1.52	41.64	41.83	2.17
4.33	4.52	.23	16.83	17.02	.88	29.33	29.52	1.53	41.83	42.02	2.18
4.52	4.72	.24	17.02	17.22	.89	29.52	29.72	1.54	42.02	42.22	2.19
4.72	4.91	.25	17.22	17.41	.90	29.72	29.91	1.55	42.22	42.41	2.20
4.91	5.10	.26	17.41	17.60	.91	29.91	30.10	1.56	42.41	42.60	2.21
5.10	5.29	.27	17.60	17.79	.92	30.10	30.29	1.57	42.60	42.79	2.22
5.29	5.49	.28	17.79	17.99	.93	30.29	30.49	1.58	42.79	42.99	2.23
5.49	5.68	.29	17.99	18.18	.94	30.49	30.68	1.59	42.99	43.18	2.24
5.68	5.87	.30	18.18	18.37	.95	30.68	30.87	1.60	43.18	43.37	2.25
5.87	6.06	.31	18.37	18.56	.96	30.87	31.06	1.61	43.37	43.56	2.26
6.06	6.25	.32	18.56	18.75	.97	31.06	31.25	1.62	43.56	43.75	2.27
6.25	6.45	.33	18.75	18.95	.98	31.25	31.45	1.63	43.75	43.95	2.28
6.45	6.64	.34	18.95	19.14	.99	31.45	31.64	1.64	43.95	44.14	2.29
6.64	6.83	.35	19.14	19.33	1.00	31.64	31.83	1.65	44.14	44.33	2.30
6.83	7.02	.36	19.33	19.52	1.01	31.83	32.02	1.66	44.33	44.52	2.31
7.02	7.22	.37	19.52	19.72	1.02	32.02	32.22	1.67	44.52	44.72	2.32
7.22	7.41	.38	19.72	19.91	1.03	32.22	32.41	1.68	44.72	44.91	2.33
7.41	7.60	.39	19.91	20.10	1.04	32.41	32.60	1.69	44.91	45.10	2.34
7.60	7.79	.40	20.10	20.29	1.05	32.60	32.79	1.70	45.10	45.29	2.35
7.79	7.99	.41	20.29	20.49	1.06	32.79	32.99	1.71	45.29	45.49	2.36
7.99	8.18	.42	20.49	20.68	1.07	32.99	33.18	1.72	45.49	45.68	2.37
8.18	8.37	.43	20.68	20.87	1.08	33.18	33.37	1.73	45.68	45.87	2.38
8.37	8.56	.44	20.87	21.06	1.09	33.37	33.56	1.74	45.87	46.06	2.39
8.56	8.75	.45	21.06	21.25	1.10	33.56	33.75	1.75	46.06	46.25	2.40
8.75	8.95	.46	21.25	21.45	1.11	33.75	33.95	1.76	46.25	46.45	2.41
8.95	9.14	.47	21.45	21.64	1.12	33.95	34.14	1.77	46.45	46.64	2.42
9.14	9.33	.48	21.64	21.83	1.13	34.14	34.33	1.78	46.64	46.83	2.43
9.33	9.52	.49	21.83	22.02	1.14	34.33	34.52	1.79	46.83	47.02	2.44
9.52	9.72	.50	22.02	22.22	1.15	34.52	34.72	1.80	47.02	47.22	2.45
9.72	9.91	.51	22.22	22.41	1.16	34.72	34.91	1.81	47.22	47.41	2.46
9.91	10.10	.52	22.41	22.60	1.17	34.91	35.10	1.82	47.41	47.60	2.47
10.10	10.29	.53	22.60	22.79	1.18	35.10	35.29	1.83	47.60	47.79	2.48
10.29	10.49	.54	22.79	22.99	1.19	35.29	35.49	1.84	47.79	47.99	2.49
10.49	10.68	.55	22.99	23.18	1.20	35.49	35.68	1.85	47.99	48.18	2.50
10.68	10.87	.56	23.18	23.37	1.21	35.68	35.87	1.86	48.18	48.37	2.51
10.87	11.06	.57	23.37	23.56	1.22	35.87	36.06	1.87	48.37	48.56	2.52
11.06	11.25	.58	23.56	23.75	1.23	36.06	36.25	1.88	48.56	48.75	2.53
11.25	11.45	.59	23.75	23.95	1.24	36.25	36.45	1.89	48.75	48.95	2.54
11.45	11.64	.60	23.95	24.14	1.25	36.45	36.64	1.90	48.95	49.14	2.55
11.64	11.83	.61	24.14	24.33	1.26	36.64	36.83	1.91	49.14	49.33	2.56
11.83	12.02	.62	24.33	24.52	1.27	36.83	37.02	1.92	49.33	49.52	2.57
12.02	12.22	.63	24.52	24.72	1.28	37.02	37.22	1.93	49.52	49.72	2.58
12.22	12.41	.64	24.72	24.91	1.29	37.22	37.41	1.94	49.72	49.91	2.59

Table X, continued

Social Security Employee Tax Table—Continued
5.2 percent employee tax deductions

Wages		Tax to be withheld	Wages		Tax to be withheld	Wages		Tax to be withheld	Wages		Tax to be withheld
At least	But less than		At least	But less than		At least	But less than		At least	But less than	
$49.91	$50.10	$2.60	$62.41	$62.60	$3.25	$74.91	$75.10	$3.90	$87.41	$87.60	$4.55
50.10	50.29	2.61	62.60	62.79	3.26	75.10	75.29	3.91	87.60	87.79	4.56
50.29	50.49	2.62	62.79	62.99	3.27	75.29	75.49	3.92	87.79	87.99	4.57
50.49	50.68	2.63	62.99	63.18	3.28	75.49	75.68	3.93	87.99	88.18	4.58
50.68	50.87	2.64	63.18	63.37	3.29	75.68	75.87	3.94	88.18	88.37	4.59
50.87	51.06	2.65	63.37	63.56	3.30	75.87	76.06	3.95	88.37	88.56	4.60
51.06	51.25	2.66	63.56	63.75	3.31	76.06	76.25	3.96	88.56	88.75	4.61
51.25	51.45	2.67	63.75	63.95	3.32	76.25	76.45	3.97	88.75	88.95	4.62
51.45	51.64	2.68	63.95	64.14	3.33	76.45	76.64	3.98	88.95	89.14	4.63
51.64	51.83	2.69	64.14	64.33	3.34	76.64	76.83	3.99	89.14	89.33	4.64
51.83	52.02	2.70	64.33	64.52	3.35	76.83	77.02	4.00	89.33	89.52	4.65
52.02	52.22	2.71	64.52	64.72	3.36	77.02	77.22	4.01	89.52	89.72	4.66
52.22	52.41	2.72	64.72	64.91	3.37	77.22	77.41	4.02	89.72	89.91	4.67
52.41	52.60	2.73	64.91	65.10	3.38	77.41	77.60	4.03	89.91	90.10	4.68
52.60	52.79	2.74	65.10	65.29	3.39	77.60	77.79	4.04	90.10	90.29	4.69
52.79	52.99	2.75	65.29	65.49	3.40	77.79	77.99	4.05	90.29	90.49	4.70
52.99	53.18	2.76	65.49	65.68	3.41	77.99	78.18	4.06	90.49	90.68	4.71
53.18	53.37	2.77	65.68	65.87	3.42	78.18	78.37	4.07	90.68	90.87	4.72
53.37	53.56	2.78	65.87	66.06	3.43	78.37	78.56	4.08	90.87	91.06	4.73
53.56	53.75	2.79	66.06	66.25	3.44	78.56	78.75	4.09	91.06	91.25	4.74
53.75	53.95	2.80	66.25	66.45	3.45	78.75	78.95	4.10	91.25	91.45	4.75
53.95	54.14	2.81	66.45	66.64	3.46	78.95	79.14	4.11	91.45	91.64	4.76
54.14	54.33	2.82	66.64	66.83	3.47	79.14	79.33	4.12	91.64	91.83	4.77
54.33	54.52	2.83	66.83	67.02	3.48	79.33	79.52	4.13	91.83	92.02	4.78
54.52	54.72	2.84	67.02	67.22	3.49	79.52	79.72	4.14	92.02	92.22	4.79
54.72	54.91	2.85	67.22	67.41	3.50	79.72	79.91	4.15	92.22	92.41	4.80
54.91	55.10	2.86	67.41	67.60	3.51	79.91	80.10	4.16	92.41	92.60	4.81
55.10	55.29	2.87	67.60	67.79	3.52	80.10	80.29	4.17	92.60	92.79	4.82
55.29	55.49	2.88	67.79	67.99	3.53	80.29	80.49	4.18	92.79	92.99	4.83
55.49	55.68	2.89	67.99	68.18	3.54	80.49	80.68	4.19	92.99	93.18	4.84
55.68	55.87	2.90	68.18	68.37	3.55	80.68	80.87	4.20	93.18	93.37	4.85
55.87	56.06	2.91	68.37	68.56	3.56	80.87	81.06	4.21	93.37	93.56	4.86
56.06	56.25	2.92	68.56	68.75	3.57	81.06	81.25	4.22	93.56	93.75	4.87
56.25	56.45	2.93	68.75	68.95	3.58	81.25	81.45	4.23	93.75	93.95	4.88
56.45	56.64	2.94	68.95	69.14	3.59	81.45	81.64	4.24	93.95	94.14	4.89
56.64	56.83	2.95	69.14	69.33	3.60	81.64	81.83	4.25	94.14	94.33	4.90
56.83	57.02	2.96	69.33	69.52	3.61	81.83	82.02	4.26	94.33	94.52	4.91
57.02	57.22	2.97	69.52	69.72	3.62	82.02	82.22	4.27	94.52	94.72	4.92
57.22	57.41	2.98	69.72	69.91	3.63	82.22	82.41	4.28	94.72	94.91	4.93
57.41	57.60	2.99	69.91	70.10	3.64	82.41	82.60	4.29	94.91	95.10	4.94
57.60	57.79	3.00	70.10	70.29	3.65	82.60	82.79	4.30	95.10	95.29	4.95
57.79	57.99	3.01	70.29	70.49	3.66	82.79	82.99	4.31	95.29	95.49	4.96
57.99	58.18	3.02	70.49	70.68	3.67	82.99	83.18	4.32	95.49	95.68	4.97
58.18	58.37	3.03	70.68	70.87	3.68	83.18	83.37	4.33	95.68	95.87	4.98
58.37	58.56	3.04	70.87	71.06	3.69	83.37	83.56	4.34	95.87	96.06	4.99
58.56	58.75	3.05	71.06	71.25	3.70	83.56	83.75	4.35	96.06	96.25	5.00
58.75	58.95	3.06	71.25	71.45	3.71	83.75	83.95	4.36	96.25	96.45	5.01
58.95	59.14	3.07	71.45	71.64	3.72	83.95	84.14	4.37	96.45	96.64	5.02
59.14	59.33	3.08	71.64	71.83	3.73	84.14	84.33	4.38	96.64	96.83	5.03
59.33	59.52	3.09	71.83	72.02	3.74	84.33	84.52	4.39	96.83	97.02	5.04
59.52	59.72	3.10	72.02	72.22	3.75	84.52	84.72	4.40	97.02	97.22	5.05
59.72	59.91	3.11	72.22	72.41	3.76	84.72	84.91	4.41	97.22	97.41	5.06
59.91	60.10	3.12	72.41	72.60	3.77	84.91	85.10	4.42	97.41	97.60	5.07
60.10	60.29	3.13	72.60	72.79	3.78	85.10	85.29	4.43	97.60	97.79	5.08
60.29	60.49	3.14	72.79	72.99	3.79	85.29	85.49	4.44	97.79	97.99	5.09
60.49	60.68	3.15	72.99	73.18	3.80	85.49	85.68	4.45	97.99	98.18	5.10
60.68	60.87	3.16	73.18	73.37	3.81	85.68	85.87	4.46	98.18	98.37	5.11
60.87	61.06	3.17	73.37	73.56	3.82	85.87	86.06	4.47	98.37	98.56	5.12
61.06	61.25	3.18	73.56	73.75	3.83	86.06	86.25	4.48	98.56	98.75	5.13
61.25	61.45	3.19	73.75	73.95	3.84	86.25	86.45	4.49	98.75	98.95	5.14
61.45	61.64	3.20	73.95	74.14	3.85	86.45	86.64	4.50	98.95	99.14	5.15
61.64	61.83	3.21	74.14	74.33	3.86	86.64	86.83	4.51	99.14	99.33	5.16
61.83	62.02	3.22	74.33	74.52	3.87	86.83	87.02	4.52	99.33	99.52	5.17
62.02	62.22	3.23	74.52	74.72	3.88	87.02	87.22	4.53	99.52	99.72	5.18
62.22	62.41	3.24	74.72	74.91	3.89	87.22	87.41	4.54	99.72	99.91	5.19

Table X, continued

Social Security Employee Tax Table—Continued

5.2 percent employee tax deductions

Wages At least	But less than	Tax to be withheld	Wages At least	But less than	Tax to be withheld	Wages At least	But less than	Tax to be withheld	Wages At least	But less than	Tax to be withheld
$99.91	$100.10	$5.20	$112.41	$112.60	$5.85	$124.91	$125.10	$6.50	$137.41	$137.60	$7.15
100.10	100.29	5.21	112.60	112.79	5.86	125.10	125.29	6.51	137.60	137.79	7.16
100.29	100.49	5.22	112.79	112.99	5.87	125.29	125.49	6.52	137.79	137.99	7.17
100.49	100.68	5.23	112.99	113.18	5.88	125.49	125.68	6.53	137.99	138.18	7.18
100.68	100.87	5.24	113.18	113.37	5.89	125.68	125.87	6.54	138.18	138.37	7.19
100.87	101.06	5.25	113.37	113.56	5.90	125.87	126.06	6.55	138.37	138.56	7.20
101.06	101.25	5.26	113.56	113.75	5.91	126.06	126.25	6.56	138.56	138.75	7.21
101.25	101.45	5.27	113.75	113.95	5.92	126.25	126.45	6.57	138.75	138.95	7.22
101.45	101.64	5.28	113.95	114.14	5.93	126.45	126.64	6.58	138.95	139.14	7.23
101.64	101.83	5.29	114.14	114.33	5.94	126.64	126.83	6.59	139.14	139.33	7.24
101.83	102.02	5.30	114.33	114.52	5.95	126.83	127.02	6.60	139.33	139.52	7.25
102.02	102.22	5.31	114.52	114.72	5.96	127.02	127.22	6.61	139.52	139.72	7.26
102.22	102.41	5.32	114.72	114.91	5.97	127.22	127.41	6.62	139.72	139.91	7.27
102.41	102.60	5.33	114.91	115.10	5.98	127.41	127.60	6.63	139.91	140.10	7.28
102.60	102.79	5.34	115.10	115.29	5.99	127.60	127.79	6.64	140.10	140.29	7.29
102.79	102.99	5.35	115.29	115.49	6.00	127.79	127.99	6.65	140.29	140.49	7.30
102.99	103.18	5.36	115.49	115.68	6.01	127.99	128.18	6.66	140.49	140.68	7.31
103.18	103.37	5.37	115.68	115.87	6.02	128.18	128.37	6.67	140.68	140.87	7.32
103.37	103.56	5.38	115.87	116.06	6.03	128.37	128.56	6.68	140.87	141.06	7.33
103.56	103.75	5.39	116.06	116.25	6.04	128.56	128.75	6.69	141.06	141.25	7.34
103.75	103.95	5.40	116.25	116.45	6.05	128.75	128.95	6.70	141.25	141.45	7.35
103.95	104.14	5.41	116.45	116.64	6.06	128.95	129.14	6.71	141.45	141.64	7.36
104.14	104.33	5.42	116.64	116.83	6.07	129.14	129.33	6.72	141.64	141.83	7.37
104.33	104.52	5.43	116.83	117.02	6.08	129.33	129.52	6.73	141.83	142.02	7.38
104.52	104.72	5.44	117.02	117.22	6.09	129.52	129.72	6.74	142.02	142.22	7.39
104.72	104.91	5.45	117.22	117.41	6.10	129.72	129.91	6.75	142.22	142.41	7.40
104.91	105.10	5.46	117.41	117.60	6.11	129.91	130.10	6.76	142.41	142.60	7.41
105.10	105.29	5.47	117.60	117.79	6.12	130.10	130.29	6.77	142.60	142.79	7.42
105.29	105.49	5.48	117.79	117.99	6.13	130.29	130.49	6.78	142.79	142.99	7.43
105.49	105.68	5.49	117.99	118.18	6.14	130.49	130.68	6.79	142.99	143.18	7.44
105.68	105.87	5.50	118.18	118.37	6.15	130.68	130.87	6.80	143.18	143.37	7.45
105.87	106.06	5.51	118.37	118.56	6.16	130.87	131.06	6.81	143.37	143.56	7.46
106.06	106.25	5.52	118.56	118.75	6.17	131.06	131.25	6.82	143.56	143.75	7.47
106.25	106.45	5.53	118.75	118.95	6.18	131.25	131.45	6.83	143.75	143.95	7.48
106.45	106.64	5.54	118.95	119.14	6.19	131.45	131.64	6.84	143.95	144.14	7.49
106.64	106.83	5.55	119.14	119.33	6.20	131.64	131.83	6.85	144.14	144.33	7.50
106.83	107.02	5.56	119.33	119.52	6.21	131.83	132.02	6.86	144.33	144.52	7.51
107.02	107.22	5.57	119.52	119.72	6.22	132.02	132.22	6.87	144.52	144.72	7.52
107.22	107.41	5.58	119.72	119.91	6.23	132.22	132.41	6.88	144.72	144.91	7.53
107.41	107.60	5.59	119.91	120.10	6.24	132.41	132.60	6.89	144.91	145.10	7.54
107.60	107.79	5.60	120.10	120.29	6.25	132.60	132.79	6.90	145.10	145.29	7.55
107.79	107.99	5.61	120.29	120.49	6.26	132.79	132.99	6.91	145.29	145.49	7.56
107.99	108.18	5.62	120.49	120.68	6.27	132.99	133.18	6.92	145.49	145.68	7.57
108.18	108.37	5.63	120.68	120.87	6.28	133.18	133.37	6.93	145.68	145.87	7.58
108.37	108.56	5.64	120.87	121.06	6.29	133.37	133.56	6.94	145.87	146.06	7.59
108.56	108.75	5.65	121.06	121.25	6.30	133.56	133.75	6.95	146.06	146.25	7.60
108.75	108.95	5.66	121.25	121.45	6.31	133.75	133.95	6.96	146.25	146.45	7.61
108.95	109.14	5.67	121.45	121.64	6.32	133.95	134.14	6.97	146.45	146.64	7.62
109.14	109.33	5.68	121.64	121.83	6.33	134.14	134.33	6.98	146.64	146.83	7.63
109.33	109.52	5.69	121.83	122.02	6.34	134.33	134.52	6.99	146.83	147.02	7.64
109.52	109.72	5.70	122.02	122.22	6.35	134.52	134.72	7.00	147.02	147.22	7.65
109.72	109.91	5.71	122.22	122.41	6.36	134.72	134.91	7.01	147.22	147.41	7.66
109.91	110.10	5.72	122.41	122.60	6.37	134.91	135.10	7.02	147.41	147.60	7.67
110.10	110.29	5.73	122.60	122.79	6.38	135.10	135.29	7.03	147.60	147.79	7.68
110.29	110.49	5.74	122.79	122.99	6.39	135.29	135.49	7.04	147.79	147.99	7.69
110.49	110.68	5.75	122.99	123.18	6.40	135.49	135.68	7.05	147.99	148.18	7.70
110.68	110.87	5.76	123.18	123.37	6.41	135.68	135.87	7.06	148.18	148.37	7.71
110.87	111.06	5.77	123.37	123.56	6.42	135.87	136.06	7.07	148.37	148.56	7.72
111.06	111.25	5.78	123.56	123.75	6.43	136.06	136.25	7.08	148.56	148.75	7.73
111.25	111.45	5.79	123.75	123.95	6.44	136.25	136.45	7.09	148.75	148.95	7.74
111.45	111.64	5.80	123.95	124.14	6.45	136.45	136.64	7.10	148.95	149.14	7.75
111.64	111.83	5.81	124.14	124.33	6.46	136.64	136.83	7.11	149.14	149.33	7.76
111.83	112.02	5.82	124.33	124.52	6.47	136.83	137.02	7.12	149.33	149.52	7.77
112.02	112.22	5.83	124.52	124.72	6.48	137.02	137.22	7.13	149.52	149.72	7.78
112.22	112.41	5.84	124.72	124.91	6.49	137.22	137.41	7.14	149.72	149.91	7.79

Table X, continued

Social Security Employee Tax Table—Continued
5.2 percent employee tax deductions

Wages		Tax to be withheld	Wages		Tax to be withheld	Wages		Tax to be withheld	Wages		Tax to be withheld
At least	But less than		At least	But less than		At least	But less than		At least	But less than	
$149.91	$150.10	$7.80	$162.41	$162.60	$8.45	$174.91	$175.10	$9.10	$187.41	$187.60	$9.75
150.10	150.29	7.81	162.60	162.79	8.46	175.10	175.29	9.11	187.60	187.79	9.76
150.29	150.49	7.82	162.79	162.99	8.47	175.29	175.49	9.12	187.79	187.99	9.77
150.49	150.68	7.83	162.99	163.18	8.48	175.49	175.68	9.13	187.99	188.18	9.78
150.68	150.87	7.84	163.18	163.37	8.49	175.68	175.87	9.14	188.18	188.37	9.79
150.87	151.06	7.85	163.37	163.56	8.50	175.87	176.06	9.15	188.37	188.56	9.80
151.06	151.25	7.86	163.56	163.75	8.51	176.06	176.25	9.16	188.56	188.75	9.81
151.25	151.45	7.87	163.75	163.95	8.52	176.25	176.45	9.17	188.75	188.95	9.82
151.45	151.64	7.88	163.95	164.14	8.53	176.45	176.64	9.18	188.95	189.14	9.83
151.64	151.83	7.89	164.14	164.33	8.54	176.64	176.83	9.19	189.14	189.33	9.84
151.83	152.02	7.90	164.33	164.52	8.55	176.83	177.02	9.20	189.33	189.52	9.85
152.02	152.22	7.91	164.52	164.72	8.56	177.02	177.22	9.21	189.52	189.72	9.86
152.22	152.41	7.92	164.72	164.91	8.57	177.22	177.41	9.22	189.72	189.91	9.87
152.41	152.60	7.93	164.91	165.10	8.58	177.41	177.60	9.23	189.91	190.10	9.88
152.60	152.79	7.94	165.10	165.29	8.59	177.60	177.79	9.24	190.10	190.29	9.89
152.79	152.99	7.95	165.29	165.49	8.60	177.79	177.99	9.25	190.29	190.49	9.90
152.99	153.18	7.96	165.49	165.68	8.61	177.99	178.18	9.26	190.49	190.68	9.91
153.18	153.37	7.97	165.68	165.87	8.62	178.18	178.37	9.27	190.68	190.87	9.92
153.37	153.56	7.98	165.87	166.06	8.63	178.37	178.56	9.28	190.87	191.06	9.93
153.56	153.75	7.99	166.06	166.25	8.64	178.56	178.75	9.29	191.06	191.25	9.94
153.75	153.95	8.00	166.25	166.45	8.65	178.75	178.95	9.30	191.25	191.45	9.95
153.95	154.14	8.01	166.45	166.64	8.66	178.95	179.14	9.31	191.45	191.64	9.96
154.14	154.33	8.02	166.64	166.83	8.67	179.14	179.33	9.32	191.64	191.83	9.97
154.33	154.52	8.03	166.83	167.02	8.68	179.33	179.52	9.33	191.83	192.02	9.98
154.52	154.72	8.04	167.02	167.22	8.69	179.52	179.72	9.34	192.02	192.22	9.99
154.72	154.91	8.05	167.22	167.41	8.70	179.72	179.91	9.35	192.22	192.41	10.00
154.91	155.10	8.06	167.41	167.60	8.71	179.91	180.10	9.36	192.41	192.60	10.01
155.10	155.29	8.07	167.60	167.79	8.72	180.10	180.29	9.37	192.60	192.79	10.02
155.29	155.49	8.08	167.79	167.99	8.73	180.29	180.49	9.38	192.79	192.99	10.03
155.49	155.68	8.09	167.99	168.18	8.74	180.49	180.68	9.39	192.99	193.18	10.04
155.68	155.87	8.10	168.18	168.37	8.75	180.68	180.87	9.40	193.18	193.37	10.05
155.87	156.06	8.11	168.37	168.56	8.76	180.87	181.06	9.41	193.37	193.56	10.06
156.06	156.25	8.12	168.56	168.75	8.77	181.06	181.25	9.42	193.56	193.75	10.07
156.25	156.45	8.13	168.75	168.95	8.78	181.25	181.45	9.43	193.75	193.95	10.08
156.45	156.64	8.14	168.95	169.14	8.79	181.45	181.64	9.44	193.95	194.14	10.09
156.64	156.83	8.15	169.14	169.33	8.80	181.64	181.83	9.45	194.14	194.33	10.10
156.83	157.02	8.16	169.33	169.52	8.81	181.83	182.02	9.46	194.33	194.52	10.11
157.02	157.22	8.17	169.52	169.72	8.82	182.02	182.22	9.47	194.52	194.72	10.12
157.22	157.41	8.18	169.72	169.91	8.83	182.22	182.41	9.48	194.72	194.91	10.13
157.41	157.60	8.19	169.91	170.10	8.84	182.41	182.60	9.49	194.91	195.10	10.14
157.60	157.79	8.20	170.10	170.29	8.85	182.60	182.79	9.50	195.10	195.29	10.15
157.79	157.99	8.21	170.29	170.49	8.86	182.79	182.99	9.51	195.29	195.49	10.16
157.99	158.18	8.22	170.49	170.68	8.87	182.99	183.18	9.52	195.49	195.68	10.17
158.18	158.37	8.23	170.68	170.87	8.88	183.18	183.37	9.53	195.68	195.87	10.18
158.37	158.56	8.24	170.87	171.06	8.89	183.37	183.56	9.54	195.87	196.06	10.19
158.56	158.75	8.25	171.06	171.25	8.90	183.56	183.75	9.55	196.06	196.25	10.20
158.75	158.95	8.26	171.25	171.45	8.91	183.75	183.95	9.56	196.25	196.45	10.21
158.95	159.14	8.27	171.45	171.64	8.92	183.95	184.14	9.57	196.45	196.64	10.22
159.14	159.33	8.28	171.64	171.83	8.93	184.14	184.33	9.58	196.64	196.83	10.23
159.33	159.52	8.29	171.83	172.02	8.94	184.33	184.52	9.59	196.83	197.02	10.24
159.52	159.72	8.30	172.02	172.22	8.95	184.52	184.72	9.60	197.02	197.22	10.25
159.72	159.91	8.31	172.22	172.41	8.96	184.72	184.91	9.61	197.22	197.41	10.26
159.91	160.10	8.32	172.41	172.60	8.97	184.91	185.10	9.62	197.41	197.60	10.27
160.10	160.29	8.33	172.60	172.79	8.98	185.10	185.29	9.63	197.60	197.79	10.28
160.29	160.49	8.34	172.79	172.99	8.99	185.29	185.49	9.64	197.79	197.99	10.29
160.49	160.68	8.35	172.99	173.18	9.00	185.49	185.68	9.65	197.99	198.18	10.30
160.68	160.87	8.36	173.18	173.37	9.01	185.68	185.87	9.66	198.18	198.37	10.31
160.87	161.06	8.37	173.37	173.56	9.02	185.87	186.06	9.67	198.37	198.56	10.32
161.06	161.25	8.38	173.56	173.75	9.03	186.06	186.25	9.68	198.56	198.75	10.33
161.25	161.45	8.39	173.75	173.95	9.04	186.25	186.45	9.69	198.75	198.95	10.34
161.45	161.64	8.40	173.95	174.14	9.05	186.45	186.64	9.70	198.95	199.14	10.35
161.64	161.83	8.41	174.14	174.33	9.06	186.64	186.83	9.71	199.14	199.33	10.36
161.83	162.02	8.42	174.33	174.52	9.07	186.83	187.02	9.72	199.33	199.52	10.37
162.02	162.22	8.43	174.52	174.72	9.08	187.02	187.22	9.73	199.52	199.72	10.38
162.22	162.41	8.44	174.72	174.91	9.09	187.22	187.41	9.74	199.72	199.91	10.39

Table X, continued

Social Security Employee Tax Table—Continued
5.2 percent employee tax deductions

Wages At least	Wages But less than	Tax to be withheld	Wages At least	Wages But less than	Tax to be withheld	Wages At least	Wages But less than	Tax to be withheld	Wages At least	Wages But less than	Tax to be withheld
$199.91	$200.10	$10.40	$212.41	$212.60	$11.05	$224.91	$225.10	$11.70	$237.41	$237.60	$12.35
200.10	200.29	10.41	212.60	212.79	11.06	225.10	225.29	11.71	237.60	237.79	12.36
200.29	200.49	10.42	212.79	212.99	11.07	225.29	225.49	11.72	237.79	237.99	12.37
200.49	200.68	10.43	212.99	213.18	11.08	225.49	225.68	11.73	237.99	238.18	12.38
200.68	200.87	10.44	213.18	213.37	11.09	225.68	225.87	11.74	238.18	238.37	12.39
200.87	201.06	10.45	213.37	213.56	11.10	225.87	226.06	11.75	238.37	238.56	12.40
201.06	201.25	10.46	213.56	213.75	11.11	226.06	226.25	11.76	238.56	238.75	12.41
201.25	201.45	10.47	213.75	213.95	11.12	226.25	226.45	11.77	238.75	238.95	12.42
201.45	201.64	10.48	213.95	214.14	11.13	226.45	226.64	11.78	238.95	239.14	12.43
201.64	201.83	10.49	214.14	214.33	11.14	226.64	226.83	11.79	239.14	239.33	12.44
201.83	202.02	10.50	214.33	214.52	11.15	226.83	227.02	11.80	239.33	239.52	12.45
202.02	202.22	10.51	214.52	214.72	11.16	227.02	227.22	11.81	239.52	239.72	12.46
202.22	202.41	10.52	214.72	214.91	11.17	227.22	227.41	11.82	239.72	239.91	12.47
202.41	202.60	10.53	214.91	215.10	11.18	227.41	227.60	11.83	239.91	240.10	12.48
202.60	202.79	10.54	215.10	215.29	11.19	227.60	227.79	11.84	240.10	240.29	12.49
202.79	202.99	10.55	215.29	215.49	11.20	227.79	227.99	11.85	240.29	240.49	12.50
202.99	203.18	10.56	215.49	215.68	11.21	227.99	228.18	11.86	240.49	240.68	12.51
203.18	203.37	10.57	215.68	215.87	11.22	228.18	228.37	11.87	240.68	240.87	12.52
203.37	203.56	10.58	215.87	216.06	11.23	228.37	228.56	11.88	240.87	241.06	12.53
203.56	203.75	10.59	216.06	216.25	11.24	228.56	228.75	11.89	241.06	241.25	12.54
203.75	203.95	10.60	216.25	216.45	11.25	228.75	228.95	11.90	241.25	241.45	12.55
203.95	204.14	10.61	216.45	216.64	11.26	228.95	229.14	11.91	241.45	241.64	12.56
204.14	204.33	10.62	216.64	216.83	11.27	229.14	229.33	11.92	241.64	241.83	12.57
204.33	204.52	10.63	216.83	217.02	11.28	229.33	229.52	11.93	241.83	242.02	12.58
204.52	204.72	10.64	217.02	217.22	11.29	229.52	229.72	11.94	242.02	242.22	12.59
204.72	204.91	10.65	217.22	217.41	11.30	229.72	229.91	11.95	242.22	242.41	12.60
204.91	205.10	10.66	217.41	217.60	11.31	229.91	230.10	11.96	242.41	242.60	12.61
205.10	205.29	10.67	217.60	217.79	11.32	230.10	230.29	11.97	242.60	242.79	12.62
205.29	205.49	10.68	217.79	217.99	11.33	230.29	230.49	11.98	242.79	242.99	12.63
205.49	205.68	10.69	217.99	218.18	11.34	230.49	230.68	11.99	242.99	243.18	12.64
205.68	205.87	10.70	218.18	218.37	11.35	230.68	230.87	12.00	243.18	243.37	12.65
205.87	206.06	10.71	218.37	218.56	11.36	230.87	231.06	12.01	243.37	243.56	12.66
206.06	206.25	10.72	218.56	218.75	11.37	231.06	231.25	12.02	243.56	243.75	12.67
206.25	206.45	10.73	218.75	218.95	11.38	231.25	231.45	12.03	243.75	243.95	12.68
206.45	206.64	10.74	218.95	219.14	11.39	231.45	231.64	12.04	243.95	244.14	12.69
206.64	206.83	10.75	219.14	219.33	11.40	231.64	231.83	12.05	244.14	244.33	12.70
206.83	207.02	10.76	219.33	219.52	11.41	231.83	232.02	12.06	244.33	244.52	12.71
207.02	207.22	10.77	219.52	219.72	11.42	232.02	232.22	12.07	244.52	244.72	12.72
207.22	207.41	10.78	219.72	219.91	11.43	232.22	232.41	12.08	244.72	244.91	12.73
207.41	207.60	10.79	219.91	220.10	11.44	232.41	232.60	12.09	244.91	245.10	12.74
207.60	207.79	10.80	220.10	220.29	11.45	232.60	232.79	12.10	245.10	245.29	12.75
207.79	207.99	10.81	220.29	220.49	11.46	232.79	232.99	12.11	245.29	245.49	12.76
207.99	208.18	10.82	220.49	220.68	11.47	232.99	233.18	12.12	245.49	245.68	12.77
208.18	208.37	10.83	220.68	220.87	11.48	233.18	233.37	12.13	245.68	245.87	12.78
208.37	208.56	10.84	220.87	221.06	11.49	233.37	233.56	12.14	245.87	246.06	12.79
208.56	208.75	10.85	221.06	221.25	11.50	233.56	233.75	12.15	246.06	246.25	12.80
208.75	208.95	10.86	221.25	221.45	11.51	233.75	233.95	12.16	246.25	246.45	12.81
208.95	209.14	10.87	221.45	221.64	11.52	233.95	234.14	12.17	246.45	246.64	12.82
209.14	209.33	10.88	221.64	221.83	11.53	234.14	234.33	12.18	246.64	246.83	12.83
209.33	209.52	10.89	221.83	222.02	11.54	234.33	234.52	12.19	246.83	247.02	12.84
209.52	209.72	10.90	222.02	222.22	11.55	234.52	234.72	12.20	247.02	247.22	12.85
209.72	209.91	10.91	222.22	222.41	11.56	234.72	234.91	12.21	247.22	247.41	12.86
209.91	210.10	10.92	222.41	222.60	11.57	234.91	235.10	12.22	247.41	247.60	12.87
210.10	210.29	10.93	222.60	222.79	11.58	235.10	235.29	12.23	247.60	247.79	12.88
210.29	210.49	10.94	222.79	222.99	11.59	235.29	235.49	12.24	247.79	247.99	12.89
210.49	210.68	10.95	222.99	223.18	11.60	235.49	235.68	12.25	247.99	248.18	12.90
210.68	210.87	10.96	223.18	223.37	11.61	235.68	235.87	12.26	248.18	248.37	12.91
210.87	211.06	10.97	223.37	223.56	11.62	235.87	236.06	12.27	248.37	248.56	12.92
211.06	211.25	10.98	223.56	223.75	11.63	236.06	236.25	12.28	248.56	248.75	12.93
211.25	211.45	10.99	223.75	223.95	11.64	236.25	236.45	12.29	248.75	248.95	12.94
211.45	211.64	11.00	223.95	224.14	11.65	236.45	236.64	12.30	248.95	249.14	12.95
211.64	211.83	11.01	224.14	224.33	11.66	236.64	236.83	12.31	249.14	249.33	12.96
211.83	212.02	11.02	224.33	224.52	11.67	236.83	237.02	12.32	249.33	249.52	12.97
212.02	212.22	11.03	224.52	224.72	11.68	237.02	237.22	12.33	249.52	249.72	12.98
212.22	212.41	11.04	224.72	224.91	11.69	237.22	237.41	12.34	249.72	249.91	12.99

Table XI: Federal Income Tax Withholding Table

SINGLE Persons — WEEKLY Payroll Period

And the wages are—		And the number of withholding exemptions claimed is—										
At least	But less than	0	1	2	3	4	5	6	7	8	9	10 or more
		The amount of income tax to be withheld shall be—										
$0	$21	$0	$0	$0	$0	$0	$0	$0	$0	$0	$0	$0
21	22	.20	0	0	0	0	0	0	0	0	0	0
22	23	.30	0	0	0	0	0	0	0	0	0	0
23	24	.50	0	0	0	0	0	0	0	0	0	0
24	25	.60	0	0	0	0	0	0	0	0	0	0
25	26	.70	0	0	0	0	0	0	0	0	0	0
26	27	.90	0	0	0	0	0	0	0	0	0	0
27	28	1.00	0	0	0	0	0	0	0	0	0	0
28	29	1.20	0	0	0	0	0	0	0	0	0	0
29	30	1.30	0	0	0	0	0	0	0	0	0	0
30	31	1.40	0	0	0	0	0	0	0	0	0	0
31	32	1.60	0	0	0	0	0	0	0	0	0	0
32	33	1.80	0	0	0	0	0	0	0	0	0	0
33	34	1.90	.10	0	0	0	0	0	0	0	0	0
34	35	2.10	.30	0	0	0	0	0	0	0	0	0
35	36	2.30	.40	0	0	0	0	0	0	0	0	0
36	37	2.50	.50	0	0	0	0	0	0	0	0	0
37	38	2.60	.70	0	0	0	0	0	0	0	0	0
38	39	2.80	.80	0	0	0	0	0	0	0	0	0
39	40	3.00	1.00	0	0	0	0	0	0	0	0	0
40	41	3.10	1.10	0	0	0	0	0	0	0	0	0
41	42	3.30	1.20	0	0	0	0	0	0	0	0	0
42	43	3.50	1.40	0	0	0	0	0	0	0	0	0
43	44	3.60	1.50	0	0	0	0	0	0	0	0	0
44	45	3.80	1.70	0	0	0	0	0	0	0	0	0
45	46	4.00	1.90	0	0	0	0	0	0	0	0	0
46	47	4.20	2.00	.20	0	0	0	0	0	0	0	0
47	48	4.30	2.20	.30	0	0	0	0	0	0	0	0
48	49	4.50	2.40	.50	0	0	0	0	0	0	0	0
49	50	4.70	2.50	.60	0	0	0	0	0	0	0	0
50	51	4.90	2.70	.70	0	0	0	0	0	0	0	0
51	52	5.10	2.90	.90	0	0	0	0	0	0	0	0
52	53	5.30	3.10	1.00	0	0	0	0	0	0	0	0
53	54	5.50	3.20	1.20	0	0	0	0	0	0	0	0
54	55	5.70	3.40	1.30	0	0	0	0	0	0	0	0
55	56	5.90	3.60	1.40	0	0	0	0	0	0	0	0
56	57	6.10	3.70	1.60	0	0	0	0	0	0	0	0
57	58	6.30	3.90	1.80	0	0	0	0	0	0	0	0
58	59	6.50	4.10	1.90	.10	0	0	0	0	0	0	0
59	60	6.70	4.20	2.10	.30	0	0	0	0	0	0	0
60	62	7.00	4.50	2.40	.50	0	0	0	0	0	0	0
62	64	7.40	4.90	2.70	.70	0	0	0	0	0	0	0
64	66	7.80	5.30	3.10	1.00	0	0	0	0	0	0	0
66	68	8.20	5.70	3.40	1.30	0	0	0	0	0	0	0
68	70	8.60	6.10	3.70	1.60	0	0	0	0	0	0	0
70	72	9.00	6.50	4.10	1.90	.10	0	0	0	0	0	0
72	74	9.40	6.90	4.40	2.30	.40	0	0	0	0	0	0
74	76	9.80	7.30	4.80	2.60	.70	0	0	0	0	0	0
76	78	10.20	7.70	5.20	3.00	1.00	0	0	0	0	0	0
78	80	10.60	8.10	5.60	3.30	1.20	0	0	0	0	0	0

Table XI, continued

SINGLE Persons — WEEKLY Payroll Period

And the wages are—		And the number of withholding exemptions claimed is—										
At least	But less than	0	1	2	3	4	5	6	7	8	9	10 or more
		The amount of income tax to be withheld shall be—										
$80	$82	$11.00	$8.50	$6.00	$3.60	$1.50	$0	$0	$0	$0	$0	$0
82	84	11.40	8.90	6.40	4.00	1.90	0	0	0	0	0	0
84	86	11.80	9.30	6.80	4.30	2.20	.30	0	0	0	0	0
86	88	12.20	9.70	7.20	4.70	2.50	.60	0	0	0	0	0
88	90	12.60	10.10	7.60	5.10	2.90	.90	0	0	0	0	0
90	92	13.00	10.50	8.00	5.50	3.20	1.20	0	0	0	0	0
92	94	13.40	10.90	8.40	5.90	3.60	1.40	0	0	0	0	0
94	96	13.80	11.30	8.80	6.30	3.90	1.80	0	0	0	0	0
96	98	14.20	11.70	9.20	6.70	4.20	2.10	.30	0	0	0	0
98	100	14.60	12.10	9.60	7.10	4.60	2.50	.50	0	0	0	0
100	105	15.20	12.80	10.30	7.80	5.30	3.10	1.00	0	0	0	0
105	110	16.10	13.80	11.30	8.80	6.30	3.90	1.80	0	0	0	0
110	115	17.00	14.80	12.30	9.80	7.30	4.80	2.60	.70	0	0	0
115	120	17.90	15.70	13.30	10.80	8.30	5.80	3.50	1.40	0	0	0
120	125	18.80	16.60	14.30	11.80	9.30	6.80	4.30	2.20	.30	0	0
125	130	19.70	17.50	15.20	12.80	10.30	7.80	5.30	3.10	1.00	0	0
130	135	20.60	18.40	16.10	13.80	11.30	8.80	6.30	3.90	1.80	0	0
135	140	21.60	19.30	17.00	14.80	12.30	9.80	7.30	4.80	2.60	.70	0
140	145	22.60	20.20	17.90	15.70	13.30	10.80	8.30	5.80	3.50	1.40	0
145	150	23.70	21.10	18.80	16.60	14.30	11.80	9.30	6.80	4.30	2.20	.30
150	160	25.30	22.60	20.20	17.90	15.70	13.30	10.80	8.30	5.80	3.50	1.40
160	170	27.40	24.70	22.10	19.70	17.50	15.20	12.80	10.30	7.80	5.30	3.10
170	180	29.50	26.80	24.20	21.60	19.30	17.00	14.80	12.30	9.80	7.30	4.80
180	190	31.60	28.90	26.30	23.70	21.10	18.80	16.60	14.30	11.80	9.30	6.80
190	200	33.70	31.00	28.40	25.80	23.20	20.60	18.40	16.10	13.80	11.30	8.80
200	210	35.80	33.10	30.50	27.90	25.30	22.60	20.20	17.90	15.70	13.30	10.80
210	220	38.00	35.20	32.60	30.00	27.40	24.70	22.10	19.70	17.50	15.20	12.80
220	230	40.40	37.40	34.70	32.10	29.50	26.80	24.20	21.60	19.30	17.00	14.80
230	240	42.80	39.80	36.80	34.20	31.60	28.90	26.30	23.70	21.10	18.80	16.60
240	250	45.20	42.20	39.20	36.30	33.70	31.00	28.40	25.80	23.20	20.60	18.40
250	260	47.60	44.60	41.60	38.60	35.80	33.10	30.50	27.90	25.30	22.60	20.20
260	270	50.00	47.00	44.00	41.00	38.00	35.20	32.60	30.00	27.40	24.70	22.10
270	280	52.40	49.40	46.40	43.40	40.40	37.40	34.70	32.10	29.50	26.80	24.20
280	290	54.80	51.80	48.80	45.80	42.80	39.80	36.80	34.20	31.60	28.90	26.30
290	300	57.20	54.20	51.20	48.20	45.20	42.20	39.20	36.30	33.70	31.00	28.40
300	310	59.60	56.60	53.60	50.60	47.60	44.60	41.60	38.60	35.80	33.10	30.50
310	320	62.00	59.00	56.00	53.00	50.00	47.00	44.00	41.00	38.00	35.20	32.60
320	330	64.40	61.40	58.40	55.40	52.40	49.40	46.40	43.40	40.40	37.40	34.70
330	340	66.80	63.80	60.80	57.80	54.80	51.80	48.80	45.80	42.80	39.80	36.80
340	350	69.20	66.20	63.20	60.20	57.20	54.20	51.20	48.20	45.20	42.20	39.20
350	360	71.60	68.60	65.60	62.60	59.60	56.60	53.60	50.60	47.60	44.60	41.60

		24 percent of the excess over $360 plus—										
$360 and over		72.80	69.80	66.80	63.80	60.80	57.80	54.80	51.80	48.80	45.80	42.80

Table XI, continued

MARRIED Persons — WEEKLY Payroll Period

And the wages are—		And the number of withholding exemptions claimed is—										
At least	But less than	0	1	2	3	4	5	6	7	8	9	10 or more
		The amount of income tax to be withheld shall be—										
$0	$21	$0	$0	$0	$0	$0	$0	$0	$0	$0	$0	$0
21	22	.20	0	0	0	0	0	0	0	0	0	0
22	23	.30	0	0	0	0	0	0	0	0	0	0
23	24	.50	0	0	0	0	0	0	0	0	0	0
24	25	.60	0	0	0	0	0	0	0	0	0	0
25	26	.70	0	0	0	0	0	0	0	0	0	0
26	27	.90	0	0	0	0	0	0	0	0	0	0
27	28	1.00	0	0	0	0	0	0	0	0	0	0
28	29	1.20	0	0	0	0	0	0	0	0	0	0
29	30	1.30	0	0	0	0	0	0	0	0	0	0
30	31	1.40	0	0	0	0	0	0	0	0	0	0
31	32	1.60	0	0	0	0	0	0	0	0	0	0
32	33	1.70	0	0	0	0	0	0	0	0	0	0
33	34	1.90	.10	0	0	0	0	0	0	0	0	0
34	35	2.00	.30	0	0	0	0	0	0	0	0	0
35	36	2.10	.40	0	0	0	0	0	0	0	0	0
36	37	2.30	.50	0	0	0	0	0	0	0	0	0
37	38	2.40	.70	0	0	0	0	0	0	0	0	0
38	39	2.60	.80	0	0	0	0	0	0	0	0	0
39	40	2.70	1.00	0	0	0	0	0	0	0	0	0
40	41	2.80	1.10	0	0	0	0	0	0	0	0	0
41	42	3.00	1.20	0	0	0	0	0	0	0	0	0
42	43	3.10	1.40	0	0	0	0	0	0	0	0	0
43	44	3.30	1.50	0	0	0	0	0	0	0	0	0
44	45	3.50	1.70	0	0	0	0	0	0	0	0	0
45	46	3.60	1.80	0	0	0	0	0	0	0	0	0
46	47	3.80	1.90	.20	0	0	0	0	0	0	0	0
47	48	4.00	2.10	.30	0	0	0	0	0	0	0	0
48	49	4.10	2.20	.50	0	0	0	0	0	0	0	0
49	50	4.30	2.40	.60	0	0	0	0	0	0	0	0
50	51	4.50	2.50	.70	0	0	0	0	0	0	0	0
51	52	4.70	2.60	.90	0	0	0	0	0	0	0	0
52	53	4.80	2.80	1.00	0	0	0	0	0	0	0	0
53	54	5.00	2.90	1.20	0	0	0	0	0	0	0	0
54	55	5.20	3.10	1.30	0	0	0	0	0	0	0	0
55	56	5.30	3.20	1.40	0	0	0	0	0	0	0	0
56	57	5.50	3.40	1.60	0	0	0	0	0	0	0	0
57	58	5.70	3.60	1.70	0	0	0	0	0	0	0	0
58	59	5.80	3.70	1.90	.10	0	0	0	0	0	0	0
59	60	6.00	3.90	2.00	.30	0	0	0	0	0	0	0
60	62	6.30	4.10	2.20	.50	0	0	0	0	0	0	0
62	64	6.60	4.50	2.50	.70	0	0	0	0	0	0	0
64	66	7.00	4.80	2.80	1.00	0	0	0	0	0	0	0
66	68	7.30	5.20	3.10	1.30	0	0	0	0	0	0	0
68	70	7.60	5.50	3.40	1.60	0	0	0	0	0	0	0
70	72	8.00	5.80	3.70	1.90	.10	0	0	0	0	0	0
72	74	8.30	6.20	4.10	2.10	.40	0	0	0	0	0	0
74	76	8.70	6.50	4.40	2.40	.70	0	0	0	0	0	0
76	78	9.00	6.90	4.70	2.70	1.00	0	0	0	0	0	0
78	80	9.30	7.20	5.10	3.00	1.20	0	0	0	0	0	0
80	82	9.60	7.50	5.40	3.30	1.50	0	0	0	0	0	0
82	84	10.00	7.90	5.80	3.60	1.80	0	0	0	0	0	0
84	86	10.30	8.20	6.10	4.00	2.10	.30	0	0	0	0	0
86	88	10.60	8.60	6.40	4.30	2.40	.60	0	0	0	0	0
88	90	10.90	8.90	6.80	4.70	2.60	.90	0	0	0	0	0
90	92	11.20	9.20	7.10	5.00	2.90	1.20	0	0	0	0	0
92	94	11.60	9.60	7.50	5.30	3.20	1.40	0	0	0	0	0
94	96	11.90	9.90	7.80	5.70	3.60	1.70	0	0	0	0	0
96	98	12.20	10.20	8.10	6.00	3.90	2.00	.30	0	0	0	0
98	100	12.50	10.50	8.50	6.40	4.20	2.30	.50	0	0	0	0

Table XI, continued

MARRIED Persons — WEEKLY Payroll Period

And the wages are—		And the number of withholding exemptions claimed is—										
At least	But less than	0	1	2	3	4	5	6	7	8	9	10 or more
		The amount of income tax to be withheld shall be—										
$100	$105	$13.10	$11.10	$9.10	$7.00	$4.80	$2.80	$1.00	$0	$0	$0	$0
105	110	13.90	11.90	9.90	7.80	5.70	3.60	1.70	0	0	0	0
110	115	14.70	12.70	10.70	8.70	6.50	4.40	2.40	.70	0	0	0
115	120	15.50	13.50	11.50	9.50	7.40	5.30	3.10	1.40	0	0	0
120	125	16.30	14.30	12.30	10.30	8.20	6.10	4.00	2.10	.30	0	0
125	130	17.10	15.10	13.10	11.10	9.10	7.00	4.80	2.80	1.00	0	0
130	135	17.90	15.90	13.90	11.90	9.90	7.80	5.70	3.60	1.70	0	0
135	140	18.70	16.70	14.70	12.70	10.70	8.70	6.50	4.40	2.40	.70	0
140	145	19.50	17.50	15.50	13.50	11.50	9.50	7.40	5.30	3.10	1.40	0
145	150	20.30	18.30	16.30	14.30	12.30	10.30	8.20	6.10	4.00	2.10	.30
150	160	21.50	19.50	17.50	15.50	13.50	11.50	9.50	7.40	5.30	3.10	1.40
160	170	23.10	21.10	19.10	17.10	15.10	13.10	11.10	9.10	7.00	4.80	2.80
170	180	25.00	22.70	20.70	18.70	16.70	14.70	12.70	10.70	8.70	6.50	4.40
180	190	26.90	24.50	22.30	20.30	18.30	16.30	14.30	12.30	10.30	8.20	6.10
190	200	28.80	26.40	24.10	21.90	19.90	17.90	15.90	13.90	11.90	9.90	7.80
200	210	30.70	28.30	26.00	23.60	21.50	19.50	17.50	15.50	13.50	11.50	9.50
210	220	32.60	30.20	27.90	25.50	23.10	21.10	19.10	17.10	15.10	13.10	11.10
220	230	34.50	32.10	29.80	27.40	25.00	22.70	20.70	18.70	16.70	14.70	12.70
230	240	36.40	34.00	31.70	29.30	26.90	24.50	22.30	20.30	18.30	16.30	14.30
240	250	38.30	35.90	33.60	31.20	28.80	26.40	24.10	21.90	19.90	17.90	15.90
250	260	40.20	37.80	35.50	33.10	30.70	28.30	26.00	23.60	21.50	19.50	17.50
260	270	42.10	39.70	37.40	35.00	32.60	30.20	27.90	25.50	23.10	21.10	19.10
270	280	44.10	41.60	39.30	36.90	34.50	32.10	29.80	27.40	25.00	22.70	20.70
280	290	46.20	43.60	41.20	38.80	36.40	34.00	31.70	29.30	26.90	24.50	22.30
290	300	48.30	45.70	43.10	40.70	38.30	35.90	33.60	31.20	28.80	26.40	24.10
300	310	50.40	47.80	45.20	42.60	40.20	37.80	35.50	33.10	30.70	28.30	26.00
310	320	52.50	49.90	47.30	44.70	42.10	39.70	37.40	35.00	32.60	30.20	27.90
320	330	54.60	52.00	49.40	46.80	44.10	41.60	39.30	36.90	34.50	32.10	29.80
330	340	56.70	54.10	51.50	48.90	46.20	43.60	41.20	38.80	36.40	34.00	31.70
340	350	58.80	56.20	53.60	51.00	48.30	45.70	43.10	40.70	38.30	35.90	33.60
350	360	60.90	58.30	55.70	53.10	50.40	47.80	45.20	42.60	40.20	37.80	35.50
360	370	63.00	60.40	57.80	55.20	52.50	49.90	47.30	44.70	42.10	39.70	37.40
370	380	65.10	62.50	59.90	57.30	54.60	52.00	49.40	46.80	44.10	41.60	39.30
380	390	67.30	64.60	62.00	59.40	56.70	54.10	51.50	48.90	46.20	43.60	41.20
390	400	69.80	66.70	64.10	61.50	58.80	56.20	53.60	51.00	48.30	45.70	43.10
400	410	72.30	69.10	66.20	63.60	60.90	58.30	55.70	53.10	50.40	47.80	45.20
410	420	74.80	71.60	68.50	65.70	63.00	60.40	57.80	55.20	52.50	49.90	47.30
420	430	77.30	74.10	71.00	67.90	65.10	62.50	59.90	57.30	54.60	52.00	49.40
430	440	79.80	76.60	73.50	70.40	67.30	64.60	62.00	59.40	56.70	54.10	51.50
440	450	82.30	79.10	76.00	72.90	69.80	66.70	64.10	61.50	58.80	56.20	53.60
450	460	84.80	81.60	78.50	75.40	72.30	69.10	66.20	63.60	60.90	58.30	55.70
460	470	87.30	84.10	81.00	77.90	74.80	71.60	68.50	65.70	63.00	60.40	57.80
470	480	89.80	86.60	83.50	80.40	77.30	74.10	71.00	67.90	65.10	62.50	59.90
480	490	92.30	89.10	86.00	82.90	79.80	76.60	73.50	70.40	67.30	64.60	62.00
490	500	94.80	91.60	88.50	85.40	82.30	79.10	76.00	72.90	69.80	66.70	64.10
500	510	97.30	94.10	91.00	87.90	84.80	81.60	78.50	75.40	72.30	69.10	66.20
510	520	99.80	96.60	93.50	90.40	87.30	84.10	81.00	77.90	74.80	71.60	68.50
520	530	102.30	99.10	96.00	92.90	89.80	86.60	83.50	80.40	77 30	74.10	71.00
		25 percent of the excess over $530 plus—										
$530 and over		103.50	100.40	97.30	94.10	91.00	87.90	84.80	81.60	78.50	75.40	72.30

TABLE XII: THE NUMBER OF EACH DAY OF THE YEAR

Day of Month	Jan.	Feb.	Mar.	Apr.	May	June	July	Aug.	Sept.	Oct.	Nov.	Dec.	Day of Month
1	1	32	60	91	121	152	182	213	244	274	305	335	1
2	2	33	61	92	122	153	183	214	245	275	306	336	2
3	3	34	62	93	123	154	184	215	246	276	307	337	3
4	4	35	63	94	124	155	185	216	247	277	308	338	4
5	5	36	64	95	125	156	186	217	248	278	309	339	5
6	6	37	65	96	126	157	187	218	249	279	310	340	6
7	7	38	66	97	127	158	188	219	250	280	311	341	7
8	8	39	67	98	128	159	189	220	251	281	312	342	8
9	9	40	68	99	129	160	190	221	252	282	313	343	9
10	10	41	69	100	130	161	191	222	253	283	314	344	10
11	11	42	70	101	131	162	192	223	254	284	315	345	11
12	12	43	71	102	132	163	193	224	255	285	316	346	12
13	13	44	72	103	133	164	194	225	256	286	317	347	13
14	14	45	73	104	134	165	195	226	257	287	318	348	14
15	15	46	74	105	135	166	196	227	258	288	319	349	15
16	16	47	75	106	136	167	197	228	259	289	320	350	16
17	17	48	76	107	137	168	198	229	260	290	321	351	17
18	18	49	77	108	138	169	199	230	261	291	322	352	18
19	19	50	78	109	139	170	200	231	262	292	323	353	19
20	20	51	79	110	140	171	201	232	263	293	324	354	20
21	21	52	80	111	141	172	202	233	264	294	325	355	21
22	22	53	81	112	142	173	203	234	265	295	326	356	22
23	23	54	82	113	143	174	204	235	266	296	327	357	23
24	24	55	83	114	144	175	205	236	267	297	328	358	24
25	25	56	84	115	145	176	206	237	268	298	329	359	25
26	26	57	85	116	146	177	207	238	269	299	330	360	26
27	27	58	86	117	147	178	208	239	270	300	331	361	27
28	28	59	87	118	148	179	209	240	271	301	332	362	28
29	29		88	119	149	180	210	241	272	302	333	363	29
30	30		89	120	150	181	211	242	273	303	334	364	30
31	31		90		151		212	243		304		365	31

Note: In leap years, after February 28, add 1 to the tabular number.

RATE
1/4%

PERIODS	AMOUNT OF 1 — How $1 left at compound interest will grow.	AMOUNT OF 1 PER PERIOD — How $1 deposited periodically will grow.	SINKING FUND — Periodic deposit that will grow to $1 at future date.	PRESENT WORTH OF 1 — What $1 due in the future is worth today.	PRESENT WORTH OF 1 PER PERIOD — What $1 payable periodically is worth today.	PARTIAL PAYMENT — Annuity worth $1 today. Periodic payment necessary to pay off a loan of $1.	PERIODS
1	1.002 500 0000	1.000 000 0000	1.000 000 0000	.997 506 2344	.997 506 2344	1.002 500 0000	1
2	1.005 006 2500	2.002 500 0000	.499 375 7803	.995 018 6877	1.992 524 9221	.501 875 7803	2
3	1.007 518 7656	3.007 506 2500	.332 501 3872	.992 537 3443	2.985 062 2664	.335 001 3872	3
4	1.010 037 5625	4.015 025 0156	.249 064 4507	.990 062 1889	3.975 124 4553	.251 564 4507	4
5	1.012 562 6564	5.025 062 5782	.199 002 4969	.987 593 2058	4.962 717 6612	.201 502 4969	5
6	1.015 094 0631	6.037 625 2346	.165 628 0344	.985 130 3799	5.947 848 0410	.168 128 0344	6
7	1.017 631 7982	7.052 719 2977	.141 789 2812	.982 673 6957	6.930 521 7367	.144 289 2812	7
8	1.020 175 8777	8.070 351 0959	.123 910 3464	.980 223 1378	7.910 744 8745	.126 410 3464	8
9	1.022 726 3174	9.090 526 9737	.110 004 6238	.977 778 6911	8.888 523 5656	.112 504 6238	9
10	1.025 283 1332	10.113 253 2911	.098 880 1498	.975 340 3402	9.863 863 9058	.101 380 1498	10
11	1.027 846 3411	11.138 536 4243	.089 778 4019	.972 908 0701	10.836 771 9759	.092 278 4019	11
12	1.030 415 9569	12.166 382 7654	.082 193 6988	.970 481 8654	11.807 253 8413	.084 693 6988	12
13	1.032 991 9968	13.196 798 7223	.075 775 9530	.968 061 7111	12.775 315 5524	.078 275 9530	13
14	1.035 574 4768	14.229 790 7191	.070 275 1024	.965 647 5921	13.740 963 1446	.072 775 1024	14
15	1.038 163 4130	15.265 365 1959	.065 507 7679	.963 239 4934	14.704 202 6380	.068 007 7679	15
16	1.040 758 8215	16.303 528 6089	.061 336 4152	.960 837 3999	15.665 040 0379	.063 836 4152	16
17	1.043 360 7186	17.344 287 4304	.057 655 8711	.958 441 2967	16.623 481 3345	.060 155 8711	17
18	1.045 969 1204	18.387 648 1490	.054 384 3341	.956 051 1687	17.579 532 5033	.056 884 3341	18
19	1.048 584 0432	19.433 617 2694	.051 457 2242	.953 667 0012	18.533 199 5045	.053 957 2242	19
20	1.051 205 5033	20.482 201 3126	.048 822 8772	.951 288 7793	19.484 488 2838	.051 322 8772	20
21	1.053 833 5170	21.533 406 8158	.046 439 4700	.948 916 4881	20.433 404 7719	.048 939 4700	21
22	1.056 468 1008	22.587 240 3329	.044 272 7835	.946 550 1128	21.379 954 8847	.046 772 7835	22
23	1.059 109 2711	23.643 708 4337	.042 294 5496	.944 189 6387	22.324 144 5234	.044 794 5496	23
24	1.061 757 0443	24.702 817 7048	.040 481 2120	.941 835 0511	23.265 979 5744	.042 981 2120	24
25	1.064 411 4369	25.764 574 7491	.038 812 9829	.939 486 3352	24.205 465 9096	.041 312 9829	25
26	1.067 072 4655	26.828 986 1859	.037 273 1192	.937 143 4765	25.142 609 3862	.039 773 1192	26
27	1.069 740 1466	27.896 058 6514	.035 847 3580	.934 806 4604	26.077 415 8466	.038 347 3580	27
28	1.072 414 4970	28.965 798 7980	.034 523 4739	.932 475 2722	27.009 891 1188	.037 023 4739	28
29	1.075 095 5332	30.038 213 2950	.033 290 9281	.930 149 8975	27.940 041 0162	.035 790 9281	29
30	1.077 783 2721	31.113 308 8283	.032 140 5867	.927 830 3217	28.867 871 3379	.034 640 5867	30
31	1.080 477 7303	32.191 092 1003	.031 064 4944	.925 516 5303	29.793 387 8682	.033 564 4944	31
32	1.083 178 9246	33.271 569 8306	.030 055 6903	.923 208 5091	30.716 596 3773	.032 555 6903	32
33	1.085 886 8719	34.354 748 7551	.029 108 0574	.920 906 2434	31.637 502 6207	.031 608 0574	33
34	1.088 601 5891	35.440 635 6270	.028 216 1982	.918 609 7192	32.556 112 3399	.030 716 1982	34
35	1.091 323 0930	36.529 237 2161	.027 375 3221	.916 318 9218	33.472 431 2617	.029 875 3221	35
36	1.094 051 4008	37.620 560 3091	.026 581 2096	.914 033 8373	34.386 465 0990	.029 081 2096	36
37	1.096 786 5293	38.714 611 7099	.025 830 0408	.911 754 4511	35.298 219 5501	.028 330 0408	37
38	1.099 528 4956	39.811 398 2392	.025 118 4345	.909 480 7493	36.207 700 2993	.027 618 4345	38
39	1.102 277 3168	40.910 926 7348	.024 443 3475	.907 212 7175	37.114 913 0168	.026 943 3475	39
40	1.105 033 0101	42.013 204 0516	.023 802 0409	.904 950 3416	38.019 863 3584	.026 302 0409	40
41	1.107 795 5927	43.118 237 0618	.023 192 0428	.902 693 6076	38.922 556 9660	.025 692 0428	41
42	1.110 565 0816	44.226 032 6544	.022 611 1170	.900 442 5013	39.822 999 4673	.025 111 1170	42
43	1.113 341 4943	45.336 597 7360	.022 057 2352	.898 197 0088	40.721 196 4761	.024 557 2352	43
44	1.116 124 8481	46.449 939 2304	.021 528 5535	.895 957 1160	41.617 153 5921	.024 028 5535	44
45	1.118 915 1602	47.566 064 0785	.021 023 3918	.893 722 8090	42.510 876 4011	.023 523 3918	45
46	1.121 712 4481	48.684 979 2387	.020 540 2162	.891 494 0738	43.402 370 4750	.023 040 2162	46
47	1.124 516 7292	49.806 691 6868	.020 077 6234	.889 270 8966	44.291 641 3715	.022 577 6234	47
48	1.127 328 0210	50.931 208 4160	.019 634 3270	.887 053 2634	45.178 694 6349	.022 134 3270	48
49	1.130 146 3411	52.058 536 4370	.019 209 1455	.884 841 1605	46.063 535 7955	.021 709 1455	49
50	1.132 971 7069	53.188 682 7781	.018 800 9920	.882 634 5741	46.946 170 3695	.021 300 9920	50
51	1.135 804 1362	54.321 654 4851	.018 408 8649	.880 433 4904	47.826 603 8599	.020 908 8649	51
52	1.138 643 6466	55.457 458 6213	.018 031 8396	.878 237 8956	48.704 841 7555	.020 531 8396	52
53	1.141 490 2557	56.596 102 2678	.017 669 0613	.876 047 7762	49.580 889 5317	.020 169 0613	53
54	1.144 343 9813	57.737 592 5235	.017 319 7384	.873 863 1184	50.454 752 6500	.019 819 7384	54
55	1.147 204 8413	58.881 936 5048	.016 983 1371	.871 683 9086	51.326 436 5586	.019 483 1371	55
56	1.150 072 8534	60.029 141 3461	.016 658 5758	.869 510 1333	52.195 946 6919	.019 158 5758	56
57	1.152 948 0355	61.179 214 1994	.016 345 4208	.867 341 7788	53.063 288 4707	.018 845 4208	57
58	1.155 830 4056	62.332 162 2349	.016 043 0822	.865 178 8317	53.928 467 3025	.018 543 0822	58
59	1.158 719 9816	63.487 992 6405	.015 751 0099	.863 021 2795	54.791 488 5810	.018 251 0099	59
60	1.161 616 7816	64.646 712 6221	.015 468 6907	.860 869 1058	55.652 357 6868	.017 968 6907	60
61	1.164 520 8235	65.808 329 4037	.015 195 6448	.858 722 3000	56.511 079 9868	.017 695 6448	61
62	1.167 432 1256	66.972 850 2272	.014 931 4237	.856 580 8479	57.367 660 8348	.017 431 4237	62
63	1.170 350 7059	68.140 282 3527	.014 675 6069	.854 444 7361	58.222 105 5708	.017 175 6069	63
64	1.173 276 5826	69.310 633 0586	.014 427 8007	.852 313 9512	59.074 419 5220	.016 927 8007	64
65	1.176 209 7741	70.483 909 6413	.014 187 6352	.850 188 4800	59.924 608 0020	.016 687 6352	65
66	1.179 150 2985	71.660 119 4154	.013 954 7632	.848 068 3092	60.772 676 3112	.016 454 7632	66
67	1.182 098 1743	72.839 269 7139	.013 728 8581	.845 953 4257	61.618 629 7369	.016 228 8581	67
68	1.185 053 4197	74.021 367 8882	.013 509 6125	.843 843 8161	62.462 473 5530	.016 009 6125	68
69	1.188 016 0533	75.206 421 3079	.013 296 7369	.841 739 4676	63.304 213 0205	.015 796 7369	69
70	1.190 986 0934	76.394 437 3612	.013 089 9583	.839 640 3665	64.143 853 3870	.015 589 9583	70
71	1.193 963 5586	77.585 423 4546	.012 889 0190	.837 546 5003	64.981 399 8873	.015 389 0190	71
72	1.196 948 4675	78.779 387 0132	.012 693 6758	.835 457 8556	65.816 857 7429	.015 193 6758	72
73	1.199 940 8387	79.976 335 4808	.012 503 6987	.833 374 4196	66.650 232 1625	.015 003 6987	73
74	1.202 940 6908	81.176 276 3195	.012 318 8701	.831 296 1791	67.481 528 3417	.014 818 8701	74
75	1.205 948 0425	82.379 217 0103	.012 138 9840	.829 223 1213	68.310 751 4630	.014 638 9840	75
76	1.208 962 9126	83.585 165 0528	.011 963 8455	.827 155 2333	69.137 906 6963	.014 463 8455	76
77	1.211 985 3199	84.794 127 9654	.011 793 2695	.825 092 5020	69.962 999 1983	.014 293 2695	77
78	1.215 015 2832	86.006 113 2853	.011 627 0805	.823 034 9147	70.786 034 1130	.014 127 0805	78
79	1.218 052 8214	87.221 128 5685	.011 465 1119	.820 982 4586	71.607 016 5716	.013 965 1119	79
80	1.221 097 9535	88.439 181 3900	.011 307 2055	.818 935 1208	72.425 951 6923	.013 807 2055	80
81	1.224 150 6984	89.660 279 3434	.011 153 2108	.816 892 8885	73.242 844 5809	.013 653 2108	81
82	1.227 211 0751	90.884 430 0418	.011 002 9848	.814 855 7492	74.057 700 3300	.013 502 9848	82
83	1.230 279 1028	92.111 641 1169	.010 856 3911	.812 823 6900	74.870 524 0200	.013 356 3911	83
84	1.233 354 8005	93.341 920 2197	.010 713 3001	.810 796 6982	75.681 320 7182	.013 213 3001	84
85	1.236 438 1876	94.575 275 0202	.010 573 5881	.808 774 7613	76.490 095 4795	.013 073 5881	85
86	1.239 529 2830	95.811 713 2078	.010 437 1372	.806 757 8666	77.296 853 3461	.012 937 1372	86
87	1.242 628 1062	97.051 242 4908	.010 303 8351	.804 746 0016	78.101 599 3478	.012 803 8351	87
88	1.245 734 6765	98.293 870 5970	.010 173 5743	.802 739 1537	78.904 338 5015	.012 673 5743	88
89	1.248 849 0132	99.539 605 2735	.010 046 2524	.800 737 3105	79.705 075 8120	.012 546 2524	89
90	1.251 971 1357	100.788 454 2867	.009 921 7714	.798 740 4593	80.503 816 2713	.012 421 7714	90
91	1.255 101 0636	102.040 425 4224	.009 800 0375	.796 748 5879	81.300 564 8592	.012 300 0375	91
92	1.258 238 8162	103.295 526 4860	.009 680 9614	.794 761 6836	82.095 326 5428	.012 180 9614	92
93	1.261 384 4133	104.553 765 3022	.009 564 4571	.792 779 7343	82.888 106 2771	.012 064 4571	93
94	1.264 537 8743	105.815 149 7155	.009 450 4426	.790 802 7275	83.678 909 0046	.011 950 4426	94
95	1.267 699 2190	107.079 687 5898	.009 338 8393	.788 830 6509	84.467 739 6555	.011 838 8393	95
96	1.270 868 4670	108.347 386 8087	.009 229 5719	.786 863 4921	85.254 603 1476	.011 729 5719	96
97	1.274 045 6382	109.618 255 2757	.009 122 5681	.784 901 2390	86.039 504 3866	.011 622 5681	97
98	1.277 230 7523	110.892 300 9139	.009 017 7586	.782 943 8793	86.822 448 2660	.011 517 7586	98
99	1.280 423 8292	112.169 531 6662	.008 915 0769	.780 991 4008	87.603 439 6668	.011 415 0769	99
100	1.283 624 8887	113.449 955 4954	.008 814 4592	.779 043 7914	88.382 483 4581	.011 314 4592	100

RATE 1/3%

P E R I O D S	AMOUNT OF 1 — How $1 left at compound interest will grow.	AMOUNT OF 1 PER PERIOD — How $1 deposited periodically will grow.	SINKING FUND — Periodic deposit that will grow to $1 at future date.	PRESENT WORTH OF 1 — What $1 due in the future is worth today.	PRESENT WORTH OF 1 PER PERIOD — What $1 payable periodically is worth today.	PARTIAL PAYMENT — Annuity worth $1 today. Periodic payment necessary to pay off a loan of $1.	P E R I O D S
1	1.003 333 3333	1.000 000 0000	1.000 000 0000	.996 677 7409	.996 677 7409	1.003 333 3333	1
2	1.006 677 7778	2.003 333 3333	.499 168 0532	.993 366 5191	1.990 044 2600	.502 501 3866	2
3	1.010 033 3704	3.010 011 1111	.332 224 6872	.990 066 2981	2.980 110 5581	.335 558 0206	3
4	1.013 400 1483	4.020 044 4815	.248 753 4664	.986 777 0413	3.966 887 5995	.252 086 7998	4
5	1.016 778 1488	5.033 444 6298	.198 671 1037	.983 498 7123	4.950 386 3118	.202 004 4370	5
6	1.020 167 4093	6.050 222 7785	.165 283 7405	.980 231 2747	5.930 617 5865	.168 616 5033	6
7	1.023 567 9673	7.070 390 1878	.141 434 9100	.976 974 6924	6.907 592 2789	.144 768 2434	7
8	1.026 979 8605	8.093 958 1551	.123 548 9461	.973 728 9293	7.881 321 2082	.126 882 2795	8
9	1.030 403 1267	9.120 938 0156	.109 637 8463	.970 493 9445	8.851 815 1577	.112 971 1796	9
10	1.033 837 8038	10.151 341 1423	.098 509 1513	.967 269 7171	9.819 084 8747	.101 842 4846	10
11	1.037 283 9298	11.185 178 9461	.089 404 0234	.964 056 1964	10.783 141 0712	.092 737 3567	11
12	1.040 741 5429	12.222 462 8759	.081 816 5709	.960 853 3519	11.743 994 4231	.085 149 9042	12
13	1.044 210 6814	13.263 204 4189	.075 396 5609	.957 661 1481	12.701 655 5712	.078 729 8943	13
14	1.047 691 3837	14.307 415 1003	.069 893 8273	.954 479 5496	13.656 135 1208	.073 227 1606	14
15	1.051 183 6883	15.355 106 4839	.065 124 9147	.951 308 5212	14.607 443 6420	.068 458 2480	15
16	1.054 687 6339	16.406 290 1722	.060 952 2317	.948 148 0278	15.555 591 6698	.064 285 5650	16
17	1.058 203 2594	17.460 977 8061	.057 270 5613	.944 998 0343	16.500 589 7041	.060 603 8946	17
18	1.061 730 6036	18.519 181 0655	.053 998 0681	.941 858 5060	17.442 448 2100	.057 331 4014	18
19	1.065 269 7056	19.580 911 6690	.051 070 1451	.938 729 4079	18.381 177 6180	.054 403 4784	19
20	1.068 820 6046	20.646 181 3746	.048 435 1068	.935 610 7056	19.316 788 3236	.051 768 4401	20
21	1.072 383 3399	21.715 001 9792	.046 051 1125	.932 502 3644	20.249 290 6879	.049 384 4459	21
22	1.075 957 9511	22.787 385 3191	.043 883 9290	.929 404 3499	21.178 695 0378	.047 217 2624	22
23	1.079 544 4776	23.863 343 2702	.041 905 2766	.926 316 6278	22.105 011 6656	.045 238 6099	23
24	1.083 142 9592	24.942 887 7477	.040 091 5888	.923 239 1639	23.028 250 8295	.043 424 9222	24
25	1.086 753 4357	26.026 030 7069	.038 423 0700	.920 171 9242	23.948 422 7537	.041 756 4033	25
26	1.090 375 9471	27.112 784 1426	.036 882 9698	.917 114 8746	24.865 537 6282	.040 216 3032	26
27	1.094 010 5336	28.203 160 0897	.035 457 0196	.914 067 9813	25.779 605 6095	.038 790 3529	27
28	1.097 657 2354	29.297 170 6233	.034 132 9889	.911 031 2106	26.690 636 8201	.037 466 3222	28
29	1.101 316 0929	30.394 827 8588	.032 900 3344	.908 004 5288	27.598 641 3490	.036 233 6677	29
30	1.104 987 1465	31.496 143 9516	.031 749 9184	.904 987 9025	28.503 629 2515	.035 083 2517	30
31	1.108 670 4370	32.601 131 0981	.030 673 7824	.901 981 2982	29.405 610 5496	.034 007 1157	31
32	1.112 366 0021	33.709 801 5351	.029 666 9625	.898 984 6826	30.304 595 2322	.032 998 2959	32
33	1.116 073 8918	34.822 167 5402	.028 717 3393	.895 998 0225	31.200 593 2547	.032 050 6726	33
34	1.119 794 1381	35.938 241 4320	.027 825 5129	.893 021 2849	32.093 614 5395	.031 158 8462	34
35	1.123 526 7852	37.058 035 5701	.026 984 7007	.890 054 4367	32.983 668 9763	.030 318 0341	35
36	1.127 271 8745	38.181 562 3554	.026 190 6517	.887 097 4453	33.870 766 4215	.029 523 9850	36
37	1.131 029 4474	39.308 834 2299	.025 439 5741	.884 150 2777	34.754 916 6992	.028 772 9074	37
38	1.134 799 5456	40.439 863 6773	.024 728 0754	.881 212 9013	35.636 129 6005	.028 061 4088	38
39	1.138 582 2107	41.574 663 2229	.024 053 1113	.878 285 2837	36.514 414 8843	.027 386 4446	39
40	1.142 377 4848	42.713 245 4337	.023 411 9414	.875 367 3924	37.389 782 2767	.026 745 2748	40
41	1.146 185 4097	43.855 622 9184	.022 802 0932	.872 459 1951	38.262 241 4718	.026 135 4265	41
42	1.150 006 0278	45.001 808 3282	.022 221 3293	.869 560 6596	39.131 802 1313	.025 554 6626	42
43	1.153 839 3812	46.151 814 3559	.021 667 6205	.866 671 7537	39.998 473 8850	.025 000 9539	43
44	1.157 685 5125	47.305 653 7371	.021 139 1223	.863 792 4456	40.862 266 3306	.024 472 4556	44
45	1.161 544 4642	48.463 339 2496	.020 634 1539	.860 922 7032	41.723 189 0338	.023 967 4872	45
46	1.165 416 2790	49.624 883 7137	.020 151 1807	.858 062 4449	42.581 251 5287	.023 484 5141	46
47	1.169 301 0000	50.790 299 9928	.019 688 7988	.855 211 7889	43.436 463 3177	.023 022 1322	47
48	1.173 198 6700	51.959 600 9928	.019 245 7213	.852 370 5538	44.288 833 8714	.022 579 0546	48
49	1.177 109 3322	53.132 799 6627	.018 820 7662	.849 538 7579	45.138 372 6293	.022 154 0995	49
50	1.181 033 0300	54.309 908 9949	.018 412 8462	.846 716 3700	45.985 088 9993	.021 746 1795	50
51	1.184 969 8067	55.490 942 0249	.018 020 9592	.843 903 3588	46.828 992 3582	.021 354 2925	51
52	1.188 919 7061	56.675 911 8317	.017 644 1802	.841 099 6923	47.670 092 0513	.020 977 5135	52
53	1.192 882 7718	57.864 831 5378	.017 281 6540	.838 305 3420	48.508 397 3933	.020 614 9874	53
54	1.196 859 0477	59.057 714 3096	.016 932 5889	.835 520 2744	49.343 917 6678	.020 265 9223	54
55	1.200 848 5779	60.254 573 3573	.016 596 2506	.832 744 4596	50.176 662 1274	.019 929 5839	55
56	1.204 851 4065	61.455 421 9351	.016 271 9573	.829 977 8667	51.006 639 9940	.019 605 2906	56
57	1.208 867 5778	62.660 273 3416	.015 959 0750	.827 220 4651	51.833 860 4592	.019 292 4083	57
58	1.212 897 1364	63.869 140 9194	.015 657 0135	.824 472 2244	52.658 332 6836	.018 990 3468	58
59	1.216 940 1269	65.082 038 0558	.015 365 2226	.821 733 1140	53.480 065 7976	.018 698 5559	59
60	1.220 996 5939	66.298 978 1826	.015 083 1887	.819 003 1037	54.299 068 9012	.018 416 5221	60
61	1.225 066 5826	67.519 974 7766	.014 810 4321	.816 282 1631	55.115 351 0644	.018 143 7654	61
62	1.229 150 1379	68.745 041 3592	.014 546 5037	.813 570 2622	55.928 921 3266	.017 879 8371	62
63	1.233 247 3050	69.974 191 4970	.014 290 9833	.810 867 3710	56.739 788 6976	.017 624 3166	63
64	1.237 358 1293	71.207 438 8020	.014 043 4926	.808 173 4595	57.547 962 1571	.017 376 8099	64
65	1.241 482 6564	72.444 796 9314	.013 803 6138	.805 488 4978	58.353 450 6549	.017 136 9472	65
66	1.245 620 9320	73.686 279 5878	.013 571 0475	.802 812 4563	59.156 263 1112	.016 904 3808	66
67	1.249 773 0017	74.931 900 5198	.013 345 4509	.800 145 3053	59.956 408 4165	.016 678 7842	67
68	1.253 938 9117	76.181 673 5215	.013 126 5166	.797 487 0152	60.753 895 4317	.016 459 8499	68
69	1.258 118 7081	77.435 612 4332	.012 913 9548	.794 837 5567	61.548 732 9884	.016 247 2881	69
70	1.262 312 4371	78.693 731 1413	.012 707 4925	.792 196 9004	62.340 929 8888	.016 040 8259	70
71	1.266 520 1453	79.956 043 5785	.012 506 8720	.789 565 0170	63.130 494 9058	.015 840 2053	71
72	1.270 741 8791	81.222 563 7237	.012 311 8497	.786 941 8774	63.917 436 7831	.015 645 1831	72
73	1.274 977 6853	82.493 305 6028	.012 122 1958	.784 327 4525	64.701 764 2357	.015 455 5291	73
74	1.279 227 6110	83.768 283 2882	.011 937 6924	.781 721 7135	65.483 485 9492	.015 271 0257	74
75	1.283 491 7030	85.047 510 8991	.011 758 1337	.779 124 6314	66.262 610 5806	.015 091 4670	75
76	1.287 770 0087	86.331 002 6021	.011 583 3243	.776 536 1775	67.039 146 7581	.014 916 6576	76
77	1.292 062 5754	87.618 772 6108	.011 413 0793	.773 956 3231	67.813 103 0811	.014 746 4126	77
78	1.296 369 4506	88.910 835 1862	.011 247 2231	.771 385 0396	68.584 488 1207	.014 580 5564	78
79	1.300 690 6821	90.207 204 6368	.011 085 5891	.768 822 2986	69.353 310 4193	.014 418 9224	79
80	1.305 026 3177	91.507 895 3189	.010 928 0188	.766 268 0717	70.119 578 4910	.014 261 3521	80
81	1.309 376 4055	92.812 921 6366	.010 774 3618	.763 722 3306	70.883 300 8216	.014 107 6952	81
82	1.313 740 9935	94.122 298 0421	.010 624 4750	.761 185 0471	71.644 485 8687	.013 957 8083	82
83	1.318 120 1301	95.436 039 0356	.010 478 2220	.758 656 1931	72.403 142 0619	.013 811 5553	83
84	1.322 513 8639	96.754 159 1657	.010 335 4730	.756 135 7407	73.159 277 8025	.013 668 8063	84
85	1.326 922 2434	98.076 673 0296	.010 196 1466	.753 623 6618	73.912 901 4643	.013 529 4378	85
86	1.331 345 3176	99.403 595 2730	.010 059 9983	.751 119 9287	74.664 021 3930	.013 393 3316	86
87	1.335 783 1353	100.734 940 5906	.009 927 0421	.748 624 5136	75.412 645 9066	.013 260 3755	87
88	1.340 235 7458	102.070 723 7259	.009 797 1285	.746 137 3890	76.158 783 2956	.013 130 4619	88
89	1.344 703 1982	103.410 959 4716	.009 670 1549	.743 658 5273	76.902 441 8229	.013 003 4883	89
90	1.349 185 5422	104.755 662 6699	.009 546 0233	.741 187 9009	77.643 629 7238	.012 879 3567	90
91	1.353 682 8274	106.104 848 2121	.009 424 6400	.738 725 4684	78.382 355 2065	.012 757 9734	91
92	1.358 195 1035	107.458 531 0395	.009 305 9154	.736 271 2452	79.118 626 4516	.012 639 2487	92
93	1.362 722 4205	108.816 726 1429	.009 189 7637	.733 825 1613	79.852 451 6129	.012 523 0970	93
94	1.367 264 8285	110.179 448 5634	.009 076 1028	.731 387 2039	80.583 838 8169	.012 409 4361	94
95	1.371 822 3780	111.546 713 3920	.008 964 8544	.728 957 3641	81.312 796 1630	.012 298 1873	95
96	1.376 395 1192	112.918 535 7699	.008 855 9420	.726 535 5609	82.039 331 7239	.012 189 2753	96
97	1.380 983 1030	114.294 930 8892	.008 749 2944	.724 121 8215	82.763 453 5454	.012 082 6277	97
98	1.385 586 3800	115.675 913 9921	.008 644 8420	.721 716 1012	83.485 169 6466	.011 978 1753	98
99	1.390 205 0012	117.061 500 3721	.008 542 5182	.719 318 3733	84.204 488 0199	.011 875 8516	99
100	1.394 839 0179	118.451 705 3733	.008 442 2592	.716 928 6112	84.921 416 6311	.011 775 5925	100

RATE
5/12%

PERIODS	XIII COMPOUND AMOUNT — AMOUNT OF 1 (How $1 left at compound interest will grow.)	XIV AMOUNT OF ANUITY — AMOUNT OF 1 PER PERIOD (How $1 deposited periodically will grow.)	XV SINKING FUND — SINKING FUND (Periodic deposit that will grow to $1 at future date.)	XVI PRESENT VALUE — PRESENT WORTH OF 1 (What $1 due in the future is worth today.)	XVII PRESENT VALUE OF ANNUITY — PRESENT WORTH OF 1 PER PERIOD (What $1 payable periodically is worth today.)	XVIII AMORTIZATION — PARTIAL PAYMENT (Annuity worth $1 today. Periodic payment necessary to pay off a loan of $1.)	PERIODS
1	1.004 166 6667	1.000 000 0000	1.000 000 0000	.995 850 6224	.995 850 6224	1.004 166 6667	1
2	1.008 350 6944	2.004 166 6667	.498 960 4990	.991 718 4621	1.987 569 0846	.503 127 1656	2
3	1.012 552 1557	3.012 517 3611	.331 948 2944	.987 603 4478	2.975 172 5323	.336 114 9611	3
4	1.016 771 1230	4.025 069 5168	.248 442 9140	.983 505 5082	3.958 678 0405	.252 609 5807	4
5	1.021 007 6693	5.041 840 6398	.198 340 2633	.979 424 5724	4.938 102 6129	.202 506 9300	5
6	1.025 261 8680	6.062 848 3091	.164 938 9774	.975 360 5701	5.913 463 1830	.169 105 6440	6
7	1.029 533 7924	7.088 110 1771	.141 081 3285	.971 313 4308	6.884 776 6138	.145 247 9951	7
8	1.033 823 5165	8.117 643 9695	.123 188 4527	.967 283 0846	7.852 059 6984	.127 355 1193	8
9	1.038 131 1145	9.151 467 4860	.109 272 0923	.963 269 6618	8.815 329 1602	.113 438 7590	9
10	1.042 456 6608	10.189 598 6005	.098 139 2927	.959 272 4931	9.774 601 6533	.102 305 9594	10
11	1.046 800 2303	11.232 055 2614	.089 030 9010	.955 292 1093	10.729 893 7626	.093 197 5677	11
12	1.051 161 8979	12.278 855 4916	.081 440 8151	.951 328 2446	11.681 222 0043	.085 607 4818	12
13	1.055 541 7919	13.330 017 3895	.075 018 6568	.947 380 8216	12.628 602 8259	.079 185 3235	13
14	1.059 939 8297	14.385 559 1286	.069 514 1559	.943 449 7808	13.572 052 6067	.073 680 8226	14
15	1.064 356 2457	15.445 498 9583	.064 743 7809	.939 535 0514	14.511 587 6581	.068 910 4475	15
16	1.068 791 0633	16.509 855 2040	.060 569 8831	.935 636 5657	15.447 224 2238	.064 736 5498	16
17	1.073 246 3594	17.578 646 2673	.056 887 2019	.931 754 2563	16.378 978 4802	.061 053 8686	17
18	1.077 716 2109	18.651 892 6268	.053 613 8679	.927 888 0561	17.306 866 5363	.057 780 5346	18
19	1.082 206 6952	19.729 608 8377	.050 685 2472	.924 037 8982	18.230 904 4344	.054 851 9139	19
20	1.086 715 8897	20.811 813 5329	.048 049 6329	.920 203 7160	19.151 108 1505	.052 216 2996	20
21	1.091 243 8726	21.898 529 4226	.045 665 1669	.916 385 4434	20.067 493 5938	.049 831 8335	21
22	1.095 790 7221	22.989 773 2952	.043 497 6016	.912 583 0141	20.980 076 6080	.047 664 2683	22
23	1.100 356 5167	24.085 564 0173	.041 518 6457	.908 796 3626	21.888 872 9706	.045 685 3124	23
24	1.104 941 3356	25.185 920 5340	.039 704 7291	.905 025 4234	22.793 898 3940	.043 871 3897	24
25	1.109 545 2578	26.290 861 8696	.038 036 0296	.901 270 1311	23.695 168 5251	.042 202 6963	25
26	1.114 168 3630	27.400 407 1273	.036 495 8081	.897 530 4211	24.592 698 9462	.040 662 4748	26
27	1.118 810 7312	28.514 575 4904	.035 069 7839	.893 806 2284	25.486 505 1746	.039 236 4506	27
28	1.123 472 4426	29.633 386 2216	.033 745 7215	.890 097 4889	26.376 602 6635	.037 912 3882	28
29	1.128 153 5778	30.756 858 6642	.032 513 0733	.886 404 1383	27.263 006 8018	.036 679 7400	29
30	1.132 854 2177	31.885 012 2419	.031 362 6977	.882 726 1129	28.145 732 9147	.035 529 3644	30
31	1.137 574 4436	33.017 866 4596	.030 286 6329	.879 063 3489	29.024 796 2636	.034 453 2995	31
32	1.142 314 3371	34.155 440 9032	.029 277 9122	.875 415 7833	29.900 212 0467	.033 444 5789	32
33	1.147 073 9802	35.297 755 2403	.028 330 4135	.871 783 3525	30.771 995 3992	.032 497 0801	33
34	1.151 853 4551	36.444 829 2205	.027 438 7347	.868 165 9942	31.640 161 3934	.031 605 4014	34
35	1.156 652 8445	37.596 682 6756	.026 598 0913	.864 563 6457	32.504 725 0391	.030 764 7580	35
36	1.161 472 2313	38.753 335 5200	.025 804 2304	.860 976 2447	33.365 701 2837	.029 970 8971	36
37	1.166 311 6990	39.914 807 7514	.025 053 3588	.857 403 7291	34.223 105 0129	.029 220 0255	37
38	1.171 171 3310	41.081 119 4503	.024 342 0825	.853 846 0373	35.076 951 0501	.028 508 7492	38
39	1.176 051 2116	42.252 290 7814	.023 667 3558	.850 303 1077	35.927 254 1578	.027 834 0225	39
40	1.180 951 4250	43.428 341 9930	.023 026 4374	.846 774 8790	36.774 029 0368	.027 193 1041	40
41	1.185 872 0559	44.609 293 4179	.022 416 8536	.843 261 2903	37.617 290 3271	.026 583 5203	41
42	1.190 813 1895	45.795 165 4738	.021 836 3661	.839 762 2808	38.457 052 6079	.026 003 0328	42
43	1.195 774 9111	46.985 978 6633	.021 282 9450	.836 277 7900	39.293 330 3979	.025 449 6117	43
44	1.200 757 3066	48.181 753 5744	.020 754 7448	.832 807 7577	40.126 138 1556	.024 921 4115	44
45	1.205 760 4620	49.382 510 8810	.020 250 0841	.829 352 1238	40.955 490 2795	.024 416 7508	45
46	1.210 784 4639	50.588 271 3430	.019 767 4278	.825 910 8287	41.781 401 1082	.023 934 0944	46
47	1.215 829 3992	51.799 055 8069	.019 305 3712	.822 483 8128	42.603 884 9210	.023 472 0379	47
48	1.220 895 3550	53.014 885 2061	.018 862 6269	.819 071 0169	43.422 955 9379	.023 029 2936	48
49	1.225 982 4190	54.235 780 5611	.018 438 0125	.815 672 3820	44.238 628 3199	.022 604 6792	49
50	1.231 090 6791	55.461 762 9801	.018 030 4402	.812 287 8493	45.050 916 1692	.022 197 1069	50
51	1.236 220 2236	56.692 853 6592	.017 638 9075	.808 917 3603	45.859 833 5295	.021 805 5741	51
52	1.241 371 1412	57.929 073 8828	.017 262 4890	.805 560 8567	46.665 394 3862	.021 429 1557	52
53	1.246 543 5209	59.170 445 0240	.016 900 3292	.802 218 2806	47.467 612 6668	.021 066 9959	53
54	1.251 737 4523	60.416 988 5449	.016 551 6360	.798 889 5740	48.266 502 2408	.020 718 3026	54
55	1.256 953 0250	61.668 725 9972	.016 215 6747	.795 574 6795	49.062 076 9203	.020 382 3414	55
56	1.262 190 3293	62.925 679 0222	.015 891 7634	.792 273 5397	49.854 350 4600	.020 058 4300	56
57	1.267 449 4556	64.187 869 3514	.015 579 2677	.788 986 0977	50.643 336 5577	.019 745 9344	57
58	1.272 730 4950	65.455 318 8071	.015 277 5973	.785 712 2964	51.429 048 8542	.019 444 2639	58
59	1.278 033 5388	66.728 049 3021	.014 986 2016	.782 452 0794	52.211 500 9336	.019 152 8683	59
60	1.283 358 6785	68.006 082 8408	.014 704 5670	.779 205 3903	52.990 706 3239	.018 871 2336	60
61	1.288 706 0063	69.289 441 5193	.014 432 2133	.775 972 1729	53.766 678 4969	.018 598 8800	61
62	1.294 075 6147	70.578 147 5257	.014 168 4915	.772 752 3714	54.539 430 8682	.018 335 3582	62
63	1.299 467 5964	71.872 223 1404	.013 913 5810	.769 545 9300	55.308 976 7982	.018 080 2477	63
64	1.304 882 0447	73.171 690 7368	.013 666 4875	.766 352 7934	56.075 329 5916	.017 833 1542	64
65	1.310 319 0533	74.476 572 7815	.013 427 0410	.763 172 9063	56.838 502 4979	.017 593 7077	65
66	1.315 778 7160	75.786 891 8348	.013 194 8939	.760 006 2137	57.598 508 7116	.017 361 5606	66
67	1.321 261 1273	77.102 670 5508	.012 969 7194	.756 852 6605	58.355 361 3721	.017 136 3860	67
68	1.326 766 3820	78.423 931 6781	.012 751 2097	.753 712 1935	59.109 073 5660	.016 917 8764	68
69	1.332 294 5753	79.750 698 0600	.012 539 0522	.750 584 7570	59.859 658 3230	.016 705 7194	69
70	1.337 845 8026	81.082 992 6353	.012 333 0426	.747 470 2974	60.607 128 6204	.016 499 7092	70
71	1.343 420 1602	82.420 838 4379	.012 132 8540	.744 368 7609	61.351 497 3813	.016 299 5207	71
72	1.349 017 7442	83.764 258 5981	.011 938 2660	.741 280 0939	62.092 777 4752	.016 104 9327	72
73	1.354 638 6514	85.113 276 3423	.011 749 0484	.738 204 2428	62.830 981 7180	.015 915 7150	73
74	1.360 282 9791	86.467 914 9937	.011 564 9834	.735 141 1547	63.566 122 8727	.015 731 6500	74
75	1.365 950 8249	87.828 197 9728	.011 385 8649	.732 090 7765	64.298 213 6492	.015 552 5316	75
76	1.371 642 2867	89.194 148 7977	.011 211 4978	.729 053 0554	65.027 266 7046	.015 378 1644	76
77	1.377 357 4629	90.565 791 0844	.011 041 6967	.726 027 9390	65.753 294 6435	.015 208 3634	77
78	1.383 096 4523	91.943 148 5472	.010 876 2862	.723 015 3749	66.476 310 0185	.015 042 9529	78
79	1.388 859 3542	93.326 244 9995	.010 715 0995	.720 015 3111	67.196 325 3296	.014 881 7662	79
80	1.394 646 2681	94.715 104 3537	.010 557 9781	.717 027 6957	67.913 353 0253	.014 724 6448	80
81	1.400 457 2943	96.109 750 6218	.010 404 7716	.714 052 4771	68.627 405 5024	.014 571 4382	81
82	1.406 292 5330	97.510 207 9161	.010 255 3366	.711 089 6037	69.338 495 1061	.014 422 0032	82
83	1.412 152 0852	98.916 500 4490	.010 109 5368	.708 139 0245	70.046 634 1306	.014 276 2035	83
84	1.418 036 0522	100.328 652 5342	.009 967 2424	.705 200 6883	70.751 834 8188	.014 133 9091	84
85	1.423 944 5358	101.746 688 5865	.009 828 3297	.702 274 5443	71.454 109 3632	.013 994 9964	85
86	1.429 877 6380	103.170 633 1223	.009 692 6807	.699 360 5421	72.153 469 9052	.013 859 3473	86
87	1.435 835 4615	104.600 510 7603	.009 560 1828	.696 458 8311	72.849 928 5363	.013 726 8494	87
88	1.441 818 1093	106.036 346 2218	.009 430 7286	.693 568 7613	73.543 497 2976	.013 597 3952	88
89	1.447 825 6847	107.478 164 3310	.009 304 2155	.690 690 8826	74.234 188 1802	.013 470 8821	89
90	1.453 858 2917	108.925 990 0157	.009 180 5454	.687 824 9453	74.922 013 1255	.013 347 2121	90
91	1.459 916 0346	110.379 848 3075	.009 059 6247	.684 970 8999	75.606 984 0254	.013 226 2914	91
92	1.465 999 0181	111.839 764 3421	.008 941 3636	.682 128 6970	76.289 112 7224	.013 108 0303	92
93	1.472 107 3473	113.305 763 3602	.008 825 6764	.679 298 2875	76.968 411 0099	.012 992 3431	93
94	1.478 241 1279	114.777 870 7075	.008 712 4808	.676 479 6224	77.644 890 6322	.012 879 1475	94
95	1.484 400 4660	116.256 111 8355	.008 601 6983	.673 672 6530	78.318 563 2852	.012 768 3650	95
96	1.490 585 4679	117.740 512 3014	.008 493 2533	.670 877 3308	78.989 440 6159	.012 659 9200	96
97	1.496 796 2407	119.231 097 7694	.008 387 0737	.668 093 6074	79.657 534 2233	.012 553 7403	97
98	1.503 032 8917	120.727 894 0101	.008 283 0899	.665 321 4348	80.322 855 6581	.012 449 7566	98
99	1.509 295 5288	122.230 926 9018	.008 181 2355	.662 560 7649	80.985 416 4230	.012 347 9022	99
100	1.515 584 2601	123.740 222 4305	.008 081 4466	.659 811 5501	81.645 227 9731	.012 248 1133	100

XIII	XIV	XV	XVI	XVII	XVIII
COMPOUND AMOUNT	AMOUNT OF ANNUITY	SINKING FUND	PRESENT VALUE	PRESENT VALUE OF ANNUITY	AMORTIZATION

RATE

½%

P E R I O D S	AMOUNT OF 1 — How $1 left at compound interest will grow.	AMOUNT OF 1 PER PERIOD — How $1 deposited periodically will grow.	SINKING FUND — Periodic deposit that will grow to $1 at future date.	PRESENT WORTH OF 1 — What $1 due in the future is worth today.	PRESENT WORTH OF 1 PER PERIOD — What $1 payable periodically is worth today.	PARTIAL PAYMENT — Annuity worth $1 today. Periodic payment necessary to pay off a loan of $1.	P E R I O D S
1	1.005 000 0000	1.000 000 0000	1.000 000 0000	.995 024 8756	.995 024 8756	1.005 000 0000	1
2	1.010 025 0000	2.005 000 0000	.498 753 1172	.990 074 5031	1.985 099 3787	.503 753 1172	2
3	1.015 075 1250	3.015 025 0000	.331 672 2084	.985 148 7593	2.970 248 1380	.336 672 2084	3
4	1.020 150 5006	4.030 100 1250	.248 132 7930	.980 247 5217	3.950 495 6597	.253 132 7930	4
5	1.025 251 2531	5.050 250 6256	.198 009 9750	.975 370 6684	4.925 866 3281	.203 009 9750	5
6	1.030 377 5094	6.075 501 8788	.164 595 4556	.970 518 0780	5.896 384 4061	.169 595 4556	6
7	1.035 529 3969	7.105 879 3881	.140 728 5355	.965 689 6298	6.862 074 0359	.145 728 5355	7
8	1.040 707 0439	8.141 408 7851	.122 828 8649	.960 885 2038	7.822 959 2397	.127 828 8649	8
9	1.045 910 5791	9.182 115 8290	.108 907 3606	.956 104 6804	8.779 063 9201	.113 907 3606	9
10	1.051 140 1320	10.228 026 4082	.097 770 5727	.951 347 9407	9.730 411 8608	.102 770 5727	10
11	1.056 395 8327	11.279 166 5402	.088 659 0331	.946 614 8664	10.677 026 7272	.093 659 0331	11
12	1.061 677 8119	12.335 562 3729	.081 066 4297	.941 905 3397	11.618 932 0668	.086 066 4297	12
13	1.066 986 2009	13.397 240 1848	.074 642 2387	.937 219 2434	12.556 151 3103	.079 642 2387	13
14	1.072 321 1319	14.464 226 3857	.069 136 0860	.932 556 4611	13.488 707 7714	.074 136 0860	14
15	1.077 682 7376	15.536 547 5176	.064 364 3640	.927 916 8768	14.416 624 6482	.069 364 3640	15
16	1.083 071 1513	16.614 230 2552	.060 189 3669	.923 300 3749	15.339 925 0231	.065 189 3669	16
17	1.088 486 5070	17.697 301 4055	.056 505 7902	.918 706 8407	16.258 631 8637	.061 505 7902	17
18	1.093 928 9396	18.785 787 9135	.053 231 7305	.914 136 1599	17.172 768 0236	.058 231 7305	18
19	1.099 398 5843	19.879 716 8531	.050 302 5273	.909 588 2188	18.082 356 2424	.055 302 5273	19
20	1.104 895 5772	20.979 115 4373	.047 666 4520	.905 062 9043	18.987 419 1467	.052 666 4520	20
21	1.110 420 0551	22.084 011 0145	.045 281 6293	.900 560 1037	19.887 979 2504	.050 281 6293	21
22	1.115 972 1553	23.194 431 0696	.043 113 7973	.896 079 7052	20.784 058 9556	.048 113 7973	22
23	1.121 552 0161	24.310 403 2250	.041 134 6530	.891 621 5972	21.675 680 5529	.046 134 6530	23
24	1.127 159 7762	25.431 955 2411	.039 320 6103	.887 185 6689	22.562 866 2218	.044 320 6103	24
25	1.132 795 5751	26.559 115 0173	.037 651 8570	.882 771 8098	23.445 638 0316	.042 651 8570	25
26	1.138 459 5530	27.691 910 5924	.036 111 6289	.878 379 9103	24.324 017 9419	.041 111 6289	26
27	1.144 151 8507	28.830 370 1453	.034 685 6456	.874 009 8610	25.198 027 8029	.039 685 6456	27
28	1.149 872 6100	29.974 521 9961	.033 361 6663	.869 661 5532	26.067 689 3561	.038 361 6663	28
29	1.155 621 9730	31.124 394 6060	.032 129 1390	.865 334 8788	26.933 024 2349	.037 129 1390	29
30	1.161 400 0829	32.280 016 5791	.030 978 9184	.861 029 7302	27.794 053 9651	.035 978 9184	30
31	1.167 207 0833	33.441 416 6620	.029 903 0394	.856 746 0002	28.650 799 9653	.034 903 0394	31
32	1.173 043 1187	34.608 623 7453	.028 894 5324	.852 483 5823	29.503 283 5475	.033 894 5324	32
33	1.178 908 3343	35.781 666 8640	.027 947 2727	.848 242 3704	30.351 525 9179	.032 947 2727	33
34	1.184 802 8760	36.960 575 1983	.027 055 8560	.844 022 2591	31.195 548 1771	.032 055 8560	34
35	1.190 726 8904	38.145 378 0743	.026 215 4958	.839 823 1434	32.035 371 3205	.031 215 4958	35
36	1.196 680 5248	39.336 104 9647	.025 421 9375	.835 644 9188	32.871 016 2393	.030 421 9375	36
37	1.202 663 9274	40.532 785 4895	.024 671 3861	.831 487 4814	33.702 503 7207	.029 671 3861	37
38	1.208 677 2471	41.735 449 4170	.023 960 4464	.827 350 7278	34.529 854 4484	.028 960 4464	38
39	1.214 720 6333	42.944 126 6640	.023 286 0714	.823 234 5550	35.353 089 0034	.028 286 0714	39
40	1.220 794 2365	44.158 847 2974	.022 645 5186	.819 138 8607	36.172 227 8641	.027 645 5186	40
41	1.226 898 2077	45.379 641 5338	.022 036 3133	.815 063 5430	36.987 291 4070	.027 036 3133	41
42	1.233 032 6987	46.606 539 7415	.021 456 2163	.811 008 5005	37.798 299 9075	.026 456 2163	42
43	1.239 197 8622	47.839 572 4402	.020 903 1969	.806 973 6323	38.605 273 5398	.025 903 1969	43
44	1.245 393 8515	49.078 770 3024	.020 375 4086	.802 958 8381	39.408 232 3779	.025 375 4086	44
45	1.251 620 8208	50.324 164 1539	.019 871 1696	.798 964 0180	40.207 196 3959	.024 871 1696	45
46	1.257 878 9249	51.575 784 9747	.019 388 9439	.794 989 0727	41.002 185 4686	.024 388 9439	46
47	1.264 168 3195	52.833 663 8996	.018 927 3264	.791 033 9031	41.793 219 3717	.023 927 3264	47
48	1.270 489 1611	54.097 832 2191	.018 485 0290	.787 098 4111	42.580 317 7828	.023 485 0290	48
49	1.276 841 6069	55.368 321 3802	.018 060 8690	.783 182 4996	43.363 500 2814	.023 060 8690	49
50	1.283 225 8149	56.645 162 9871	.017 653 7580	.779 286 0683	44.142 786 3497	.022 653 7580	50
51	1.289 641 9440	57.928 388 8020	.017 262 6931	.775 409 0231	44.918 195 3728	.022 262 6931	51
52	1.296 090 1537	59.218 030 7460	.016 886 7486	.771 551 2668	45.689 746 6396	.021 886 7486	52
53	1.302 570 6045	60.514 120 8997	.016 525 0686	.767 712 7033	46.457 459 3429	.021 525 0686	53
54	1.309 083 4575	61.816 691 5042	.016 176 8606	.763 893 2371	47.221 352 5800	.021 176 8606	54
55	1.315 628 8748	63.125 774 9618	.015 841 3897	.760 092 7732	47.981 445 3532	.020 841 3897	55
56	1.322 207 0192	64.441 403 8366	.015 517 9735	.756 311 2171	48.737 756 5704	.020 517 9735	56
57	1.328 818 0543	65.763 610 8558	.015 205 9777	.752 548 4748	49.490 305 0452	.020 205 9777	57
58	1.335 462 1446	67.092 428 9100	.014 904 8114	.748 804 4525	50.239 109 4977	.019 904 8114	58
59	1.342 139 4553	68.427 891 0546	.014 613 9240	.745 079 0572	50.984 188 5549	.019 613 9240	59
60	1.348 850 1525	69.770 030 5099	.014 332 8015	.741 372 1962	51.725 560 7511	.019 332 8015	60
61	1.355 594 4033	71.118 880 6624	.014 060 9637	.737 683 7774	52.463 244 5285	.019 060 9637	61
62	1.362 372 3753	72.474 475 0657	.013 797 9613	.734 013 7088	53.197 258 2373	.018 797 9613	62
63	1.369 184 2372	73.836 847 4411	.013 543 3735	.730 361 8993	53.927 620 1366	.018 543 3735	63
64	1.376 030 1584	75.206 031 6783	.013 296 8058	.726 728 2580	54.654 348 3946	.018 296 8058	64
65	1.382 910 3092	76.582 061 8366	.013 057 8882	.723 112 6946	55.377 461 0892	.018 057 8882	65
66	1.389 824 8607	77.964 972 1458	.012 826 2728	.719 515 1190	56.096 976 2082	.017 826 2728	66
67	1.396 773 9850	79.354 797 0066	.012 601 6326	.715 935 9418	56.812 911 6499	.017 601 6326	67
68	1.403 757 8550	80.751 570 9916	.012 383 6600	.712 373 5739	57.525 285 2238	.017 383 6600	68
69	1.410 776 6442	82.155 328 8466	.012 172 0650	.708 829 4267	58.234 114 6505	.017 172 0650	69
70	1.417 830 5275	83.566 105 4908	.011 966 5742	.705 302 9122	58.939 417 5627	.016 966 5742	70
71	1.424 919 6801	84.983 936 0182	.011 766 9297	.701 793 9425	59.641 211 5052	.016 766 9297	71
72	1.432 044 2785	86.408 855 6983	.011 572 8879	.698 302 4303	60.339 513 9355	.016 572 8879	72
73	1.439 204 4999	87.840 899 9768	.011 384 2185	.694 828 2889	61.034 342 2244	.016 384 2185	73
74	1.446 400 5224	89.280 104 4767	.011 200 7037	.691 371 4317	61.725 713 6561	.016 200 7037	74
75	1.453 632 5250	90.726 504 9991	.011 022 1374	.687 931 7729	62.413 645 4290	.016 022 1374	75
76	1.460 900 6876	92.180 137 5241	.010 848 3240	.684 509 2267	63.098 154 6557	.015 848 3240	76
77	1.468 205 1911	93.641 038 2117	.010 679 0785	.681 103 7082	63.779 258 3639	.015 679 0785	77
78	1.475 546 2170	95.109 243 4028	.010 514 2252	.677 715 1325	64.456 973 4964	.015 514 2252	78
79	1.482 923 9481	96.584 789 6198	.010 353 5971	.674 343 4154	65.131 316 9118	.015 353 5971	79
80	1.490 338 5678	98.067 713 5679	.010 197 0359	.670 988 4731	65.802 305 3849	.015 197 0359	80
81	1.497 790 2607	99.558 052 1357	.010 044 3910	.667 650 2220	66.469 955 6069	.015 044 3910	81
82	1.505 279 2120	101.055 842 3964	.009 895 5189	.664 328 5791	67.134 284 1859	.014 895 5189	82
83	1.512 805 6080	102.561 121 6084	.009 750 2834	.661 023 4618	67.795 307 6477	.014 750 2834	83
84	1.520 369 6361	104.073 927 2164	.009 608 5545	.657 734 7878	68.453 042 4355	.014 608 5545	84
85	1.527 971 4843	105.594 296 8525	.009 470 2084	.654 462 4754	69.107 504 9110	.014 470 2084	85
86	1.535 611 3417	107.122 268 3368	.009 335 1272	.651 206 4432	69.758 711 3542	.014 335 1272	86
87	1.543 289 3984	108.657 879 6784	.009 203 1982	.647 966 6102	70.406 677 9644	.014 203 1982	87
88	1.551 005 8454	110.201 169 0768	.009 074 3139	.644 742 8957	71.051 420 8601	.014 074 3139	88
89	1.558 760 8746	111.752 174 9222	.008 948 3717	.641 535 2196	71.692 956 0797	.013 948 3717	89
90	1.566 554 6790	113.310 935 7968	.008 825 2735	.638 343 5021	72.331 299 5818	.013 825 2735	90
91	1.574 387 4524	114.877 490 4758	.008 704 9255	.635 167 6638	72.966 467 2455	.013 704 9255	91
92	1.582 259 3896	116.451 877 9282	.008 587 2381	.632 007 6256	73.598 474 8712	.013 587 2381	92
93	1.590 170 6866	118.034 137 3178	.008 472 1253	.628 863 3091	74.227 338 1803	.013 472 1253	93
94	1.598 121 5400	119.624 308 0044	.008 359 5050	.625 734 6359	74.853 072 8162	.013 359 5050	94
95	1.606 112 1477	121.222 429 5445	.008 249 2984	.622 621 5283	75.475 694 3445	.013 249 2984	95
96	1.614 142 7085	122.828 541 6922	.008 141 4302	.619 523 9087	76.095 218 2532	.013 141 4302	96
97	1.622 213 4220	124.442 684 4006	.008 035 8279	.616 441 7002	76.711 659 9535	.013 035 8279	97
98	1.630 324 4891	126.064 897 8226	.007 932 4222	.613 374 8261	77.325 034 7796	.012 932 4222	98
99	1.638 476 1116	127.695 222 3118	.007 831 1466	.610 323 2101	77.935 357 9896	.012 831 1466	99
100	1.646 668 4921	129.333 698 4233	.007 731 9369	.607 286 7762	78.542 644 7658	.012 731 9369	100

	XIII COMPOUND AMOUNT	XIV AMOUNT OF ANUITY	XV SINKING FUND	XVI PRESENT VALUE	XVII PRESENT VALUE OF ANNUITY	XVIII AMORTIZATION	
P E R I O D S	AMOUNT OF 1 *How $1 left at compound interest will grow.*	AMOUNT OF 1 PER PERIOD *How $1 deposited periodically will grow.*	SINKING FUND *Periodic deposit that will grow to $1 at future date.*	PRESENT WORTH OF 1 *What $1 due in the future is worth today.*	PRESENT WORTH OF 1 PER PERIOD *What $1 payable periodically is worth today.*	PARTIAL PAYMENT *Annuity worth $1 today. Periodic payment necessary to pay of a loan of $1.*	P E R I O D S
1	1.007 500 0000	1.000 000 0000	1.000 000 0000	.992 555 8313	.992 555 8313	1.007 500 0000	1
2	1.015 056 2500	2.007 500 0000	.498 132 0050	.985 167 0782	1.977 722 9094	.505 632 0050	2
3	1.022 669 1719	3.022 556 2500	.330 845 7866	.977 833 3282	2.955 556 2377	.338 345 7866	3
4	1.030 339 1907	4.045 225 4219	.247 205 0123	.970 554 1719	3.926 110 4096	.254 705 0123	4
5	1.038 066 7346	5.075 564 6125	.197 022 4155	.963 329 2029	4.889 439 6125	.204 522 4155	5
6	1.045 852 2351	6.113 631 3471	.163 568 9074	.956 158 0178	5.845 597 6303	.171 068 9074	6
7	1.053 696 1269	7.159 483 5822	.139 674 8786	.949 040 2162	6.794 637 8464	.147 174 8786	7
8	1.061 598 8478	8.213 179 7091	.121 755 5241	.941 975 4006	7.736 613 2471	.129 255 5241	8
9	1.069 560 8392	9.274 778 5569	.107 819 2858	.934 963 1768	8.671 576 4239	.115 319 2858	9
10	1.077 582 5455	10.344 339 3961	.096 671 0532	.928 003 1532	9.599 579 5771	.104 171 2287	10
11	1.085 664 4146	11.421 921 9416	.087 550 9398	.921 094 9411	10.520 674 5182	.095 050 9398	11
12	1.093 806 8977	12.507 586 3561	.079 951 6768	.914 238 1550	11.434 912 6731	.087 451 6768	12
13	1.102 010 4494	13.601 393 2538	.073 521 8798	.907 432 4119	12.342 345 0850	.081 021 8798	13
14	1.110 275 5278	14.703 403 7032	.068 011 4632	.900 677 3319	13.243 022 4169	.075 511 4632	14
15	1.118 602 5942	15.813 679 2310	.063 236 3908	.893 972 5378	14.136 994 9547	.070 736 3908	15
16	1.126 992 1137	16.932 281 8252	.059 058 7855	.887 317 6554	15.024 312 6101	.066 558 7855	16
17	1.135 444 5545	18.059 273 9389	.055 373 2118	.880 712 3131	15.905 024 9232	.062 873 2118	17
18	1.143 960 3887	19.194 718 4934	.052 097 6643	.874 156 1420	16.779 181 0652	.059 597 6643	18
19	1.152 540 0916	20.338 678 8821	.049 167 4020	.867 648 7762	17.646 829 8414	.056 667 4020	19
20	1.161 184 1423	21.491 218 9738	.046 530 6319	.861 189 8523	18.508 019 6937	.054 030 6319	20
21	1.169 893 0234	22.652 403 1161	.044 145 4266	.854 779 0097	19.362 798 7034	.051 645 4266	21
22	1.178 667 2210	23.822 296 1394	.041 977 4817	.848 415 8905	20.211 214 5940	.049 477 4817	22
23	1.187 507 2252	25.000 963 3605	.039 998 4587	.842 100 1395	21.053 314 7335	.047 498 4587	23
24	1.196 413 5294	26.188 470 5857	.038 184 7423	.835 831 4040	21.889 146 1374	.045 684 7423	24
25	1.205 386 6309	27.384 884 1151	.036 516 4956	.829 609 3340	22.718 755 4714	.044 016 4956	25
26	1.214 427 0306	28.590 270 7459	.034 976 9355	.823 433 5821	23.542 189 0535	.042 476 9335	26
27	1.223 535 2333	29.804 697 7765	.033 551 7578	.817 303 8036	24.359 492 8571	.041 051 7578	27
28	1.232 711 7476	31.028 233 0099	.032 228 7125	.811 219 6562	25.170 712 5132	.039 728 7125	28
29	1.241 957 0857	32.260 944 7574	.030 997 2323	.805 180 8001	25.975 893 3134	.038 497 2323	29
30	1.251 271 7638	33.502 901 8431	.029 848 1608	.799 186 8984	26.775 080 2118	.037 348 1608	30
31	1.260 656 3021	34.754 173 6069	.028 773 5226	.793 237 6163	27.568 317 8281	.036 273 5226	31
32	1.270 111 2243	36.014 829 9090	.027 766 3397	.787 332 6216	28.355 650 4497	.035 266 3397	32
33	1.279 637 0585	37.284 941 1333	.026 820 4795	.781 471 5847	29.137 122 0344	.034 320 4795	33
34	1.289 234 3364	38.564 578 1918	.025 930 5313	.775 654 1784	29.912 776 2128	.033 430 5313	34
35	1.298 903 5940	39.853 812 5282	.025 091 7023	.769 880 0778	30.682 656 2907	.032 591 7023	35
36	1.308 645 3709	41.152 716 1222	.024 299 7327	.764 148 9606	31.446 805 2513	.031 799 7327	36
37	1.318 460 2112	42.461 361 4931	.023 550 8228	.758 460 5068	32.205 265 7581	.031 050 8228	37
38	1.328 348 6628	43.779 821 7043	.022 841 5732	.752 814 3988	32.958 080 1569	.030 341 5732	38
39	1.338 311 2778	45.108 170 3671	.022 168 9329	.747 210 3214	33.705 290 4783	.029 668 9329	39
40	1.348 348 6123	46.446 481 6449	.021 530 1561	.741 647 9617	34.446 938 4400	.029 030 1561	40
41	1.358 461 2269	47.794 830 2572	.020 922 7650	.736 127 0091	35.183 065 4492	.028 422 7650	41
42	1.368 649 6861	49.153 291 4841	.020 344 5175	.730 647 1555	35.913 712 6046	.027 844 5175	42
43	1.378 914 5588	50.521 941 1703	.019 793 3804	.725 208 0948	36.638 920 6994	.027 293 3804	43
44	1.389 256 4180	51.900 855 7290	.019 267 5051	.719 809 5233	37.358 730 2227	.026 767 5051	44
45	1.399 675 8411	53.290 112 1470	.018 765 2073	.714 451 1398	38.073 181 3625	.026 265 2073	45
46	1.410 173 4099	54.689 787 9881	.018 284 9493	.709 132 6449	38.782 314 0074	.025 784 9493	46
47	1.420 749 7105	56.099 961 3980	.017 825 3242	.703 853 7419	39.486 167 7493	.025 325 3242	47
48	1.431 405 3333	57.520 711 1085	.017 385 0424	.698 614 1359	40.184 781 8852	.024 885 0424	48
49	1.442 140 8733	58.952 116 4418	.016 962 9194	.693 413 5344	40.878 195 4195	.024 462 9194	49
50	1.452 956 9299	60.394 257 3151	.016 557 8657	.688 251 6470	41.566 447 0665	.024 057 8657	50
51	1.463 854 1068	61.847 214 2450	.016 168 8770	.683 128 1856	42.249 575 2521	.023 668 8770	51
52	1.474 833 0126	63.311 068 3518	.015 795 0265	.678 042 8641	42.927 618 1163	.023 295 0265	52
53	1.485 894 2602	64.785 901 3645	.015 435 4571	.672 995 3986	43.600 613 5149	.022 935 4571	53
54	1.497 038 4672	66.271 795 6247	.015 089 3754	.667 985 5073	44.268 599 0222	.022 589 3754	54
55	1.508 266 2557	67.768 834 0919	.014 756 0455	.663 012 9105	44.931 611 9327	.022 256 0455	55
56	1.519 578 2526	69.277 100 3476	.014 434 7843	.658 077 3305	45.589 689 2633	.021 934 7843	56
57	1.530 975 0895	70.796 678 6002	.014 124 9564	.653 178 4918	46.242 867 7551	.021 624 9564	57
58	1.542 457 4027	72.327 653 6897	.013 825 9704	.648 316 1209	46.891 183 8760	.021 325 9704	58
59	1.554 025 8332	73.870 111 0923	.013 537 2749	.643 489 9463	47.534 673 8224	.021 037 2749	59
60	1.565 681 0269	75.424 136 9255	.013 258 3552	.638 699 6986	48.173 373 5210	.020 758 3552	60
61	1.577 423 6346	76.989 817 9525	.012 988 7305	.633 945 1103	48.807 318 6312	.020 488 7305	61
62	1.589 254 3119	78.567 241 5871	.012 727 9510	.629 225 9159	49.436 544 5471	.020 227 9510	62
63	1.601 173 7192	80.156 495 8990	.012 475 5953	.624 541 8520	50.061 086 3991	.019 975 5953	63
64	1.613 182 5221	81.757 669 6183	.012 231 2684	.619 892 6571	50.680 979 0562	.019 731 2684	64
65	1.625 281 3911	83.370 852 1404	.011 994 5997	.615 278 0715	51.296 257 1278	.019 494 5997	65
66	1.637 471 0015	84.996 133 5315	.011 765 2411	.610 697 8378	51.906 954 9655	.019 265 2411	66
67	1.649 762 0340	86.633 604 5329	.011 542 8650	.606 151 7000	52.513 106 6655	.019 042 8650	67
68	1.662 125 1743	88.283 356 5669	.011 327 1633	.601 639 4045	53.114 746 0700	.018 827 1633	68
69	1.674 591 1131	89.945 481 7412	.011 117 8458	.597 160 6992	53.711 906 7692	.018 617 8458	69
70	1.687 150 5464	91.620 072 8543	.010 914 6388	.592 715 3342	54.304 622 1035	.018 414 6388	70
71	1.699 804 1755	93.307 223 4007	.010 717 2839	.588 303 0613	54.892 925 1647	.018 217 2839	71
72	1.712 552 7068	95.007 027 5762	.010 525 5372	.583 923 6340	55.476 848 7987	.018 025 5372	72
73	1.725 396 8521	96.719 580 2830	.010 339 1681	.579 576 8079	56.056 425 6067	.017 839 1681	73
74	1.738 337 3285	98.444 977 1351	.010 157 9586	.575 262 3404	56.631 687 9471	.017 657 9586	74
75	1.751 374 8585	100.183 314 4636	.009 981 7021	.570 979 9905	57.202 667 9375	.017 481 7021	75
76	1.764 510 1699	101.934 689 3221	.009 810 2030	.566 729 5191	57.769 397 4566	.017 310 2030	76
77	1.777 743 9962	103.699 199 4920	.009 643 2760	.562 510 6889	58.331 908 1455	.017 143 2760	77
78	1.791 077 0762	105.476 943 4882	.009 480 7450	.558 323 2644	58.890 231 4099	.016 980 7450	78
79	1.804 510 1542	107.268 020 5644	.009 322 4429	.554 167 0118	59.444 398 4218	.016 822 4429	79
80	1.818 043 9804	109.072 530 7186	.009 168 2112	.550 041 6991	59.994 440 1209	.016 668 2112	80
81	1.831 679 5102	110.890 574 6990	.009 017 8990	.545 947 0959	60.540 387 2168	.016 517 8990	81
82	1.845 416 9051	112.722 254 0092	.008 871 3627	.541 882 9736	61.082 270 1903	.016 371 3627	82
83	1.859 257 5319	114.567 670 9143	.008 728 4658	.537 849 1053	61.620 119 2956	.016 228 4658	83
84	1.873 201 9633	116.426 928 4462	.008 589 0783	.533 845 2668	62.153 964 5614	.016 089 0783	84
85	1.887 250 9781	118.300 130 4095	.008 453 0761	.529 871 2316	62.683 835 7930	.015 953 0761	85
86	1.901 405 3604	120.187 381 3876	.008 320 3410	.525 926 7807	63.209 762 5736	.015 820 3410	86
87	1.915 665 9006	122.088 786 7480	.008 190 7604	.522 011 6930	63.731 774 2666	.015 690 7604	87
88	1.930 033 3949	124.004 452 6486	.008 064 2266	.518 125 7499	64.249 900 0165	.015 564 2266	88
89	1.944 508 6453	125.934 486 0435	.007 940 6367	.514 268 7344	64.764 168 7509	.015 440 6367	89
90	1.959 092 4602	127.878 994 6888	.007 819 8926	.510 440 4031	65.274 609 1820	.015 319 8926	90
91	1.973 785 6536	129.838 087 1490	.007 701 9003	.506 640 6264	65.781 249 8085	.015 201 9003	91
92	1.988 589 0460	131.811 872 8026	.007 586 5700	.502 869 1081	66.284 118 9166	.015 086 5700	92
93	2.003 503 4639	133.800 461 8486	.007 473 8158	.499 125 6656	66.783 244 5822	.014 973 8158	93
94	2.018 529 7398	135.803 965 3125	.007 363 5552	.495 410 0900	67.278 654 6722	.014 863 5552	94
95	2.033 668 7129	137.822 495 0523	.007 255 7096	.491 722 1737	67.770 376 8458	.014 755 7096	95
96	2.048 921 2282	139.856 163 7652	.007 150 2033	.488 061 7038	68.258 438 5567	.014 650 2033	96
97	2.064 288 1375	141.905 084 9934	.007 046 9638	.484 428 4971	68.742 867 0538	.014 546 9638	97
98	2.079 770 2985	143.969 373 1309	.006 945 9217	.480 822 3296	69.223 689 3834	.014 445 9217	98
99	2.095 368 5757	146.049 143 4294	.006 847 0104	.477 243 0071	69.700 932 3905	.014 347 0104	99
100	2.111 083 8400	148.144 512 0051	.006 750 1657	.473 690 3296	70.174 622 7201	.014 250 1657	100

RATE 1%

P E R I O D S	AMOUNT OF 1 *How $1 left at compound interest will grow.*	AMOUNT OF 1 PER PERIOD *How $1 deposited periodically will grow.*	SINKING FUND *Periodic deposit that will grow to $1 at future date.*	PRESENT WORTH OF 1 *What $1 due in the future is worth today.*	PRESENT WORTH OF 1 PER PERIOD *What $1 payable periodically is worth today.*	PARTIAL PAYMENT *Annuity worth $1 today. Periodic payment necessary to pay off a loan of $1.*	P E R I O D S
1	1.010 000 0000	1.000 000 0000	1.000 000 0000	.990 099 0099	.990 099 0099	1.010 000 0000	1
2	1.020 100 0000	2.010 000 0000	.497 512 4378	.980 296 0494	1.970 395 0593	.507 512 4378	2
3	1.030 301 0000	3.030 100 0000	.330 022 1115	.970 590 1479	2.940 985 2072	.340 022 1115	3
4	1.040 604 0100	4.060 401 0000	.246 281 0939	.960 980 3445	3.901 965 5517	.256 281 0939	4
5	1.051 010 0501	5.101 005 0100	.196 039 7996	.951 465 6876	4.853 431 2393	.206 039 7996	5
6	1.061 520 1506	6.152 015 0601	.162 548 3667	.942 045 2353	5.795 476 4746	.172 548 3667	6
7	1.072 135 3521	7.213 535 2107	.138 628 2829	.932 718 0547	6.728 194 5293	.148 628 2829	7
8	1.082 856 7056	8.285 670 5628	.120 690 2920	.923 483 2225	7.651 677 7518	.130 690 2920	8
9	1.093 685 2727	9.368 527 2684	.106 740 3628	.914 339 8242	8.566 017 5760	.116 740 3628	9
10	1.104 622 1254	10.462 212 5411	.095 582 0766	.905 286 9547	9.471 304 5307	.105 582 0766	10
11	1.115 668 3467	11.566 834 6665	.086 454 0757	.896 323 7175	10.367 628 2482	.096 454 0757	11
12	1.126 825 0301	12.682 503 0132	.078 848 7887	.887 449 2253	11.255 077 4735	.088 848 7887	12
13	1.138 093 2804	13.809 328 0433	.072 414 8197	.878 662 5993	12.133 740 0728	.082 414 8197	13
14	1.149 474 2132	14.947 421 3238	.066 901 1717	.869 962 9696	13.003 703 0423	.076 901 1717	14
15	1.160 968 9554	16.096 895 5370	.062 123 7802	.861 349 4748	13.865 052 5172	.072 123 7802	15
16	1.172 578 6449	17.257 864 4924	.057 944 5968	.852 821 2622	14.717 873 7794	.067 944 5968	16
17	1.184 304 4314	18.430 443 1373	.054 258 0551	.844 377 4873	15.562 251 2667	.064 258 0551	17
18	1.196 147 4757	19.614 747 5687	.050 982 0479	.836 017 3142	16.398 268 5809	.060 982 0479	18
19	1.208 108 9504	20.810 895 0444	.048 051 7536	.827 739 9150	17.226 008 4959	.058 051 7536	19
20	1.220 190 0399	22.019 003 9948	.045 415 3149	.819 544 4703	18.045 552 9663	.055 415 3149	20
21	1.232 391 9403	23.239 194 0347	.043 030 7522	.811 430 1687	18.856 983 1349	.053 030 7522	21
22	1.244 715 8598	24.471 585 9751	.040 863 7185	.803 396 2066	19.660 379 3415	.050 863 7185	22
23	1.257 163 0183	25.716 301 8348	.038 885 8401	.795 441 7887	20.455 821 1302	.048 885 8401	23
24	1.269 734 6485	26.973 464 8532	.037 073 4722	.787 566 1274	21.243 387 2576	.047 073 4722	24
25	1.282 431 9950	28.243 199 5017	.035 406 7534	.779 768 4430	22.023 155 7006	.045 406 7534	25
26	1.295 256 3150	29.525 631 4967	.033 868 8776	.772 047 9634	22.795 203 6640	.043 868 8776	26
27	1.308 208 8781	30.820 887 8117	.032 445 5287	.764 403 9241	23.559 607 5881	.042 445 5287	27
28	1.321 290 9669	32.129 096 6898	.031 124 4356	.756 835 5684	24.316 443 1565	.041 124 4356	28
29	1.334 503 8766	33.450 387 6567	.029 895 0198	.749 342 1470	25.065 785 3035	.039 895 0198	29
30	1.347 848 9153	34.784 891 5333	.028 748 1132	.741 922 9178	25.807 708 2213	.038 748 1132	30
31	1.361 327 4045	36.132 740 4486	.027 675 7309	.734 577 1463	26.542 285 3676	.037 675 7309	31
32	1.374 940 6785	37.494 067 8531	.026 670 8857	.727 304 1053	27.269 589 4729	.036 670 8857	32
33	1.388 690 0853	38.869 008 5316	.025 727 4378	.720 103 0745	27.989 692 5474	.035 727 4378	33
34	1.402 576 9862	40.257 698 6170	.024 839 9694	.712 973 3411	28.702 665 8885	.034 839 9694	34
35	1.416 602 7560	41.660 275 6031	.024 003 6818	.705 914 1991	29.408 580 0876	.034 003 6818	35
36	1.430 768 7836	43.076 878 3592	.023 214 3098	.698 924 9496	30.107 505 0373	.033 214 3098	36
37	1.445 076 4714	44.507 647 1427	.022 468 0491	.692 004 9006	30.799 509 9379	.032 468 0491	37
38	1.459 527 2361	45.952 723 6142	.021 761 4958	.685 153 3670	31.484 663 3048	.031 761 4958	38
39	1.474 122 5085	47.412 250 8503	.021 091 5951	.678 369 6702	32.163 032 9751	.031 091 5951	39
40	1.488 863 7336	48.886 373 3588	.020 455 5980	.671 653 1389	32.834 686 1140	.030 455 5980	40
41	1.503 752 3709	50.375 237 0924	.019 851 0232	.665 003 1078	33.499 689 2217	.029 851 0232	41
42	1.518 789 8946	51.878 989 4633	.019 275 6260	.658 418 9186	34.158 108 1403	.029 275 6260	42
43	1.533 977 7936	53.397 779 3580	.018 727 3705	.651 899 9194	34.810 008 0597	.028 727 3705	43
44	1.549 317 5715	54.931 757 1515	.018 204 4058	.645 445 4648	35.455 453 5245	.028 204 4058	44
45	1.564 810 7472	56.481 074 7231	.017 705 0455	.639 054 9156	36.094 508 4401	.027 705 0455	45
46	1.580 458 8547	58.045 885 4703	.017 227 7499	.632 727 6392	36.727 236 0793	.027 227 7499	46
47	1.596 263 4432	59.626 344 3250	.016 771 1103	.626 463 0091	37.353 699 0884	.026 771 1103	47
48	1.612 226 0777	61.222 607 7682	.016 333 8354	.620 260 4051	37.973 959 4935	.026 333 8354	48
49	1.628 348 3385	62.834 833 8459	.015 914 7393	.614 119 2129	38.588 078 7064	.025 914 7393	49
50	1.644 631 8218	64.463 182 1844	.015 512 7309	.608 038 8247	39.196 117 5311	.025 512 7309	50
51	1.661 078 1401	66.107 814 0062	.015 126 8048	.602 018 6383	39.798 136 1694	.025 126 8048	51
52	1.677 688 9215	67.768 892 1463	.014 756 0329	.596 058 0577	40.394 194 2271	.024 756 0329	52
53	1.694 465 8107	69.446 581 0678	.014 399 5570	.590 156 4908	40.984 350 7199	.024 399 5570	53
54	1.711 410 4688	71.141 046 8784	.014 056 5826	.584 313 3592	41.568 664 0791	.024 056 5826	54
55	1.728 524 5735	72.852 457 3472	.013 726 3730	.578 528 0784	42.147 192 1576	.023 726 3730	55
56	1.745 809 8192	74.580 981 9207	.013 408 2440	.572 800 0776	42.719 992 2352	.023 408 2440	56
57	1.763 267 9174	76.326 791 7399	.013 101 5595	.567 128 7898	43.287 121 0250	.023 101 5595	57
58	1.780 900 5966	78.090 059 6573	.012 805 7272	.561 513 6532	43.848 634 6782	.022 805 7272	58
59	1.798 709 6025	79.870 960 2539	.012 520 1950	.555 954 1121	44.404 588 7903	.022 520 1950	59
60	1.816 696 6986	81.669 669 8564	.012 244 4477	.550 449 6159	44.955 038 4062	.022 244 4477	60
61	1.834 863 6655	83.486 366 5550	.011 978 0036	.544 999 6197	45.500 038 0260	.021 978 0036	61
62	1.853 212 3022	85.321 230 2205	.011 720 4123	.539 603 5839	46.039 641 6099	.021 720 4123	62
63	1.871 744 4252	87.174 442 5227	.011 471 2520	.534 260 9742	46.573 902 5840	.021 471 2520	63
64	1.890 461 8695	89.046 186 9480	.011 230 1271	.528 971 2615	47.102 873 8456	.021 230 1271	64
65	1.909 366 4882	90.936 648 8174	.010 996 6665	.523 733 9223	47.626 607 7679	.020 996 6665	65
66	1.928 460 1531	92.846 015 3056	.010 770 5215	.518 548 4379	48.145 156 2058	.020 770 5215	66
67	1.947 744 7546	94.774 475 4587	.010 551 3641	.513 414 2950	48.658 570 5008	.020 551 3641	67
68	1.967 222 2021	96.722 220 2133	.010 338 8859	.508 330 9851	49.166 901 4860	.020 338 8859	68
69	1.986 894 4242	98.689 442 4154	.010 132 7961	.503 298 0051	49.670 199 4911	.020 132 7961	69
70	2.006 763 3684	100.676 336 8395	.009 932 8207	.498 314 8565	50.168 514 3476	.019 932 8207	70
71	2.026 831 0021	102.683 100 2079	.009 738 7009	.493 381 0461	50.661 895 3936	.019 738 7009	71
72	2.047 099 3121	104.709 931 2100	.009 550 1925	.488 496 0852	51.150 391 4789	.019 550 1925	72
73	2.067 570 3052	106.757 030 5221	.009 367 0646	.483 659 4903	51.634 050 9692	.019 367 0646	73
74	2.088 246 0083	108.824 600 8273	.009 189 0987	.478 870 7825	52.112 921 7516	.019 189 0987	74
75	2.109 128 4684	110.912 846 8356	.009 016 0881	.474 129 4876	52.587 051 2393	.019 016 0881	75
76	2.130 219 7530	113.021 975 3040	.008 847 8369	.469 435 1362	53.056 486 3755	.018 847 8369	76
77	2.151 521 9506	115.152 195 0570	.008 684 1593	.464 787 2636	53.521 273 6391	.018 684 1593	77
78	2.173 037 1701	117.303 717 0076	.008 524 8791	.460 185 4095	53.981 459 0486	.018 524 8791	78
79	2.194 767 5418	119.476 754 1776	.008 369 8290	.455 629 1183	54.437 088 1670	.018 369 8290	79
80	2.216 715 2172	121.671 521 7194	.008 218 8501	.451 117 9389	54.888 206 1059	.018 218 8501	80
81	2.238 882 3694	123.888 236 9366	.008 071 7914	.446 651 4247	55.334 857 5306	.018 071 7914	81
82	2.261 271 1931	126.127 119 3060	.007 928 5090	.442 229 1334	55.777 086 6639	.017 928 5090	82
83	2.283 883 9050	128.388 390 4990	.007 788 8662	.437 850 6271	56.214 937 2910	.017 788 8662	83
84	2.306 722 7440	130.672 274 4040	.007 652 7328	.433 515 4724	56.648 452 7634	.017 652 7328	84
85	2.329 789 9715	132.978 997 1481	.007 519 9845	.429 223 2400	57.077 676 0034	.017 519 9845	85
86	2.353 087 8712	135.308 787 1196	.007 390 5030	.424 973 5049	57.502 649 5083	.017 390 5030	86
87	2.376 618 7499	137.661 874 9908	.007 264 1754	.420 765 8465	57.923 415 3547	.017 264 1754	87
88	2.400 384 9374	140.038 493 7407	.007 140 8937	.416 599 8480	58.340 015 2027	.017 140 8937	88
89	2.424 388 7868	142.438 878 6781	.007 020 5551	.412 475 0970	58.752 490 2997	.017 020 5551	89
90	2.448 632 6746	144.863 267 4648	.006 903 0612	.408 391 1852	59.160 881 4849	.016 903 0612	90
91	2.473 119 0014	147.311 900 1395	.006 788 3178	.404 347 7081	59.565 229 1929	.016 788 3178	91
92	2.497 850 1914	149.785 019 1409	.006 676 2351	.400 344 2654	59.965 573 4584	.016 676 2351	92
93	2.522 828 6933	152.282 869 3323	.006 566 7268	.396 380 4608	60.361 953 9192	.016 566 7268	93
94	2.548 056 9803	154.805 698 0256	.006 459 7105	.392 455 9018	60.754 409 8210	.016 459 7105	94
95	2.573 537 5501	157.353 755 0059	.006 355 1073	.388 570 1998	61.142 980 0207	.016 355 1073	95
96	2.599 272 9256	159.927 292 5559	.006 252 8414	.384 722 9701	61.527 702 9908	.016 252 8414	96
97	2.625 265 6548	162.526 565 4815	.006 152 8403	.380 913 8318	61.908 616 8226	.016 152 8403	97
98	2.651 518 3114	165.151 831 1363	.006 055 0343	.377 142 4077	62.285 759 2303	.016 055 0343	98
99	2.678 033 4945	167.803 349 4477	.005 959 3566	.373 408 3245	62.659 167 5548	.015 959 3566	99
100	2.704 813 8294	170.481 382 9422	.005 865 7431	.369 711 2123	63.028 878 7671	.015 865 7431	100

	XIII COMPOUND AMOUNT	XIV AMOUNT OF ANNUITY	XV SINKING FUND	XVI PRESENT VALUE	XVII PRESENT VALUE OF ANNUITY	XVIII AMORTIZATION	
P E R I O D S	AMOUNT OF 1 — How $1 left at compound interest will grow.	AMOUNT OF 1 PER PERIOD — How $1 deposited periodically will grow.	SINKING FUND — Periodic deposit that will grow to $1 at future date.	PRESENT WORTH OF 1 — What $1 due in the future is worth today.	PRESENT WORTH OF 1 PER PERIOD — What $1 payable periodically is worth today.	PARTIAL PAYMENT — Annuity worth $1 today. Periodic payment necessary to pay off a loan of $1.	P E R I O D S
1	1.012 500 0000	1.000 000 0000	1.000 000 0000	.987 654 3210	.987 654 3210	1.012 500 0000	1
2	1.025 156 2500	2.012 500 0000	.496 894 4099	.975 461 0578	1.963 115 3788	.509 394 4099	2
3	1.037 970 7031	3.037 656 2500	.329 201 1728	.963 418 3287	2.926 533 7076	.341 701 1728	3
4	1.050 945 3369	4.075 626 9531	.245 361 0233	.951 524 2752	3.878 057 9826	.257 861 0233	4
5	1.064 082 1536	5.126 572 2900	.195 062 1084	.939 777 0619	4.817 835 0446	.207 562 1084	5
6	1.077 383 1805	6.190 654 4437	.161 533 8102	.928 174 8760	5.746 009 9206	.174 033 8102	6
7	1.090 850 4703	7.268 037 6242	.137 588 7209	.916 715 9269	6.662 725 8475	.150 088 7209	7
8	1.104 486 1012	8.358 888 0945	.119 633 1365	.905 398 4463	7.568 124 2938	.132 133 1365	8
9	1.118 292 1774	9.463 374 1957	.105 670 5546	.894 220 6877	8.462 344 9815	.118 170 5546	9
10	1.132 270 8297	10.581 666 3731	.094 503 0740	.883 180 9262	9.345 525 9077	.107 003 0740	10
11	1.146 424 2150	11.713 937 2028	.085 368 3935	.872 277 4579	10.217 803 3656	.097 868 3935	11
12	1.160 754 5177	12.860 361 4178	.077 758 3123	.861 508 6004	11.079 311 9660	.090 258 3123	12
13	1.175 263 9492	14.021 115 9356	.071 320 9993	.850 872 6918	11.930 184 6578	.083 820 9993	13
14	1.189 954 7486	15.196 379 8848	.065 805 1462	.840 368 0906	12.770 552 7485	.078 305 1462	14
15	1.204 829 1829	16.386 334 6333	.061 026 4603	.829 993 1759	13.600 545 9244	.073 526 4603	15
16	1.219 889 5477	17.591 163 8162	.056 846 7221	.819 746 3466	14.420 292 2710	.069 346 7221	16
17	1.235 138 1670	18.811 053 3639	.053 160 2341	.809 626 0213	15.229 918 2924	.065 660 2341	17
18	1.250 577 3941	20.046 191 5310	.049 884 7873	.799 630 6384	16.029 548 9307	.062 384 7873	18
19	1.266 209 6116	21.296 768 9251	.046 955 4797	.789 758 6552	16.819 307 5859	.059 455 4797	19
20	1.282 037 2317	22.562 978 5367	.044 320 3896	.780 008 5483	17.599 316 1342	.056 820 3896	20
21	1.298 062 6971	23.845 015 7684	.041 937 4854	.770 378 8132	18.369 694 9474	.054 437 4854	21
22	1.314 288 4808	25.143 078 4655	.039 772 3772	.760 867 9636	19.130 562 9110	.052 272 3772	22
23	1.330 717 0868	26.457 366 9463	.037 796 6561	.751 474 5320	19.882 037 4430	.050 296 6561	23
24	1.347 351 0504	27.788 084 0331	.035 986 6480	.742 197 0686	20.624 234 5116	.048 486 6480	24
25	1.364 192 9385	29.135 435 0836	.034 322 4667	.733 034 1418	21.357 268 6534	.046 822 4667	25
26	1.381 245 3503	30.499 628 0221	.032 787 2851	.723 984 3376	22.081 252 9910	.045 287 2851	26
27	1.398 510 9172	31.880 873 3724	.031 366 7693	.715 046 2594	22.796 299 2504	.043 866 7693	27
28	1.415 992 3036	33.279 384 2895	.030 048 6329	.706 218 5278	23.502 517 7782	.042 548 6329	28
29	1.433 692 2074	34.695 376 5932	.028 822 2841	.697 499 7805	24.200 017 5587	.041 322 2841	29
30	1.451 613 3600	36.129 068 8006	.027 678 5434	.688 888 6721	24.888 906 2308	.040 178 5434	30
31	1.469 758 5270	37.580 682 1606	.026 609 4159	.680 383 8737	25.569 290 1045	.039 109 4159	31
32	1.488 130 5066	39.050 440 6876	.025 607 9056	.671 984 0728	26.241 274 1773	.038 107 9056	32
33	1.506 732 1400	40.538 571 1962	.024 667 8650	.663 687 9731	26.904 962 1504	.037 167 8650	33
34	1.525 566 2917	42.045 303 3361	.023 783 8693	.655 494 2944	27.560 456 4448	.036 283 8693	34
35	1.544 635 8703	43.570 869 6278	.022 951 1141	.647 401 7723	28.207 858 2171	.035 451 1141	35
36	1.563 943 8187	45.115 505 4982	.022 165 3285	.639 409 1578	28.847 267 3749	.034 665 3285	36
37	1.583 493 1165	46.679 449 3169	.021 422 7035	.631 515 2176	29.478 782 5925	.033 922 7035	37
38	1.603 286 7804	48.262 942 4334	.020 719 8308	.623 718 7334	30.102 501 3259	.033 219 8308	38
39	1.623 327 8652	49.866 229 2138	.020 053 6519	.616 018 5021	30.718 519 8281	.032 553 6519	39
40	1.643 619 4635	51.489 557 0790	.019 421 4139	.608 413 3355	31.326 933 1635	.031 921 4139	40
41	1.664 164 7068	53.133 176 5424	.018 820 6327	.600 902 0597	31.927 835 2233	.031 320 6327	41
42	1.684 966 7656	54.797 341 2492	.018 249 0606	.593 483 5158	32.521 318 7390	.030 749 0606	42
43	1.706 028 8502	56.482 308 0148	.017 704 6589	.586 156 5588	33.107 475 2978	.030 204 6589	43
44	1.727 354 2108	58.188 336 8650	.017 185 5745	.578 920 0581	33.686 395 3558	.029 685 5745	44
45	1.748 946 1384	59.915 691 0758	.016 690 1188	.571 772 8968	34.258 168 2527	.029 190 1188	45
46	1.770 807 9652	61.664 637 2143	.016 216 7499	.564 713 9722	34.822 882 2249	.028 716 7499	46
47	1.792 943 0647	63.435 445 1795	.015 764 0574	.557 742 1948	35.380 624 4196	.028 264 0574	47
48	1.815 384 8531	65.228 388 2442	.015 330 7443	.550 856 4886	35.931 480 9083	.027 830 7443	48
49	1.838 046 7887	67.043 743 0973	.014 915 6350	.544 055 7913	36.475 536 6995	.027 415 6350	49
50	1.861 022 3736	68.881 789 8860	.014 517 6251	.537 339 0531	37.012 875 7526	.027 017 6251	50
51	1.884 285 1532	70.742 812 2596	.014 135 7117	.530 705 2376	37.543 580 9902	.026 635 7117	51
52	1.907 838 7177	72.627 097 4128	.013 768 9655	.524 153 3211	38.067 734 3114	.026 268 9655	52
53	1.931 686 7016	74.534 936 1305	.013 416 5272	.517 682 2925	38.585 416 6038	.025 916 5272	53
54	1.955 832 7854	76.466 622 8321	.013 077 6012	.511 291 1530	39.096 707 7568	.025 577 6012	54
55	1.980 280 6952	78.422 455 6175	.012 751 4497	.504 978 9166	39.601 686 6734	.025 251 4497	55
56	2.005 034 2039	80.402 736 3127	.012 437 3877	.498 744 6090	40.100 431 2824	.024 937 3877	56
57	2.030 097 1315	82.407 770 5166	.012 134 7780	.492 587 2681	40.593 018 5505	.024 634 7780	57
58	2.055 473 3456	84.437 867 6481	.011 843 0276	.486 505 9438	41.079 524 4943	.024 343 0276	58
59	2.081 166 7624	86.493 340 9937	.011 561 5837	.480 499 6976	41.560 024 1919	.024 061 5837	59
60	2.107 181 3470	88.574 507 7561	.011 289 9301	.474 567 6026	42.034 591 7945	.023 789 9301	60
61	2.133 521 1138	90.681 689 1031	.011 027 5846	.468 708 7843	42.503 300 5378	.023 527 5846	61
62	2.160 190 1277	92.815 210 2168	.010 774 0962	.462 922 2156	42.966 222 7534	.023 274 0962	62
63	2.187 192 5043	94.975 400 3445	.010 529 0422	.457 207 1265	43.423 429 8799	.023 029 0422	63
64	2.214 532 4106	97.162 592 8489	.010 292 0267	.451 562 5941	43.874 992 4739	.022 792 0267	64
65	2.242 214 0657	99.377 125 2595	.010 062 6779	.445 987 7474	44.320 980 2212	.022 562 6779	65
66	2.270 241 7416	101.619 339 3252	.009 840 6465	.440 481 7257	44.761 461 9468	.022 340 6465	66
67	2.298 619 7633	103.889 581 0668	.009 625 6043	.435 043 6797	45.196 505 6265	.022 125 6043	67
68	2.327 352 5104	106.188 200 8301	.009 417 2421	.429 672 7700	45.626 178 3966	.021 917 2421	68
69	2.356 444 4168	108.515 553 3405	.009 215 2689	.424 368 1679	46.050 546 5645	.021 715 2689	69
70	2.385 899 9720	110.871 997 7572	.009 019 4100	.419 129 0548	46.469 675 6193	.021 519 4100	70
71	2.415 324 9467	113.257 897 7292	.008 829 4063	.413 954 6220	46.883 630 2412	.021 329 4063	71
72	2.445 920 2681	115.673 621 4508	.008 645 0133	.408 844 0711	47.292 474 3123	.021 145 0133	72
73	2.476 494 2715	118.119 541 7190	.008 465 9997	.403 796 6134	47.696 270 9258	.020 965 9997	73
74	2.507 450 4499	120.596 035 9904	.008 292 1465	.398 811 4701	48.095 082 3958	.020 792 1465	74
75	2.538 793 5805	123.103 486 4403	.008 123 2468	.393 887 8717	48.488 970 2675	.020 623 2468	75
76	2.570 528 5003	125.642 280 0208	.007 959 1042	.389 025 0584	48.877 995 3259	.020 459 1042	76
77	2.602 660 1065	128.212 808 5211	.007 799 5328	.384 222 2799	49.262 217 6058	.020 299 5328	77
78	2.635 193 3578	130.815 468 6276	.007 644 3559	.379 478 7950	49.641 696 4008	.020 144 3559	78
79	2.668 133 2748	133.450 661 9854	.007 493 4061	.374 793 8716	50.016 490 2724	.019 993 4061	79
80	2.701 484 9408	136.118 795 2603	.007 346 5240	.370 166 7868	50.386 657 0592	.019 846 5240	80
81	2.735 253 5025	138.820 280 2010	.007 203 5584	.365 596 8264	50.752 253 8856	.019 703 5584	81
82	2.769 444 1713	141.555 533 7035	.007 064 3653	.361 083 2854	51.113 337 1710	.019 564 3653	82
83	2.804 062 2234	144.324 977 8748	.006 928 8076	.356 625 4670	51.469 962 6380	.019 428 8076	83
84	2.839 113 0012	147.129 040 0983	.006 796 7547	.352 222 6835	51.822 185 3215	.019 296 7547	84
85	2.874 601 9137	149.968 153 0995	.006 668 0824	.347 874 2553	52.170 059 5768	.019 168 0824	85
86	2.910 534 4377	152.842 755 0132	.006 542 6719	.343 579 5114	52.513 639 0882	.019 042 6719	86
87	2.946 916 1181	155.753 289 4509	.006 420 4101	.339 337 7890	52.852 976 8772	.018 920 4101	87
88	2.983 752 5696	158.700 205 5690	.006 301 1891	.335 148 4356	53.188 125 3108	.018 801 1891	88
89	3.021 049 4767	161.683 958 1386	.006 184 9055	.331 010 7986	53.519 136 1094	.018 684 9055	89
90	3.058 812 5952	164.705 007 6154	.006 071 4608	.326 924 2456	53.846 060 3550	.018 571 4608	90
91	3.097 047 7526	167.763 820 2106	.005 960 7608	.322 888 1438	54.168 948 4988	.018 460 7608	91
92	3.135 760 8495	170.860 867 9632	.005 852 7152	.318 901 8704	54.487 850 3692	.018 352 7152	92
93	3.174 957 8602	173.996 628 8127	.005 747 2378	.314 964 8103	54.802 815 1794	.018 247 2378	93
94	3.214 644 8334	177.171 586 6729	.005 644 2459	.311 076 3558	55.113 891 5352	.018 144 2459	94
95	3.254 827 8938	180.386 231 5063	.005 543 6604	.307 235 9070	55.421 127 4422	.018 043 6604	95
96	3.295 513 2425	183.641 059 4001	.005 445 4053	.303 442 8711	55.724 570 3133	.017 945 4053	96
97	3.336 707 1580	186.936 572 6426	.005 349 4080	.299 696 6628	56.024 266 9761	.017 849 4080	97
98	3.378 415 9975	190.273 279 8007	.005 255 5987	.295 996 7040	56.320 263 6801	.017 755 5987	98
99	3.420 645 1975	193.651 695 7982	.005 163 9104	.292 342 4237	56.612 606 1038	.017 663 9104	99
100	3.463 404 2749	197.072 341 9957	.005 074 2788	.288 733 2580	56.901 339 3618	.017 574 2788	100

	XIII COMPOUND AMOUNT	XIV AMOUNT OF ANNUITY	XV SINKING FUND	XVI PRESENT VALUE	XVII PRESENT VALUE OF ANNUITY	XVIII AMORTIZATION	
P E R I O D S	AMOUNT OF 1 *How $1 left at compound interest will grow.*	AMOUNT OF 1 PER PERIOD *How $1 deposited periodically will grow.*	SINKING FUND *Periodic deposit that will grow to $1 at future date.*	PRESENT WORTH OF 1 *What $1 due in the future is worth today.*	PRESENT WORTH OF 1 PER PERIOD *What $1 payable periodically is worth today.*	PARTIAL PAYMENT *Annuity worth $1 today. Periodic payment necessary to pay off a loan of $1.*	P E R I O D S
1	1.015 000 0000	1.000 000 0000	1.000 000 0000	.985 221 6749	.985 221 6749	1.015 000 0000	1
2	1.030 225 0000	2.015 000 0000	.496 277 9156	.970 661 7486	1.955 883 4235	.511 277 9156	2
3	1.045 678 3750	3.045 225 0000	.328 382 9602	.956 316 9937	2.912 200 4173	.343 382 9602	3
4	1.061 363 5506	4.090 903 3750	.244 444 7860	.942 184 2303	3.854 384 6476	.259 444 7860	4
5	1.077 284 0039	5.152 266 9256	.194 089 3231	.928 260 3254	4.782 644 9730	.209 089 3231	5
6	1.093 443 2639	6.229 550 9295	.160 525 2146	.914 542 1925	5.697 187 1655	.175 525 2146	6
7	1.109 844 9129	7.322 994 1935	.136 556 1645	.901 026 7907	6.598 213 9561	.151 556 1645	7
8	1.126 492 5866	8.432 839 1064	.118 584 0246	.887 711 1238	7.485 925 0799	.133 584 0246	8
9	1.143 389 9754	9.559 331 6929	.104 609 8234	.874 592 2402	8.360 517 3201	.119 609 8234	9
10	1.160 540 8250	10.702 721 6683	.093 434 1779	.861 667 2317	9.222 184 5519	.108 434 1779	10
11	1.177 948 9374	11.863 262 4934	.084 293 8442	.848 933 2332	10.071 117 7851	.099 293 8442	11
12	1.195 618 1715	13.041 211 4308	.076 679 9929	.836 387 4219	10.907 505 2070	.091 679 9929	12
13	1.213 552 4440	14.236 829 6022	.070 240 3574	.824 027 0166	11.731 532 2236	.085 240 3574	13
14	1.231 755 7307	15.450 382 0463	.064 723 3186	.811 849 2775	12.543 381 5011	.079 723 3186	14
15	1.250 232 0667	16.682 137 7770	.059 944 3557	.799 851 5049	13.343 233 0060	.074 944 3557	15
16	1.268 985 5477	17.932 369 8436	.055 765 0778	.788 031 0393	14.131 264 0453	.070 765 0778	16
17	1.288 020 3309	19.201 355 3913	.052 079 6569	.776 385 2604	14.907 649 3057	.067 079 6569	17
18	1.307 340 6358	20.489 375 7221	.048 805 7818	.764 911 5866	15.672 560 8924	.063 805 7818	18
19	1.326 950 7454	21.796 716 3580	.045 878 4701	.753 607 4745	16.426 168 3669	.060 878 4701	19
20	1.346 855 0066	23.123 667 1033	.043 245 7559	.742 470 4182	17.168 638 7851	.058 245 7359	20
21	1.367 057 8316	24.470 522 1099	.040 865 4950	.731 497 9490	17.900 136 7341	.055 865 4950	21
22	1.387 563 6991	25.837 579 9415	.038 703 3152	.720 687 6345	18.620 824 3685	.053 703 3152	22
23	1.408 377 1546	27.225 143 6407	.036 730 7520	.710 037 0783	19.330 861 4468	.051 730 7520	23
24	1.429 502 8119	28.633 520 7953	.034 924 1020	.699 543 9195	20.030 405 3663	.049 924 1020	24
25	1.450 945 3541	30.063 023 6072	.033 263 4539	.689 205 8320	20.719 611 1984	.048 263 4539	25
26	1.472 709 5344	31.513 968 9613	.031 731 9599	.679 020 5242	21.398 631 7225	.046 731 9599	26
27	1.494 800 1774	32.986 678 4957	.030 315 2680	.668 985 7381	22.067 617 4606	.045 315 2680	27
28	1.517 222 1801	34.481 478 6732	.029 001 0765	.659 099 2494	22.726 716 7100	.044 001 0765	28
29	1.539 980 5128	35.998 700 8533	.027 778 7802	.649 358 8664	23.376 075 5763	.042 778 7802	29
30	1.563 080 2205	37.538 681 3661	.026 639 1883	.639 762 4299	24.015 838 0062	.041 639 1883	30
31	1.586 526 4238	39.101 761 5865	.025 574 2954	.630 307 8127	24.646 145 8189	.040 574 2954	31
32	1.610 324 3202	40.688 288 0103	.024 577 0970	.620 992 9189	25.267 138 7379	.039 577 0970	32
33	1.634 479 1850	42.298 612 3305	.023 641 4375	.611 815 6857	25.878 954 4216	.038 641 4375	33
34	1.658 996 3727	43.933 091 5155	.022 761 8855	.602 774 0726	26.481 728 4941	.037 761 8855	34
35	1.683 881 3183	45.592 087 8882	.021 933 6303	.593 866 0814	27.075 594 5755	.036 933 6303	35
36	1.709 139 5381	47.275 969 2065	.021 152 3955	.585 089 7353	27.660 684 3109	.036 152 3955	36
37	1.734 776 6312	48.985 108 7446	.020 414 3673	.576 443 0890	28.237 127 3999	.035 414 3673	37
38	1.760 798 2806	50.719 885 3758	.019 716 1329	.567 924 2256	28.805 051 6255	.034 716 1329	38
39	1.787 210 2548	52.480 683 6564	.019 054 6298	.559 531 2568	29.364 582 8822	.034 054 6298	39
40	1.814 018 4087	54.267 893 9113	.018 427 1017	.551 262 3219	29.915 845 2042	.033 427 1017	40
41	1.841 228 6848	56.081 912 3199	.017 831 0610	.543 115 5881	30.458 960 7923	.032 831 0610	41
42	1.868 847 1151	57.923 141 0047	.017 264 2571	.535 089 2494	30.994 050 0417	.032 264 2571	42
43	1.896 879 8218	59.791 988 1198	.016 724 6488	.527 181 5265	31.521 231 5681	.031 724 6488	43
44	1.925 333 0191	61.688 867 9416	.016 210 3801	.519 390 6665	32.040 622 2346	.031 210 3804	44
45	1.954 213 0144	63.614 200 9607	.015 719 7604	.511 714 9423	32.552 337 1770	.030 719 7604	45
46	1.983 526 2096	65.568 413 9751	.015 251 2458	.504 152 6526	33.056 489 8295	.030 251 2458	46
47	2.013 279 1028	67.551 940 1848	.014 803 4238	.496 702 1207	33.553 191 9503	.029 803 4238	47
48	2.043 478 2893	69.565 219 2875	.014 374 9996	.489 361 6953	34.042 553 6456	.029 374 9996	48
49	2.074 130 4637	71.608 697 5768	.013 964 7841	.482 129 7491	34.524 683 3947	.028 964 7841	49
50	2.105 242 4206	73.682 828 0405	.013 571 6832	.475 004 6789	34.999 688 0736	.028 571 6832	50
51	2.136 821 0569	75.788 070 4611	.013 194 6887	.467 984 9053	35.467 672 9789	.028 194 6887	51
52	2.168 873 3728	77.924 891 5180	.012 832 8700	.461 068 8722	35.928 741 8511	.027 832 8700	52
53	2.201 406 4734	80.093 764 8908	.012 485 3664	.454 255 0465	36.382 996 8977	.027 485 3664	53
54	2.234 427 5705	82.295 171 3642	.012 151 3812	.447 541 9178	36.830 538 8154	.027 151 3812	54
55	2.267 943 9840	84.529 598 9346	.011 830 1756	.440 927 9978	37.271 466 8132	.026 830 1756	55
56	2.301 963 1438	86.797 542 9186	.011 521 0635	.434 411 8205	37.705 878 6337	.026 521 0635	56
57	2.336 492 5909	89.099 506 0624	.011 223 4068	.427 991 9414	38.133 870 5751	.026 223 4068	57
58	2.371 539 9798	91.435 998 6534	.010 936 6116	.421 666 9373	38.555 537 5124	.025 936 6116	58
59	2.407 113 0795	93.807 538 6332	.010 660 1241	.415 435 4062	38.970 972 9186	.025 660 1241	59
60	2.443 219 7757	96.214 651 7126	.010 393 4274	.409 295 9667	39.380 268 8853	.025 393 4274	60
61	2.479 868 0723	98.657 871 4883	.010 136 0387	.403 247 2579	39.783 516 1432	.025 136 0387	61
62	2.517 066 0934	101.137 739 5607	.009 887 5059	.397 287 9388	40.180 804 0820	.024 887 5059	62
63	2.554 822 0848	103.654 805 6541	.009 647 4061	.391 416 6886	40.572 220 7704	.024 647 4061	63
64	2.593 144 4161	106.209 627 7389	.009 415 3423	.385 632 2054	40.957 852 9758	.024 415 3423	64
65	2.632 041 5823	108.802 772 1550	.009 190 9423	.379 933 2073	41.337 786 1830	.024 190 9423	65
66	2.671 522 2061	111.434 813 7373	.008 973 8563	.374 318 4308	41.712 104 6138	.023 973 8563	66
67	2.711 595 0392	114.106 335 9434	.008 763 7552	.368 786 6313	42.080 891 2451	.023 763 7552	67
68	2.752 268 9647	116.817 930 9825	.008 560 3297	.363 336 5826	42.444 227 8277	.023 560 3297	68
69	2.793 552 9992	119.570 199 9472	.008 363 2878	.357 967 0764	42.802 194 9042	.023 363 2878	69
70	2.835 456 2942	122.363 752 9464	.008 172 3548	.352 676 9226	43.154 871 8268	.023 172 3548	70
71	2.877 988 1386	125.199 209 2406	.007 987 2709	.347 464 9484	43.502 336 7751	.022 987 2709	71
72	2.921 157 9607	128.077 197 3793	.007 807 7911	.342 329 9984	43.844 666 7735	.022 807 7911	72
73	2.964 975 3301	130.998 355 3399	.007 633 6836	.337 270 9344	44.181 937 7079	.022 633 6836	73
74	3.009 449 9601	133.963 330 6700	.007 464 7293	.332 286 6349	44.514 224 3428	.022 464 7293	74
75	3.054 591 7095	136.972 780 6301	.007 300 7206	.327 375 9949	44.841 600 3377	.022 300 7206	75
76	3.100 410 5851	140.027 372 3395	.007 141 4609	.322 537 9260	45.164 138 2638	.022 141 4609	76
77	3.146 916 7439	143.127 782 9246	.006 986 7637	.317 771 3557	45.481 909 6195	.021 986 7637	77
78	3.194 120 4950	146.274 699 6685	.006 836 4523	.313 075 2273	45.794 984 8468	.021 836 4523	78
79	3.242 032 3025	149.468 820 1635	.006 690 3586	.308 448 4998	46.103 433 3466	.021 690 3586	79
80	3.290 662 7870	152.710 852 4660	.006 548 3231	.303 890 1476	46.407 323 4941	.021 548 3231	80
81	3.340 022 7288	156.001 515 2530	.006 410 1941	.299 399 1602	46.706 722 6543	.021 410 1941	81
82	3.390 123 0697	159.341 537 9818	.006 275 8275	.294 974 5421	47.001 697 1964	.021 275 8275	82
83	3.440 974 9158	162.731 661 0515	.006 145 0857	.290 615 3124	47.292 312 5088	.021 145 0857	83
84	3.492 589 5395	166.172 635 9673	.006 017 8380	.286 320 5048	47.578 633 0136	.021 017 8380	84
85	3.544 978 3826	169.665 225 5068	.005 893 9597	.282 089 1673	47.860 722 1808	.020 893 9597	85
86	3.598 153 0583	173.210 203 8894	.005 773 3319	.277 920 3619	48.138 642 5427	.020 773 3319	86
87	3.652 125 3542	176.808 356 9477	.005 655 8413	.273 813 1644	48.412 455 7071	.020 655 8413	87
88	3.706 907 2345	180.460 482 3019	.005 541 3794	.269 766 6644	48.682 222 3715	.020 541 3794	88
89	3.762 510 8430	184.167 389 5365	.005 429 8429	.265 779 9650	48.948 002 3365	.020 429 8429	89
90	3.818 948 5057	187.929 900 3795	.005 321 1330	.261 852 1822	49.209 854 5187	.020 321 1330	90
91	3.876 232 7333	191.748 848 8852	.005 215 1552	.257 982 4455	49.467 836 9642	.020 215 1552	91
92	3.934 376 2243	195.625 081 6185	.005 111 8190	.254 169 8971	49.722 006 8613	.020 111 8190	92
93	3.993 391 8676	199.559 457 8428	.005 011 0379	.250 413 6917	49.972 420 5530	.020 011 0379	93
94	4.053 292 7457	203.552 849 7104	.004 912 7291	.246 712 9968	50.219 133 5498	.019 912 7291	94
95	4.114 092 1368	207.606 142 4561	.004 816 8132	.243 066 9919	50.462 200 5416	.019 816 8132	95
96	4.175 803 5189	211.720 234 5929	.004 723 2141	.239 474 8688	50.701 675 4105	.019 723 2141	96
97	4.238 440 5717	215.896 038 1118	.004 631 8590	.235 935 8314	50.937 611 2419	.019 631 8590	97
98	4.302 017 1803	220.134 478 6835	.004 542 6778	.232 449 0949	51.170 060 3368	.019 542 6778	98
99	4.366 547 4380	224.436 495 8637	.004 455 6033	.229 013 8866	51.399 074 2235	.019 455 6033	99
100	4.432 045 6495	228.803 043 3017	.004 370 5712	.225 629 4450	51.624 703 6684	.019 370 5712	100

	XIII COMPOUND AMOUNT	XIV AMOUNT OF ANNUITY	XV SINKING FUND	XVI PRESENT VALUE	XVII PRESENT VALUE OF ANNUITY	XVIII AMORTIZATION	

RATE 1¾%

PERIODS	AMOUNT OF 1 How $1 left at compound interest will grow.	AMOUNT OF 1 PER PERIOD How $1 deposited periodically will grow.	SINKING FUND Periodic deposit that will grow to $1 at future date.	PRESENT WORTH OF 1 What $1 due in the future is worth today.	PRESENT WORTH OF 1 PER PERIOD What $1 payable periodically is worth today.	PARTIAL PAYMENT Annuity worth $1 today. Periodic payment necessary to pay off a loan of $1.	PERIODS
1	1.017 500 0000	1.000 000 0000	1.000 000 0000	.982 800 9828	.982 800 9828	1.017 500 0000	1
2	1.035 306 2500	2.017 500 0000	.495 662 9492	.965 897 7718	1.948 698 7546	.513 162 9492	2
3	1.053 424 1094	3.052 806 2500	.327 567 4635	.949 285 2794	2.897 984 0340	.345 067 4635	3
4	1.071 859 0313	4.106 230 3594	.243 532 3673	.932 958 5056	3.830 942 5396	.261 032 3673	4
5	1.090 616 5643	5.178 089 3907	.193 121 4246	.916 912 5362	4.747 855 0757	.210 621 4246	5
6	1.109 702 3542	6.268 705 9550	.159 522 5565	.901 142 5417	5.648 997 6174	.177 022 5565	6
7	1.129 122 1454	7.378 408 3092	.135 530 5857	.885 643 7756	6.534 641 3930	.153 030 5857	7
8	1.148 881 7830	8.507 530 4546	.117 542 9233	.870 411 5731	7.405 052 9661	.135 042 9233	8
9	1.168 987 2142	9.656 412 2376	.103 558 1306	.855 441 3495	8.260 494 3156	.121 058 1306	9
10	1.189 444 4904	10.825 399 4517	.092 375 3442	.840 728 5959	9.101 222 9146	.109 875 3442	10
11	1.210 259 7690	12.014 843 9421	.083 230 3778	.826 268 8934	9.927 491 8080	.100 730 3778	11
12	1.231 439 3149	13.225 103 7111	.075 613 7738	.812 057 8805	10.739 549 6884	.093 113 7738	12
13	1.252 989 5030	14.456 543 0261	.069 172 8305	.798 091 2830	11.537 640 9714	.086 672 8305	13
14	1.274 916 8193	15.709 532 5290	.063 655 6179	.784 364 8973	12.322 005 8687	.081 155 6179	14
15	1.297 227 8636	16.984 449 3483	.058 877 3872	.770 874 5919	13.092 880 4607	.076 377 3872	15
16	1.319 929 3512	18.281 677 2119	.054 699 5764	.757 616 3066	13.850 496 7672	.072 199 5764	16
17	1.343 028 1149	19.601 606 5631	.051 016 2265	.744 586 0507	14.595 082 8179	.068 516 2265	17
18	1.366 531 1069	20.944 634 6779	.047 744 9244	.731 779 9024	15.326 862 7203	.065 244 9244	18
19	1.390 445 4012	22.311 165 7848	.044 820 6073	.719 194 0073	16.046 056 7276	.062 320 6073	19
20	1.414 778 1958	23.701 611 1860	.042 191 2246	.706 824 5772	16.752 881 3048	.059 691 2246	20
21	1.439 536 8142	25.116 389 3818	.039 814 6399	.694 667 8891	17.447 549 1939	.057 314 6399	21
22	1.464 728 7084	26.555 926 1960	.037 656 3782	.682 720 2841	18.130 269 4780	.055 156 3782	22
23	1.490 361 4608	28.020 654 9044	.035 687 9596	.670 978 1662	18.801 247 6442	.053 187 9596	23
24	1.516 442 7864	29.511 016 3652	.033 885 6510	.659 438 0012	19.460 685 6454	.051 385 6510	24
25	1.542 980 5352	31.027 459 1516	.032 229 5163	.648 096 3157	20.108 781 9611	.049 729 5163	25
26	1.569 882 6945	32.570 439 6868	.030 702 6865	.636 949 6960	20.745 731 6571	.048 202 6865	26
27	1.597 457 3917	34.140 422 3813	.029 290 7917	.625 994 7872	21.371 726 4443	.046 790 7917	27
28	1.625 412 8960	35.737 879 7730	.027 981 5145	.615 228 2992	21.986 954 7364	.045 481 5145	28
29	1.653 857 6217	37.363 292 6690	.026 764 2365	.604 646 9701	22.591 601 7066	.044 264 2365	29
30	1.682 800 1303	39.017 150 2907	.025 629 7954	.594 247 6365	23.185 849 3431	.043 129 7954	30
31	1.712 249 1324	40.699 950 4208	.024 570 0545	.584 027 1612	23.769 876 5042	.042 070 0545	31
32	1.742 213 4922	42.412 199 5532	.023 578 1216	.573 982 4680	24.343 858 9722	.041 078 1216	32
33	1.772 702 2283	44.154 413 0453	.022 647 7928	.564 110 5336	24.907 969 5059	.040 147 7928	33
34	1.803 724 5173	45.927 115 2736	.021 773 6297	.554 408 3893	25.462 377 8928	.039 273 6297	34
35	1.835 289 6963	47.730 839 7909	.020 950 8151	.544 873 1075	26.007 251 0003	.038 450 8151	35
36	1.867 407 2660	49.566 129 4873	.020 175 0673	.535 501 8255	26.542 752 8258	.037 675 0673	36
37	1.900 086 8932	51.433 536 7533	.019 442 5673	.526 291 7204	27.069 044 5462	.036 942 5673	37
38	1.933 338 4138	53.333 623 6465	.018 749 8979	.517 240 0201	27.586 284 5663	.036 249 8979	38
39	1.967 171 8361	55.266 962 0603	.018 093 9926	.508 344 0001	28.094 628 5664	.035 593 9926	39
40	2.001 597 3432	57.234 133 8963	.017 472 0911	.499 600 9829	28.594 229 5493	.034 972 0911	40
41	2.036 625 2967	59.235 731 2395	.016 881 7026	.491 008 3370	29.085 237 8863	.034 381 7026	41
42	2.072 266 2394	61.272 356 5362	.016 320 5735	.482 563 4762	29.567 801 3625	.033 820 5735	42
43	2.108 530 8986	63.344 622 7756	.015 786 6596	.474 263 8586	30.042 065 2211	.033 286 6596	43
44	2.145 430 1893	65.453 153 6742	.015 278 1026	.466 106 9864	30.508 172 2075	.032 778 1026	44
45	2.182 975 2176	67.598 583 8635	.014 793 2093	.458 090 4043	30.966 262 6117	.032 293 2093	45
46	2.221 177 2839	69.781 559 0811	.014 330 4336	.450 211 6996	31.416 474 3113	.031 830 4336	46
47	2.260 047 8864	72.002 736 3650	.013 888 3611	.442 468 5008	31.858 942 8121	.031 388 3611	47
48	2.299 598 7244	74.262 784 2514	.013 465 6950	.434 858 4774	32.293 801 2895	.030 965 6950	48
49	2.339 841 7021	76.562 382 9758	.013 061 2445	.427 379 3390	32.721 180 6285	.030 561 2445	49
50	2.380 788 9319	78.902 224 6779	.012 673 9139	.420 028 8304	33.141 209 4629	.030 173 9139	50
51	2.422 452 7382	81.283 013 6097	.012 302 6935	.412 804 7513	33.554 014 2142	.029 802 6935	51
52	2.464 845 6611	83.705 466 3479	.011 946 6511	.405 704 9163	33.959 719 1294	.029 446 6511	52
53	2.507 980 4602	86.170 312 0090	.011 604 9249	.398 727 1894	34.358 446 3188	.029 104 9249	53
54	2.551 870 1182	88.678 292 4691	.011 276 7169	.391 869 4734	34.750 315 7925	.028 776 7169	54
55	2.596 527 8453	91.230 162 5874	.010 961 2871	.385 129 7038	35.135 445 4963	.028 461 2871	55
56	2.641 967 0826	93.826 690 4326	.010 657 9481	.378 505 8614	35.513 951 3477	.028 157 9481	56
57	2.688 201 5065	96.468 657 5152	.010 366 0611	.371 995 9228	35.885 947 2705	.027 866 0611	57
58	2.735 245 0329	99.156 859 0217	.010 085 0310	.365 597 9585	36.251 545 2290	.027 585 0310	58
59	2.783 111 8210	101.892 104 0546	.009 814 3032	.359 310 0329	36.610 855 2619	.027 314 3032	59
60	2.831 816 2778	104.675 215 8756	.009 553 3598	.353 130 2535	36.963 985 5154	.027 053 3598	60
61	2.881 373 0627	107.507 032 1534	.009 301 7171	.347 056 7602	37.311 042 2755	.026 801 7171	61
62	2.931 797 0913	110.388 405 2161	.009 058 9224	.341 087 7250	37.652 130 0005	.026 558 9224	62
63	2.983 103 5404	113.320 202 3073	.008 824 5518	.335 221 3513	37.987 351 3519	.026 324 5518	63
64	3.035 307 8523	116.303 305 8477	.008 598 2079	.329 455 8736	38.316 807 2254	.026 098 2079	64
65	3.088 425 7398	119.338 613 7001	.008 379 5175	.323 789 5056	38.640 596 7817	.025 879 5175	65
66	3.142 473 1902	122.427 039 4398	.008 168 1302	.318 220 6942	38.958 817 4759	.025 668 1302	66
67	3.197 466 4710	125.569 512 6300	.007 963 7165	.312 747 6110	39.271 565 0869	.025 463 7165	67
68	3.253 422 1343	128.766 979 1010	.007 765 9661	.307 368 6594	39.578 933 7463	.025 265 9661	68
69	3.310 357 0216	132.020 401 2353	.007 574 5869	.302 082 2206	39.881 015 9669	.025 074 5869	69
70	3.368 288 2695	135.330 758 2569	.007 389 3032	.296 886 7033	40.177 902 6702	.024 889 3032	70
71	3.427 233 3142	138.699 046 5264	.007 209 8549	.291 780 5438	40.469 683 2139	.024 709 8549	71
72	3.487 209 8972	142.126 279 8406	.007 035 9964	.286 762 2052	40.756 445 4191	.024 535 9964	72
73	3.548 236 0704	145.613 489 7378	.006 867 4956	.281 830 1771	41.038 275 5962	.024 367 4956	73
74	3.610 330 2016	149.161 725 8083	.006 704 1327	.276 982 9750	41.315 258 5712	.024 204 1327	74
75	3.673 510 9802	152.772 056 0099	.006 545 6997	.272 219 1401	41.587 477 7112	.024 045 6997	75
76	3.737 797 4223	156.445 566 9901	.006 391 9996	.267 537 2384	41.855 014 9496	.023 891 9996	76
77	3.803 208 8772	160.183 364 4124	.006 242 8455	.262 935 8608	42.117 950 8104	.023 742 8455	77
78	3.869 765 0326	163.986 573 2896	.006 098 0602	.258 413 6224	42.376 364 4329	.023 598 0602	78
79	3.937 485 9206	167.856 338 3222	.005 957 4754	.253 969 1621	42.630 333 5949	.023 457 4754	79
80	4.006 391 9242	171.793 824 2428	.005 820 9310	.249 601 1421	42.879 934 7370	.023 320 9310	80
81	4.076 503 7829	175.800 216 1671	.005 688 2751	.245 308 2478	43.125 242 9848	.023 188 2751	81
82	4.147 842 5991	179.876 719 9500	.005 559 3631	.241 089 1870	43.366 332 1718	.023 059 3631	82
83	4.220 429 8446	184.024 562 5491	.005 434 0572	.236 942 6899	43.603 274 8617	.022 934 0572	83
84	4.294 287 3669	188.244 992 3937	.005 312 2263	.232 867 5085	43.836 142 3702	.022 812 2263	84
85	4.369 437 3958	192.539 279 7606	.005 193 7454	.228 862 4142	44.065 004 7845	.022 693 7454	85
86	4.445 902 5502	196.908 717 1564	.005 078 4953	.224 926 2076	44.289 930 9941	.022 578 4953	86
87	4.523 705 8449	201.354 619 7067	.004 966 3623	.221 057 6979	44.510 988 6920	.022 466 3623	87
88	4.602 870 6972	205.878 325 5515	.004 857 2379	.217 255 7227	44.728 244 4147	.022 357 2379	88
89	4.683 420 9344	210.481 196 2487	.004 751 0182	.213 519 1378	44.941 763 5525	.022 251 0182	89
90	4.765 380 8007	215.164 617 1830	.004 647 6043	.209 846 8185	45.151 610 3711	.022 147 6043	90
91	4.848 774 9647	219.929 997 9837	.004 546 9013	.206 237 6595	45.357 848 0305	.022 046 9013	91
92	4.933 628 5266	224.778 772 9485	.004 448 8187	.202 690 5744	45.560 538 6049	.021 948 8187	92
93	5.019 967 0258	229.712 401 4751	.004 353 2695	.199 204 4957	45.759 743 1007	.021 853 2695	93
94	5.107 816 4488	234.732 368 5009	.004 260 1709	.195 778 3742	45.955 521 4749	.021 760 1709	94
95	5.197 203 2366	239.840 184 9496	.004 169 4431	.192 411 1786	46.147 932 6534	.021 669 4431	95
96	5.288 154 2933	245.037 388 1863	.004 081 0099	.189 101 8954	46.337 034 5488	.021 581 0099	96
97	5.380 696 9934	250.325 542 4795	.003 994 7981	.185 849 5286	46.522 884 0775	.021 494 7981	97
98	5.474 859 1908	255.706 239 4729	.003 910 7376	.182 653 0994	46.705 537 1769	.021 410 7376	98
99	5.570 669 2266	261.181 098 6637	.003 828 7610	.179 511 6456	46.885 048 8225	.021 328 7610	99
100	5.668 155 9381	266.751 767 8903	.003 748 8036	.176 424 2217	47.061 473 0442	.021 248 8036	100

	XIII COMPOUND AMOUNT	XIV AMOUNT OF ANUITY	XV SINKING FUND	XVI PRESENT VALUE	XVII PRESENT VALUE OF ANNUITY	XVIII AMORTIZATION	
P E R I O D S	AMOUNT OF 1 How $1 left at compound interest will grow.	AMOUNT OF 1 PER PERIOD How $1 deposited periodically will grow.	SINKING FUND Periodic deposit that will grow to $1 at future date.	PRESENT WORTH OF 1 What $1 due in the future is worth today.	PRESENT WORTH OF 1 PER PERIOD What $1 payable periodically is worth today.	PARTIAL PAYMENT Annuity worth $1 today. Periodic payment necessary to pay off a loan of $1.	P E R I O D S
1	1.020 000 0000	1.000 000 0000	1.000 000 0000	.980 392 1569	.980 392 1569	1.020 000 0000	1
2	1.040 400 0000	2.020 000 0000	.495 049 5050	.961 168 7812	1.941 560 9381	.515 049 5050	2
3	1.061 208 0000	3.060 400 0000	.326 754 6726	.942 322 3345	2.883 883 2726	.346 754 6726	3
4	1.082 432 1600	4.121 608 0000	.242 623 7527	.923 845 4260	3.807 728 6987	.262 623 7527	4
5	1.104 080 8032	5.204 040 1600	.192 158 3941	.905 730 8098	4.713 459 5085	.212 158 3941	5
6	1.126 162 4193	6.308 120 9632	.158 525 8123	.887 971 3822	5.601 430 8907	.178 525 8123	6
7	1.148 685 6676	7.434 283 3825	.134 511 9561	.870 560 1786	6.471 991 0693	.154 511 9561	7
8	1.171 659 3810	8.582 969 0501	.116 509 7991	.853 490 3712	7.325 481 4405	.136 509 7991	8
9	1.195 092 5686	9.754 628 4311	.102 515 4374	.836 755 2659	8.162 236 7064	.122 515 4374	9
10	1.218 994 4200	10.949 720 9997	.091 326 5279	.820 348 2999	8.982 585 0062	.111 326 5279	10
11	1.243 374 3084	12.168 715 4197	.082 177 9428	.804 263 0391	9.786 848 0453	.102 177 9428	11
12	1.268 241 7946	13.412 089 7281	.074 559 5966	.788 493 1756	10.575 341 2209	.094 559 5966	12
13	1.293 606 6305	14.680 331 5227	.068 118 3527	.773 032 5251	11.348 373 7460	.088 118 3527	13
14	1.319 478 7631	15.973 938 1531	.062 601 9702	.757 875 0246	12.106 248 7706	.082 601 9702	14
15	1.345 868 3383	17.293 416 9162	.057 825 4723	.743 014 7300	12.849 263 5006	.077 825 4723	15
16	1.372 785 7051	18.639 285 2545	.053 650 1259	.728 445 8137	13.577 709 3143	.073 650 1259	16
17	1.400 241 4192	20.012 070 9596	.049 969 8408	.714 162 5625	14.291 871 8768	.069 969 8408	17
18	1.428 246 2476	21.412 312 3788	.046 702 1022	.700 159 3750	14.992 031 2517	.066 702 1022	18
19	1.456 811 1725	22.840 558 6264	.043 781 7663	.686 430 7598	15.678 462 0115	.063 781 7663	19
20	1.485 947 3960	24.297 369 7989	.041 156 7181	.672 971 3331	16.351 433 3446	.061 156 7181	20
21	1.515 666 3439	25.783 317 1949	.038 784 7689	.659 775 8168	17.011 209 1614	.058 784 7689	21
22	1.545 979 6708	27.298 983 5388	.036 631 4005	.646 839 0361	17.658 048 1974	.056 631 4005	22
23	1.576 899 2642	28.844 963 2096	.034 668 0976	.634 155 9177	18.292 204 1151	.054 668 0976	23
24	1.608 437 2495	30.421 862 4738	.032 871 0975	.621 721 4879	18.913 925 6031	.052 871 0975	24
25	1.640 605 9945	32.030 299 7232	.031 220 4384	.609 530 8705	19.523 456 4736	.051 220 4384	25
26	1.673 418 1144	33.670 905 7177	.029 699 2308	.597 579 2848	20.121 035 7584	.049 699 2308	26
27	1.706 886 4766	35.344 323 8321	.028 293 0862	.585 862 0440	20.706 897 8024	.048 293 0862	27
28	1.741 024 2062	37.051 210 3087	.026 989 6716	.574 374 5523	21.281 272 3553	.046 989 6716	28
29	1.775 844 6903	38.792 234 5149	.025 778 3552	.563 112 3068	21.844 384 6620	.045 778 3552	29
30	1.811 361 5841	40.568 079 2052	.024 649 9223	.552 070 8890	22.396 455 5510	.044 649 9223	30
31	1.847 588 8158	42.379 440 7893	.023 596 3472	.541 245 9696	22.937 701 5206	.043 596 3472	31
32	1.884 540 5921	44.227 029 6051	.022 610 6073	.530 633 3035	23.468 334 8241	.042 610 6073	32
33	1.922 231 4039	46.111 570 1972	.021 686 5311	.520 228 7289	23.988 563 5530	.041 686 5311	33
34	1.960 676 0320	48.033 801 6010	.020 818 6728	.510 028 1656	24.498 591 7187	.040 818 6728	34
35	1.999 889 5527	49.994 477 6331	.020 002 2092	.500 027 6134	24.998 619 3320	.040 002 2092	35
36	2.039 887 3437	51.994 367 1858	.019 232 8526	.490 223 1504	25.488 842 4824	.039 232 8526	36
37	2.080 685 0906	54.034 254 5295	.018 506 7789	.480 610 9317	25.969 453 4141	.038 506 7789	37
38	2.122 298 7924	56.114 939 6201	.017 820 5663	.471 187 1880	26.440 640 6021	.037 820 5663	38
39	2.164 744 7682	58.237 238 4125	.017 171 1439	.461 948 2235	26.902 588 8256	.037 171 1439	39
40	2.208 039 6636	60.401 983 1807	.016 555 7478	.452 890 4152	27.355 479 2407	.036 555 7478	40
41	2.252 200 4569	62.610 022 8444	.015 971 8836	.444 010 2110	27.799 489 4517	.035 971 8836	41
42	2.297 244 4660	64.862 223 3012	.015 417 2945	.435 304 1284	28.234 793 5801	.035 417 2945	42
43	2.343 189 3553	67.159 467 7673	.014 889 9334	.426 768 7533	28.661 562 3334	.034 889 9334	43
44	2.390 053 1425	69.502 657 1226	.014 387 9391	.418 400 7386	29.079 963 0720	.034 387 9391	44
45	2.437 854 2053	71.892 710 2651	.013 909 6161	.410 196 8025	29.490 159 8745	.033 909 6161	45
46	2.486 611 2894	74.330 564 4704	.013 453 4159	.402 153 7280	29.892 313 6025	.033 453 4159	46
47	2.536 343 5152	76.817 175 7598	.013 017 9220	.394 268 3607	30.286 581 9632	.033 017 9220	47
48	2.587 070 3855	79.353 519 2750	.012 601 8355	.386 537 6086	30.673 119 5718	.032 601 8355	48
49	2.638 811 7932	81.940 589 6605	.012 203 9639	.378 958 4398	31.052 078 0115	.032 203 9639	49
50	2.691 588 0291	84.579 401 4537	.011 823 2097	.371 527 8821	31.423 605 8937	.031 823 2097	50
51	2.745 419 7897	87.270 989 4828	.011 458 5615	.364 243 0217	31.787 848 9153	.031 458 5615	51
52	2.800 328 1854	90.016 409 2724	.011 109 0856	.357 101 0017	32.144 949 9170	.031 109 0856	52
53	2.856 334 7492	92.816 737 4579	.010 773 9189	.350 099 0212	32.495 048 9382	.030 773 9189	53
54	2.913 461 4441	95.673 072 2070	.010 452 2618	.343 234 3345	32.838 283 2728	.030 452 2618	54
55	2.971 730 6730	98.586 533 6512	.010 143 3732	.336 504 2496	33.174 787 5223	.030 143 3732	55
56	3.031 165 2865	101.558 264 3242	.009 846 5645	.329 906 1271	33.504 693 6494	.029 846 5645	56
57	3.091 788 5922	104.589 429 6107	.009 561 1957	.323 437 3794	33.828 131 0288	.029 561 1957	57
58	3.153 624 3641	107.681 218 2029	.009 286 6706	.317 095 4700	34.145 226 4988	.029 286 6706	58
59	3.216 696 8513	110.834 842 5669	.009 022 4335	.310 877 9118	34.456 104 4106	.029 022 4335	59
60	3.281 030 7884	114.051 539 4183	.008 767 9658	.304 782 2665	34.760 886 6770	.028 767 9658	60
61	3.346 651 4041	117.332 570 2066	.008 522 7827	.298 806 1436	35.059 692 8206	.028 522 7827	61
62	3.413 584 4322	120.679 221 6108	.008 286 4306	.292 947 1996	35.352 640 0202	.028 286 4306	62
63	3.481 856 1209	124.092 806 0430	.008 058 4849	.287 203 1369	35.639 843 1571	.028 058 4849	63
64	3.551 493 2433	127.574 662 1638	.007 838 5471	.281 571 7028	35.921 414 8599	.027 838 5471	64
65	3.622 523 1081	131.126 155 4071	.007 626 2436	.276 050 6890	36.197 465 5489	.027 626 2436	65
66	3.694 973 5703	134.748 678 5153	.007 421 2231	.270 637 9304	36.468 103 4793	.027 421 2231	66
67	3.768 873 0417	138.443 652 0856	.007 223 1543	.265 331 3043	36.733 434 7837	.027 223 1543	67
68	3.844 250 5025	142.212 525 1273	.007 031 7294	.260 128 7297	36.993 563 5134	.027 031 7294	68
69	3.921 135 5126	146.056 775 6298	.006 846 6526	.255 028 1664	37.248 591 6798	.026 846 6526	69
70	3.999 558 2228	149.977 911 1424	.006 667 6485	.250 027 6141	37.498 619 2939	.026 667 6485	70
71	4.079 549 3873	153.977 469 3653	.006 494 4567	.245 125 1119	37.743 744 4058	.026 494 4567	71
72	4.161 140 3751	158.057 018 7526	.006 326 8307	.240 318 7371	37.984 063 1429	.026 326 8307	72
73	4.244 363 1826	162.218 159 1276	.006 164 5380	.235 606 6050	38.219 669 7480	.026 164 5380	73
74	4.329 250 4462	166.462 522 3102	.006 007 3582	.230 986 8677	38.450 656 6157	.026 007 3582	74
75	4.415 835 4551	170.791 772 7564	.005 855 0830	.226 457 7134	38.677 114 3291	.025 855 0830	75
76	4.504 152 1642	175.207 608 2115	.005 707 5147	.222 017 3661	38.899 131 6952	.025 707 5147	76
77	4.594 235 2075	179.711 760 3757	.005 564 6461	.217 664 0844	39.116 795 7796	.025 564 6461	77
78	4.686 119 9117	184.305 995 5833	.005 425 7595	.213 396 1612	39.330 191 9408	.025 425 7595	78
79	4.779 842 3099	188.992 115 4949	.005 291 2260	.209 211 9227	39.539 403 8635	.025 291 2260	79
80	4.875 439 1561	193.771 957 8048	.005 160 7055	.205 109 7282	39.744 513 5917	.025 160 7055	80
81	4.972 947 9392	198.647 396 9609	.005 034 0453	.201 087 9688	39.945 601 5605	.025 034 0453	81
82	5.072 406 8980	203.620 344 9001	.004 911 1006	.197 145 0674	40.142 746 6279	.024 911 1006	82
83	5.173 855 0360	208.692 751 7981	.004 791 7333	.193 279 4779	40.336 026 1058	.024 791 7333	83
84	5.277 332 1367	213.866 606 8341	.004 675 8118	.189 489 6842	40.525 515 7900	.024 675 8118	84
85	5.382 878 7794	219.143 938 9708	.004 563 2108	.185 774 2002	40.711 289 9902	.024 563 2108	85
86	5.490 536 3550	224.526 817 7502	.004 453 8110	.182 131 5688	40.893 421 5590	.024 453 8110	86
87	5.600 347 0821	230.017 354 1052	.004 347 4981	.178 560 3616	41.071 981 9206	.024 347 4981	87
88	5.712 354 0237	235.617 701 1873	.004 244 1633	.175 059 1780	41.247 041 0986	.024 244 1633	88
89	5.826 601 1042	241.330 055 2111	.004 143 7027	.171 626 6451	41.418 667 7437	.024 143 7027	89
90	5.943 133 1263	247.156 656 3153	.004 046 0169	.168 261 4168	41.586 929 1605	.024 046 0169	90
91	6.061 995 7888	253.099 789 4416	.003 951 0108	.164 962 1733	41.751 891 3339	.023 951 0108	91
92	6.183 235 7046	259.161 785 2304	.003 858 5936	.161 727 6209	41.913 618 9548	.023 858 5936	92
93	6.306 900 4187	265.345 020 9350	.003 768 6782	.158 556 4911	42.072 175 4458	.023 768 6782	93
94	6.433 038 4271	271.651 921 3537	.003 681 1814	.155 447 5403	42.227 622 9861	.023 681 1814	94
95	6.561 699 1956	278.084 959 7808	.003 596 0233	.152 399 5493	42.380 022 5354	.023 596 0233	95
96	6.692 933 1795	284.646 658 9764	.003 513 1275	.149 411 3228	42.529 433 8582	.023 513 1275	96
97	6.826 791 8431	291.339 592 1559	.003 432 4205	.146 481 6891	42.675 915 5473	.023 432 4205	97
98	6.963 327 6800	298.166 383 9991	.003 353 8321	.143 609 4991	42.819 525 0464	.023 353 8321	98
99	7.102 594 2336	305.129 711 6790	.003 277 2947	.140 793 6265	42.960 318 6729	.023 277 2947	99
100	7.244 646 1183	312.232 305 9126	.003 202 7435	.138 032 9672	43.098 351 6401	.023 202 7435	100

RATE 2%

	XIII COMPOUND AMOUNT	XIV AMOUNT OF ANNUITY	XV SINKING FUND	XVI PRESENT VALUE	XVII PRESENT VALUE OF ANNUITY	XVIII AMORTIZATION	
P E R I O D S	AMOUNT OF 1 *How $1 left at compound interest will grow.*	AMOUNT OF 1 PER PERIOD *How $1 deposited periodically will grow.*	SINKING FUND *Periodic deposit that will grow to $1 at future date.*	PRESENT WORTH OF 1 *What $1 due in the future is worth today.*	PRESENT WORTH OF 1 PER PERIOD *What $1 payable periodically is worth today.*	PARTIAL PAYMENT *Annuity worth $1 today. Periodic payment necessary to pay off a loan of $1.*	P E R I O D S
1	1.022 500 0000	1.000 000 0000	1.000 000 0000	.977 995 1100	.977 995 1100	1.022 500 0000	1
2	1.045 506 2500	2.022 500 0000	.494 437 5773	.956 474 4352	1.934 469 5453	.516 937 5773	2
3	1.069 030 1406	3.068 006 2500	.325 944 5772	.935 427 3205	2.869 896 8658	.348 444 5772	3
4	1.093 083 3188	4.137 036 3906	.241 718 9277	.914 843 3453	3.784 740 2110	.264 218 9277	4
5	1.117 617 6935	5.230 119 7094	.191 200 2125	.894 712 3181	4.679 452 5291	.213 700 2125	5
6	1.142 825 4416	6.347 797 4029	.157 534 9584	.875 024 2720	5.554 476 8011	.180 034 9584	6
7	1.168 539 0140	7.490 622 8444	.133 500 2470	.855 769 4591	6.410 246 2602	.156 000 2470	7
8	1.194 831 1418	8.659 161 8584	.115 484 6181	.836 938 3464	7.247 184 6066	.137 984 6181	8
9	1.221 714 8425	9.853 993 0003	.101 481 7039	.818 521 6101	8.065 706 2167	.123 981 7039	9
10	1.249 053 4265	11.075 707 8428	.090 287 6831	.800 510 1322	8.866 216 3489	.112 787 6831	10
11	1.277 310 5036	12.324 911 2692	.081 136 4868	.782 894 9948	9.649 111 3436	.103 636 4868	11
12	1.306 049 9899	13.602 221 7728	.073 517 4015	.765 667 4765	10.414 778 8202	.096 017 4015	12
13	1.335 436 1147	14.908 271 7627	.067 076 8561	.748 819 0349	11.163 597 8681	.089 576 8561	13
14	1.365 483 4272	16.243 707 8773	.061 562 2989	.732 341 3672	11.895 939 2354	.084 062 2989	14
15	1.396 206 8044	17.609 191 3046	.056 788 5250	.716 226 2760	12.612 165 5113	.079 288 5250	15
16	1.427 621 4575	19.005 398 1089	.052 616 6300	.700 465 7956	13.312 631 3069	.075 116 6300	16
17	1.459 742 9402	20.433 019 5664	.048 940 3926	.685 052 1228	13.997 683 4298	.071 440 3926	17
18	1.492 587 1564	21.892 762 5066	.045 677 1958	.669 977 6262	14.667 661 0560	.068 177 1958	18
19	1.526 170 3674	23.385 349 6630	.042 761 8152	.655 234 8423	15.322 895 8983	.065 261 8152	19
20	1.560 509 2007	24.911 520 0304	.040 142 0708	.640 816 4717	15.963 712 3700	.062 642 0708	20
21	1.595 620 6577	26.472 029 2311	.037 775 7214	.626 715 3757	16.590 427 7457	.060 275 7214	21
22	1.631 522 1225	28.067 649 8888	.035 628 2056	.612 924 5728	17.203 352 3185	.058 128 2056	22
23	1.668 231 3703	29.699 172 0113	.033 670 9724	.599 437 2350	17.802 789 5536	.056 170 9724	23
24	1.705 766 5761	31.367 403 3816	.031 880 2289	.586 246 6846	18.389 036 2382	.054 380 2289	24
25	1.744 146 3240	33.073 169 9577	.030 235 9889	.573 346 3908	18.962 382 6291	.052 735 9889	25
26	1.783 389 6163	34.817 316 2817	.028 721 3406	.560 729 9066	19.523 112 5957	.051 221 3406	26
27	1.823 515 8827	36.600 705 8980	.027 321 8774	.548 391 1654	20.071 503 7610	.049 821 8774	27
28	1.864 544 9901	38.424 221 7807	.026 025 2506	.536 323 8781	20.607 827 6392	.048 525 2506	28
29	1.906 497 2523	40.288 766 7708	.024 820 8143	.524 522 1302	21.132 349 7693	.047 320 8143	29
30	1.949 393 4405	42.195 264 0232	.023 699 4922	.512 980 0784	21.645 329 8478	.046 199 3422	30
31	1.993 254 7929	44.144 657 4637	.022 652 7978	.501 692 0082	22.147 021 8560	.045 152 7978	31
32	2.038 103 0258	46.137 912 2566	.021 674 1493	.490 652 3308	22.637 674 1868	.044 174 1493	32
33	2.083 960 3439	48.176 015 2824	.020 757 2169	.479 855 5802	23.117 529 7670	.043 257 2169	33
34	2.130 849 4516	50.259 975 6262	.019 896 5477	.469 296 4110	23.586 826 1780	.042 396 5477	34
35	2.178 793 5643	52.390 825 0778	.019 087 3115	.458 969 5951	24.045 795 7731	.041 587 3115	35
36	2.227 816 4194	54.569 618 6421	.018 325 2151	.448 870 0197	24.494 665 7928	.040 825 2151	36
37	2.277 942 2889	56.797 435 0615	.017 606 4289	.438 992 6843	24.933 658 4771	.040 106 4289	37
38	2.329 195 9904	59.075 377 3504	.016 927 5262	.429 332 6985	25.362 991 1756	.039 427 5262	38
39	2.381 602 9002	61.404 573 3408	.016 285 4319	.419 885 2798	25.782 876 4554	.038 785 4319	39
40	2.435 188 9654	63.786 176 2410	.015 677 3781	.410 645 7504	26.193 522 2057	.038 177 3781	40
41	2.489 980 7171	66.221 365 2064	.015 100 8666	.401 609 5358	26.595 131 7416	.037 600 8666	41
42	2.546 005 2833	68.711 345 9235	.014 553 6372	.392 772 1622	26.987 903 9037	.037 053 6372	42
43	2.603 290 4022	71.257 351 2068	.014 033 6398	.384 129 2540	27.372 033 1577	.036 533 6398	43
44	2.661 864 4362	73.860 641 6090	.013 539 0105	.375 676 5320	27.747 709 6897	.036 039 0105	44
45	2.721 756 3860	76.522 506 0452	.013 068 0508	.367 409 8112	28.115 119 5009	.035 568 0508	45
46	2.782 995 9047	79.244 262 4312	.012 619 2101	.359 324 9988	28.474 444 4997	.035 119 2101	46
47	2.845 613 3126	82.027 258 3359	.012 191 0694	.351 418 0917	28.825 862 5913	.034 691 0694	47
48	2.909 639 6121	84.872 871 6484	.011 782 3279	.343 685 1753	29.169 547 7666	.034 282 3279	48
49	2.975 106 5034	87.782 511 2605	.011 391 7908	.336 122 4208	29.505 670 1874	.033 891 7908	49
50	3.042 046 3997	90.757 617 7639	.011 018 3588	.328 726 0039	29.834 396 2713	.033 518 3588	50
51	3.110 492 4437	93.799 664 1636	.010 661 0190	.321 492 5026	30.155 888 7739	.033 161 0190	51
52	3.180 478 5237	96.910 156 6073	.010 318 8359	.314 418 0954	30.470 306 8693	.032 818 8359	52
53	3.252 039 2904	100.090 635 1309	.009 990 9447	.307 499 3598	30.777 806 2291	.032 490 9447	53
54	3.325 210 1745	103.342 674 4214	.009 676 5446	.300 732 8703	31.078 539 0994	.032 176 5446	54
55	3.400 027 4034	106.667 884 5958	.009 374 8930	.294 115 2765	31.372 654 3760	.031 874 8930	55
56	3.476 528 0200	110.067 911 9993	.009 085 3000	.287 643 3022	31.660 297 6782	.031 585 3000	56
57	3.554 749 9004	113.544 440 0192	.008 807 1243	.281 313 7430	31.941 611 4212	.031 307 1243	57
58	3.634 731 7732	117.099 189 9197	.008 539 7687	.275 123 4651	32.216 734 8863	.031 039 7687	58
59	3.716 513 2381	120.733 921 6929	.008 282 6764	.269 069 4035	32.485 804 2898	.030 782 6764	59
60	3.800 134 7859	124.450 434 9310	.008 035 3275	.263 148 5609	32.748 952 8506	.030 535 3275	60
61	3.885 637 8186	128.250 569 7169	.007 797 2363	.257 358 0057	33.006 310 8563	.030 297 2363	61
62	3.973 064 6695	132.136 207 5355	.007 567 9484	.251 694 8711	33.258 005 7275	.030 067 9484	62
63	4.062 458 6246	136.109 272 2051	.007 347 0380	.246 156 3532	33.504 162 0807	.029 847 0380	63
64	4.153 863 9437	140.171 730 8297	.007 134 1061	.240 739 7097	33.744 901 7904	.029 634 1061	64
65	4.247 325 8824	144.325 594 7734	.006 928 7780	.235 442 2589	33.980 344 0493	.029 428 7780	65
66	4.342 890 7148	148.572 920 6558	.006 730 7016	.230 261 3779	34.210 605 4272	.029 230 7016	66
67	4.440 605 7558	152.915 811 3705	.006 539 5461	.225 194 5016	34.435 799 9288	.029 039 5461	67
68	4.540 519 3853	157.356 417 1264	.006 354 9998	.220 239 1214	34.656 039 0501	.028 854 9998	68
69	4.642 681 0715	161.896 936 5117	.006 176 7691	.215 392 7837	34.871 431 8339	.028 676 7691	69
70	4.747 141 3956	166.539 617 5832	.006 004 5773	.210 653 0892	35.082 084 9231	.028 504 5773	70
71	4.853 952 0770	171.286 758 9788	.005 838 1629	.206 017 6912	35.288 102 6143	.028 338 1629	71
72	4.963 165 9988	176.140 711 0559	.005 677 2792	.201 484 2946	35.489 586 9088	.028 177 2792	72
73	5.074 837 2337	181.103 877 0546	.005 521 6929	.197 050 6548	35.686 637 5637	.028 021 6929	73
74	5.189 021 0715	186.178 714 2883	.005 371 1833	.192 714 5768	35.879 352 1405	.027 871 1833	74
75	5.305 774 0463	191.367 735 3598	.005 225 5413	.188 473 9318	36.067 826 0543	.027 725 5413	75
76	5.425 153 9616	196.673 509 4054	.005 084 5689	.184 326 5660	36.252 152 6203	.027 584 5689	76
77	5.547 219 9258	202.098 663 3670	.004 948 0782	.180 270 4082	36.432 423 1006	.027 448 0782	77
78	5.672 032 3741	207.645 883 2928	.004 815 8913	.176 303 6482	36.608 726 7487	.027 315 8913	78
79	5.799 653 1025	213.317 915 6669	.004 687 8388	.172 424 1068	36.781 150 8545	.027 187 8388	79
80	5.930 145 2973	219.117 568 7694	.004 563 7600	.168 629 9323	36.949 780 7868	.027 063 7600	80
81	6.063 573 5665	225.047 714 0667	.004 443 5021	.164 919 2942	37.114 700 0360	.026 943 5021	81
82	6.200 003 9717	231.111 287 6332	.004 326 9198	.161 290 2193	37.275 990 2552	.026 826 9198	82
83	6.339 504 0611	237.311 291 6050	.004 213 8745	.157 741 0407	37.433 731 3010	.026 713 8745	83
84	6.482 142 9025	243.650 795 6661	.004 104 2345	.154 269 9714	37.588 001 2723	.026 604 2345	84
85	6.627 991 1178	250.132 938 5686	.003 997 8741	.150 875 2776	37.738 876 5500	.026 497 8741	85
86	6.777 120 9179	256.760 929 6863	.003 894 6735	.147 555 2837	37.886 431 8337	.026 394 6735	86
87	6.929 606 1386	263.538 050 6043	.003 794 5185	.144 308 3640	38.030 740 1977	.026 294 5185	87
88	7.085 522 2767	270.467 656 7429	.003 697 2998	.141 132 8567	38.171 873 0363	.026 197 2998	88
89	7.244 946 5279	277.553 179 0196	.003 602 9132	.138 027 2437	38.309 900 2800	.026 102 9132	89
90	7.407 957 8248	284.798 125 5475	.003 511 2591	.134 989 9694	38.444 890 2494	.026 011 2591	90
91	7.574 636 8759	292.206 083 3724	.003 422 2422	.132 019 5300	38.576 909 7794	.025 922 2422	91
92	7.745 066 2056	299.780 720 2482	.003 335 7716	.129 114 4547	38.706 024 2341	.025 835 7716	92
93	7.919 330 1952	307.525 786 4538	.003 251 7598	.126 273 3054	38.832 297 5395	.025 751 7598	93
94	8.097 515 1246	315.445 116 6490	.003 170 1236	.123 494 6752	38.955 792 2147	.025 670 1236	94
95	8.279 709 2149	323.542 631 7736	.003 090 7828	.120 777 1886	39.076 569 4031	.025 590 7828	95
96	8.466 002 6722	331.822 340 9885	.003 013 6609	.118 119 4997	39.194 688 9028	.025 513 6609	96
97	8.656 487 7324	340.288 343 6608	.002 938 6843	.115 520 2931	39.310 209 1959	.025 438 6843	97
98	8.851 258 7063	348.944 831 3932	.002 865 7825	.112 978 2818	39.423 187 4776	.025 365 7825	98
99	9.050 412 0272	357.796 090 0995	.002 794 8880	.110 492 2071	39.533 679 6847	.025 294 8880	99
100	9.254 046 2979	366.846 502 1267	.002 725 9358	.108 060 8382	39.641 740 5229	.025 225 9358	100

RATE 2½%

PERIODS	AMOUNT OF 1 *How $1 left at compound interest will grow.*	AMOUNT OF 1 PER PERIOD *How $1 deposited periodically will grow.*	SINKING FUND *Periodic deposit that will grow to $1 at future date.*	PRESENT WORTH OF 1 *What $1 due in the future is worth today.*	PRESENT WORTH OF 1 PER PERIOD *What $1 payable periodically is worth today.*	PARTIAL PAYMENT *Annuity worth $1 today. Periodic payment necessary to pay off a loan of $1.*	PERIODS
1	1.025 000 0000	1.000 000 0000	1.000 000 0000	.975 609 7561	.975 609 7561	1.025 000 0000	1
2	1.050 625 0000	2.025 000 0000	.493 827 1605	.951 814 3962	1.927 424 1523	.518 827 1605	2
3	1.076 890 6250	3.075 625 0000	.325 137 1672	.928 599 4109	2.856 023 5632	.350 137 1672	3
4	1.103 812 8906	4.152 515 6250	.240 817 8777	.905 950 6448	3.761 974 2080	.265 817 8777	4
5	1.131 408 2129	5.256 328 5156	.190 246 8609	.883 854 2876	4.645 828 4956	.215 246 8609	5
6	1.159 693 4182	6.387 736 7285	.156 549 9711	.862 296 8660	5.508 125 3616	.181 549 9711	6
7	1.188 685 7537	7.547 430 1467	.132 495 4296	.841 265 2351	6.349 390 5967	.157 495 4296	7
8	1.218 402 8975	8.736 115 9004	.114 467 3458	.820 746 5708	7.170 137 1675	.139 467 3458	8
9	1.248 862 9699	9.954 518 7979	.100 456 8900	.800 728 3618	7.970 865 5292	.125 456 8900	9
10	1.280 084 5442	11.203 381 7679	.089 258 7632	.781 198 4017	8.752 063 9310	.114 258 7632	10
11	1.312 086 6578	12.483 466 3121	.080 105 9558	.762 144 7822	9.514 208 7131	.105 105 9558	11
12	1.344 888 8242	13.795 552 9699	.072 487 1270	.743 555 8850	10.257 764 5982	.097 487 1270	12
13	1.378 511 0449	15.140 441 7941	.066 048 2708	.725 420 3757	10.983 184 9738	.091 048 2708	13
14	1.412 973 8210	16.518 952 8390	.060 536 5249	.707 727 1958	11.690 912 1696	.085 536 5249	14
15	1.448 298 1665	17.931 926 6599	.055 766 4561	.690 465 5568	12.381 377 7264	.080 766 4561	15
16	1.484 505 6207	19.380 224 8264	.051 598 9886	.673 624 9335	13.055 002 6599	.076 598 9886	16
17	1.521 618 2612	20.864 730 4471	.047 927 7699	.657 195 0571	13.712 197 7170	.072 927 7699	17
18	1.559 658 7177	22.386 348 7083	.044 670 0805	.641 165 9093	14.353 363 6264	.069 670 0805	18
19	1.598 650 1856	23.946 007 4260	.041 760 6151	.625 527 7164	14.978 891 3428	.066 760 6151	19
20	1.638 616 4403	25.544 657 6116	.039 147 1287	.610 270 9429	15.589 162 2856	.064 147 1287	20
21	1.679 581 8513	27.183 274 0519	.036 787 3273	.595 386 2857	16.184 548 5714	.061 787 3273	21
22	1.721 571 3976	28.862 855 9032	.034 646 6061	.580 864 6609	16.765 413 2404	.059 646 6061	22
23	1.764 610 6825	30.584 427 3008	.032 696 3781	.566 697 2380	17.332 110 4784	.057 696 3781	23
24	1.808 725 9496	32.349 037 9833	.030 912 8204	.552 875 3542	17.884 985 8326	.055 912 8204	24
25	1.853 944 0983	34.157 763 9329	.029 275 9210	.539 390 5894	18.424 376 4220	.054 275 9210	25
26	1.900 292 7008	36.011 708 0312	.027 768 7457	.526 234 7214	18.950 611 1434	.052 768 7457	26
27	1.947 800 0183	37.912 000 7320	.026 376 8722	.513 399 7282	19.464 010 8717	.051 376 8722	27
28	1.996 495 0188	39.859 800 7503	.025 087 9327	.500 877 7836	19.964 888 6553	.050 087 9327	28
29	2.046 407 3942	41.856 295 7690	.023 891 2685	.488 661 2523	20.453 549 9076	.048 891 2685	29
30	2.097 567 5791	43.902 703 1633	.022 777 6407	.476 742 6852	20.930 292 5928	.047 777 6407	30
31	2.150 006 7686	46.000 270 7424	.021 739 0025	.465 114 8148	21.395 407 4076	.046 739 0025	31
32	2.203 756 9378	48.150 277 5109	.020 768 3123	.453 770 5510	21.849 177 9586	.045 768 3123	32
33	2.258 850 8612	50.354 034 4487	.019 859 3819	.442 702 9766	22.291 880 9352	.044 859 3819	33
34	2.315 322 1327	52.612 885 3099	.019 006 7508	.431 905 3430	22.723 786 2783	.044 006 7508	34
35	2.373 205 1861	54.928 207 4426	.018 205 5823	.421 371 0664	23.145 157 3447	.043 205 5823	35
36	2.432 535 3157	57.301 412 6287	.017 451 5767	.411 093 7233	23.556 251 0680	.042 451 5767	36
37	2.493 348 6986	59.733 947 9444	.016 740 8992	.401 067 0471	23.957 318 1151	.041 740 8992	37
38	2.555 682 4161	62.227 296 6430	.016 070 1180	.391 284 9240	24.348 603 0391	.041 070 1180	38
39	2.619 574 4765	64.782 979 0591	.015 436 1534	.381 741 3893	24.730 344 4284	.040 436 1534	39
40	2.685 063 8384	67.402 553 5356	.014 836 2332	.372 430 6237	25.102 775 0521	.039 836 2332	40
41	2.752 190 4343	70.087 617 3740	.014 267 8555	.363 346 9499	25.466 122 0020	.039 267 8555	41
42	2.820 995 1952	72.839 807 8083	.013 728 7567	.354 484 8292	25.820 606 8313	.038 728 7567	42
43	2.891 520 0751	75.660 803 0035	.013 216 8833	.345 838 8578	26.166 445 6890	.038 216 8833	43
44	2.963 808 0770	78.552 323 0786	.012 730 3683	.337 403 7637	26.503 849 4527	.037 730 3683	44
45	3.037 903 2789	81.516 131 1556	.012 267 5106	.329 174 4036	26.833 023 8563	.037 267 5106	45
46	3.113 850 8609	84.554 034 4345	.011 826 7568	.321 145 7596	27.154 169 6159	.036 826 7568	46
47	3.191 697 1324	87.667 885 2954	.011 406 6855	.313 312 9362	27.467 482 5521	.036 406 6855	47
48	3.271 489 5607	90.859 582 4277	.011 005 9938	.305 671 1573	27.773 153 7094	.036 005 9938	48
49	3.353 276 7997	94.131 071 9884	.010 623 4847	.298 215 7632	28.071 369 4726	.035 623 4847	49
50	3.437 108 7197	97.484 348 7881	.010 258 0569	.290 942 2080	28.362 311 6805	.035 258 0569	50
51	3.523 036 4377	100.921 457 5078	.009 908 6956	.283 846 0566	28.646 157 7371	.034 908 6956	51
52	3.611 112 3486	104.444 493 9455	.009 574 4635	.276 922 9820	28.923 080 7191	.034 574 4635	52
53	3.701 390 1574	108.055 606 2942	.009 254 4944	.270 168 7629	29.193 249 4821	.034 254 4944	53
54	3.793 924 9113	111.756 996 4515	.008 947 9856	.263 579 2809	29.456 828 7630	.033 947 9856	54
55	3.888 773 0341	115.550 921 3628	.008 654 1932	.257 150 5180	29.713 979 2810	.033 654 1932	55
56	3.985 992 3599	119.439 694 3969	.008 372 4260	.250 878 5541	29.964 857 8351	.033 372 4260	56
57	4.085 642 1689	123.425 686 7568	.008 102 0412	.244 759 5650	30.209 617 4001	.033 102 0412	57
58	4.187 783 2231	127.511 328 9257	.007 842 4404	.238 789 8195	30.448 407 2196	.032 842 4404	58
59	4.292 477 8037	131.699 112 1489	.007 593 0656	.232 965 6776	30.681 372 8972	.032 593 0656	59
60	4.399 789 7488	135.991 589 9526	.007 353 3959	.227 283 5879	30.908 656 4851	.032 353 3959	60
61	4.509 784 4925	140.391 379 7014	.007 122 9445	.221 740 0857	31.130 396 5708	.032 122 9445	61
62	4.622 529 1048	144.901 164 1940	.006 901 2558	.216 331 7910	31.346 728 3617	.031 901 2558	62
63	4.738 092 3325	149.523 693 2988	.006 687 9033	.211 055 4058	31.557 783 7676	.031 687 9033	63
64	4.856 544 6408	154.261 785 6313	.006 482 4869	.205 907 7130	31.763 691 4805	.031 482 4869	64
65	4.977 958 2568	159.118 330 2721	.006 284 6311	.200 885 5736	31.964 577 0542	.031 284 6311	65
66	5.102 407 2132	164.096 288 5289	.006 093 9830	.195 985 9255	32.160 562 9797	.031 093 9830	66
67	5.229 967 3936	169.198 695 7421	.005 910 2110	.191 205 7810	32.351 768 7607	.030 910 2110	67
68	5.360 716 5784	174.428 663 1358	.005 733 0027	.186 542 2253	32.538 310 9860	.030 733 0027	68
69	5.494 734 4929	179.789 379 7140	.005 562 0638	.181 992 4150	32.720 303 4010	.030 562 0638	69
70	5.632 102 8552	185.284 114 2069	.005 397 1168	.177 553 5756	32.897 856 9766	.030 397 1168	70
71	5.772 905 4266	190.916 217 0620	.005 237 8997	.173 223 0006	33.071 079 9772	.030 237 8997	71
72	5.917 228 0622	196.689 122 4886	.005 084 1652	.168 998 0493	33.240 078 0265	.030 084 1652	72
73	6.065 158 7638	202.606 350 5508	.004 935 6794	.164 876 1457	33.404 954 1722	.029 935 6794	73
74	6.216 787 7329	208.671 509 3146	.004 792 2211	.160 854 7763	33.565 808 9485	.029 792 2211	74
75	6.372 207 4262	214.888 297 0474	.004 653 5806	.156 931 4891	33.722 740 4375	.029 653 5806	75
76	6.531 512 6118	221.260 504 4736	.004 519 5594	.153 103 8918	33.875 844 3293	.029 519 5594	76
77	6.694 800 4271	227.792 017 0855	.004 389 9695	.149 369 6505	34.025 213 9798	.029 389 9695	77
78	6.862 170 4378	234.486 817 5126	.004 264 6321	.145 726 4881	34.170 940 4681	.029 264 6321	78
79	7.033 724 6988	241.348 987 9504	.004 143 3776	.142 172 1837	34.313 112 6518	.029 143 3776	79
80	7.209 567 8162	248.382 712 6492	.004 026 0451	.138 704 5695	34.451 817 2213	.029 026 0451	80
81	7.389 807 0116	255.592 280 4654	.003 912 4812	.135 321 5312	34.587 138 7525	.028 912 4812	81
82	7.574 552 1869	262.982 087 4770	.003 802 5404	.132 021 0060	34.719 159 7585	.028 802 5404	82
83	7.763 915 9916	270.556 639 6640	.003 696 0838	.128 800 9815	34.847 960 7400	.028 696 0838	83
84	7.958 013 8914	278.320 555 6556	.003 592 9793	.125 659 4941	34.973 620 2342	.028 592 9793	84
85	8.156 964 2387	286.278 569 5470	.003 493 1011	.122 594 6284	35.096 214 8626	.028 493 1011	85
86	8.360 888 3446	294.435 533 7856	.003 396 3292	.119 604 5155	35.215 819 3781	.028 396 3292	86
87	8.569 910 5533	302.796 422 1303	.003 302 5489	.116 687 3322	35.332 506 7014	.028 302 5489	87
88	8.784 158 3171	311.366 332 6835	.003 211 6510	.113 841 2997	35.446 348 0101	.028 211 6510	88
89	9.003 762 2750	320.150 491 0006	.003 123 5311	.111 064 6827	35.557 412 6928	.028 123 5311	89
90	9.228 856 3319	329.154 253 2756	.003 038 0893	.108 355 7880	35.665 768 4808	.028 038 0893	90
91	9.459 577 7402	338.383 109 6075	.002 955 2302	.105 712 9639	35.771 481 4447	.027 955 2302	91
92	9.696 067 1837	347.842 687 3477	.002 874 8628	.103 134 5989	35.874 616 0436	.027 874 8628	92
93	9.938 468 8633	357.538 754 5314	.002 796 8996	.100 619 1209	35.975 235 1645	.027 796 8996	93
94	10.186 930 5849	367.477 223 3947	.002 721 2571	.098 164 9960	36.073 400 1605	.027 721 2571	94
95	10.441 603 8495	377.664 153 9796	.002 647 8552	.095 770 7278	36.169 170 8882	.027 647 8552	95
96	10.702 643 9457	388.105 757 8290	.002 576 6173	.093 434 8564	36.262 605 7446	.027 576 6173	96
97	10.970 210 0444	398.808 401 7748	.002 507 4697	.091 155 9574	36.353 761 7021	.027 507 4697	97
98	11.244 465 2955	409.778 611 8191	.002 440 3421	.088 932 6414	36.442 694 3435	.027 440 3421	98
99	11.525 576 9279	421.023 077 1146	.002 375 1667	.086 763 5526	36.529 457 8961	.027 375 1667	99
100	11.813 716 3511	432.548 654 0425	.002 311 8787	.084 647 3684	36.614 105 2645	.027 311 8787	100

		XIII COMPOUND AMOUNT	XIV AMOUNT OF ANUITY	XV SINKING FUND	XVI PRESENT VALUE	XVII PRESENT VALUE OF ANNUITY	XVIII AMORTIZATION	
P E R I O D S		AMOUNT OF 1 How $1 left at compound interest will grow.	AMOUNT OF 1 PER PERIOD How $1 deposited periodically will grow.	SINKING FUND Periodic deposit that will grow to $1 at future date.	PRESENT WORTH OF 1 What $1 due in the future is worth today.	PRESENT WORTH OF 1 PER PERIOD What $1 payable periodically is worth today.	PARTIAL PAYMENT Annuity worth $1 today. Periodic payment necessary to pay off a loan of $1.	P E R I O D S
1		1.027 500 0000	1.000 000 0000	1.000 000 0000	.973 236 0097	.973 236 0097	1.027 500 0000	1
2		1.055 756 2500	2.027 500 0000	.493 218 2491	.947 188 3306	1.920 424 3404	.520 718 2491	2
3		1.084 789 5469	3.083 256 2500	.324 332 4326	.921 837 7914	2.842 262 1317	.351 832 4326	3
4		1.114 621 2594	4.168 045 7969	.239 920 5884	.897 165 7937	3.739 427 8654	.267 420 5884	4
5		1.145 273 3440	5.282 667 0563	.189 298 3202	.873 153 9987	4.612 581 8642	.216 798 3202	5
6		1.176 768 3610	6.427 940 4003	.155 570 8264	.849 784 9136	5.462 366 7778	.183 070 8264	6
7		1.209 129 4909	7.604 708 7613	.131 497 4750	.827 041 2785	6.289 408 0562	.158 997 4750	7
8		1.242 380 5519	8.813 838 2523	.113 457 9478	.804 906 3537	7.094 314 4100	.140 957 9478	8
9		1.276 546 0171	10.056 218 8042	.099 440 9548	.783 363 8479	7.877 678 2579	.126 940 9548	9
10		1.311 651 0326	11.332 764 8213	.088 239 7205	.762 397 9055	8.640 076 1634	.115 739 7205	10
11		1.347 721 4360	12.644 415 8539	.079 086 2948	.741 993 0954	9.382 069 2588	.106 586 2948	11
12		1.384 783 7755	13.992 137 2899	.071 468 7098	.722 134 3994	10.104 203 6582	.098 968 7098	12
13		1.422 865 3293	15.376 921 0654	.065 032 5248	.702 807 2014	10.807 010 8595	.092 532 5248	13
14		1.461 994 1259	16.799 786 3947	.059 524 5664	.683 997 2763	11.491 008 1358	.087 024 5664	14
15		1.502 198 9643	18.261 780 5205	.054 759 1731	.665 690 7798	12.156 698 9156	.082 259 1731	15
16		1.543 509 4358	19.763 979 4848	.050 597 0977	.647 874 2383	12.804 573 1539	.078 097 0977	16
17		1.585 955 9453	21.307 488 9207	.046 931 8559	.630 534 5385	13.435 107 6923	.074 431 8559	17
18		1.629 569 7338	22.893 444 8660	.043 680 6259	.613 658 9182	14.048 766 6106	.071 180 6259	18
19		1.674 382 9015	24.523 014 5998	.040 778 0208	.597 234 9569	14.646 001 5675	.068 278 0208	19
20		1.720 428 4313	26.197 397 5013	.038 171 7306	.581 250 5663	15.227 252 1338	.065 671 7306	20
21		1.767 740 2131	27.917 825 9326	.035 819 4081	.565 693 9818	15.792 946 1156	.063 319 4081	21
22		1.816 353 0690	29.685 566 1457	.033 686 4049	.550 553 7536	16.343 499 8692	.061 186 4049	22
23		1.866 302 7784	31.501 919 2147	.031 744 0977	.535 818 7383	16.879 318 6075	.059 244 0977	23
24		1.917 626 1048	33.368 221 9532	.029 968 6330	.521 478 0009	17.400 796 6093	.057 468 6330	24
25		1.970 360 8227	35.285 848 0980	.028 339 9735	.507 521 2563	17.908 317 9545	.055 839 9735	25
26		2.024 545 7453	37.256 208 9207	.026 841 1636	.493 937 9623	18.402 255 9168	.054 341 1636	26
27		2.080 220 7533	39.280 754 6660	.025 457 7594	.480 718 2115	18.882 974 1283	.052 957 7594	27
28		2.137 146 8240	41.360 975 4193	.024 177 3795	.467 852 2739	19.350 826 4022	.051 677 3795	28
29		2.196 206 0617	43.498 402 2433	.022 989 3501	.455 330 6802	19.806 157 0825	.050 489 3501	29
30		2.256 601 7284	45.694 608 3050	.021 884 4200	.443 144 2143	20.249 301 2968	.049 384 4200	30
31		2.318 658 2759	47.951 210 0334	.020 854 5311	.431 283 9069	20.680 585 2037	.048 354 5311	31
32		2.382 621 3785	50.269 868 3093	.019 892 6322	.419 741 0286	21.100 326 2323	.047 392 6322	32
33		2.447 937 9664	52.652 289 6878	.018 992 5264	.408 507 0838	21.508 833 3161	.046 492 5264	33
34		2.515 256 2605	55.100 227 6542	.018 148 7453	.397 573 8042	21.906 407 1203	.045 648 7453	34
35		2.584 425 8077	57.615 483 9147	.017 356 4454	.386 933 1428	22.293 340 2631	.044 856 4454	35
36		2.655 497 5174	60.199 909 7224	.016 611 3206	.376 577 2679	22.669 917 5310	.044 111 3206	36
37		2.728 523 6991	62.855 407 2398	.015 909 5302	.366 498 5576	23.036 416 0885	.043 409 5302	37
38		2.803 558 1008	65.583 930 9388	.015 247 6374	.356 689 5937	23.393 105 6823	.042 747 6374	38
39		2.880 655 9486	68.387 489 0397	.014 622 5576	.347 143 1569	23.740 248 8392	.042 122 5576	39
40		2.959 873 9872	71.268 144 9883	.014 031 5144	.337 852 2200	24.078 101 0600	.041 531 5144	40
41		3.041 270 5218	74.228 018 9754	.013 472 0017	.328 809 9473	24.406 911 0073	.040 972 0017	41
42		3.124 905 4612	77.269 289 4973	.012 941 7522	.320 009 6811	24.726 920 6884	.040 441 7522	42
43		3.210 840 3614	80.394 194 9584	.012 438 7090	.311 444 9451	25.038 365 6335	.039 938 7090	43
44		3.299 138 4713	83.605 035 3198	.011 961 0021	.303 109 4336	25.341 475 0691	.039 461 0021	44
45		3.389 864 7793	86.904 173 7911	.011 506 9272	.294 997 0176	25.636 472 0867	.039 006 9272	45
46		3.483 086 0607	90.294 038 5703	.011 074 9283	.287 101 7203	25.923 573 8070	.038 574 9283	46
47		3.578 870 9274	93.777 124 6310	.010 663 5814	.279 417 7327	26.202 991 5397	.038 163 5814	47
48		3.677 289 8779	97.355 995 5584	.010 271 5811	.271 939 3992	26.474 930 9389	.037 771 5811	48
49		3.778 415 3495	101.033 285 4362	.009 897 7282	.264 661 2157	26.739 592 1546	.037 397 7282	49
50		3.882 321 7716	104.811 700 7857	.009 540 9195	.257 577 8255	26.997 169 9802	.037 040 9195	50
51		3.989 085 6203	108.694 022 5573	.009 200 1379	.250 684 0151	27.247 853 9953	.036 700 1379	51
52		4.098 785 4749	112.683 108 1777	.008 874 4446	.243 974 7106	27.491 828 7059	.036 374 4446	52
53		4.211 502 0754	116.781 893 6525	.008 562 9713	.237 444 9738	27.729 273 6797	.036 062 9713	53
54		4.327 318 3825	120.993 395 7280	.008 264 9139	.231 089 9988	27.960 363 6785	.035 764 9139	54
55		4.446 319 6380	125.320 714 1105	.007 979 5268	.224 905 1084	28.185 268 7869	.035 479 5268	55
56		4.568 593 4281	129.767 033 7485	.007 706 1174	.218 885 7502	28.404 154 5371	.035 206 1174	56
57		4.694 229 7474	134.335 627 1766	.007 444 0416	.213 027 4941	28.617 182 0312	.034 944 0416	57
58		4.823 321 0654	139.029 856 9240	.007 192 6996	.207 326 0296	28.824 508 0596	.034 692 6996	58
59		4.955 962 3947	143.853 177 9894	.006 951 5322	.201 777 1566	29.026 285 2162	.034 451 5322	59
60		5.092 251 3606	148.809 140 3841	.006 720 0173	.196 376 7947	29.222 662 0109	.034 220 0173	60
61		5.232 288 2730	153.901 391 7447	.006 497 6670	.191 120 9681	29.413 782 9789	.033 997 6670	61
62		5.376 176 2005	159.133 680 0177	.006 284 0249	.186 005 8083	29.599 788 7873	.033 784 0249	62
63		5.524 021 0460	164.509 856 2181	.006 078 6631	.181 027 5507	29.780 816 3380	.033 578 6631	63
64		5.675 931 6248	170.033 877 2641	.005 881 1810	.176 182 5311	29.956 998 8691	.033 381 1810	64
65		5.832 019 7444	175.709 808 8889	.005 691 2019	.171 467 1836	30.128 466 0527	.033 191 2019	65
66		5.992 400 2874	181.541 828 6333	.005 508 3724	.166 878 0375	30.295 344 0902	.033 008 3724	66
67		6.157 191 2953	187.534 228 9208	.005 332 3599	.162 411 7153	30.457 755 8055	.032 832 3599	67
68		6.326 514 0559	193.691 420 2161	.005 162 8513	.158 064 9298	30.615 820 7353	.032 662 8513	68
69		6.500 493 1925	200.017 934 2720	.004 999 5517	.153 834 4815	30.769 655 2168	.032 499 5517	69
70		6.679 256 7553	206.518 427 4645	.004 842 1829	.149 717 2570	30.919 372 4788	.032 342 1829	70
71		6.862 936 3160	213.197 684 2198	.004 690 4825	.145 710 2258	31.065 082 6996	.032 190 4825	71
72		7.051 667 0647	220.060 620 5358	.004 544 2024	.141 810 4387	31.206 893 1383	.032 044 2024	72
73		7.245 587 9090	227.112 287 6006	.004 403 1083	.138 015 0255	31.344 908 1638	.031 903 1083	73
74		7.444 841 5765	234.357 875 5096	.004 266 9784	.134 321 1927	31.479 229 3565	.031 766 9784	74
75		7.649 574 7199	241.802 717 0861	.004 135 6028	.130 726 2216	31.609 955 5781	.031 635 6028	75
76		7.859 938 0247	249.452 291 8060	.004 008 7826	.127 227 4663	31.737 183 0443	.031 508 7826	76
77		8.076 086 3203	257.312 229 8306	.003 886 3291	.123 822 3516	31.861 005 3960	.031 386 3291	77
78		8.298 178 6942	265.388 316 1510	.003 768 0634	.120 508 3714	31.981 513 7674	.031 268 0634	78
79		8.526 378 6082	273.686 494 8451	.003 663 8157	.117 283 0865	32.098 796 8539	.031 153 8157	79
80		8.760 854 0200	282.212 873 4534	.003 543 4245	.114 144 1291	32.212 940 9770	.031 043 4245	80
81		9.001 777 5055	290.973 727 4733	.003 436 7364	.111 089 1990	32.324 030 1479	.030 936 7364	81
82		9.249 326 3869	299.975 504 9788	.003 333 6055	.108 115 9814	32.432 146 1294	.030 833 6055	82
83		9.503 682 8626	309.224 831 3658	.003 233 8929	.105 222 3664	32.537 368 4957	.030 733 8929	83
84		9.765 034 1413	318.728 514 2283	.003 137 4664	.102 406 1960	32.639 774 6917	.030 637 4664	84
85		10.033 572 5802	328.493 548 3696	.003 044 1998	.099 665 3975	32.739 440 0893	.030 544 1998	85
86		10.309 495 8261	338.527 120 9498	.002 953 9731	.096 997 9538	32.836 438 0431	.030 453 9731	86
87		10.593 006 9613	348.836 616 7759	.002 866 6715	.094 401 9015	32.930 839 9446	.030 366 6715	87
88		10.884 314 6528	359.429 623 7372	.002 782 1858	.091 875 3299	33.022 715 2746	.030 282 1858	88
89		11.183 633 3057	370.313 938 3900	.002 700 4115	.089 416 7995	33.112 131 6541	.030 200 4115	89
90		11.491 183 2216	381.497 571 6957	.002 621 2487	.087 023 2404	33.199 154 8945	.030 121 2487	90
91		11.807 190 7602	392.988 754 9173	.002 544 6021	.084 694 1513	33.283 849 0457	.030 044 6021	91
92		12.131 888 5061	404.795 945 6776	.002 470 3805	.082 427 3978	33.366 276 4435	.029 970 3805	92
93		12.465 515 4401	416.927 834 1837	.002 398 4496	.080 221 3117	33.446 497 7552	.029 898 4966	93
94		12.808 317 1147	429.393 349 6238	.002 328 8670	.078 074 2693	33.524 572 0246	.029 828 8670	94
95		13.160 545 8353	442.201 666 7386	.002 261 4116	.075 984 6909	33.600 556 7154	.029 761 4116	95
96		13.522 460 8458	455.362 212 5737	.002 196 0540	.073 951 0368	33.674 507 7517	.029 696 0540	96
97		13.894 328 5209	468.884 673 4195	.002 132 7206	.071 971 8120	33.746 479 5637	.029 632 7206	97
98		14.276 422 5533	482.779 001 9385	.002 071 3411	.070 045 5591	33.816 525 1229	.029 571 3411	98
99		14.669 024 1735	497.055 424 4918	.002 011 8481	.068 170 8605	33.884 695 9833	.029 511 8481	99
100		15.072 422 3383	511.724 448 6654	.001 954 1767	.066 346 3362	33.951 042 3195	.029 454 1767	100

	XIII COMPOUND AMOUNT	XIV AMOUNT OF ANNUITY	XV SINKING FUND	XVI PRESENT VALUE	XVII PRESENT VALUE OF ANNUITY	XVIII AMORTIZATION	
PERIODS	AMOUNT OF 1 How $1 left at compound interest will grow.	AMOUNT OF 1 PER PERIOD How $1 deposited periodically will grow.	SINKING FUND Periodic deposit that will grow to $1 at future date.	PRESENT WORTH OF 1 What $1 due in the future is worth today.	PRESENT WORTH OF 1 PER PERIOD What $1 payable periodically is worth today.	PARTIAL PAYMENT Annuity worth $1 today. Periodic payment necessary to pay off a loan of $1.	PERIODS
1	1.030 000 0000	1.000 000 0000	1.000 000 0000	.970 873 7864	.970 873 7864	1.030 000 0000	1
2	1.060 900 0000	2.030 000 0000	.492 610 8374	.942 595 9091	1.913 469 6955	.522 610 8374	2
3	1.092 727 0000	3.090 000 0000	.323 530 3633	.915 141 6594	2.828 611 3549	.353 530 3633	3
4	1.125 508 8100	4.183 627 0000	.239 027 0452	.888 487 0479	3.717 098 4028	.269 027 0452	4
5	1.159 274 0743	5.309 135 8100	.188 354 5714	.862 608 7844	4.579 707 1872	.218 354 5714	5
6	1.194 052 2965	6.468 409 8843	.154 597 5005	.837 484 2567	5.417 191 4439	.184 597 5005	6
7	1.229 873 8654	7.662 462 1808	.130 506 3538	.813 091 5113	6.230 282 9552	.160 506 3538	7
8	1.266 770 0814	8.892 336 0463	.112 456 3888	.789 409 2343	7.019 692 1895	.142 456 3888	8
9	1.304 773 1838	10.159 106 1276	.098 433 8570	.766 416 7323	7.786 108 9219	.128 433 8570	9
10	1.343 916 3793	11.463 879 3115	.087 230 5066	.744 093 9149	8.530 202 8368	.117 230 5066	10
11	1.384 233 8707	12.807 795 6908	.078 077 4478	.722 421 2766	9.252 624 1134	.108 077 4478	11
12	1.425 760 8868	14.192 029 5615	.070 462 0855	.701 379 8802	9.954 003 9936	.100 462 0855	12
13	1.468 533 7135	15.617 790 4484	.064 029 5440	.680 951 3400	10.634 955 3336	.094 029 5440	13
14	1.512 589 7249	17.086 324 1618	.058 526 3390	.661 117 8058	11.296 073 1394	.088 526 3390	14
15	1.557 967 4166	18.598 913 8867	.053 766 5805	.641 861 9474	11.937 935 0868	.083 766 5805	15
16	1.604 706 4391	20.156 881 3033	.049 610 8493	.623 166 9392	12.561 102 0260	.079 610 8493	16
17	1.652 847 6323	21.761 587 7424	.045 952 5294	.605 016 4458	13.166 118 4718	.075 952 5294	17
18	1.702 433 0612	23.414 435 3747	.042 708 6959	.587 394 6076	13.753 513 0795	.072 708 6959	18
19	1.753 506 0531	25.116 868 4359	.039 813 8806	.570 286 0268	14.323 799 1063	.069 813 8806	19
20	1.806 111 2347	26.870 374 4890	.037 215 7076	.553 675 7542	14.877 474 8605	.067 215 7076	20
21	1.860 294 5717	28.676 485 7236	.034 871 7765	.537 549 2759	15.415 024 1364	.064 871 7765	21
22	1.916 103 4089	30.536 780 2954	.032 747 3948	.521 892 5009	15.936 916 6372	.062 747 3948	22
23	1.973 586 5111	32.452 883 7042	.030 813 9027	.506 691 7484	16.443 608 3857	.060 813 9027	23
24	2.032 794 1065	34.426 470 2153	.029 047 4159	.491 933 7363	16.935 542 1220	.059 047 4159	24
25	2.093 777 9297	36.459 264 3218	.027 427 8710	.477 605 5693	17.413 147 6913	.057 427 8710	25
26	2.156 591 2675	38.553 042 2515	.025 938 2903	.463 694 7274	17.876 842 4187	.055 938 2903	26
27	2.221 289 0056	40.709 633 5190	.024 564 2103	.450 189 0558	18.327 031 4745	.054 564 2103	27
28	2.287 927 6757	42.930 922 5246	.023 293 2334	.437 076 7532	18.764 108 2277	.053 293 2334	28
29	2.356 565 5060	45.218 850 2003	.022 114 6711	.424 346 3623	19.188 454 5900	.052 114 6711	29
30	2.427 262 4712	47.575 415 7063	.021 019 2593	.411 986 7595	19.600 441 3495	.051 019 2593	30
31	2.500 080 3453	50.002 678 1775	.019 998 9288	.399 987 1452	20.000 428 4946	.049 998 9288	31
32	2.575 082 7557	52.502 758 5228	.019 046 6183	.388 337 0341	20.388 765 5288	.049 046 6183	32
33	2.652 335 2384	55.077 841 2785	.018 156 1219	.377 026 2467	20.765 791 7755	.048 156 1219	33
34	2.731 905 2955	57.730 176 5169	.017 321 9633	.366 044 8977	21.131 836 6752	.047 321 9633	34
35	2.813 862 4544	60.462 081 8124	.016 539 2916	.355 383 3978	21.487 220 0731	.046 539 2916	35
36	2.898 278 3280	63.275 944 2668	.015 803 7942	.345 032 4251	21.832 252 4981	.045 803 7942	36
37	2.985 226 6778	66.174 222 5948	.015 111 6244	.334 982 9369	22.167 235 4351	.045 111 6244	37
38	3.074 783 4782	69.159 449 2726	.014 459 3401	.325 226 1524	22.492 461 5874	.044 459 3401	38
39	3.167 026 9825	72.234 232 7508	.013 843 8516	.315 753 5460	22.808 215 1334	.043 843 8516	39
40	3.262 037 7920	75.401 259 7333	.013 262 3779	.306 556 8408	23.114 771 9742	.043 262 3779	40
41	3.359 898 9258	78.663 297 5253	.012 712 4089	.297 628 0008	23.412 399 9750	.042 712 4089	41
42	3.460 695 8935	82.023 196 4511	.012 191 6731	.288 959 2240	23.701 359 1990	.042 191 6731	42
43	3.564 516 7703	85.483 892 3446	.011 698 1103	.280 542 9360	23.981 902 1349	.041 698 1103	43
44	3.671 452 2734	89.048 409 1149	.011 229 8469	.272 371 7825	24.254 273 9174	.041 229 8469	44
45	3.781 595 8417	92.719 861 3884	.010 785 1757	.264 438 6238	24.518 712 5412	.040 785 1757	45
46	3.895 043 7169	96.501 457 2300	.010 362 5378	.256 736 5279	24.775 449 0691	.040 362 5378	46
47	4.011 895 0284	100.396 500 9469	.009 960 5065	.249 258 7650	25.024 707 8341	.039 960 5065	47
48	4.132 251 8793	104.408 395 9753	.009 577 7738	.241 998 8009	25.266 706 6350	.039 577 7738	48
49	4.256 219 4356	108.540 647 8546	.009 213 1383	.234 950 2922	25.501 656 9272	.039 213 1383	49
50	4.383 906 0187	112.796 867 2902	.008 865 4944	.228 107 0799	25.729 764 0070	.038 865 4944	50
51	4.515 423 1993	117.180 773 3089	.008 533 8232	.221 463 1843	25.951 227 1913	.038 533 8232	51
52	4.650 885 8952	121.696 196 5082	.008 217 1837	.215 012 8003	26.166 239 9915	.038 217 1837	52
53	4.790 412 4721	126.347 082 4035	.007 914 7059	.208 750 2915	26.374 990 2830	.037 914 7059	53
54	4.934 124 8463	131.137 494 8756	.007 625 5841	.202 670 1893	26.577 660 4690	.037 625 5841	54
55	5.082 148 5917	136.071 619 7218	.007 349 0710	.196 767 1708	26.774 427 6398	.037 349 0710	55
56	5.234 613 0494	141.153 768 3135	.007 084 4726	.191 036 0882	26.965 463 7279	.037 084 4726	56
57	5.391 651 4409	146.388 381 3629	.006 831 1432	.185 471 9303	27.150 935 6582	.036 831 1432	57
58	5.553 400 9841	151.780 032 8038	.006 588 4819	.180 069 8352	27.331 005 4934	.036 588 4819	58
59	5.720 003 0136	157.333 433 7879	.006 355 9281	.174 825 0827	27.505 830 5761	.036 355 9281	59
60	5.891 603 1040	163.053 436 8015	.006 132 9587	.169 733 0900	27.675 563 6661	.036 132 9587	60
61	6.068 351 1972	168.945 039 9056	.005 919 0847	.164 789 4078	27.840 353 0739	.035 919 0847	61
62	6.250 401 7331	175.013 391 1027	.005 713 8485	.159 989 7163	28.000 342 7902	.035 713 8485	62
63	6.437 913 7851	181.263 792 8358	.005 516 8216	.155 329 8216	28.155 672 6118	.035 516 8216	63
64	6.631 051 1986	187.701 706 6209	.005 327 6021	.150 805 6521	28.306 478 2639	.035 327 6021	64
65	6.829 982 7346	194.332 757 8195	.005 145 8128	.146 413 2544	28.452 891 5184	.035 145 8128	65
66	7.034 882 2166	201.162 740 5541	.004 971 0995	.142 148 7907	28.595 040 3091	.034 971 0995	66
67	7.245 928 6831	208.197 622 7707	.004 803 1288	.138 008 5347	28.733 048 8438	.034 803 1288	67
68	7.463 306 5436	215.443 551 4539	.004 641 5871	.133 988 8686	28.867 037 7124	.034 641 5871	68
69	7.687 205 7399	222.906 857 9975	.004 486 1787	.130 086 2802	28.997 123 9926	.034 486 1787	69
70	7.917 821 9121	230.594 063 7374	.004 336 6251	.126 297 3594	29.123 421 3521	.034 336 6251	70
71	8.155 356 5695	238.511 885 6495	.004 192 6632	.122 618 7956	29.246 040 1476	.034 192 6632	71
72	8.400 017 2666	246.667 242 2190	.004 054 0446	.119 047 3743	29.365 087 5220	.034 054 0446	72
73	8.652 017 7846	255.067 259 4856	.003 920 5345	.115 579 9751	29.480 667 4971	.033 920 5345	73
74	8.911 578 3181	263.719 277 2701	.003 791 9109	.112 213 5680	29.592 881 0651	.033 791 9109	74
75	9.178 925 6676	272.630 855 5882	.003 667 9634	.108 945 2117	29.701 826 2768	.033 667 9634	75
76	9.454 293 4377	281.809 781 2559	.003 548 4929	.105 772 0502	29.807 598 3270	.033 548 4929	76
77	9.737 922 2408	291.264 074 6936	.003 433 3105	.102 691 3109	29.910 289 6379	.033 433 3105	77
78	10.030 059 9080	301.001 996 9344	.003 322 2371	.099 700 3018	30.009 989 9397	.033 322 2371	78
79	10.330 961 7053	311.032 056 8424	.003 215 1027	.096 796 4095	30.106 786 3492	.033 215 1027	79
80	10.640 890 5564	321.363 018 5477	.003 111 7457	.093 977 0966	30.200 763 4458	.033 111 7457	80
81	10.960 117 2731	332.003 909 1041	.003 012 0127	.091 239 8906	30.292 003 3465	.033 012 0127	81
82	11.288 920 7913	342.964 026 3772	.002 915 7577	.088 582 4268	30.380 585 7723	.032 915 7577	82
83	11.627 588 4151	354.252 947 1685	.002 822 8417	.086 002 3561	30.466 588 1284	.032 822 8417	83
84	11.976 416 0675	365.880 535 5836	.002 733 1325	.083 497 4332	30.550 085 5616	.032 733 1325	84
85	12.335 708 5495	377.856 951 6511	.002 646 5042	.081 065 4692	30.631 151 0307	.032 646 5042	85
86	12.705 779 8060	390.192 660 2006	.002 562 8365	.078 704 3389	30.709 855 3696	.032 562 8365	86
87	13.086 953 2002	402.898 440 0067	.002 482 0151	.076 411 9795	30.786 267 3491	.032 482 0151	87
88	13.479 561 7962	415.985 393 2069	.002 403 9306	.074 186 3879	30.860 453 7370	.032 403 9306	88
89	13.883 948 6501	429.464 955 0031	.002 328 4787	.072 025 6193	30.932 479 3563	.032 328 4787	89
90	14.300 467 1096	443.348 903 6532	.002 255 5599	.069 927 7857	31.002 407 1421	.032 255 5599	90
91	14.729 481 1229	457.649 370 7628	.002 185 0789	.067 891 0541	31.070 298 1962	.032 185 0789	91
92	15.171 365 5566	472.378 851 8856	.002 116 9449	.065 913 6448	31.136 211 8409	.032 116 9449	92
93	15.626 506 5233	487.550 217 4422	.002 051 0708	.063 993 8299	31.200 205 6708	.032 051 0708	93
94	16.095 301 7190	503.176 723 9655	.001 987 3733	.062 129 9319	31.262 335 6027	.031 987 3733	94
95	16.578 160 7705	519.272 025 6844	.001 925 7729	.060 320 3223	31.322 655 9250	.031 925 7729	95
96	17.075 505 5936	535.850 186 4550	.001 866 1932	.058 563 4197	31.381 219 3446	.031 866 1932	96
97	17.587 770 7615	552.925 692 0486	.001 808 5613	.056 857 6890	31.438 077 0336	.031 808 5613	97
98	18.115 403 8843	570.513 462 8101	.001 752 8070	.055 201 6398	31.493 278 6734	.031 752 8070	98
99	18.658 866 0008	588.628 866 6944	.001 698 8633	.053 593 8250	31.546 872 4985	.031 698 8633	99
100	19.218 631 9809	607.287 732 6952	.001 646 6659	.052 032 8399	31.598 905 3383	.031 646 6659	100

	XIII COMPOUND AMOUNT	XIV AMOUNT OF ANNUITY	XV SINKING FUND	XVI PRESENT VALUE	XVII PRESENT VALUE OF ANNUITY	XVIII AMORTIZATION	
PERIODS	AMOUNT OF 1 — How $1 left at compound interest will grow.	AMOUNT OF 1 PER PERIOD — How $1 deposited periodically will grow.	SINKING FUND — Periodic deposit that will grow to $1 at future date.	PRESENT WORTH OF 1 — What $1 due in the future is worth today.	PRESENT WORTH OF 1 PER PERIOD — What $1 payable periodically is worth today.	PARTIAL PAYMENT — Annuity worth $1 today. Periodic payment necessary to pay off a loan of $1.	PERIODS
1	1.035 000 0000	1.000 000 0000	1.000 000 0000	.966 183 5749	.966 183 5749	1.035 000 0000	1
2	1.071 225 0000	2.035 000 0000	.491 400 4914	.933 510 7004	1.899 694 2752	.526 400 4914	2
3	1.108 717 8750	3.106 225 0000	.321 934 1806	.901 942 7057	2.801 636 9809	.356 934 1806	3
4	1.147 523 0006	4.214 942 8750	.237 251 1395	.871 442 2277	3.673 079 2086	.272 251 1395	4
5	1.187 686 3056	5.362 465 8756	.186 481 3732	.841 973 1669	4.515 052 3755	.221 481 3732	5
6	1.229 255 3263	6.550 152 1813	.152 668 2087	.813 500 6443	5.328 553 0198	.187 668 2087	6
7	1.272 279 2628	7.779 407 5076	.128 544 4938	.785 990 9607	6.114 543 9805	.163 544 4938	7
8	1.316 809 0370	9.051 686 7704	.110 476 6465	.759 411 5562	6.873 955 5367	.145 476 6465	8
9	1.362 897 3533	10.368 495 8073	.096 446 0051	.733 730 9722	7.607 686 5089	.131 446 0051	9
10	1.410 598 7606	11.731 393 1606	.085 241 0674	.708 918 8137	8.316 605 3226	.120 241 3679	10
11	1.459 969 7172	13.141 991 9212	.076 091 9658	.684 945 7137	9.001 551 0363	.111 091 9658	11
12	1.511 068 6573	14.601 961 6385	.068 483 9493	.661 783 2983	9.663 334 3346	.103 483 9493	12
13	1.563 956 0604	16.113 030 2959	.062 061 5726	.639 404 1529	10.302 738 4875	.097 061 5726	13
14	1.618 694 5225	17.676 986 3562	.056 570 7287	.617 781 7903	10.920 520 2778	.091 570 7287	14
15	1.675 348 8308	19.295 680 8786	.051 825 0694	.596 890 6186	11.517 410 8964	.086 825 0694	15
16	1.733 986 0398	20.971 029 7094	.047 684 8306	.576 705 9117	12.094 116 8081	.082 684 8306	16
17	1.794 675 5512	22.705 015 7492	.044 043 1317	.557 203 7794	12.651 320 5876	.079 043 1317	17
18	1.857 489 1955	24.499 691 3004	.040 816 8408	.538 361 1396	13.189 681 7271	.075 816 8408	18
19	1.922 501 3174	26.357 180 4960	.037 940 3252	.520 155 6904	13.709 837 4175	.072 940 3252	19
20	1.989 788 8635	28.279 681 8133	.035 361 0768	.502 565 8844	14.212 403 3020	.070 361 0768	20
21	2.059 431 4737	30.269 470 6768	.033 036 5870	.485 570 9028	14.697 974 2048	.068 036 5870	21
22	2.131 511 5753	32.328 902 1505	.030 932 0742	.469 150 6308	15.167 124 8355	.065 932 0742	22
23	2.206 114 4804	34.460 413 7257	.029 018 8042	.453 285 6336	15.620 410 4691	.064 018 8042	23
24	2.283 328 4872	36.666 528 2061	.027 272 8303	.437 957 1339	16.058 367 6030	.062 272 8303	24
25	2.363 244 9843	38.949 856 6933	.025 674 0354	.423 146 9893	16.481 514 5923	.060 674 0354	25
26	2.445 958 5587	41.313 101 6776	.024 205 3963	.408 837 6708	16.890 352 2631	.059 205 3963	26
27	2.531 567 1083	43.759 060 2363	.022 852 4103	.395 012 2423	17.285 364 5054	.057 852 4103	27
28	2.620 171 9571	46.290 627 3446	.021 602 6452	.381 654 3404	17.667 018 8458	.056 602 6452	28
29	2.711 877 9756	48.910 799 3017	.020 445 3825	.368 748 1550	18.035 767 0008	.055 445 3825	29
30	2.806 793 7047	51.622 677 2772	.019 371 3316	.356 278 4114	18.392 045 4114	.054 371 3316	30
31	2.905 031 4844	54.429 470 9819	.018 372 3998	.344 230 3484	18.736 275 7598	.053 372 3998	31
32	3.006 707 5863	57.334 502 4663	.017 441 5048	.332 589 7086	19.068 865 4684	.052 441 5048	32
33	3.111 942 3518	60.341 210 0526	.016 572 4221	.321 342 7136	19.390 208 1820	.051 572 4221	33
34	3.220 860 3342	63.453 152 4044	.015 759 6583	.310 476 0518	19.700 684 2338	.050 759 6583	34
35	3.333 590 4459	66.674 012 7386	.014 998 3473	.299 976 8617	20.000 661 0955	.049 998 3473	35
36	3.450 266 1115	70.007 603 1845	.014 284 1628	.289 832 7166	20.290 493 8121	.049 284 1628	36
37	3.571 025 4254	73.457 869 2959	.013 613 2454	.280 031 6102	20.570 525 4223	.048 613 2454	37
38	3.696 011 3152	77.028 894 7213	.012 982 1414	.270 561 9422	20.841 087 3645	.047 982 1414	38
39	3.825 371 7113	80.724 906 0365	.012 387 7506	.261 412 5046	21.102 499 8691	.047 387 7506	39
40	3.959 259 7212	84.550 277 7478	.011 827 2823	.252 572 4682	21.355 072 3373	.046 827 2823	40
41	4.097 833 8114	88.509 537 4690	.011 298 2174	.244 031 3702	21.599 103 7075	.046 298 2174	41
42	4.241 257 9948	92.607 371 2804	.010 798 2765	.235 779 1017	21.834 882 8092	.045 798 2765	42
43	4.389 702 0246	96.848 629 2752	.010 325 3914	.227 805 8953	22.062 688 7046	.045 325 3914	43
44	4.543 341 5955	101.238 331 2998	.009 877 6816	.220 102 3143	22.282 791 0189	.044 877 6816	44
45	4.702 358 5513	105.781 672 8953	.009 453 4334	.212 659 2409	22.495 450 2598	.044 453 4334	45
46	4.866 941 1006	110.484 031 4467	.009 051 0817	.205 467 8656	22.700 918 1254	.044 051 0817	46
47	5.037 284 0392	115.350 972 5473	.008 669 1944	.198 519 6769	22.899 437 8023	.043 669 1944	47
48	5.213 588 9805	120.388 256 5865	.008 306 4580	.191 806 4511	23.091 244 2535	.043 306 4580	48
49	5.396 064 5948	125.601 845 5670	.007 961 6665	.185 320 2426	23.276 564 4961	.042 961 6665	49
50	5.584 926 8557	130.997 910 1618	.007 633 7096	.179 053 3745	23.455 617 8706	.042 633 7096	50
51	5.780 399 2956	136.582 837 0175	.007 321 5641	.172 998 4295	23.628 616 3001	.042 321 5641	51
52	5.982 713 2710	142.363 236 3131	.007 024 2854	.167 148 2421	23.795 764 5412	.042 024 2854	52
53	6.192 108 2354	148.345 949 5840	.006 740 9997	.161 495 8851	23.957 260 4263	.041 740 9997	53
54	6.408 832 0237	154.538 057 8195	.006 470 8979	.156 034 6716	24.113 295 0978	.041 470 8979	54
55	6.633 141 1445	160.946 889 8432	.006 213 2297	.150 758 1368	24.264 053 2346	.041 213 2297	55
56	6.865 301 0846	167.580 030 9877	.005 967 2981	.145 660 0335	24.409 713 2702	.040 967 2981	56
57	7.105 586 6225	174.445 332 0722	.005 732 4549	.140 734 3339	24.550 447 6040	.040 732 4549	57
58	7.354 282 1543	181.550 918 6948	.005 508 0966	.135 975 2018	24.686 422 8058	.040 508 0966	58
59	7.611 682 0297	188.905 200 8491	.005 293 6605	.131 377 0066	24.817 799 8124	.040 293 6605	59
60	7.878 090 9008	196.516 882 8788	.005 088 6213	.126 934 3099	24.944 734 1182	.040 088 6213	60
61	8.153 824 0823	204.394 973 7796	.004 892 4882	.122 641 8414	25.067 375 9597	.039 892 4882	61
62	8.439 207 9252	212.548 797 8619	.004 704 8020	.118 494 5328	25.185 870 4924	.039 704 8020	62
63	8.734 580 2025	220.988 005 7870	.004 525 1325	.114 487 4713	25.300 357 9637	.039 525 1325	63
64	9.040 290 5096	229.722 585 9896	.004 353 0765	.110 615 9143	25.410 973 8780	.039 353 0765	64
65	9.356 700 6775	238.762 876 4992	.004 188 2558	.106 875 2795	25.517 849 1575	.039 188 2558	65
66	9.684 185 2012	248.119 577 1767	.004 030 3148	.103 261 1396	25.621 110 2971	.039 030 3148	66
67	10.023 131 6832	257.803 762 3779	.003 878 9193	.099 769 2170	25.720 879 5141	.038 878 9193	67
68	10.373 941 2921	267.826 894 0611	.003 733 7550	.096 395 3988	25.817 274 8928	.038 733 7550	68
69	10.737 029 2374	278.200 835 3532	.003 594 5255	.093 135 6316	25.910 410 5245	.038 594 5255	69
70	11.112 825 2607	288.937 864 5906	.003 460 9517	.089 986 1175	26.000 396 6420	.038 460 9517	70
71	11.501 774 1448	300.050 689 8512	.003 332 7702	.086 943 1087	26.087 339 7507	.038 332 7702	71
72	11.904 336 2399	311.552 463 9960	.003 209 7323	.084 003 0036	26.171 342 7543	.038 209 7323	72
73	12.320 988 0083	323.456 800 2359	.003 091 6030	.081 162 3223	26.252 505 0766	.038 091 6030	73
74	12.752 222 5885	335.777 788 2442	.002 978 1601	.078 417 7207	26.330 922 7794	.037 978 1601	74
75	13.198 550 3791	348.530 010 8327	.002 869 1934	.075 765 8964	26.406 688 6757	.037 869 1934	75
76	13.660 499 6424	361.728 561 2119	.002 764 5038	.073 203 7646	26.479 892 4403	.037 764 5038	76
77	14.138 617 1299	375.389 060 8543	.002 663 9029	.070 728 2750	26.550 620 7153	.037 663 9029	77
78	14.633 468 7294	389.527 677 9842	.002 567 2117	.068 336 4976	26.618 957 2128	.037 567 2117	78
79	15.145 640 1350	404.161 146 7136	.002 474 2606	.066 025 6015	26.684 982 8143	.037 474 2606	79
80	15.675 737 5397	419.306 786 8486	.002 384 8887	.063 792 8517	26.748 775 6660	.037 384 8887	80
81	16.224 388 3536	434.982 524 3883	.002 298 9429	.061 635 6055	26.810 411 2715	.037 298 9429	81
82	16.792 241 9460	451.206 912 7419	.002 216 2781	.059 551 3097	26.869 962 5812	.037 216 2781	82
83	17.379 970 4141	467.999 154 6878	.002 136 7560	.057 537 4973	26.927 500 0784	.037 136 7560	83
84	17.988 269 3786	485.379 125 1019	.002 060 2452	.055 591 7848	26.983 091 8632	.037 060 2452	84
85	18.617 858 8068	503.367 394 4805	.001 986 6205	.053 711 8694	27.036 803 7326	.036 986 6205	85
86	19.269 483 8651	521.985 253 2873	.001 915 7629	.051 895 5260	27.088 699 2585	.036 915 7629	86
87	19.943 915 8003	541.254 737 1524	.001 847 5589	.050 140 6048	27.138 839 8633	.036 847 5589	87
88	20.641 952 8533	561.198 652 9527	.001 781 9002	.048 445 0288	27.187 284 8921	.036 781 9002	88
89	21.364 421 2032	581.840 605 8060	.001 718 6838	.046 806 7911	27.234 091 6832	.036 718 6838	89
90	22.112 175 9453	603.205 027 0092	.001 657 8111	.045 223 9527	27.279 315 6359	.036 657 8111	90
91	22.886 102 1034	625.317 202 9546	.001 599 1884	.043 694 6403	27.323 010 2762	.036 599 1884	91
92	23.687 115 6770	648.203 305 0580	.001 542 7259	.042 217 0438	27.365 227 3200	.036 542 7259	92
93	24.516 164 7257	671.890 420 7350	.001 488 3379	.040 789 4143	27.406 016 7343	.036 488 3379	93
94	25.374 230 4911	696.406 585 4607	.001 435 9428	.039 410 0621	27.445 426 7965	.036 435 9428	94
95	26.262 328 5583	721.780 815 9519	.001 385 4621	.038 077 3504	27.483 504 1512	.036 385 4621	95
96	27.181 510 0579	748.043 144 5102	.001 336 8213	.036 789 7147	27.520 293 8659	.036 336 8213	96
97	28.132 862 9099	775.224 654 5680	.001 289 9487	.035 545 6181	27.555 839 4839	.036 289 9487	97
98	29.117 513 1117	803.357 517 4779	.001 244 7758	.034 343 5923	27.590 183 0763	.036 244 7758	98
99	30.136 626 0706	832.475 030 5896	.001 201 2372	.033 182 2148	27.623 365 2911	.036 201 2372	99
100	31.191 407 9831	862.611 656 6603	.001 159 2702	.032 060 1109	27.655 425 4020	.036 159 2702	100

	XIII COMPOUND AMOUNT	XIV AMOUNT OF ANNUITY	XV SINKING FUND	XVI PRESENT VALUE	XVII PRESENT VALUE OF ANNUITY	XVIII AMORTIZATION	
PERIODS	AMOUNT OF 1 How $1 left at compound interest will grow.	AMOUNT OF 1 PER PERIOD How $1 deposited periodically will grow.	SINKING FUND Periodic deposit that will grow to $1 at future date.	PRESENT WORTH OF 1 What $1 due in the future is worth today.	PRESENT WORTH OF 1 PER PERIOD What $1 payable periodically is worth today.	PARTIAL PAYMENT Annuity worth $1 today. Periodic payment necessary to pay off a loan of $1.	PERIODS
1	1.040 000 0000	1.000 000 0000	1.000 000 0000	.961 538 4615	.961 538 4615	1.040 000 0000	1
2	1.081 600 0000	2.040 000 0000	.490 196 0784	.924 556 2130	1.886 094 6746	.530 196 0784	2
3	1.124 864 0000	3.121 600 0000	.320 348 5392	.888 996 3587	2.775 091 0332	.360 348 5392	3
4	1.169 858 5600	4.246 464 0000	.235 490 0454	.854 804 1910	3.629 895 2243	.275 490 0454	4
5	1.216 652 9024	5.416 322 5600	.184 627 1135	.821 927 1068	4.451 822 3310	.224 627 1135	5
6	1.265 319 0185	6.632 975 4624	.150 761 9025	.790 314 5257	5.242 136 8567	.190 761 9025	6
7	1.315 931 7792	7.898 294 4809	.126 609 6120	.759 917 8132	6.002 054 6699	.166 609 6120	7
8	1.368 569 0504	9.214 226 2601	.108 527 8320	.730 690 2050	6.732 744 8750	.148 527 8320	8
9	1.423 311 8124	10.582 795 3105	.094 492 9927	.702 586 7356	7.435 331 6105	.134 492 9927	9
10	1.480 244 2849	12.006 107 1230	.083 290 9443	.675 564 1688	8.110 895 7794	.123 290 9443	10
11	1.539 454 0563	13.486 351 4079	.074 149 0393	.649 580 9316	8.760 476 7109	.114 149 0393	11
12	1.601 032 2186	15.025 805 4642	.066 552 1727	.624 597 0496	9.385 073 7605	.106 552 1727	12
13	1.665 073 5073	16.626 837 6828	.060 143 7278	.600 574 0861	9.985 647 8466	.100 143 7278	13
14	1.731 676 4476	18.291 911 1901	.054 668 9731	.577 475 0828	10.563 122 9295	.094 668 9731	14
15	1.800 943 5055	20.023 587 6377	.049 941 1004	.555 264 5027	11.118 387 4322	.089 941 1004	15
16	1.872 981 2457	21.824 531 1432	.045 819 9992	.533 908 1757	11.652 295 6079	.085 819 9992	16
17	1.947 900 4956	23.697 512 3889	.042 198 5221	.513 373 2459	12.165 668 8537	.082 198 5221	17
18	2.025 816 5154	25.645 412 8845	.038 993 3281	.493 628 1210	12.659 296 9747	.078 993 3281	18
19	2.106 849 1760	27.671 229 3998	.036 138 6184	.474 642 4240	13.133 939 3988	.076 138 6184	19
20	2.191 123 1430	29.778 078 5758	.033 581 7503	.456 386 9462	13.590 326 3450	.073 581 7503	20
21	2.278 768 0688	31.969 201 7189	.031 280 1054	.438 833 6021	14.029 159 9471	.071 280 1054	21
22	2.369 918 7915	34.247 969 7876	.029 198 8111	.421 955 3867	14.451 115 3337	.069 198 8111	22
23	2.464 715 5432	36.617 888 5791	.027 309 0568	.405 726 3333	14.856 841 6671	.067 309 0568	23
24	2.563 304 1649	39.082 604 1223	.025 586 8313	.390 121 4743	15.246 963 1414	.065 586 8313	24
25	2.665 836 3315	41.645 908 2872	.024 011 9628	.375 116 8023	15.622 079 9437	.064 011 9628	25
26	2.772 469 7847	44.311 744 6187	.022 567 3805	.360 689 2329	15.982 769 1766	.062 567 3805	26
27	2.883 368 5761	47.084 214 4034	.021 238 5406	.346 816 5701	16.329 585 7467	.061 238 5406	27
28	2.998 703 3192	49.967 582 9796	.020 012 9752	.333 477 4713	16.663 063 2180	.060 012 9752	28
29	3.118 651 4519	52.966 286 2987	.018 879 9342	.320 651 4147	16.983 714 6327	.058 879 9342	29
30	3.243 397 5100	56.084 937 7507	.017 830 0991	.308 318 6680	17.292 033 3007	.057 830 0991	30
31	3.373 133 4104	59.328 335 2607	.016 855 3524	.296 460 2577	17.588 493 5583	.056 855 3524	31
32	3.508 058 7468	62.701 468 6711	.015 948 5897	.285 057 9401	17.873 551 4984	.055 948 5897	32
33	3.648 381 0967	66.209 527 4180	.015 103 5665	.274 094 1731	18.147 645 6715	.055 103 5665	33
34	3.794 316 3406	69.857 908 5147	.014 314 7715	.263 552 0896	18.411 197 7611	.054 314 7715	34
35	3.946 088 9942	73.652 224 8553	.013 577 3224	.253 415 4707	18.664 613 2318	.053 577 3224	35
36	4.103 932 5540	77.598 313 8495	.012 886 8780	.243 668 7219	18.908 281 9537	.052 886 8780	36
37	4.268 089 8561	81.702 246 4035	.012 239 5655	.234 296 8479	19.142 578 8016	.052 239 5655	37
38	4.438 813 4504	85.970 336 2596	.011 631 9191	.225 285 4307	19.367 864 2323	.051 631 9191	38
39	4.616 365 9884	90.409 149 7100	.011 060 8274	.216 620 6064	19.584 484 8388	.051 060 8274	39
40	4.801 020 6279	95.025 515 6984	.010 523 4893	.208 289 0447	19.792 773 8384	.050 523 4893	40
41	4.993 061 4531	99.826 536 3264	.010 017 3765	.200 277 9276	19.993 051 8110	.050 017 3765	41
42	5.192 783 9112	104.819 597 7794	.009 540 2007	.192 574 9303	20.185 626 7413	.049 540 2007	42
43	5.400 495 2676	110.012 381 6906	.009 089 8859	.185 168 2023	20.370 794 9436	.049 089 8859	43
44	5.616 515 0783	115.412 876 9582	.008 664 5444	.178 046 3483	20.548 841 2919	.048 664 5444	44
45	5.841 175 6815	121.029 392 0365	.008 262 4558	.171 198 4118	20.720 039 7038	.048 262 4558	45
46	6.074 822 7087	126.870 567 7180	.007 882 0488	.164 613 8575	20.884 653 5613	.047 882 0488	46
47	6.317 815 6171	132.945 390 4267	.007 521 8855	.158 282 5553	21.042 936 1166	.047 521 8855	47
48	6.570 528 2418	139.263 206 0438	.007 180 6476	.152 194 7647	21.195 130 8814	.047 180 6476	48
49	6.833 349 3714	145.833 734 2855	.006 857 1240	.146 341 1199	21.341 472 0013	.046 857 1240	49
50	7.106 683 3463	152.667 083 6570	.006 550 2004	.140 712 6153	21.482 184 6167	.046 550 2004	50
51	7.390 950 6801	159.773 767 0032	.006 258 8497	.135 300 5917	21.617 485 2083	.046 258 8497	51
52	7.686 588 7073	167.164 717 6834	.005 982 1236	.130 096 7228	21.747 581 9311	.045 982 1236	52
53	7.994 052 2556	174.851 306 3907	.005 719 1451	.125 093 0027	21.872 674 9337	.045 719 1451	53
54	8.313 814 3459	182.845 358 6463	.005 469 1025	.120 281 7333	21.992 956 6671	.045 469 1025	54
55	8.646 366 9197	191.159 172 9922	.005 231 2426	.115 655 5128	22.108 612 1799	.045 231 2426	55
56	8.992 221 5965	199.805 539 9119	.005 004 8662	.111 207 2239	22.219 819 4037	.045 004 8662	56
57	9.351 910 4603	208.797 761 5083	.004 789 3234	.106 930 0229	22.326 749 4267	.044 789 3234	57
58	9.725 986 8787	218.149 671 9687	.004 584 0087	.102 817 3297	22.429 566 7564	.044 584 0087	58
59	10.115 026 3539	227.875 658 8474	.004 388 3581	.098 862 8171	22.528 429 5735	.044 388 3581	59
60	10.519 627 4081	237.990 685 2013	.004 201 8451	.095 060 4010	22.623 489 9745	.044 201 8451	60
61	10.940 412 5044	248.510 312 6094	.004 023 9779	.091 404 2318	22.714 894 2062	.044 023 9779	61
62	11.378 029 0045	259.450 725 1137	.003 854 2964	.087 888 6844	22.802 782 8906	.043 854 2964	62
63	11.833 150 1647	270.828 754 1183	.003 692 3701	.084 508 3504	22.887 291 2410	.043 692 3701	63
64	12.306 476 1713	282.661 904 2830	.003 537 7955	.081 258 0292	22.968 549 2702	.043 537 7955	64
65	12.798 735 2182	294.968 380 4544	.003 390 1939	.078 132 7204	23.046 681 9905	.043 390 1939	65
66	13.310 684 6269	307.767 115 6725	.003 249 2100	.075 127 6157	23.121 809 6063	.043 249 2100	66
67	13.843 112 0120	321.077 800 2994	.003 114 5099	.072 238 0921	23.194 047 6984	.043 114 5099	67
68	14.396 836 4925	334.920 912 3114	.002 985 7795	.069 459 7039	23.263 507 4023	.042 985 7795	68
69	14.972 709 9522	349.317 748 8039	.002 862 7231	.066 788 1768	23.330 295 5791	.042 862 7231	69
70	15.571 618 3502	364.290 458 7560	.002 745 0623	.064 219 4008	23.394 514 9799	.042 745 0623	70
71	16.194 483 0843	379.862 077 1063	.002 632 5344	.061 749 4238	23.456 264 4038	.042 632 5344	71
72	16.842 262 4076	396.056 560 1905	.002 524 8919	.059 374 4460	23.515 638 8498	.042 524 8919	72
73	17.515 952 9039	412.898 822 5981	.002 421 9008	.057 090 8135	23.572 729 6632	.042 421 9008	73
74	18.216 591 0201	430.414 775 5021	.002 323 3403	.054 895 0130	23.627 624 6762	.042 323 3403	74
75	18.945 254 6609	448.631 366 5221	.002 229 0015	.052 783 6663	23.680 408 3425	.042 229 0015	75
76	19.703 064 8473	467.576 621 1830	.002 138 6869	.050 753 5253	23.731 161 8678	.042 138 6869	76
77	20.491 187 4412	487.279 686 0303	.002 052 2095	.048 801 4646	23.779 963 3344	.042 052 2095	77
78	21.310 834 9389	507.770 873 4716	.001 969 3922	.046 924 4871	23.826 887 8215	.041 969 3922	78
79	22.163 268 3364	529.081 708 4104	.001 890 0672	.045 119 6992	23.872 007 5207	.041 890 0672	79
80	23.049 799 0699	551.244 976 7468	.001 814 0755	.043 384 3261	23.915 391 8468	.041 814 0755	80
81	23.971 791 0327	574.294 775 8167	.001 741 2661	.041 715 6982	23.957 107 5450	.041 741 2661	81
82	24.930 662 6740	598.266 566 8494	.001 671 4957	.040 111 2483	23.997 218 7933	.041 671 4957	82
83	25.927 889 1809	623.197 229 5233	.001 604 6284	.038 568 5079	24.035 787 3013	.041 604 6284	83
84	26.965 004 7482	649.125 118 7043	.001 540 5351	.037 085 1038	24.072 872 4050	.041 540 5351	84
85	28.043 604 9381	676.090 123 4525	.001 479 0928	.035 658 7537	24.108 531 1587	.041 479 0928	85
86	29.165 349 1356	704.133 728 3906	.001 420 1848	.034 287 2631	24.142 818 4218	.041 420 1848	86
87	30.331 963 1010	733.299 077 5262	.001 363 7001	.032 968 5222	24.175 786 9441	.041 363 7001	87
88	31.545 241 6251	763.631 040 6272	.001 309 5329	.031 700 5022	24.207 487 4462	.041 309 5329	88
89	32.807 051 2901	795.176 282 2523	.001 257 5828	.030 481 2521	24.237 968 6983	.041 257 5828	89
90	34.119 333 3417	827.983 333 5424	.001 207 7538	.029 308 8962	24.267 277 5945	.041 207 7538	90
91	35.484 106 6754	862.102 666 8841	.001 159 9547	.028 181 6310	24.295 459 2255	.041 159 9547	91
92	36.903 470 9424	897.586 773 5595	.001 114 0984	.027 097 7221	24.322 556 9476	.041 114 0984	92
93	38.379 609 7801	934.490 244 5018	.001 070 1021	.026 055 5020	24.348 612 4496	.041 070 1021	93
94	39.914 794 1713	972.869 854 2819	.001 027 8867	.025 053 3673	24.373 665 8169	.041 027 8867	94
95	41.511 385 9381	1012.784 648 4532	.000 987 3767	.024 089 7763	24.397 755 5932	.040 987 3767	95
96	43.171 841 3757	1054.296 034 3913	.000 948 5002	.023 163 2464	24.420 918 8396	.040 948 5002	96
97	44.915 715 0307	1097.467 875 7670	.000 911 1884	.022 272 3523	24.443 191 1919	.040 911 1884	97
98	46.694 663 6319	1142.366 590 7976	.000 875 3757	.021 415 7234	24.464 606 9153	.040 875 3757	98
99	48.562 450 1772	1189.061 254 4296	.000 840 9996	.020 592 0417	24.485 198 9570	.040 840 9996	99
100	50.504 948 1843	1237.623 704 6067	.000 808 0000	.019 800 0401	24.504 998 9972	.040 808 0000	100

	XIII COMPOUND AMOUNT	XIV AMOUNT OF ANNUITY	XV SINKING FUND	XVI PRESENT VALUE	XVII PRESENT VALUE OF ANNUITY	XVIII AMORTIZATION	
P E R I O D S	AMOUNT OF 1 *How $1 left at compound interest will grow.*	AMOUNT OF 1 PER PERIOD *How $1 deposited periodically will grow.*	SINKING FUND *Periodic deposit that will grow to $1 at future date.*	PRESENT WORTH OF 1 *What $1 due in the future is worth today.*	PRESENT WORTH OF 1 PER PERIOD *What $1 payable periodically is worth today.*	PARTIAL PAYMENT *Annuity worth $1 today. Periodic payment necessary to pay off a loan of $1.*	P E R I O D S
1	1.050 000 0000	1.000 000 0000	1.000 000 0000	.952 380 9524	.952 380 9524	1.050 000 0000	1
2	1.102 500 0000	2.050 000 0000	.487 804 8780	.907 029 4785	1.859 410 4308	.537 804 8780	2
3	1.157 625 0000	3.152 500 0000	.317 208 5646	.863 837 5985	2.723 248 0294	.367 208 5646	3
4	1.215 506 2500	4.310 125 0000	.232 011 8326	.822 702 4748	3.545 950 5042	.282 011 8326	4
5	1.276 281 5625	5.525 631 2500	.180 974 7981	.783 526 1665	4.329 476 6706	.230 974 7981	5
6	1.340 095 6406	6.801 912 8125	.147 017 4681	.746 215 3966	5.075 692 0673	.197 017 4681	6
7	1.407 100 4227	8.142 008 4531	.122 819 8184	.710 681 3301	5.786 373 3974	.172 819 8184	7
8	1.477 455 4438	9.549 108 8758	.104 721 8136	.676 839 3620	6.463 212 7594	.154 721 8136	8
9	1.551 328 2160	11.026 564 3196	.090 690 0800	.644 608 9162	7.107 821 6756	.140 690 0800	9
10	1.628 894 6268	12.577 892 5355	.079 504 5750	.613 913 2535	7.721 734 9292	.129 504 5750	10
11	1.710 339 3581	14.206 787 1623	.070 388 8915	.584 679 2891	8.306 414 2183	.120 388 8915	11
12	1.795 856 3260	15.917 126 5204	.062 825 4100	.556 837 4182	8.863 251 6364	.112 825 4100	12
13	1.885 649 1423	17.712 982 8465	.056 455 7652	.530 321 3506	9.393 572 9871	.106 455 7652	13
14	1.979 931 5994	19.598 631 9888	.051 023 9695	.505 067 9530	9.898 640 9401	.101 023 9695	14
15	2.078 928 1794	21.578 563 5882	.046 342 2876	.481 017 0981	10.379 658 0382	.096 342 2876	15
16	2.182 874 5884	23.657 491 7676	.042 269 9080	.458 111 5220	10.837 769 5602	.092 269 9080	16
17	2.292 018 3178	25.840 366 3560	.038 699 1417	.436 296 6876	11.274 066 2478	.088 699 1417	17
18	2.406 619 2337	28.132 384 6738	.035 546 2223	.415 520 6549	11.689 586 9027	.085 546 2223	18
19	2.526 950 1954	30.539 003 9075	.032 745 0104	.395 733 9570	12.085 320 8597	.082 745 0104	19
20	2.653 297 7051	33.065 954 1029	.030 242 5872	.376 889 4829	12.462 210 3425	.080 242 5872	20
21	2.785 962 5904	35.719 251 8080	.027 996 1071	.358 942 3646	12.821 152 7072	.077 996 1071	21
22	2.925 260 7199	38.505 214 3984	.025 970 5086	.341 849 8713	13.163 002 5783	.075 970 5086	22
23	3.071 523 7559	41.430 475 1184	.024 136 8219	.325 571 3058	13.488 573 8841	.074 136 8219	23
24	3.225 099 9437	44.501 998 8743	.022 470 9008	.310 067 9103	13.798 641 7943	.072 470 9008	24
25	3.386 354 9409	47.727 098 8180	.020 952 4573	.295 302 7717	14.093 944 5660	.070 952 4573	25
26	3.555 672 6879	51.113 453 7589	.019 564 3207	.281 240 7350	14.375 185 3010	.069 564 3207	26
27	3.733 456 3223	54.669 126 4468	.018 291 8599	.267 848 3190	14.643 033 6200	.068 291 8599	27
28	3.920 129 1385	58.402 582 7692	.017 122 5304	.255 093 6371	14.898 127 2571	.067 122 5304	28
29	4.116 135 5954	62.322 711 9076	.016 045 5149	.242 946 3211	15.141 073 5782	.066 045 5149	29
30	4.321 942 3752	66.434 847 5030	.015 051 4351	.231 377 4487	15.372 451 0269	.065 051 4351	30
31	4.538 039 4939	70.760 789 8782	.014 132 1204	.220 359 4749	15.592 810 5018	.064 132 1204	31
32	4.764 941 4686	75.298 829 3721	.013 280 4189	.209 866 1666	15.802 676 6684	.063 280 4189	32
33	5.003 188 5420	80.063 770 8407	.012 490 0437	.199 872 5396	16.002 549 2080	.062 490 0437	33
34	5.253 347 9691	85.066 959 3827	.011 755 4454	.190 354 7996	16.192 904 0076	.061 755 4454	34
35	5.516 015 3676	90.320 307 3518	.011 071 7072	.181 290 2854	16.374 194 2929	.061 071 7072	35
36	5.791 816 1360	95.836 322 7194	.010 434 4571	.172 657 4146	16.546 851 7076	.060 434 4571	36
37	6.081 406 9428	101.628 138 8554	.009 839 7945	.164 435 6330	16.711 287 3405	.059 839 7945	37
38	6.385 477 2899	107.709 545 7982	.009 284 2282	.156 605 3647	16.867 892 7053	.059 284 2282	38
39	6.704 751 1544	114.095 023 0881	.008 764 6242	.149 147 9664	17.017 040 6717	.058 764 6242	39
40	7.039 988 7121	120.799 774 2425	.008 278 1612	.142 045 6823	17.159 086 3540	.058 278 1612	40
41	7.391 988 1477	127.839 762 9546	.007 822 2924	.135 281 6022	17.294 367 9562	.057 822 2924	41
42	7.761 587 5551	135.231 751 1023	.007 394 7131	.128 839 6211	17.423 207 5773	.057 394 7131	42
43	8.149 666 9329	142.993 338 6575	.006 993 3328	.122 704 4011	17.545 911 9784	.056 993 3328	43
44	8.557 150 2795	151.143 005 5903	.006 616 2506	.116 861 3344	17.662 773 3128	.056 616 2506	44
45	8.985 007 7935	159.700 155 8699	.006 261 7347	.111 296 5089	17.774 069 8217	.056 261 7347	45
46	9.434 258 1832	168.685 163 6633	.005 928 2036	.105 996 6752	17.880 066 4968	.055 928 2036	46
47	9.905 971 0923	178.119 421 8465	.005 614 2109	.100 949 2144	17.981 015 7113	.055 614 2109	47
48	10.401 269 6469	188.025 392 9388	.005 318 4306	.096 142 1090	18.077 157 8203	.055 318 4306	48
49	10.921 333 1293	198.426 662 5858	.005 039 6453	.091 563 9133	18.168 721 7336	.055 039 6453	49
50	11.467 399 7858	209.347 995 7151	.004 776 7355	.087 203 7270	18.255 925 4606	.054 776 7355	50
51	12.040 769 7750	220.815 395 5008	.004 528 6697	.083 051 1685	18.338 976 6291	.054 528 6697	51
52	12.642 808 2638	232.856 165 2759	.004 294 4966	.079 096 3510	18.418 072 9801	.054 294 4966	52
53	13.274 948 6770	245.498 973 5397	.004 073 3368	.075 329 8581	18.493 402 8382	.054 073 3368	53
54	13.938 696 1108	258.773 922 2166	.003 864 3770	.071 742 7220	18.565 145 5602	.053 864 3770	54
55	14.635 630 9164	272.712 618 3275	.003 666 8637	.068 326 4019	18.633 471 9621	.053 666 8637	55
56	15.367 412 4622	287.348 249 2439	.003 480 0978	.065 072 7637	18.698 544 7258	.053 480 0978	56
57	16.135 783 0853	302.715 661 7060	.003 303 4300	.061 974 0607	18.760 518 7865	.053 303 4300	57
58	16.942 572 2396	318.851 444 7913	.003 136 2568	.059 022 9149	18.819 541 7014	.053 136 2568	58
59	17.789 700 8515	335.794 017 0309	.002 978 0161	.056 212 2999	18.875 754 0013	.052 978 0161	59
60	18.679 185 8941	353.583 717 8825	.002 828 1845	.053 535 5237	18.929 289 5251	.052 828 1845	60
61	19.613 145 1888	372.262 903 7766	.002 686 2736	.050 986 2131	18.980 275 7382	.052 686 2736	61
62	20.593 802 4483	391.876 048 9654	.002 551 8273	.048 558 2982	19.028 834 0363	.052 551 8273	62
63	21.623 492 5707	412.469 851 4137	.002 424 4196	.046 245 9983	19.075 080 0346	.052 424 4196	63
64	22.704 667 1992	434.093 343 9844	.002 303 6520	.044 043 8079	19.119 123 8425	.052 303 6520	64
65	23.839 900 5592	456.798 011 1836	.002 189 1514	.041 946 4837	19.161 070 3262	.052 189 1514	65
66	25.031 895 5871	480.637 911 7428	.002 080 5683	.039 949 0321	19.201 019 3583	.052 080 5683	66
67	26.283 490 3655	505.669 807 3299	.001 977 5751	.038 046 6972	19.239 066 0555	.051 977 5751	67
68	27.597 664 8848	531.953 297 6964	.001 879 8643	.036 234 9497	19.275 301 0052	.051 879 8643	68
69	28.977 548 1291	559.550 962 5812	.001 787 1473	.034 509 4759	19.309 810 4812	.051 787 1473	69
70	30.426 425 5355	588.528 510 7103	.001 699 1530	.032 866 1676	19.342 676 6487	.051 699 1530	70
71	31.947 746 8123	618.954 936 2458	.001 615 6265	.031 301 1120	19.373 977 7607	.051 615 6265	71
72	33.545 134 1529	650.902 683 0581	.001 536 3280	.029 810 5828	19.403 788 3435	.051 536 3280	72
73	35.222 390 8605	684.447 817 2110	.001 461 0318	.028 391 0313	19.432 179 3748	.051 461 0318	73
74	36.983 510 4036	719.670 208 0715	.001 389 5254	.027 039 0774	19.459 218 4522	.051 389 5254	74
75	38.832 685 9238	756.653 718 4751	.001 321 6085	.025 751 5023	19.484 969 9545	.051 321 6085	75
76	40.774 320 2199	795.486 404 3989	.001 257 0925	.024 525 2403	19.509 495 1947	.051 257 0925	76
77	42.813 036 2309	836.260 724 6188	.001 195 7993	.023 357 3717	19.532 852 5664	.051 195 7993	77
78	44.953 688 0425	879.073 760 8497	.001 137 5610	.022 245 1159	19.555 097 6823	.051 137 5610	78
79	47.201 372 4446	924.027 448 8922	.001 082 2189	.021 185 8247	19.576 283 5069	.051 082 2189	79
80	49.561 441 0668	971.228 821 3368	.001 029 6235	.020 176 9759	19.596 460 4828	.051 029 6235	80
81	52.039 513 1202	1020.790 262 4037	.000 979 6332	.019 216 1675	19.615 676 6503	.050 979 6332	81
82	54.641 488 7762	1072.829 775 5239	.000 932 1143	.018 301 1119	19.633 977 7622	.050 932 1143	82
83	57.373 563 2150	1127.471 264 3001	.000 886 9406	.017 429 6304	19.651 407 3925	.050 886 9406	83
84	60.242 241 3758	1184.844 827 5151	.000 843 9924	.016 599 6480	19.668 007 0405	.050 843 9924	84
85	63.254 353 4445	1245.087 068 8908	.000 803 1567	.015 809 1885	19.683 816 2291	.050 803 1567	85
86	66.417 071 1168	1308.341 422 3354	.000 764 3265	.015 056 3700	19.698 872 5991	.050 764 3265	86
87	69.737 924 6726	1374.758 493 4521	.000 727 4005	.014 339 4000	19.713 211 9992	.050 727 4005	87
88	73.224 820 9062	1444.496 418 1247	.000 692 2828	.013 656 5715	19.726 868 5706	.050 692 2828	88
89	76.886 061 9515	1517.721 239 0310	.000 658 8825	.013 006 2585	19.739 874 8292	.050 658 8825	89
90	80.730 365 0491	1594.607 300 9825	.000 627 1136	.012 386 9129	19.752 261 7421	.050 627 1136	90
91	84.766 883 3016	1675.337 666 0317	.000 596 8946	.011 797 0599	19.764 058 8020	.050 596 8946	91
92	89.005 227 4667	1760.104 549 3332	.000 568 1481	.011 235 2951	19.775 294 0971	.050 568 1481	92
93	93.455 488 8400	1849.109 776 7999	.000 540 8008	.010 700 2811	19.785 994 3782	.050 540 8008	93
94	98.128 263 2820	1942.565 265 6399	.000 514 7832	.010 190 7439	19.796 185 1221	.050 514 7832	94
95	103.034 676 4461	2040.693 528 9219	.000 490 0295	.009 705 4704	19.805 890 5925	.050 490 0295	95
96	108.186 410 2684	2143.728 205 3680	.000 466 4770	.009 243 3051	19.815 133 8976	.050 466 4770	96
97	113.595 730 7818	2251.914 615 6364	.000 444 0666	.008 803 1477	19.823 937 0453	.050 444 0666	97
98	119.275 517 3209	2365.510 346 4182	.000 422 7418	.008 383 9502	19.832 320 9955	.050 422 7418	98
99	125.239 293 1870	2484.785 863 7391	.000 402 4492	.007 984 7145	19.840 305 7100	.050 402 4492	99
100	131.501 257 8463	2610.025 156 9261	.000 383 1381	.007 604 4900	19.847 910 2000	.050 383 1381	100

	XIII COMPOUND AMOUNT	XIV AMOUNT OF ANNUITY	XV SINKING FUND	XVI PRESENT VALUE	XVII PRESENT VALUE OF ANNUITY	XVIII AMORTIZATION	
P E R I O D S	AMOUNT OF 1 *How $1 left at compound interest will grow.*	AMOUNT OF 1 PER PERIOD *How $1 deposited periodically will grow.*	SINKING FUND *Periodic deposit that will grow to $1 at future date.*	PRESENT WORTH OF 1 *What $1 due in the future is worth today.*	PRESENT WORTH OF 1 PER PERIOD *What $1 payable periodically is worth today.*	PARTIAL PAYMENT *Annuity worth $1 today. Periodic payment necessary to pay off a loan of $1.*	P E R I O D S
1	1.060 000 0000	1.000 000 0000	1.000 000 0000	.943 396 2264	.943 396 2264	1.060 000 0000	1
2	1.123 600 0000	2.060 000 0000	.485 436 8932	.889 996 4400	1.833 392 6664	.545 436 8932	2
3	1.191 016 0000	3.183 600 0000	.314 109 8128	.839 619 2830	2.673 011 9495	.374 109 8128	3
4	1.262 476 9600	4.374 616 0000	.228 591 4924	.792 093 6632	3.465 105 6127	.288 591 4924	4
5	1.338 225 5776	5.637 092 9600	.177 396 4004	.747 258 1729	4.212 363 7856	.237 396 4004	5
6	1.418 519 1123	6.975 318 5376	.143 362 6285	.704 960 5404	4.917 324 3260	.203 362 6285	6
7	1.503 630 2590	8.393 837 6499	.119 135 0181	.665 057 1136	5.582 381 4396	.179 135 0181	7
8	1.593 848 0745	9.897 467 9088	.101 035 9426	.627 412 3713	6.209 793 8110	.161 035 9426	8
9	1.689 478 9590	11.491 315 9834	.087 022 2350	.591 898 4635	6.801 692 2745	.147 022 2350	9
10	1.790 847 6965	13.180 794 9424	.075 867 9582	.558 394 7769	7.360 087 0514	.135 867 9582	10
11	1.898 298 5583	14.971 642 6389	.066 792 9381	.526 787 5254	7.886 874 5768	.126 792 9381	11
12	2.012 196 4718	16.869 941 1973	.059 277 0294	.496 969 3636	8.383 843 9404	.119 277 0294	12
13	2.132 928 2601	18.882 137 6691	.052 960 1053	.468 839 0222	8.852 682 9626	.112 960 1053	13
14	2.260 903 9558	21.015 065 9292	.047 584 9090	.442 300 9644	9.294 983 9270	.107 584 9090	14
15	2.396 558 1931	23.275 969 8850	.042 962 7640	.417 265 0607	9.712 248 9877	.102 962 7640	15
16	2.540 351 6847	25.672 528 0781	.038 952 1436	.393 646 2837	10.105 895 2715	.098 952 1436	16
17	2.692 772 7858	28.212 879 7628	.035 444 8042	.371 364 4186	10.477 259 6901	.095 444 8042	17
18	2.854 339 1529	30.905 652 5485	.032 356 5406	.350 343 7911	10.827 603 4812	.092 356 5406	18
19	3.025 599 5021	33.759 991 7015	.029 620 8604	.330 513 0105	11.158 116 4917	.089 620 8604	19
20	3.207 135 4722	36.785 591 2035	.027 184 5570	.311 804 7269	11.469 921 2186	.087 184 5570	20
21	3.399 563 6005	39.992 726 6758	.025 004 5467	.294 155 4027	11.764 076 6213	.085 004 5467	21
22	3.603 537 4166	43.392 290 2763	.023 045 5685	.277 505 0969	12.041 581 7182	.083 045 5685	22
23	3.819 749 6616	46.995 827 6929	.021 278 4847	.261 797 2612	12.303 378 9794	.081 278 4847	23
24	4.048 934 6413	50.815 577 3545	.019 679 0050	.246 978 5483	12.550 357 5278	.079 679 0050	24
25	4.291 870 7197	54.864 511 9957	.018 226 7182	.232 998 6305	12.783 356 1583	.078 226 7182	25
26	4.549 382 9629	59.156 382 7155	.016 904 3467	.219 810 0288	13.003 166 1870	.076 904 3467	26
27	4.822 345 9407	63.705 765 6784	.015 697 1663	.207 367 9517	13.210 534 1387	.075 697 1663	27
28	5.111 686 6971	68.528 111 6191	.014 592 5515	.195 630 1431	13.406 164 2818	.074 592 5515	28
29	5.418 387 8990	73.639 798 3162	.013 579 6135	.184 556 7388	13.590 721 0206	.073 579 6135	29
30	5.743 491 1729	79.058 186 2152	.012 648 9115	.174 110 1309	13.764 831 1515	.072 648 9115	30
31	6.088 100 6433	84.801 677 3881	.011 792 2196	.164 254 8405	13.929 085 9920	.071 792 2196	31
32	6.453 386 6819	90.889 778 0314	.011 002 3374	.154 957 3967	14.084 043 3887	.071 002 3374	32
33	6.840 589 8828	97.343 164 7133	.010 272 9350	.146 186 2233	14.230 229 6119	.070 272 9350	33
34	7.251 025 2758	104.183 754 5961	.009 598 4254	.137 911 5314	14.368 141 1433	.069 598 4254	34
35	7.686 086 7923	111.434 779 8719	.008 973 8590	.130 105 2183	14.498 246 3616	.068 973 8590	35
36	8.147 251 9999	119.120 866 6642	.008 394 8348	.122 740 7720	14.620 987 1336	.068 394 8348	36
37	8.636 087 1198	127.268 118 6640	.007 857 4274	.115 793 1811	14.736 780 3147	.067 857 4274	37
38	9.154 252 3470	135.904 205 7839	.007 358 1240	.109 238 8501	14.846 019 1648	.067 358 1240	38
39	9.703 507 4879	145.058 458 1309	.006 893 7724	.103 055 5190	14.949 074 6838	.066 893 7724	39
40	10.285 717 9371	154.761 965 6188	.006 461 5359	.097 222 1877	15.046 296 8715	.066 461 5359	40
41	10.902 861 0134	165.047 683 5559	.006 058 8551	.091 719 0450	15.138 015 9165	.066 058 8551	41
42	11.557 032 6742	175.950 544 5693	.005 683 4152	.086 527 4010	15.224 543 3175	.065 683 4152	42
43	12.250 454 6346	187.507 577 2434	.005 333 1178	.081 629 6235	15.306 172 9410	.065 333 1178	43
44	12.985 481 9127	199.758 031 8780	.005 006 0565	.077 009 0788	15.383 182 0198	.065 006 0565	44
45	13.764 610 8274	212.743 513 7907	.004 700 4958	.072 650 0743	15.455 832 0942	.064 700 4958	45
46	14.590 487 4771	226.508 124 6181	.004 414 8527	.068 537 8060	15.524 369 9002	.064 414 8527	46
47	15.465 916 7257	241.098 612 0952	.004 147 6805	.064 658 3075	15.589 028 2077	.064 147 6805	47
48	16.393 871 7293	256.564 528 8209	.003 897 6549	.060 998 4033	15.650 026 6110	.063 897 6549	48
49	17.377 504 0330	272.958 400 5502	.003 663 5619	.057 545 6635	15.707 572 2746	.063 663 5619	49
50	18.420 154 2750	290.335 904 5832	.003 444 2864	.054 288 3618	15.761 860 6364	.063 444 2864	50
51	19.525 363 5315	308.756 058 8582	.003 238 8028	.051 215 4357	15.813 076 0721	.063 238 8028	51
52	20.696 885 3434	328.281 422 3897	.003 046 1669	.048 316 4488	15.861 392 5208	.063 046 1669	52
53	21.938 698 4640	348.978 307 7331	.002 865 5076	.045 581 5554	15.906 974 0762	.062 865 5076	53
54	23.255 020 3718	370.917 006 1971	.002 696 0209	.043 001 4574	15.949 975 5436	.062 696 0209	54
55	24.650 321 5941	394.172 026 5689	.002 536 9634	.040 567 4221	15.990 542 9657	.062 536 9634	55
56	26.129 340 8898	418.822 348 1630	.002 387 6472	.038 271 1529	16.028 814 1186	.062 387 6472	56
57	27.697 101 3432	444.951 689 0528	.002 247 4350	.036 104 8612	16.064 918 9798	.062 247 4350	57
58	29.358 927 4238	472.648 790 3959	.002 115 7359	.034 061 1898	16.098 980 1696	.062 115 7359	58
59	31.120 463 0692	502.007 717 8197	.001 992 0012	.032 133 1979	16.131 113 3676	.061 992 0012	59
60	32.987 690 8533	533.128 180 8889	.001 875 7215	.030 314 3377	16.161 427 7052	.061 875 7215	60
61	34.966 952 3045	566.115 871 7422	.001 766 4228	.028 598 4318	16.190 026 1370	.061 766 4228	61
62	37.064 969 4428	601.082 824 0467	.001 663 6642	.026 979 6526	16.217 005 7896	.061 663 6642	62
63	39.288 867 6094	638.147 793 4895	.001 567 0351	.025 452 5025	16.242 458 2921	.061 567 0351	63
64	41.646 199 6659	677.436 661 0989	.001 476 1528	.024 011 7948	16.266 470 0869	.061 476 1528	64
65	44.144 971 6459	719.082 860 7649	.001 390 6603	.022 652 6366	16.289 122 7235	.061 390 6603	65
66	46.793 669 9446	763.227 832 4107	.001 310 2248	.021 370 4119	16.310 493 1354	.061 310 2248	66
67	49.601 290 1413	810.021 502 3554	.001 234 5351	.020 160 7652	16.330 653 9013	.061 234 5351	67
68	52.577 367 5498	859.622 792 4967	.001 163 3009	.019 019 5905	16.349 673 4918	.061 163 3009	68
69	55.732 009 6028	912.200 160 0465	.001 096 2506	.017 943 0099	16.367 616 5017	.061 096 2506	69
70	59.075 930 1790	967.932 169 6493	.001 033 1302	.016 927 3678	16.384 543 8695	.061 033 1302	70
71	62.620 485 9897	1027.008 099 8283	.000 973 7022	.015 969 2149	16.400 513 0844	.060 973 7022	71
72	66.377 715 1491	1089.628 585 8180	.000 917 7439	.015 065 2971	16.415 578 3816	.060 917 7439	72
73	70.360 378 0580	1156.006 300 9670	.000 865 0472	.014 212 5464	16.429 790 9260	.060 865 0472	73
74	74.582 000 7415	1226.366 679 0251	.000 815 4168	.013 408 0608	16.443 198 9868	.060 815 4168	74
75	79.056 920 7860	1300.948 679 7666	.000 768 6698	.012 649 1140	16.455 848 1007	.060 768 6698	75
76	83.800 336 0332	1380.005 600 5526	.000 724 6347	.011 933 1264	16.467 781 2271	.060 724 6347	76
77	88.828 356 1951	1463.805 936 5857	.000 683 1507	.011 257 6646	16.479 038 8935	.060 683 1507	77
78	94.158 057 5669	1552.634 292 7808	.000 644 0667	.010 620 4400	16.489 659 3335	.060 644 0667	78
79	99.807 541 0209	1646.792 350 3477	.000 607 2411	.010 019 2830	16.499 678 6165	.060 607 2411	79
80	105.795 993 4821	1746.599 891 3686	.000 572 5410	.009 452 1538	16.509 130 7703	.060 572 5410	80
81	112.143 753 0910	1852.395 884 8507	.000 539 8414	.008 917 1262	16.518 047 8965	.060 539 8414	81
82	118.872 378 2765	1964.539 637 9417	.000 509 0251	.008 412 3832	16.526 460 2797	.060 509 0251	82
83	126.004 720 9731	2083.412 016 2182	.000 479 9819	.007 936 2016	16.534 396 4903	.060 479 9819	83
84	133.565 004 2315	2209.416 737 1913	.000 452 6081	.007 486 9911	16.541 883 4814	.060 452 6081	84
85	141.578 904 4854	2342.981 741 4228	.000 426 8066	.007 063 1992	16.548 946 6806	.060 426 8066	85
86	150.073 638 7545	2484.560 645 9082	.000 402 4856	.006 663 3954	16.555 610 0760	.060 402 4856	86
87	159.078 057 0798	2634.634 284 6626	.000 379 5593	.006 286 2221	16.561 896 2981	.060 379 5593	87
88	168.622 740 5045	2793.712 341 7424	.000 357 9467	.005 930 3982	16.567 826 6963	.060 357 9467	88
89	178.740 104 9348	2962.335 082 2469	.000 337 5715	.005 594 7153	16.573 421 4116	.060 337 5715	89
90	189.464 511 2309	3141.075 187 1818	.000 318 3623	.005 278 0333	16.578 699 4450	.060 318 3623	90
91	200.832 381 9048	3330.539 698 4127	.000 300 2516	.004 979 2767	16.583 678 7217	.060 300 2516	91
92	212.882 324 8190	3531.372 080 3174	.000 283 1761	.004 697 4308	16.588 376 1525	.060 283 1761	92
93	225.655 264 3082	3744.254 405 1365	.000 267 0759	.004 431 5385	16.592 807 6910	.060 267 0759	93
94	239.194 580 1667	3969.909 669 4447	.000 251 8949	.004 180 6967	16.596 988 3878	.060 251 8949	94
95	253.546 254 9767	4209.104 249 6113	.000 237 5802	.003 944 0535	16.600 932 4413	.060 237 5802	95
96	268.759 030 2753	4462.650 504 5880	.000 224 0821	.003 720 8052	16.604 653 2465	.060 224 0821	96
97	284.884 572 0918	4731.409 534 8633	.000 211 3535	.003 510 1936	16.608 163 4401	.060 211 3535	97
98	301.977 646 4173	5016.294 106 9551	.000 199 3504	.003 311 5034	16.611 474 9435	.060 199 3504	98
99	320.096 305 2023	5318.271 753 3724	.000 188 0310	.003 124 0598	16.614 599 0033	.060 188 0310	99
100	339.302 083 5145	5638.368 058 5748	.000 177 3563	.002 947 2262	16.617 546 2295	.060 177 3563	100

RATE **7%**

	XIII COMPOUND AMOUNT	XIV AMOUNT OF ANUITY	XV SINKING FUND	XVI PRESENT VALUE	XVII PRESENT VALUE OF ANNUITY	XVIII AMORTIZATION	
PERIODS	**AMOUNT OF 1** — How $1 left at compound interest will grow.	**AMOUNT OF 1 PER PERIOD** — How $1 deposited periodically will grow.	**SINKING FUND** — Periodic deposit that will grow to $1 at future date.	**PRESENT WORTH OF 1** — What $1 due in the future is worth today.	**PRESENT WORTH OF 1 PER PERIOD** — What $1 payable periodically is worth today.	**PARTIAL PAYMENT** — Annuity worth $1 today. Periodic payment necessary to pay off a loan of $1.	**PERIODS**
1	1.070 000 0000	1.000 000 0000	1.000 000 0000	.934 579 4393	.934 579 4393	1.070 000 0000	1
2	1.144 900 0000	2.070 000 0000	.483 091 7874	.873 438 7283	1.808 018 1675	.553 091 7874	2
3	1.225 043 0000	3.214 900 0000	.311 051 6657	.816 297 8769	2.624 316 0444	.381 051 6657	3
4	1.310 796 0100	4.439 943 0000	.225 228 1167	.762 895 2120	3.387 211 2565	.295 228 1167	4
5	1.402 551 7307	5.750 739 0100	.173 890 6944	.712 986 1795	4.100 197 4359	.243 890 6944	5
6	1.500 730 3518	7.153 290 7407	.139 795 7998	.666 342 2238	4.766 539 6598	.209 795 7998	6
7	1.605 781 4765	8.654 021 0925	.115 553 2196	.622 749 7419	5.389 289 4016	.185 553 2196	7
8	1.718 186 1798	10.259 802 5690	.097 467 7625	.582 009 1046	5.971 298 5062	.167 467 7625	8
9	1.838 459 2124	11.977 988 7489	.083 486 4701	.543 933 7426	6.515 232 2488	.153 486 4701	9
10	1.967 151 3573	13.816 447 9613	.072 377 5027	.508 349 2921	7.023 581 5409	.142 377 5027	10
11	2.104 851 9523	15.783 599 3186	.063 356 9048	.475 092 7964	7.498 674 3373	.133 356 9048	11
12	2.252 191 5890	17.888 451 2709	.055 901 9887	.444 011 9592	7.942 686 2966	.125 901 9887	12
13	2.409 845 0002	20.140 642 8599	.049 650 8481	.414 964 4479	8.357 650 7444	.119 650 8481	13
14	2.578 534 1502	22.550 487 8600	.044 344 9386	.387 817 2410	8.745 467 9855	.114 344 9386	14
15	2.759 031 5407	25.129 022 0102	.039 794 6247	.362 446 0196	9.107 914 0051	.109 794 6247	15
16	2.952 163 7486	27.888 053 5509	.035 857 6477	.338 734 5978	9.446 648 6029	.105 857 6477	16
17	3.158 815 2110	30.840 217 2995	.032 425 1931	.316 574 3905	9.763 222 9934	.102 425 1931	17
18	3.379 932 2757	33.999 032 5105	.029 412 6017	.295 863 9163	10.059 086 9097	.099 412 6017	18
19	3.616 527 5350	37.378 964 7862	.026 753 0148	.276 508 3330	10.335 595 2427	.096 753 0148	19
20	3.869 684 4625	40.995 492 3212	.024 392 9257	.258 419 0028	10.594 014 2455	.094 392 9257	20
21	4.140 562 3749	44.865 176 7837	.022 289 0017	.241 513 0867	10.835 527 3323	.092 289 0017	21
22	4.430 401 7411	49.005 739 1586	.020 405 7732	.225 713 1652	11.061 240 4974	.090 405 7732	22
23	4.740 529 8630	53.436 140 8997	.018 713 9263	.210 946 8833	11.272 187 3808	.088 713 9263	23
24	5.072 366 9534	58.176 670 7627	.017 189 0207	.197 146 6199	11.469 334 0007	.087 189 0207	24
25	5.427 432 6401	63.249 037 7160	.015 810 5172	.184 249 1775	11.653 583 1783	.085 810 5172	25
26	5.807 352 9249	68.676 470 3562	.014 561 0279	.172 195 4930	11.825 778 6713	.084 561 0279	26
27	6.213 867 6297	74.483 823 2811	.013 425 7340	.160 930 3673	11.986 709 0386	.083 425 7340	27
28	6.648 838 3638	80.697 690 9108	.012 391 9283	.150 402 2214	12.137 111 2510	.082 391 9283	28
29	7.114 257 0492	87.346 529 2745	.011 448 6518	.140 562 8154	12.277 674 0664	.081 448 6518	29
30	7.612 255 0427	94.460 786 3237	.010 586 4035	.131 367 1172	12.409 041 1835	.080 586 4035	30
31	8.145 112 8956	102.073 041 3664	.009 796 9061	.122 773 0067	12.531 814 1902	.079 796 9061	31
32	8.715 270 7983	110.218 154 2621	.009 072 9155	.114 741 1277	12.646 555 3179	.079 072 9155	32
33	9.325 339 7542	118.933 425 0604	.008 408 0653	.107 234 6988	12.753 790 0168	.078 408 0653	33
34	9.978 113 5370	128.258 764 8146	.007 796 7381	.100 219 3447	12.854 009 3615	.077 796 7381	34
35	10.676 581 4846	138.236 878 3516	.007 233 9596	.093 662 9390	12.947 672 3004	.077 233 9596	35
36	11.423 942 1885	148.913 459 8363	.006 715 3097	.087 535 4570	13.035 207 7574	.076 715 3097	36
37	12.223 618 1417	160.337 402 0248	.006 236 8480	.081 808 8383	13.117 016 5957	.076 236 8480	37
38	13.079 271 4117	172.561 020 1665	.005 795 0515	.076 456 8582	13.193 473 4539	.075 795 0515	38
39	13.994 820 4105	185.640 291 5782	.005 386 7616	.071 455 0077	13.264 928 4616	.075 386 7616	39
40	14.974 457 8392	199.635 111 9887	.005 009 1389	.066 780 3810	13.331 708 8426	.075 009 1389	40
41	16.022 669 8880	214.609 569 8279	.004 659 6245	.062 411 5710	13.394 120 4137	.074 659 6245	41
42	17.144 256 7801	230.632 239 7158	.004 335 9072	.058 328 5711	13.452 448 9847	.074 335 9072	42
43	18.344 354 7547	247.776 496 4959	.004 035 8953	.054 512 6832	13.506 961 6680	.074 035 8953	43
44	19.628 459 5875	266.120 851 2507	.003 757 6913	.050 946 4329	13.557 908 1009	.073 757 6913	44
45	21.002 451 7587	285.749 310 8382	.003 499 5710	.047 613 4887	13.605 521 5896	.073 499 5710	45
46	22.472 623 3818	306.751 762 5969	.003 259 9650	.044 498 5876	13.650 020 1772	.073 259 9650	46
47	24.045 707 0185	329.224 385 9787	.003 037 4421	.041 587 4650	13.691 607 6423	.073 037 4421	47
48	25.728 906 5098	353.270 092 9972	.002 830 6953	.038 866 7898	13.730 474 4320	.072 830 6953	48
49	27.529 929 9655	378.998 999 5070	.002 638 5294	.036 324 1026	13.766 798 5346	.072 638 5294	49
50	29.457 025 0631	406.528 929 4724	.002 459 8495	.033 947 7594	13.800 746 2940	.072 459 8495	50
51	31.519 016 8175	435.985 954 5355	.002 293 6519	.031 726 8780	13.832 473 1720	.072 293 6519	51
52	33.725 347 9947	467.504 971 3530	.002 139 0147	.029 651 2878	13.862 124 4598	.072 139 0147	52
53	36.086 122 3543	501.230 319 3477	.001 995 0908	.027 711 4839	13.889 835 9437	.071 995 0908	53
54	38.612 150 9191	537.316 441 7021	.001 861 1007	.025 898 5831	13.915 734 5269	.071 861 1007	54
55	41.315 001 4835	575.928 592 6212	.001 736 3264	.024 204 2833	13.939 938 8102	.071 736 3264	55
56	44.207 051 5873	617.243 594 1047	.001 620 1059	.022 620 8255	13.962 559 6357	.071 620 1059	56
57	47.301 545 1984	661.450 645 6920	.001 511 8286	.021 140 9584	13.983 700 5941	.071 511 8286	57
58	50.612 653 3623	708.752 190 8905	.001 410 9304	.019 757 9051	14.003 458 4991	.071 410 9304	58
59	54.155 539 0977	759.364 844 2528	.001 316 8900	.018 465 3318	14.021 923 8310	.071 316 8900	59
60	57.946 426 8345	813.520 383 3505	.001 229 2255	.017 257 3395	14.039 181 1504	.071 229 2255	60
61	62.002 676 7130	871.466 810 1850	.001 147 4906	.016 128 3360	14.055 309 4864	.071 147 4906	61
62	66.342 864 0829	933.469 486 8980	.001 071 2723	.015 073 2112	14.070 382 6976	.071 071 2723	62
63	70.986 864 5687	999.812 350 9808	.001 000 1877	.014 087 1132	14.084 469 8108	.071 000 1877	63
64	75.955 945 0885	1070.799 215 5495	.000 933 8819	.013 165 5264	14.097 635 3372	.070 933 8819	64
65	81.272 861 2447	1146.755 160 6379	.000 872 0257	.012 304 2303	14.109 939 5675	.070 872 0257	65
66	86.961 961 5318	1228.028 021 8826	.000 814 3137	.011 499 2806	14.121 438 8481	.070 814 3137	66
67	93.049 298 8390	1314.989 983 4144	.000 760 4621	.010 746 9912	14.132 185 8394	.070 760 4621	67
68	99.562 749 7577	1408.039 282 2534	.000 710 2075	.010 043 9171	14.142 229 7564	.070 710 2075	68
69	106.532 142 2408	1507.602 032 0111	.000 663 3050	.009 386 8384	14.151 616 5948	.070 663 3050	69
70	113.989 392 1976	1614.134 174 2519	.000 619 5272	.008 772 7461	14.160 389 3409	.070 619 5272	70
71	121.968 649 6515	1728.123 566 4495	.000 578 6623	.008 198 8282	14.168 588 1691	.070 578 6623	71
72	130.506 455 1271	1850.092 216 1010	.000 540 5136	.007 662 4562	14.176 250 6253	.070 540 5136	72
73	139.641 906 9860	1980.598 671 2281	.000 504 8978	.007 161 1740	14.183 411 7993	.070 504 8978	73
74	149.416 840 4750	2120.240 578 2140	.000 471 6446	.006 692 6860	14.190 104 4854	.070 471 6446	74
75	159.876 019 3082	2269.657 418 6890	.000 440 5951	.006 254 8468	14.196 359 3321	.070 440 5951	75
76	171.067 340 6598	2429.533 437 9973	.000 411 6017	.005 845 6512	14.202 204 9833	.070 411 6017	76
77	183.042 054 5060	2600.600 778 6571	.000 384 5265	.005 463 2264	14.207 668 2087	.070 384 5265	77
78	195.854 998 3214	2783.642 833 1631	.000 359 2415	.005 105 8181	14.212 774 0268	.070 359 2415	78
79	209.564 848 2039	2979.497 831 4845	.000 335 6270	.004 771 7926	14.217 545 8194	.070 335 6270	79
80	224.234 387 5782	3189.062 679 6884	.000 313 5718	.004 459 6193	14.222 005 4387	.070 313 5718	80
81	239.930 794 7087	3413.297 067 2666	.000 292 9719	.004 167 8685	14.226 173 3072	.070 292 9719	81
82	256.725 950 3383	3653.227 861 9752	.000 273 7305	.003 895 2042	14.230 068 5114	.070 273 7305	82
83	274.696 766 8619	3909.953 812 3135	.000 255 7575	.003 640 3778	14.233 708 8892	.070 255 7575	83
84	293.925 540 5423	4184.650 579 1754	.000 238 9686	.003 402 2222	14.237 111 1114	.070 238 9686	84
85	314.500 328 3802	4478.576 119 7177	.000 223 2853	.003 179 6649	14.240 290 7583	.070 223 2853	85
86	336.515 351 3669	4793.076 448 0980	.000 208 6343	.002 971 6326	14.243 262 3909	.070 208 6343	86
87	360.071 425 9625	5129.591 799 4648	.000 194 9473	.002 777 2268	14.246 039 6177	.070 194 9473	87
88	385.276 425 7799	5489.663 225 4273	.000 182 1605	.002 595 5390	14.248 635 1567	.070 182 1605	88
89	412.245 775 5845	5874.939 651 2073	.000 170 2145	.002 425 7374	14.251 060 8941	.070 170 2145	89
90	441.102 979 8754	6287.185 426 7918	.000 159 0537	.002 267 0443	14.253 327 9384	.070 159 0537	90
91	471.980 188 4667	6728.288 406 6672	.000 148 6262	.002 118 7393	14.255 446 6778	.070 148 6262	91
92	505.018 801 6594	7200.268 595 1339	.000 138 8837	.001 980 1243	14.257 426 7957	.070 138 8837	92
93	540.370 117 7755	7705.287 396 7933	.000 129 7810	.001 850 5835	14.259 277 3792	.070 129 7810	93
94	578.196 026 0198	8245.657 514 5688	.000 121 2760	.001 729 5172	14.261 006 8965	.070 121 2760	94
95	618.669 747 8412	8823.853 540 5886	.000 113 3292	.001 616 3713	14.262 623 2677	.070 113 3292	95
96	661.976 630 1901	9442.523 288 4298	.000 105 9039	.001 510 6273	14.264 133 8951	.070 105 9039	96
97	708.314 994 3034	10104.499 918 6199	.000 098 9658	.001 411 8013	14.265 545 6963	.070 098 9658	97
98	757.897 043 9046	10812.814 912 9233	.000 092 4829	.001 319 4404	14.266 865 1367	.070 092 4829	98
99	810.949 836 9780	11570.711 956 8279	.000 086 4251	.001 233 1219	14.268 098 2586	.070 086 4251	99
100	867.716 325 5664	12381.661 793 8059	.000 080 7646	.001 152 4504	14.269 250 7090	.070 080 7646	100

	XIII COMPOUND AMOUNT	XIV AMOUNT OF ANNUITY	XV SINKING FUND	XVI PRESENT VALUE	XVII PRESENT VALUE OF ANNUITY	XVIII AMORTIZATION	
P E R I O D S	**AMOUNT OF 1** How $1 left at compound interest will grow.	**AMOUNT OF 1 PER PERIOD** How $1 deposited periodically will grow.	**SINKING FUND** Periodic deposit that will grow to $1 at future date.	**PRESENT WORTH OF 1** What $1 due in the future is worth today.	**PRESENT WORTH OF 1 PER PERIOD** What $1 payable periodically is worth today.	**PARTIAL PAYMENT** Annuity worth $1 today. Periodic payment necessary to pay off a loan of $1.	**P E R I O D S**
1	1.080 000 0000	1.000 000 0000	1.000 000 0000	.925 925 9259	.925 925 9259	1.080 000 0000	1
2	1.166 400 0000	2.080 000 0000	.480 769 2308	.857 338 8203	1.783 264 7462	.560 769 2308	2
3	1.259 712 0000	3.246 400 0000	.308 033 5140	.793 832 2410	2.577 096 9872	.388 033 5140	3
4	1.360 488 9600	4.506 112 0000	.221 920 8045	.735 029 8528	3.312 126 8400	.301 920 8045	4
5	1.469 328 0768	5.866 600 9600	.170 456 4546	.680 583 1970	3.992 710 0371	.250 456 4546	5
6	1.586 874 3229	7.335 929 0368	.136 315 3862	.630 169 6269	4.622 879 6640	.216 315 3862	6
7	1.713 824 2688	8.922 803 3597	.112 072 4014	.583 490 3953	5.206 370 0592	.192 072 4014	7
8	1.850 930 2103	10.636 627 6285	.094 014 7606	.540 268 8845	5.746 638 9437	.174 014 7606	8
9	1.999 004 6271	12.487 557 8388	.080 079 7092	.500 248 9671	6.246 887 9109	.160 079 7092	9
10	2.158 924 9973	14.486 562 4659	.069 029 4887	.463 193 4881	6.710 081 3989	.149 029 4887	10
11	2.331 638 9971	16.645 487 4632	.060 076 3421	.428 882 8593	7.138 964 2583	.140 076 3421	11
12	2.518 170 1168	18.977 126 4602	.052 695 0169	.397 113 7586	7.536 078 0169	.132 695 0169	12
13	2.719 623 7262	21.495 296 5771	.046 521 8052	.367 697 9247	7.903 775 9416	.126 521 8052	13
14	2.937 193 6243	24.214 920 3032	.041 296 8528	.340 461 0414	8.244 236 9830	.121 296 8528	14
15	3.172 169 1142	27.152 113 9275	.036 829 5449	.315 241 7050	8.559 478 6879	.116 829 5449	15
16	3.425 942 6433	30.324 283 0417	.032 976 8720	.291 890 4676	8.851 369 1555	.112 976 8720	16
17	3.700 018 0548	33.750 225 6850	.029 629 4315	.270 268 9514	9.121 638 1069	.109 629 4315	17
18	3.996 019 4992	37.450 243 7398	.026 702 0959	.250 249 0291	9.371 887 1360	.106 702 0959	18
19	4.315 701 0591	41.446 263 2390	.024 127 6275	.231 712 0640	9.603 599 2000	.104 127 6275	19
20	4.660 957 1438	44.761 964 2981	.021 852 2088	.214 548 2074	9.818 147 4074	.101 852 2088	20
21	5.033 833 7154	50.422 921 4420	.019 832 2503	.198 655 7476	10.016 803 1550	.099 832 2503	21
22	5.436 540 4126	55.456 755 1573	.018 032 0684	.183 940 5070	10.200 743 6621	.098 032 0684	22
23	5.871 463 6456	60.893 295 5699	.016 422 1692	.170 315 2843	10.371 058 9464	.096 422 1692	23
24	6.341 180 7372	66.764 759 2155	.014 977 9616	.157 699 3373	10.528 758 2837	.094 977 9616	24
25	6.848 475 1962	73.105 939 9527	.013 678 7791	.146 017 9049	10.674 776 1886	.093 678 7791	25
26	7.396 353 2119	79.954 415 1490	.012 507 1267	.135 201 7638	10.809 977 9524	.092 507 1267	26
27	7.988 061 4689	87.350 768 3609	.011 448 0962	.125 186 8183	10.935 164 7707	.091 448 0962	27
28	8.627 106 3864	95.338 829 8297	.010 488 9057	.115 913 7207	11.051 078 4914	.090 488 9057	28
29	9.317 274 8973	103.965 936 2161	.009 618 5350	.107 327 5192	11.158 406 0106	.089 618 5350	29
30	10.062 656 8891	113.283 211 1134	.008 827 4334	.099 377 3325	11.257 783 3431	.088 827 4334	30
31	10.867 669 4402	123.345 868 0025	.008 107 2841	.092 016 0487	11.349 799 3918	.088 107 2841	31
32	11.737 082 9954	134.213 537 4427	.007 450 8132	.085 200 0451	11.434 999 4368	.087 450 8132	32
33	12.676 049 6350	145.950 620 4381	.006 851 6324	.078 888 9306	11.513 888 3674	.086 851 6324	33
34	13.690 133 6059	158.626 670 0732	.006 304 1011	.073 045 3061	11.586 933 6736	.086 304 1011	34
35	14.785 344 2943	172.316 803 6790	.005 803 2646	.067 634 5427	11.654 568 2163	.085 803 2646	35
36	15.968 171 8379	187.102 147 9733	.005 344 6741	.062 624 5766	11.717 192 7928	.085 344 6741	36
37	17.245 625 5849	203.070 319 8112	.004 924 4025	.057 985 7190	11.775 178 5119	.084 924 4025	37
38	18.625 275 6317	220.315 945 3961	.004 538 9361	.053 690 4806	11.828 868 9925	.084 538 9361	38
39	20.115 297 6822	238.941 221 0278	.004 185 1297	.049 713 4080	11.878 582 4004	.084 185 1297	39
40	21.724 521 4968	259.056 518 7100	.003 860 1615	.046 030 9333	11.924 613 3337	.083 860 1615	40
41	23.462 483 2165	280.781 040 2068	.003 561 4940	.042 621 2345	11.967 234 5683	.083 561 4940	41
42	25.339 481 8739	304.243 523 4233	.003 286 8407	.039 464 1061	12.006 698 6743	.083 286 8407	42
43	27.366 640 4238	329.583 005 2972	.003 034 1370	.036 540 8389	12.043 239 5133	.083 034 1370	43
44	29.555 971 6577	356.949 645 7210	.002 801 5156	.033 834 1101	12.077 073 6234	.082 801 5156	44
45	31.920 449 3903	386.505 617 3787	.002 587 2845	.031 327 8791	12.108 401 5032	.082 587 2845	45
46	34.474 085 3415	418.426 066 7690	.002 389 9085	.029 007 2961	12.137 408 7992	.082 389 9085	46
47	37.232 012 1688	452.900 152 1105	.002 207 9922	.026 858 6075	12.164 267 4067	.082 207 9922	47
48	40.210 573 1423	490.132 164 2793	.002 040 2606	.024 869 0810	12.189 136 4877	.082 040 2606	48
49	43.427 418 9937	530.342 737 4217	.001 885 5731	.023 026 9268	12.212 163 4145	.081 885 5731	49
50	46.901 612 5337	573.770 156 4154	.001 742 8582	.021 321 2286	12.233 484 6431	.081 742 8582	50
51	50.653 741 5143	620.671 768 9286	.001 611 1575	.019 741 8783	12.253 226 5214	.081 611 1575	51
52	54.706 040 8354	671.325 510 4429	.001 489 5903	.018 279 5169	12.271 506 0383	.081 489 5903	52
53	59.082 524 1023	726.031 551 2783	.001 377 3506	.016 925 4786	12.288 431 5169	.081 377 3506	53
54	63.809 126 0304	785.114 075 3806	.001 273 7003	.015 671 7395	12.304 103 2564	.081 273 7003	54
55	68.913 856 1129	848.923 201 4111	.001 177 9629	.014 510 8699	12.318 614 1263	.081 177 9629	55
56	74.426 964 6019	917.837 057 5239	.001 089 5180	.013 435 9906	12.332 050 1170	.081 089 5180	56
57	80.381 121 7701	992.264 022 1259	.001 007 7963	.012 440 7321	12.344 490 8490	.081 007 7963	57
58	86.811 611 5117	1072.645 143 8959	.000 932 2748	.011 519 1964	12.356 010 0454	.080 932 2748	58
59	93.756 540 4326	1159.456 755 4076	.000 862 4729	.010 665 9226	12.366 675 9680	.080 862 4729	59
60	101.257 063 6672	1253.213 295 8402	.000 797 9488	.009 875 8542	12.376 551 8222	.080 797 9488	60
61	109.357 628 7606	1354.470 359 5074	.000 738 2960	.009 144 3095	12.385 696 1317	.080 738 2960	61
62	118.106 239 0614	1463.827 988 2680	.000 683 1404	.008 466 9532	12.394 163 0849	.080 683 1404	62
63	127.554 738 1864	1581.934 227 3295	.000 632 1375	.007 839 7715	12.402 002 8564	.080 632 1375	63
64	137.759 117 2413	1709.488 965 5158	.000 584 9701	.007 259 0477	12.409 261 9040	.080 584 9701	64
65	148.779 846 6206	1847.248 082 7571	.000 541 3458	.006 721 3404	12.415 983 2445	.080 541 3458	65
66	160.682 234 3502	1996.027 929 3777	.000 500 9950	.006 223 4634	12.422 206 7079	.080 500 9950	66
67	173.536 813 0982	2156.710 163 7279	.000 463 6692	.005 762 4661	12.427 969 1739	.080 463 6692	67
68	187.419 758 1461	2330.246 976 8261	.000 429 1391	.005 335 6167	12.433 304 7907	.080 429 1391	68
69	202.413 338 7978	2517.666 734 9722	.000 397 1932	.004 940 3859	12.438 245 1766	.080 397 1932	69
70	218.606 405 9016	2720.080 073 7700	.000 367 6362	.004 574 4314	12.442 819 6079	.080 367 6362	70
71	236.094 918 3737	2938.686 479 6716	.000 340 2881	.004 235 5846	12.447 055 1925	.080 340 2881	71
72	254.982 511 8436	3174.781 398 0453	.000 314 9823	.003 921 8376	12.450 977 0301	.080 314 9823	72
73	275.381 112 7911	3429.763 909 8889	.000 291 5653	.003 631 3311	12.454 608 3612	.080 291 5653	73
74	297.411 601 8144	3705.145 022 6800	.000 269 8950	.003 362 3436	12.457 970 7048	.080 269 8950	74
75	321.204 529 9596	4002.556 624 4944	.000 249 8403	.003 113 2811	12.461 083 9860	.080 249 8403	75
76	346.900 892 3563	4323.761 154 4540	.000 231 2801	.002 882 6677	12.463 966 6537	.080 231 2801	76
77	374.652 963 7448	4670.662 046 8103	.000 214 1024	.002 669 1368	12.466 635 7904	.080 214 1024	77
78	404.625 200 8444	5045.315 010 5551	.000 198 2037	.002 471 4229	12.469 107 2134	.080 198 2037	78
79	436.995 216 9120	5449.940 211 3995	.000 183 4883	.002 288 3546	12.471 395 5679	.080 183 4883	79
80	471.954 834 2649	5886.935 428 3115	.000 169 8677	.002 118 8468	12.473 514 4147	.080 169 8677	80
81	509.711 221 0061	6358.890 262 5764	.000 157 2601	.001 961 8952	12.475 476 3099	.080 157 2601	81
82	550.488 118 6866	6868.601 483 5825	.000 145 5900	.001 816 5696	12.477 292 8795	.080 145 5900	82
83	594.527 168 1815	7419.089 602 2691	.000 134 7874	.001 682 0089	12.478 974 8885	.080 134 7874	83
84	642.089 341 6361	8013.616 770 4506	.000 124 7876	.001 557 4157	12.480 532 3042	.080 124 7876	84
85	693.456 488 9669	8655.706 112 0867	.000 115 5307	.001 442 0515	12.481 974 3557	.080 115 5307	85
86	748.933 008 0843	9349.162 601 0536	.000 106 9615	.001 335 2329	12.483 309 5886	.080 106 9615	86
87	808.847 648 7310	10098.095 609 1379	.000 099 0286	.001 236 3268	12.484 545 9154	.080 099 0286	87
88	873.555 460 6295	10906.943 257 8690	.000 091 6847	.001 144 7470	12.485 690 6624	.080 091 6847	88
89	943.439 897 4799	11780.498 718 4985	.000 084 8860	.001 059 9509	12.486 750 6133	.080 084 8860	89
90	1018.915 089 2783	12723.938 615 9783	.000 078 5920	.000 981 4360	12.487 732 0494	.080 078 5920	90
91	1100.428 296 4205	13742.853 705 2566	.000 072 7651	.000 908 7371	12.488 640 7865	.080 072 7651	91
92	1188.462 560 1342	14843.282 001 6771	.000 067 3705	.000 841 4232	12.489 482 2097	.080 067 3705	92
93	1283.539 564 9449	16031.744 561 8113	.000 062 3762	.000 779 0956	12.490 261 3053	.080 062 3762	93
94	1386.222 730 1405	17315.284 126 7562	.000 057 7524	.000 721 3848	12.490 982 6901	.080 057 7524	94
95	1497.120 548 5517	18701.506 856 8967	.000 053 4716	.000 667 9489	12.491 650 6389	.080 053 4716	95
96	1616.890 192 4359	20198.627 405 4485	.000 049 5083	.000 618 4712	12.492 269 1101	.080 049 5083	96
97	1746.241 407 8307	21815.517 597 8843	.000 045 8389	.000 572 6585	12.492 841 7686	.080 045 8389	97
98	1885.940 720 4572	23561.759 005 7151	.000 042 4417	.000 530 2394	12.493 372 0080	.080 042 4417	98
99	2036.815 978 0938	25447.699 726 1723	.000 039 2963	.000 490 9624	12.493 862 9704	.080 039 2963	99
100	2199.761 256 3413	27484.515 704 2661	.000 036 3841	.000 454 5948	12.494 317 5652	.080 036 3841	100

Table XIX: Interest From Day of Deposit

At 5% Compounded Daily
(for one quarter)

Quarter	1st Month	2nd Month	3rd Month
1st	January	February	March
2nd	April	May	June
3rd	July	August	September
4th	October	November	December

1st Month		2nd Month		3rd Month	
Dep. Date	Factor	Dep. Date	Factor	Dep. Date	Factor
1	0.0125 7757	1	0.0083 6757	1	0.0041 7507
2	0.0124 3696	2	0.0082 2754	2	0.0040 3562
3	0.0122 9636	3	0.0080 8753	3	0.0038 9619
4	0.0121 5578	4	0.0079 4753	4	0.0037 5678
5	0.0120 1523	5	0.0078 0756	5	0.0036 1739
6	0.0118 7469	6	0.0076 6761	6	0.0034 7802
7	0.0117 3417	7	0.0075 2767	7	0.0033 3866
8	0.0115 9367	8	0.0073 8776	8	0.0031 9933
9	0.0114 5319	9	0.0072 4786	9	0.0030 6002
10	0.0113 1273	10	0.0071 0798	10	0.0029 2072
11	0.0111 7229	11	0.0069 6813	11	0.0027 8145
12	0.0110 3187	12	0.0068 2829	12	0.0026 4219
13	0.0108 9147	13	0.0066 8847	13	0.0025 0295
14	0.0107 5108	14	0.0065 4867	14	0.0023 6374
15	0.0106 1072	15	0.0064 0890	15	0.0022 2454
16	0.0104 7038	16	0.0062 6914	16	0.0020 8536
17	0.0103 3006	17	0.0061 2940	17	0.0019 4620
18	0.0101 8975	18	0.0059 8968	18	0.0018 0706
19	0.0100 4947	19	0.0058 4997	19	0.0016 6794
20	0.0099 0920	20	0.0057 1029	20	0.0015 2884
21	0.0097 6896	21	0.0055 7063	21	0.0013 8976
22	0.0096 2873	22	0.0054 3099	22	0.0012 5069
23	0.0094 8852	23	0.0052 9136	23	0.0011 1165
24	0.0093 4834	24	0.0051 5176	24	0.0009 7263
25	0.0092 0817	25	0.0050 1217	25	0.0008 3362
26	0.0090 6802	26	0.0048 7261	26	0.0006 9464
27	0.0089 2789	27	0.0047 3306	27	0.0005 5567
28	0.0087 8778	28	0.0045 9353	28	0.0004 1672
29	0.0086 4769	29	0.0044 5403	29	0.0002 7780
30	0.0085 0762	30	0.0043 1454	30	0.0001 3889

Tables for interest compounded daily are reprinted here through the courtesy of California Federal Savings and Loan Association.

Table XX: Interest to Date of Withdrawal

At 5% Compounded Daily
(for one quarter)

	1st Month			2nd Month			3rd Month	
W/D Date	Factor		W/D Date	Factor		W/D Date	Factor	
1	0.0001	3889	1	0.0043	1454	1	0.0085	0762
2	0.0002	7780	2	0.0044	5403	2	0.0086	4769
3	0.0004	1672	3	0.0045	9353	3	0.0087	8778
4	0.0005	5567	4	0.0047	3306	4	0.0089	2789
5	0.0006	9464	5	0.0048	7261	5	0.0090	6802
6	0.0008	3362	6	0.0050	1217	6	0.0092	0817
7	0.0009	7263	7	0.0051	5176	7	0.0093	4834
8	0.0011	1165	8	0.0052	9136	8	0.0094	8852
9	0.0012	5069	9	0.0054	3099	9	0.0096	2873
10	0.0013	8976	10	0.0055	7063	10	0.0097	6896
11	0.0015	2884	11	0.0057	1029	11	0.0099	0920
12	0.0016	6794	12	0.0058	4997	12	0.0100	4947
13	0.0018	0706	13	0.0059	8968	13	0.0101	8975
14	0.0019	4620	14	0.0061	2940	14	0.0103	3006
15	0.0020	8536	15	0.0062	6914	15	0.0104	7038
16	0.0022	2454	16	0.0064	0890	16	0.0106	1072
17	0.0023	6374	17	0.0065	4867	17	0.0107	5108
18	0.0025	0295	18	0.0066	8847	18	0.0108	9147
19	0.0026	4219	19	0.0068	2829	19	0.0110	3187
20	0.0027	8145	20	0.0069	6813	20	0.0111	7229
21	0.0029	2072	21	0.0071	0798	21	0.0113	1273
22	0.0030	6002	22	0.0072	4786	22	0.0114	5319
23	0.0031	9933	23	0.0073	8776	23	0.0115	9367
24	0.0033	3866	24	0.0075	2767	24	0.0117	3417
25	0.0034	7802	25	0.0076	6761	25	0.0118	7469
26	0.0036	1739	26	0.0078	0756	26	0.0120	1523
27	0.0037	5678	27	0.0079	4753	27	0.0121	5578
28	0.0038	9619	28	0.0080	8753	28	0.0122	9636
29	0.0040	3562	29	0.0082	2754	29	0.0124	3696
30	0.0041	7507	30	0.0083	6757	30	0.0125	7757

Tables for interest compounded daily are reprinted here through the courtesy of California Federal Savings and Loan Association.

Table XXI: Annual Percentage Rate Table

ANNUAL PERCENTAGE RATE TABLE FOR MONTHLY PAYMENT PLANS
SEE INSTRUCTIONS FOR USE OF TABLES   FRB-103-M

(FINANCE CHARGE PER $100 OF AMOUNT FINANCED)

NUMBER OF PAYMENTS	10.00%	10.25%	10.50%	10.75%	11.00%	11.25%	11.50%	11.75%	12.00%	12.25%	12.50%	12.75%	13.00%	13.25%	13.50%	13.75%
1	0.83	0.85	0.87	0.90	0.92	0.94	0.96	0.98	1.00	1.02	1.04	1.06	1.08	1.10	1.12	1.15
2	1.25	1.28	1.31	1.35	1.38	1.41	1.44	1.47	1.50	1.53	1.57	1.60	1.63	1.66	1.69	1.72
3	1.67	1.71	1.76	1.80	1.84	1.88	1.92	1.96	2.01	2.05	2.09	2.13	2.17	2.22	2.26	2.30
4	2.09	2.14	2.20	2.25	2.30	2.35	2.41	2.46	2.51	2.57	2.62	2.67	2.72	2.78	2.83	2.88
5	2.51	2.58	2.64	2.70	2.77	2.83	2.89	2.96	3.02	3.08	3.15	3.21	3.27	3.34	3.40	3.46
6	2.94	3.01	3.08	3.16	3.23	3.31	3.38	3.45	3.53	3.60	3.68	3.75	3.83	3.90	3.97	4.05
7	3.36	3.45	3.53	3.62	3.70	3.78	3.87	3.95	4.04	4.12	4.21	4.29	4.38	4.47	4.55	4.64
8	3.79	3.88	3.98	4.07	4.17	4.26	4.36	4.46	4.55	4.65	4.74	4.84	4.94	5.03	5.13	5.22
9	4.21	4.32	4.43	4.53	4.64	4.75	4.85	4.96	5.07	5.17	5.28	5.39	5.49	5.60	5.71	5.82
10	4.64	4.76	4.88	4.99	5.11	5.23	5.35	5.46	5.58	5.70	5.82	5.94	6.05	6.17	6.29	6.41
11	5.07	5.20	5.33	5.45	5.58	5.71	5.84	5.97	6.10	6.23	6.36	6.49	6.62	6.75	6.88	7.01
12	5.50	5.64	5.78	5.92	6.06	6.20	6.34	6.48	6.62	6.76	6.90	7.04	7.18	7.32	7.46	7.60
13	5.93	6.08	6.23	6.38	6.53	6.68	6.84	6.99	7.14	7.29	7.44	7.59	7.75	7.90	8.05	8.20
14	6.36	6.52	6.69	6.85	7.01	7.17	7.34	7.50	7.66	7.82	7.99	8.15	8.31	8.48	8.64	8.81
15	6.80	6.97	7.14	7.32	7.49	7.66	7.84	8.01	8.19	8.36	8.53	8.71	8.88	9.06	9.23	9.41
16	7.23	7.41	7.60	7.78	7.97	8.15	8.34	8.53	8.71	8.90	9.08	9.27	9.46	9.64	9.83	10.02
17	7.67	7.86	8.06	8.25	8.45	8.65	8.84	9.04	9.24	9.44	9.63	9.83	10.03	10.23	10.43	10.63
18	8.10	8.31	8.52	8.73	8.93	9.14	9.35	9.56	9.77	9.98	10.19	10.40	10.61	10.82	11.03	11.24
19	8.54	8.76	8.98	9.20	9.42	9.64	9.86	10.08	10.30	10.52	10.74	10.96	11.18	11.41	11.63	11.85
20	8.98	9.21	9.44	9.67	9.90	10.13	10.37	10.60	10.83	11.06	11.30	11.53	11.76	12.00	12.23	12.46
21	9.42	9.66	9.90	10.15	10.39	10.63	10.88	11.12	11.36	11.61	11.85	12.10	12.34	12.59	12.84	13.08
22	9.86	10.12	10.37	10.62	10.88	11.13	11.39	11.64	11.90	12.16	12.41	12.67	12.93	13.19	13.44	13.70
23	10.30	10.57	10.84	11.10	11.37	11.63	11.90	12.17	12.44	12.71	12.97	13.24	13.51	13.78	14.05	14.32
24	10.75	11.02	11.30	11.58	11.86	12.14	12.42	12.70	12.98	13.26	13.54	13.82	14.10	14.38	14.66	14.95
25	11.19	11.48	11.77	12.06	12.35	12.64	12.93	13.22	13.52	13.81	14.10	14.40	14.69	14.98	15.28	15.57
26	11.64	11.94	12.24	12.54	12.85	13.15	13.45	13.75	14.06	14.36	14.67	14.97	15.28	15.59	15.89	16.20
27	12.09	12.40	12.71	13.03	13.34	13.66	13.97	14.29	14.60	14.92	15.24	15.56	15.87	16.19	16.51	16.83
28	12.53	12.86	13.18	13.51	13.84	14.16	14.49	14.82	15.15	15.48	15.81	16.14	16.47	16.80	17.13	17.46
29	12.98	13.32	13.66	14.00	14.33	14.67	15.01	15.35	15.70	16.04	16.38	16.72	17.07	17.41	17.75	18.10
30	13.43	13.78	14.13	14.48	14.83	15.19	15.54	15.89	16.24	16.60	16.95	17.31	17.66	18.02	18.38	18.74
31	13.89	14.25	14.61	14.97	15.33	15.70	16.06	16.43	16.79	17.16	17.53	17.90	18.27	18.63	19.00	19.38
32	14.34	14.71	15.09	15.46	15.84	16.21	16.59	16.97	17.35	17.73	18.11	18.49	18.87	19.25	19.63	20.02
33	14.79	15.18	15.57	15.95	16.34	16.73	17.12	17.51	17.90	18.29	18.65	19.08	19.47	19.87	20.26	20.66
34	15.25	15.65	16.05	16.44	16.85	17.25	17.65	18.05	18.46	18.86	19.27	19.67	20.08	20.49	20.90	21.31
35	15.70	16.11	16.53	16.94	17.35	17.77	18.18	18.60	19.01	19.43	19.85	20.27	20.69	21.11	21.53	21.95
36	16.16	16.58	17.01	17.43	17.86	18.29	18.71	19.14	19.57	20.00	20.43	20.87	21.30	21.73	22.17	22.60
37	16.62	17.06	17.49	17.93	18.37	18.81	19.25	19.69	20.13	20.58	21.02	21.46	21.91	22.36	22.81	23.25
38	17.08	17.53	17.98	18.43	18.88	19.33	19.78	20.24	20.69	21.15	21.61	22.07	22.52	22.99	23.45	23.91
39	17.54	18.00	18.46	18.93	19.39	19.86	20.32	20.79	21.26	21.73	22.20	22.67	23.14	23.61	24.09	24.56
40	18.00	18.48	18.95	19.43	19.90	20.38	20.86	21.34	21.82	22.30	22.79	23.27	23.76	24.25	24.73	25.22
41	18.47	18.95	19.44	19.93	20.42	20.91	21.40	21.89	22.39	22.88	23.38	23.88	24.38	24.88	25.38	25.88
42	18.93	19.43	19.93	20.43	20.93	21.44	21.94	22.45	22.96	23.47	23.98	24.49	25.00	25.51	26.03	26.55
43	19.40	19.91	20.42	20.94	21.45	21.97	22.49	23.01	23.53	24.05	24.57	25.10	25.62	26.15	26.68	27.21
44	19.86	20.39	20.91	21.44	21.97	22.50	23.03	23.57	24.10	24.64	25.17	25.71	26.25	26.79	27.33	27.88
45	20.33	20.87	21.41	21.95	22.49	23.03	23.58	24.12	24.67	25.22	25.77	26.32	26.88	27.43	27.99	28.55
46	20.80	21.35	21.90	22.46	23.01	23.57	24.13	24.69	25.25	25.81	26.37	26.94	27.51	28.08	28.65	29.22
47	21.27	21.83	22.40	22.97	23.53	24.10	24.68	25.25	25.82	26.40	26.98	27.56	28.14	28.72	29.31	29.89
48	21.74	22.32	22.90	23.48	24.06	24.64	25.23	25.81	26.40	26.99	27.58	28.18	28.77	29.37	29.97	30.57
49	22.21	22.80	23.39	23.99	24.58	25.18	25.78	26.38	26.98	27.59	28.19	28.80	29.41	30.02	30.63	31.24
50	22.69	23.29	23.89	24.50	25.11	25.72	26.33	26.95	27.56	28.18	28.80	29.42	30.04	30.67	31.29	31.92
51	23.16	23.78	24.40	25.02	25.64	26.26	26.89	27.52	28.15	28.78	29.41	30.05	30.68	31.32	31.96	32.60
52	23.64	24.27	24.90	25.53	26.17	26.81	27.45	28.09	28.73	29.38	30.02	30.67	31.32	31.98	32.63	33.29
53	24.11	24.76	25.40	26.05	26.70	27.35	28.00	28.66	29.32	29.98	30.64	31.30	31.97	32.63	33.30	33.97
54	24.59	25.25	25.91	26.57	27.23	27.90	28.56	29.23	29.91	30.58	31.25	31.93	32.61	33.29	33.98	34.66
55	25.07	25.74	26.41	27.09	27.77	28.44	29.13	29.81	30.50	31.18	31.87	32.56	33.26	33.95	34.65	35.35
56	25.55	26.23	26.92	27.61	28.30	28.99	29.69	30.39	31.09	31.79	32.49	33.20	33.91	34.62	35.33	36.04
57	26.03	26.73	27.43	28.13	28.84	29.54	30.25	30.97	31.68	32.39	33.11	33.83	34.56	35.28	36.01	36.74
58	26.51	27.23	27.94	28.66	29.37	30.10	30.82	31.55	32.27	33.00	33.74	34.47	35.21	35.95	36.69	37.43
59	27.00	27.72	28.45	29.18	29.91	30.65	31.39	32.13	32.87	33.61	34.36	35.11	35.86	36.62	37.37	38.13
60	27.48	28.22	28.96	29.71	30.45	31.20	31.96	32.71	33.47	34.23	34.99	35.75	36.52	37.29	38.06	38.83

Table XXI, continued

ANNUAL PERCENTAGE RATE TABLE FOR MONTHLY PAYMENT PLANS
SEE INSTRUCTIONS FOR USE OF TABLES

FRB-104-M

NUMBER OF PAYMENTS	ANNUAL PERCENTAGE RATE															
	14.00%	14.25%	14.50%	14.75%	15.00%	15.25%	15.50%	15.75%	16.00%	16.25%	16.50%	16.75%	17.00%	17.25%	17.50%	17.75%
	(FINANCE CHARGE PER $100 OF AMOUNT FINANCED)															
1	1.17	1.19	1.21	1.23	1.25	1.27	1.29	1.31	1.33	1.35	1.37	1.40	1.42	1.44	1.46	1.48
2	1.75	1.78	1.82	1.85	1.88	1.91	1.94	1.97	2.00	2.04	2.07	2.10	2.13	2.16	2.19	2.22
3	2.34	2.38	2.43	2.47	2.51	2.55	2.59	2.64	2.68	2.72	2.76	2.80	2.85	2.89	2.93	2.97
4	2.93	2.99	3.04	3.09	3.14	3.20	3.25	3.30	3.36	3.41	3.46	3.51	3.57	3.62	3.67	3.73
5	3.53	3.59	3.65	3.72	3.78	3.84	3.91	3.97	4.04	4.10	4.16	4.23	4.29	4.35	4.42	4.48
6	4.12	4.20	4.27	4.35	4.42	4.49	4.57	4.64	4.72	4.79	4.87	4.94	5.02	5.09	5.17	5.24
7	4.72	4.81	4.89	4.98	5.06	5.15	5.23	5.32	5.40	5.49	5.58	5.66	5.75	5.83	5.92	6.00
8	5.32	5.42	5.51	5.61	5.71	5.80	5.90	6.00	6.09	6.19	6.29	6.38	6.48	6.58	6.67	6.77
9	5.92	6.03	6.14	6.25	6.35	6.46	6.57	6.68	6.78	6.89	7.00	7.11	7.22	7.32	7.43	7.54
10	6.53	6.65	6.77	6.88	7.00	7.12	7.24	7.36	7.48	7.60	7.72	7.84	7.96	8.08	8.19	8.31
11	7.14	7.27	7.40	7.53	7.66	7.79	7.92	8.05	8.18	8.31	8.44	8.57	8.70	8.83	8.96	9.09
12	7.74	7.89	8.03	8.17	8.31	8.45	8.59	8.74	8.88	9.02	9.16	9.30	9.45	9.59	9.73	9.87
13	8.36	8.51	8.66	8.81	8.97	9.12	9.27	9.43	9.58	9.73	9.89	10.04	10.20	10.35	10.50	10.66
14	8.97	9.13	9.30	9.46	9.63	9.79	9.96	10.12	10.29	10.45	10.62	10.78	10.95	11.11	11.28	11.45
15	9.59	9.76	9.94	10.11	10.29	10.47	10.64	10.82	11.00	11.17	11.35	11.53	11.71	11.88	12.06	12.24
16	10.20	10.39	10.58	10.77	10.95	11.14	11.33	11.52	11.71	11.90	12.09	12.28	12.46	12.65	12.84	13.03
17	10.82	11.02	11.22	11.42	11.62	11.82	12.02	12.22	12.42	12.62	12.83	13.03	13.23	13.43	13.63	13.83
18	11.45	11.66	11.87	12.08	12.29	12.50	12.72	12.93	13.14	13.35	13.57	13.78	13.99	14.21	14.42	14.64
19	12.07	12.30	12.52	12.74	12.97	13.19	13.41	13.64	13.86	14.09	14.31	14.54	14.76	14.99	15.22	15.44
20	12.70	12.93	13.17	13.41	13.64	13.88	14.11	14.35	14.59	14.82	15.06	15.30	15.54	15.77	16.01	16.25
21	13.33	13.58	13.82	14.07	14.32	14.57	14.82	15.06	15.31	15.56	15.81	16.06	16.31	16.56	16.81	17.07
22	13.96	14.22	14.48	14.74	15.00	15.26	15.52	15.78	16.04	16.30	16.57	16.83	17.09	17.36	17.62	17.88
23	14.59	14.87	15.14	15.41	15.68	15.96	16.23	16.50	16.78	17.05	17.32	17.60	17.88	18.15	18.43	18.70
24	15.23	15.51	15.80	16.08	16.37	16.65	16.94	17.22	17.51	17.80	18.09	18.37	18.66	18.95	19.24	19.53
25	15.87	16.17	16.46	16.76	17.06	17.35	17.65	17.95	18.25	18.55	18.85	19.15	19.45	19.75	20.05	20.36
26	16.51	16.82	17.13	17.44	17.75	18.06	18.37	18.68	18.99	19.30	19.62	19.93	20.24	20.56	20.87	21.19
27	17.15	17.47	17.80	18.12	18.44	18.76	19.09	19.41	19.74	20.06	20.39	20.71	21.04	21.37	21.69	22.02
28	17.80	18.13	18.47	18.80	19.14	19.47	19.81	20.15	20.48	20.82	21.16	21.50	21.84	22.18	22.52	22.86
29	18.45	18.79	19.14	19.49	19.83	20.18	20.53	20.88	21.23	21.58	21.94	22.29	22.64	22.99	23.35	23.70
30	19.10	19.45	19.81	20.17	20.54	20.90	21.26	21.62	21.99	22.35	22.72	23.09	23.45	23.81	24.18	24.55
31	19.75	20.12	20.49	20.87	21.24	21.61	21.99	22.37	22.74	23.12	23.50	23.88	24.25	24.64	25.02	25.40
32	20.40	20.79	21.17	21.56	21.95	22.33	22.72	23.11	23.50	23.89	24.28	24.68	25.07	25.46	25.86	26.25
33	21.06	21.46	21.85	22.25	22.65	23.06	23.46	23.86	24.26	24.67	25.07	25.48	25.88	26.29	26.70	27.11
34	21.72	22.13	22.54	22.95	23.37	23.78	24.19	24.61	25.03	25.44	25.86	26.28	26.70	27.12	27.54	27.97
35	22.38	22.80	23.23	23.65	24.08	24.51	24.94	25.36	25.79	26.23	26.66	27.09	27.52	27.96	28.39	28.83
36	23.04	23.48	23.92	24.35	24.80	25.24	25.68	26.12	26.57	27.01	27.46	27.90	28.35	28.80	29.25	29.70
37	23.70	24.16	24.61	25.06	25.51	25.97	26.42	26.88	27.34	27.80	28.26	28.72	29.18	29.64	30.10	30.57
38	24.37	24.84	25.30	25.77	26.24	26.70	27.17	27.64	28.11	28.59	29.06	29.53	30.01	30.49	30.96	31.44
39	25.04	25.52	26.00	26.48	26.96	27.44	27.92	28.41	28.89	29.38	29.87	30.36	30.85	31.34	31.83	32.32
40	25.71	26.20	26.70	27.19	27.69	28.18	28.68	29.18	29.68	30.18	30.69	31.19	31.69	32.19	32.69	33.20
41	26.39	26.89	27.40	27.91	28.41	28.92	29.44	29.95	30.46	30.97	31.49	32.01	32.52	33.04	33.55	34.08
42	27.06	27.58	28.10	28.62	29.15	29.67	30.19	30.72	31.25	31.78	32.31	32.84	33.37	33.90	34.44	34.97
43	27.74	28.27	28.81	29.34	29.88	30.42	30.96	31.50	32.04	32.58	33.13	33.67	34.22	34.76	35.31	35.86
44	28.42	28.97	29.52	30.07	30.62	31.17	31.72	32.28	32.83	33.39	33.95	34.51	35.07	35.63	36.19	36.76
45	29.11	29.67	30.23	30.79	31.36	31.92	32.49	33.06	33.63	34.20	34.77	35.35	35.92	36.50	37.08	37.66
46	29.79	30.36	30.94	31.52	32.10	32.68	33.26	33.84	34.43	35.01	35.60	36.19	36.78	37.37	37.96	38.56
47	30.48	31.07	31.66	32.25	32.84	33.44	34.03	34.63	35.23	35.83	36.43	37.04	37.64	38.25	38.86	39.46
48	31.17	31.77	32.37	32.98	33.59	34.20	34.81	35.42	36.03	36.65	37.27	37.88	38.50	39.13	39.75	40.37
49	31.86	32.48	33.09	33.71	34.34	34.96	35.59	36.21	36.84	37.47	38.10	38.74	39.37	40.01	40.65	41.29
50	32.55	33.18	33.82	34.45	35.09	35.73	36.37	37.01	37.65	38.30	38.94	39.59	40.24	40.89	41.55	42.20
51	33.25	33.89	34.54	35.19	35.84	36.49	37.15	37.81	38.46	39.12	39.79	40.45	41.11	41.78	42.45	43.12
52	33.95	34.61	35.27	35.93	36.60	37.27	37.94	38.61	39.28	39.96	40.63	41.31	41.99	42.67	43.36	44.04
53	34.65	35.32	36.00	36.68	37.36	38.04	38.72	39.41	40.10	40.79	41.48	42.17	42.87	43.57	44.27	44.97
54	35.35	36.04	36.73	37.42	38.12	38.82	39.52	40.22	40.92	41.63	42.33	43.04	43.75	44.47	45.18	45.90
55	36.05	36.76	37.46	38.17	38.88	39.60	40.31	41.03	41.74	42.47	43.19	43.91	44.64	45.37	46.10	46.83
56	36.76	37.48	38.20	38.92	39.65	40.38	41.11	41.84	42.57	43.31	44.05	44.79	45.53	46.27	47.02	47.77
57	37.47	38.20	38.94	39.68	40.42	41.16	41.91	42.65	43.40	44.15	44.91	45.66	46.42	47.18	47.94	48.71
58	38.18	38.93	39.68	40.43	41.19	41.95	42.71	43.47	44.23	45.00	45.77	46.54	47.32	48.09	48.87	49.65
59	38.89	39.66	40.42	41.19	41.96	42.74	43.51	44.29	45.07	45.85	46.64	47.42	48.21	49.01	49.80	50.60
60	39.61	40.39	41.17	41.95	42.74	43.53	44.32	45.11	45.91	46.71	47.51	48.31	49.12	49.92	50.73	51.56

Table XXI, continued

ANNUAL PERCENTAGE RATE TABLE FOR MONTHLY PAYMENT PLANS
SEE INSTRUCTIONS FOR USE OF TABLES   FRB-105-M

ANNUAL PERCENTAGE RATE

(FINANCE CHARGE PER $100 OF AMOUNT FINANCED)

NUMBER OF PAYMENTS	18.00%	18.25%	18.50%	18.75%	19.00%	19.25%	19.50%	19.75%	20.00%	20.25%	20.50%	20.75%	21.00%	21.25%	21.50%	21.75%
1	1.50	1.52	1.54	1.56	1.58	1.60	1.62	1.65	1.67	1.69	1.71	1.73	1.75	1.77	1.79	1.81
2	2.26	2.29	2.32	2.35	2.38	2.41	2.44	2.48	2.51	2.54	2.57	2.60	2.63	2.66	2.70	2.73
3	3.01	3.06	3.10	3.14	3.18	3.23	3.27	3.31	3.35	3.39	3.44	3.48	3.52	3.56	3.60	3.65
4	3.78	3.83	3.88	3.94	3.99	4.04	4.10	4.15	4.20	4.25	4.31	4.36	4.41	4.47	4.52	4.57
5	4.54	4.61	4.67	4.74	4.80	4.86	4.93	4.99	5.06	5.12	5.18	5.25	5.31	5.37	5.44	5.50
6	5.32	5.39	5.46	5.54	5.61	5.69	5.76	5.84	5.91	5.99	6.06	6.14	6.21	6.29	6.36	6.44
7	6.09	6.18	6.26	6.35	6.43	6.52	6.60	6.69	6.78	6.86	6.95	7.04	7.12	7.21	7.29	7.38
8	6.87	6.96	7.06	7.16	7.26	7.35	7.45	7.55	7.64	7.74	7.84	7.94	8.03	8.13	8.23	8.33
9	7.65	7.76	7.87	7.97	8.08	8.19	8.30	8.41	8.52	8.63	8.73	8.84	8.95	9.06	9.17	9.28
10	8.43	8.55	8.67	8.79	8.91	9.03	9.15	9.27	9.39	9.51	9.63	9.75	9.88	10.00	10.12	10.24
11	9.22	9.35	9.49	9.62	9.75	9.88	10.01	10.14	10.28	10.41	10.54	10.67	10.80	10.94	11.07	11.20
12	10.02	10.16	10.30	10.44	10.59	10.73	10.87	11.02	11.16	11.31	11.45	11.59	11.74	11.88	12.02	12.17
13	10.81	10.97	11.12	11.28	11.43	11.59	11.74	11.90	12.05	12.21	12.36	12.52	12.67	12.83	12.99	13.14
14	11.61	11.78	11.95	12.11	12.28	12.45	12.61	12.78	12.95	13.11	13.28	13.45	13.62	13.79	13.95	14.12
15	12.42	12.59	12.77	12.95	13.13	13.31	13.49	13.67	13.85	14.03	14.21	14.39	14.57	14.75	14.93	15.11
16	13.22	13.41	13.60	13.80	13.99	14.18	14.37	14.56	14.75	14.94	15.13	15.33	15.52	15.71	15.90	16.10
17	14.04	14.24	14.44	14.64	14.85	15.05	15.25	15.46	15.66	15.86	16.07	16.27	16.48	16.68	16.89	17.09
18	14.85	15.07	15.28	15.49	15.71	15.93	16.14	16.36	16.57	16.79	17.01	17.22	17.44	17.66	17.88	18.09
19	15.67	15.90	16.12	16.35	16.58	16.81	17.03	17.26	17.49	17.72	17.95	18.18	18.41	18.64	18.87	19.10
20	16.49	16.73	16.97	17.21	17.45	17.69	17.93	18.17	18.41	18.66	18.90	19.14	19.38	19.63	19.87	20.11
21	17.32	17.57	17.82	18.07	18.33	18.58	18.83	19.09	19.34	19.60	19.85	20.11	20.36	20.62	20.87	21.13
22	18.15	18.41	18.68	18.94	19.21	19.47	19.74	20.01	20.27	20.54	20.81	21.08	21.34	21.61	21.88	22.15
23	18.98	19.26	19.54	19.81	20.09	20.37	20.65	20.93	21.21	21.49	21.77	22.05	22.33	22.61	22.90	23.18
24	19.82	20.11	20.40	20.69	20.98	21.27	21.56	21.86	22.15	22.44	22.74	23.03	23.33	23.62	23.92	24.21
25	20.66	20.96	21.27	21.57	21.87	22.18	22.48	22.79	23.10	23.40	23.71	24.02	24.32	24.63	24.94	25.25
26	21.50	21.82	22.14	22.45	22.77	23.09	23.41	23.73	24.04	24.36	24.68	25.01	25.33	25.65	25.97	26.29
27	22.35	22.68	23.01	23.34	23.67	24.00	24.33	24.67	25.00	25.33	25.67	26.00	26.34	26.67	27.01	27.34
28	23.20	23.55	23.89	24.23	24.58	24.92	25.27	25.61	25.96	26.30	26.65	27.00	27.35	27.70	28.05	28.40
29	24.06	24.41	24.77	25.13	25.49	25.84	26.20	26.56	26.92	27.28	27.64	28.00	28.37	28.73	29.09	29.46
30	24.92	25.29	25.66	26.03	26.40	26.77	27.14	27.52	27.89	28.26	28.64	29.01	29.39	29.77	30.14	30.52
31	25.78	26.16	26.55	26.93	27.32	27.70	28.09	28.47	28.86	29.25	29.64	30.03	30.42	30.81	31.20	31.59
32	26.65	27.04	27.44	27.84	28.24	28.64	29.04	29.44	29.84	30.24	30.64	31.05	31.45	31.85	32.26	32.67
33	27.52	27.93	28.34	28.75	29.16	29.57	29.99	30.40	30.82	31.23	31.65	32.07	32.49	32.91	33.33	33.75
34	28.39	28.81	29.24	29.66	30.09	30.52	30.95	31.37	31.80	32.23	32.67	33.10	33.53	33.96	34.40	34.83
35	29.27	29.71	30.14	30.58	31.02	31.47	31.91	32.35	32.79	33.24	33.68	34.13	34.58	35.03	35.47	35.92
36	30.15	30.60	31.05	31.51	31.96	32.42	32.87	33.33	33.79	34.25	34.71	35.17	35.63	36.09	36.56	37.02
37	31.03	31.50	31.97	32.43	32.90	33.37	33.84	34.32	34.79	35.26	35.74	36.21	36.69	37.16	37.64	38.12
38	31.92	32.40	32.88	33.37	33.85	34.33	34.82	35.30	35.79	36.28	36.77	37.26	37.75	38.24	38.73	39.23
39	32.81	33.31	33.80	34.30	34.80	35.30	35.80	36.30	36.80	37.30	37.81	38.31	38.82	39.32	39.83	40.34
40	33.71	34.22	34.73	35.24	35.75	36.26	36.78	37.29	37.81	38.33	38.85	39.37	39.89	40.41	40.93	41.46
41	34.61	35.13	35.66	36.18	36.71	37.24	37.77	38.30	38.83	39.36	39.89	40.43	40.96	41.50	42.04	42.58
42	35.51	36.05	36.59	37.13	37.67	38.21	38.76	39.30	39.85	40.40	40.95	41.50	42.05	42.60	43.15	43.71
43	36.42	36.97	37.52	38.08	38.63	39.19	39.75	40.31	40.87	41.44	42.00	42.57	43.13	43.70	44.27	44.84
44	37.33	37.89	38.46	39.03	39.60	40.18	40.75	41.33	41.90	42.48	43.06	43.64	44.22	44.81	45.39	45.98
45	38.24	38.82	39.41	39.99	40.58	41.17	41.75	42.35	42.94	43.53	44.13	44.72	45.32	45.92	46.52	47.12
46	39.16	39.75	40.35	40.95	41.55	42.16	42.76	43.37	43.98	44.58	45.20	45.81	46.42	47.03	47.65	48.27
47	40.08	40.69	41.30	41.92	42.54	43.15	43.77	44.40	45.02	45.64	46.27	46.90	47.53	48.16	48.79	49.42
48	41.00	41.63	42.26	42.89	43.52	44.15	44.79	45.43	46.07	46.71	47.35	47.99	48.64	49.28	49.93	50.58
49	41.93	42.57	43.22	43.86	44.51	45.16	45.81	46.46	47.12	47.77	48.43	49.09	49.75	50.41	51.08	51.74
50	42.86	43.52	44.18	44.84	45.50	46.17	46.83	47.50	48.17	48.84	49.52	50.19	50.87	51.55	52.23	52.91
51	43.79	44.47	45.14	45.82	46.50	47.18	47.86	48.55	49.23	49.92	50.61	51.30	51.99	52.69	53.38	54.08
52	44.73	45.42	46.11	46.80	47.50	48.20	48.89	49.59	50.30	51.00	51.71	52.41	53.12	53.83	54.55	55.26
53	45.67	46.38	47.08	47.79	48.50	49.22	49.93	50.65	51.37	52.09	52.81	53.53	54.26	54.98	55.71	56.44
54	46.62	47.34	48.06	48.79	49.51	50.24	50.97	51.70	52.44	53.17	53.91	54.65	55.39	56.14	56.88	57.63
55	47.57	48.30	49.04	49.78	50.52	51.27	52.02	52.76	53.52	54.27	55.02	55.78	56.54	57.30	58.06	58.82
56	48.52	49.27	50.03	50.78	51.54	52.30	53.06	53.83	54.60	55.37	56.14	56.91	57.68	58.46	59.24	60.02
57	49.47	50.24	51.01	51.79	52.56	53.34	54.12	54.90	55.68	56.47	57.25	58.04	58.84	59.63	60.43	61.22
58	50.43	51.22	52.00	52.79	53.58	54.38	55.17	55.97	56.77	57.57	58.38	59.18	59.99	60.80	61.62	62.43
59	51.39	52.20	53.00	53.80	54.61	55.42	56.23	57.05	57.87	58.68	59.51	60.33	61.15	61.98	62.81	63.64
60	52.36	53.18	54.00	54.82	55.64	56.47	57.30	58.13	58.96	59.80	60.64	61.48	62.32	63.17	64.01	64.86

Table XXI, continued

ANNUAL PERCENTAGE RATE TABLE FOR MONTHLY PAYMENT PLANS
SEE INSTRUCTIONS FOR USE OF TABLES

FRB-106-M

NUMBER OF PAYMENTS	ANNUAL PERCENTAGE RATE															
	22.00%	22.25%	22.50%	22.75%	23.00%	23.25%	23.50%	23.75%	24.00%	24.25%	24.50%	24.75%	25.00%	25.25%	25.50%	25.75%
	(FINANCE CHARGE PER $100 OF AMOUNT FINANCED)															
1	1.83	1.85	1.87	1.90	1.92	1.94	1.96	1.98	2.00	2.02	2.04	2.06	2.08	2.10	2.12	2.15
2	2.76	2.79	2.82	2.85	2.88	2.92	2.95	2.98	3.01	3.04	3.07	3.10	3.14	3.17	3.20	3.23
3	3.69	3.73	3.77	3.82	3.86	3.90	3.94	3.98	4.03	4.07	4.11	4.15	4.20	4.24	4.28	4.32
4	4.62	4.68	4.73	4.78	4.84	4.89	4.94	5.00	5.05	5.10	5.16	5.21	5.26	5.32	5.37	5.42
5	5.57	5.63	5.69	5.76	5.82	5.89	5.95	6.02	6.08	6.14	6.21	6.27	6.34	6.40	6.46	6.53
6	6.51	6.59	6.66	6.74	6.81	6.89	6.96	7.04	7.12	7.19	7.27	7.34	7.42	7.49	7.57	7.64
7	7.47	7.55	7.64	7.73	7.81	7.90	7.99	8.07	8.16	8.24	8.33	8.42	8.51	8.59	8.68	8.77
8	8.42	8.52	8.62	8.72	8.82	8.91	9.01	9.11	9.21	9.31	9.40	9.50	9.60	9.70	9.80	9.90
9	9.39	9.50	9.61	9.72	9.83	9.94	10.04	10.15	10.26	10.37	10.48	10.59	10.70	10.81	10.92	11.03
10	10.36	10.48	10.60	10.72	10.84	10.96	11.08	11.21	11.33	11.45	11.57	11.69	11.81	11.93	12.06	12.18
11	11.33	11.47	11.60	11.73	11.86	12.00	12.13	12.26	12.40	12.53	12.66	12.80	12.93	13.06	13.20	13.33
12	12.31	12.46	12.60	12.75	12.89	13.04	13.18	13.33	13.47	13.62	13.76	13.91	14.05	14.20	14.34	14.49
13	13.30	13.46	13.61	13.77	13.93	14.08	14.24	14.40	14.55	14.71	14.87	15.03	15.18	15.34	15.50	15.66
14	14.29	14.46	14.63	14.80	14.97	15.13	15.30	15.47	15.64	15.81	15.98	16.15	16.32	16.49	16.66	16.83
15	15.29	15.47	15.65	15.83	16.01	16.19	16.37	16.56	16.74	16.92	17.10	17.28	17.47	17.65	17.83	18.02
16	16.29	16.48	16.68	16.87	17.06	17.26	17.45	17.65	17.84	18.03	18.23	18.42	18.62	18.81	19.01	19.21
17	17.30	17.50	17.71	17.92	18.12	18.33	18.53	18.74	18.95	19.16	19.36	19.57	19.78	19.99	20.20	20.40
18	18.31	18.53	18.75	18.97	19.19	19.41	19.62	19.84	20.06	20.28	20.50	20.72	20.95	21.17	21.39	21.61
19	19.33	19.56	19.79	20.02	20.26	20.49	20.72	20.95	21.19	21.42	21.65	21.89	22.12	22.35	22.59	22.82
20	20.35	20.60	20.84	21.09	21.33	21.58	21.82	22.07	22.31	22.56	22.81	23.05	23.30	23.55	23.79	24.04
21	21.38	21.64	21.90	22.16	22.41	22.67	22.93	23.19	23.45	23.71	23.97	24.23	24.49	24.75	25.01	25.27
22	22.42	22.69	22.96	23.23	23.50	23.77	24.04	24.32	24.59	24.86	25.13	25.41	25.68	25.96	26.23	26.50
23	23.46	23.74	24.03	24.31	24.60	24.88	25.17	25.45	25.74	26.02	26.31	26.60	26.88	27.17	27.46	27.75
24	24.51	24.80	25.10	25.40	25.70	25.99	26.29	26.59	26.89	27.19	27.49	27.79	28.09	28.39	28.69	29.00
25	25.56	25.87	26.18	26.49	26.80	27.11	27.43	27.74	28.05	28.36	28.68	28.99	29.31	29.62	29.94	30.25
26	26.62	26.94	27.26	27.59	27.91	28.24	28.56	28.89	29.22	29.55	29.87	30.20	30.53	30.86	31.19	31.52
27	27.68	28.02	28.35	28.69	29.03	29.37	29.71	30.05	30.39	30.73	31.07	31.42	31.76	32.10	32.45	32.79
28	28.75	29.10	29.45	29.80	30.15	30.50	30.86	31.22	31.57	31.93	32.28	32.64	33.00	33.35	33.71	34.07
29	29.82	30.19	30.55	30.92	31.28	31.65	32.02	32.39	32.76	33.13	33.50	33.87	34.24	34.61	34.98	35.36
30	30.90	31.28	31.66	32.04	32.42	32.80	33.18	33.57	33.95	34.33	34.72	35.10	35.49	35.88	36.26	36.65
31	31.98	32.38	32.77	33.17	33.56	33.96	34.35	34.75	35.15	35.55	35.95	36.35	36.75	37.15	37.55	37.95
32	33.07	33.48	33.89	34.30	34.71	35.12	35.53	35.94	36.35	36.77	37.18	37.60	38.01	38.43	38.84	39.26
33	34.17	34.59	35.01	35.44	35.86	36.29	36.71	37.14	37.57	37.99	38.42	38.85	39.28	39.71	40.14	40.58
34	35.27	35.71	36.14	36.58	37.02	37.46	37.90	38.34	38.78	39.23	39.67	40.11	40.56	41.01	41.45	41.90
35	36.37	36.83	37.28	37.73	38.18	38.64	39.09	39.55	40.01	40.47	40.92	41.38	41.84	42.31	42.77	43.23
36	37.49	37.95	38.42	38.89	39.35	39.82	40.29	40.77	41.24	41.71	42.19	42.66	43.14	43.61	44.09	44.57
37	38.60	39.08	39.56	40.05	40.53	41.02	41.50	41.99	42.48	42.96	43.45	43.94	44.43	44.93	45.42	45.91
38	39.72	40.22	40.72	41.21	41.71	42.21	42.71	43.22	43.72	44.22	44.73	45.23	45.74	46.25	46.75	47.26
39	40.85	41.36	41.87	42.39	42.90	43.42	43.93	44.45	44.97	45.49	46.01	46.53	47.05	47.57	48.10	48.62
40	41.98	42.51	43.04	43.56	44.09	44.62	45.16	45.69	46.22	46.76	47.29	47.83	48.37	48.91	49.45	49.99
41	43.12	43.66	44.20	44.75	45.29	45.84	46.39	46.94	47.48	48.03	48.59	49.14	49.69	50.25	50.80	51.36
42	44.26	44.82	45.38	45.94	46.50	47.06	47.62	48.19	48.75	49.32	49.89	50.46	51.03	51.60	52.17	52.74
43	45.41	45.98	46.56	47.13	47.71	48.29	48.87	49.45	50.03	50.61	51.19	51.78	52.36	52.95	53.54	54.13
44	46.56	47.15	47.74	48.33	48.93	49.52	50.11	50.71	51.31	51.91	52.51	53.11	53.71	54.31	54.92	55.52
45	47.72	48.33	48.93	49.54	50.15	50.76	51.37	51.98	52.59	53.21	53.82	54.44	55.06	55.68	56.30	56.92
46	48.89	49.51	50.13	50.75	51.37	52.00	52.63	53.26	53.89	54.52	55.15	55.78	56.42	57.05	57.69	58.33
47	50.06	50.69	51.33	51.97	52.61	53.25	53.89	54.54	55.18	55.83	56.48	57.13	57.78	58.44	59.09	59.75
48	51.23	51.88	52.54	53.19	53.85	54.51	55.16	55.83	56.49	57.15	57.82	58.49	59.15	59.82	60.50	61.17
49	52.41	53.08	53.75	54.42	55.09	55.77	56.44	57.12	57.80	58.48	59.16	59.85	60.53	61.22	61.91	62.60
50	53.59	54.28	54.96	55.65	56.34	57.03	57.73	58.42	59.12	59.81	60.51	61.21	61.92	62.62	63.33	64.03
51	54.78	55.48	56.19	56.89	57.60	58.30	59.01	59.73	60.44	61.15	61.87	62.59	63.31	64.03	64.75	65.47
52	55.98	56.69	57.41	58.13	58.86	59.58	60.31	61.04	61.77	62.50	63.23	63.97	64.70	65.44	66.18	66.92
53	57.18	57.91	58.65	59.38	60.12	60.87	61.61	62.35	63.10	63.85	64.60	65.35	66.11	66.86	67.62	68.38
54	58.38	59.13	59.88	60.64	61.40	62.16	62.92	63.68	64.44	65.21	65.98	66.75	67.52	68.29	69.07	69.84
55	59.59	60.36	61.13	61.90	62.67	63.45	64.23	65.01	65.79	66.57	67.36	68.14	68.93	69.72	70.52	71.31
56	60.80	61.59	62.38	63.17	63.96	64.75	65.54	66.34	67.14	67.94	68.74	69.55	70.36	71.16	71.97	72.79
57	62.02	62.83	63.63	64.44	65.25	66.06	66.87	67.68	68.50	69.32	70.14	70.96	71.78	72.61	73.44	74.27
58	63.25	64.07	64.89	65.71	66.54	67.37	68.20	69.03	69.86	70.70	71.54	72.38	73.22	74.06	74.91	75.76
59	64.48	65.32	66.15	67.00	67.84	68.68	69.53	70.38	71.23	72.09	72.94	73.80	74.66	75.52	76.39	77.25
60	65.71	66.57	67.42	68.28	69.14	70.01	70.87	71.74	72.61	73.48	74.35	75.23	76.11	76.99	77.87	78.76

Table XXI, continued

ANNUAL PERCENTAGE RATE TABLE FOR MONTHLY PAYMENT PLANS
SEE INSTRUCTIONS FOR USE OF TABLES   FRB-107-M

ANNUAL PERCENTAGE RATE

(FINANCE CHARGE PER $100 OF AMOUNT FINANCED)

NUMBER OF PAYMENTS	26.00%	26.25%	26.50%	26.75%	27.00%	27.25%	27.50%	27.75%	28.00%	28.25%	28.50%	28.75%	29.00%	29.25%	29.50%	29.75%
1	2.17	2.19	2.21	2.23	2.25	2.27	2.29	2.31	2.33	2.35	2.37	2.40	2.42	2.44	2.46	2.48
2	3.26	3.29	3.32	3.36	3.39	3.42	3.45	3.48	3.51	3.54	3.58	3.61	3.64	3.67	3.70	3.73
3	4.36	4.41	4.45	4.49	4.53	4.58	4.62	4.66	4.70	4.74	4.79	4.83	4.87	4.91	4.96	5.00
4	5.47	5.53	5.58	5.63	5.69	5.74	5.79	5.85	5.90	5.95	6.01	6.06	6.11	6.17	6.22	6.27
5	6.59	6.66	6.72	6.79	6.85	6.91	6.98	7.04	7.11	7.17	7.24	7.30	7.37	7.43	7.49	7.56
6	7.72	7.79	7.87	7.95	8.02	8.10	8.17	8.25	8.32	8.40	8.48	8.55	8.63	8.70	8.78	8.85
7	8.85	8.94	9.03	9.11	9.20	9.29	9.37	9.46	9.55	9.64	9.72	9.81	9.90	9.98	10.07	10.16
8	9.99	10.09	10.19	10.29	10.39	10.49	10.58	10.68	10.78	10.88	10.98	11.08	11.18	11.28	11.38	11.47
9	11.14	11.25	11.36	11.47	11.58	11.69	11.80	11.91	12.03	12.14	12.25	12.36	12.47	12.58	12.69	12.80
10	12.30	12.42	12.54	12.67	12.79	12.91	13.03	13.15	13.28	13.40	13.52	13.64	13.77	13.89	14.01	14.14
11	13.46	13.60	13.73	13.87	14.00	14.13	14.27	14.40	14.54	14.67	14.81	14.94	15.08	15.21	15.35	15.48
12	14.64	14.78	14.93	15.07	15.22	15.37	15.51	15.66	15.81	15.95	16.10	16.25	16.40	16.54	16.69	16.84
13	15.82	15.97	16.13	16.29	16.45	16.61	16.77	16.93	17.09	17.24	17.40	17.56	17.72	17.88	18.04	18.20
14	17.00	17.17	17.35	17.52	17.69	17.86	18.03	18.20	18.37	18.54	18.72	18.89	19.06	19.23	19.41	19.58
15	18.20	18.38	18.57	18.75	18.93	19.12	19.30	19.48	19.67	19.85	20.04	20.22	20.41	20.59	20.78	20.96
16	19.40	19.60	19.79	19.99	20.19	20.38	20.58	20.78	20.97	21.17	21.37	21.57	21.76	21.96	22.16	22.36
17	20.61	20.82	21.03	21.24	21.45	21.66	21.87	22.08	22.29	22.50	22.71	22.92	23.13	23.34	23.55	23.77
18	21.83	22.05	22.27	22.50	22.72	22.94	23.16	23.39	23.61	23.83	24.06	24.28	24.51	24.73	24.96	25.18
19	23.06	23.29	23.53	23.76	24.00	24.23	24.47	24.71	24.94	25.18	25.42	25.65	25.89	26.13	26.37	26.61
20	24.29	24.54	24.79	25.04	25.28	25.53	25.78	26.03	26.28	26.53	26.78	27.04	27.29	27.54	27.79	28.04
21	25.53	25.79	26.05	26.32	26.58	26.84	27.11	27.37	27.63	27.90	28.16	28.43	28.69	28.96	29.22	29.49
22	26.78	27.05	27.33	27.61	27.88	28.16	28.44	28.71	28.99	29.27	29.55	29.82	30.10	30.38	30.66	30.94
23	28.04	28.32	28.61	28.90	29.19	29.48	29.77	30.07	30.36	30.65	30.94	31.23	31.53	31.82	32.11	32.41
24	29.30	29.60	29.90	30.21	30.51	30.82	31.12	31.43	31.73	32.04	32.34	32.65	32.96	33.27	33.57	33.88
25	30.57	30.89	31.20	31.52	31.84	32.16	32.48	32.80	33.12	33.44	33.76	34.08	34.40	34.72	35.04	35.37
26	31.85	32.18	32.51	32.84	33.18	33.51	33.84	34.18	34.51	34.84	35.18	35.51	35.85	36.19	36.52	36.86
27	33.14	33.48	33.83	34.17	34.52	34.87	35.21	35.56	35.91	36.26	36.61	36.96	37.31	37.66	38.01	38.36
28	34.43	34.79	35.15	35.51	35.87	36.23	36.59	36.96	37.32	37.68	38.05	38.41	38.78	39.15	39.51	39.88
29	35.73	36.10	36.48	36.85	37.23	37.61	37.98	38.36	38.74	39.12	39.50	39.88	40.26	40.64	41.02	41.40
30	37.04	37.43	37.82	38.21	38.60	38.99	39.38	39.77	40.17	40.56	40.95	41.35	41.75	42.14	42.54	42.94
31	38.35	38.76	39.16	39.57	39.97	40.38	40.79	41.19	41.60	42.01	42.42	42.83	43.24	43.65	44.06	44.48
32	39.68	40.10	40.52	40.94	41.36	41.78	42.20	42.62	43.05	43.47	43.90	44.32	44.75	45.17	45.60	46.03
33	41.01	41.44	41.88	42.31	42.75	43.19	43.62	44.06	44.50	44.94	45.38	45.82	46.26	46.70	47.15	47.59
34	42.35	42.80	43.25	43.70	44.15	44.60	45.05	45.51	45.96	46.42	46.87	47.33	47.79	48.24	48.70	49.16
35	43.69	44.16	44.62	45.09	45.56	46.02	46.49	46.96	47.43	47.90	48.37	48.85	49.32	49.79	50.27	50.74
36	45.05	45.53	46.01	46.49	46.97	47.45	47.94	48.42	48.91	49.40	49.88	50.37	50.86	51.35	51.84	52.33
37	46.41	46.90	47.40	47.90	48.39	48.89	49.39	49.89	50.40	50.90	51.40	51.91	52.41	52.92	53.42	53.93
38	47.77	48.29	48.80	49.31	49.82	50.34	50.86	51.37	51.89	52.41	52.93	53.45	53.97	54.49	55.02	55.54
39	49.15	49.68	50.20	50.73	51.26	51.79	52.33	52.86	53.39	53.93	54.46	55.00	55.54	56.08	56.62	57.16
40	50.53	51.07	51.62	52.16	52.71	53.26	53.81	54.35	54.90	55.46	56.01	56.56	57.12	57.67	58.23	58.79
41	51.92	52.48	53.04	53.60	54.16	54.73	55.29	55.86	56.42	56.99	57.56	58.13	58.70	59.28	59.85	60.42
42	53.32	53.89	54.47	55.05	55.63	56.21	56.79	57.37	57.95	58.54	59.12	59.71	60.30	60.89	61.48	62.07
43	54.72	55.31	55.90	56.50	57.09	57.69	58.29	58.89	59.49	60.09	60.69	61.30	61.90	62.51	63.11	63.72
44	56.13	56.74	57.35	57.96	58.57	59.19	59.80	60.42	61.03	61.65	62.27	62.89	63.51	64.14	64.76	65.39
45	57.55	58.17	58.80	59.43	60.06	60.69	61.32	61.95	62.59	63.22	63.86	64.50	65.13	65.77	66.42	67.06
46	58.97	59.61	60.26	60.90	61.55	62.20	62.84	63.49	64.15	64.80	65.45	66.11	66.76	67.42	68.08	68.74
47	60.40	61.06	61.72	62.38	63.05	63.71	64.38	65.05	65.71	66.38	67.06	67.73	68.40	69.08	69.75	70.43
48	61.84	62.52	63.20	63.87	64.56	65.24	65.92	66.60	67.29	67.98	68.67	69.36	70.05	70.74	71.44	72.13
49	63.29	63.98	64.68	65.37	66.07	66.77	67.47	68.17	68.87	69.58	70.29	70.99	71.70	72.41	73.13	73.84
50	64.74	65.45	66.16	66.88	67.59	68.31	69.03	69.75	70.47	71.19	71.91	72.64	73.37	74.10	74.83	75.56
51	66.20	66.93	67.66	68.39	69.12	69.86	70.59	71.33	72.07	72.81	73.55	74.29	75.04	75.78	76.53	77.28
52	67.67	68.41	69.16	69.91	70.66	71.41	72.16	72.92	73.67	74.43	75.19	75.95	76.72	77.48	78.25	79.02
53	69.14	69.90	70.67	71.43	72.20	72.97	73.74	74.52	75.29	76.07	76.85	77.62	78.41	79.19	79.97	80.76
54	70.62	71.40	72.18	72.97	73.75	74.54	75.33	76.12	76.91	77.71	78.50	79.30	80.10	80.90	81.71	82.51
55	72.11	72.91	73.71	74.51	75.31	76.12	76.92	77.73	78.55	79.36	80.17	80.99	81.81	82.63	83.45	84.27
56	73.60	74.42	75.24	76.06	76.88	77.70	78.53	79.35	80.18	81.02	81.85	82.68	83.52	84.36	85.20	86.04
57	75.10	75.94	76.77	77.61	78.45	79.29	80.14	80.98	81.83	82.68	83.53	84.39	85.24	86.10	86.96	87.82
58	76.61	77.46	78.32	79.17	80.03	80.89	81.75	82.62	83.48	84.35	85.22	86.10	86.97	87.85	88.72	89.60
59	78.12	78.99	79.87	80.74	81.62	82.50	83.38	84.26	85.15	86.03	86.92	87.81	88.71	89.60	90.50	91.40
60	79.64	80.53	81.42	82.32	83.21	84.11	85.01	85.91	86.81	87.72	88.63	89.54	90.45	91.37	92.28	93.20

Table XXI, continued

ANNUAL PERCENTAGE RATE TABLE FOR MONTHLY PAYMENT PLANS
SEE INSTRUCTIONS FOR USE OF TABLES

FRB-108-M

NUMBER OF PAYMENTS	30.00%	30.25%	30.50%	30.75%	31.00%	31.25%	31.50%	31.75%	32.00%	32.25%	32.50%	32.75%	33.00%	33.25%	33.50%	33.75%
							(FINANCE CHARGE PER $100 OF AMOUNT FINANCED)									
1	2.50	2.52	2.54	2.56	2.58	2.60	2.62	2.65	2.67	2.69	2.71	2.73	2.75	2.77	2.79	2.81
2	3.77	3.80	3.83	3.86	3.89	3.92	3.95	3.99	4.02	4.05	4.08	4.11	4.14	4.18	4.21	4.24
3	5.04	5.08	5.13	5.17	5.21	5.25	5.30	5.34	5.38	5.42	5.46	5.51	5.55	5.59	5.63	5.68
4	6.33	6.38	6.43	6.49	6.54	6.59	6.65	6.70	6.75	6.81	6.86	6.91	6.97	7.02	7.08	7.13
5	7.62	7.69	7.75	7.82	7.88	7.95	8.01	8.08	8.14	8.20	8.27	8.33	8.40	8.46	8.53	8.59
6	8.93	9.01	9.08	9.16	9.23	9.31	9.39	9.46	9.54	9.61	9.69	9.77	9.84	9.92	9.99	10.07
7	10.25	10.33	10.42	10.51	10.60	10.68	10.77	10.86	10.95	11.03	11.12	11.21	11.30	11.39	11.47	11.56
8	11.57	11.67	11.77	11.87	11.97	12.07	12.17	12.27	12.37	12.47	12.57	12.67	12.77	12.87	12.97	13.07
9	12.91	13.02	13.13	13.24	13.36	13.47	13.58	13.69	13.80	13.91	14.02	14.14	14.25	14.36	14.47	14.58
10	14.26	14.38	14.50	14.63	14.75	14.87	15.00	15.12	15.24	15.37	15.49	15.62	15.74	15.86	15.99	16.11
11	15.62	15.75	15.89	16.02	16.16	16.29	16.43	16.56	16.70	16.84	16.97	17.11	17.24	17.38	17.52	17.65
12	16.98	17.13	17.28	17.43	17.58	17.72	17.87	18.02	18.17	18.32	18.47	18.61	18.76	18.91	19.06	19.21
13	18.36	18.52	18.68	18.84	19.00	19.16	19.33	19.49	19.65	19.81	19.97	20.13	20.29	20.45	20.62	20.78
14	19.75	19.92	20.10	20.27	20.44	20.62	20.79	20.96	21.14	21.31	21.49	21.66	21.83	22.01	22.18	22.36
15	21.15	21.34	21.52	21.71	21.89	22.08	22.27	22.45	22.64	22.83	23.01	23.20	23.39	23.58	23.76	23.95
16	22.56	22.76	22.96	23.16	23.35	23.55	23.75	23.95	24.15	24.35	24.55	24.75	24.96	25.16	25.36	25.56
17	23.98	24.19	24.40	24.61	24.83	25.04	25.25	25.47	25.68	25.89	26.11	26.32	26.53	26.75	26.96	27.18
18	25.41	25.63	25.86	26.08	26.31	26.54	26.76	26.99	27.22	27.44	27.67	27.90	28.13	28.35	28.58	28.81
19	26.85	27.08	27.32	27.56	27.80	28.04	28.28	28.52	28.76	29.00	29.25	29.49	29.73	29.97	30.21	30.45
20	28.29	28.55	28.80	29.05	29.31	29.56	29.81	30.07	30.32	30.58	30.83	31.09	31.34	31.60	31.86	32.11
21	29.75	30.02	30.29	30.55	30.82	31.09	31.36	31.62	31.89	32.16	32.43	32.70	32.97	33.24	33.51	33.78
22	31.22	31.50	31.78	32.06	32.35	32.63	32.91	33.19	33.48	33.76	34.04	34.33	34.61	34.89	35.18	35.46
23	32.70	33.00	33.29	33.59	33.88	34.18	34.48	34.77	35.07	35.37	35.66	35.96	36.26	36.56	36.86	37.16
24	34.19	34.50	34.81	35.12	35.43	35.74	36.05	36.36	36.67	36.99	37.30	37.61	37.92	38.24	38.55	38.87
25	35.69	36.01	36.34	36.66	36.99	37.31	37.64	37.96	38.29	38.62	38.94	39.27	39.60	39.93	40.26	40.59
26	37.20	37.54	37.88	38.21	38.55	38.89	39.23	39.58	39.92	40.26	40.60	40.94	41.29	41.63	41.97	42.32
27	38.72	39.07	39.42	39.78	40.13	40.49	40.84	41.20	41.56	41.91	42.27	42.63	42.99	43.34	43.70	44.06
28	40.25	40.61	40.98	41.35	41.72	42.09	42.46	42.83	43.20	43.58	43.95	44.32	44.70	45.07	45.45	45.82
29	41.78	42.17	42.55	42.94	43.32	43.71	44.09	44.48	44.87	45.25	45.64	46.03	46.42	46.81	47.20	47.59
30	43.33	43.73	44.13	44.53	44.93	45.33	45.73	46.13	46.54	46.94	47.34	47.75	48.15	48.56	48.96	49.37
31	44.89	45.30	45.72	46.13	46.55	46.97	47.38	47.80	48.22	48.64	49.06	49.48	49.90	50.32	50.74	51.17
32	46.46	46.89	47.32	47.75	48.18	48.61	49.05	49.48	49.91	50.35	50.78	51.22	51.66	52.09	52.53	52.97
33	48.04	48.48	48.93	49.37	49.82	50.27	50.72	51.17	51.62	52.07	52.52	52.97	53.43	53.88	54.33	54.79
34	49.62	50.08	50.55	51.01	51.47	51.94	52.40	52.87	53.33	53.80	54.27	54.74	55.21	55.68	56.15	56.62
35	51.22	51.70	52.17	52.65	53.13	53.61	54.09	54.58	55.06	55.54	56.03	56.51	57.00	57.48	57.97	58.46
36	52.83	53.32	53.81	54.31	54.80	55.30	55.80	56.30	56.80	57.30	57.80	58.30	58.80	59.30	59.81	60.31
37	54.44	54.95	55.46	55.97	56.49	57.00	57.51	58.03	58.54	59.06	59.58	60.10	60.62	61.14	61.66	62.18
38	56.07	56.59	57.12	57.65	58.18	58.71	59.24	59.77	60.30	60.84	61.37	61.90	62.44	62.98	63.52	64.06
39	57.70	58.24	58.79	59.33	59.88	60.42	60.97	61.52	62.07	62.62	63.17	63.72	64.28	64.83	65.39	65.94
40	59.34	59.90	60.47	61.03	61.59	62.15	62.72	63.28	63.85	64.42	64.99	65.56	66.13	66.70	67.27	67.84
41	61.00	61.57	62.15	62.73	63.31	63.89	64.47	65.06	65.64	66.22	66.81	67.40	67.99	68.57	69.16	69.76
42	62.66	63.25	63.85	64.44	65.04	65.64	66.24	66.84	67.44	68.04	68.65	69.25	69.86	70.46	71.07	71.68
43	64.33	64.94	65.56	66.17	66.78	67.40	68.01	68.63	69.25	69.87	70.49	71.11	71.74	72.36	72.99	73.62
44	66.01	66.64	67.27	67.90	68.53	69.17	69.80	70.43	71.07	71.71	72.35	72.99	73.63	74.27	74.91	75.56
45	67.70	68.35	69.00	69.64	70.29	70.94	71.60	72.25	72.90	73.56	74.21	74.87	75.53	76.19	76.85	77.52
46	69.40	70.07	70.73	71.40	72.06	72.73	73.40	74.07	74.74	75.42	76.09	76.77	77.44	78.12	78.80	79.48
47	71.11	71.79	72.47	73.16	73.84	74.53	75.22	75.90	76.60	77.29	77.98	78.67	79.37	80.07	80.76	81.46
48	72.83	73.53	74.23	74.93	75.63	76.34	77.04	77.75	78.46	79.17	79.88	80.59	81.30	82.02	82.74	83.45
49	74.55	75.27	75.99	76.71	77.43	78.15	78.88	79.60	80.33	81.06	81.79	82.52	83.25	83.98	84.72	85.45
50	76.29	77.02	77.76	78.50	79.24	79.98	80.72	81.46	82.21	82.96	83.70	84.45	85.20	85.96	86.71	87.47
51	78.03	78.79	79.54	80.30	81.06	81.81	82.58	83.34	84.10	84.87	85.63	86.40	87.17	87.94	88.71	89.49
52	79.79	80.56	81.33	82.11	82.88	83.66	84.44	85.22	86.00	86.79	87.57	88.36	89.15	89.94	90.73	91.52
53	81.55	82.34	83.13	83.92	84.72	85.51	86.31	87.11	87.91	88.72	89.52	90.33	91.13	91.94	92.75	93.57
54	83.32	84.13	84.94	85.75	86.56	87.38	88.19	89.01	89.83	90.66	91.48	92.30	93.13	93.96	94.79	95.62
55	85.10	85.93	86.75	87.58	88.42	89.25	90.09	90.92	91.76	92.60	93.45	94.29	95.14	95.99	96.83	97.69
56	86.89	87.73	88.58	89.43	90.28	91.13	91.99	92.84	93.70	94.56	95.43	96.29	97.15	98.02	98.89	99.76
57	88.68	89.55	90.41	91.28	92.15	93.02	93.90	94.77	95.65	96.53	97.41	98.30	99.18	100.07	100.96	101.85
58	90.49	91.37	92.26	93.14	94.03	94.92	95.82	96.71	97.61	98.51	99.41	100.31	101.22	102.12	103.03	103.94
59	92.30	93.20	94.11	95.01	95.92	96.83	97.75	98.66	99.58	100.50	101.42	102.34	103.26	104.19	105.12	106.05
60	94.12	95.04	95.97	96.89	97.82	98.75	99.68	100.62	101.56	102.49	103.43	104.38	105.32	106.27	107.21	108.16

Table XXI, continued

ANNUAL PERCENTAGE RATE TABLE FOR MONTHLY PAYMENT PLANS
SEE INSTRUCTIONS FOR USE OF TABLES

FRB-109-M

NUMBER OF PAYMENTS	ANNUAL PERCENTAGE RATE															
	34.00%	34.25%	34.50%	34.75%	35.00%	35.25%	35.50%	35.75%	36.00%	36.25%	36.50%	36.75%	37.00%	37.25%	37.50%	37.75%
	(FINANCE CHARGE PER $100 OF AMOUNT FINANCED)															
1	2.83	2.85	2.87	2.90	2.92	2.94	2.96	2.98	3.00	3.02	3.04	3.06	3.08	3.10	3.12	3.15
2	4.27	4.30	4.33	4.36	4.40	4.43	4.46	4.49	4.52	4.55	4.59	4.62	4.65	4.68	4.71	4.74
3	5.72	5.76	5.80	5.85	5.89	5.93	5.97	6.02	6.06	6.10	6.14	6.19	6.23	6.27	6.31	6.36
4	7.18	7.24	7.29	7.34	7.40	7.45	7.50	7.56	7.61	7.66	7.72	7.77	7.83	7.88	7.93	7.99
5	8.66	8.72	8.79	8.85	8.92	8.98	9.05	9.11	9.18	9.24	9.31	9.37	9.44	9.50	9.57	9.63
6	10.15	10.22	10.30	10.38	10.45	10.53	10.61	10.68	10.76	10.83	10.91	10.99	11.06	11.14	11.22	11.29
7	11.65	11.74	11.83	11.91	12.00	12.09	12.18	12.27	12.35	12.44	12.53	12.62	12.71	12.80	12.88	12.97
8	13.17	13.27	13.36	13.46	13.56	13.66	13.76	13.86	13.97	14.07	14.17	14.27	14.37	14.47	14.57	14.67
9	14.69	14.81	14.92	15.03	15.14	15.25	15.37	15.48	15.59	15.70	15.82	15.93	16.04	16.15	16.27	16.38
10	16.24	16.36	16.48	16.61	16.73	16.86	16.98	17.11	17.23	17.36	17.48	17.60	17.73	17.85	17.98	18.10
11	17.79	17.93	18.06	18.20	18.34	18.47	18.61	18.75	18.89	19.02	19.16	19.30	19.43	19.57	19.71	19.85
12	19.36	19.51	19.66	19.81	19.96	20.11	20.25	20.40	20.55	20.70	20.85	21.00	21.15	21.31	21.46	21.61
13	20.94	21.10	21.26	21.43	21.59	21.75	21.91	22.08	22.24	22.40	22.56	22.73	22.89	23.05	23.22	23.38
14	22.53	22.71	22.88	23.06	23.23	23.41	23.59	23.76	23.94	24.11	24.29	24.47	24.64	24.82	25.00	25.17
15	24.14	24.33	24.52	24.71	24.89	25.08	25.27	25.46	25.65	25.84	26.03	26.22	26.41	26.60	26.79	26.98
16	25.76	25.96	26.16	26.37	26.57	26.77	26.97	27.17	27.38	27.58	27.78	27.99	28.19	28.39	28.60	28.80
17	27.39	27.61	27.82	28.04	28.25	28.47	28.69	28.90	29.12	29.34	29.55	29.77	29.99	30.20	30.42	30.64
18	29.04	29.27	29.50	29.73	29.96	30.19	30.42	30.65	30.88	31.11	31.34	31.57	31.80	32.03	32.26	32.49
19	30.70	30.94	31.18	31.43	31.67	31.91	32.16	32.40	32.65	32.89	33.14	33.38	33.63	33.87	34.12	34.36
20	32.37	32.63	32.88	33.14	33.40	33.66	33.91	34.17	34.43	34.69	34.95	35.21	35.47	35.73	35.99	36.25
21	34.05	34.32	34.60	34.87	35.14	35.41	35.68	35.96	36.23	36.50	36.78	37.05	37.33	37.60	37.88	38.15
22	35.75	36.04	36.32	36.61	36.89	37.18	37.47	37.76	38.04	38.33	38.62	38.91	39.20	39.49	39.78	40.07
23	37.46	37.76	38.06	38.36	38.66	38.96	39.27	39.57	39.87	40.18	40.48	40.78	41.09	41.39	41.70	42.00
24	39.18	39.50	39.81	40.13	40.44	40.76	41.08	41.40	41.71	42.03	42.35	42.67	42.99	43.31	43.63	43.95
25	40.92	41.25	41.58	41.91	42.24	42.57	42.90	43.24	43.57	43.90	44.24	44.57	44.91	45.24	45.58	45.91
26	42.66	43.01	43.36	43.70	44.05	44.40	44.74	45.09	45.44	45.79	46.14	46.49	46.84	47.19	47.54	47.89
27	44.42	44.78	45.15	45.51	45.87	46.23	46.60	46.96	47.32	47.69	48.05	48.42	48.78	49.15	49.52	49.88
28	46.20	46.57	46.95	47.33	47.70	48.08	48.46	48.84	49.22	49.60	49.98	50.36	50.75	51.13	51.51	51.89
29	47.98	48.37	48.77	49.16	49.55	49.95	50.34	50.74	51.13	51.53	51.93	52.32	52.72	53.12	53.52	53.92
30	49.78	50.19	50.60	51.00	51.41	51.82	52.23	52.65	53.06	53.47	53.88	54.30	54.71	55.13	55.54	55.96
31	51.59	52.01	52.44	52.86	53.29	53.71	54.14	54.57	55.00	55.43	55.85	56.28	56.72	57.15	57.58	58.01
32	53.41	53.85	54.29	54.73	55.17	55.62	56.06	56.50	56.95	57.39	57.84	58.29	58.73	59.18	59.63	60.08
33	55.24	55.70	56.16	56.62	57.07	57.53	57.99	58.45	58.92	59.38	59.84	60.30	60.77	61.23	61.70	62.16
34	57.09	57.56	58.04	58.51	58.99	59.46	59.94	60.42	60.89	61.37	61.85	62.33	62.81	63.30	63.78	64.26
35	58.95	59.44	59.93	60.42	60.91	61.40	61.90	62.39	62.89	63.38	63.88	64.38	64.88	65.37	65.87	66.37
36	60.82	61.33	61.83	62.34	62.85	63.36	63.87	64.38	64.89	65.41	65.92	66.43	66.95	67.47	67.98	68.50
37	62.70	63.22	63.75	64.27	64.80	65.33	65.85	66.38	66.91	67.44	67.97	68.51	69.04	69.57	70.11	70.64
38	64.59	65.14	65.68	66.22	66.76	67.31	67.85	68.40	68.95	69.49	70.04	70.59	71.14	71.69	72.25	72.80
39	66.50	67.06	67.62	68.18	68.74	69.30	69.86	70.43	70.99	71.56	72.12	72.69	73.26	73.83	74.40	74.97
40	68.42	68.99	69.57	70.15	70.73	71.31	71.89	72.47	73.05	73.63	74.22	74.80	75.39	75.98	76.56	77.15
41	70.35	70.94	71.53	72.13	72.73	73.32	73.92	74.52	75.12	75.72	76.32	76.93	77.53	78.14	78.74	79.35
42	72.29	72.90	73.51	74.12	74.74	75.35	75.97	76.59	77.20	77.82	78.44	79.07	79.69	80.31	80.94	81.56
43	74.24	74.87	75.50	76.13	76.76	77.40	78.03	78.67	79.30	79.94	80.58	81.22	81.86	82.50	83.14	83.79
44	76.20	76.85	77.50	78.15	78.80	79.45	80.10	80.76	81.41	82.07	82.72	83.38	84.04	84.70	85.36	86.03
45	78.18	78.84	79.51	80.18	80.85	81.52	82.19	82.86	83.53	84.21	84.88	85.56	86.24	86.92	87.60	88.28
46	80.17	80.85	81.53	82.22	82.91	83.60	84.28	84.98	85.67	86.36	87.06	87.75	88.45	89.15	89.85	90.55
47	82.16	82.87	83.57	84.27	84.98	85.69	86.39	87.10	87.81	88.53	89.24	89.95	90.67	91.39	92.11	92.83
48	84.17	84.89	85.61	86.34	87.06	87.79	88.52	89.24	89.97	90.70	91.44	92.17	92.91	93.64	94.38	95.12
49	86.19	86.93	87.67	88.41	89.16	89.90	90.65	91.40	92.14	92.89	93.65	94.40	55.15	95.91	96.67	97.42
50	88.22	88.98	89.74	90.50	91.26	92.03	92.79	93.56	94.33	95.10	95.87	96.64	97.41	98.19	98.96	99.74
51	90.26	91.04	91.82	92.60	93.38	94.16	94.95	95.74	96.52	97.31	98.10	98.89	99.69	100.48	101.28	102.07
52	92.32	93.11	93.91	94.71	95.51	96.31	97.12	97.92	98.73	99.54	100.35	101.16	101.97	102.79	103.60	104.42
53	94.38	95.20	96.01	96.83	97.65	98.47	99.30	100.12	100.95	101.78	102.61	103.44	104.27	105.10	105.94	106.78
54	96.45	97.29	98.13	98.96	99.80	100.64	101.49	102.33	103.18	104.03	104.87	105.73	106.58	107.43	108.29	109.14
55	98.54	99.39	100.25	101.11	101.97	102.83	103.69	104.55	105.42	106.29	107.16	108.03	108.90	109.77	110.65	111.53
56	100.63	101.51	102.38	103.26	104.14	105.02	105.90	106.79	107.67	108.56	109.45	110.34	111.23	112.13	113.02	113.92
57	102.74	103.63	104.53	105.43	106.32	107.22	108.13	109.03	109.94	110.85	111.75	112.67	113.58	114.49	115.41	116.33
58	104.85	105.77	106.68	107.60	108.52	109.44	110.36	111.29	112.21	113.14	114.07	115.00	115.93	116.87	117.81	118.74
59	106.98	107.91	108.85	109.79	110.73	111.67	112.61	113.55	114.50	115.45	116.40	117.35	118.30	119.26	120.22	121.17
60	109.12	110.07	111.02	111.98	112.94	113.90	114.87	115.83	116.80	117.77	118.74	119.71	120.68	121.66	122.64	123.62

Answers

1. (a) 2,880
    (b) 14,040
    (c) 69,000
    (d) 33,600
    (e) 858,600
    (f) 573,872
    (g) 295,962
    (h) 50,460,618
    (i) 568,080
    (j) 171.0
    (k) 36.9
    (l) 12.740
    (m) 12.88
    (n) 7.12
    (o) 1,024
    (p) 16
    (q) 125
    (r) 1.1025

3. (a) 81
    (b) 4
    (c) 5
    (d) 40
    (e) 3.6
    (f) −$750
    (g) −$75
    (h) −$1,700
    (i) −$400

5. (a) $\frac{104}{100}$
    (b) $\frac{293}{300}$
    (c) $\frac{395}{400}$
    (d) $\frac{407}{400}$
    (e) $\frac{304}{300}$
    (f) $\frac{195}{200}$
    (g) 515
    (h) 584
    (i) $300 + 21t$
    (j) $640 - 160r$
    (k) $a + abc$

7. (a) 24.3
         6.2
         154.6
    (b) 7.48
         12.39
         0.67
    (c) 117.634
         5.080
         24.307
    (d) 8.0; 16.7
         7.99; 16.67
         7.988; 16.675

9. (a) 109.6; 110
   (b) 30.3; 30
   (c) 5.2; 5.2
   (d) 450.5; 450

11. (a) $654.99
    (b) $1,240.54
    (c) $777.14
    (d) $15,053.78

CHAPTER TWO

**Section
One
Page 21**

1. $x = 14$
3. $x = 40$
5. $y = 4$
7. $k = 64$
9. $r = 5$
11. $p = 8$
13. $t = 9$
15. $n = 6$
17. $g = 7$

19. $x = 3$
21. $p = \frac{3}{2}$
23. $y = 1$
25. $s = \frac{5}{2}$
27. $c = \frac{17}{3}$
29. $r = 28$
31. $t = 48$
33. $d = 18$
35. $k = 32$

**Section
Two
Page 25**

1. 24
3. $49
5. $75
7. $1,400
9. 30
11. $15

13. $15,000
15. Depr.—$600; Overhd.—$2,400
17. Grounds—$2,000; Building—$9,000
19. Lounges—12; chairs—30
21. 35

**Section
Three
Page 28**

1. (a) 1 to 3; 1:3; $\frac{1}{3}$
   (b) 2 to 5; 2:5; $\frac{2}{5}$
   (c) 1 to 6; 1:6; $\frac{1}{6}$
   (d) 5 to 4; 5:4; $\frac{5}{4}$ or
       1.25 to 1; 1.25:1; $\frac{1.25}{1}$

   (e) 8 to 5; 8:5; $\frac{8}{5}$ or
       1.6 to 1; 1.6:1; $\frac{1.6}{1}$

3. 4 to 5

5. $\frac{3}{2}$

7. 3 to 7

9. $ 5,000 son
   $12,500 mother

11. 60 Bob
    48 Frank

13. $43,750 first
    17,500 second
    8,750 third

15. $5,600 1st
    2,400 2nd
    1,600 3rd
    3,200 4th

1. (a) $\frac{8}{9}$
   (b) $\frac{23}{33}$
   (c) $\frac{118}{333}$

   (d) $\frac{19}{45}$
   (e) $\frac{109}{150}$
   (f) $\frac{17}{99}$

CHAPTER THREE

Section
One
Page 38

1. $\frac{3}{25}$
3. $\frac{2}{25}$
5. $\frac{59}{100}$
7. $\frac{169}{500}$
9. $\frac{141}{2000}$
11. $\frac{253}{400}$
13. $\frac{31}{20}$
15. $\frac{31}{2000}$
17. $\frac{1}{250}$
19. $\frac{9}{1250}$
21. $\frac{13}{8}$
23. $\frac{1}{400}$
25. $\frac{1}{125}$
27. $\frac{2}{11}$
29. $\frac{3}{7}$
31. $\frac{1}{14}$

1. 45%
3. 5%
5. 81.3%
7. 6.7%
9. 128%
11. 159.8%
13. 1.2%
15. 37.5%
17. 0.8%
19. 0.72%
21. 260%
23. 40%
25. $16\frac{2}{3}\%$
27. $42\frac{2}{19}\%$
29. 212.5%
31. $146\frac{2}{3}\%$

Section
Two
Page 41

1. 10.5
3. 1.4
5. 47.6
7. 2.1
9. 45
11. 2.8
13. 80%
15. 125%
17. 55%
19. 25%
21. 4%
23. 160%

25. 150
27. 280
29. 63
31. 600
33. 70
35. 350
37. $33\frac{1}{3}\%$
39. 25%
41. 45%
43. 60%
45. $16\frac{2}{3}\%$
47. 0.8%

Section Three
Page 43

1.	41.2%
3.	36%
5.	$4,500
7.	$7,340
9.	$24
11.	$37,500
13.	40%
15.	$8\frac{1}{3}$%
17.	$22\frac{2}{9}$%

19.	32
21.	$3,000
23.	$2,000
25.	$50
27.	$15,000
29.	$140
31.	$42,000
33.	$37\frac{1}{2}$%
35.	30%

Section Four
Page 48

1.	$93
3.	$90
5.	$75
7.	$18
9.	$320
11.	$52
13.	$57
15.	$7

17.	$48
19.	$180
21.	$54
23.	$54
25.	$36
27.	$138
29.	$156

CHAPTER FOUR

Section One
Page 57

		Mean	Median	Mode
1.	(a)	62	62	72
	(b)	18	17	24
3.	(a)	2.80		
	(b)	3.00		
5.	(a)	$19.54		
	(b)	$18.50		
7.	(a)	$120		
	(b)	$100		
9.		$6,750		

11.		$445
13.		Model 1210
15.	(a)	38 years
	(b)	34.5 years
	(c)	No mode
17.	(a)	$21
	(b)	$18
	(c)	$16

1. (a) 72
   (b) 70
   (c) 60–79
3. (a) $9\frac{1}{3}$ years
   (b) 8 years
   (c) 6–8 years

5. (a) $8,680
   (b) $8,250
   (c) $6,200–$6,999

1. (a) $115.70
   (b) 120.70
   (c) 12.03
   (d) New York
   (e) Cannot be determined

Year	Index, 1964 = 100
3. 1964	100
1966	96
1968	102
1970	110
1972	116

Year	Index, 1963 = 100
5. 1963	100
1965	95
1967	105
1969	115
1971	125

CHAPTER FIVE

		Marked Price	Sales Tax	Total Price
1.	(a)	—	$ .24	$ 6.03
	(b)	—	.55	18.88
	(c)	—	.00	46.55
	(d)	—	.97	33.22
	(e)	$27.50	—	28.60
	(f)	43.00	—	43.86
	(g)	68.00	3.40	—
	(h)	24.50	.98	—

3. (a) $5.03; $130.53
   (b) $1.47; $50.36
   (c) .00; $73.29
5. $1.16; $30.11
7. (a) $47
   (b) $48.41
9. (a) $65
   (b) $74.75

11. (a) $32
    (b) $1.60
13. (a) $125
    (b) $5
15. (a) $118.20
    (b) $3.55

17. (a) $78.54
    (b) $3.93
19. (a) $8.40
    (b) $.42
    (c) $.84

**Section
Two
Page 92**

1. (a) 1.84%
   (b) $1.84 per C
   (c) $18.35 per M
   (d) 19 mills
3. (a) 1.448%
   (b) $1.45 per C
   (c) $14.48 per M
   (d) 14.5 mills

7. $371
9. $84
11. $32,500
13. $23,000
15. $1.88 per C
17. $16.25 per M
19. $600 increase

		Rate	Assessed Value	Tax
5.	(a)	—	—	$119
	(b)	—	—	252
	(c)	—	—	165
	(d)	—	—	248
	(e)	—	$12,500	—
	(f)	—	14,000	—
	(g)	—	8,000	—
	(h)	—	11,500	—
	(i)	2.5%	—	—
	(j)	$1.25 per C	—	—
	(k)	$14.80 per M	—	—
	(l)	17.2 mills	—	—

CHAPTER SIX

**Section
One
Page 105**

1. (a) $208.00
   (b) 178.20
   (c) 192.40

		Premium	Refund
3.	(a)	$ 51.30	—
	(b)	64.80	$ 7.20
	(c)	189.00	135.00

		Insurance Required	Compensation
5.	(a)	$24,000	$15,000
	(b)	52,000	9,000
	(c)	36,000	24,000
	(d)	42,000	28,000
	(e)	36,000	30,000

		Ratio of Coverage	Compensation
7.	(a)	4/7	$20,000
		3/7	15,000
	(b)	1/4	20,000
		2/5	32,000
		3/20	12,000
		1/5	16,000
9.	(a)	$ 663.00	
	(b)	1,790.10	
	(c)	198.90	
11.	(a)	$222.00	
	(b)	599.40	
	(c)	66.60	

13. $97.44
15. (a) $61.05
    (b) 55.00
17. (a) $17,000
    (b) 25,000
    (c) 35,000
19. (a) $14,000
    (b) 31,500
    (c) 56,000
21. (a) $24,000
    (b) 48,000
    (c) 72,000
23. (a) $ 9,000; $36,000; $27,000
    (b) $15,000; $60,000; $45,000
25. (a) $80,000; $60,000;
         20,000; 40,000
    (b) 180,000; 135,000;
         45,000; 90,000
    (c) 240,000; 180,000;
         60,000; 120,000

**Section Two
Page 117**

1. (a) $ 93.80
  (b) 126.85
  (c) 361.60
3. (a) $ 35.20
  (b) 92.40
  (c) 122.00
5. $87.00
7. $99.00
9. $190

11. $176.40
13. (a) $23,000
    (b) 7,000
15. (a) $135
    (b) $ 0
17. (a) $27,000
    (b) $ 3,100
19. (a) $65,900
    (b) 10,100

**Section Three
Page 136**

1. (a) $ 987.90
  (b) 441.75
  (c) 460.10
  (d) 1,037.60

3. (a) $260
  (b) 32 yrs. 164 da.
  (c) $26,500
  (d) 4,740

5. (a) $94.10
   (b) 12 yrs.
   (c) $34.10
   (d) 60.16
7. (a) $ 1,613.60
   (b) 1,130.40
   (c) 32,272.00
   (d) 32,781.60
9. (a) $1,436.00
   (b) 5,726.00
   (c) The 20-payment life policy
       would earn nonforfeiture
       values (cash value, paid-up
       insurance, extended term
       insurance) which have not
       yet been given consideration.
       Also, future term insurance
       could be purchased only at an
       increased rate.
17. (a) $2,130
    (b) 2,958
    (c) The 20-pay life is $828 higher.
    (d) The 20-payment life policy
        will continue at the same
        rate, whereas a new term
        policy could be purchased
        only at an increased rate.
19. (a) $ 258.30; $298.20
    (b) 1,767.00
    (c) 1,203.00
    (d) Mr. X is $564 higher.

21. (a) $4,123
    (b) Net profit = $4,718
    (c) Straight life; $8,841 more
23. (a) $133
    (b) 14 years ($7.05 monthly)
25. (a) $249
    (b) 234
27. (a) $30,208
    (b) 22,500
    (c) Gained $3,208
        (Gained $5,208 over the
        face value.)
11. (a) $ 193.44
    (b) 8,109.60
    (c) 8,269.56
13. (a) $ 1,202.50
    (b) 14,750.00
    (c) 19,300.00
    (d) 35 yrs. 290 da.
15. $4,428
29. (a) $ 166
    (b) 69,720
    (c) 211.60
    (d) 50,784
    (e) Gained $18,936
        (Gained $29,720 over
        the face value.)

CHAPTER SEVEN

Page 151

1. $1,308.80
3. $1,987.76
5. $1,824.24
7. (a) $1,331.23
       1,276.43
   (b) 1,251.64
   (c) 24.79

CHAPTER EIGHT

1. (a) $232
   (b) $2,580
   (c) $4\frac{1}{2}\%$
   (d) $105; $135
   (e) $4,800; $120
   (f) $90
   (g) $68; $108
   (h) $5,400; $114
   (i) $40; $117
3. $570

5. $2,200
7. (a) $788
   (b) 363
9. $4\frac{1}{2}\%$
11. $168
13. $151
15. $635.57
17. $977.80
19. $1,692.27
21. $4,437.98

1. $573.90
3. $653.60
5. $301.96
7. $110.40; $86.00; $110.00

9. $ 98.00 A
   90.30 B
   131.30 C
11. $940.60

1. $67.65
3. $72.48
5. $595.27

7. $457.13
9. $534.15

	Gross Wages	Deductions				Total Wages Due
		FICA	Inc. Tax	Other	Tot. Deds.	
1.	$640.00	$33.28	$ 68.50	$ 6.40	$108.18	$531.82
3.	489.90	25.47	35.00	15.50	75.97	413.93
5.	849.00	44.15	106.00	84.90	235.05	613.95
7.	454.40	23.63	32.90	13.50	70.03	384.37

	Reg. Wages	Over-time	Gross Wages	Deductions				Net Wages Due
				FICA	Inc. tax	Other	Tot. Deds.	
9.	$540.00	$133.50	$673.50	$23.19	$73.30	$ 6.75	$103.24	$570.26
11.	568.00	89.40	657.40	24.04	71.50	13.14	108.68	548.72

Section Six Page 196

	$20	$10	$5	$1	50¢	25¢	10¢	5¢	1¢
1.	$20	$10	$5	$1	50¢	25¢	10¢	5¢	1¢
	20	4	4	13	2	3	4	4	12

3. $475.47

Section Seven Page 208

1. 1. $3,640
   2. $ 320
   3. —
   4. $320
   5. $3,640 × 10.4% = $378.56
   6. —
   7. $378.56
   8. —
   9. $378.56
   10. $698.56
   11. 517.56
   12a. $181.00

3. $1,800; $700; $2,200

			FICA Taxable Wage			
		Name	1st Qtr	2nd Qtr	3rd Qtr	4th Qtr
5.	(a)	Boyd	$ 1,600	$ 2,000	$ 1,900	$2,200
		Caldwell	2,500	2,100	2,200	2,200
		Dyson	2,800	2,500	2,500	1,200
		Eaton	2,900	3,400	2,700	—
		Fisher	3,100	3,300	2,600	—
	(b)	Totals	$12,900	$13,300	$11,900	$5,600

7. (12a) = $0
9. (12a) = $0

		Taxable Wages for Unemployment			
	Name	1st Qtr	2nd Qtr	3rd Qtr	4th Qtr
11. (a)	X	$2,600	$1,600	—	—
	Y	2,500	1,700	—	—
	Z	3,300	900	—	¢
(b)	Total	$8,400	$4,200	—	—
(c)	State	$151.20	$75.60	—	—
	Federal	—	—	—	$63.00 (for year)
13. (a)	Boyd	$ 1,600	$2,000	$600	—
	Caldwell	2,500	1,700	—	—
	Dyson	2,800	1,400	—	—
	Eaton	2,900	1,300	—	—
	Fisher	3,100	1,100	—	—
(b)	Total	$12,900	$7,500	$600	—
(c)	State	$154.80	$90.00	$7.20	—
	Federal	—	—	—	$105.00 (for year)

CHAPTER NINE

Section
One
Page 224

The final year of each schedule would read as follows:

		Book Value (End of Year)	Annual Depreciation	Accumulated Depreciation
1.	(a)	$600	$600	$2,400
	(b)	600	240	2,400
	(c)	388.80	259.20	4,611.20

		First Year	Second Year
3.	(a)	$2,400	$ 800
	(b)	1,900	700
	(c)	4,200	1,600

Entries for the last year of each schedule are given:

		Book Value (End of Year)	Annual Depreciation	Accumulated Depreciation		
5.		$400	$250	$2,000		
7.		320	80	1,680		
9.	(a)	756	504	2,744	(b)	$756
11.		600	300	2,400		
13.		800	200	9,200		
15.		421.40	210.70	5,578.60		

17. (a) $2,000
    (b) $3,000
    (c) $2,800; $800
19. (a) $2,000
    (b) $1,200
    (c) $2,900; $900

**Section
Two
Page 228**

1.	(a)	$4,000		(b)	$18,000	
		6,000			45,000	
		5,000			9,000	
		9,000			36,000	
	(b)	$16,000			27,000	
		8,000		7.	$3,600	
		12,000			2,700	
		20,000			1,800	
		24,000			900	
					3,000	
3.	(a)	$ 500			4,500	
		1,500			1,200	
		2,000			300	
		1,000		9.	$ 640	
	(b)	$1,200			1,920	
		600			1,280	
		1,800			2,400	
		900			160	
		300		11.	$3,200	
5.	(a)	$24,000			1,600	
		9,000			4,800	
		12,000			4,000	
		27,000			2,400	

1. **GEM APPLIANCE SALES, INC.**

   Income Statement for Year Ending December 31, 1971

			%	
Income from sales:				
Gross sales		$510,000	102.0%	
Sales returns & allowances		10,000	2.0	
Net sales		$500,000		100.0%
Cost of goods sold:				
Inventory, January 1		$ 80,000		
Purchases	$302,000			
Less: Returns				
& allowances	5,000			
Net purchases	$297,000			
Add: freight in	1,000			
Net purchase cost		298,000		
Goods available for sale		$378,000		
Inventory, December 31		78,000		
Cost of goods sold		300,000	60.0	
Gross profit on operations		$200,000	40.0%	
Expenses:				
Salaries		$ 80,000	16.0%	
Rent and utilities		20,000	4.0	
Maintenance		9,000	1.8	
Office supplies		6,500	1.3	
Insurance		5,000	1.0	
Advertising		10,000	2.0	
Depreciation		7,000	1.4	
Other		2,500	0.5	
Total operating expenses		140,000	28.0	
Net profit on operation		$ 60,000	12.0%	
Income taxes		35,000	7.0	
Net income		$ 25,000	5.0%	

3. W. D. CRENSHAW CO.

Balance Sheet, September 30, 1972

			%
Assets			
Current assets:			
Cash	$ 4,000		5.0%
Accounts receivable	22,000		27.5
Notes receivable	2,000		2.5
Merchandise inventory	20,000		25.0
Total current assets		$48,000	60.0%
Fixed assets:			
Building (less depreciation)	$16,000		20.0%
Furnishings and fixtures			
(less depreciation)	3,200		4.0
Delivery truck	2,800		3.5
Land	10,000		12.5
Total fixed assets		32,000	40.0
Total assets		$80,000	100.0%
Liabilities and proprietorship			
Current liabilities:			
Accounts payable	$20,000		25.0%
Taxes payable	1,600		2.0
Note payable	2,400		3.0
Total current liabilities		$24,000	30.0%
Fixed liabilities:			
Mortgage (due 1978)		32,000	40.0
Total liabilities		$56,000	70.0%
Proprietorship:			
W. D. Crenshaw, capital		24,000	30.0
Total liabilities and proprietorship		$80,000	100.0%

5. SANFORD AND GRIER ELECTRONICS

Comparative Income Statement
for Years Ending June 30, 1972 and 1971

	1972	1971	Increase (or Decrease) Amount	%	% of Net Sales 1972	1971
Income						
Net sales	$480,000	$400,000	$80,000	20.0%	100.0%	100.0%
Cost of goods:						
Inventory, July 1	$ 40,000	$ 60,000	($20,000)	(33.3)	8.3%	15.0%
Purchases	320,000	240,000	80,000	33.3	66.7	60.0
Goods available for sale	$360,000	$300,000	$60,000	20.0%	75.0%	75.0%
Inventory, June 30	60,000	40,000	20,000	50.0	12.5	10.0
Cost of goods sold	300,000	260,000	40,000	15.4	62.5	65.0
Gross Profit	$180,000	$140,000	$40,000	28.6%	37.5%	35.0%
Expenses:						
Salaries	$ 60,000	$ 48,000	$12,000	25.0%	12.5%	12.0%
Occupancy	32,000	28,000	4,000	14.3	6.7	7.0
Promotion	24,000	12,000	12,000	100.0	5.0	3.0
Depreciation	12,000	16,000	(4,000)	(25.0)	2.5	4.0
Miscellaneous	12,000	8,000	4,000	50.0	2.5	2.0
Total expenses	140,000	112,000	28,000	25.0	29.2	28.0
Net profit on operations	$ 40,000	$ 28,000	$12,000	42.9	8.3%	7.0%

7. GEM APPLIANCE SALES, INC.

Comparative Balance Sheet
for Years Ending December 31, 1971 and 1970

	1971	1970	Increase (or Decrease) Amount	%	% of Total Assets 1971	1970
Assets						
Cash	$ 24,000	$ 30,000	($ 6,000)	20.0%	7.5%	10.0%
Accounts receivable	48,000	40,000	8,000	20.0	15.0	13.3
Inventory	143,000	130,000	13,000	10.0	44.7	43.3
Current assets	$215,000	$200,000	$15,000	7.5	67.2	66.7%
Fixed assets	105,000	100,000	5,000	5.0	32.8	33.3
Total assets	$320,000	$300,000	$20,000	6.7	100.0%	100.0%
Liabilities and net worth						
Current liabilities	$ 60,000	$ 75,000	($15,000)	20.0	18.8%	25.0%
Fixed liabilities	45,000	40,000	5,000	12.5	14.1	13.3
Total liabilities	$105,000	$115,000	($10,000)	(8.7)	32.8%	38.3%
Retained earnings	50,000	50,000	—	—	15.6%	16.7%
Common stock	165,000	135,000	30,000	22.2	51.6	45.0
Total net worth	215,000	185,000	30,000	16.2	67.2	61.7
Total liabilities and net worth	$320,000	$300,000	$20,000	6.7	100.0%	100.0%

9. (a) 2.0 to 1
   (b) 1.2 to 1
   (c) 60%
   (d) 40%
   (e) 70%
   (f) 30%
11. (a) 3.6 to 1
   (b) 1.2 to 1
   (c) 12.5%
   (d) 1.6 to 1

   (e) 11.4 times
   (f) 32 days
   (g) 60%
   (h) 40%
   (i) 28%
   (j) 1.2%; 5%
   (k) 67.2%
   (l) 32.8%
   (m) 32.8%
   (n) 67.2%

CHAPTER ELEVEN

Section
One
Page 261

1. (a) $3.50
   (b) $2.50 common
       $3.00 preferred

   (c) $4.30 common
       $14.00 preferred
3. $4.75

5. $5.15 common
    $6.00 preferred
7. $6.50 common
    $8.00 preferred

9. $1.60 common
    $7.00 preferred
11. $4.20 common
    $22.50 preferred

Section
Two
Page 267

1. (a) $ 8,000
         12,000
    (b) $ 6,000
         9,000
         3,000
    (c) $12,450
         9,480
         6,270
    (d) $12,720
         15,480
3. $8,500
5. (a) $8,400
         3,600
         6,000
    (b) $2,100
         900
         1,500

7. $16,000
    12,000
9. $20,500
    22,000
11. (a) $ 8,000
    (b) $ 5,400
         10,800
13. (a) $9,000
    (b) $8,560
         8,630
15. (a) $ 8,260
         14,340
    (b) $ 360
         6,440
17. (a) $12,750
         14,000
    (b) $ 7,750
         11,000

CHAPTER TWELVE

Section
One
Page 278

1. (a) 90%; $18
    (b) 65%; $26
    (c) 75%; $56
    (d) 45%; $60
    (e) .72; $36; 28%
    (f) $\frac{3}{4}$; $51; 25%
    (g) .595; $20; 40.5%
    (h) .504; $95; 49.6%
3. (a) $ 4.50
    (b) 13.60
    (c) 6.00
    (d) 63.00
5. $499.80

7. (a) $16; .64; 36%
    (b) $32; $\frac{2}{3}$; $33\frac{1}{3}$%
    (c) $9.18; .612; 38.8%
    (d) $11.34; .567; 43.3%
9. National: 40.5% vs. 39.2%
11. $40
13. $75
15. $28\frac{4}{7}$%
17. 20%; 40%
19. (a) $40; $36
    (b) 10%
21. (a) $54; $43.20
    (b) 20%

1. (a) $225.40
   (b)   174.60
   (c)   125.00
   (d)   444.99
   (e)   281.06
   (f)   510.77
3. (a) $245; $90
   (b) $116.40; $300
   (c) $400; $392
   (d) $150; $130
   (e) $270; $100

5. $174.34
7. $1,296.30
9. $388
11. (a) $349.20
    (b)   360.00
    (c)   709.20
13. (a) $450
    (b)   180

CHAPTER THIRTEEN

1. (a) $ 6; $ 3; $3 profit
   (b)   4;   5; 1 loss
   (c)   10;   5; 5 profit
   (d)   5;   7; 2 loss
   (e)   9;   12; 3 loss
3. (a) $60; $12; 20%
   (b) $56; $21; $37\frac{1}{2}$%
   (c) $76; $19; 25%
   (d) $25; $7.50; $23\frac{1}{13}$%
   (e) $63; $7; 10%
   (f) $14\frac{2}{7}$%; $8; $12\frac{1}{2}$%
   (g) $16\frac{2}{3}$%; $72; $14\frac{2}{7}$%
5. (a) 1.38
   (b) $69
   (c) $19

7. (a) 50%
   (b) $33\frac{1}{3}$%
9. (a) 1.6
   (b) $560; $8; $12.40; $7.12
   (c) $37\frac{1}{2}$%
11. (a) $24
    (b) $3.20; $11\frac{1}{9}$%
13. (a) $60; $90
    (b) 50%
    (c) $33\frac{1}{3}$%
15. (a) $48
    (b) 25%

1. (a) $30; $12; $66\frac{2}{3}$%
   (b) $72; $24; 50%
   (c) $64; $16; 25%
   (d) $45; $27; 60%
   (e) $16\frac{2}{3}$%; $84; 20%

3. (a) $\frac{7}{5}$
   (b) $49
   (c) $14
5. (a) $25
   (b) $15.50

7. (a) $\frac{5}{4}$
   (b) $4.50; $7.50; $6.50; $6.00
   (c) 25%
9. (a) $200
   (b) $33\frac{1}{3}$%
   (c) 25%
11. (a) 20% on selling price
   (1.2 vs. 1.25)

(b) $37\frac{1}{2}$% on selling price
   (1.45 vs. 1.6)
13. (a) 2
   (b) $36
   (c) 100%
15. (a) 1.75
   (b) $20
17. $600

Section
Three
Page 303

1. (a) $40; $50
   (b) $24; $28
   (c) $60; $45; 20%
   (d) $75; $60; $16\frac{2}{3}$%
   (e) $35; 30%; $50
   (f) $35; $44\frac{4}{9}$%; $63
   (g) $324; $600; $432
   (h) $272; $500; $340
3. (a) $60
   (b) $72

5. (a) $80
   (b) $64
   (c) $12\frac{1}{2}$%
7. (a) $400
   (b) $250
   (c) $37\frac{1}{2}$%
9. (a) $300
   (b) $480
   (c) $750

Section
Four
Page 306

1. (a) $30; $36; 90 lb.; 40¢
   (b) $150; $210; 72 doz.; $2.92
       doz.
   (c) $400; $550; 235; $2.35
3. (a) $120; $144; 380; 20; 37¢
   (b) $200; $288; 47; 3; $6

5. (a) $7.80
   (b) 52%
   (c) 34.2%
7. 15¢ lb.
9. 84¢ per box
11. $45

CHAPTER FOURTEEN

Section
One
Page 313

1. (a) $9; $36; $34; $2
   (b) $33\frac{1}{3}$%; $40; $48; ($8)
   (c) 25%; $6; $12; $15
   (d) $37\frac{1}{2}$%; $6; $10; $11
   (e) $50; 30%; $35; $7
   (f) $35; $10; $20; $24

3. (a) 25%; $36; $45; ($9); ($4); 10%
   (b) $14; $56; $5; ($12); ($7); $11\frac{1}{9}$%
   (c) $25; $8; $20; ($7); ($3); 15%
   (d) $36; $18; $21; $30; ($12); $14\frac{2}{7}$%
5. ($3)

7. (a) $33\frac{1}{3}\%$
    (b) $6
9. (a) $40
    (b) ($11)
    (c) ($3); 12%
11. (a) $5.60

(b) $.72
(c) 9%
13. (a) $560; $644; $670
    (b) Net profit
    (c) $26; $4\frac{9}{14}\%$

**Section
Two
Page 317**

1. 5¢ short
3. $1.09 short

Page 319

1. $36,000
3. $21,500

5. 3.85
7. 3.8

CHAPTER FIFTEEN

**Section
One
Page 327**

1. (a) $30; $630
    (b) $15; $615
    (c) $12.60; $372.60
    (d) $11.25; $461.25
    (e) $39.90; $799.90

5. 7%
7. $\frac{1}{2}$ year or 6 mos.
9. 6.5%
11. $1,200
13. $8\frac{1}{3}\%$

**Section
Two
Page 330**

1. (a) 233 da.
    (b) 164 da.
    (c) 108 da.
    (d) 106 da.
    (e)   97 da.
    (f) 237 da.
    (g) 226 da.
    (h) 224 da.

3. (a) Sept. 25; Sept. 24
    (b) July 10; July 9
    (c) Nov. 3; Oct. 31
5. (a) Dec. 15; 90 da.; 91 da.
    (b) Nov. 19; 180 da.; 184 da.
    (c) Nov. 16, 1972; 270 da.; 274 da.
    (d) Sept. 8, 1973; 240 da.; 243 da.
    (e) Apr. 10, 1975; 300 da.; 304 da.

1. (a) $29.20; $28.80
   (b) $7.30; $7.20
3. (a) $7.30
   (b) $7.20
   (c) $7.48
   (d) $7.38
5. (a) $36.60
   (b) $18.30
   (c) $9.15
   (d) $27.45

7. (a) $28
   (b) $14
   (c) $7
   (d) $42
9. (a) $6.30
   (b) $18.90
   (c) $9.45
11. (a) $9.15
    (b) $12.20
    (c) $27.45

1. $5.35; $540.35
3. $3.40; $683.40
5. $4.80; $644.80
7. $6.30; $356.30
9. $4.50; $544.50
11. $14.80; $1,679.80

13. $12.50; $612.50
15. $8.94; $604.94
17. $15.30; $1,290.30
19. $7.64; $772.00
21. $3.39; $342.63

1. (a) $500
   (b) George D. Rogers
   (c) North Austin State Bank
   (d) July 7
   (e) October 5
   (f) $500
   (g) 8%
   (h) 90 days
   (i) $10
   (j) $510
3. (a) 180 da.; $23.40; $803.40

   (b) Nov. 15; $6.15; $456.15
   (c) Sept. 30; $24.00; $744.00
   (d) $1,500; March 29; $1,548
5. $14; $494
7. $313.75
9. $276.75
11. 8%
13. 144 days
15. 210 da.
17. $450
19. $540

1. (a) $600
   (b) $800

3. (a) $912; $902.97
   (b) $1,025; $990.34

5. (a) $309; $302.20
   (b) $636; $632.84
7. $450
9. $585.87
11. (a) less
   (b) more
   (c) If money is invested at a rate higher than the rate money is worth, its present value is greater than the principal. If the investment rate is less than the rate money is worth, the present value is less than the principal.
13. $731.09
15. $10,200 in 4 mos.

CHAPTER SIXTEEN

Section One
Page 358

1. (a) $1,000
   (b) Charles N. Oxford
   (c) North Carolina National Bank
   (d) March 19
   (e) June 17
   (f) 8%
   (g) 90 days
   (h) $20
   (i) $980
   (j) $1,000
3. (a) Sept. 14; $18; $382
   (b) Aug. 24; $4; $796
   (c) 60 da.; $9; $711
   (d) May 16; $11; $539

5. (a) $4; $446
   (b) $4.20; $275.80
   (c) $16; $624
7. (a) Sept. 10; $863.20
   (b) July 17; $476
   (c) Nov. 25; $515.43
   (d) Nov. 8; $310.16
9. $386
11. 5 mos. or 150 da.
13. 5%
15. $575.70
17. $700; $699.72

Section Two
Page 363

1. (a) Oct. 19; $600
   (b) Sept. 14; $640
   (c) June 23; $800
   (d) Sept. 7; $400
3. (a) $595; $598; $3
   (b) $1,160; $1,182; $22
   (c) $1,482; $1,490; $8
5. (a) $510; $504.90; $4.90
   (b) $615; $604.75; $4.75
7. $900
9. $420

11. (a) $435
   (b) $447
   (c) $12
   (d) $3
13. (a) $730.62
   (b) $10.62
   (c) $7.38
15. (a) $593
   (b) $598
   (c) $5
   (d) $2

1. (a) $598; 20 da.; $600; $10.20
    (b) $1,792; 20 da.; $1,800; $28.57
    (c) $958; 15 da.; $960; $27.63

3. (a) $1,600
    (b) $26.53

5. (a) $720
    (b) $11.59

1. $12; $612
3. $45; $955
5. (a) $6; $6
    (b) $450; $444
    (c) $456; $450
7. $600
9. $500; $500
11. (a) $800; $799.50
    (b) $800; $799.50
    (c) $20; $20.50

13. $537.30
15. $724.94
17. (a) $609.15
    (b) $9.15
    (c) $6.15
19. (a) $763.40
    (b) $792
    (c) $28.60
    (d) $8

CHAPTER SEVENTEEN

1. (a) $404
    (b) $605
    (c) $454

3. $1,530
5. $1,606

1. (a) $2.20
    (b) $4.71
3. (a) $24 per month
    (b) $3.50 per week
    (c) $31 per month
5. (a) 17.5%
    (b) 19.25%
    (c) 18.25%
    (d) 19.0%
9. $2.81

11. $25
13. $23
15. (a) $108
    (b) $56
    (c) $1,108
    (d) 14.75%
17. (a) $10
    (b) 35.0%
19. (a) $108
    (b) 28.5%

21. (a) $1,016
    (b) $216
    (c) 18.0%
23. (a) $3,624
    (b) $624
    (c) 23.25%
25. (a) 18.0%
    (b) 18.25%
    (c) 17.0%

27. (a) $3.92
    (b) $12.56
    (c) 13.75%
29. (a) $4
    (b) $26

CHAPTER EIGHTEEN

**Section
One
Page 398**

1. (a) 60; $\frac{1}{2}$%
   (b) 28; 1%
   (c) 20; $3\frac{1}{2}$%
   (d) 14; 8%
   (e) 16; $2\frac{3}{4}$%
3. (a) $108.24; $8.24
   (b) $108.28; $8.28
5. (a) $503.88; $103.88
   (b) $506.14; $106.14

7. (a) $636; $36
   (b) $636.82; $36.82
9. (a) $206.04; $6.04
   (b) $206.08; $6.08
11. More interest is earned when interest is compounded more often.

**Section
Two
Page 403**

1. (a) $108.24; $8.24
   (b) $108.29; $8.29
3. (a) $503.88; $103.88
   (b) $506.13; $106.13
5. (a) $636.00; $36.00
   (b) $636.82; $36.82
7. (a) $206.04; $6.04
   (b) $206.08; $6.08
9. (a) $1,349.02; $349.02
   (b) $1,826.66; $1,026.66
   (c) $3,080.53; $1,480.53
   (d) $619.38; $169.38
   (e) $4,280.14; $1,880.14
11. (a) $610.50; $110.50

   (b) $1,221; $221
   (c) $2,441.99; $441.99
   (d) When the principal is doubled, the interest also doubles.
13. (a) $1,346.86; $346.86
    (b) $1,806.11; $806.11
    (c) $3,207.14; $2,207.14
    (d) No
15. (a) $1,319.93; $319.93
    (b) $1,742.21; $742.21
    (c) $3,035.31; $2,035.31
    (d) No

17. (a) $1,025.16
    (b) $374.84
    (c) $1,471.32
    (d) $96.48
19. (a) $320.71
    (b) $556.65
    (c) $56.65

21. (a) $1,055.76
    (b) $1,136.94
    (c) $136.94
23. (a) $1,015.00
    (b) $1,061.60
    (c) $61.60

**Section
Three
Page 411**

1. (a) $10.61; $1,010.61
   (b) $2.09; $502.09
   (c) $10.03; $1,810.03
   (d) $50.31; $4,050.31
3. (a) $3.62; $4.18
   (b) $5.69; $6.69
   (c) $35.20; $37.73
5. (a) $12.58; $12.50
   (b) $56.60; $56.25

7. (a) $50.50; $4,650.50
   (b) $26.80; $2,426.80
9. (a) $13.81; $1,013.81
   (b) $56.01; $4,056.01
11. (a) $26.55; $2,026.55
    (b) $42.25; $3,442.25
    (c) $31.55; $2,111.55

**Section
Four
Page 415**

1. (a) $788.03; $211.97
   (b) $444.77; $155.26
   (c) $585.18; $914.82
   (d) $1,642.58; $2,357.42
   (e) $1,578.56; $821.44
3. (a) $3,660.45
   (b) $6,339.55
5. (a) $5,930.98
   (b) $2,069.02

7. (a) $14,568.92
   (b) $5,431.08
9. (a) $6,321.54
   (b) $2,801.35
11. (a) $1,300
    (b) $1,024.44
13. (a) $900
    (b) $784.30

CHAPTER NINETEEN

**Section
One
Page 423**

1. (a) $23,123.67; $20,000;
       $3,123.67
   (b) $5,459.80; $4,400;
       $1,059.80

   (c) $5,233.76; $3,000;
       $2,233.76
   (d) $37,100.42; $33,600;
       $3,510.42

(e) $30,649.87; $25,200;
$5,449.87

3. (a) $2,100
(b) $5,042.29
(c) $2,942.29

5. (a) $8,336.43
(b) $7,200
(c) $1,136.43

7. (a) $18,000
(b) $19,405.23
(c) $1,405.23

**Section
Two
Page 428**

1. (a) $6,033.95; $7,200;
$1,166.05
(b) $13,677.74; $20,000;
$6,322.26
(c) $16,058.37; $24,000;
$7,941.63
(d) $2,605.38; $2,880;
$274.62
(e) $21,521.43; $42,000;
$20,478.57
(1)
3. (a) $4,115.27; $515.27
(b) $40,688.29; $8,688.29
(c) $51,089.32; $11,089.32
(2)
$3,144.68; $455.32
$25,267.14; $6,732.86
$31,178.32; $8,821.68

5. (a) $13,753.51
(b) $18,000
(c) $4,246.49

7. (a) $110,891.96
(b) $180,000
(c) $69,108.04

9. (a) $1,331.26
(b) $653.17
(c) $946.83

11. (a) $70,668.08
(b) $28,891.77
(c) $83,108.23

13. (a) $87,000
(b) $70,476.85

15. (a) $92,000
(b) $51,585.55

CHAPTER TWENTY

**Section
One
Page 436**

1. (a) $256.08; $8,194.56;
$1,805.44
(b) $1,768.05; $35,361.00;
$14,639
(c) $92.58; $6,665.76;
$1,334.24
(d) $4,955.62; $69,378.68;
$50,621.32

(e) $1,815.76; $65,367.36;
$24,632.64

3. (a) $62,833.09
(b) $502,664.72
(c) $97,335.28

5. (a) $2,429.97
(b) $12,521.08

7. (a) $24,446.87   9. (a) $2,285.91
    (b) $113,275.12   (b) $466.04

	Payment	Periodic Interest	Periodic Payment	Total Increase	Balance, End of Period
9. (a)	4	436.65	2,285.91	2,722.56	9,999.98
	Totals	$856.34	$9,143.64		
(b)	8	69.29	466.04	535.33	4,000.02
	Totals	$271.70	$3,728.32		

Section
Two
Page 445

1. (a) $180.26; $12,978.72;   5. (a) $2,253.50
         $2,978.72   (b) $6,056
    (b) $1,276.86; $51,074.40;   7. (a) $1,705.35
         $11,074.40   (b) $45,267.50
    (c) $5,035.37; $161,131.84;   (c) $93,267.50
         $71,131.84   9. (a) $1,509.70
    (d) $140.91; $6,763.68;   (b) $10,582
         $763.68   (c) $107,582
    (e) $3,006.65; $180,399;   11. (a) $288.59
         $105,399   (b) $1,652.94
3. (a) $2,872.92
    (b) $72,154.32

	Payment	Principal Owed	Interest	Payment Toward Principal
11. (a)	4	272.26	16.34	272.25
	Totals	$154.37	$999.99	
		$1,154.36	=	Total paid
(b)	4	1,589.36	63.57	1,589.37
	Totals	$611.75	$6,000.01	
		$6,611.76	=	Total paid

Section
Three
Page 448

1. (a) $2,025.82; $1,025.82   3. (a) $1,642.58; $2,357.42
    (b) $674.51; $174.51   (b) $8,207.47; $1,792.53

5. (a) $79,353.52; $48,000;
        $31,353.52
   (b) $10,407.39; $8,400;
        $2,007.39

7. (a) $30,673.12; $48,000;
        $17,326.88
   (b) $6,845.30; $8,400;
        $1,554.70

9. (a) $132.58; $7,954.80;
        $2,045.20
   (b) $196.62; $6,291.84;
        $1,708.16

11. (a) $126.60; $12,153.60;
        $2,153.60
    (b) $646.45; $51,716;
        $21,716

13. (a) $5,013.87
    (b) $986.13

15. (a) $59,022.03
    (b) $11,022.03

17. (a) $2,644.34
    (b) $45,196.24

19. (a) $48,156.20
    (b) $80,000
    (c) $31,843.80

21. (a) $75.45
    (b) $3,621.60
    (c) $378.40

23. (a) $24,351.89
    (b) $14,351.89

APPENDIX A

Section
One
Page 455

1. (a) 10,000,000
   (b) 2
   (c) 300,000,000
   (d) 40,000,000,000
   (e) 5,000,000

3. (a) Fifty-five million, two
       hundred eighteen thous-
       and, three hundred
       forty-nine.
   (b) Four billion, six hundred
       twenty-three million,
       three hundred fifty-two
       thousand, seven hundred
       eighty-seven.
   (c) Eighty-three billion, four
       million, two hundred
       sixty thousand, four
       hundred nine.

(d) Six hundred twenty-five
    billion, seven hundred
    eighty million, two
    hundred eleven thous-
    and, seven.
(e) Thirty-six billion, five
    hundred million, four
    thousand, seven hundred
    eight
(f) Two hundred three bil-
    lion, seven hundred
    thousand, six hundred
    ninety-five.
(g) Seventy-four billion,
    thirty.

1. (a) $g + h = h + g$
   (b) $15 + 47 \overset{?}{=} 47 + 15$
       $62 = 62$
   (c) $(d + e) + f = d + (e + f)$
   (d) $(9 + 28) + 16 \overset{?}{=} 9 + (28 + 16)$
       $37 + 16 \overset{?}{=} 9 + 44$
       $53 = 53$
   (e) $x \cdot y = y \cdot x$
   (f) $38 \times 25 \overset{?}{=} 25 \times 38$
       $950 = 950$
   (g) $(l \cdot m)n = l(m \cdot n)$
   (h) $(7 \cdot 3)9 \overset{?}{=} 7(3 \cdot 9)$
       $(21)9 \overset{?}{=} 7(27)$
       $189 = 189$
   (i) $r(s + t) = r \cdot s + r \cdot t$
   (j) $5(3 + 6) \overset{?}{=} 5 \cdot 3 + 5 \cdot 6$
       $5(9) \overset{?}{=} 15 + 30$
       $45 = 45$

3. (a) 20
   (b) 23
   (c) 25
   (d) 27
   (e) 24
   (f) 33
   (g) 31
   (h) 239
   (i) 225

5. (a) 33
   (b) 28
   (c) 31

   (d) 30
   (e) 267
   (f) 225
   (g) 276
   (h) 368
   (i) 298

7. (a) 237
   (b) 262
   (c) 2,084
   (d) 3,209
   (e) 27,574
   (f) 52,945

9. (a) 2,470
   (b) 39,000
   (c) 46,300
   (d) 7,980
   (e) 438,600
   (f) 7,560,000
   (g) 3,770,000
   (h) 10,440,000
   (i) 432,999
   (j) 3,054,510
   (k) 46,660,926
   (l) 5,020,645,938

11. (a) 598
    (b) 748
    (c) 2,709
    (d) 6,004
    (e) 4,975 R3
    (f) 4,802 R8

13.

Dept.	Mon.	Tues.	Wed.	Thur.	Fri.	Sat.	Dept. Totals
#1							$ 2,404.35
#2							3,002.09
#3							2,651.89
#4							1,991.98
#5							1,962.61
#6							2,671.48
Daily Totals	$2,457.47	$2,315.53	$2,189.82	$2,361.51	$2,732.17	$2,627.90	$14,684.40

15.

$43.68	5.04
42.60	19.32
61.50	636.00
29.25	476.35
74.88	505.14
5.25	419.90
5.00	269.96
4.50	Total $2,598.37

Section Three
Page 482

1. (a) $p + q = q + p$

(b) $3\frac{1}{2} + 5\frac{2}{3} \stackrel{?}{=} 5\frac{2}{3} + 3\frac{1}{2}$

$3\frac{3}{6} + 5\frac{4}{6} \stackrel{?}{=} 5\frac{4}{6} + 3\frac{3}{6}$

$8\frac{7}{6} = 8\frac{7}{6}$

$9\frac{1}{6} = 9\frac{1}{6}$

(c) $(d + e) + f = d + (e + f)$

(d) $(\frac{3}{4} + \frac{1}{2}) + \frac{3}{5} \stackrel{?}{=} \frac{3}{4} + (\frac{1}{2} + \frac{3}{5})$

$(\frac{3}{4} + \frac{2}{4}) + \frac{3}{5} \stackrel{?}{=} \frac{3}{4} + (\frac{5}{10} + \frac{6}{10})$

$\frac{5}{4} + \frac{3}{5} \stackrel{?}{=} \frac{3}{4} + \frac{11}{10}$

$\frac{25}{20} + \frac{12}{20} \stackrel{?}{=} \frac{15}{20} + \frac{22}{20}$

$\frac{37}{20} = \frac{37}{20}$

$1\frac{17}{20} = 1\frac{17}{20}$

(e) $r \cdot s = s \cdot r$

(f) $4\frac{4}{5} \times 3\frac{3}{4} \stackrel{?}{=} 3\frac{3}{4} \times 4\frac{4}{5}$

$\frac{24}{5} \times \frac{15}{4} \stackrel{?}{=} \frac{15}{4} \times \frac{24}{5}$

$18 = 18$

(g) $(u \cdot v)w = u(v \cdot w)$

(h) $(\frac{5}{6} \cdot \frac{2}{7})\frac{7}{8} \stackrel{?}{=} \frac{5}{6}(\frac{2}{7} \cdot \frac{7}{8})$

$(\frac{5}{21})\frac{7}{8} \stackrel{?}{=} \frac{5}{6}(\frac{1}{4})$

$\frac{5}{24} = \frac{5}{24}$

(i) $j(k + l) = j \cdot k + j \cdot l$

(j) $\frac{2}{3}(\frac{3}{4} + \frac{6}{5}) \stackrel{?}{=} \frac{2}{3} \cdot \frac{3}{4} + \frac{2}{3} \cdot \frac{6}{5}$

$\frac{2}{3}(\frac{39}{20}) \stackrel{?}{=} \frac{1}{2} + \frac{4}{5}$

$\frac{2}{3}(\frac{39}{20}) \stackrel{?}{=} \frac{5}{10} + \frac{8}{10}$

$\frac{13}{10} = \frac{13}{10}$

$1\frac{3}{10} = 1\frac{3}{10}$

3. (a) $\frac{2}{3}$

(b) $\frac{9}{4}$

(c) $\frac{7}{12}$

(d) $\frac{3}{5}$

(e) $\frac{1}{3}$

(f) $\frac{3}{2}$

(g) $\frac{3}{4}$

(h) $\frac{8}{5}$

(i) $\frac{11}{13}$

(j) $\frac{5}{12}$

5. (a) $\frac{7}{15}, \frac{7}{12}, \frac{2}{3}, \frac{3}{4}, \frac{4}{5}, \frac{5}{6}$

(b) $\frac{5}{9}, \frac{11}{18}, \frac{5}{8}, \frac{17}{24}, \frac{3}{4}, \frac{5}{6}$

7. (a) $3\frac{1}{2}$

(b) $4\frac{3}{4}$

(c) $5\frac{1}{3}$

(d) $3\frac{2}{3}$

(e) $8\frac{3}{7}$

(f) $4\frac{1}{7}$

(g) $11\frac{2}{3}$

(h) $4\frac{1}{2}$

(i) $5\frac{8}{11}$

(j) $11\frac{1}{2}$

(k) $5\frac{4}{7}$

(l) $18\frac{1}{3}$

9. (a) $\frac{1}{3}$

(b) $\frac{3}{8}$

(c) $\frac{8}{21}$

(d) $\frac{9}{40}$

(e) $\frac{1}{12}$

(f) $3\frac{11}{24}$

(g) $7\frac{6}{35}$

(h) $5\frac{7}{16}$

(i) $7\frac{5}{18}$

(j) $8\frac{37}{56}$

(k) $6\frac{46}{63}$

(l) $7\frac{23}{30}$

(m) $8\frac{6}{11}$

(n) $21\frac{41}{56}$

(o) $13\frac{17}{36}$

11. (a) $\frac{3}{5}$　　　　　　　　(i) 6
　　(b) $\frac{7}{6}$　　　　　　　　(j) $\frac{1}{14}$
　　(c) $\frac{15}{14}$　　　　　　　(k) $\frac{6}{5}$
　　(d) $\frac{9}{10}$　　　　　　　(l) $\frac{5}{4}$
　　(e) $\frac{3}{2}$　　　　　　　　(m) $\frac{6}{7}$
　　(f) 4　　　　　　　　　(n) $\frac{16}{45}$
　　(g) $\frac{3}{4}$　　　　　　　　(o) $\frac{20}{7}$
　　(h) $\frac{8}{15}$

**Section
Four
Page 498**

1. (a) $r + f = f + r$
　　(b) $4.82 + 7.35 \overset{?}{=} 7.35 + 4.82$
　　　　　$12.17 = 12.17$
　　(c) $(x + y) + z = x + (y + z)$
　　(d) $(1.3 + 5.2) + 0.6 \overset{?}{=} 1.3 + (5.2 + 0.6)$
　　　　　$6.5 + 0.6 \overset{?}{=} 1.3 + 5.8$
　　　　　　　$7.1 = 7.1$
　　(e) $m \cdot n = n \cdot m$
　　(f) $.6 \times .9 \overset{?}{=} .9 \times .6$
　　　　　$.54 = .54$
　　(g) $(g \cdot h)k = g(h \cdot k)$
　　(h) $(.3 \times .4).7 \overset{?}{=} .3(.4 \times .7)$
　　　　　$(.12).7 \overset{?}{=} .3(.28)$
　　　　　　$.084 = .084$
　　(i) $b(d + g) = bd + bg$
　　(j) $.5(.3 + .8) \overset{?}{=} .5 \times .3 + .5 \times .8$
　　　　　$.5(1.1) \overset{?}{=} .15 + .40$
　　　　　　$.55 = .55$

3. (a) $\frac{1}{1000}$　　　　　　　(f) 0.116
　　(b) $\frac{2}{10}$　　　　　　　(g) 0.375
　　(c) 30　　　　　　　(h) $0.42\frac{6}{9}$
　　(d) $\frac{4}{100}$　　　　　　　(i) $0.36\frac{4}{11}$
　　(e) 5　　　　　　　　(j) $0.41\frac{2}{3}$
　　(f) $\frac{6}{100,000}$　　　　　(k) $0.35\frac{5}{7}$
　　(g) 700　　　　　　(l) $0.21\frac{7}{8}$
　　(h) $\frac{8}{10,000}$　　　　　(m) $3.16\frac{2}{3}$
　　(i) 9,000　　　　　(n) 18.375

5. (a) 0.6　　　　　　　(o) 5.35
　　(b) 0.25　　　　　　(p) $15.44\frac{4}{9}$
　　(c) 0.35　　　　　　(q) $6.28\frac{4}{7}$
　　(d) 0.72　　　　　　(r) 5.492
　　(e) 0.425

7. (a) 1.462
    (b) 375.2
    (c) 0.2271
    (d) 723.3
    (e) 418.8
    (f) 0.3589
    (g) 4,980
    (h) 1.6
    (i) 7.28
    (j) 0.003827
    (k) 0.00615
    (l) 125,000
    (m) 529,000
    (n) 0.0004
    (o) 0.00138

9. (a) 59.45
    (b) 2.737
    (c) 8.568
    (d) 219.307
    (e) 26.8569
    (f) 28.679
    (g) 263.512
    (h) 7.371
    (i) 35.3487

(j) 227.23
(k) 38.201
(l) 71.677
(m) 26.746
(n) 41.54
(o) 74.65
(p) 247.491
(q) 5.0279

11. (a) 14
    (b) 3.4
    (c) 26.8
    (d) 0.52
    (e) 0.023
    (f) 0.0623
    (g) 0.00617
    (h) 0.36
    (i) 32
    (j) 564
    (k) 1.25
    (l) 816
    (m) $4.73\frac{5}{13}$
    (n) $0.65\frac{5}{18}$
    (o) $48.93\frac{31}{33}$
    (p) $3.67\frac{4}{63}$

Index

215
60 / 135

320 6
10 / 13
2